D1084964

A SOCIOLOGY OF AGE STRATIFICATION

AGING AND SOCIETY *consists of three volumes:*

Volume one: An inventory of research findings
Volume two: Aging and the professions
Volume three: A sociology of age stratification

Under the direction of Matilda White Riley

AGING AND SOCIETY

Volume three: A sociology of age stratification

by Matilda White Riley,
Marilyn Johnson, and Anne Foner

with contributions by: John A. Clausen,
Richard Cohn, Beth Hess, Robert K. Merton,
Edward E. Nelson, Talcott Parsons,
Gerald Platt, Norman B. Ryder, Harris Schrank,
Bernice C. Starr, Harriet Zuckerman

RUSSELL SAGE FOUNDATION   NEW YORK

PUBLICATIONS OF RUSSELL SAGE FOUNDATION

Russell Sage Foundation was established in 1907 by Mrs. Russell Sage for the improvement of social and living conditions in the United States. In carrying out its purpose the Foundation conducts research under the direction of members of the staff or in close collaboration with other institutions, and supports programs designed to improve the utilization of social science knowledge. As an integral part of its operations, the Foundation from time to time publishes books or pamphlets resulting from these activities. Publication under the imprint of the Foundation does not necessarily imply agreement by the Foundation, its Trustees, or its staff with the interpretations or conclusions of the authors.

Contents

Foreword

This body of work on age stratification stands in its own right beside earlier studies of religion, nationality, economic class, and more recently race and sex. Each of these areas of inquiry has shown how one or another place in the social structure powerfully influences the actions, feelings, and aspirations of people. Now, as the capstone of more than a half-dozen years of study on age and aging, *The Sociology of Age Stratification* puts into focus this area of social science inquiry, essential to the understanding of social life and to policy decisions affecting social life.

The major theoretical chapters of this volume systematically develop the elements and processes fundamental to a model of age stratification. They stress the inevitable connections between history and the changing opportunities, rewards and constraints holding for the young, middle-aged and old. Age, of course, has been long recognized as a basis for differentiation of social relations and for distribution of societal resources. Indeed, the very universality and visibility of age serving in this capacity, as well as the biological aspects of age, may actually have hindered examination of the variability and change-ability of age as a social role. But, as the authors point out, age is a significant position in social structure, affecting every process and product of that structure. It involves continuous replenishment of the varied social strata and categories of the population through the successive birth, aging, and death of new cohorts (or generations). And these cohorts, as they age, go through continuing processes of socialization and allocation to a role structure which is itself responding both to the fluctuations in personnel and to many other exigencies and historical events. Thus age, with its biological roots and its inexorable linkages with time and circumstance, is intrinsically bound up with social change.

Several of the substantive essays, in exploring the operation of age in selected social institutions, illustrate and extend the emphasis on variability that emerges in this theoretical model of age stratification. For example, the chapter on science moves beyond the long-familiar question of the most creative ages of scientists at work in the various disciplines to advance the central idea that widely-shared anticipations about the years of peak performance affect the actual allocation, and hence the age structure, of roles within the social structure of science. In this way, age stratification is utilized as a dependent variable rather than, as is often the case, as an independent one. Or again, the changing age patterns of labor force participation are shown to accompany changes in the technological development of the society. Or entirely new life stages are held to arise historically, as, for example, when "studentry" comes to be regarded as a new stage in the process of differentiation and institutionalization, much as adolescence became differentiated in an earlier period.

Thus, common to the many-faceted analyses carried out by the authors and contributors to this volume, is the insight that constraints on thought and action associated with age are, in large measure, not inherent but reflect the normative expectations of particular societies. Norms both prescribe and proscribe throughout the life course. The pervasive injunction "Act your age!" regulates attitudes and behavior with respect to talent, sex, careers, and most other areas of life. We hear, "grow up" but also "don't get too big for your britches." And, "be a man" but not a "dirty old man." One is told that he is "falling behind," and another that he is "too old to start over." But the meaning of such norms, and the degree of conformity to them, is variable throughout history, from one society to another, and among individuals within a society.

As the emerging field of age stratification develops, one task must be to discern the beliefs and judgments and rules and laws involving age that seem most durable, and those that are most open to change. Comparative studies of normative age patterns by ethnic groups, economic strata, professions, and types of families may further document the extent of variation. The limits of variation need to be identified through studies of individual differences in conformity to age norms along with exploration of the sources and consequences of deviance from these norms. One might study, for example, the young conservative and the old liberal, happy marriage across age gaps, successful new careers launched late in life, and youth who are most comfortable with adults.

Specifically, then, in what practical ways can knowledge about age stratification be valuable? First, the description of age-related social norms, and the processes by which norms are linked to the endless renewal of the population and to changes over the life course of individuals, can lead us to better understanding of self and to better understanding of social institutions. Second, and still more important, this knowledge provides the means to intervene in our own affairs, and possibly to change parts of our destinies which may seem on the surface to be determined by chronological age. Some will say that age-related norms are less subject to deliberate intervention than other norms, because they are tied more closely to the biological facts of life. But we said the same thing about ethnicity some decades ago, before we learned differently. And we said the same thing about sex-related norms which are now under critical scrutiny.

Similarly, research that charts the malleability of age-related norms can also develop the potential for deliberate change. And such change could contribute both to general societal welfare and to greater freedom for individuals to nurture and direct their capacities. A powerful illustration of what can be done, drawn from the comparable field of social stratification, is the change in the socioeconomic characteristics of college students during the past forty years, a change to which social science research contributed in no small way. Research on social class and social mobility in the United States described college attendance by income, ethnicity, and religion, and examined also the beliefs about achievements, opportunities, and intellectual abilities which seemed to justify the status quo. At about the same time historically, the development of standardized tests of abilities and their use in national studies demonstrated that substantial numbers of young people of high ability in lower socioeconomic groups did not attend college. This research provided a basis for several decades of intervention and deliberate effort to change opportunities for mobility through a great variety of scholarship programs and through changes in criteria for admission to college. As a consequence, as the Educational Testing Service points out,

> . . . in the Ivy League Colleges . . . the undergraduate body of the 1920's was a homogeneous group with respect to socioeconomic background and a heterogeneous one with respect to intellectual ability. Today the picture is almost reversed—undergraduates in these colleges come from a widely varying socioeconomic background and possess a generally high intellectual ability. (Annual Report 1961–1962, pp. 45–46.)

In summary, *The Sociology of Age Stratification* is an important contribution on three counts. It sharpens a focus of interest in social science by describing how age stratification informs and is informed by social life. It directs us to the methods of analysis needed for the further accumulation of knowledge in the field. Finally, it is a major contribution of the kind that, quite surely, will lead in time to an increase in direct social action, and in the numbers of persons seeking to alter some of the social constraints of age to accord with their views of the better world.

Orville G. Brim, Jr.

Preface

Age is a household word in sociology, though not often used to full advantage. In empirical analysis, age is often a crucial variable, accounting to a conspicuous degree for the variance in attitudes and behavior. In sociological theory, assumptions about aging (as biological, psychological, and social process) are fundamental to analyses of socialization, for example, or of the family cycle. The current literature is replete with sociological studies of discrete phases of the life course, notably childhood, adolescence, and old age. There is, however, still little unity or coherence in these ideas and analyses. Nor has age been systematically related to general sociological theory. No conceptual framework is at hand for interpreting age as a structural element in the society, for isolating the social components of the aging process from birth to death, or for assessing the impact of age upon societal stability and change.

Yet the absence of such a conceptual framework limits comprehension of both aging and society. How can we understand social cleavages or the unequal distribution of power or wealth—without taking into account the differences and the relationships among age strata? How can we apprehend such central topics as socialization over the life course, or the continual allocation of people to new roles—without considering the related exigencies imposed by aging and by the endless succession of cohorts (generations)? How can we investigate the course of human events without assessing our own *cohort-centrism*—the circumscription of our viewpoint by the particular generation to which we were born?

To begin to fill this need, we announce in this book a theory of age stratification. It is our contention that age stratification is an essential aspect of both social structure and social dynamics, influencing—and being influenced by— the behavior and attitudes of individual members of the society. Age stratification parallels class stratification in certain respects, such as the differing relationships within and between strata, or the strains attendant upon mobility from one stratum to another. In other respects, however, age stratification is unique: for the dual processes that form the strata, aging and cohort succession, are universal, inevitable, and irreversible (in contrast to class mobility, for example, in which some, but not all, individuals move, and can move either upward or downward across class lines). Indeed, we believe that age stratification gives promise of becoming a special field of sociology, cutting across, yet related to, other sociological fields.

Our present aim is to suggest and explore such a theory, not to formulate or elaborate it; for, despite several years of study and interchange with scholars and students, the work is still far from definitive or systematic. (As Robert Merton reminds us, it took generations of preliminary work before sociologists finally evolved a special field of class stratification.) A sociological view of age is set forth in the first part of the book, and then examined in subsequent parts with reference both to the society generally and to selected social institutions. The chapters range from paradigmatic outlines of abstract ideas to informal essays devoted to special topics or to special issues. Data are used primarily to illustrate or to suggest extensions of the theory, rather than as basis for generalization, since the comprehensive facts available on old age or on aging in contemporary societies are not equalled in certain other areas. There is a paucity of cross-cultural and cross-temporal materials, for example, of knowledge that is up-to-date, or of information about the middle years of the life course. And, while empirically based generalization is impeded too by certain logical problems, we suggest the high potential of a theory of age for solutions to the problems, for example, of disentangling the processes of aging from the processes of social change. By providing a framework for analysis of society using age as a central focus, we hope to illuminate the value of such an approach and to point out the scientific and practical importance of further empirical and theoretical development along these lines. Since the innovative aspects of our topic require that certain familiar terms be given special meaning in this book, and that occasional new terms be introduced, the subject index emphasizes pages containing relevant definitions or usages.

The book is written in particular for sociologists. It is also addressed to others who may find new insights from a sociological view of age. Thus it is addressed to general readers or students seeking to apprehend the generation gap or to assess the situation of particular age groups; to scientists in social or biological fields who are charged with testing and amplifying numerous theories on which age impinges; to policy makers needing guidelines to the probable outcome of alternative courses affecting people of diverse ages; and to practitioners in those professions concerned with prevention and treatment of the varied problems associated with age and human development.

History of the project   As the third volume in the series on AGING AND SOCIETY, this book began as a companion piece to the two earlier volumes— the inventory of social science findings and the essays on aging and the practicing professions—devoted to the current situation of people in their middle and later years. As Volume III has developed, however, its distinctive feature is its focus, not exclusively upon older people in the contemporary scene, but upon the broad spectrum of connections between age in general and society as a whole. The *theory* developed here extends current thinking in three directions: (1) it examines old age as only one phase of the total life course of the individual; (2) it points to variations occurring in the aging process as social conditions vary from time to time and from place to place; and (3) it locates age, aging, and the succession of cohorts as integral parts of the changing society. In parallel fashion, the *data* required to aid theory development, though in considerable measure available from the inventory in Volume I, cannot be restricted to older Americans today, but must be supplemented by findings on earlier life stages of the individual, on age within varied social settings at other times and other places, and on the patterning of relationships within the society among individuals of different ages. Many such findings are still to be gleaned from related research or from sorely needed compilations similar to our Volume I.

In short, the sociological importance of age has been forced upon us. In empirical studies generally, age clamors for the attention of social scientists. And in the massive outpourings of scholarship and practice in the special field of gerontology, social factors insinuate themselves that require broader vision. Thus we are led to a new plateau of problems—concerning the similarities and the differences between young and old, the cohesion and the conflicts between them, or the social dynamics of aging and the succession of generations— problems that await solution for a better understanding of both individual and society.

Acknowledgments   The program of study which this volume brings to completion was made possible by a grant from The Ford Foundation to Russell

Sage Foundation. The foresight that initiated this program and the enthusiasm that has sustained it are attributable in large part to Stacey H. Widdicombe, Jr., and Ollie A. Randall of The Ford Foundation and to Donald R. Young, Orville G. Brim, Jr., and Eleanor Bernert Sheldon of Russell Sage Foundation.

The following advisers, who have participated in planning conferences and edited various portions of the manuscript, have contributed overall guidance on the project as well as many specific ideas and suggestions: John A. Clausen, Beth Hess, Robert K. Merton, Talcott Parsons, John W. Riley, Jr., and Bernice C. Starr. Special advisers include: John C. Beresford, Richard Cohn, Robert Gutman, Carl-Gunnar Janson, John Knodel, Edward Nelson, Harris Schrank, Zena Stein, Mervyn Susser, and Jackson Toby. Among the many scholars kind enough to react critically to selected portions of the manuscript are: Hubert M. Blalock, Harry C. Bredemeier, Harvey Brooks, Joseph H. Bunzel, James S. Coleman, Ruth E. Eckert, Zelda Gamson, Bernard Goldstein, Kenneth Keniston, Bruce Mazlish, Robert A. Nisbet, Edward Sagarin, Karl E. Taeuber, and Kenichi Tominga.

Research assistants and members of seminars who have assisted in the project are: Thomas J. Agnello, Jr., Paula Alexander, Mildred G. Aurelius, Robert D. Cecil, Zelda Cohen, Betty Conley, Patricia Fillingham, Richard B. Greenhouse, Phillip Hughes, Fred Kasner, Patricia Mysak, Elizabeth Nelson, Susan Niehaus, Stephen H. Paul, Daniel J. Phelan, Nura Resh, Daniel J. Smyth, and Douglas E. Trainor. Editorial and technical help on the manuscript was provided by Mildred G. Aurelius, who also compiled the bibliography. Successive revisions of the manuscript were typed by Marion F. Erhart, Ann Bondira and Irene Zulandt.

To all these persons and agencies the authors express their profound appreciation.

M.W.R.
M.J.
A.F.

Processes related to structural elements

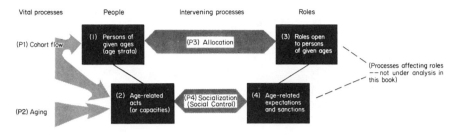

Processes of cohort formation and aging showing selected cohorts over time

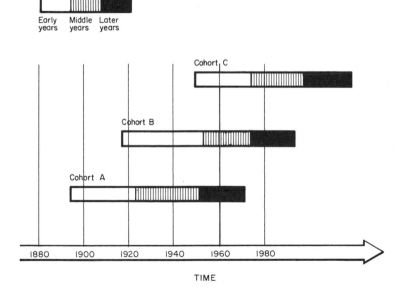

Figures 1.2 (top) and 1.3 (bottom) appear, respectively, on pages 9 and 10 of the text. They are reproduced here for easy reference.

PART 1

INTRODUCTION

Part 1 is intended to aid the reader at various points as he develops and organizes his own understanding of age stratification. It provides an analytical framework for dealing with this emerging field at several levels: with age as an individual attribute, with collectivities bounded by age-related criteria, and with the age structure of a society composed of multiple, coexisting cohorts (or generations). Above all, this framework stresses the dynamic potential of examining the relations between the rhythm of men's birth, aging, and death, and the less predictable timing of social stability and change.

Chapter 1 is a synopsis of the book. It outlines a working model of conceptual elements and propositions, designed for heuristic purposes. Its style is highly compact and schematic, utilizing outlines and diagrams. The reader may choose to scan Chapter 1 first, or last, or preferably at both points with different objectives.

Whereas Chapter 1 stresses the conceptual aspects of age stratification, Chapter 2 deals with the logical and methodological aspects. Age stratification is formally similar to class stratification in certain respects, requiring comparisons within and between strata, examination of the overall structure of society, and tracing of mobility across strata. In other respects, however, age stratification requires a unique approach, one that takes into account its linkage with biology and demography, on the one hand, and its inherence to social change, on the other hand. Both aging (or mobility through the age strata) and the flow of cohorts are inevitable processes, and both are tied to history by the crucial fact that the life span of a society is far longer than the life span of its members. Thus there are difficulties of avoiding fallacious interpretations, constituting a challenge to develop and utilize appropriate methodological approaches. A mathematical formulation of some intrinsic difficulties was prepared for this chapter by Richard Cohn.

The possibilities for a demographic approach are eloquently set forth in Chapter 3 by Norman B. Ryder. This essay, one of several written by Ryder on cohorts (and the only chapter not prepared especially for this book), defines the concept of a cohort and amplifies the nature of its utility for sociologists wishing to understand the demographic view and to go beyond it toward a sociological view of the actors who flow continuously through the roles in the social structure.

An Appendix to Chapters 2 and 3 outlines special difficulties confronted by the student of age stratification who, with vast stores of data now available and computer techniques for processing them, must nevertheless solve numerous problems of sampling, data collection, and analysis of age-specific elements and processes.

1

Elements in a model of age stratification

Age is an essential, though little understood, ingredient of the social system. Every society is divided into strata according to the age of its members. On the one hand, people at varying ages (or stages of development) differ in their capacity to perform key social roles. On the other hand, the age strata differ in the roles members are expected to play and in the rights and privileges accorded to them by society. Thus the social system, which depends upon the continuing performance of numerous age-specific functions, must accommodate the endless succession of cohorts (generations) that are born, grow old, and die within it.

Not only is age fundamental to the social system (see, e.g., Parsons, 1942; Linton, 1942; Eisenstadt, 1956). Age also serves as an important link, on the one hand, between the individual and his biological life cycle and, on the other hand, between the society and its history. Thus one peculiarity of the age structure of society is its *physiological* base, its dependence upon the organic maturation and inevitable decay of the constituent members. The mobility or succession of individuals through the age strata, unlike social mobility through the class structure, is not primarily contingent upon motivation or recruitment: to a certain extent it is biologically determined. Moreover, this mobility is irreversible; no matter how hard people try, they cannot grow younger. The particular individuals constituting any given age category are continuously moving on and being replaced.

In addition, the age strata within the society rest upon an *historical* base. Each new cohort, starting its life course at a unique point in time, has unique characteristics because of the particular historical events undergone or the particular knowledge and attitudes acquired in childhood (cf. Mannheim [1928], 1952; Cain, 1964; Ryder, 1965). The society with which each new cohort of individuals interacts is not the same, nor is the nature of the individuals constant. Hence the sequence of cohorts, marked by the imprint of history and each in turn leaving its own imprint, is inextricably involved in societal processes of stability and change.

The purpose of this book is to explore society from the perspective of its age strata, much as other approaches have examined ethnic structure, for example, or the division into classes along lines of money, power, or prestige. This introductory chapter—of necessity highly abstract—outlines a conceptual model of age stratification, and points to certain implications of age for an understanding of the society and its members. (The reader may wish to treat this chapter as a synopsis at the beginning and as a summary at the end of his perusal of the book.)

Many of the definitions and assumptions upon which the conceptual model rests are arbitrary, since there are numerous ways of simplifying the complex phenomena at hand. Thus the model is heuristic, designed to stimulate investigation and debate and to invite revision. With no intention of espousing any narrow or parochial position, then, we have made use of many basic ideas about the social system borrowed from a single theoretical tradition, that of Parsons and his associates, as this tradition organizes the relevant thinking of such earlier scholars as Durkheim, Mead, or Freud and as it relates to much present-day thinking. Certain of the traditional concepts are modified, however, for the sake of parsimony in relating age to society. Additional concepts have been adapted from methodological work in such fields as demography, epidemiology, and developmental psychology, because of the vagueness or the impoverishment of the pertinent sociological language. For example, the word "generation," which has several meanings, will ordinarily be used here in its kinship reference to the parent-child relationship, while the word "cohort" will be regularly applied to persons born (or entering the system) at the same time. (Special usage of terms is indicated by pages listed in bold face type in the subject index.)

These definitions and assumptions, to be used as a working model, will be utilized and illustrated where relevant in the essays in Part 2 of the book; and they will be discussed, expanded, and formulated in Part 3 as principles, hypotheses, or questions for further analysis.

1 Age-specific elements in the model

Age, in the sociological view, affects both the *roles* in the social system and the *people* who act in these roles. Thus the conceptual scheme to be outlined in Section 1 of this chapter will assume the existence of a role system[1] and of a population of actors, and will concentrate on age-specific structural elements and processes in these two complementary aspects of the social system. This section will deal first with *structural* (or synchronic) elements, then with the *processes* inherent in this age structure, and finally, with the kinds of *changes* that can occur in the age structure over time. These structural elements are convenient categories for describing in cross section the same processes that can also be viewed diachronically over time. However, the

[1] In this book, a role is heuristically defined as a part to be played by individuals, which typically carries with it certain normative expectations (rights and obligations), sanctions (rewards or punishments for performance), and facilities and resources necessary for performance (including other people or groups acting as socializers, allocators, or role-partners of various kinds). Since the role as a position and its characteristics as defined can either change or remain relatively unchanged regardless of the succession of the particular role-occupants, the role is considered to be a constituent of the group structure or the social system. While we recognize the limitations of our usage (in examining many not-yet-crystallized or fully institutionalized roles, for example, or in emphasizing the importance of situational factors in performance), we have found it convenient for our immediate purposes to avoid many of the more refined terminological distinctions (such as the distinction between role and status) that other theorists have required in their work.

structural or synchronic focus has a special significance for the sociology of age stratification, since it locates processes affecting individuals within the framework of stability or change in the larger society.

The relationships between these age-specific elements in the social system and the associated factors in the social, physical, and biological environment will be reserved for Section 2 of this chapter; and certain implications of the model will be suggested in Section 3.

1 · A STRUCTURAL ELEMENTS

See Chapter 10

Viewed in cross section at given periods of time, both *people* (the population structure) and *roles* (the role structure) are differentiated by age, and both make age-differentiated contributions to the social system. Thus two pairs of structural elements can be identified, as diagrammed in Figure 1 · 1.

1 · A · 1 Age strata in the population People (conceived here in sociological terms as actors in the social system) form strata composed of persons of similar age; and the total population is made up of a series of such age strata.

Within a population, the several age strata can vary in *size* and *composition*. For example, there may be more people in the younger than in the older strata; or the ratio of females to males may increase steadily from younger to older strata.

More specific aspects of our model of the age strata in the population include the following:

An aggregate of individuals (or of groups) who are of similar age at a particular time is called an *age stratum* (or an age category).

The *divisions* between strata may be variously specified, either precisely or approximately, and in terms either of the chronological age of the members (as in census age categories) or of their stage of biological, psychological, or social development.

FIGURE 1 · 1 *Elements in the age structure of a society*

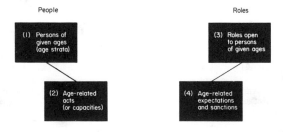

The strata within a population form an *ordered series*, along a dimension from younger to older.

The *focus* of attention can be either on the stratum, the population as composed of age strata, or the individual as a member of either or both.

$1 \cdot A \cdot 2$ *Age-related acts* Not only do the age strata differ from one another at any given period of time in size and composition, but they differ also in the *contributions* they can make to the activities and processes of society (see Riley, Foner, Hess, and Toby, 1969, pp. 954–959). That is, both actual performances and orientations, and the capacity and motivation to perform, are affected by age (in complex ways to be outlined later). For example, older people may be less responsive than younger people to technical retraining for various reasons, perhaps because they have forgotten the strategy for learning or because they start with a generally poorer educational background.

$1 \cdot A \cdot 3$ *Age structure of roles* Just as age divides the population into age strata (or age categories), age is also built into the social structure as a *criterion* for entering or relinquishing certain roles. Age can operate *directly* as a criterion; for example, in the United States a man cannot vote until a certain age or become President until age 35; or he may be required to retire at age 65. Age can also operate *indirectly* as a role criterion through association with other factors; for example, biological stage limits motherhood, or being old enough to have completed high school tends to limit entry into college; or the rapid reaction time required for certain occupations can exclude the aged.

The roles open to persons in the several age strata vary in *type* (so that particular complexes or constellations of role types are simultaneously accessible), and they vary in the *numbers* of each type available (e.g., in the number of jobs open to workers under age 20 or over age 60).

More specific aspects of our model of the age structure of roles include the following:

As an aspect of the social structure, most age criteria are *normative*, permitting or requiring people of given ages to perform particular activities (as in the prescribed ages for school attendance or the minimum ages for entering the work force). Normative age criteria reflect the values and perceived exigencies of a particular society. Other criteria, though they are often translated into normative standards, constitute *factual* regularities in the age strata, such as average or modal ages of entering or leaving roles (e.g., the age of first marriage).

Age as a criterion for role assignment may be variously *specified* in terms of chronological age, either precisely (as in the age of becoming a voter) or approximately (as in age of entry into college); or age limits may be indirectly specified, for example, in terms of stage of biological development (as in becoming a parent). The age criterion may set a lower limit (to the role of voter or of "drinker") or an upper limit (to the role of draftee or of worker where there is mandatory retirement), or an age range may be applied.

Age is a criterion that links together *complexes of roles* that are otherwise differentiated. For example, adolescence places individuals simultaneously in the roles of high school student, peer group member, and dependent offspring in a family.

Complexes of age-linked roles form an *ordered series* within the society. However, the ordering of roles by age—though it often results in inequalities—does not necessarily constitute a social hierarchy in the sense that socioeconomic strata, for example, may be ranked in terms of control over social sanctions. [*See Section 3D of this chapter.*]

The *focus* of attention can be either on the total system of age-related roles, on the complex of roles appropriate to a given age (stratum), or on particular roles as parts either of the total system or of the complex.

1 · A · 4 Age-related expectations and sanctions Age enters into role definition as well as into role assignment. Thus age affects not only *what* roles are open to the several strata, but also the societal *contributions*—the performance expectations, opportunities, and rewards—afforded to incumbents of particular roles (see Riley, Foner, Hess, and Toby, 1969, pp. 959–970). For example, role expectations as to appropriate behavior and sanctions (whether rewards or punishments) may differ for the infant son and the son in his teens, or for the young worker and the worker nearing the end of his career, or for age-heterogeneous and age-homogeneous friendship.

1 · B PROCESSES
See Chapters 11 and 12

These four elements in the age structure of the society at any given period are the product of separate but intertwined processes operating within the population and the role system, respectively. Apart from broad changes in the role system itself, two sets of age-related processes are continuously at work, corresponding to the two pairs of structural elements in our model (see Figure 1 · 2). First, in regard to people (the members of the society), the vital processes of (P1) cohort flow yield the age strata, while the processes of (P2) aging over the life course (including biological, psychological, and social aging) produce mobility across these strata and thus affect performance at each age. Second, linking people with roles, the dual process of (P3) allocation and (P4) socialization enable the role structure to persist and the performance of age-specific functions to continue, despite the succession of role-incumbents.

1 · B · 1 Cohort flow The essential process underlying the changing size and composition of the age strata (element 1 in Figure 1 · 2) consists

FIGURE 1 · 2 *Processes related to structural elements*

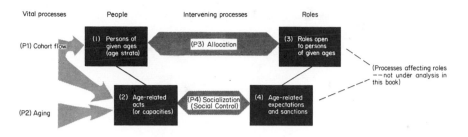

of the formation of successive cohorts, their modification through migration, and the gradual reduction and eventual dissolution of each cohort through the death of individual members.

A cohort is *defined* here as an aggregate of individuals who were born (or who entered a particular system) in the same time interval and who age together.

Each cohort starts out with a given *size,* which (except for additions from immigration) is the maximum size it can ever attain.

Over its life course, a portion of its members survive, while others move away or die out until the entire cohort is destroyed.

Each cohort starts out with a given *composition;* that is, it consists of members born with certain characteristics and dispositions.

Certain of these characteristics are relatively stable in that they are unlikely to change over the life course of the individual (such as sex, color, genetic make-up, country of birth, or—at entry into adulthood—level of educational attainment). [*See Section 2 · B · 1 in Chapter 2.*]

Even in respect to such stable characteristics, however, the composition of the cohort changes over its life course, since certain segments tend to survive longer than others (e.g., women longer than men, whites longer than Negroes).

The succession of cohorts (barring the complete disruption of the society) is an inevitable and irreversible process. Successive cohorts can differ from one another in initial size and composition and in age-specific patterns of survival (or longevity). Moreover, since their respective life spans cover different periods of history, each cohort encounters a unique sequence of social and environmental events.

In Figure 1 · 3, which represents schematically the life spans of three selected cohorts, the age strata at a given time (such as 1960) can be conceptualized in terms of a cross-sectional view of the several cohorts. Thus the cohort is the dynamic counterpart of the age stratum as a structural element.

1 · B · 2 Aging   The individual members of every cohort (irrespective of

FIGURE 1 · 3 *Processes of cohort formation and aging showing selected cohorts over time*

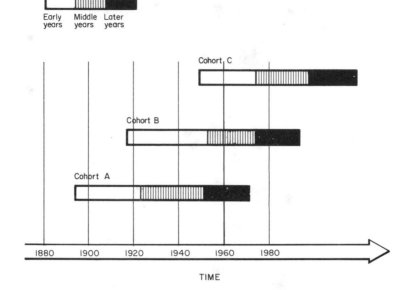

Stages in life course

Early years | Middle years | Later years

Cohort C

Cohort B

Cohort A

1880 · 1900 · 1920 · 1940 · 1960 · 1980

TIME

date of birth) proceed over their life course from birth to death, undergoing changes in performance and attitudes (element 2 in Figure 1 · 2).

> *Aging* involves the accumulation of experience through participation in a succession of social roles, and through psychological change and development (as well as through various organically based changes noted in Section 2 below).
>
> Aging constitutes *mobility* from one age stratum to the next—an inevitable and irreversible process.
>
>> Over the life course, individuals enter certain roles but relinquish others, acquire certain capacities and motivations but lose others.
>
> Note that, unlike much popular usage, we do not confine the term to later stages of the life course.

Despite the inevitability of chronological aging, however, the character of the aging process is far from uniform. Even biologists have difficulty in establishing an aging process that is inherent in the organism apart from its environment (see, e.g., Strehler, 1962). The nature of aging among human beings as members of society is markedly affected by many factors—psychological and social, as well as biological: by the individual's characteristics and dispositions, by the modifications of these characteristics through socialization, by the particular role sequences in which he participates, and by the particular social situations and environmental events he encounters. Hence it follows that patterns of aging can differ, not only from one society to another and from one century to another (see Section 2 of this Chapter), but also among successive cohorts in a single society. For any given cohort, the pattern of aging will reflect the unique historical background of the cohort, and the special patterns of its compositional segments (by sex, color, or socioeconomic status, for example).

Thus the two processes of aging (P2) and cohort succession and survival (P1) are linked together, and both processes have important implications for the age structure of the society. Not all of the differences among strata in action and orientation (element 2) can be accounted for by aging alone. As can be seen from Figure 1 · 3, the age strata at any given period differ not only in age but also in the cohorts to which they belong. A central problem (and a source of many fallacies) in interpreting empirical findings on age is to disentangle patterns of aging from patterns of cohort succession; and also to discover how these two sets of processual patterns are connected with structured shifts in the age strata, and with social and environmental change [*as discussed in Chapter 2 and also in Volume I, Chapter 1*].

1 · B · 3 Allocation   The facts of aging, death, and the infusion of new cohorts into the population mean a continuing flow of manpower into age-specific roles and the training of new recruits to meet expectations (see Figure 1 · 2). Of the two processes involved, one is allocation—a set of mechanisms for the continual assignment and reassignment of individuals of given ages to the appropriate roles. Allocative processes can operate, either on the basis of ascription or of achievement, through various agencies and devices that range from personnel managers or pension plans in a firm to the control of contraception or of bereavement.

1 · B · 4 Socialization   The second articulating process, socialization, serves to teach individuals at each stage of the life course how to perform new roles, how to adjust to changing roles, and how to relinquish old ones. Like allocation, it appears with fresh lucidity from the viewpoint of a sociology of age.

The processes of allocation and socialization combine, then, to bring into conjunction the four sets of elements within the age structure.

1 · B · 5 Role changes   In sum, both persistence and change in the population and in the role structure depend upon the operation of the two sets of age-related processes just described. Whereas the population processes (P1 and P2) bear directly upon people, allocation and socialization (P3 and P4) are intervening processes operating to connect people with roles. In addition, a postulated third set of processes is also at work to affect the role system directly. Such role processes often produce shifts in the number of roles open to given age groups and in the age criteria of roles (element 3), and they produce shifts in the age-related expectations and sanctions (element 4). However, the range of these processes affecting the system of roles far exceeds our immediate focus on age. Unlike the processes of cohort flow and aging, which invariably impinge upon age[2] as a characteristic of the population, age is by no means always a salient property of the role system processes (which involve many criteria other than age, or bear upon the entire system without regard to age). Hence the role structure at any particular period of time will be taken as "given," while shifts in the age criteria for role assignment or for role definition will be brought to attention in Section 1 · C and treated, not as continuous processes, but as structural *changes*.

1 · B · 6 Differences in timing Of central importance to our analysis, however, are the differences in rhythm and timing in these three sets of processes. These differences arise from the crucial fact that the life span of a society or of its population is far longer than the life span of its members. Not only do aging and cohort succession differ in their timing; but, still more important, there is a fundamental asymmetry or lack of synchronization between the sets of processes affecting people and those affecting roles. The wide range of factors influencing the role structure, though less clearly understood[3] than the population processes, are patently less regular or definable in periodicity. Thus a constant tension—a potential source of immanent change—inheres in the articulating processes whereby the rhythmic flow of people is channeled through an unpredictable structure of roles. Recognition of this tension casts a new light upon socialization and allocation [*discussed in Chapter 12*], and points to certain strains and imbalances between population and role structure that are beyond the reach of these articulating processes [*Chapter 10 · 4*].

1 · C **STRUCTURAL CHANGE**

See Chapter 10 and Chapter 12.4

Apart from the continuous processes set in motion by cohort flow and aging, processes that persist even when the population structure and the role structure approach stability, age-specific changes in these structures can also

---

[2] In a subgroup or subpopulation where members enter at differing ages, these processes have a different meaning—dependent not on specific chronological age but on aging (duration) within the subsystem.

[3] Among the numerous treatments of the phasing of social change, Sorokin, 1941, pp. 505 ff., cites and evaluates many "cyclical" explanations; Nisbet, 1969, analyzes the many analogies drawn between the life course of a role system and particular organic models; and Smelser, 1968, pp. 266 ff., has proposed a phasing of social change that might serve as a common theoretical framework for further studies.

occur.[4] Such alterations, viewed as changes in the state of the social system from one period of time to another, can arise in *any one* of the four elements shown in Figure 1 · 2. Moreover, a change in one element of the age structure can generate pressures for changes in *other elements* as well. A few examples will illustrate these principles:

An increase in the numbers of school-age children (element 1), as in the recent United States experience, can increase the number of places required for them (3) in the schools.

An increase in the numbers of senescent persons (1) can increase the number of geriatric caretakers required (3).

An increase in the performance capacity of an age category (2), as through improved levels of health or through retraining of older workers, can allow more roles for an age stratum by mitigating the age restrictions on hiring (3).

Modified expectations for performance by older workers (4), as in wartime, can also serve to relax age restrictions in hiring (3).

Higher rewards (4) for an age stratum, as for school children, can increase motivation and raise performance levels (2) for that stratum.

Such changes in the structural elements arise out of changes in the corresponding processes. The four age-related processes, as diagrammed in Figure 1 · 2, can be viewed as an intricate feedback system in which each process interacts with the others, with changes in the role structure, and with the environment (to be outlined in Sections 2 · A and 2 · B). Although these complex interrelationships will be discussed further in Chapter 12, a few moments of reflection will suggest how, for example:

Changes in allocation (P3) or in socialization (P4) each affect the processes (social or psychological as well as biological) by which people age (P2). And, in turn, changes in aging influence the nature of socialization and of allocation.

Meanwhile, allocation (P3) and socialization (P4) clearly influence each other.

Changes in cohort flow (P1) by affecting who lives and for how long, can alter the life-course patterns by which individuals age (P2). Thus, if longevity increases, more people confront problems of old age; or, if males are killed in a war, marriage patterns change.

Changes in cohort flow (P1), by affecting the numbers and capacities of individuals in the several strata, can modify the processes of allocation (P3) and of socialization (P4).

The cohort flow (P1) can, in turn, be influenced by various changes in each of the other processes. Thus changes in allocation (P3) of the young, or of the

[4] While process and change are useful largely as ideal types, with the boundary between them often indistinguishable (cf. Parsons and Shils, 1951, p. 233, e.g.) in this book we emphasize the distinction between the age-specific *processes* in our model and the *changes* affecting the state of the society.

old, to work roles can alter the incentive to produce children (see e.g., Bogue, 1969, pp. 839–841). Or longevity can be affected by changes in socialization for health care, or by reductions in the will to live imposed by senescence (P2).

These interdependent changes in the age-specific processes operate only rarely to maintain the age structure by equilibrating imbalances among the several elements (Parsons, 1961, p. 37). And, once disequilibria have developed, they can persist. For example, the numbers of the superannuated (or of the recently trained) who aspire to occupational roles may consistently exceed the numbers of roles available to them; or the irreversibility of age mobility can limit the possibilities of redressing imbalances in the age structure through socialization or allocation. And persistent imbalances can result in various forms of strain, conflict, and deviance and can press for the establishment of new or altered structures.

1 · D ELABORATIONS OF THE MODEL

As this model of age stratification develops in the ensuing chapters, many elaborations and variations will be required for understanding the selected elements briefly outlined here.

For example, at the outset the population is viewed, in the simplest terms, as consisting of *individuals*. Age is, indeed, a property of the individual; and through aggregation of individuals it becomes a *collective* property of strata or cohorts (e.g., Riley, 1963, pp. 23–24). For many purposes, however, sociologists want to deal with age as a property of more complex units. For example:

> Strata (or cohorts) can be composed of age-homogeneous *groups* (rather than individuals). Here age of the group can be measured: as an average for all group members; by the age of a single member, such as the wife in the husband-wife pair; or by the duration (of a marriage or of a university) from the time of formation of the group.

> In networks of individuals, age can be regarded as a *relational*, rather than an absolute, characteristic. Thus particular analyses can focus on the relative age of an individual's role-partners, such as his spouse, his friends, or "peers," or his parents or offspring (where the age gap between strata is a "generation" in the kinship sense of the word).

A different type of elaboration can focus, not on the entire population of a society, but upon the population of a smaller group (such as inmates of a hospital) or upon selected population *segments* (or quasi-populations) such as the population of scientists, members of the labor force, voters, or inmates of a hospital. Here the cohort is defined as an aggregate of individuals who share, not a common date of birth, but a common date of entry into the particular segment. Quite different definitions must then be given to the processes of cohort succession and survival, especially if individuals are of dif-

fering ages at time of entry (for example, at time of entry into the popula
of a long-stay mental hospital).

1 · E SUMMARY OF AGE-SPECIFIC ELEMENTS

Section 1 has defined age stratification, then, in terms of those selected
pects of a social system in which age appears to be importantly implicat
Structurally, age has been emphasized as a factor for:

Dividing the *population* into strata, with differentiated contributions.

Defining criteria for occupying *roles;* and defining the expectations, facilit
and sanctions associated with particular roles.

Correspondingly, two sets of processes that underlie this age structure ;
described as:

Those impinging upon the *population* to produce age strata and mobil
across strata.

Those effecting the allocation and the socialization to *roles* of people at t
various ages.

Moreover, both the structural and the processual elements in age stratific
tion can change over time in diverse ways.

2 *Age stratification and the environment*

Our model of the age-specific elements in society does not, of course, form
closed system. The elements, while interdependent (as described in Sectic
1 · C), are also open to the influences of the environment. Two broad types (
environmental factors are at work: first, factors that operate, irrespective (
age, *within* the boundaries of the society or social system; and second, fac
tors that impinge upon the age structure from *outside* the social systen
boundaries (cf. Parsons, 1961, pp. 70–72).

Thus, in the first place, the age-specific elements do not form a complet
system in themselves, but are part and parcel of the social system as ;
whole. The model refers to just one aspect of society: age. It is a device fo
viewing society along the dimensions of age stratification, cohort flow, anc
aging (defined as mobility across the age strata from infancy to old age), some
what parallel to the more familiar model for viewing society along the dimen
sions of class stratification and social mobility (both intergenerational anc
intragenerational). Hence, the age-specific elements are subject to many variations, processes, and changes that are *inherent* in the social system, though
not themselves specifically tied to age, such as variations in the norms, or in
the degree of urbanization or of industrialization.

In the second place, the age structure is subject to numerous *exogenous*

events and conditions that intrude from outside the boundaries of any particular social system. These boundaries separate the social system not only from its physical, cultural, or social environment, but also from the purely organic system of its individual members; and entirely 'different sets of exogenous factors operate respectively at the two levels of society and individual. On the one hand, those environmental factors affecting the *society* can occur in the physical environment (for example, climate, or productivity of the soil); in the cultural climate (for example, values or technology); or in the social environment (for example, the relations of the society to neighboring societies).

On the other hand, that set of exogenous factors affecting *individuals* as members of the society can operate through the biological systems of which these individuals are constituted. In our model, each individual in the age strata is regarded as an actor within the social system, one who is socially conditioned and socially oriented. In addition, of course, he is a biological organism, born with certain innate capacities, and characterized by biological and physiological changes with age. As an organism, he is subject to genetic changes, for example, or to changes in health as a consequence of medical practice. This biological component, though outside the *social* boundaries of the society or system is importantly implicated in the individual's longevity, in his capacity to perform age-specific social roles, and in his social development over the life course.

While the dividing lines are far from clear, then, the model of age stratification focuses only on those elements that are both age-related and social. All other elements, including the biological, are treated for purposes of this discussion as external to the model, hence as "environmental" in this sense.

A major objective of this book is to trace some of the connections between changes (or variations) in age stratification and the related changes (or variations) in the environing factors, both those inside and outside the social system. These changes are two-directional, so that we can examine particular environmental factors as operating sometimes as "cause," sometimes as "effect," of particular elements in the age structure. Moreover, although we shall not attempt to explore the full interdependence among the many elements in the age structure and its environment, each change presumably has repercussions throughout the system and is in turn influenced by them.

2 · A ENVIRONMENTAL CHANGES AS CAUSAL FACTORS

Social changes, and changes in the environment more generally, often operate to *produce* changes in the age structure of the society. Such external changes can impinge directly upon any one of the four structural elements (or the underlying processes) shown in Figure 1 · 2, typically initiating a subse-

quent chain of reactions within the age structure itself, as suggested in Section 1 · C.

$2 \cdot A \cdot 1$ *Factors affecting the age structure of roles*   The following are examples of these factors:

> Annual or seasonal variations in crop yields in an agricultural society, as these might affect demands for the field labor of very young or very old people otherwise exempted (element 3).

> A war that, by reducing the ratio of young adult males to females (1), produces changes in age-specific sex norms (4), such as those surrounding the appropriate age of marriage.

> The general tendency toward increasing role differentiation in the United States, as it affects the numbers or types of age-specific roles available (3).

> A general increase in freedom of individual expression, as this can press for redefinition of age-appropriate expectations, facilities, or sanctions (4), such as those defining the role of student.

$2 \cdot A \cdot 2$ *Factors affecting the age structure of the population*[5]   The following are examples of these factors:

> An epidemic among infants (P1) affects the sizes of the age strata (element 1); or a war affects these sizes by influencing nuptiality and fertility.

> Changes in science or technology (in medicine, air pollution, or atomic radiation), in public health practices, or in standard of living, can influence the aging process (P2) with consequent effects on age-related performances (element 2).

> Changes in the norms of family life can modify role behavior (element 2) as well as socialization (P4) at various stages of marriage and childrearing.

> The imprint of social change upon successive cohorts (P1) can affect the gap between age strata in performance levels (element 2). For example, the gap between young and old in educational attainment results from the general upgrading of the population.

2 · B ENVIRONMENTAL CHANGES AS CONSEQUENCE

Broad societal and environmental changes, as well as specific changes in biological and physiological functioning, can occur not only as the causes, but also as the *consequences* of changes in the age-stratification of society. A few examples will suggest the principles of such relationships:

> A change in the absolute sizes of certain age strata (element 1) can influence the overall structure of societal roles. For example, the increasing joint survival

---

[5] Here again, as in Section 1 · B, the processes producing such changes in the age structure of the population are specified, whereas those affecting the age structure of roles are simply taken as given.

of husband and wife into the middle years may strengthen the autonomy of the nuclear family at all ages.

A change in the *relative* sizes (element 1) of the age strata (i.e., a change in the age distribution of the total population), by changing the societal distribution of such age-related characteristics as health, can influence the *overall* performance capacity of the society and change its dependency burden (cf. Hawley, 1959, pp. 378–380).

A further institutionalization of expectations and rewards (4) in the leisure-time roles available to older people could affect leisure facilities and roles available in the total society, and could result in changing the values for all age strata.

Enhancement of age-related role opportunities (3), as these opportunities may increase motivation and involvement, can have possible biological consequences for health and physical functioning. For example, if more old people became engaged in active occupations, this engagement might heighten their vitality and reduce certain of the deficits of senescence.

Upgrading of the capacities of the young (2), as through modern education, can influence the technological and cultural development of an entire society.

Apart from such specific examples, the dynamic processes underlying the age structure are of dramatic significance for any full understanding of social change. Time is the dimension along which both social change and the age-related processes occur. And innovation can be fostered not only by the succession of new cohorts (P1) and by the plasticity of the aging individual (P2) (see Ryder, 1965), but also through the mechanisms of allocation (P3) and socialization (P4).

2 · C SITUATIONAL VARIATION

Sections 2 · A and 2 · B have illustrated the impact of the environment on our age-specific model by focusing on change over time and on the single society as a unified system. But, of course, the age structure at a single point of time can also show variations among different societies, or (through compositional analysis) among different subpopulations within the same society [*see the discussion of compositional analysis in Chapter 2 · 1 · B and 2 · 4 · B*]. In the United States today, for example:

Age-related expectations and sanctions (as well as socialization practices) differ between lower and middle classes.

Roles open to persons at various ages differ between blacks and whites.

Thus an understanding of the place of age in society requires analysis of the interrelationships of environmental factors both to *changes* in the age-specific aspects of society and to *variations* that occur in different collectivities under varied socio-temporal conditions.

FIGURE 1 · 4 *Personal life course in relation to history of society*

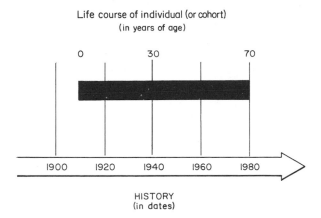

Life course of individual (or cohort)
(in years of age)

HISTORY
(in dates)

3 *Some implications of the model*

Such a preliminary examination of the age structure, necessarily condensed and abstract, begins to suggest the complexity of age as a sociological concept. While a fuller understanding awaits the discussions in the ensuing chapters, certain implications of age for individual and for society, and certain key questions requiring investigation, are readily apparent at the outset.

3 · A THE MEANING OF AGE

For the individual, or for the cohort of individuals,[6] the concept of age includes two parallel dimensions of time, one indexed by years of age as applied to the life course of a person (or cohort of persons), and the second indexed by calendar years as applied to the *history* of the society in which the person lives. Each dimension has at least three segments (see Figure 1 · 4): a present, a past, and a future. Thus the life course of the individual is demarcated by his present age, the number of years since birth, and the probable number of years until death. The corresponding dates and time intervals in the history of the society demarcate major segments of the environment in which the individual lives.

Each of these points and time intervals in the life course of the *individual* is an indicant of personal (biological, psychological, and social) experiences that carry varying probabilities of behavior and attitudes; and the parallel points and time intervals in his changing environment reflect the particular sociocultural and physical conditions and events—present, past, and future—to which the individual is exposed.

[6] Here again, and throughout the book, situational and subpopulation variability within age strata are taken for granted.

For the *society* as a whole, these six time segments have special implications for both the structural and the processual elements in age stratification (as outlined in Section 1).

3 · B STRUCTURAL IMPLICATIONS

See Chapter 10 · **3**

At any given time, age serves to link persons who are of similar age as well as roles that have similar age criteria, and to segregate (or differentiate) those that differ in age.

3 · B · 1 Age integration Within particular strata, age often operates as an integrative mechanism for both society and for its individual members.

Members of a particular age stratum tend to be alike in all six time segments in Figure 1 · 4.

> Thus, in biological stage and in participation in the role structure, they tend as individuals to share a common past, present, and future. They are alike in the sheer number of years behind and the potential years ahead.

> They also share a common historical (environmental) past, present, and future. For example, those aged 30 in 1940 had all experienced World War I and the Great Depression, were currently exposed to World War II, and confronted the future of the 1940's through the 1970's.

> As Mannheim ([1928], 1952) puts it, they share common positions in society.

Similarly, age links together *complexes of roles* that are otherwise differentiated.

> For example, middle age is a life stage that often links together the roles of worker, spouse, and parent of dependent offspring.

> Moreover, characteristic sequences of roles precede and follow the particular complex available in the middle years.

> And these complexes and sequences of roles, quite apart from patterns of *individual* variation are also responsive to history—as history affects the role system and its age-specific elements.

Thus at a given period in history, individuals of similar age find their way into, and learn to play, roughly similar sets of roles. What pressures ensue, then, to produce solidarity among age peers? What counterpressures generate competition or conflict? To what degree do the consistency and congruence of role expectations lessen, rather than increase, malintegration within given age strata?

3 · B · 2 Age segregation Between strata, age operates quite differently, by segregating sets of people from one another and differentiating many of the roles they play.

Persons in different age strata hold different positions in five of the six time segments, as can be seen by comparing any two cohorts in Figure 1–3.

They share the same *present situation.*

They *differ* in all of the other five segments. However, there is a degree of overlap, depending upon such factors as the size of the time gap between the particular cohorts; or the rate of social change (e.g., there may have been more shared experiences in some respects between persons 30 and 50 in 1840 than between persons 30 and 50 in 1940).

Note also that, even when persons of differing age may encounter the same historical situation, they may experience it differently.

Roles and role complexes are also differentiated by age. For example, the roles of student, worker, and retiree (though somewhat overlapping) are typically separated by differences in age criteria.

Moreover, certain *relational* roles, such as parent and his offspring, are inherently differentiated by age.

Such age gaps between roles tend to persist in the social structure over time (history).

What mechanisms operate to articulate the structural gap between age strata? Is articulation between strata related to the degree and rigidity of age-grading within a society? Is there a perennial revolt of young against old, endemic to strains within the age structure?[7] To what extent does the constant shifting of personnel from one age stratum to the next (discussed in Section 3 · C) constitute a continuing threat to such articulation as may develop?

3 · C PROCESSUAL IMPLICATIONS

See Chapter 12

Over time, the cohort is the link between the life course of individuals and the sweep of history. Yet, the marked asymmetry between life course and history as dimensions of time stresses the divergent implications for age stratification of the two different sets of time segments. The differences can be seen by considering the past, present, and future of different cohorts—that is, by comparing (in Figure 1 · 3) individuals who are of similar age but who belong to sequential cohorts. On the life-course dimension, such individuals share many aspects of all three segments, since they tend to be *alike* in present life stage and in various of the biological, psychological, and social experiences of their personal lives, past and future. In all three segments of the historical dimension, however, the two cohorts—exposed as they were to differ-

---

[7] Compare the discussion by Eisenstadt (1956) of types of societies characterized by such revolt. [*See also Chapter 10 · 3.*]

ent eras—*differ* from one another. Subsequent chapters will explore various aspects of the processes along these two dimensions, and the differences between them, which can only be suggested in this Introduction.

3 · C · 1 The life-course dimension The process of aging on this dimension comprises the steady flow of personnel both through the age strata in the population and through the age-differentiated succession of roles (and role complexes).

> Sequential roles over the life course may be more or less *continuous* (cf. Benedict, 1938) with one another [*as discussed in Chapter 11*].

> Persons in one age category at a given time are the *same* individuals who are in another age category at another time. In this way age-differentiated roles are linked together by the passage through them of particular individuals. For example, a student revolt cannot develop permanent personnel and leadership, because individual members move out of the role of student and into adult roles.

> Processes of allocation and socialization, operating to articulate the flow of personnel, are themselves limited by the *irreversible* character of the aging process.

3 · C · 2 The dimension of history The aging process on this dimension differs markedly in rhythm and periodicity[8] from social change, on the one hand, and, on the other hand, from the changes in population strata resulting from the processes of cohort succession and survival. These differing rhythms have dramatic consequences, as the following examples[9] can only begin to illustrate:

> Social (historical) changes tend to set off the cohorts from one another, creating gaps between the age strata due to "cohort effects" as distinct from "aging effects."

> Imbalances between numbers of roles and the supply of age-appropriate role players (between "supply" and "demand" within age strata) may be slow to remedy, insofar as such imbalances must await either structural changes in the role system or the formation and maturation of new cohorts of the requisite size. Note, however, that socialization can redress certain imbalances and that migration can sometimes operate comparatively rapidly to offset a deficit of role players in a particular age category.

3 · D AGE STRATIFICATION VERSUS CLASS STRATIFICATION

The potential value of age as a perspective for understanding society can be further suggested through a comparison between age stratification and the

---

[8] This phrasing appears in Sorokin (1941, p. 505).

[9] The examples under Section 2 · B also suggest some of the consequences in terms of social change.

more widely explored societal division according to socioeconomic status. (Similar comparisons might also be drawn with divisions in terms of sex, race, or ethnic background, which resemble age in having a biological base, but differ from age in not permitting mobility of individuals across strata.)

Both age strata and class strata may be conceived as ordering not only the people but also the roles in the society. And both tend to persist over time, or to change together in an orderly fashion, even though the individual incumbents may be shifting. However, the two types of strata differ in several respects, such as the following:

The criteria for class stratification are largely social (stated variously in terms of inequality of income, influence, power, etc.);[10] in contrast, the criteria for age stratification are in part *biological.*

Whereas socioeconomic strata are *ranked* to form a *social hierarchy,* age strata are typically ordered by time (hence, are more akin to geological strata).

Mobility of individuals across the age strata, but not across the class strata (Sorokin, 1959), is both *universal* and *irreversible.*

Thus all members of an age cohort move together over the life course.

And all members of different age cohorts maintain parallel distances from one another (e.g., the chronological age distance[11] between parents and their children remains constant), although the social class mobility of parents and children can diverge markedly.

Whereas both aging and class mobility locate individuals in current social processes (Mannheim [1928], 1952), the irreversibility of aging and cohort flow also ties individuals inevitably to the historical process.

Within a society, age strata and socioeconomic strata are, to be sure, intertwined. Since the particular roles in the complex occupied by persons of a given age are themselves differentially placed in the class hierarchy, that complex of roles can tend to confer a greater or lesser degree of prestige (or deference) upon the age group as a whole. In the United States today, for example, where many older people belong in the lower socioeconomic echelons (with low education and low income), old age is often stereotyped as a life stage carrying low esteem. However, the degree of esteem seems not to inhere in the age stratum per se, since individuals of the same age can have markedly different class positions depending upon what roles they play (or have played in the past). Old age could not in itself confer low prestige upon an Einstein, an Eisenhower, or a Casals.

---

[10] For a summary of the theories of Marx, Weber, the functionalists, and others, see, for example, Lipset (1968). See also Riley, 1971, for a comparison of age and class stratification.

[11] Though the social distance indexed by an age gap of, say, 20 years may have quite different meanings when the parents are at age 65 rather than at age 45.

4 Synopsis of the book

The chapters of this book will explore from several points of view the nature and implications of a sociological theory of age stratification.

Part 1 is a conceptual and methodological introduction that investigates various types of empirical approaches for developing and testing such a theory. Chapter 2 discusses the data used to index the several structural and processual elements in the conceptual model outlined in Chapter 1, and examines the possibilities and problems of interpreting such data (while the numerous biases arising from procedures of sampling, data collection, and analysis that characterize much available research on age are examined in an Appendix at the end of the book). In Chapter 3, Ryder describes the notion of population, pointing to applications of this demographic frame of reference to several problems of concern to sociology.

Before examining (in Part 3) the full complexity of roles and role sequences confronting the differentiated and ever-changing age strata in the population, the chapters in Part 2 treat society segmentally, concentrating respectively upon discrete institutions. This part consists of essays by several different authors that interpret the principles of age stratification in selected fields of sociological inquiry. These chapters test the relevance to particular aspects of the society of a sociological view of age; and they serve, in turn, to revise, specify, and amplify the more general formulations outlined in the other parts of the book.

Part 3 proceeds to specify and exemplify the elements in our conceptual model of age stratification, and to explore their interrelationships. Underlying the discussion of this model in Chapters 10 through 12, are two cross-cutting dimensions that stress respectively:

1. A *microlevel* focus on the individual role or person, versus a *macrolevel* focus on the social system as a whole (role system and population);
2. A *synchronic* (cross-sectional) view that cuts through time at various historical periods, versus a *diachronic* view that traces processes over time.

Thus Chapter 10 views the age strata at given points of time dealing both with the society that contains these strata and with the individual persons who occupy roles and role complexes within these strata. Chapter 11 by Clausen takes a longitudinal perspective, tracing the life course of the individual (or the cohort of individuals) and the sequence of roles through which he passes. Chapter 12 reverts to the societal view, dealing processually with the composite of cohorts as they flow through, affect, and are affected by, the role structure, and with allocation and socialization as processes articulating role structure and cohort flow. This final chapter draws attention to the kinds of imbalance, strain, and deviance that can accrue from the operation of these processes and can sometimes produce shifts both in social structure and in the underlying processes. Thus it brings together, from various parts of the book, diverse strands of the emerging theory of intimate relationship between age stratification and social stability or change.

Works cited in Chapter 1

Benedict, Ruth, 1938. "Continuities and Discontinuities in Cultural Conditioning," *Psychiatry*, 1, pp. 161–167.

Bogue, Donald J., 1969. *Principles of Demography*, New York: Wiley.

Cain, Leonard D., Jr., 1964. "Life Course and Social Structure," in Faris, Robert E. L., editor, *Handbook of Modern Sociology*, Chicago: Rand McNally, pp. 272–309.

Eisenstadt, S. N., 1956. *From Generation to Generation: Age Groups and Social Structure*, Glencoe, Ill.: Free Press.

Hawley, Amos H., 1959. "Population Composition," in Hauser, Philip M., and Otis Dudley Duncan, editors, *The Study of Population*, Chicago: University of Chicago Press, pp. 361–382.

Linton, Ralph, 1942. "Age and Sex Categories," *American Sociological Review*, 7, pp. 589–603.

Lipset, Seymour M., 1968. "Stratification, Social: Social Class," in Sills, David L., editor, *International Encyclopedia of the Social Sciences*, 17 vols., New York: Macmillan and Free Press, 15, pp. 296–315.

Mannheim, Karl (1928), 1952. "The Problem of Generations," in *Essays on the Sociology of Knowledge*, edited and translated by Paul Kecskemeti, London: Routledge and Kegan Paul, pp. 276–322.

Nisbet, Robert A., 1969. *Social Change and History*, New York: Oxford University Press.

Parsons, Talcott, 1942. "Age and Sex in the Social Structure of the United States," *American Sociological Review*, 7, pp. 604–616.

―――――, 1961. "An Outline of the Social System," in Parsons, Talcott, et al., editors, *Theories of Society*, New York: Free Press, pp. 30–79.

―――――, and Edward A. Shils, 1951. "Values, Motives and Systems of Action," in Parsons, Talcott, and Edward A. Shils, editors, *Toward a General Theory of Action*, Cambridge, Mass.: Harvard University Press, pp. 45–275.

Riley, Matilda White, 1963. *Sociological Research, Volume I, A Case Approach*, New York: Harcourt, Brace & World.

―――――, 1971. "Social Gerontology and the Age Stratification of Society," *The Gerontologist*, 11, No. 1, Part 1, pp. 79–87.

―――――, Anne Foner, Beth Hess, and Marcia L. Toby, 1969. "Socialization for the Middle and Later Years," in Goslin, David A., editor, *Handbook of Socialization Theory and Research*, Chicago: Rand McNally, pp. 951–982.

Ryder, Norman B., 1965. "The Cohort as a Concept in the Study of Social Change," *American Sociological Review*, 30, pp. 843–861.

Smelser, Neil J., 1968. *Essays in Sociological Explanation*, Englewood Cliffs. N.J.: Prentice-Hall.

Sorokin, Pitirim A., 1941. *Social and Cultural Dynamics, Vol. IV, Basic Problems, Principles and Methods,* New York: American Book Company.

————, 1959. *Social and Cultural Mobility,* Glencoe, Ill.: Free Press.

Strehler, Bernard L., 1962. *Time, Cells, and Aging,* New York: Academic Press.

2

Interpretation of research on age

IN ASSOCIATION WITH **EDWARD E. NELSON AND BERNICE C. STARR**
WITH A MATHEMATICAL NOTE BY **RICHARD COHN**

Age stratification, cohort flow, and aging are all areas abounding in misapprehensions. In this era of data banks, the accumulation of age-relevant material is far outstripping the development of relevant theory or the application of appropriate methods of analysis and interpretation. Yet the precise form in which any particular set of data is presented and analyzed places certain constraints upon the interpretation that can be made legitimately. And data on the age structure of a society, on the changes in this structure, and on the processes underlying stability and change take diverse forms. Any given set of data is a selection from the full information that is potentially available, at least in principle, to the investigator. It is a partial set, gathered and analyzed in line with a particular objective. The age data used by sociologists (often from other fields, compiled by scholars such as demographers, epidemiologists, psychologists, economists, or public opinion experts) differ widely both in their research objectives and in the methods used for securing and manipulating the material.

This chapter attempts to cut through certain confusions and difficulties of interpreting data on age by starting with elementary examples and applications of well-established research procedures [*further details are noted in the Appendix*], and then by formulating a few general principles that emerge from the general welter, once the nature and limitations of various kinds of data are firmly understood.

THEORETICAL RELEVANCE

Throughout, the emphasis is upon appropriate, in contrast to potentially fallacious, interpretations. If we seem to repeat some rather basic methodological points, we do so because unless the researcher grasps these clearly, he may begin with mistaken assumptions about what his data can tell him.

The chapter will stress the potentialities of analyses in terms of the dimensions set forth in Chapter 1. One dimension involves the interpretation of data on the *structural* elements in our age-specific model in contrast to data on the underlying *processes*. By providing cross-sectional views of the age-related processes, structural data are useful for describing the society at given periods and for describing the changes in this society as the age strata move concurrently over time. Data on processes help to explain particular states, and changes in state, of the age-stratified society. A second dimension that is generally pertinent for interpreting most sets of data concerns the *level* of the social system to which the data refer (cf. Riley, 1963, Volume I, Unit 12): to the society as a whole, to the age stratum (or cohort), or to the individual or role. While structural data, for example, are peculiarly germane to age stratification of the total society, they may also pertain to the composition of a single stratum (or cohort), or to the responses of an individual to his location within a stratum or a cohort. Another dimension of relevance to many analyses concerns the *inclusiveness* of the population to which the data refer: whether to the entire population of a society, within which most inhabitants live out their full life span, or to the selected population of a group or social category (such as members of the labor force, scientists, inmates of an institution); in the latter case, important adjustments of the usual forms of demographic analysis and interpretation are often required (underscoring our sociological definition of people as actors performing in social roles). Above all, the phrasing of interpretations depends upon the central distinction between *societal timing*, as the age strata move concurrently through history, and *cohort timing*, as cohorts enter the society and age—not together—but following one another. [*See Chapter 1 · B · 6.*]

Theory and data   One major source of difficulty in the interpretation of data on age is that many important conceptual distinctions [*as in Chapter 1*], while separable in the abstract, are merged in the empirical reality. The age-specific elements in our model are bonded to the historical, social, or organic elements in the "environment" excluded from the model. Moreover, the usual research difficulty of transpositions between fact and theory is aggravated in sociological analyses of age because of the intractability of certain of our key distinctions. The conceptual distinction between people and roles, for example, is essential to interpretations in terms of our model, since the two undergo differing processes and can be understood only at differing levels of discourse. Yet concrete individuals can be observed in research only as they act in and respond to their particular set of roles. Thus many findings that may appear to focus largely on the people in our model actually reflect the mutual interaction (within the given environment) between certain people and their varied roles. Even the newborn infant, as Clausen suggests in Chapter 11, starts out, not simply as an organism or a person, but as a "bundle of statuses."

Because of this coalescence in the data of the discrete elements in our model, Chapter 2 substitutes for the conceptual terminology of Chapter 1 a new terminology that refers to empirically observed patterns and regularities. We shall now speak, for example, of the life-course differences (Ld) of specific cohorts of individuals, in recognition of the fact that the concrete patterns of lifetime change (or stability) observed in research do not result simply from the idealized process of aging ($P2$) or from the historical era marked by the birthdate of the cohort (one aspect of $P1$). Instead, the specific individuals age in the way they do as the result of many additional factors, including their physical environment and the particular sequence of roles in which they happened to take part.

Thus the challenge to the investigator is to find data and means of interpreting them that will permit inferences from the confusion of observed facts to the conceptually distinct elements. In a research area beset by difficulties (where, for example, time is an essential ingredient, and where the key variable—age—is not amenable to experimental control), the present chapter can offer only selected illustrations.

Many of our illustrations seem to focus especially on people—on the population of actors—viewed in cross section or in a sequence of cross sections. In some parts of the discussion, examples deal exclusively with age-related *characteristics* of people, disregarding the equally important data on the *numbers* of component individuals who contribute their differential characteristics to the society as a whole. Selection of certain aspects of the model for illustration is not intended, of course, to underemphasize the importance of other aspects.

Roles, for example, to which less methodological heed has been paid, require attention equal to that devoted in our present discussion to people. Yet data that refer to the conjunction of people and roles allow indirect inferences about each one. Indirectly, a great deal of information can be inferred about the role structure from the data about particular populations as discussed here. Indirect inferences from population data do, of course, require certain assumptions as to the correspondence between normative expectations and behavioral enactment. For most roles, a range of permissible performances is defined, although the boundary distinguishing deviance from adequacy may be unclear. Unless some disturbance develops in the equilibrium of the social system,[1] the researcher, or even the members of the system, typically cannot draw this boundary. Thus, within the range of role behaviors known or assumed to be permitted, the knowledge provided by population data shows which performances actually are typical. For many purposes the actual performances of individuals at given ages[2] are more useful indicators of normative patterns than are explicitly stated role prescriptions. For example, actual labor force participation rates show the average age of entry to be considerably higher than the permitted minimum, or the average age of withdrawal to be well below the widely specified retirement age of 65. Moreover, many of the factors grossly interpreted as historical or environmental influences upon the life course of individuals or cohorts (loosely described in Section 4 as "cohort effects" or "period effects" without identification of the age-related role

[1] On the general methodological principle that a slight disturbance in a system is sometimes necessary to reveal the workings of the system, see, for example, Riley (1963, Volume I, pp. 65–66).

[2] Defined in Chapter 10 as factual criteria for role incumbency.

mechanisms involved) are undoubtedly specifiable as age criteria that define aspects of the environing structure of social roles.

Inferences about *people,* as well as those about roles, are of course also indirect when drawn from a single set of concrete data. Hence much attention will be paid to studying age-specific aspects of populations under widely varying times and conditions.

There are also various direct sources of potential information about age as an ingredient of the role structure and about the role processes of allocation and socialization that articulate people and roles [*see Chapters 10 and 12*]. For example, analyses of legislation can show ages at which voting or labor force participation are permitted, or at which military service may be required. Analysis of pension agreements, or of the openings available in the files of employment agencies, can indicate the approximate ages of exit from the labor force or the maximum ages for rehiring. Analysis of mass media content can suggest age-related norms of various kinds. Much information can be gleaned also from new research that focuses on norms and definitions affecting persons at different ages—although such new research cannot reach into the past beyond the recollection of respondents still alive today.

Using selected examples from the many possible types of data, then, the first two sections of this chapter deal with the empirical implications of the heuristic distinction in our conceptual model [*Chapter 1*] between structural and processual elements.[3] Section 1 outlines uses of data to describe the structural (or more precisely, the cross-sectional) elements: the differing numbers and characteristics of the people (or roles) in the age strata (called Sd) at given periods of observation, and the structural changes occurring in sequential periods (Pd). Section 2 outlines uses of data to describe the processual elements underlying this structure: the life-course patterns (Ld) of particular cohorts and the differences in these patterns (Cd) among successive cohorts with differing dates of birth. Section 3, which becomes less technical and more speculative than previous sections, suggests, both by example and in more formal terms, certain relationships between data on the age-related processes outlined in Section 2 and data on societal structure and change outlined in Section 1. Finally, Section 4 discusses some special possibilities and problems of relating empirical findings on age to

---

[3] The terms Sd, Pd, Ld, and Cd are used throughout to indicate which comparisons are being made, whether or not the particular data reveal differences or lack of differences.

Structural elements and change	{ Age strata differences at a given point in time	Sd
	Period differences across two or more periods of time	Pd
Process	{ Life course differences (within a given cohort)	Ld
	Cohort differences (age-by-age comparison among cohorts)	Cd

history and the environment [*as defined in Chapter 1, section 2*], and of analyzing connections between cohort flow and social change.

1 *Structural elements and changes*

See Chapter 1, Sections 1 · A · 1 and 1 · A · 2 and Chapter 10

Cross-sectional data (also called period data or synchronic data) are essential for understanding the age stratification of society and the stabilities and changes in these strata over time. In this section, we shall outline various forms in which data are used to represent empirically the two major structural elements in the population: element 1, the age strata and element 2, the characteristics of these strata. In interpreting such data, however, we recognize that elements 1 and 2 (referring to people) are empirically observed only in their conjunction with the given role structure (elements 3 and 4) in the particular situation.

> Data referring to element 1 show the *size* of (or number of people in) each of the several strata. These data are sometimes separated into substrata (by sex, for example) according to the *kinds* (and numbers) of people of which the several strata are composed.
>
> Data referring to element 2 show the proportions of people in the several strata who have a particular *characteristic* (or express a certain attitude or behave in a certain way).[4]

Both sets of data can be analyzed to compare strata, hence to observe *differences or lack of differences among age strata* (called Sd) at a given period of observation. Such analysis is used to index the age structure of a population.

In addition, comparisons of age-specific cross-sectional data across two or more periods of observation indicate *period differences* (called Pd).[5] Analysis of either structural element—size or characteristics of strata—at different time periods shows shifts or stabilities in the age structure. These data assume special vitality as a basis for studying social change.

Seemingly simple data can be used to suggest various aspects of the structural elements and changes. A few elementary examples will illustrate the nature of the data, the diversity of information that can be extracted, and the potential of period data for describing the age structure and indicating structural changes. These examples review certain rudiments of research design in application to our special subject matter.

[4] Certain characteristics may be treated, depending upon the research objective, either as constitutive of the strata or as the focus for comparison among strata, as discussed below.
[5] Note: The expressions Sd and Pd include those patterns in which the differences may be equal to zero.

Table 2 · 1 illustrates data that can be referred conceptually to element 1. The table shows the absolute size of age strata in the United States, the relative size of the several strata, and the size of strata for two subpopulations (males and females). All these measures can be compared at two points in time (1960 and 1950) to discover period differences. The age-specific data, both absolute numbers and percentages, refer to all three system levels: the distribution shows the picture for the society as a whole, the number in a given age category refers to the stratum, individuals can be analyzed by age as an index of location within a stratum. However, the totals refer only to the society (or to each subpopulation) as a whole.

Absolute size   The use of absolute numbers to measure the sizes of the several age strata for the United States is shown in column 5. Absolute size is relevant to such questions as: What is the fit between the size of particular age strata and the number of appropriate role opportunities available? For example, are there enough places in school to match the absolute number of school-age children? What is the impact of a large (or small) stratum on the role structure? Thus measures of absolute size relate to our concern with the age-specific "supply" and "demand" for role players, and with the strains and potential changes resulting from imbalances between supply and demand [*see Chapter 10 · 4*].

Changes over time in the sizes of particular strata can be seen by compar-

TABLE 2 · 1   *Age of United States population, 1960 and 1950*

In millions

Age	Males N (1)	Males % (2)	Females N (3)	Females % (4)	Total N (5)	Total % (6)
1960						
0–19	(34.9)	40	(33.8)	37	(68.7)	39
20–44	(27.9)	32	(29.4)	33	(57.3)	32
45–64	(17.7)	20	(18.5)	20	(36.2)	20
65+	(7.1)	8	(8.8)	10	(15.9)	9
Total (as percentage base)	(87.6)	100	(90.5)	100	(178.1)	100
1950						
0–19	(25.9)	35	(25.3)	33	(51.2)	34
20–44	(27.3)	37	(28.7)	38	(56.0)	38
45–64	(15.0)	20	(15.2)	20	(30.2)	20
65+	(5.7)	8	(6.4)	9	(12.1)	8
Total (as percentage base)	(73.9)	100	(75.6)	100	(149.5)	100

Source: 1960 Census of Population, Vol. I, Part 1, Table 158, pp. 359–360 (adapted).

ing 1950 with 1960 in column 5. For example, the stratum aged 0–19 grew from 51.2 million to 68.7 million, whereas the stratum aged 20–44 barely increased at all. While this table shows that the number of people 65 and over increased from 12.1 million to 15.9 million in that decade, another set of data for several periods (and wider intervals between periods) indicates even more dramatically that the number of people in that stratum has increased sharply since 1900; see Figure 2 · 1.

Relative size Proportional measures can be used to index the size of one stratum relative to other strata or to the population as a whole. In column 6 of Table 2 · 1, for example, the age distribution of the United States is shown in percentages, rather than in absolute frequencies, thus focusing on the *share* of the total population located in each stratum. This focus is achieved by disregarding the total size of the population (treating it always

FIGURE 2 · 1   *Growth of United States population 65 and over*

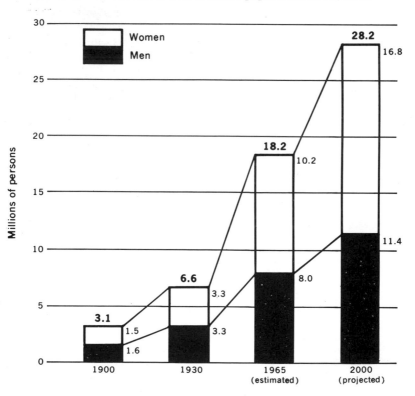

Source: United States Administration on Aging, January, 1966; based on data from **United States** Bureau of the Census.

as 100). Again, period differences are apparent. A comparison of the percentages for 1950 and 1960, by disregarding the general increase for the population as a whole, points to the relative stability of the 45–64 stratum and to the relative decline in the 20–44 stratum. The utility of proportional measures is illustrated by the studies (see, e.g., Kiser, 1962; Rosset, 1964) of the "aging" of human populations [*compare Chapter 10 · 2*], which are based on the proportion of the population that is old (65 and over, for example). Thus measures of relative size permit examination of such issues as the actual or potential contributions of particular age strata to phenomena in the society as a whole, or the effects of varying size of strata on complementary or interdependent role relationships.

Figure 2 · 2 dramatizes the differing results obtained from absolute as compared with relative data [*similar to Figure 10 · 2 in Chapter 10*].

Summary measures Various types of summary measures can be derived from either the absolute or the proportional data to refer to the society as a whole. One such measure, which collapses a great deal of information, is the median age. The median can be compared at different time periods (for 1950 and 1960 in Table 2 · 1), or for several societies. Another widely used measure is the dependency ratio (see, e.g., Bogue, 1969, pp. 154–156). This ratio is obtained in several ways, as by taking the ratio of the old (or the young, or of the old and young combined) over those in the middle years. Thus a single figure can be derived to describe the societal balance between those in their productive middle years and those who are not economically active. One use of this measure has been to test hypotheses about its relationship to industrialization and other factors in a series of countries (see, e.g., Rosset, 1964).

Composition Similar sets of data can be used to describe the kinds of people of which the age strata are composed. In Table 2 · 1, for example, the sex composition is shown in columns 1 through 4. Here again the absolute figures (columns 1 and 3) show the numbers of men and women in the several strata, and the relative (percentage) figures (columns 2 and 4) highlight the differences between males and females in their respective shares of the very young and the very old.

Whether absolute or relative numbers are used, composition is basic to age stratification from two points of view. First, the society may be viewed as divided into subpopulations according to any given compositional characteristic (such as sex, race, or country of birth), in order to examine the age strata within each subpopulation separately. Second, and often by using the same data, particular age strata may be viewed as divided into substrata according to the compositional characteristics, in order to examine the composition of the strata. Here at the outset we note that compositional data may be used *descriptively,* from either point of view. In later sections, we shall empha-

FIGURE 2·2 *Age distribution of the white population, United States, 1830–1950*

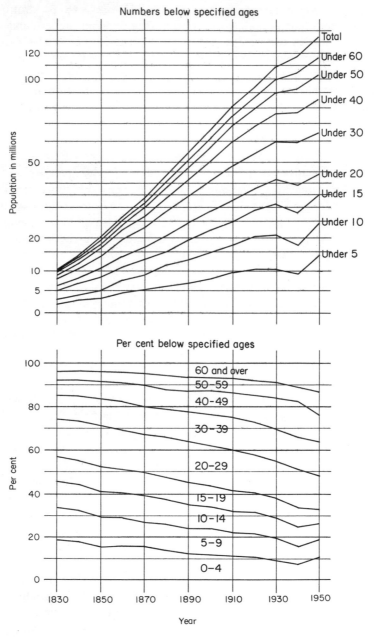

Numbers below specified ages

Per cent below specified ages

Source: Taeuber and Taeuber, 1958, p. 28.

size the utility for many *analyses* of taking into account both what kinds of people, and how many of each kind, compose the age strata.

Data on compositional characteristics of the strata are often simplified through visual presentation in the form of age pyramids, as in Figure 2 · 3, which shows the absolute sizes of the age strata for males and females at two time periods. A variety of such pyramids appears later in the book. (See also Volume I, Exhibit 2 · 7, pp. 22–23.)

1 · B CHARACTERISTICS OF STRATA

When the conceptual model directs attention to the characteristics (element 2), rather than the size (or composition) of the strata, the analysis and presentation of data take a different form. In Table 2 · 2, for example, the objective is to examine one selected characteristic of the age strata, participation in the labor force. Here the most useful figures are those in column 2, which hold constant the sizes of the strata in order to focus on the proportion of males in each stratum who participate in the labor force. With the percentages based on the age categories (and running across the rows[6])—in contrast to Table 2 · 1, where the percentages were based on the subpopulations—age is no longer a dependent variable, but has now become the independent variable. The figures, by disregarding the size of the strata, constitute age-specific rates (in this instance, the widely used labor force participation rate). In this form, they provide an essential tool for comparing age strata and for uncovering age-related similarities and differences in capacities, orientations, performance, and many other characteristics.

However, let us note one caveat. The control of size in analyzing the characteristics of the strata (or cohorts) can obscure the key role that size can often play. Therefore, in any full analysis, the focus on characteristics is complemented by an analysis of differences, or similarities, in the sizes of strata (or in the size of a given cohort over its life course).

Summary measures Not all data on characteristics are simple percentages, as in Table 2 · 2. A variety of procedures (some too complex to be readily comprehensible) are used to summarize information on characteristics, to allow wider scope for generalization through comparisons of many societies or of many time periods. Table 2 · 3 illustrates summary measures (Bogue, 1969, pp. 120–122) for comparing two countries in respect to their age-specific fertility rates (number of births per 1,000 women in each stratum). One measure, the rate differences, subtracts one set of rates from the other set. A second measure converts these differences into ratios, in order to show the relative differences. Still another measure for each country (not shown) subtracts each of the age-specific fertility rates from the average of all

[6] Whether rows or columns are used for any particular set of percentages is, of course, purely a matter of convention.

FIGURE 2 · 3 *Population of the United States, by single years of age and sex: 1960 and 1950*

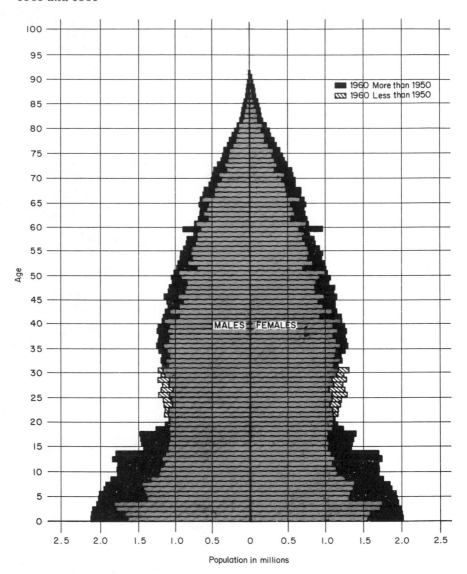

Population in millions

Source: 1960 Census of Population, Vol. I, Part 1, Fig. 47, p. S37.

TABLE 2 · 2 *Labor force participation of United States males, 1960 and 1950*

In millions

Age	In labor force N (1)	% (2)	Not in labor force N (3)	% (4)	Total (as percentage base) N (5)
1960					
14–19	(3.0)	38	(5.0)	62	(8.0)
20–44	(26.3)	94	(1.6)	6	(27.9)
45–64	(15.6)	89	(1.9)	11	(17.5)
65+	(2.3)	32	(5.0)	68	(7.3)
Total	(47.2)	78	(13.5)	22	(60.7)
1950					
14–19	(2.5)	40	(3.8)	60	(6.3)
20–44	(25.1)	91	(2.4)	9	(27.5)
45–64	(13.3)	89	(1.7)	11	(15.0)
65+	(2.3)	40	(3.4)	60	(5.7)
Total	(43.2)	79	(11.3)	21	(54.5)

Source: 1960 Census of Population, Vol. I, Part 1, Table 195, p. 499 (adapted).

TABLE 2 · 3 *Illustrative computation of differences and relative differences between schedules of fertility rates: El Salvador, 1961, and Spain, 1960*

Age	Age-specific birth rates Spain (1)	El Salvador (2)	Differences (3)[a]	Relative difference (4)[b]
Total 15–49 years	82.7	210.5	127.8	155
15–19 years	9.1	143.0	133.9	1471
20–24 years	104.7	323.3	218.6	209
25–29 years	185.2	316.6	131.4	71
30–34 years	140.2	264.8	124.6	89
35–39 years	78.7	188.9	110.2	140
40–44 years	28.8	69.9	41.1	143
45–49 years	3.1	16.8	13.7	442

[a] Column (3) equals column (2) minus column (1).
[b] Column (4) equals column (3) divided by column (1) times 100.
Source: Bogue, 1969, p. 121.

rates, thus showing the differing age patterns for each country after the general fertility level is controlled.[7]

Compositional analysis of characteristics However a characteristic of the age strata may be measured, the analysis often takes into account the

[7] Carl-Gunnar Janson has suggested in a personal communication that another example to illustrate the many possibilities of age variables in describing social systems may lie in factor analytical studies of spatial urban structure. Together with family household variables they, as items, build up family cycle variables (see, e.g., Sweetser, 1965).

numbers and kinds of people of which the strata are composed. Thus although Table 2 · 2 does not utilize compositional analysis, it might do so by subdividing each age stratum by sex or by color, for example, to allow comparison of the age patterns of labor force participation between males and females, or between blacks and whites. Here the compositional analysis would hold constant the differing numbers of males and females (or of blacks and whites) in the several strata, as a means of focusing on age-specific differences in selected characteristics, attitudes, or behavior (compare Section 4 · B of this chapter).

A variable is defined as compositional, as we have said, when it is employed to divide age strata into substrata. Whether any given property is treated as a compositional variable (referring to element 1) or as an age-related characteristic (referring to element 2) depends on the focus of the analysis. Most properties (such as sex, labor force status, fertility in a given year) may be treated either as a subdivision of the strata, or as a characteristic to be examined in relation to age. But these alternative ways of treating the property affect both the nature and the interpretation of the analysis. Table 2 · 1, for example, treats sex as a compositional variable. That is, by dividing the population into male and female subsets, it holds the sex variable constant, focusing on the dependent variable (size of strata in this exhibit) for each sex separately. For other purposes, however, these same data could be reanalyzed (in Table 2 · 1 by percentaging in the other direction) to treat sex as a characteristic proportional to each stratum. This reanalysis would highlight the predominance of women over men in the older, but not in the youngest, strata—a finding of great import for many aspects of age stratification today. Table 2 · 2 could be repercentaged to control labor force status as a compositional variable, in order to examine the sizes of the age strata within the respective subsets of participants and nonparticipants in the labor force.

The age pyramid, as employed in Figure 2 · 4, allows visual inspection of the relationship between age and two other properties—both sex and labor force participation in this example. Even though absolute numbers are used, simply by inspection one can analyze the data in various ways. For example, both sex and labor force status can be treated as cross-classified compositional variables, in order to focus on the sizes of the age strata in each of four subpopulations. Or the labor force participation rate can be viewed as a characteristic of the several age strata, but *within* each sex category (that is, with sex composition controlled).

Total rates　In an analysis of the characteristics of strata, a rate for the total population (or the total of each subpopulation) can be derived in alternative ways: either by averaging the age-specific rates or by computing a crude total rate from the sums of the absolute numbers (as in Table 2 · 2). The

FIGURE 2·4 *Labor force status of persons 14 to 74 years old, by single years of age and sex, 1950*

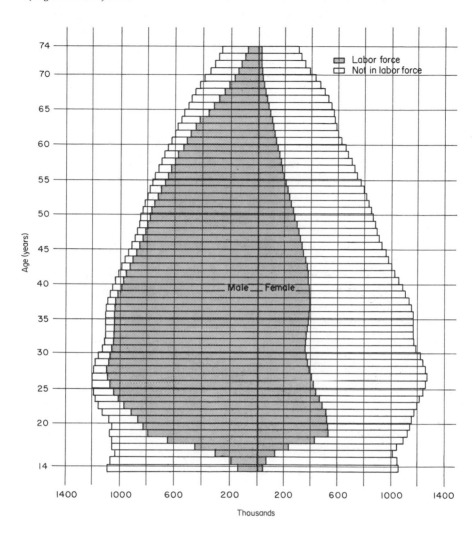

Source: Taeuber and Taeuber, 1958, p. 214.

crude rate is, in effect, an average of the age-specific rates *weighted* by the sizes of the several strata. When the crude rate is used, an increase over time in the total crime rate, for example, might be produced simply by an increasing proportion of the population who are young—without any increase in the extent to which young people themselves commit crimes. Similarly, an increase in the crude total rate of chronic illness might result from an increasing proportion of the population who are old, without a concomitant increase in the prevalence of chronic illness in any particular age stratum.

Either these total rates or the age-specific rates can be compared over two or more periods in order to observe structural change from one period to another (Pd). Column 2 of Table 2 · 2, for example, shows that the labor force participation rate for men in one stratum, those over 65, fell from 40 to 32 per cent between 1950 and 1960, although the crude total rate for all age categories combined showed little change (79 as compared with 78 per cent).

In such period comparisons, the different methods of computing the total rates can sometimes have quite different meanings, both of which may be useful for particular purposes. The crude totals reflect a composite of the period changes in the rates for each stratum, weighted by any changes in the sizes of the strata; whereas the age-specific totals reflect only the period changes in the rates, with any changes in the sizes of the strata held constant. In either case, the total rate refers to the population as a whole, and no longer to particular strata. Thus an increase in the total rate could result either from consistent increases in all age strata, or from increases in certain strata that are partially offset by decreases in other strata.

Our purpose in explicating this set of deceptively simple tables has been twofold. First, to outline certain rudimentary tools for a distinctively sociological analysis of age as a component of the changing society; and second, to lay groundwork for the task, to which we now turn, of examining the processual elements that fit together to produce the societal structure.

2 *Processes*

See Chapter 1, Sections 1 · B · 1 and 1 · B · 2; and Chapter 3 by Ryder

Diachronic data that trace the life course of successive cohorts are essential for understanding the special regularities and rhythms in the flow of people who form the age-stratified society. In contrast to data referring to societal timing (as in the Pd noted in Section 1), we now turn to data referring to cohort timing—that is, to data used in various forms to represent empirically the processes that underlie the age structure of the populations. [*See Chapter 1, Section 1.*] Among the four main sets of *processes* conceptualized in our model, we shall deal especially with $P1$, cohort succession and survival, and

P2, aging (or life-course changes) of members of particular cohorts.[8] Many of the same principles could also be applied to P3, allocation, and P4, socialization.

When P1 is the focus of interest, two types of information can be used for each of a *series of cohorts:* first, its date of birth (or entry into a group or system), which indexes the unique period of history through which the cohort survives; and second, its size and composition at time of birth and at consecutive ages until the entire cohort is dissolved through the death of all its members.

When P2 is the focus of interest, the data used may show either the life-course patterns of *individuals* within given cohorts; or, for *given cohorts,* the proportions of members who, at consecutive ages, have certain characteristics. The aging process is conceived here [*see Chapter 1*] as including social, as well as biological, factors, although specific analyses may attempt to disentangle the two.

As will become apparent in our discussion, diachronic *data* cannot reflect these processes directly but can permit two sets of comparisons of cohort size, composition, or characteristics: first, comparisons at differing ages over the life course *within* a cohort (Ld); and second, age-by-age comparisons *among* cohorts (Cd). In this section, we shall point to a number of ways in which such comparisons can aid the search for understanding of these underlying processes of cohort flow and aging.

2 · A COHORT SUCCESSION AND SURVIVAL

Of the two sets of postulated processes, the cohort processes (P1) are more complex, since they refer not only to each single cohort of individuals as they undergo the aging process (P2), but also to the overall succession of cohorts that comprise the changing society. Both sets, which extend over time, can be viewed in cross section at selected periods of observation to reveal the structural elements and changes discussed in Section 1. [*See Figure 1 · 3 in Chapter 1.*] The two structural elements, the size or composition of the age strata and the characteristics of these strata, are both affected by the cohort processes. [*See Figure 1 · 2 in Chapter 1 and Chapter 12 · 1.*]

(1) *Size of strata* Let us start with the three fundamental demographic processes determining size: natality (or the number of persons born at each successive point or interval of time), mortality (or conversely, survival), and migration in or out of the population. The schematic outline in Table 2 · 4 can be used to trace these processes as they produce the numbers of people in the several age strata at a particular period of observation. (In this

[8] As with data referring to structural elements, empirical observations of cohorts take as given the age-specific role structure and its changes.

TABLE 2 · 4 *Cohort processes underlying the* size *of selected age strata*[a]

(Age in parentheses)

P (*period of observation*)

C (*date of birth*)	1900	1920	1940	1960	1980	2000	2020
1940[b]			(0)	(20) 2.2	(40)	(60)	(80)
1920		(0)	(20)	(40) 2.4	(60)	(80)	
1900	(0)	(20)	(40)	(60) 1.5	(80)		

a United States, 1960, single years of age in millions.
b More precisely, this date (and each of the others in comparable fashion) should be 1939–1940, since those aged 20 at the date of Census-taking in 1960 would be drawn from both of these cohorts.
Source: 1960 Census of Population, Vol. I, Part 1, p. 349 (adapted).

example, which shows selected strata only, the period of observation is 1960, and it is assumed that a new cohort is born each year, though the interval is arbitrary.)

We can think of the processes as starting with *natality*. Thus the data for each cohort will show, along with the date of birth which identifies the cohort, the number who were born.

Natality can, of course, be traced back to the earlier set of processes affecting the *parental* cohorts: their ages of marriage, fertility, and child spacing.

If it could be assumed that all the members of each cohort survived together and died at the same time (and if nobody moved in or out of the country), then the sizes of the age strata at the period of observation (1960) would be entirely determined by natality. A cross section of the population would simply include the set of cohorts already born and still surviving, each a year younger than its predecessor (if the full set were shown in the diagram), and each with its respective size. The differences among age strata (Sd) would be a direct reflection of the difference in natality among the several cohorts.

In fact, of course, this oversimplified picture must be modified because the size of each cohort does not remain constant over the life course but changes, primarily as the result of *mortality*. Every year some members die, so that fewer and fewer members survive. Each cohort has its distinctive pattern of survival. Thus at a given period the sizes of the several strata depend not only upon natality, but also upon the age-specific survival rates of the respective cohorts. Further modifications must also be made because each cohort expands and contracts somewhat over its life course through (external) *migration,* as some individuals move in or out of the society.[9]

(2) *Composition of strata*   Not only the size but also the composition of the age strata reflects the distinctive demographic processes undergone by successive cohorts. The composition of cohorts at birth may differ from one another because of the *differential* fertility patterns of the parents (as, for example, between whites and nonwhites, Catholics and non-Catholics, or urban and rural residents). Within a cohort, moreover, mortality and migration differentially select members, with the result that differing kinds of people do not have equal propensities to enter (through immigration) or leave (through emigration or death) the cohort at consecutive ages. Mortality rates tend to differ, for example, by sex, race, occupational level, or marital status. (See Volume I, Chapter 2 · 3). Those subpopulations having the lower mortality rates (such as females, whites, or members of high status occupations) will, then, constitute increasingly high proportions of the successively older age strata.

Differential fertility, mortality, and migration affect the composition of the cross-sectional age strata in still another way, because these differentials, rather than remaining constant, may *vary* over time. In the United States in recent decades, for example, the age-specific mortality differentials by geographical region and by race have declined, while those by sex have increased. In like manner, changing patterns of immigration have affected the proportions of foreign-born in the age strata. Thus, in 1960, about one in five persons aged 65 and over was foreign-born, in contrast to only one in twenty for the United States as a whole (see Volume I, Chapters 2 · 1 · e and 5 · 1 · c). Such changes over time produce marked differences among the kinds of people who compose the several age strata at given periods of time.

(3) *Characteristics of strata*   Cohort processes can influence the cross-sectional age strata in respect to their characteristics as well as their size, because mortality and migration are selective, and also because successive cohorts are born at different points in history. For example, more recent cohorts are more likely than those born earlier to have been born in a city, to have graduated from high school, or to have other characteristics associated with long-term trends toward industrialization or urbanization. However, this connection between cohort succession and the characteristics of strata is mediated through the differential effects of history on still another process— aging (P2); accordingly we shall defer examination of this complex connection until Section 3, after we have considered the data for analysis of aging.

---

[9] Such modifications become especially necessary if the research case is some subsystem (such as a city or a hospital), other than the total society.

In terms of our conceptual model, the characteristics (element 2) of each age stratum at a given period of observation depend, not only upon the size and composition and on the unique history of the respective cohort (P1), but also on the current stage of the cohort members in the aging process (P2). [*See Chapter 11 by Clausen and Figure 1 · 2 in Chapter 1.*] Data relevant to this aging process reflect the progress of individuals over their own lifetime. This progress will, of course, vary somewhat for different cohorts of individuals as they encounter the particular role sequences and the particular environmental events and conditions of the differing eras in which they live.

The rows in the schematic diagram shown in Table 2 · 5 can be used to trace the empirically observed life course patterns (*Ld*) of selected cohorts. Thus the figures for the cohort born in 1900, for example, indicate the proportions having the given characteristic at the consecutive ages 20, 40, and 60. The form of presentation shown in Table 2 · 5 (already suggested in Table 2 · 4, and to be described more fully later as a basis for cohort analysis) is only one of many possible forms used for studying sets of individuals as they age. These forms can be classified on such dimensions as: whether or not the data reflect individual shifts within the cohort; whether the data refer to just one cohort or to several cohorts (so that differences in life-course patterns among cohorts can be observed); or whether or not the numbers of people (size) of the cohort and the interrelated compositional factors are held constant in the analysis of the characteristics of interest.

TABLE 2 · 5   *Characteristics of successive cohorts*

Fictitious figures show proportions of persons in each stratum having a given characteristic

(Age in parentheses)

			P (*period of observation*)			
C (*date of birth*)	1900	1920	1940	1960	1980	2000
1940				(20) 50	(40) 50	(60) 50
1920			(20) 40	(40) 40	(60) 40	
1900		(20) 30	(40) 30	(60) 30		
1880	(20) 20	(40) 20	(60) 20			

(1) *Individual shifts*   When the members of a cohort[10] are to be studied over their life course (or over some portion of it), it is not ordinarily feasible to maintain continuous observation. Instead, the researcher usually makes observations at successive points in time, drawing inferences about how the individuals age during the intervening intervals.[11]

Two main types of data can be used at these successive points in time: either aggregate data for all individuals in the cohort (in the sequence-of-cross-sections design), or data that trace the *same* individuals from one time to the next (in the panel or longitudinal design).[12] With the first type of data it is possible to observe only net shifts for the cohort as a whole. Table 2·5, which illustrates aggregate data of this type, shows only that there is no net change in a cohort over its life course; it does not show whether some individuals have shifted in one direction while other individuals have shifted in the other direction (shifts that, in this example, would have to counteract one another completely). This fuller picture of the "turnover" or shifting of individuals within the cohort can be observed only in the second type of data, through panel (or longitudinal) analysis that maintains the identity of the same individuals over time.

Data on internal shifting of individuals within the cohort can reveal changes at two system levels. Such data are often essential for an understanding of the ways in which *individuals* change over their life course, as they may switch political party allegiance, for example, or as individual women may move in and out of the labor force. At the *cohort* level also, information on the internal rearrangements of individuals may sometimes be useful. Thus two cohorts might show the same net shifts in income between age 20 and 30; but intracohort analysis might distinguish clearly between one cohort in which the income of nearly all individuals remained the same or went up, and a second cohort in which rises in income for a great many individuals were counterbalanced by drops in income for many other individuals (see Riley, 1963, Volume II, pp. 134–135).

As a further means of specifying the nature of such internal changes, mathematical models can be developed. One widely applied model is stochastic (probabilistic), utilizing a Markov process in which the transition probabilities

[10] Much of this discussion is equally applicable to data based on samples or on complete counts.

[11] A sometimes satisfactory alternative to study of individuals at successive time periods is to ask individuals for self-reports of past events or attitudes. Data on changes of residence, for example, are often gathered in this manner (Volume I, Chapter 6·C·2·c; see also Back and Bourque, 1970). But, as Clausen points out in Chapter 11, the tendency of individuals to reconstruct their past in the light of subsequent experiences imposes serious limitations on the purposes for which the retrospective longitudinal design is useful.

[12] See, for example, Riley (1963, Volume I, pp. 555–559; 560–561). Of course, not all panel or longitudinal studies are based upon cohorts of individuals who, as in the present discussion, are of similar age.

of moving from one to another of a set of specified states are defined for members of a closed population [*compare Chapter 3 · 3 by Ryder*].[13] As Coleman (1964, pp. 103–188) points out, however, this model assumes that change takes place at discrete points in time. For example, the model might be appropriate to an analysis of voting shifts in presidential election years. Though examples of discrete-time changes are to be found, many—perhaps even most—types of change are more appropriately conceived as occurring continuously. Thus various forms of migration, or shifts in attitudes toward political issues, may occur continuously through a period of time. For such processes, Coleman has proposed a continuous-time model to allow analysis of continual transitions between two or more specific states.

Despite the obvious advantages of data or models that do reflect internal shifts within the cohort, these advantages apply especially to analysis of certain kinds of characteristics: namely, to those characteristics that are *reversible* over the life course of the individual. In studies of irreversible characteristics—on which individuals do not change[14] or change in one direction only—the net shifts tend to approximate the gross shifts. For irreversible characteristics, then, the complexities of panel analysis or other designs for studying intracohort shifts can usually be avoided; however, even here it is necessary to control for those factors that may selectively change the composition of a cohort over its life course.[15]

Many age-related characteristics are irreversible in this sense.[16] Some are single events, such as college attendance, ever having married, birth of first child, or dying. Others may *cumulate* or change, but in one direction only, as, for example, number of children ever born, or number of years of schooling. Still others may be logically reversible but known empirically to be largely unidirectional (at least for major segments of the life course). Thus certain organic functions may deteriorate but seldom or never improve with aging. Or individual commitment to a political party may be known, on the basis of prior research, to tend toward increase rather than decrease over time.

(2) *Single versus multiple cohorts*   Studies of the aging process also differ according to the number of cohorts examined. Many longitudinal studies

[13] For an application of this model by Lazarsfeld, see Riley (1963, Volume I, pp. 520–530, 558–561); see also Goodman (1962).

[14] Demographers frequently distinguish a category of characteristics that are "stationary" or "fixed" over the full life course, such as sex or color; and the composition of a cohort is often demographically defined in terms of such stationary characteristics. [*See Section 2 in Chapter 3 by Ryder.*]

[15] Note that the Coleman model described above assumes a closed system in which the same individuals are present at the successive periods of observation.

[16] Clearly, whether an event defines a reversible or irreversible characteristic may vary. Thus many reversible *current* statuses, such as being married or being in the labor force, become irreversible once they are referred to the individual's *past* as having occurred or not.

refer only to a single cohort. As such, they may provide detailed information about the life course of that particular set of individuals. Yet they have severe limitations. The particular cohort examined may be atypical, in size and composition, or in historical and environmental background. Thus, for example, the early experiences of the Depression cohort or the size of the baby boom cohort following World War II may constitute a unique condition affecting the life-course patterns of persons born in those particular periods. Or the aging of an earlier cohort with a high proportion of foreign-born may differ in important aspects from that of more recent, largely native-born, cohorts. It is only by comparing cohorts from different times and places and under varied conditions that one can begin to generalize about life-course patterns. And it is only by comparing a sequence of cohorts that one can contrast and explain the differences in life-course patterns from one cohort to the next (Cd) within a single society.

2 · C COHORT ANALYSIS

Studies that compare the life-course patterns of one or more successive cohorts are often referred to as "cohort analyses," in contrast to the "period analyses" described in Section 1. A cohort analysis has the special property of allowing simultaneous examination of life-course differences (Ld) and differences among cohorts (Cd), thus helping to map the complicated interrelationship between the two.[17] Moreover, cohort analysis holds great promise for the sociologist who would understand how the consecutive cohorts, each one lagging behind its predecessor in the process of aging, all fit together to form the changing structure of the society. [*See Section 3 and, for a fuller discussion, Chapter 12.*]

　　(1) *The form of cohort analysis*　　Table 2 · 5 is a simplified example of a cohort analysis.[18] The patterns associated with the life course of each cohort (Ld) are observed by reading across each row. In these fictitious data (which show percentages having a given characteristic), there are no changes across the rows. By comparing several rows, one can also observe Cd—the similarities and differences in the ways the various cohorts behave over their respective lifetimes. (Since each cohort starts at a different date, differences among rows are observed by reading along the diagonals from lower left to upper right, so as to compare cohorts when they are at similar ages.) Cohorts can differ from one another in a great variety of ways: in the shape of their life-course patterns, for example, or the rates at which they change with aging. In this simplified example, the age patterns for the several cohorts have clearly

[17] Note: The expressions Ld and Cd (like Sd and Pd) include those patterns in which the differences may be equal to zero.
[18] Of the various ways of presenting such data, the one generally used in this book corresponds visually to the cohort diagram, Figure 1 · 3, in Chapter 1.

TABLE 2 · 6 *A period analysis of death rates[a] from all forms of tuberculosis: for males, Massachusetts, 1880–1950[b]*

Age group	Year of death							
	1880	1890	1900	1910	1920	1930	1940	1950
0–4	760[c]	578	309	209	108	41	10	4
5–9	43	49	31	21	24	11	2	1
10–19	126	115	90	63	49	21	6	1
20–29	444	361	288	207	149	81	36	7
30–39	378	368	296	253	164	115	55	25
40–49	364	336	253	253	175	118	86	42
50–59	366	325	267	252	171	127	95	69
60–69	475	346	304	246	172	95	108	87

[a] Rates are annual death rates per 100,000 male population.
[b] Data from Frost (1939) and Pope and Gordon (1955).
[c] Rates for the cohort of 1875 are italicized.
Source: MacMahon et al., 1960, p. 89.

apparent differences and similarities. They *differ* in general level: at the starting age (which happens to be 20) each more recent cohort is increasingly likely to have the characteristic in question. But beyond the starting age, the age patterns of all cohorts are *alike* in their stability.

A technical point that must be made clear at the onset is that while such an analysis can yield distinctive results that apply to cohort processes, it is based simply on a rearrangement of the *same data* (see, e.g., Spiegelman, 1968, pp. 153–154) that can alternatively be used in a period analysis to apply to societal-level structure or structural change (as described in Section 1). For example, in Table 2 · 5, the cross-sectional data for each period of observation appear in the columns; thus the differences among strata (*Sd*) at each period can be observed by reading down each column. For the cohort analysis, these columns have been staggered, as an aid to extracting an entirely new set of insights by tracing each cohort over its life course.

(2) *A classic example*   An actual example, which deals with death rates from tuberculosis,[19] will begin to suggest the special utility of cohort analysis versus period analysis of the same data. This example is selected from the field of epidemiology where sociologically useful procedures for comparing these two approaches have become well-established as a means of seeking empirical regularities that can help to develop or to test particular theories. (*See Volume 2, Chapter 5 by Susser, especially pp. 137–143;* see also MacMahon, Pugh, and Ipsen, 1960, pp. 88–97).

The data are first arranged, as in Table 2 · 6, by period of observation— in this instance, by time of death. A first inspection of the *Pd* (from column to

[19] This analysis, which has been successively updated by more recent scholars, was published by Frost in 1939. Frost (who also gives credit to Andvord, 1930) gives a brilliant explanation of the differences in the two approaches under conditions of secular change, and of the possible misinterpretations if cross-sectional data alone are employed.

column) shows a steady decline in the death rates for each age stratum—a finding that reflects the secular decline in tuberculosis. However, the differences among the strata (Sd), as graphed for period analysis in Figure 2 · 5, panel a, reveal a baffling complexity from one period to the next: apart from the expected general tendency for rates to peak in infancy, there is also a secondary peak within each column, which shifts to increasingly higher strata over the more recent decades. While various intricate hypotheses might be invented, of course, the period data alone seem insufficient to explain why (counter to the overall decline) the disease should appear to attack people at older and older ages.

As an alternative, then, the data are rearranged for cohort analysis, as graphically presented in panel b of Figure 2 · 5. Each of the curves in this figure describes the life course of a single cohort (Ld).[20] (The data for these curves are taken from the diagonals of the period analysis, Table 2 · 6, reading from upper left to lower right.) The virtue of the cohort analysis is readily apparent from this graph. Here the complexities of the period analysis have disappeared and the life-course patterns do show a consistent tendency: beyond a peak at age 30 there is a regular decline with age (rather than any tendency toward increase in old age). Moreover, when the curves for the several cohorts are compared age for age (Cd), each has a lower level of death rates than its predecessor, thus reflecting the long-term decline indicated in the period analysis.

(3) *Alternative interpretations*   This example points to the potential benefits of combining period analysis with cohort analysis,[21] and to a difference in interpretation of the two sets of results. When both approaches are used, either one may prove more successful than the other in uncovering regularities or meaningful patterns in a particular set of data. But if one is more successful, this outcome can guide the further search for reasonable explanations. In the tuberculosis example, it is the cohort analysis that uncovered the more consistent curves. Moreover, this outcome is compatible with the secular trend of primary infection in early life, and with the theory that this primary infection is an important determinant of the once highly fatal secondary form of the disease among adults. Thus the cross-sectional finding that old people from the earliest cohorts maintain high death rates as recently as 1950 no longer appears anomalous. According to this explanation, their death rates reflect infection in early life near the beginning of the century, when rates of infection were still high.

More generally, when regularities are observed in the life-course patterns

[20] These curves correspond to the rows in our schematic diagram in Table 2 · 5.

[21] Richard Cohn suggests in a personal communication that, for some problems, an alternative set of tables might be based on rates per members born in each cohort, rather than per members living at a given time. One would expect that, in most cases, such tables would show the cohort pattern more clearly.

FIGURE 2 · 5 *Comparison of period analysis with cohort analysis: rearrangements of data from Table 2 · 6*

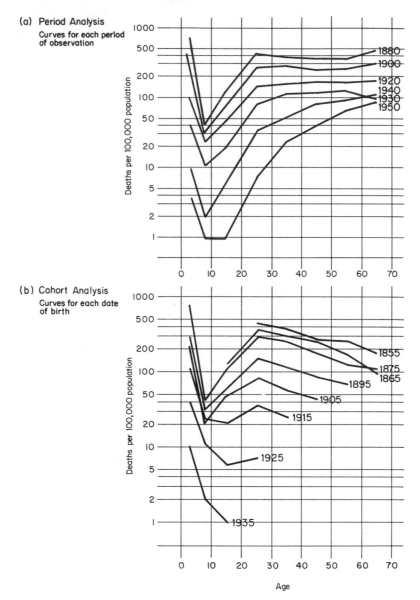

(a) Period Analysis
Curves for each period of observation

(b) Cohort Analysis
Curves for each date of birth

Source: MacMahon et al., 1960, pp. 90, 91.

of successive cohorts, it seems reasonable to look for effects of history (or environment) that impinge upon people at similar points in their own lifetime —as successive cohorts may, for example, be infected in childhood with a chronic disease affecting their later lives. By contrast, when regularities are observed in a period analysis, it seems more reasonable to look for effects of history or environment that impinge upon all age strata simultaneously—as the state of medical care in a given era may apply equally to the entire population, irrespective of age. The search for possible explanations in terms of "cohort effects" or "period effects," fraught with the difficulties discussed in Section 4 · A, can often be aided, as in the tuberculosis example, by attempting both types of analysis, and hoping to isolate one set of findings that shows greater empirical regularity and is, at the same time, consistent with an acceptable theory.

3 *Processes related to structure*

See Chapter 1 and Chapter 12 · 4

The foregoing example of an epidemiological analysis points to a basic difference between period analysis and cohort analysis, and begins to suggest their combined potential for deeper understanding of sociological process and change. Period analysis (sometimes called current analysis), by examining age-specific structural elements and changes in these elements, focuses on our concept of societal timing. Cohort analysis, by examining the underlying processes of cohort succession and aging, focuses on our concept of cohort timing. Because of this crucial divergence in conceptual focus, the two analyses, even when performed on the same data, can sometimes yield dramatically different results. Moreover, these differing results often lead the researcher to look for quite different sources of historical or environmental explanation, a point to be considered in Section 4.

Despite the differences in pattern and in interpretation often observable between period data and cohort data, however, the two have a definite, if sometimes confusing, relation to each other. On the one hand, the structural information about societal age strata and period changes (Sd and Pd discussed in Section 1) can be viewed as the resultant of the processual information about cohort flow and the life course of successive cohorts (Cd and Ld discussed in Section 2). In this sense, structure can be explained in terms of process. The schematic connections will be clarified through a brief review of Tables 2 · 4 and 2 · 5 (or Figure 1 · 3 in Chapter 1). As we pointed out in our discussion of the form that cohort analysis takes, the structure is seen in these schematic representations as simply a cross-sectional view of the processes at a given period of observation. Conversely, if the cross-sectional strata are viewed as a set of points at a moment of time, each point can be extended into a line referring to the aging of a single cohort over its lifetime, and the entire set of points can be extended into staggered lines referring to the succession of cohorts through the society over historical time.

As we consider more generally in this section how cohort and life-course processes relate, first, to age structure (Sd) at a given time period, and second, to structural change (Pd) over successive time periods, we shall start with a suggestive example that points to the essential analytical problems to be confronted.

3 · A AN EXAMPLE

A comparison of Figures 2 · 6 and 2 · 7 illustrates (National Manpower Council, 1957, pp. 125–129) both the potentialities and the difficulties of relating structural change to the underlying processes.

In the *period analysis*, Figure 2 · 6, each curve portrays the differences by age strata (Sd) in the percentage of women in the labor force; and a comparison of these curves indicates the period differences (Pd) in this respect. In the two earlier periods, when 1940 is contrasted with 1890, the proportions are substantially higher for all strata (except the youngest and the oldest). But the shapes of the two curves are strikingly similar: in both years, labor force participation rates were highest among women about 20 years old and then fell off sharply for successively older strata. By 1956, however, a revolutionary change has occurred:[22] the participation rate stops declining at around age 30, and then shows a pronounced rise until about age 50. Thus, during the years between 1940 and 1956, the rates nearly doubled in the strata of women aged 45 to 54 and women aged 55 to 64.

What might such an analysis indicate about the underlying processes? Inferences from the period analysis about the "typical" contemporary work-life patterns of women would suggest the following tendencies: withdrawal from the labor force during the childrearing years, subsequent re-entry, followed by withdrawal again after the age of 50.[23] In fact, the *cohort analysis* in Figure 2 · 7 uncovers quite different sets of patterns for a sequence of several cohorts. This analysis reveals that only one of the cohorts—the cohort of women born in the decade 1886–1895 and in their 60's in 1955—exhibits a work-life history approaching the shape of the current cross-sectional pattern! The shape of the curves for the more recent cohorts points to the emergence of quite different patterns. In the cohort born in 1896–1905, no tendency to withdraw as early as age 50 appears. And in the two most recent cohorts for which data are presented, the tendencies toward high initial rates of entry followed by withdrawal during the childrearing years have both dis-

[22] For the persistence of this pattern, see Volume I, Chapter 3 · A · 2 · b and 3 · A · 2 · c.
[23] The data in Figure 2 · 7 represent net shifts. Hence the life course of *individual* women, as they may enter, leave, and re-enter the labor force, cannot be traced.

FIGURE 2 · 6 *A period analysis of female labor force participation rates*

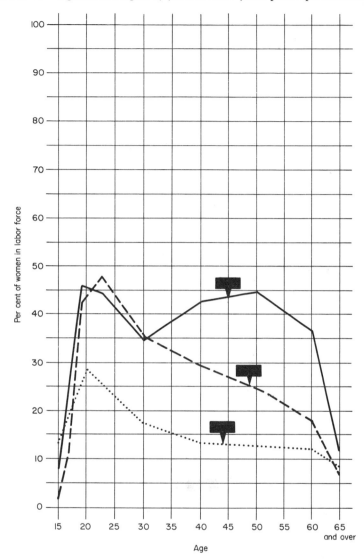

Source: National Manpower Council, 1957, p. 126; estimates based on data from United States Bureau of the Census.

FIGURE 2·7 *A cohort analysis of female labor force participation rates, United States, 1900–1955*

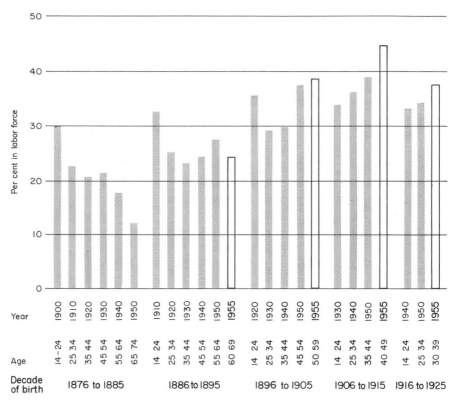

Source: National Manpower Council, 1957, p. 128; estimates based on data from United States Bureau of the Census.

appeared. Here the not-yet-completed cohort data indicate, instead, consistently rising rates over the life course (in contrast to the declining rates over the life course of the earliest cohort, born between 1876 and 1885). Thus the cross-sectional view, though in itself an important composite of the age strata in the society, does not immediately reveal this remarkable and ongoing transformation in the working lives of the people involved.

This example dramatizes the elaborate and entirely unpredictable processes that may sometimes underlie apparently straightforward period changes. It also demonstrates once again how a cohort analysis can sometimes redirect the search for underlying explanations. A period analysis alone might lead the researcher to explain the emergence of the characteristic cross-sectional age-curve through factors having a differential impact on different age strata today. For example, he might cite continuing normative restrictions against the employment of young mothers; the increased leisure and adjustment problems of "empty nest" mothers for whom work provides a temporary palliative; the age discrimination against hiring women in their 50's; or the development of new leisure pursuits to encourage retirement. The cohort data make clear, however, that such explanations will not suffice. Rather, these data, by disclosing a continuing revolution in the work-life cycle of women, require consideration of societal trends affecting women over their life course, such as rising educational attainment or the radical restructuring of expectations governing the feminine role (Cf. Riley, Johnson, and Boocock, 1963).

The example serves also as an antidote against the many simplified illustrations that follow, and against many facile modes of statistical manipulation that may obscure significant complexities in the data. The two analyses in Figures $2 \cdot 6$ and $2 \cdot 7$ suffer from lack of comparability, employing different time periods and different age categories. But, even if they were comparable, it would be a difficult task to account precisely for these particular period changes in terms of the complex cohort and life-course processes here at work.

In order now to elucidate certain selected principles, we shall turn to less intricate examples, considering situations in which the patterns observable in one type of analysis can be readily inferred from patterns observable in the other type.

3 · B PROCESSES AND STRUCTURE (Sd)

It is possible to state—though typically difficult to apply—a few rudimentary principles as to how cross-sectional (period) data reflect certain kinds of life-course and cohort patterns. We continue, of course, to utilize our definitions of Sd, Ld, and Cd as referring to the full complexity of empirically observed patterns; and we focus attention here on selected characteristics, holding size constant and disregarding variations in composition. Any particular set of cross-sectional data on the characteristics of the age strata (Sd) (similar principles could be developed for size—cf. Ryder, 1964b) is merely a snapshot of the life course patterns (Ld) of the cohorts involved and the differences among these patterns (Cd). That is, the differences (or similarities) among old, middle-aged, and young at a given time can be completely described in terms of Ld and Cd (or, in other words, in terms of intracohort and intercohort differences). Thus we can start by stating:

Principal 1. Sd are determined by Ld and Cd.[24]

[24] This principle, and its corollaries as discussed later, assume a closed population. As John Knodel points out in personal communication, this restriction could be important when looking at a city, for example, or a small area in a mobile population where migration is appreciable.

The nature of this relationship is suggested in Table 2 · 7, which shows how selected cohort and life-course tendencies are translated into cross-sectional age patterns.

Cohort differences and structure   The translation into Sd of certain types of Cd is illustrated in cases (a) and (b) of this table. If, as in case (a), there is an increasing trend over time, so that successive cohorts are marked by *rising* levels of a characteristic—educational attainment, for example—then a slice through the age strata at a particular time will reflect a consequent heightening of the educational levels for the *younger,* as compared with the older, strata. (Such a situation of a rising trend among the more recent cohorts is shown in the fictitious Example 1 in Table 2 · 8.) Conversely, as in case (b) of Table 2 · 7, if successive cohorts experience *declining* levels of a characteristic—such as *declining* death rates from tuberculosis—then the consequence for the cross-sectional picture will be to heighten the effects of the disease in the *older,* as compared with the younger, strata (cf. Volume II, Chapter 5 by Susser, p. 139).

Life-course patterns and structure   Not only intercohort differences but also life-course patterns (Ld) are reflected in cross-sectional data, as illustrated in cases (c) and (d) of Table 2 · 7. For example, if knowledge of vocabulary *rises* over the life course, as in case (c), then this characteristic will tend to rise with increasing age among the strata; whereas, if speed of response *declines* over the life course, as in case (d), the strata will tend to show a decrease by age. (Table 2 · 8 shows a fictitious Example 2, in which increases with age over the life course translate into a rising pattern of Sd at each period of observation.)

Combined intercohort and intracohort differences   Since both sets of diachronic patterns (Cd and Ld) are at work here (Principle 1), as suggested in Table 2 · 7, their consequences for particular sets of cross-sectional data can combine either to reinforce or to counteract one another. (In

TABLE 2 · 7   *Translation of processual data into cross-sectional data*

	Tendency in cross-sectional data (Sd) for:
If trends have produced:	
a. Increases in successive cohorts (Cd are $+$)	Younger $>$ older
b. Decreases in successive cohorts (Cd are $-$)	Younger $<$ older
If life-course patterns show:	
c. Increases with aging (Ld are $+$)	Younger $<$ older
d. Decreases with aging (Ld are $-$)	Younger $>$ older

Note: The apparent anomaly that Cd and Ld seem to have opposite effects on Sd occurs simply because, among "successive cohorts," the more recent cohorts constitute the younger (rather than the older) strata.

more complicated situations, of course, the two can interact with each other, as when different cohorts respond in different ways to similar life-stage experiences. Here the nature of the cross-sectional patterns would not be predictable from an examination of each source of diachronic variation separately.)

Thus a combination of the processes indicated in cases (a) and (d) can jointly increase the tendency for younger strata to exceed older strata; for example, if genetic increments in response speed among the more recent cohorts were coupled with decrements accompanying aging over the life course; or if cohort increases in the tendency to drink alcoholic beverages were coupled with a decline in drinking over the life course. However, if the decline (as in drinking) over the life course (d) were to be coupled with *decreases* over successive cohorts (b), then the cross-sectional differences between young and old produced by (d) would tend to be reduced by (b); indeed (if the two sets of decrements were equal), the strata differences might disappear entirely, or they might become the reverse of the life course decline (cf. Schaie, 1965b, p. 5).

In converse fashion, the joint operation of cases (b) and (c) can heighten the tendency for the younger strata to be *lower* than the older strata in cross-sectional measurements, as would occur, for example, if a cohort decline in religiosity were accompanied by increases with aging. If, however, an increase associated with aging (c), as in the tendency to vote, were to be accompanied by cohort *increases* (a)—perhaps rising education—associated positively with the tendency to vote [*see Chapter 4 by Foner on this point*], then the cross-sectional differences would tend to be reduced.

An illustration of the translation of certain cohort and life course differences into cross-sectional age patterns has been developed by the epidemiologist MacMahon and his collaborators, and is diagrammed in Figure 2 · 8. Each solid line represents the life course of a cohort (as in the cohort graphs shown in Figure 2 · 5). In this example, the incidence of the disease is assumed to rise over the life course of each cohort by similar ratios—but by different absolute amounts, thus creating the fan-like series of curves shown in the diagram. Two alternative trend situations are then considered in the example. First, if incidence is *decreasing* over time and affecting successive cohorts, then the more recent cohorts will be those lower on the incidence scale, hence nearer the bottom of the diagram. Under these conditions, a cross-sectional view is represented by the line of long dashes running from lower left to upper right, which intersects the cohorts at the ages when they respectively reach this period of observation. And it can be readily seen that this cross-sectional curve rises with age—and rises far more sharply than the slopes of any of the life course curves. Second, conversely, if *increasing* incidence is raising the level of the more recent cohorts, then the slope of the

FIGURE 2·8 *Diagram of cohort versus cross-section patterns*

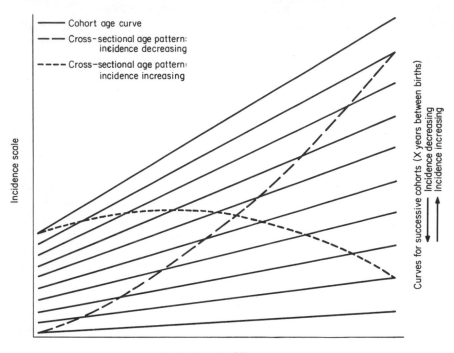

NOTE: If incidence is decreasing, age curves for
the more recent cohorts appear near the bottom
of diagram; if incidence is increasing, they appear
near the top

Source: MacMahon et al., 1960, p. 96 (adapted).

cross-sectional curve (the line of short dashes from upper left to lower right)
is reduced relative to the life curves and, in this case, tends to decline by age
categories.

Various modifications of this situation might be similarly diagrammed.
Suppose, for example, that the several cohorts started at different points
(sequentially higher or lower), but that each maintained the same absolute
amounts of change over the life course. Then the life-course curves in the
diagram would be parallel, rather than fan-shaped, and both of the cross-sectional (dotted) curves, though differing in direction, would have the same
slope. Note that the slope of the cross-sectional curve in such a diagram depends on the distances between the life-course curves at successive ages.

There is, of course, an immense variety of possible combinations. The life-
course curves might take many different shapes. Or the heights of the several

curves, instead of being successively higher or lower, might be ordered in many different ways.

Despite this potential complexity, however, certain corollaries to Principle 1, though they refer to special situations, are often useful:

Principle 1a. If there are no variations over the life course (Ld equals zero), then Sd will be determined by Cd.

Principle 1b. If there are no differences among cohorts (Cd equals zero), then Sd will be determined by Ld.

Principle 1c. If there are no cross-sectional differences among strata (Sd equals zero), this could occur:

either because both Cd and Ld are zero (show no differences)
or because Cd and Ld balance each other precisely.

Interpretations and fallacies These principles can be applied to measures of size (and composition) or to characteristics, but *only* if one is held constant while the other is under scrutiny. For example, changes in size or composition of a cohort over its life course may affect the proportions exhibiting a given characteristic, even though *individuals* do not change in respect to that characteristic as they age. Despite this limitation, Principles 1a and 1b have important applications, often making it possible to draw inferences about underlying processes from the data of a single cross-sectional study. Such inferences are obviously appropriate in situations where there is a reasonable basis to assume that there are *no* appreciable variations either in Ld or in Cd in the measure under scrutiny. Consider the example of educational attainment (beyond early adulthood). Here it has seemed safe to assume, at least up to the present time, that most people do not change their level of education over the life course. Accordingly, since Ld has little influence on the cross-sectional pattern (if size and composition are held constant for consecutive ages) the Sd can be used effectively as a measure of the differing amounts of schooling experienced by the successive cohorts (Cd). In parallel fashion, if cohorts can be assumed to be substantially alike in a certain respect, then differences among strata in this respect (Sd) might properly be attributed to changes over the life course (Ld). For example, if there is indication that a particular series of cohorts entered the voting role (or the occupational role) at approximately the same starting ages, then strata differences in the duration of experience in the role, or perhaps in role commitment, might reasonably be interpreted in terms of differing experiences over the life course.

However, in a great many situations there is no reasonable basis for such assumptions. And here there is considerable danger of fallacious interpretation. For, strange as it may seem, scholars in various social science fields persistently overlook Principle 1, as we have stated it: that cross-sectional findings typically reflect a *combination* of cohort and life-course processes.

On the one hand, by overlooking the possibility of Ld, scholars run into the danger of what we might call a "generational fallacy" (though fallacies in this direction seem comparatively rare). For example, cross-sectional differences in political attitudes might be explained entirely by a theory of "political generations," when in fact the differences were not wholly attributable to the differing eras in which the cohorts were reared (Cd), but also to certain changes in opinion over the life course (Ld).[25]

On the other hand, by overlooking the possibility of Cd, scholars can—and all too frequently do—run into the alternative danger of a "life-course fallacy." Thus cross-sectional data on intelligence were long interpreted to mean a decline (beyond the late teens) due to aging, until a few longitudinal studies opened this interpretation to serious question. Here, as it turned out, a probable source of the fallacy is the sharp differences in educational level among successive cohorts (Cd); since educational level is highly correlated with performance on intelligence tests, these cohort differences would affect the cross-sectional findings (Sd) profoundly. There are many similar instances where age-specific cross-sectional patterns—for example, in family income, or in organizational participation, or in social class identification—are ascribed by social scientists to life-course processes.[26] That the tenability of these life-course explanations requires supplementary assumptions about cohort differences is often unstated; and even less often are such assumptions put to empirical test. The danger of this type of fallacy is particularly acute because of the pervasiveness of social change in many areas under study: it is precisely in these areas, of course, that the assumption of slight or insignificant differences among cohorts is most questionable.

3 · C PROCESSES AND STRUCTURAL CHANGE (Pd)

We have been discussing the processes underlying differences among age strata (Sd) as observed at a single period of time. Now we turn to the relationship of these processes to period differences (Pd)—that is, to the structural change (or stability) observable in cross-sectional age data when two or more periods are compared. After a re-examination of the data employed for relating process to structural change, we shall contrast the uses of these data in cohort analysis versus period analysis.

Identities in the data   Starting with a given set of Sd, one might, perhaps, look for additional principles for explaining Pd (age-specific differences among periods) in terms of Cd or Ld. A moment's reflection shows, however, that Pd are themselves simply a rearrangement of age-specific differences among cohorts. The same data, though differently organized, are used to study

[25] [*For a discussion of political generations, see Section 2 of Chapter 4 by Foner.*]
[26] See Volume I, Chapter 1, pp. 7–9; and Chapter 4 · A · 4. See also such examples as Lipset (1963, p. 284); or the discussion by Wilensky (1961, p. 217).

both Pd and Cd. As noted in connection with Table 2·5 above, for example, the cross-sectional data for successive periods appear in the columns of the same table where the longitudinal data for successive cohorts appear in the rows. Any age-for-age comparison between two rows also constitutes an age-for-age comparison between two columns. For example, in the upper right portion of Table 2·5, the numbers 40 and 50 for persons aged 60 can be used either to compare the rows for the 1940 versus the 1920 cohorts, or to compare the columns for the periods 1980 versus 2000. However, since these comparisons are differently organized in period analysis versus cohort analysis (a matter that we shall examine in detail below), this identity is often obscured by various confusing rearrangements and reinterpretations of the same data. Thus it seems useful to state as a principle:

> *Principle 2.* An age-specific change between two or more periods of observation (Pd) is the same as the differences (Cd) in the life-course patterns of those cohorts existing at the particular time periods.

At the risk of redundancy, two sets of fictitious data in Table 2·8 illustrate this identity between Pd and Cd, indicating also the place of Ld (or intracohort patterns). Example 1 shows zero Ld (across the rows), but consistent cohort increases (Cd) at each age level (on the diagonals from lower left to upper right). Here the age-specific period differences[27] simply repeat the previously observed Cd: thus they show an increase over time at each age. Example 2 is the reverse: it shows consistent increases over the life course (Ld), but zero Cd. Here, as a result, there are *no* differences from period to period, again simply repeating the pattern of Cd. Example 2 illustrates an important warning and a useful corollary to Principle 2:

> Caution: Beware of thinking that, for comparisons of a single measure, Ld enter into Pd. Since Pd are identical with Cd, life-course patterns (Ld) cannot in themselves produce Pd (in the absence of any changes in these patterns from one cohort to another).

> *Principle 2a.* If there are no differences among cohorts (Cd equals zero), then there will be no differences among periods (Pd equals zero), regardless of the life-course patterns.

In sum, Pd are produced, not by intracohort, but by intercohort, patterns. Differences in the age strata from one period to another are the consequences of intercohort differences—in level, slope, or shape—of life-course patterns. As Ryder puts it in Chapter 3, social change occurs to the extent that "successive cohorts do something other than merely repeat the patterns of behavior of their predecessors."

---

[27] In the usual form for period analysis, the columns, which are staggered in Table 2·8, would be realigned to create a row (instead of a diagonal) for each age stratum.

TABLE 2 · 8 *Analyses reflecting different life course* (Ld) *and cohort* (Cd) *patterns*

Fictitious figures show proportions of persons in each stratum having the characteristic

(Age in parentheses)

Example 1 (Cd, zero Ld)

C (date of birth)	P (period of observation)		
	1930	1940	1950
1920			(30) 50
1910		(30) 40	(40) 40
1900	(30) 30	(40) 30	(50) 30
1890	(40) 20	(50) 20	
1880	(50) 10		

Example 2 (Ld, zero Cd)

C (date of birth)	P (period of observation)		
	1930	1940	1950
1920			(30) 20
1910		(30) 20	(40) 25
1900	(30) 20	(40) 25	(50) 30
1890	(40) 25	(50) 30	
1880	(50) 30		

Cohort analysis versus period analysis   Since every age-specific period change constitutes an age-specific difference between cohorts, how can period analysis and cohort analysis produce such widely differing results? The answer lies, of course, in the differing ways in which the data are organized for analysis.

This difference in organization is shown in Table 2 · 9. Cohort analysis arranges longitudinal data according to date of birth; thus it compares cohorts, without regard to the particular periods at which observations were made. By contrast, period analysis organizes cross-sectional data according to date of observation; thus it compares historical periods, without regard to the particular cohorts involved.

Various types of comparisons can then be made simultaneously within

TABLE 2 · 9   *Patterns of cohort and period analysis*
(Age in parentheses)

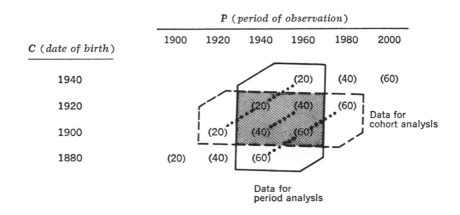

these two organizational patterns,[28] always making *age-for-age* comparisons in this table between pairs of numbers along the dotted diagonals. Thus the period differences (Pd) focus on two dates of observation, comparing, for example, the data for persons aged 20 in 1940 with those aged 20 in 1960, and so on for each age level. In parallel fashion, the cohort differences (Cd) focus on two dates of birth, comparing, for example, the 1900 cohort at age 20 with the 1920 cohort at age 20, and so on for each age level. But note that the paths of these two analyses intersect at only one of these comparisons: for persons aged 40, who were born respectively in 1900 and 1920 and observed in 1940 and 1960. Otherwise, the two analyses differ in their selection of the data to be utilized.

Comparisons between *summary indexes*, such as averages or totals of the age-specific data, can also be made. Thus a summary index of the strata differences (Sd) could be prepared from the data in each column, and the period differences obtained by contrasting the summaries for 1940 and 1960. Similarly, a summary index of the life-course differences (Ld) could be prepared from the data in each row, and the cohort differences obtained by contrasting the summaries for the 1900 cohort and the 1920 cohort. But here again it is very clear that different sets of data are selected for the two types of summary indexes.

To be sure, the example in Table 2 · 9 is only a *partial* set of data: infor-

---

[28] For greater effectiveness, graphs of both types of analysis can be plotted either with ages along the abscissa (as in Figure 2 · 5 above) or with dates along the abscissa (as in Figure 2 · 10 below). The appropriate comparisons are then made either down or across. Compare Figures 6, 8, and 9 in Volume II, Chapter 5 by Susser, pp. 140, 142, 144–145.

mation on all three age categories, while available for four cohorts, is complete for only two time periods. In practice, many attempts to compare cohort and period results are restricted by the data. Data from sequential cross-sectional studies or censuses provide only truncated information about most cohorts (as in Table 2 · 8). Moreover, at any current period of observation, the future life course of cohorts recently born is still unknown and can, at best, be estimated.[29] But quite apart from such perennial difficulties of execution, problems of comparability persist. Even where full data for several time periods and several cohorts are available, there is a basic difference, as Ryder describes it, between the behavior manifested by a series of *cohorts* through time, and the manifestations of that behavior in the age strata at successive periods, as two modes of representation of the same experience (Ryder, 1964b, p. 79).

What can be said, then, about the *relationship* between cohort processes and period change? In general, very little. In the limiting case, a set of data that shows no Cd (where the life-course patterns are all alike) will show no Pd either, following Principle 2a above; here there would be no differences between the results of a cohort analysis and those of a period analysis. Beyond this, the difficulty of making cohort-type inferences from a sequence of cross-sectional studies has already been suggested in the foregoing examples of death rates from tuberculosis or of female labor force participation. For particular sets of data, the nature of the relationship can often be seen through graphic or tabular procedures, as in these examples. More generally, Ryder (1964b, p. 80; see also MacMahon, Pugh, and Ipsen, 1960, pp. 88, 95–97) has begun to develop mathematical formulae for translation from period indexes into cohort indexes (or, in the other direction, from cohort indexes to period indexes).[30] These formulae can be used to indicate the implications for each set of indexes entailed by certain kinds of changes in the other.

Interpretations and fallacies   The obvious difference between cohort analysis and period analysis, and the complexity of their interrelationship, points to important differences of interpretation and to the dangers of any naive interpretation of one in terms of the other.

For example, computations of the expectation of life are typically based (at least for human beings, in contrast to fruit flies or other short-lived species) on mortality rates in current cross-sectional data. To be sure, the differences between current life tables and cohort life tables have long been recognized,[31] and it seems clear that the one refers to the risks of dying for all age strata in

[29] Such truncated data create special difficulties when age-by-age comparisons are replaced by total, or summary, measures where the information is not comparable. See, for example, the attempts to use such data in Cutler (1968, 1970).

[30] The solutions are general for all moment-type functions (Ryder, personal communication).

[31] Lotka (1931); Dublin and Spiegelman (1941); see also the comparison between the two different sets of curves for Massachusetts between 1890 and 1940 presented by Merrell (1956).

particular calendar years, while the other refers to the pattern of survival of a cohort over the life span. Nevertheless, since the future life course of existing cohorts is problematical, the usual estimates of life expectancy are cross-sectional, assuming that babies born today will encounter in due course the mortality conditions of older people today. Since there has been a long-term decline in mortality rates, these estimates have in fact continually tended to underestimate actual longevity (Volume I, Chapter 2 · 3; Spiegelman, 1968, Chapter 6). Thus, to use the current (period-specific) life table for prognosis would constitute an extension to trend data of the error (either witting or unwitting) that we have called the "life-course fallacy." Yet, as Margaret Merrell (1956, p. 114) has said, "The very form in which the life table is put, that of survivorship, tempts us . . . to think of the curve as giving us a flow of people through their lives."

Another example of the utility of cohort analysis is afforded by the various studies of fertility in this country since World War II. The extremely high rates of period fertility between 1947 and 1957 overestimated the increases in family size that were taking place.[32] Careful cohort analysis (Kiser, Grabill, and Campbell, 1968, pp. 258–269) revealed that part of the increase during these years could be attributed to births and marriages that had been postponed among older childbearing cohorts from the depression and war years, and to younger marriage, a higher proportion marrying, and earlier childbearing within marriage among younger cohorts. The result was an unusual degree of temporal overlap in the childbearing experience of older and younger cohorts, contributing to the high period fertility rates. The downturn in fertility rates after 1957, which was in part due to the dissipation of this overlap, could have been anticipated from an understanding of the shifting cohort patterns of childbearing (Ryder, 1969; see also Kiser, Grabill, and Campbell, 1968, pp. 257, 264; U.S. Department of Health, Education and Welfare, 1969, pp. 1–2).

4 *Explanation: Possibilities and Problems*

See Mathematical Note to Chapter 2 by Cohn

The same body of data can move in different paths across history and across the human lifetime, a fact that opens a wide door to a clearer understanding of the connections between cohort processes and social change (see, e.g., Ryder, 1965). This fact also raises critical problems of interpretation. As the previous section has shown (Principle 2), changes in the age structure of the society are direct reflections of *differences* in size, composition, or character-

---

[32] This was particularly true of such indexes as the total fertility rate, which are free from the influence of age distribution.

istics in the life course of successive cohorts, while structural stabilities reflect tendencies for different cohorts to age in *similar* fashion. But why do cohorts age in different (or in similar) ways?[33] What clues can be teased out of data to explicate the nature of the abstract processes we have defined in Chapter 1 as cohort flow $(P1)$ and aging $(P2)$? Finally, how can such specific explanations contribute to a fuller understanding of the age-stratified society as a whole?

There are no ready answers to such questions, and a variety of approaches must be tailor-made for the research objective at hand. In this final section, we shall first outline two types of analysis that are sometimes useful as aids to explanation of particular sets of data. One type seeks answers in the nature of history and the environment; a second, in the internal composition of the cohorts themselves. Finally, a third analysis will reinforce the importance of size—of the numbers of people in particular cohorts at particular times—as fundamental to any explanation of age as a factor in societal stratification and change. For variables like age and date have little meaning until they can be translated into social phenomena and their interrelationships.

4 · A ANALYSIS OF HISTORICAL EFFECTS

Differences (or similarities) among cohorts can be related to history in diverse ways. In the data on structure and on process examined in Sections 1 to 3, the many historical (or more generally, the many environmental) effects are built in. We have been observing age strata and the related processes *as* they occur in particular environmental and historical contexts [*see Chapter 1 · 2*]. We now want to probe into these relationships to history by using two sets of dates: either the dates that bound the lifetime of each cohort or the dates at which the age strata are observed. These dates are of interest as indicators of situations or factors in the social environment that are potentially relevant to the problem under study. We speak of the "effects" of such factors, though the direction of any causal relationship varies with the particular problem. Remember that this discussion of "effects" no longer refers to the cohort differences (Cd) and life-course patterns (Ld) as these are actually observed in the data; it refers instead to postulated tendencies presumed to underlie these observed patterns, and to the ways in which these two types of observed regularities can help focus theoretical explanation.

Types of effects The environmental factors conceived as potential cause or consequence of the Ld and Cd observed in a given analysis[34] can be roughly divided into two broad categories: First, one category of environ-

---

[33] The important question of the causal linkages between cohort processes and structural changes will be discussed in Chapter 12.

[34] The environmental factors may, of course, be associated with either a widening or a reduction of the observed Ld and Cd in a sequence of observations.

mental factors (usually indexed by dates of birth) impinges upon successive cohorts at *similar* points in the life course. For example, cohorts might be distinguished from one another by the state of public health to which infants are exposed, the practices by which children are socialized, or the condition of the economy at entry into the labor force. We label the influence of such environmental factors "cohort effects" (noting again that cohorts are intrinsically distinguished not only by their unique historical backgrounds, but also by their size and by their composition in respect to sex, race, and so on (as discussed in later sections).

Second, another broad category of environmental factors (usually indexed by dates of observation) affects successive cohorts concurrently; for example, long-term changes in income level or short-term fluctuations in employment can cut across all the age strata at given periods. We refer to the influence of such factors as "period effects." Even when a period effect has the same impact on all the strata, it produces differences in the life curves of successive cohorts since it strikes them at *different* stages of the life course. Moreover, many period effects act differently on the several strata, both because the cohorts involved differ in composition and historical background, and because they differ in age and hence in length of exposure to the environment.

Of course, a third set of factors also operates *within* each cohort to produce these life-course patterns. We shall speak of the consequences of these factors (indexed by chronological age) as the "effects of aging." At the *individual* level certain effects of aging are biologically based, but even the biological changes are importantly conditioned by the particular range of sociocultural situations that individuals experience. In addition, many aspects of individual aging are purely social, since age reflects not only the number of years that an individual has been exposed to other people (we are not considering human beings in isolation) but also the sequence of roles through which he has passed.

The distinction between cohort effects and period effects as postulated tendencies is suggested by the differing points of impact of the arrows in Figure 2 · 9. Ideally, one might imagine the trace lines representing the life curves of these successive cohorts if only one set of factors were operating at a time, or if the effects of the others could be controlled. Thus a constantly rising period effect, producing a steady increase over time for everybody regardless of age, could be diagrammed by a single upward trace line—in which the curves for the successive cohorts would coincide. By contrast, if an aging effect were tending to produce decrements over the life course, the trace line for each cohort would be downward. And a cohort effect might, in addition, operate to start each cohort at a point above (or below) its predecessor. In principle, if it were possible for the researcher to control all factors

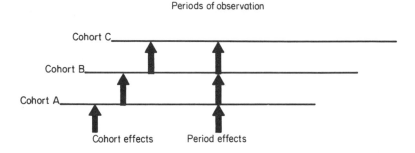

actually operating as period effects and as cohort effects (including the effects of cohort size and composition), the several cohorts would show similar life-course patterns (Principle 2 in Section 3). In actuality, a complex of many specific forces is undoubtedly at work in intricate combinations, sometimes reinforcing and sometimes counteracting one another.

In the effort to explore such possible effects, various research approaches have attempted to disentangle the two main types of historical (environmental) effects and to separate these from the effects of aging. (See, for example, Kessen, 1960; Schaie, 1965a, 1965b; and the Mathematical Note by Richard Cohn at the end of this chapter.) For example, to the extent that potentially confounding period effects can be ruled out, the focus can be more closely directed to the processes of cohort succession (P1) and aging (P2). In such a situation, the *differences* that are observed in the life-course patterns of successive cohorts may often be traceable to environmental cohort effects, while the *similarities* observed often suggest explanation in terms of persistent factors governing the aging process.

We shall now illustrate some of the research attempts to isolate these three effects, first reviewing the use of cohort analysis versus period analysis to uncover empirical regularities that seem more nearly attributable to one than to another; and then considering the use of various assumptions as an aid to interpretation.

The search for empirical regularities The analyses previously shown in Figures 2 · 5 and 2 · 7 have provided examples of explanations adduced from regularities in the *cohort data*. In the tuberculosis example (Figure 2 · 5), the similarity in the shape of the life-course curves suggested a disposition to contract the disease early in life (interpreted as an aging effect), regardless of the age at which death might ensue; whereas the differing heights of the curves reflected the long-term decline in incidence (interpreted as a cohort effect). In the labor force example (Figure 2 · 7), data for the successive cohorts show not only the steady rise in female participation in the labor force, but also a marked reversal over this century in the life-course patterns of participation (interpreted as cohort effects). In these instances, cohort analysis is used to uncover possible "cohort effects" that impinge upon the basic processes of cohort succession and aging, and that can, in turn, be explained through further inspection of the related historical circumstances. In both cases, the life-course patterns show certain regularities (in Ld or in long-term Cd) within which aberrations can be detected, interpreted as probable aging effects or cohort effects, and subjected to scrutiny.

The limiting case would be the finding of *no difference among cohorts.* Such a finding, which implies no change either in biological aging or in social conditions influencing the life course, seems quite possible in studies of restricted temporal, cultural, and situational range.[35] It would be uncovered equally well by either a period or a cohort analysis (Principle 2). However, the very lack of variation in this situation precludes explanation through correlation with historical or environmental factors, except as their persistence indexes societal stability or cultural universality.

In contrast to such instances in which regularities appear in the cohort data, in others the clearest patterns are revealed through period analysis in the *cross-sectional data.* These patterns signal possible period effects that impinge upon the entire society, irrespective of age, or that produce simultaneous changes in a wide range of age strata. One type of period effect that can be readily seen when sufficient data are available is the impact on the age structure of short-run events or fluctuations, such as epidemics, wars, or depressions.[36] As an example, Figure 2 · 10 shows the suicide rate for white males in the United States over several decades (cf. Volume II, Chapter 5 by Susser, p. 143). (Here, in order to show the trends over many time periods, the dates of observation are shown along the abscissa and the curves plotted for each age separately.) On the whole, the period data for the several age strata, which rise sharply by age, show a general stability over time; but this stability is disturbed at various points—by a rise in rates at the depth of the Depression following 1929, and by a fall during World War II. It is clear from the period analysis that all the age strata tend to rise and fall together;[37] and

[35] The finding (which could reflect some complex pattern of equal but opposite period and age effects) would be less likely if many cohorts were compared across a wide range of temporal and cultural settings. Even biologists are not agreed about the nature, causes, or indeed the inevitability of an inherent aging process apart from the onslaughts of the environment. See Volume I, Chapter 8, especially p. 187.

[36] Obviously, not all consequences of such environmental events are best conceptualized as period effects, since cohort effects may also arise. For example, one effect of war is to create cohort differences in performance of military roles.

[37] Of course, these fluctuations might be comparatively greater or less (or even reversed) in some age strata than in others.

FIGURE 2·10   *Suicide death rates, by age, cross-section curves, for each age stratum, United States, 1921–1964*

Per 100,000 White Males

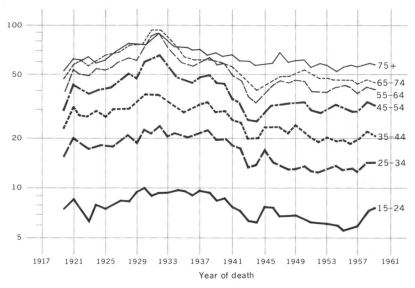

Source: MacMahon, Johnson, and Pugh, 1963, p. 289.

this finding supports the hypothesis that the phenomenon is affected by conditions associated with the time of observation.

Short-term changes of this kind could be observed equally well, but in a different form, in a cohort analysis of the same data. (Here the dates of birth would appear on the abscissa, and the age curves from Figure 2·10 would be fanned out to show the earliest cohorts near the upper left of the figure, the most recent cohorts near the lower right.) Thus the peaks and dips, instead of occurring simultaneously, would be staggered across the successive cohorts. This staggering would again call attention to a probable period effect, because of the consistent pattern appearing in the various cohorts at *different* ages.

This possibility of detecting short-run period effects arises when the data are of sufficient scope to reveal aberrations in otherwise regular patterns. Of course, the researcher could also look for regularities indicating various longer-range period effects.

One attempt to "control" period fluctuations is used by Crittenden (1962, pp. 651–654) in tracing shifts in party identification over the life course of cohorts between presidential election polls. [*See also Chapter 4·2 by Foner.*] Crittenden corrects each cohort shift by the amount of shift in the total electorate, using the latter to index the period effects produced by par-

FIGURE 2 · 11 *Cohort analysis of cigarette smoking among men, 1959–1965*

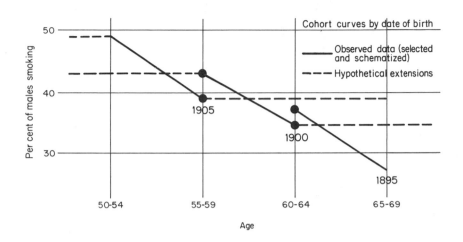

Source: Hammond and Garfinkel, 1968, p. 32 (adapted).

ticular candidates and by changes in the political climate. This total shift[38] combines the separate shifts for all cohorts with the change due to replacement—because the more recent period excludes some very old people who died in the interval, but includes the very young who have entered the electorate since the previous period.

Problems of inadequate data   What happens when the data are of insufficient scope to reveal the underlying regularities and deviations reflective of cohort effects or period effects?

An interesting case in point is afforded by a sequence of two cross-sectional surveys of cigarette smoking made in 1959 and 1965.[39] The samples (all over age 30) were large enough to allow subdivisions within each sex by five-year date-of-birth groups for cohort analysis. The outcome of the analysis is a decline over the life course for every cohort, for each sex, without exception.[40] A portion of the data for males is diagrammed by the solid lines in Figure 2 · 11. These lines portray the life-course declines over the interval between surveys.

[38] Note also that the totals can either be averages of the age-specific data, or crude totals weighted by the changing sizes of the age strata to reflect the changing "climate of opinion."

[39] Hammond and Garfinkel (1968, esp. pp. 31–34); this particular study supplements the cohort data with a panel analysis and various additional sets of information.

[40] The decline is reportedly due only to a slight extent to selective mortality since death rates are higher among cigarette smokers than among nonsmokers and subjects who died between surveys were excluded from the analysis (pp. 35, 36).

How, then, is the result to be interpreted? Do all these simultaneous declines constitute a unique response to the propaganda against smoking at that particular time (a period effect)? Or do the declines simply reflect a tendency for people, quite apart from propaganda, to cut down on smoking as they grow older (an age effect)? This question cannot be answered from these data alone because, as the Figure makes clear, there is no way to examine the many life-course patterns for consistency. Because measures were obtained at only two time periods, there is no overlap between the curves for the successive cohorts. Thus two extreme situations are among those possible:

> *Hypothesis 1*, as suggested by the dotted extensions of two of the age curves in Figure 2 · 11, postulates that levels of smoking ordinarily remain constant over the life course, deflected downward only under the special circumstances at the time interval 1959–1965.
>
> Under this hypothesis, the situation would reflect a period effect that would be consistent with the impact of the propaganda across all age strata.
>
> *Hypothesis 2*, which could be diagrammed by extending the life course of each cohort along the curve indicated by the observed data, postulates a usual decline over the life course at the same rates observed between the two surveys.
>
> Under this hypothesis, there would be no evidence of any period effect.

What *additional* information would be required to rule out either of these hypotheses as less likely than the other? Clearly, more extensive information on actual life-course patterns would be pertinent; and, this particular study presents additional evidence that smoking patterns tend to be established in youth and to persist unless there is strong motivation to change.

A second piece of information that could aid the interpretation of these data concerns the direction of the long-term trend in smoking for the population as a whole. If the trend has been consistently upward (and here again this particular study affords additional evidence of a trend in this direction), then one would probably expect a general tendency for the more recent cohorts to have higher levels of smoking than the earlier cohorts. For the periods observed in the surveys, however, the more recent cohorts (of males) are not higher, but consistently lower. These drops can be visualized by comparing the vertically aligned dots in Figure 2 · 11. For example, at age 55–59, the cohort born in 1905 has a lower rate than the previous cohort born in 1900. If Hypothesis 2 were true, the projections of these curves would maintain this unlikely general pattern of cohort differences; whereas Hypothesis 1 would reverse the pattern, as the diagram shows, producing the more likely situation in which each cohort starts out with a higher level of smoking than its predecessor.

In any full explanation of the results of this study, the cohort differences as actually observed are relevant to the research objective because they constitute the period differences between the two surveys (each age-specific period difference reflects a corresponding cohort difference—Principle 2 in Section 3). At every age level, there is a drop between 1959 and 1965 in the proportions of men smoking. And, since there is outside evidence to suggest that Hypothesis 1 is consistent with more of the facts than Hypothesis 2, this period drop can now be interpreted to reflect a 1959–1965 curtailment of smoking that more than offsets any rise in smoking among successive cohorts of young men.

Interestingly enough, among women these age-specific period differences tend to be reversed (data not shown). That is, women at given ages were more likely to smoke in 1965 than in 1959. Here the parallel explanation would be that the 1959–1965 curtailment was *not* sufficient to offset the rising tendency to smoke among successive cohorts of young women.

We have dwelt on this example because it seems highly instructive. Since a detailed set of supporting materials were brought to bear in this study, there is considerable basis for deciding between alternative hypotheses. Without such outside evidence, however, the researcher is faced with a dilemma. He is forced to make a priori assumptions. And different assumptions can lead, as in this example, to diametrically opposed interpretations. Thus the search for empirical regularities that suggest, or seem compatible with, reasonable theories can often prove abortive because of insufficient information, especially since studies frequently cover only limited numbers of cohorts or of time periods.

The need for assumptions   There is, however, a peculiar need to make the assumptions explicit in the types of analyses we have been discussing where data are arranged by age and date. As we have seen, it is often useful for particular research objectives to specify at the conceptual level *three* distinct and independent sets of factors—which can be loosely classified as producing the broad categories of "aging effects," "cohort effects," and "period effects." Ideally, each factor would be measured directly. But, in the absence of direct measures, the researcher postulates that his factors are associated respectively with the empirical indicants: age, date of birth, and date of observation. For example, income may increase with experience (indexed by age); it may increase with the secular rise in prosperity (indexed by date of birth); and it may fluctuate with the business cycle (indexed by date of observation). With three factors in the theory, the researcher wishes to proceed, of course, to a joint analysis of the simultaneous effects of all three. Unfortunately, however, this procedure is impossible, because *only two* independent pieces of information are available to measure these three factors. For each of the empirical indicants is completely defined in terms of the other two. In other words, age (A) is defined as the period of observation (P)

minus the year of birth (C); likewise, C is defined as $P - A$; and P is defined as $C + A$.

The researcher is confronted by a problem, then, whenever he wants to use two pieces of information for analysis of the three types of causal factors specified in the theory. How is he to decide which theoretical factors correspond to the empirical elements? How is he to distinguish among the three effects of age (A), cohort (C), and period (P)?

Fortunately, this dilemma is not peculiar to studies of age, but represents a special case of the *identification problem*, which arises more generally when there are too many unknowns for solution. The basic problem, widely recognized in the fields of biometrics and econometrics, has been subjected to sociological scrutiny by Blalock with reference to such topics as social mobility and status inconsistency.[41] Here the difficulty arises when, in addition to two status variables, a third variable is also conceptualized but is defined as a perfect mathematical function of the other two. For example, social mobility may be defined as the difference between father's status and son's status; or status inconsistency as the difference between the status variables of income and education. In order to identify which of the component factors are affecting the dependent variable, certain assumptions are ordinarily required.[42] The danger lies in unwitting assumptions—as when students of social mobility may unintentionally use a form of analysis that assumes that the main effects of the two status variables are zero even when they do not believe that such assumptions are correct (cf. Blalock, 1967a, pp. 794–795). Thus, one obvious approach to the identification problem is to spell out the relevant assumptions clearly in advance.

Three types of analysis   The nature of the identification problem and of the required assumptions can be understood by considering three types of analysis (or rearrangements) of any given set of data, as Schaie (1965a) has suggested in his studies of psychological development. In addition to the period (cross-sectional) designs and the cohort (longitudinal) designs we have been discussing, there is logically a third design which, following Schaie's terminology, we call the "cross-sequential." In each type of analysis, the period factor (P) is indexed by date of observation; the cohort factor (C) by

[41] Blalock (1966); see also Blalock (1967a and 1967b). In addition to the regression approach used by Blalock, the difficulty can be readily seen by the student who attempts to apply the familiar procedures of cross-classification and percentaging (Blalock, 1966, pp. 58–60).

[42] There are, of course, additional ways to solve this identification problem. Ideally the problem can be avoided if each of the specific factors defined in the theory (e.g., strain due to status inconsistency or age) can be measured directly. For example, Blalock suggests directly measuring the strain associated with status inconsistency, rather than using the difference between two status variables as an indicant of such strain (see Blalock, 1966, pp. 56–57). Another attempt to solve the identification problem might utilize nonlinear models (see Blalock, 1967a, pp. 800–801).

date of birth; and the age factor (A) by chronological age. Each type of analysis attempts to examine the joint effects of just two of these factors at a time.

First, the *period analysis* focuses on the pair of factors, P and A, but is potentially confounded by the uncontrolled effects of C. The data as arranged for this analysis (discussed in detail in Section 3 · B above) refer to age strata (Sd) at multiple periods of observation, as diagrammed in the columns of Table 2 · 9. This design has proved useful for *describing* particular structural changes as these relate to particular period changes in the environment. But how can this description be restated in terms of *effects*? According to Principle 1 (Section 3), each cross section is the composite of life-course differences and cohort differences $(Ld$ and $Cd)$, and hence potentially explainable in terms of some unknown mix of aging effects and cohort effects. Thus, if it can be assumed (Principle 1b) that the excluded factor, C, has no effects, the results as shown in the analysis can be attributed to the two factors, P and A. Alternatively, if C is assumed to have an effect, then additional assumptions are required for interpreting the results without perpetrating a life-course fallacy.

Second, in parallel fashion, the *cohort analysis* focuses on the pair of factors, C and A, but is potentially confounded by uncontrolled effects of P. The data as arranged for this analysis examine multiple cohorts over a range of ages, diagrammed in the rows of Table 2 · 9. This design has proved useful for describing differences in life-course patterns (Ld) among particular cohorts, as these differences may relate to the particular historical circumstances surrounding the several cohorts. But here again the age patterns may be attributable to two types of effects: to aging and to the impact of the particular periods at which these cohorts were observed. Thus, the factors in the analysis can be interpreted directly only if the excluded factor, P, can be assumed to have no effect. Otherwise, additional assumptions are required to avoid fallacious interpretation.

It is important to note the limitations of the *single* cross-sectional study and of the longitudinal study based on a *single* cohort, as specially restricted cases of period analysis and cohort analysis respectively. Both run the risk of the confounding effects of the excluded factor. For, as Schaie (1965a, p. 95) makes clear, the cross-sectional study, like period analysis, rests on the assumption that C has no effect; and the longitudinal study, on the assumption that P has no effect. As a further limitation, in each instance one of the main variables in the analysis, though it is controlled, cannot even be examined. In a cross-sectional study where P is restricted to a single period, there is no possibility of generalizing across periods, studying period differences, or assessing period effects. And, in a longitudinal study where C is restricted to a single cohort, there is no possibility of generalizing across cohorts, studying cohort differences, or assessing cohort effects. Thus, in both these commonly used designs, important information is missing; consequently there is less opportunity for analysis, and greater danger of fallacious interpretation, than in the more extensive designs we have been discussing.

A third, or cross-sequential, analysis completes the examination of relationships between pairs of factors. It focuses on P and C, but is potentially confounded by the uncontrolled effects of A. The data it employs are diagrammed in the shaded area of Table $2 \cdot 9$. Here the factors P and C can be interpreted directly only if A can be assumed to have no effect.

To sum up, in each of these three analyses the difficulty is patent: because of the impossibility of a simultaneous analysis of all three factors, each set of results is potentially confounded by the effects of the excluded third factor. Hence the dilemma: which effects are appropriate for phrasing the interpretation? Even though the factors are conceptually distinct and may, indeed, have independent effects, how can the true situation be teased out of these data? The answer is that a clear decision is possible only in special empirical situations or when special assumptions can reasonably be made: namely, in those situations where there is a basis—either in a priori reasoning or in outside information—for assuming that a particular one (or two) of the factors has no effect. Thus it seems useful to state:

> *Principle 3.* In an analysis of effects (A, P, C), the findings can be interpreted directly in terms of any particular two factors, only if the third factor can be assumed to have approximately zero effect.

Otherwise, there is a perennial danger that uncontrolled factors are confounding the results.

The use of models Where there is no clear basis for assuming in advance that one of the three factors has zero effect, valid interpretation generally depends upon the formulation of restrictive assumptions of various kinds. As an aid to identifying which effects are actually operating in particular research problems, special mathematical or statistical models might be developed that state appropriate assumptions and provide rules for testing the consistency of the data with these assumptions.[43]

The limiting case, in which a model is scarcely needed, is instructive. This is the case where, in fact, *only one* of the three factors is producing the effect. The problem is: How can the researcher identify this factor? And the answer is: This situation can be readily seen in either of the two forms of analysis using the factor.

---

[43] Schaie, 1965a, makes a bold attempt at a general model; but his overall strategy breaks down because he does not come to grips with the implications of the exact mathematical relationships among the variables. (See Baltes, 1967, 1968; Baltes and Nesselroade, 1970; and Schaie, 1970.)

For example, if age alone is making a difference in the dependent variable, Y, then Y will be associated with age in both the $A \times C$ analysis and in the $A \times P$ analysis; while in both analyses the effect of the second factor (C or P) will equal zero, showing no appreciable relationship to Y. A fictitious example of such a situation appears in Table 2 · 10. From either the cohort analysis or the period analysis, it can be stated mathematically that Y (as measured

TABLE 2 · 10   *Three types of analyses of a set of fictitious data*

(Age in parentheses)

Data

		Period of observation		
	Date of birth	1920	1940	1960
	1940			(20) 70
	1920		(20) 70	(40) 80
	1900	(20) 70	(40) 80	(60) 90

		Age		Age difference
Cohort analysis	Cohort	20	40	
	1920	70	80	+10
	1900	70	80	+10
	Cohort difference	0	0	

		Period		Period difference
Period analysis	Age	1940	1960	
	20	70	70	0
	40	80	80	0
	Age difference	+10	+10	

		Period		Period difference
Cross-sequential analysis	Cohort	1940	1960	
	1920	70	80	+10
	1900	80	90	+10
	Cohort difference	+10	+10	

in the cells of the table) is a function of this one variable, A. To be sure, this function can always be mathematically restated to say that Y is also a function of $P - C$, and the researcher must choose, as usual, between these mathematically equivalent statements. But in this limiting case, the data themselves can prove helpful to the decision, since the alternative explanation would mean that P and C tend to balance each other precisely—a possibility that would, in most situations, seem unlikely.[44] This equivalence between the period effects and the counteracting cohort effects is apparent from the cross-sequential analysis in Table 2 · 10.

To make the example less abstract, the researcher might find that the incidence of a particular disease is the function of A alone. Alternatively, he might consider formulating his interpretation in terms of a trend toward increasing air pollution that fosters the disease (a period effect) counterbalanced by an increasing resistance to the disease among the more recent cohorts as perinatal care improves (a cohort effect). But, in order to choose this alternative interpretation, the researcher must be willing to accept the empirical datum as indicating that the effects of air pollution are exactly equivalent to the countervailing effects of perinatal care.

When *two (or three) factors* are actually operative, rather than just one, the problem of deciding which ones to use in the interpretation becomes more complex. Here assumptions can be made and tested to see, for instance, whether one particular pair of variables must be used, whether either a particular pair or all three may be used, or whether all three are required. Blalock (1966, 1967a), for example, suggests such assumptions regarding the signs or magnitudes of some of the coefficients, or regarding certain kinds of nonlinear relationships. Since many combinations of assumptions are possible, which can lead to entirely different interpretations of the same data, every effort must be made to formulate assumptions that are appropriate to the particular data, and to conduct all possible tests of these assumptions. An illustrative example of such a decision procedure appears in Cohn's Mathematical Note to this chapter.

Moreover, many of the situations we examine in this book (e.g., the analysis of women's labor force participation shown in Figure 2 · 7 and in various examples in Chapter 12 and elsewhere) are too complex to be handled by any simple mathematical model. In general, then, it is clearly important, not only to consider the implicit assumptions, but also to examine the full array of available data before subjecting them to any standardized statistical procedures and tests.

[44] Suppose $Y = mP - nC$
$\qquad A = \quad P - \quad C$
$\quad$ If $m = \quad n$
$\quad$ Then $Y = mA$

We have been considering how certain differences in the life-course patterns of particular cohorts may be attributed to the effects of aging and to the diverse effects of history. In addition, a fuller explanation requires information about the *mechanisms* connecting both the aging process (P2) and the historical circumstances with the changes observed over the life course of the respective cohorts. Indications of such mechanisms can be obtained by various approaches. Exploratory panel analyses that trace the same individuals over time can delve beneath the surface for details and clues as to who changes at various life stages, what environmental factors appear to condition the changes, and why people themselves say that they change (or do not change).[45] Or, as special theories develop to account for given phenomena, the powerful experimental design can be used to test hypotheses that specify certain causal linkages—although the central variable of age itself cannot be experimentally manipulated. Still another highly useful approach, with the advantage over new research that it can be applied to data already collected about the past, utilizes the type of compositional analysis described in Section 1.

Each cohort has not only a starting date, which indexes its historical environment, but also certain intrinsic aspects (namely, size and composition), which influence the way it ages (Ld) and its relation to other cohorts (Cd). The cohort is heterogeneous, composed of individuals who, as organisms and as social actors, respond in diverse ways to age-associated biological and social changes and to historical events. Because males and females age differently, for example, the sex composition of a cohort can affect its life-course pattern, and successive cohorts can have divergent patterns to the extent that they differ in sex composition. Similarly, many other compositional variables—such as race, education, occupation, or marital status—serve to mediate the effects on particular cohorts of aging and of the environment. Compositional analysis, by treating relevant properties of cohorts as intervening variables, attempts to uncover such linkages, thereby suggesting possible clues to the underlying mechanisms either at the level of the component individuals, or at the level of the cohort as an aggregate. Moreover, by performing compositional analysis, the researcher can often avoid a special type of fallacy—what might be termed the "compositional fallacy"—of viewing changes in a characteristic (Y), either within or between cohorts, as representing changes in individual propensities or capacities when the changes are actually artifacts of changes in composition of the population under examination. For example, changes in the age-specific divorce rate may reflect changes

---

[45] For a classic statement of this procedure, see Lazarsfeld, Berelson, and Gaudet (1944, pp. 1–27).

in the proportion who are married at a particular age rather than actual age differences in tendencies for married couples to divorce. By examining divorce rates for a given time interval only among those classified as married at the beginning of the interval, and excluding other marital statuses, a compositional fallacy may be avoided.

Analysis of single cohorts Compositional analysis of relevant variables can often be applied to a particular cohort to explain the association between age and a given characteristic under study (call it Y). To revert to the example of sex (since sex has great power as an explanatory variable in many analyses), a cohort typically changes its sex composition over the life course as the result of the greater longevity of females. Thus if the characteristic Y, such as church attendance, is generally more pronounced among females than males, there will be an increasing tendency for the cohort as it ages to manifest Y. In such instances, the researcher can subdivide the cohort into males and females and perform the life course analysis separately for each subset.

As this example indicates, two objectives can be met by such a procedure. First, the researcher can control the effect of sex in further analyses (as in examination of period or cohort effects, or in cross-classification with additional variables), in order to focus more nearly upon the relationship between aging and the characteristic Y. Second, the researcher can use the procedure to uncover any differences in the life-course patterns of males and females, in order to suggest possible explanations as to how aging affects Y.[46]

In some situations, once the compositional variable is controlled, the original relationship between age and Y may disappear entirely. This type of possibility is illustrated by the finding[47] that, although responses to poll questions on political knowledge or awareness may show declines with age for the sample as a whole, there is *no* such relationship to age once educational level is controlled. [*See Chapter 4·1 by Foner.*] Such findings completely change the focus of analysis: the problem is no longer to describe the relationship of age to Y (political knowledge), but to explain this relationship by showing (a) that education is age-related and that (b) education accounts for part or all of the relationship of age to Y.

[46] A frequently employed alternative to control of a variable through separate analyses of subsets is standardization. As applied to analysis of a single cohort, a "standard composition" (which is fixed) is substituted at each age for the actual composition (which may be changing); and the changes in the characteristic of interest (Y) are then recomputed to show what they *would have been* if the actual cohort had the same composition at each consecutive age as the standard (cf. Hawley, 1959, p. 376; Bogue, 1969, pp. 121–123). Unlike compositional analysis, however, standardization does not have the advantage of enabling the researcher to look for differences in life course patterns within each subset of the compositional variable.

[47] Glenn (1969, pp. 27–28). Although these particular data actually refer to cross-sectional analysis, similar findings on voting appear in panel analyses too; see Glenn and Grimes (1968, pp. 565–567).

Certain kinds of characteristics seem to lend themselves to compositional analysis, apart from the obvious criterion that they must be associated with the particular dependent variable involved. First, since mortality operates selectively, it produces not only a continual reduction in the size of the cohort over its life course, but also a continual change in its composition. Thus factors, like sex, on which mortality rates differ (Volume I, Chapter 2 · 3) may be important sources of explanation for certain observed differences between old and young (Glenn and Zody, 1970). Second, irreversible characteristics can be utilized more conveniently as intervening variables than characteristics on which individuals tend to switch back and forth over the life course. When populations are stratified for compositional analysis by reversible characteristics, particular individuals may appear in different columns at different time periods, thus complicating the interpretation.

Analysis of successive cohorts   Compositional analysis can also be used with a sequence of cohorts as an aid to explaining why cohorts age in different ways. Thus cohorts might perhaps show divergent life-course patterns on IQ tests. However, one might imagine that these differences would be reduced if the educational composition of the respective cohorts were controlled so as to allow comparisons age-for-age between persons born at different dates but alike in their educational background.[48]

Many elaborations of compositional analysis are possible as conceptualization becomes increasingly precise and as more of the relevant properties and experiences of each cohort can be controlled. In certain studies of fertility, for example, cohorts are simultaneously cross-classified by several variables, including marital status and parity (the number of children already in the family). (See, e.g., Whelpton, 1954.)

Limitations and elaborations   We have been discussing examples of situations in which the effects of a compositional variable are explored by subdividing the *individuals* within each cohort. Obviously, this procedure is possible only where individuals within the cohort differ in terms of the variable at hand. Moreover, there are distinguishing aspects of a cohort often indexed by "global" measures, that are not compositional in the strict sense because they refer more nearly to the *cohort as a whole* than to discrete individuals. For example, certain historical conditions—such as the general level of economic productivity, or a Durkheimian state of anomie—are conceived as impinging on the entire cohort, though they may differentially affect the component individuals. In some other situations differences in composition of successive cohorts, or within a single cohort as it ages, may produce changes that

---

[48] As noted, standardization may be employed to control the effects of the compositional variable. As applied to analysis of successive cohorts, a fixed "standard cohort" composition over the life course of the cohort would be substituted for the actual life-course composition of each cohort to be compared.

ramify through other cohorts but that are not manifest in the cohort exhibiting change, or that are manifest only at some later period of the cohort's life course. In all such instances, the search for explanation, for empirical patterns that can be referred to postulated conceptual processes, and the tracing of intervening mechanisms will require far more complex and sophisticated designs for measurement and analysis than those described by our simple illustrations.[49] Nevertheless, whatever the age phenomenon under study, the search for understanding requires that the ever-changing composition of cohorts be accounted for.

4 · C SIZE AS A FACTOR

Throughout much of this essay, the analytical problems presented have focused on the *characteristics* of age strata or cohorts, with little regard for the ways in which the *size* of these strata or cohorts enters the analysis. As long as research interest centers on aspects of individuals, or categories of individuals, the convention of proportional representation of characteristics, in which size is "held constant," is useful in making age comparisons. Understanding at the *societal* level, however, requires knowledge of the joint contributions of size and characteristics to relations among the age strata and to societal change.

What might be termed a "fallacy of proportional representation" interprets societal phenomena without regard to variations in size of the age strata involved. Thus a series of age-specific crime *rates* (or summary measures based on such rates) might conceal major changes in the amount of crime in the total society, if the adolescent age stratum, which contributes the bulk of official crime, were to change its size. Or the lesser *tendency* of young adults to vote might lead political analysts to discount their electoral impact on the polity, if the large size of young adult cohorts is overlooked. Or the *proportions* in the several age strata playing interdependent roles—such as teacher and student, or physician and patient—might obscure the effects of their relative size in contributing to imbalances between people and roles.

Such fallacies may be avoided through the simple device of permitting size to vary in the empirical analysis. Either the proportions displaying a particular characteristic may be weighted by size to assess the combined effects of the two; or, if the analyst wishes to separate the variations in size on the total age structure, he may "hold constant" the proportions having the given characteristic.

This chapter has sketched in broad outline research that can disclose essential, if little understood, aspects of society. In much of the current work,

---

[49] Cohort or group measures that attempt to reflect differential individual behaviors are suggested in Riley and Nelson (1971); see also Riley (1963, Volume I, Unit 12).

however, the designs tend to be exploratory, the variables are frequently restricted to gross categories of age and time, and the interpretations are typically ad hoc. In order to advance this field of inquiry, what seems needed is not only improved methods of analysis and interpretation, but also a more sophisticated theory. As more detailed conceptual formulations develop, it will become increasingly possible to define intervening variables, to postulate connecting mechanisms, and to design research and experimentation that can test mutually supporting hypotheses. And, in turn, as a body of knowledge is systematically accumulated, it will begin to support a rounded conceptualization that can specify the place of age in the social structure and clarify the relationships among aging, cohort flow, and the forces of social stability and change.

On interpretation of cohort and period analyses: A mathematical note

RICHARD COHN

As discussed in Chapter 2, one of the crucial problems facing the researcher in the typical cohort or period analysis is that of deciding which of three conceptually defined factors—aging (A), cohort (C), and period (P)—may actually be operating in a particular situation.[1] A basic difficulty arises because each factor is defined empirically in terms of the other two,[2] limiting the extent to which empirical analysis can guide interpretation. Which of the three factors the researcher selects as operative must depend upon the additional assumptions—based in theory or prior knowledge—he is willing to make about the nature of the relationships under scrutiny.

The researcher confronted by a particular set of data may be aided in such decisions by a mathematical conceptualization that enables him systematically to scrutinize the ways in which his assumptions affect the choice of interpretations open to him. The procedure can be described as a sequence of steps in which (1) a formula that describes a particular set of data is first expressed and then (2) defined generally as the full set of formulas exressing a relationship of the dependent variable, Y, to A, P, and C consistent with the data. As guides in analysis and interpretation, the researcher (3) introduces

---

[1] One approach to this problem is suggested by the work of Schaie (1965a), who makes a suggestive, though abortive, attempt to formulate a complete set of decision rules applicable under specific assumptions.

[2] It has already been pointed out that this is one more example of the identification problem which has been discussed by Blalock, 1967a. Essentially we illustrate in detail Blalock's statement on p. 799: "In general, the simplest way to obtain solutions to identification problems is to make *a priori* assumptions to the effect that certain of the parameters are zero (or some other known value)." Blalock goes on to suggest a number of more sophisticated methods, and it is unfortunate that the data available to the researcher on age do not ordinarily seem to permit their use. [*See also Chapter 2 · 4 · A.*]

one or more assumptions about the nature of this relationship, each of which produces a selection from among the full set of formulas. The resultant selections are then (4) examined for consistency with one another and with the data, to determine which formulas from among the full set of alternatives may be ruled out by the set of assumptions. Any assumption or combination of assumptions that reduces the set of formulas descriptive of the data to zero is found to be in some way inappropriate to the data. When this occurs, the process may be repeated with an altered set of assumptions.

We shall now illustrate this procedure with a simple hypothetical example:

Step 1. Find the formula for the dependent variable (Y) that fits the data. Suppose we find in a particular set of data that Y is related to A and P by the simple formula $Y = 3A - 2P$.

Step 2. Determine the full set of alternatives to this formula for Y. Restricting ourselves for simplicity to linear formulas, we can restate the formula $Y = 3A - 2P$ in a number of ways. For example, we can write $Y = (4A - A) - (3P - P) = 4A - 3P + (P - A)$, which (since $C = P - A$) enables us to write $Y = 4A - 3P + C$. Alternatively we can write $Y = (5A - 2A) - (4P - 2P) = 5A - 4P + 2(P - A) = 5A - 4P + 2C$. What, then, is the full set of possible formulas? The full set of linear formulas defining Y in terms of A, P, and C can be expressed as $Y = (3 + x)A - (2 + x)P + xP - xA = (3 + x)A - (2 + x)P + xC$. Thus, (x) can be chosen in any way and the formula for Y would still fit the data, resulting in an infinite number of possible formulations.

Step 3. Decide on certain restrictive assumptions. In this particular example we shall make assumptions dealing with directionality and the number of factors actually operating.

Suppose we believe that the value of Y is determined by three factors indexed by A, P, and C and that the relationship is such that Y increases with (or is unaffected by) the first of these factors (A), but decreases with (or is unaffected by) the other two $(C$ and $P)$. Then, the coefficient for A (i.e., $3 + x$) must be positive or zero; the coefficient for P (i.e., $2 + x$) must be positive or zero; and the coefficient for C (i.e., x) must be negative or zero. These conditions now restrict (x) to the range from 0 to -2, redefining the set of possible formulas for Y (Step 2).

Now suppose further that we believe that only two of the factors actually operate (or that, for simplicity, we want to express the formula in this way). This assumption leaves us with the following alternatives:

Choice 1: A and P only are operative. Then $x = 0$, so $Y = 3A - 2P$ (our original formula).

Choice 2: A and C only are operative. Then $2 + x = 0$ or $x = -2$, so $Y = A - 2C$.

Choice 3: P and C only are operative. Then $3 + x = 0$ or $x = -3$, so $Y = P - 3C$.

Step 4. Determine whether any of the full set of alternative formulas (Step 2) can be ruled out by the assumptions introduced (Step 3). In our example, if only P and C are operative (choice 3 above), then $Y = P - 3C$. However, this is inconsistent with our assumption about the direction of the effect of the "P" factor. (This inconsistency can be ascertained immediately by observing that the choice of $x = -3$ defines a formula outside the range, 0 to -2, permitted by the assumption of directionality.) We must now either discard choice 3 or alter the assumptions regarding directionality. Which shall we do? If we feel confident that only two factors are operating and that our assumption about the direction of the effects is the most reasonable available, then we have narrowed our selection to two alternatives: Either A and P only *or* A and C only are operating.

Suppose, however, we wish to explore various particular assumptions about the direction of the effects, under the assumption that only two factors are operating.[3] We find that, with different assumptions, we are led to different selections of factors.

Repetitions of Steps 3 and 4 with altered assumptions of directionality. Suppose we decide (Step 3) that Y decreases with (or is unaffected by) A and C, but increases with (or is unaffected by) P. Then the coefficients for A (i.e., $3 + x$), P (i.e., $2 + x$) and C (i.e., x) must all be negative or zero. These conditions now restrict (x) to the range -3 or less. We now find (Step 4) that, if only two factors are operating, we are restricted to choice 3 above, in which P and C only are operative, $x = -3$, and $Y = P - 3C$.

As another example, we might assume (Step 3) that Y decreases with (or is unaffected by) each of the three factors A, P, and C. Now the coefficient for A must be negative or zero; the coefficient for P must be positive or zero; and the coefficient for C must be negative or zero. We find, however, that *no* choice of (x) will fulfill these conditions. We decide, therefore (Step 4), that we have made an assumption inconsistent with the data.

These simple examples serve to illustrate the complex process of decision-making in which the statement of assumptions determines the alternative selections that can be made in interpreting a particular set of data. Very often, the researcher finds that his assumptions do not enable him to rule out all formulations but one, that several formulations fit his empirical findings under his assumptions. In other circumstances, he may even find that his assumptions are not consistent with the data and must be revised. Thus translation of the interpretive decision-making process into the framework of mathe-

---

[3] With three factors, each of which may have positive (or zero) *or* negative (or zero) effects, there are eight possible assumptions regarding directionality.

matics provides no simple answer to the basic difficulty in interpreting cohort or period analyses. Such translation may, however, make the researcher more fully aware of the way in which his decisions must be guided by his asumptions.

Works cited in Chapter 2

Andvord, K. F., 1930. "What Can We Learn by Studying Tuberculosis by Generations?" *Norsk Magazin for Laegevidenskaben*, 91, pp. 642–660.

Back, Kurt W., and Linda Brookover Bourque, 1970. "Life Graphs: Aging and Cohort Effect," *Journal of Gerontology*, 25, pp. 249–255.

Baltes, P. B., 1967. "Laengsschnitt- und Querschnittsequenzen zur Erfassung von Alters- und Generationseffekten." Unpublished doctoral dissertation, University of Saarland, Saarbruecken, Germany.

————, 1968. "Longitudinal and Cross-Sectional Sequences in the Study of Age and Generation Effects," *Human Development*, 11, pp. 145–171.

————, and J. R. Nesselroade, 1970. "Multivariate Longitudinal and Cross-Sectional Sequences for Analyzing Ontogenetic and Generational Change: A Methodolcgical Note," *Developmental Psychology*, 2, pp. 163–168.

Blalock, Hubert M., Jr., 1966. "The Identification Problem and Theory Building: The Case of Status Inconsistency," *American Sociological Review*, 31, pp. 52–61.

————, 1967a. "Status Inconsistency, Social Mobility, Status Integration and Structural Effects," *American Sociological Review*, 32, pp. 790–801.

————, 1967b. "Status Inconsistency and Interaction: Some Alternative Models," *American Journal of Sociology*, 73, pp. 305–315.

Bogue, Donald J., 1969. *Principles of Demography*, New York: Wiley.

Coleman, James S., 1964. *Introduction to Mathematical Sociology*, New York: Free Press of Glencoe.

Crittenden, John, 1962. "Aging and Party Affiliation," *Public Opinion Quarterly*, 26, pp. 648–657.

Cutler, Neal E., 1968. *The Alternative Effects of Generations and Aging Upon Political Behavior: A Cohort Analysis of American Attitudes Toward Foreign Policy, 1946–1966.* Oak Ridge, Tenn.: Oak Ridge National Laboratory.

————, 1970. "Generation, Maturation, and Party Affiliation: A Cohort Analysis," *Public Opinion Quarterly*, 33, pp. 583–588.

Dublin, Louis I., and Mortimer Spiegelman, 1941. "Current versus Generation Life Tables," *Human Biology*, 13, pp. 439–459.

Frost, Wade Hampton, 1939. "The Age Selection of Mortality from Tuberculosis in Successive Decades," *American Journal of Hygiene*, Section A, 30, pp. 91–96.

Glenn, Norval D., 1969. "Aging, Disengagement, and Opinionation," *Public Opinion Quarterly*, 33, pp. 17–33.

————, and Michael Grimes, 1968. "Aging, Voting and Political Interest," *American Sociological Review*, 33, pp. 563–575.

————, and Richard E. Zody, 1970. "Cohort Analysis with National Survey Data," *The Gerontologist*, 10, pp. 233–240.

Goodman, Leo A., 1962. "Statistical Methods for Analyzing Process of Change," *American Journal of Sociology*, 68, pp. 57–87.

Hammond, E. Cuyler, and Lawrence Garfinkel, 1968. "Changes in Cigarette Smoking 1959–1965," *American Journal of Public Health*, 58, pp. 30–45.

Hawley, Amos H., 1959. "Population Composition," in Hauser, Philip M., and Otis Dudley Duncan, editors, *The Study of Population*, Chicago: University of Chicago Press, pp. 361–382.

Kessen, W., 1960. "Research Design in the Study of Developmental Problems," in Mussen, Paul, editor, *Handbook of Research Methods in Child Development*, New York: Wiley.

Kiser, Clyde V., 1962. "The Aging of Human Populations: Mechanisms of Change," in Tibbitts, Clark, and Wilma Donahue, editors, *Social and Psychological Aspects of Aging*, New York: Columbia University Press, pp. 18–35.

————, Wilson Grabill, and Arthur Campbell, 1968. *Trends and Variations in Fertility in the United States*, Cambridge, Mass.: Harvard University Pess.

Lazarsfeld, Paul F., Bernard Berelson, and Hazel Gaudet, 1944. *The People's Choice*, New York: Duell, Sloan & Pearce, pp. 40–51.

Lipset, Seymour Martin, 1963. *Political Man*, Garden City, N.Y.: Doubleday, Anchor Books.

Lotka, A. J., 1931. "The Structure of a Growing Population," *Human Biology*, 3, pp. 459–493.

MacMahon, Brian, S. Johnson, and Thomas F. Pugh, 1963. "Relation of Suicide Rates to Social Conditions," *Public Health Reports*, 78, pp. 285–293.

————, Thomas F. Pugh, and Johannes Ipsen, 1960. *Epidemiologic Methods*, Boston: Little, Brown.

Merrell, Margaret, 1956. "Time-Specific Life Tables Contrasted with Observed Survivorship," in Spengler, Joseph J., and Otis Dudley Duncan, editors, *Demographic Analysis*, Glencoe, Ill: Free Press, pp. 108–114.

National Manpower Council, 1957. *Womanpower*, A Statement by the National Manpower Council, New York: Columbia University Press

Riley, Matilda White, 1963. *Sociological Research, Volume I, A Case Approach; Volume II, Exercises and Manual*, New York: Harcourt, Brace & World.

————, Marilyn E. Johnson, and Sarane S. Boocock, 1963. "Woman's Changing Occupational Role—A Research Report," *The American Behavioral Scientist*, 6, pp. 33–37.

————, and Edward E. Nelson, 1971. "Research on Stability and Change in Social Systems," in Barber, Bernard, and Alex Inkeles, editors, *Stability and Social Change: A Volume in Honor of Talcott Parsons*, Boston: Little, Brown, pp. 407–449.

Rosset, Edward, 1964. *Aging Process of Population*, New York: Macmillan.

Ryder, Norman B., 1964a. "Notes on the Concept of a Population," *American Journal of Sociology*, 69, pp. 447–463.

————, 1964b. "The Process of Demographic Translation," *Demography*, Vol. 1, No. 1, pp. 74–82.

————, 1965. "The Cohort as a Concept in the Study of Social Change," *American Sociological Review*, 30, pp. 843–861.

————, 1969. "The Emergence of a Modern Fertility Pattern: United States 1917–66," in Behrman, S. J., Leslie Corsa, and Ronald Freedman, editors, *Fertility and Family Planning*, Ann Arbor: University of Michigan Press, pp. 99–123.

Schaie, K. Warner, 1965a. "A General Model for the Study of Develpomental Problems," *Psychological Bulletin*, 64, pp. 92–107.

————, 1965b. "Age Changes and Age Differences." Presented at a symposium of the Gerontological Society, Los Angeles.

————, 1970. "A Reinterpretation of Age-Related Changes in Cognitive Structure and Functioning," in Goulet, L. R., and P. B. Baltes, editors, *Theory and Research in Life-span Developmental Psychology*, New York: Academic Press.

Spiegelman, Mortimer, 1968. *Introduction to Demography*, rev. ed. Cambridge, Mass.: Harvard University Press.

Sweetser, Frank L., 1965. "Factorial Ecology: Helsinki, 1960," *Demography*, 2, pp. 372–385.

Taeuber, Conrad, and Irene Taeuber, 1958. *The Changing Population of the United States*, New York: Wiley.

United States Bureau of the Census, 1960 Census of Population, Vol. I, Part 1.

United States Department of Health, Education and Welfare, *Monthly Vital Statistics Report*, Vol. 17, No. 13 (August 15, 1969), pp. 1–2.

Whelpton, Pascal K., 1954. *Cohort Fertility: Native White Women in the United States*, Princeton, N.J.: Princeton University Press.

Wilensky, Harold L., 1961. "Life Cycle, Work Situation, and Participation in Formal Associations" in Kleemeier, R. W., editor, *Aging and Leisure*, New York: Oxford University Press, pp. 213–242.

3

Notes on the concept of a population

NORMAN B. RYDER

Introduction
1   The basic population model
2   Population composition
3   Population processes
4   Macroanalysis and microanalysis
5   Social change from a demographic perspective
6   Conclusion

This essay is an attempt to identify some distinctive characteristics of the demographic approach to social analysis with emphasis on the contributions that can be made by the concept of a population. The effort has been prompted

Reprinted in part and in slightly altered form from *The American Journal of Sociology*, Vol. LXIX, No. 5, March 1964, pp. 447–463, with permission of The University of Chicago Press. Copyright 1964 by the University of Chicago.

Revised version of a paper entitled "The Demographer's Ken," which was delivered at the annual meetings of the Population Association of America, Madison, Wisconsin, May 1962. The writer wishes to acknowledge the financial support of the Social Systems Research Institute, University of Wisconsin, and the intellectual support of O. Dudley Duncan and George J. Stolnitz in the preparation of this paper.

by several publications with similar intent but somewhat different conclusions. (See Hauser and Duncan, 1959; Grauman, 1959; Hawley, 1959; and also Schnore, 1961.) In the first section of this essay the basic population model is introduced and described. This model is then used to provide a basis for distinguishing the demographer's special contribution to the study of population composition and population processes. The penultimate section introduces the concept of a population into the controversy concerning the interrelationships of microanalysis and macroanalysis. Finally, some suggestions are made concerning the contributions a demographic approach can make to the study of social change. The pervasive theme of the article is the way in which the concept of a population forces the sociologist to give time a central place in his theory and research.

1 *The basic population model*

The backbone of population study is formal demography. The demographer is equipped with a special type of mathematical model, which is adaptable to a wide range of problems and which yields proposals that particular kinds of data be studied with particular techniques of description and measurement. Formal demography is the deductive study of the necessary relationships between the quantities serving to describe the state of a population and those serving to describe changes in that state, in abstraction from their association with other phenomena (Lotka, 1939). The central features of demography as a body of knowledge and methods may be approached by considering the population as a model. The generic concept of a population is an abstract view of a universe of phenomena comprising recognizable individual elements. Although demography is concerned substantively with humans, it has formal affinity with the analysis of all such collectivities. The first contribution by Alfred J. Lotka (1907), the man most responsible for modern demography, was a study of "the mode of growth of material aggregates."[1] In that paper, he presented the essence of demography in his opening observation that, in a material system, certain individual constituent elements may each have a limited life-period, but the aggregate of a number of such individuals may nevertheless have a prolonged existence, provided there is some process for the formation of new individuals as the old ones are eliminated.

The elements of the basic population model may be specified as follows:

1. The population is characterized as an aggregate of individuals who conform to a given definition. This definition is ordinarily at least spatial and temporal in specificity.

2. The central question concerns the change of the aggregate number of

[1] The author emphasized the generality he intended by using biological terms like "birth" and "death" only in quotation marks.

constituent elements through time. Population research is dynamic in this elementary sense.

3. The change through time in the aggregate number is conceptualized as the difference between the number of additions to, and number of subtractions from, that total during the time interval of observation.[2] Decomposition in this way is so characteristic of the demographer's behavior that it is often specified in a definition of the field (Hauser and Duncan, 1959). If additions and subtractions are further distinguished as births and immigrations on the one hand, and deaths and emigrations on the other, the proposition becomes the so-called demographic equation (Davis, 1949). In this section of the paper, the population is assumed to be closed to migration; in a subsequent section migration is given special attention.

4. The model is microdynamic as well as macrodynamic. That is to say, the passage of time is identified for the individual constituent elements as well as for the population as a whole. This emphasizes, in Lotka's terms, the distinction between persistence of the individual and persistence of the aggregate. Individual entries and exits are dated, and the difference between date of entry and date of observation, for the individual, is his age at that time. Age is the central variable in the demographic model. It identifies birth cohort membership (as discussed below). It is a measure of the interval of time spent within the population, and thus of exposure to the risk of occurrence of the event of leaving the population, and more generally is a surrogate for the experience that causes changing probabilities of behavior of various kinds. Age as the passage of personal time is, in short, the link between the history of the individual and the history of the population.[3]

5. Once increases and decreases are identified in terms of both personal and population time, attention is focused on properties of the system that determine the limitation of the life-period of the constituents and the formation of new constituents. The emphasis passes from the deaths and births that occur to the individuals, to mortality and fertility, which are cohort processes.[4]

6. The population model is completed by linking together three kinds of functions. The first of these is the number of person-years of exposure of the population within each age interval and time interval; the second is the num-

[2] Boulding has called this proposition perhaps the most fundamental of all science (Boulding, 1950, p. 190).

[3] Age is only the most useful case of the general category of intervals, measured from the time of entry into particular kinds of subpopulations or quasi-populations. These are discussed in Section 2.

[4] An important distinction can be made between biological populations, to which new members are added as a consequence of the event of parenthood occurring to existing members of the population, and other situations in which the population concept is applicable, but the additions are properties of the population as a whole and its total environment. Immigration is a case in point.

ber of births occurring within each age interval and time interval per person-year of exposure; the third is the number of deaths occurring within each age interval and time interval per person-year of exposure. In brief, they are the age-time structure of the population, and the age-time processes of fertility and mortality. These three functions represent a network of identities within a complete deterministic model. The formal theory of demography is concerned with working out the logico-mathematical relationships among these components and elaborating schemes for their analysis in terms suggested by the structure of the model.

At several points above, reference has been made to the distinction between individual occurrences and cohort processes. The significance of this may be exemplified by reference to mortality. An individual has a lifetime of, say, x years, which is begun at birth and terminated by death. In the population accounts this is recorded as an addition to, and then, x years later, as a subtraction from, the aggregate of one unit. From the standpoint of population size as a function of time, the age of the individual at death is irrelevant. Only the fact and time of death enter the accounting procedure, since the question of which individual dies does not affect the size of the population. The individual is assigned to a temporal aggregate on the basis of his time of birth, because this offers some obvious arithmetical conveniences. Such an aggregate is termed a (birth) cohort.[5] The mortality process for the cohort is the distribution of its membership by age at death (and, since time of birth is identical among the members, by the time of death as well). This distribution is a characteristic of the cohort as an aggregate, but the argument of the function representing it is individual time. Thus the events of subtraction of individuals from the aggregate are transformed into rates for each age-time interval, the numerator of the rate being the number of occurrences of the event of death, and the denominator the area of person-years of exposure of the aggregate to the risk of occurrence of that event during the particular time interval. By this form of calculation the event that characterizes the individual is transformed into the process that characterizes the cohort.

In considering the demographic history of a cohort, there is an obvious cause-and-effect relationship between its mortality process and its age-time structure, that is, the distribution through time of the person-years of exposure. Considered as an age structure, the population at any moment of time is a cross section of cohorts as age structures, when the cohorts are viewed diagrammatically as if they were stacked in uniformly staggered fashion, each atop its predecessor in time. The procedure for relating the parameters of these two kinds of age structures has been developed by the writer and named the process of "demographic translation" (Ryder, 1964b).

---

[5] The cohort approach has analytical as well as arithmetical advantages (see Ryder, 1968).

To complete the basic population model as a web of structures and processes, some fertility mechanism is required. The size of any cohort at birth is provided by the number of births in the period that dates the cohort. Those births that occur in any period may be viewed as a product sum of the age structure of the population in the period and the fertility rates of the cohorts that occupy the various ages of parenthood at that time. These rates are of the occurrence-exposure type elaborated for mortality.[6] Now the period age structure is a cross-sectional translation of the age structures of the successive participant cohorts, and the fertility rates are a cross-sectional translation of the fertility rates of the same cohorts. Thus the process of demographic translation between period and cohort functions is intrinsic to the establishment of interdependencies among all three functions of the basic population model.

To summarize, the system provides a way of generating changes in population size through time, because of the continual destruction and creation of members, as a joint product of population structures and cohort processes. As noted, the population structure in any period is a translation of cohort age structures, and these are in turn the outcome of cohort mortality processes. The circle of formal analysis moves from (1) individual acts of procreation and death to (2) cohort processes of fertility and mortality, and thence to (3) cohort age structures. These are translated into (4) period age structures, which combine with period translations of the cohort vital processes to yield (5) the births and deaths that change the size of the population. This mode of analysis presents the problem of structural transformation in terms of the processes that shape and reshape the structure. Thus it is attuned to the tendency of present-day science to regard events rather than things, processes rather than states, as the ultimate components of the world of reality.[7] The contributions of Lotka (1939) have established the determinacy of the population structure implicit in fixed processes of cohort fertility and mortality and have provided, at this level, a comprehensive representation of the stable equilibrium model. Work is now proceeding on the establishment of the structural consequences of systematic change in the cohort processes, in order to develop models that are dynamic in the customary sense of the term (see Ryder, 1963).

2 Population composition

The basic population model presented above can be used in consideration of social composition and social mobility as topics for demographic inquiry.[8]

[6] The process is purposely described here as if parenthood were monosexual or nonsexual, for reasons to be amplified in Section 3.
[7] The philosophical term for this view is "actuality theory" (see "Actuality Theory" in *Encyclopaedia Britannica* (1957).
[8] See Schnore (1961) for the ideas that prompted this section.

Population composition has been defined as the relative frequency of any enumerable or measurable characteristic, quality, trait, attribute, or variable observed for individuals in a population, that is, as any view of an aggregate that recognizes any differences among its individual components. A list of such components would include residential location; ethnic group membership; religion; education; employment; occupation; industry; social roles and memberships; anthropometric, biometric, and psychometric traits; genetic constitution; health status; and attained skills (United Nations, 1958; Hauser and Duncan, 1959). From this vantage point the demographer's ken seems boundless. The concern in this section is to attempt to identify some criteria for drawing a line between demographic and nondemographic variables, in order to arrive at an understanding of what it is about demographic analysis that could distinguish it from any other kind of statistical social analysis.[9] The position to be advanced is that limits can be established for the sphere of demographic competence by considering not so much the substance of any characteristic as its adaptability to formulation in the terms of the basic population model.[10]

The argument begins with consideration of a distinction that has been proposed between characteristics that are fixed and characteristics that are changeable.[11] Some characteristics are determinable at birth and fixed for life. These may be distinguished for convenience as the genetic inheritance and the cultural inheritance, in both cases derivative from the parents. The most prominent representatives of the former are sex and color. Under the latter heading come such nonbiological characteristics of parents as ethnic origin, mother tongue, and place and date of birth. The last of these, which identifies cohort membership, is usually represented by age, which is, of course, an invariant function of time and in this sense a fixed variable. Other characteristics are subject to change throughout the course of an individual's life, such as educational attainment, marital status, and the various attributes associated with economic activities.

Now this distinction between changeable and unchangeable characteristics is an important convenience at an operational level, but it is scarcely defensible from the standpoint of the significance of such identifications for behavior, and it conceals a facet of almost all census questions that can be exploited by the demographer. Thus there is merely a distinction of degree

[9] One of the beginnings of sociology as an academic discipline in the United States was the quantitative treatment of social problems. Some such departments were first called "Statistics" but later changed their name to "Sociology." "Population problems" gradually became identified as a major subdivision of these departments (Lorimer, 1959).

[10] An analogous approach has been adopted in the study of the economics of capital (see Boulding, 1950, p. 189).

[11] Grauman (1959); Schnore (1961). Status ascription is a process that ties some changeable characteristics to some fixed characteristics. Status achievement is a process that ties some changeable characteristics to other changeable characteristics.

rather than kind between inherited and acquired characteristics, since virtually all phenotypic characters manifest the interaction of genetic and environmental factors. From a sociological standpoint sex, race, age, and other "biological" characteristics are learned roles. Although the various types of nonbiological identification that can be used to label a person at birth may be regarded as having a persistent influence on his lifetime behavior, their fixity is only a convenient approximation to a much more complex and dynamic reality.

There are several senses in which the changeable characteristics are fixed. Many of them endure for extended periods of time, and are frequently permanent within or beyond particular age limits. Thus educational attainment is by and large established during prematurity; marital status tends to be fixed for lengthy periods within each stage of the sequence of single, married, and widowed; labor force participation for many involves a single entry early in life and a single departure late in life; religion and citizenship are fixed for life for the majority. Now it is not disputed that changes can and do occur in these variables. But the significant point for the student of the population as an aggregate is that these changes tend to occur within a narrow age range for most of the population.

This aspect of temporal persistence in most census characteristics is manifest in and enhanced by census practice. Thus it is accepted procedure to attempt to record those who habitually live in an area (including absentees and excluding transients) in order to get at "usual residence"—the place where a person "lives." A population is considered as consisting of inhabitants, a term that implies both spatial fixity and temporal endurance. Occupation and place of residence are among the characteristics that a person changes most frequently. But census procedures ordinarily involve the attempt to establish what these are usually rather than momentarily. This is a partial explanation for the fact that the census is primarily a classificatory rather than a measuring instrument. In the same way, migration is identified as only those changes of residence that carry some implication of permanency. In summary, population characteristics are for the most part the results of attempts to achieve relatively enduring labels by definitional devices and changeable characteristics may be distinguished by the extent to which they manifest temporal persistence.

A further type of fixity in the realm of changeable characteristics concerns fixity of sequence. Several important population characteristics have high probabilities of change, but in relatively restricted ways. The classic case is age (which departs from its fixed sequence only through age misstatement, a form of intercohort migration). Reproductive parity and educational attainment in terms of years of schooling fall under the same heading. Likewise, specific marital statuses can only be changed, by law, into a limited number of particular other marital statuses. Some occupations can be arranged in career sequence, particularly if the earlier occupation is in some sense apprenticeship for the later. Sometimes one variable is characteristically sequential with another, for example, the close relationship between certain levels of education and certain categories of occupation, which in turn are closely related to income levels.

The aspect of fixity of characteristics and sequences has been stressed here because it makes possible the application in analysis of the array of demographic techniques based on the concept of a population. The argument is, in a sense, a generalization of the implications of Grauman's (1959) observation that the principal relevance of the distinction between fixed and changeable characteristics is that population segments that have the same fixed characteristics can be treated by estimating methods analogous to those employed in estimating population totals. It is the writer's view that the special contribution of the demographer to social analysis is focused on those items of individual information that can be thought of as defining quasi-populations, because they endure. Thus a characteristic may be viewed as an individual's residence over a period of time. The time interval has a beginning and an end for the individual—an entry into and an exit from that particular quasi-population—and within the interval the individual is exposed to the risk of occurrence of various events, in particular, that of departure from that quasi-population. It is at least operationally conceivable that not only an enumeration of the individuals within these quasi-populations at successive times can be obtained, but also a registration of entries and exits. Full utilization of the power of the population model would also require determination of the length of time each individual has spent within the quasi-population. The most commonly used interval is age, and it ordinarily serves as a surrogate for more precise interval determination. Age is the outstanding representative of a large class of measurements of the length of time elapsing since the occurrence of a cohort-defining event, but is a satisfactory substitute for the particular duration only to the extent that there is small variance in age at entry into the quasi-population in question.

3 Population processes

The present section examines the applicability of the population concept in the study of the three processes that are clearly integral to the field of demography considered substantively—fertility, mortality, and migration—and to the closely associated process of nuptiality. The outcome of the presentation is that the basic population model is tailor-made for mortality analysis, plays an important but incomplete role in the measurement of nuptiality, has proliferated in several analytically advantageous ways in fertility research, and finally is appropriate for answering questions about one kind of migration but not about another.

The prototype of statistical analysis in demography is the life table. A cohort is taken from birth throughout the life span, with its numbers reduced age by age on the basis of the mortality rates, the ratios of occurrences of death to person-years of exposure to the risk of death. The area of exposure in each age and time interval is reduced successively by occurrences that depend in turn on previous areas of exposure and their mortality rates. Whatever other subpopulation or quasi-population may be studied, the events that reduce membership must include mortality as well as the departures that are specific to the particular definition of membership. The elegance of the system of life-table functions has inspired the whole array of attempts to convert other processes, often substantively quite dissimilar, into analogues of mortality.

In the sphere of nuptiality analysis, the parallel with mortality is readily drawn and the basic population model successfully applied. Every person begins life single and most persons suffer "death" as a single person by experiencing the event of first marriage, an event that is irreversible provided a strict definition of the single state is maintained. Similarly, the successive stages of married life may be studied as attrition processes, for example, the dissolution of marriage by divorce or widowhood. But the population model is restricted in its usefulness to the situation in which the event may reasonably be considered as occurring to an individual. Now marriage is in fact an event that occurs to two persons simultaneously, and the exposure to the risk of occurrence of marriage is a function not only of the personal characteristics of the man and woman involved, but also of the general state of the marriage market—the relative availability of spouses of either sex. This problem has proven completely intractable to conventional modes of demographic analysis (see Ryder, 1961). This is the reason for specifying above that the basic population model is nonsexual or monosexual. The relationships between probabilities of marriage and the sex-age composition of the unmarried population are not expressible in terms of formal interconnections between occurrences and exposures. This is a clear-cut case of the need for measurements of properties of the aggregate in determination of probabilities of individual behavior, as discussed in more detail in Section 4.

In fertility research, one important improvement in methodology has been the extension and generalization of the basic notion of a cohort from its original signification of birth cohort to cohorts identified by common date of occurrence of other significant events. The variables that have been exploited in modern fertility measurement are number, age, marital status, marital duration, parity, and birth interval. These six variables may be grouped in three pairs, in order, each pair consisting of a status (which identifies quasi-population membership) and a time interval since acquiring that status ("age" within the quasi-population). The demographic characteristics pertinent to the act of parenthood are most succinctly identified as a series of time points: date of birth of the prospective mother; date of her marriage; date of birth of each preceding child; and date of current birth. The intervals, then, are the differences between pairs of successive time points. The statuses imply membership in various types of cohort: the birth cohort, the marriage cohort, the first parity cohort, and so forth. Temporal aggregation afresh on the basis of the most recent event in the reproductive history provides a mode of efficient analysis of the frequency and the time distribution of the next succeeding event (see Ryder, 1956). The only formal problem in this sequence is the formation of marriage cohorts out of birth cohorts, as discussed in the preceding paragraph.

Migration is clearly the most complex demographic process to discuss from the standpoint of the basic population model. The problems that arise are discussed here first for external migration and then for internal migration. Immigration and emigration, the terms generally used in distinguishing the two directions of external migration, are on an equal footing with fertility and mortality as modes of entry and exit from the total population. This circumstance follows from the fact that the population is customarily defined in spatiotemporal terms: immigration and emigration represent the crossing of spatial boundaries just as fertility and mortality represent the crossing of temporal boundaries. The parallel may be extended to the conceptualization of emigration as a type of mortality. There are no unique difficulties of a formal kind in considering exposure to the risk of occurence of emigration from the population, with a determination of the probabilities of emigration in each time interval, for members of successive birth cohorts, following the life-table format. Furthermore, emigration, like mortality, is a process of exit from the total population, and therefore from every constituent subpopulation or quasi-population.

When attention is turned to immigration, the analogy immediately dissolves. This may indeed be an important mode of addition of new members to the receiving population, but the events that constitute it do not occur to members of the receiving population. In contradistinction to fertility, the initiation of immigration is exogenous to the population being studied and can be built into the model only on an ad hoc basis because the exposure to the risk of immigration lies outside the defined population. For this reason, immigration research has not been able to exploit the measurement techniques that emanate from the basic population model. The characteristics of the population which yield various patterns of immigration are characteristics of the aggregate rather than of individuals within the aggregate. In this sense, immigration is a subdivision of the general study of ecosystem interchange, a branch of population theory that is much more developed for nonhuman than for human populations (Boulding, 1950, Chapter 1).

The process of internal migration may be regarded on the one hand as a special application of the quasi-population concept, or on the other hand as the prototype of a different but related kind of population model. If the territory that defines a population is divided into subterritories, each with its own subpopulation, then the movement of an individual from one subterritory to another is formally analogous to passage from any one status to another. If the focus of interest is the subpopulation itself, then in-migration and out-migration are at that level analogous to the processes of immigration and emigration as discussed above for the total population. But if the total population within which the movements are occurring is the focus of attention, then it is more natural to speak of the movements not so much in terms of entry into and exit from particular subpopulations, as in terms of interstitial movement between subpopulations.[12] This way of describing the process places the subject within the reach of the theory of Markov chains, a type of mathematics that possesses great potentialities in demographic research. An initial distribution and a terminal distribution, termed column vectors, are related to one another by a square matrix of transition probabilities. These are the conditional probabilities of moving to a particular terminal location, given a particular initial location.[13]

The basic population model and the transition matrix model are variants of a single formal system, which have their own special advantages for two different categories of problems. The basic concept of a population has been characterized as spatiotemporal. Accordingly, two types of changes may be distinguished: metabolism, or replacement in time, characterized by the processes of fertility and mortality; and migration, or replacement in space. An emphasis on metabolic transformation leads to a preference for the model of entry, exposure, and exit, as discussed above. An emphasis on migratory transformation leads to a preference for the transition matrix model. The two types of models share one important feature. If the matrix of transition probabilities is held fixed, it may be shown that the column vectors move toward an equilibrium state, which represents the latent structural propensities of the processes characterized by the matrix. This is, of course, a precise analogy to

[12] Similarly, immigration and emigration may be considered as species of internal migration from the standpoint of the population of the world. Indeed, the world population as a model has considerable theoretical convenience because, thus far at least, there is only one mode of entry and one mode of exit.

[13] The approach has been applied with success in solving some residual difficulties in stable population theory (see Kendall, 1949; Lopez, 1961). Applications to the study of intergenerational occupational mobility have been less successful because the column vectors can be uniquely specified neither in temporal location nor in constituents (see, e.g., Prais, 1955a and 1955b; Matras, 1960 and 1961).

stable population theory. Both mathematical models direct analytic attention away from the consequent structures and toward the determinant processes. But a distinction of degree or emphasis remains. In considering the various census characteristics in the preceding section, it became clear that some of them were more adaptable to the quasi-population concept than others, and that the degree of adaptability hinged on the frequency of entry and exit, or, in other words, on the degree of temporal persistence. It seems reasonable to propose that those characteristics that are too variable from time to time to be usefully conceptualized in quasi-population terms can be accommodated methodologically within the transition matrix approach. As an alternative mode of division of labor between the two models, it may be suggested that the transition matrix approach is more suitable for comparative cross-sectional analysis, which focuses on short-run period-by-period changes in the population structure, while the population approach is more suitable for the study of behavior associated with the life cycle, which focuses on long-run cohort-by-cohort transformation. But these should be considered as tentative and probably premature forays beyond a fecund methodological frontier.

4 *Macroanalysis and Microanalysis*

The study of population comprises not only a system of formal relations but also various systems of substantive relations between parameters of the population model and other variables.

The writer has described elsewhere (Ryder, 1959) an example of the way in which a concrete object of the demographer's attention may have its various aspects allocated among different abstract disciplines. Research on fertility can be divided into the contribution of substantive analysis in the biological realm—using data about fecundity and fertility regulation to explain observed fertility—and the contribution of substantive analysis in the realm of the social sciences—using data about individuals and groups to explain observed fertility regulation (and even to some extent fecundity). Within the latter realm it is useful to distinguish between psychosocial and sociocultural research, or—to identify more precisely the point to be discussed—between microanalytic and macroanalytic inquiries. The relationships between these two levels of inquiry deserve attention because they are of peculiar relevance to the demographer and because the concept of a population contributes to their clarification. Much of the discussion of analytic strategies in fertility research has consisted of assertions of the relative importance of microanalytic and macroanalytic levels of inquiry for the explanation of fertility. Thus Vance (1959) has called macroanalytic explanations inadequate because they fail to specify the ways in which macrovariables are translated into individual motivations. In their commentary on this assertion, Hauser and Duncan

(1959) have labeled the psychosocial variables as superficial, and proposed that the deep-seated macroanalytic causes underlie them. The difficulty of adjudicating competing claims like these is that the criteria of relative success differ. If the individual is the unit of analysis, then success is measured by explanation of variance among individuals; if the population is the unit of analysis, then success is measured by explanation of variance among populations. The issue has not been confined to the field of fertility. Several influential demographers have decried the circumstance that most migration analysis ignores the study of the motivations behind particular individual movements by its macroanalytic focus on net migration (Bogue, 1952; Vance, 1959; Hamilton, 1961). Schnore (1961) has taken the opposite stand concerning sociological interest in mobility. He has expressed concern that the majority interest in the correlates of individual behavior means short shrift for macroanalytic inquiries into interdependencies of population composition and social structure. In the field of mortality research, the microanalytic approach is winning by default, because almost no student of the subject seems interested in asking macroanalytic questions.

A final controversy deserves mention. The variables in individual correlation are descriptive properties of individuals; the variables in ecological correlation are descriptive properties of populations (although they are computed by deriving summary indexes of the properties of individual members of the respective populations). (See Riley, 1963, Volume I, pp. 700–788; Volume II, pp. 89–90.) Robinson has asserted correctly that individual correlations cannot be inferred from ecological correlations, and has asserted incorrectly that the purpose of ecological correlations must be to discover something about the behavior of individuals (Robinson, 1950; Menzel, 1950; see also Goodman, 1953; Duncan and Duncan, 1953). This debate has special pertinence for the demographer because of one characteristic feature of the population concept. Given the definition of a population as an aggregate of members, it appears superficially that the characteristics of the population are merely derivative from the characteristics of individuals by summation. The situation is in fact much more complex. Just as the properties of individual members may be used in aggregate form as properties of the population, so the properties of a population may be used as properties of its individual members (Davis, Spaeth, and Huson, 1961). The macroanalytic level of inquiry consists of propositions or statements of relationships among the properties of the population as the unit of reference. The microanalytic level of inquiry consists of propositions or statements of relationships among the properties of the individual as the unit of reference. In general, it is invalid either to transform a proposition about populations into a proposition about individuals or to transform a proposition about individuals into a proposition about populations. The relationship among individual characteristics, expressed as a regression equation linking individual variables, will generally have different parameters from one population to another. Most sociological theory is pitched at the micro-analytic level and therefore requires a test based on observations of individuals. This does not imply that macroanalytic theory is a lesser breed of theorizing, nor that it is merely derivative and a temporary substitute employed for the sake of convenience.

The question of the relationships between macroanalysis and microanalysis is important in current economic thought. Most theories in economics (as in sociology) are microtheories, while most empirical descriptions contain measurements of macrovariables, which are functions, such as averages, of microvariables. The parameters in the macroanalytic regression equations are weighted averages of the parameters in the microanalytic regression equations because the former system is dependent not only on the latter but also on the composition of the population (Theil, 1954). One prominent direction of resolution of this and other problems, which exploits the magnitude of the latest computers, is the microanalysis of socioeconomic systems, an attempt to generate aggregate properties from properties of individuals (Orcutt, Greenberger, Korbel, and Rivlin, 1961). As a general rule, the theoretical systems of the economists have not encompassed the problems of differences between systems *qua* systems through time or space.[14]

The microanalytic and macroanalytic levels of inquiry differ in character in another respect, one that leads to an important example of the utility of the population concept. The properties of distributions of variables are specific to populations rather than to individuals. An important question about a population is how to explain the differential distributions of various populations in terms of some individual-specific characteristic. Microanalytic relationships are of the form: If an individual has characteristic A, then he has a probability p of having another individual characteristic B. This may be used to predict the distribution of B, given the distribution of A, but it does not answer the question: What determines the distribution of A? The approach that uses the basic population model emphasizes the events of acquiring and losing some characteristic. From the standpoint of the individual, movement into and out of categorical locations is placed in the perspective of the life cycle; from the standpoint of the population, the distribution by categories is viewed as a consequence of processual parameters of fertility and mortality, using these terms in the broad as well as the narrow sense. More specifically, attention is directed to the movement from one structure to another by means of two questions: Given this kind of exposure, what is the probability of the occurrence of departure from exposure? and Given departure from exposure,

[14] The problems of distinction between analyses of individuals and of aggregates are not confined to the social sciences. For a brief view of the parallel dilemma in physics, see Feller (1957).

what is the consequence for subsequent exposure? Thus this approach places emphasis on changes through time. More precisely, the emphasis is on long-run time, or time as the biology of evolution considers it, as distinct from short-run time, or time as used in the equations of physics. The latter is the analogy for the study of covariation of individual and population characteristics; the former is the analogy for the study of population dynamics.

In the area of conjuncture between the macroanalytic and microanalytic approaches to the study of behavior, the cohort as a population element plays a crucial role. It is a device for providing a macroscopic link between movements of the population and movements of individuals. The conceptual gap between individual behavior and population behavior is provided with a convenient bridge, in the form of the cohort aggregate, within which individuals are located and out of which the population as a function of time is constructed from the sequence of cohort behavior patterns. Thus the cohort is a macroanalytic entity like the population, but it has the same temporal location and pattern of development as the individuals that constitute it. It seems to the writer that the analysis of cohort structures and processes is a valuable intermediary between the analysis of individual behavior and the analysis of population behavior, in attempting to increase the possibilities of cross-fertilization. The concept of a population, which is closely allied with the concept of a society, is brought closer to the concept of an individual, when the latter is viewed as a member of a cohort aggregate, which is in turn a constituent of a population. Thus one avenue is provided in sociology for the perplexing questions of the relationships between the individual and the society.

5 Social change from a demographic perspective

The purpose of this section is to present some ways in which the concept of a population may contribute to the analysis of social change. The first type of contribution is related to the definition of change. It is common in discussions of the topic to confine the term "social change" to transformation of the social structure, in contradistinction to the patterned sets of phases in the life cycles of individuals and other relatively invariant systems of action and interaction (Parsons, 1961; Hawley, 1950). Two contributions to this distinction may be drawn from stable population theory. In the first place, structural transformation is caused by a discrepancy at any point of time between the extant structure and the processes that are responsible for creating that structure. In the second place, life-cycle changes for individuals can be summarized by various indexes of cohort behavior as a function of age (or other appropriate interval). The definition of social change prompted by these considerations is the modification of processual parameters from cohort to cohort. Thus social change occurs to the extent that successive cohorts do something other than merely repeat the patterns of behavior of their predecessors. Given the far greater availability of structural than of processual data of all kinds, knowledge of the nuances of interdependency of period and cohort functions of fertility, mortality, and age distribution (or their analogous forms, if a quasi-population concept is employed) is likely to be essential in research on social change.

The proposed definition of social change is incomplete because it does not distinguish long-run from short-run change. Statistical contributions to the separate measurement of each for quantitative materials have been unimpressive because the distinction to be drawn does not actually hinge on the length of time elapsing but on the consideration that such changes have different determinants, and this can only be supplied by a person with knowledge of the content rather than the form of the data. Again the basic population model provides one direction of resolution of the difficulty. If functions of process are examined for a series of cohorts over their age spans, two distinct types of changes may be observed. One of these is the manifestation of a period-specific event or situation that "marks" the successive cohort functions at the same time, and thus at successive ages of the cohorts in question. Frequently such manifestations take the form of fluctuations, in the sense that a counteracting movement occurs subsequently, which erases the impact of the situation in the eventual summary for the cohort. The other type of change is characterized by differences in functional form from cohort to cohort other than those betraying the characteristic age pattern of the period-specific event. With full recognition of the incompleteness of the view, it is suggested that among the various sense of "short run" and "long run," an important part of the distinction can be captured by statistical operations designed to segregate the period-specific and cohort-specific variations as functions of age and time. As a not entirely parenthetical remark, it may be suggested that one contrast between demography and other types of quantitative sociology has been the emphasis of the former on long-run change and of the latter on short-run or no change (Boulding, 1950, p. 26; Lorimer, 1959, *passim*).

Throughout this essay, attention has been focused almost exclusively if implicitly on the level of the total population and its less tangible partner, the society. But the concepts introduced are clearly applicable with little modification to the other levels of social organization. In particular, the demographic approach provides some methodological resources for a dynamic approach to organizational structure. Any organization experiences social metabolism: since its individual components are exposed to "mortality," the survival of the organization requires a process of "fertility." The problem of replacement is posed not only for the total organization but also for every one of its differentiated components.[15] The ineluctability of social metabolism is from one view a problem that any organization must solve in the interests of continuity and from another view a continual opportunity for adaptation and change (Ryder, 1968). Furthermore, a plausible case can be made that the processes of "fertility" and "mortality" provide revealing insights into the present character of an organization as well as predictions of its future shape. As a final note on the demography of organizations, it is evident that they themselves can be treated as individuals within a population of organizations of like type, to approach the changing structure of the larger society from another viewpoint.

It is probably true that many sociologists view population data with less than excitement because these seem to provide distributive descriptions of aggregates rather than structural information about groups. This perspective ignores the interdependency that must exist between the functioning of organizations and the demographic characteristics of the aggregates of members of these organizations. The institutional structure rests on a population base, in the sense that particular functions are dependent for their performance on the presence of particular categories of persons. The most elementary recognition of the point comes in the commonplace research practice of distinguishing three types of variables—dependent, independent, and control variables—with demographic data falling under the third heading. The implication is that the composition of the population plays a necessary role (almost tautologically so), but not a sufficient one, as a set of constraints on the degree and direction of change in the institutional structure (Hawley, 1950). Now abstracting from the population composition through the use of the control technique may be a useful practice in the static analysis of covariation, but these parameters become variables as time passes and the questions of social change arise. For analogous reasons, economic theory was able to progress without demographic variables only so long as economists failed to raise questions about economic development. Inquiry into the relationships between population composition and institutional structure promises large rewards for the person interested in developing a dynamic theory of society.

Finally, the population model offers a strategy for helping to resolve one of the most frustrating methodological issues in the study of social change. Two modes of conceptualizing and describing change may be distinguished, termed loosely the qualitative and the quantitative. The former mode ordinarily appears as an approximately ordered sequence of discrete complexes, which somehow replace or displace or merge with their temporal neighbors.

---

[15] A penetrating early contribution to this discussion, which seems to have been ignored, is Sorokin and Anderson (1931). Cf. Simmel (1897–1898), abridged in Borgatta and Meyer (1956).

Analysis relies on before-and-after comparisons or at the most on some variant of the idea of stages. With such conceptualizations it is most difficult to achieve operational precision, let alone statistical data. The latter mode of the study of change most commonly yields a precisely dated series of measurements of one or another particular element of a qualitatively homogeneous type. Precision of observation is achieved at the cost of qualitative richness. In some ways the demographic approach is a combination of these two procedures. The concept of a population suggests the examination of a succession of overlapping stages, based on elements of various qualitative (categorical) types, quantified in terms of the frequency of each and the temporal distribution of individuals within the type, and the progression of aggregate indexes for the total population. A satisfactory dynamic theory of society requires a frame of reference that can establish propositions relating quantitative changes in "inputs and outputs" to the organizational transformations that they manifest and induce (Parsons and Smelser, 1956). One such frame of reference is the concept of a population.

The case for the demographic contribution to the study of social change can easily be overstated. Clearly there are alternative procedures of great promise that have no particular connection with the population model. For example, there are many aggregate data of major significance for structural transformations such as the content of material and normative technology, and there are compositional data based on units of observation such as roles or norms rather than individuals, which require different kinds of model. But at the very least, population change provides a reflection of social change, conceived in any way, a reflection that deserves a place in efficient research because its data are well defined and well measured and its methodology is sophisticated.

6 Conclusion

In this essay the demographer has been characterized as an agent for a particular type of model, the use of which implies particular kinds of measurements and particular directions of substantive inquiry. The influence the population concept might have on the shape of social analysis is threefold. In the first place, the demographer's mode of conceptualization never strays far from the mathematical in substance if not in language. This emphasis implies not only quantification but also persistent attention to some of the necessary components of explanation of societal behavior. Second, the demographic approach is both aggregative and distributive. The basic model is macroanalytic in form, and inclines the student toward a view of social systems in their totality. Nevertheless, the model is so designed that it offers a convenient confrontation with some central issues of theorizing at different levels of organized reality. In particular the cohort provides an aggregative format within which the phases and facets of the individual life cycle are imbedded, and through which the events experienced by the individual may be translated into the population processes that shape population structures. Finally the questions that are of central interest to the demographer are by definition dynamic. He is forced by his methodology to ask not so much about the association of characteristics as about the correlates of changes in characteristics, or, in his terms, about the perpetual interplay between occurrence and exposure. The central place of time in the demographic schema is most evident in the conceptualization of structure as a consequence of evolving process. Now these emphases all require qualifications, and particularly warnings, about what they neglect, but the same is true of any model. In the long run the utility of any approach to research is determined by the test of survival as measured by the fruits of inquiry in its image. To this writer the concept of a population has a high probability of high fertility.

Works cited in Chapter 3

Bogue, Donald J., 1952. "The Quantitative Study of Social Dynamics and Social Change," *American Journal of Sociology*, 57, pp. 565–568.

Boulding, Kenneth E., 1950. *A Reconstruction of Economics*, New York: Wiley.

Davis, J. A., J. L. Spaeth, and C. Huson, 1961. "A Technique for Analyzing the Effects of Group Composition," *American Sociological Review*, 26, pp. 215–225.

Davis, Kingsley, 1949. "The Demographic Equation," in Davis, Kingsley, *Human Society*, New York: Macmillan, pp. 551–594.

Duncan, O. Dudley, and B. Duncan, 1953. "An Alternative to Ecological Correlation," *American Sociological Review*, 18, pp. 665–666.

Encyclopaedia Britannica, 1957. "Actuality Theory," I, p. 138.

Feller, William, 1957. *An Introduction to Probability Theory and Its Applications*, 2nd ed., New York: Wiley, I, p. 356.

Goodman, L. A., 1953. "Ecological Regressions and Behavior of Individuals," *American Sociological Review*, 18, pp. 663–664.

Grauman, John V., 1959. "Population Estimates and Projections," in Hauser, Philip M., and Otis Dudley Duncan, editors, *The Study of Population*, Chicago: University of Chicago Press, pp. 544–575.

Hamilton, C. Horace, 1961. "Some Problems of Method in Internal Migration Research," *Population Index*, 27, pp. 297–307.

Hauser, Philip M., and Otis Dudley Duncan, 1959. "Demography as a Science," in Hauser, Philip M., and Otis Dudley Duncan, editors, *The Study of Population*, Chicago: University of Chicago Press, Part I, pp. 29–120.

Hawley, Amos H., 1950. *Human Ecology*, New York: Ronald Press, Part IV, Change and Development, p. 319.

——— ,1959. "Population Composition," in Hauser, Philip M., and Otis Dudley

Duncan, editors, *The Study of Population,* Chicago: University of Chicago Press, pp. 361–382.

Kendall, D. G., 1949. "Stochastic Processes and Population Growth," *Journal of the Royal Statistical Society,* XI, pp. 230–265.

Lopez, Alvaro, 1961. *Problems in Stable Population Theory,* Princeton, N.J.: Office of Population Research.

Lorimer, F., 1959. "The Development of Demography," in Hauser, Philip M., and Otis Dudley Duncan, editors, *The Study of Population,* Chicago: University of Chicago Press, pp. 124–179.

Lotka, Alfred J., 1907. "Studies on the Mode of Growth of Material Aggregates," *American Journal of Science,* 24, pp. 199–216.

————, 1939. *Théorie Analytique des Associations Biologique,* Part 2: Analyse Demographique avec Application Particulière a l'Espèce Humaine, Paris: Hermann & Cie.

Matras, Judah, 1960. "Comparison of Intergenerational Occupational Mobility Patterns: An Application of the Formal Theory of Social Mobility," *Population Studies,* 14, pp. 163–169.

————, 1961. "Differential Fertility, Intergenerational Occupational Mobility, and Change in the Occupational Distribution: Some Elementary Interrelationships," *Population Studies,* 15, pp. 187–197.

Menzel, H., 1950. "Comment on Robinson's 'Ecological Correlations and the Behavior of Individuals,' " *American Sociological Review,* 15, p. 674.

Orcutt, Guy H., Martin Greenberger, John Korbel, and Alice M. Rivlin, 1961. *Microanalysis of Socioeconomic Systems,* New York: Harper & Brothers.

Parsons, Talcott, 1961. "Some Considerations on the Theory of Social Change," *Rural Sociology,* 26, pp. 219–239.

————, and Neil J. Smelser, 1956. "The Problems of Growth and Institutional Change in the Economy," in Parsons, Talcott, and Neil J. Smelser, *Economy and Society,* Glencoe, Ill.: Free Press, pp. 246–294.

Prais, S. J., 1955a. "The Formal Theory of Social Mobility," *Population Studies,* 9, pp. 72–81.

————, 1955b. "Measuring Social Mobility," *Journal of the Royal Statistical Society,* Series A, CXVIII, pp. 56–66.

Riley, Matilda White, 1963. *Sociological Research, Volume I, A Case Approach,* pp. 700–788; *Volume II, Exercises and Manual,* pp. 89–90, New York: Harcourt, Brace & World.

Robinson, W. S., 1950. "Ecological Correlations and the Behavior of Individuals," *American Sociological Review,* 15, pp. 351–357.

Ryder, Norman B, 1956. "La Mesure des Variations de la Fécondité au cours du Temps," *Population,* XI, pp. 29–46.

————, 1959. "Fertility," in Hauser, Philip M., and Otis Dudley Duncan, editors, *The Study of Population,* Chicago: University of Chicago Press, pp. 400–436.

————, 1961. "Bisexual Marriage Rates," Paper read at the annual meetings of the Population Association of America, 1961.

————, 1963. "The Translation Model of Demographic Change," in Ryder, Norman B., editor, *Emerging Techniques in Population Research,* New York: Milbank Memorial Fund, pp. 65–81.

————, 1964b. "The Process of Demographic Translation," *Demography*, Vol. 1, pp. 74–82.

————, 1968. "Cohort Analysis," in Sills, David L., *International Encyclopedia of the Social Sciences*, 17 vols., New York: Macmillan and Free Press, 2, pp. 546–550.

Schnore, Leo F., 1961. "Social Mobility in Demographic Perspective," *American Sociological Review*, 26, pp. 407–423.

Simmel, Georg [1897–1898], 1956. "The Persistence of Social Groups," *American Journal of Sociology*, translated by Albion W. Small; abridged in Borgatta, Edgar F., and Henry J. Meyer, editors, *Sociological Theory: Present-Day Sociology from the Past*, New York: Knopf, pp. 364–398.

Sorokin, Pitirim, and C. Arnold Anderson, 1931. "Metabolism of Different Strata of Social Institutions and Institutional Continuity" (Comitato Italiano per lo studio dei problemi della popolazione) Rome: Istituto Polligrafico dello Stato.

Theil, H., 1954. *Linear Aggregation and Economic Relations*, Amsterdam: North-Holland Publishing Company.

United Nations, 1958. Department of Economic and Social Affairs, *Multilingual Demographic Dictionary*, English Section ("Population Studies," No. 29 [New York, 1958]).

Vance, Rupert B., 1959. "The Development and Status of American Demography," in Hauser, Philip M., and Otis Dudley Duncan, editors, *The Study of Population*, Chicago: University of Chicago Press, pp. 286–313.

PART 2

AGE STRATIFICATION IN SELECTED ASPECTS OF SOCIETY

Part 2 consists of six interpretative essays on age stratification in selected social institutions. Contributed by authors with widely varied background and interests, these chapters utilize in diverse fashion the general theoretical orientations of this book. In the main, each chapter suggests hypotheses, raises questions, or supplies new material concerning the nature of age stratification, its variability under differing conditions, its underlying processes, and its intimate connection with social change. The combined chapters should begin to demonstrate the light to be shed on particular fields of sociological inquiry through the development of a sociological view of age.

4

The polity

ANNE FONER

Observations of political differences between youth and their elders are perhaps as old as political thought itself, though whether youth are viewed as corrupters of cherished tradition or as bearers of the ideal society has, of course, depended upon the political philosophy (and probably age!) of the particular commentator. Despite frequently observed instances of age conflict, only in recent years has age come to be a variable of central and systematic interest in political analysis. This essay demonstrates how a diverse literature—on political participation and apathy, consensus and cleavage, socialization and deviance, issues and ideologies, process and change—can be organized, and its findings extended, within a theory and methodology of age stratification. The exposition attempts to show how seemingly disparate findings can be reconciled, established concepts can achieve new clarification, and published research findings, as reanalyzed here, can yield new insights. Among the problems considered are: why young adults, despite their superior education, are less likely than middle-aged and older citizens to participate in institutionalized political processes; why conservatism generally seems to increase with aging while on certain specific issues, liberalism increases; why age conflict occasionally emerges, even though socialization tends to result in striking similarity of political views between offspring and their parents.

Throughout the essay, careful note is taken of the age elements that must be distinguished in analysis and interpretation of research findings. One set of findings is tied to the consequences of aging as a process, identifying certain age-related factors that stimulate change in political orientation and action as the individual, moving through his life course, changes, in Mannheim's terms, his "location" in society. A second set of findings is interpreted in the light of differential exposure of age cohorts to social trends and the events of history. Existing age strata, precisely because they were born at different times, differ in characteristics that affect the polity: in education; in exposure to various childrearing practices; in experiences of war or peace, of affluence or deprivation. Thus both aging and cohort differences shape the political character of the age strata at any given time. The essay points to distinctive regularities in the changing political profile of the age strata, going on then to examine the structural conditions under which these differences become fertile ground for active conflict.

A number of questions for the future emerge from this treatment of age and the polity. If ways are devised of involving the young earlier and more fully in the central adult roles of the society, can we expect the age of entry into conventional political activity to drop correspondingly? Does the political activity of youth in the 1960's presage a new awareness and acceptance of the political role as an important element in the total role complex of the older adult? Can we expect oncoming cohorts of youth to be increasingly active in politics? If not, then the youth of the 1960's will be known to historians as the "activist" generation, just as those of the 1950's have been labeled the "silent" generation. What are the implications for the polity of rising education? To what extent would the closing of the "education gap" between age strata contribute to the closing of the "generation gap"?

RELEVANCE OF VOLUME I

In addition to the material presented in this essay to illustrate the potentialities for secondary analysis of the accumulating files of data from opinion polls, an extensive set of age-related findings appears in Chapter 19 of the Inventory. This chapter discloses the importance of age as an aspect of the political role, dealing with such topics as political participation and interest, political commitment, party affiliation, political ideology, and leadership in public affairs.

The polity, in which behavior and attitudes differ dramatically by age and where age cleavage often finds open expression, provides an important sphere of social life for exploring the impact of age on social structure and on social change. Several facts are well-documented (see Volume I, Chapter 19). For many years, in many countries, and in analyses of both upper and lower classes (cf. Lipset, 1963, p. 221; Tingsten, 1963, p. 82), younger people have had lower voting rates than older adults. Age also relates, though in less consistent fashion, to the way people vote: for example, in recent decades in the United States, the young have been more likely than the old to vote Democratic; but in Germany in the 1930's, it was the young who supported the Nazis more than their older counterparts did. And young and old have often disagreed about many political issues—of late in this country there have been notable age differences in attitudes towards blacks or toward college protests, for example.

Why? What is there about age that might account for such differences? The theory of age stratification [*See Chapter 1*] points to three sets of causal factors: the aging process, differential cohort experience, and special events in history. Using this framework, this essay will consider such questions as: Do people become more conservative as they grow older? What is the effect of starting one's political career at a given period in history? How do the several age strata relate to each other? What are their respective responses to particular political events? Why is it that, even though the potential for political age differences may be omnipresent, political conflict between age strata erupts at certains periods but not others?

The answers to such questions could illuminate the nature of political processes and the consequences of these processes for the society. And, fortunately, not all the answers need be entirely speculative. Politics is one of the rare fields in which age-related data on both behavior and attitudes are widely available for entire societies.[1] Some of these data, from political surveys and public opinion polls, take the special form required for cohort analysis [*described in Chapters 2 and 12*] and can serve as models to illustrate the potential of the cohort approach for exploring processes that underlie the changing political scene.[2] In order to relate our discussion to the readily available empirical base, we shall focus mainly on modern Western democracy (many of the examples are drawn from the United States since World War II) and on the public or citizenry, as distinct from the leaders and officials within the more formally organized government.

The citizens in a democracy, who select decision-makers or influence decision-making processes, are of special interest as a field for investigating age as a possible factor in cleavage and conflict. Citizens are divided on many specific issues and among political parties that vie with one another for power and influence. The three main aspects of age and the polity that will be discussed in this essay all relate to this underlying theme of the effects of age on these divisions. The first section will describe the age pattern of political participation of the citizenry, the relative failure of young adults to utilize the established channels, and certain possible implications of this failure for the society as a whole. The second section will deal with political attitudes and ideologies, casting new light on accepted notions about "political generations" and about the connections between aging and conservatism. Finally, the third section will explore the conditions under which age differences in political attitudes and behavior can lead to deep-seated political rifts between generations.

1 Political participation

Age is variously implicated in political behavior. While research has dealt largely with voting[3] as the major institutionalized means for the public to

[1] See, for example, Cantril (1951); the periodic summaries reported by Erskine in the *Public Opinion Quarterly;* Tingsten (1963); and the data banks maintained in the United States Bureau of the Census and in many government and university centers here and abroad.

[2] However, the findings from cohort analysis must be interpreted with great caution. Problems of biased sampling often require careful controls for sex, education, or race. And, because the samples through time are not composed of the same individuals, cohort analysis does not go beyond the *net* shifts from period to period to a turnover analysis that would take full account of the reversible aspects of the political role by identifying individual changes over time. For further discussion of problems of interpreting data from these sources, see Appendix.

[3] See, e.g., the massive analyses of voting in Berelson, Lazarsfeld, and McPhee (1954); or in Campbell et al. (1960).

exercise influence on political leaders and the decisions they make,[4] age is also connected with other forms of political activity. For example, although less than 5 per cent of the United States population (1955) belong to political associations, this proportion tends to increase by age (see Volume I, Chapter 19 · 1 · e). On an index of political activity that combines voting with discussing public issues, writing to Congressmen, and the like (United States, late 1940's), young people 21–34 were considerably more likely to be rated "very inactive" than people in the age categories 35–49 or 50 and over (Woodward and Roper, 1950, p. 877). Moreover, age may be associated with other modes of political participation, such as protest politics, which can be utilized outside the regular machinery of government and are hence available—not only to disaffected groups or disadvantaged minorities of all kinds—but also to persons below the voting age.

AGE STRATIFICATION OF THE POLITY

The structural elements outlined in our conceptual model [*See Chapter 1, Figure 1 · 1*], with their distinction between the people themselves (the citizens) and the rights and duties of the citizen role, provide a starting point— but only a starting point—for analyzing the pronounced differences among age strata in political participation.

In any society, the numbers and kind of people in the several strata (element 1 in the model) constitute the basis from which the citizenry is drawn. Thus the wide variations from time to time and from place to place in the age structure of the population [*see Chapter 10*] impose differing limits on the age structure of the public or of the electorate. The large numbers and proportions of mature people available to participate in the polity in modern Western nations contrasts with the comparatively few older people at earlier periods of history or in underdeveloped countries today.[5] And within a society the composition of the strata can vary in sex, race, and other characteristics that can affect availability to the polity.

However, not all potential participants engage in political activities, of course, and the proportions who do vary by age strata.[6] Nonetheless, the

---

[4] We leave open the question of how much influence the voting public actually has, a question that has been subject to various interpretations. See, for example, Andrew Hacker (1961, p. 300); Robert E. Lane (1965, p. 3); Talcott Parsons (1959, pp. 86–90).

[5] A correspondence has been noted—though the causal connections are highly complex— between the age structure of nations in the mid-twentieth century and their form of government: the Western democracies tend to have "old" populations, the Communist countries to have a mixture of "mature" and of "young" populations, and the "neutral" countries to have "young" populations; Hauser and Vargas (1960, p. 52). See also Sheppard (1962, p. 49); Dickinson (1958), for a discussion of "aging" of the United States electorate.

[6] That there is no necessary relationship between aging of a population and aging of its elite has been shown through an analysis of several abstract models. United Nations, 1956, *Aging*, pp. 60–61.

sheer numbers of participants in the strata determine the weights of the respective strata within the polity as a whole. Thus, in assessing the total political impact of age, it is important to take into account not only the differences among the strata, but also their relative numerical contributions.

Apart from the size and composition of the several strata, the capacities of people to perform many kinds of political activity (element 2) do not vary greatly by age—at least beyond childhood and prior to senescence. While certain leadership roles do require considerable physical endurance and prior training and experience, adults in most age categories seem equally capable of voting or of performing other functions of citizenship.

Examination of the rights and duties of the political role in modern democracies also contributes little to the understanding of age differences in role performance. Indeed, this role has a peculiarly flexible or volitional character that frees it from many of the direct and obvious constraints of age. To be sure, there are a few political activities for which the age of eligibility (element 3) is legally prescribed. A minimum—but no maximum—age for voting and for holding certain offices is established by law, variously set at such ages as 18, 21, or 30 (and increasingly modified downward in recent years in several countries and states). While ages below which a person cannot be held legally responsible for specified acts of political disobedience or resistance are explicitly set, there are few age restrictions applying to participation in spontaneous demonstrations, public expression of opinion, responses to mass media campaigns, or membership in organized movements. School children are encouraged to develop an interest in public affairs through curricula and such proto-political behavior as straw votes or exposure to campaign propaganda. Increasingly, high school students are politically active both inside and outside the classroom.

By and large, then, the distinctive age patterns of political behavior are not governed directly by societal rules, expectations, or sanctions (element 4) associated with the role of citizen. Instead, the role allows wide latitude. Political behavior can be intermittent. It is often transitory, as in the expression of an opinion or in the decision about how to vote in a presidential election. Furthermore, performance in the role is reversible over the life course: a person can vote[7] or hold office at one stage of his life but not at some later stage; or he can change political attitudes or behaviors that have not had an opportunity to crystallize into habit patterns.

This section of the essay will explore certain factors that may operate within this flexible, volitional role to produce differences among age strata. Clearly, it is not only the structural elements in our conceptual model that

[7] Except in countries where voting is obligatory or where there is social pressure for various types of political participation.

must be considered, but also the dynamic processes [*see Chapter 1, Figure 1 · 2*]. Nor can the analysis be restricted to the polity alone, but must refer also to age-related behaviors in groups and other social spheres connected with the polity [*compare Chapter 10*]. In the search for explanatory clues, we shall examine the age pattern of voting as one index of political participation, weighing possible causes of the differences among strata, and considering potential societal consequences.

AGE PATTERNS OF VOTING

Voting turnout in the United States and in other Western democracies tends to be highest in the middle age strata, falling off among the very young and the very old. This pattern is persistent, having been observed in many countries and at various periods during the twentieth century where available data have been reanalyzed (see Volume 1, Chapter 19 · 1; see also Tingsten, 1963). For example, approximately three-fourths of the population in each of the ten-year age categories between 35 and 74 voted in the United States national election of November 1964 (United States Bureau of the Census, 1965, pp. 1, 9). However, by age 75 and over, participation in this election dropped to 57 percent. And at the other end of the age scale the rate fell to less than two-thirds at age 25 to 34 and to only about half at age 21 to 24. Thus it is the mature strata in a democracy who in effect contribute most to the total impact of voter influence upon the polity.

Compositional factors   Some of this difference is accounted for by the differential composition of the strata in respect to characteristics (such as education or sex) that affect the propensity to vote. The significance of *education* as a compositional factor has been demonstrated for the United States, where the proportions of highly educated people decrease sharply from the younger to the older strata. Since education is itself highly associated with voting turnout, a compositional analysis, as shown in Table 4 · 1, can focus more directly on the relation of voting to age by holding education constant. This analysis reveals[8] that, within each educational subset of the population, the tendency persists for voting rates to drop among the youngest strata; among the oldest strata, however, the drop has now become less pronounced, almost disappearing among males (see also Glenn and Grimes, 1968, p. 565).

Further insight into the relation of age to voting is gleaned by controlling the differences in *sex* composition of the older strata, where women outnumber men. Thus an analysis of the United States data for the 1964 elections (United States Bureau of the Census, 1965, p. 9) shows again, for each sex,

---

[8] The table also points out that differences among the strata are less pronounced among the college-educated than among the grammar-school educated segments of the population.

TABLE 4 · 1 *Voter participation, by age and education, United States, November 1964*

Per cent voting

Age	Years of education						Total
	Elementary		High school		College		
	0–7 years	8 years	1–3 years	4 years	1–3 years	4 years or more	
Males							
21–24	14	30	34	56	70	80	53
25–44	43	58	65	76	82	87	71
45–64	63	79	81	88	88	93	79
65+	66	79	80	88	91	88	74
Total 21+	58	73	69	80	82	88	73
Females							
21–24	22	21	33	55	69	78	52
25–44	34	52	58	76	85	87	68
45–64	52	69	75	84	87	92	74
65+	46	63	72	76	82	93	61
Total 21+	45	63	63	76	83	89	68

Source: Current Population Reports, 1965, P-20, No. 143, pp. 16–19 (adapted).

the low rates among the young; but in old age, the drop is less pronounced and comes later for men (who start to drop at age 75) than for women (whose drop starts at 65). In explaining the lower voting rates among old people, then, particular attention should be focused on women. Are old women deterred from voting because many of them, now widowed, had formerly voted with their husbands?[9] Are they kept from the polls by the fact that their health is generally poorer (and their average age higher) than that of old men? Is this particular cohort of old women a special case—unused to voting because many of them were socialized before the introduction of woman suffrage? Although we have not sought answers to such questions, there is little evidence of a special cohort effect on the current generation of old people in the United States: for similar age patterns distinguishing old men from old women have been observed in a variety of national and local elections in Western Europe over the years between 1911 and 1935—when woman suffrage was new in many countries and would have exerted its influence on the young as well as the old (Volume I, Chapter 19 · 1 · b).

In such ways, compositional analysis can help to explain the low voting rates among old people (especially among old men), but not among young people. The low turnout of the *old* may be largely a function of their comparatively low educational level and the high proportion of females among them; but the

[9] Data for both men and women in Hanover, Germany, 1929, show voting rates higher for the married than for the widowed, divorced, or never married (Tingsten, 1963, pp. 94–95).

young voters, even in those sex or educational statuses where high turnout is predictable, still lag behind the mature adults.

Life-course differences and trends   Since the poor voting record of the younger strata so far have not been explained through compositional analysis, is it attributable to the aging process? Is there something about the stage of young adulthood that interferes with voting? Are there impediments to *becoming* a voter that disappear as people grow older? Such a possibility can be examined only by following voting patterns over the life course (*P2* in our conceptual model).

Fortunately, an analysis is available[10] that provides, at least for the United States, a crude approximation of the shifts in voting turnout over the life course. (Such analyses, while they can afford only limited insights, are presented here as illustrations of the untapped potential of the extensive data series now available in many countries. The investigators, Glenn and Grimes, piece together data from 23 Gallup polls in order to trace voter turnout for each of six different cohorts in the successive presidential elections from 1944 through 1964. And indeed, their findings are consistent with the hypothesis that individuals do tend to increase their voting participation from their early 20's to their early 30's (although evidence here is for only two cohorts), and then to maintain this participation at a fairly even level into their 60's and 70's. People may be slow to enter into the voting role; but once entered, they are likely to persist up to the age where disability sets in.

So far our examination of the differential voting rates among age strata has served to focus attention on certain key factors: The lower rates among older people at any one point in time seem related to the lower educational attainment of older people; but among younger people, the low rates appear to stem from conditions that change over the life course.

Before turning to a scrutiny of such possible accompaniments to the aging process, we must inquire whether the differences among age strata may also be affected by secular trends in the propensity to vote. Has there been a long-term decline in participation rates generally, which would be reflected in successive cohorts as they flow through the polity (*P1* in our model)? If so, then the consequences for the cross-sectional picture (according to the principles described in Chapter 2 · 3 · B and Table 2 · 7) would be to depress voting rates among the younger, as compared with the older, strata. In this event, both the cohort differences and the life-course shifts would be operating jointly to shape the strata differences in voting behavior, and both would require explanation. On this point, the evidence, though scanty, is largely nega-

---

[10] Glenn and Grimes (1968, pp. 565–569). These investigators offset some of the sampling difficulties by controlling on sex and race and by standardizing for several educational levels. Such analyses, which may have greater heuristic value than inherent validity, must be interpreted with great caution as indicated previously.

tive. Two studies,[11] both using Gallup poll data for roughly commensurate periods and both controlling for education, show very slight (though somewhat contradictory) differences among successive cohorts in proportions exercising the franchise as they come of age. It would thus appear that the lower turnout of young persons is related to the process of first becoming a voter.

OBSTACLES TO BECOMING A VOTER

That so many young people postpone assumption of the voting role, while older people cling to it until late in life, suggests impediments in the process of becoming a voter. We shall examine such possible barriers as: a general lack of motivation to participate in politics at all, legal restrictions impinging on youthful voters, role conflicts that lead to political withdrawal, or competing pressures of other role obligations.

a. Political interest and awareness   No simple explanation for the age differences in voting is afforded by the various cross-sectional studies of opinion, information, and concern about current events. Interest in politics has several dimensions, of course—only some of which may lead to political action, or to voting rather than to some other mode of participation (such as campaigning, lobbying, or demonstrating). But on most of these dimensions, the available data suggest that the young are no less interested in politics than mature adults. However, these similarities among the strata are a function not so much of age as of the comparatively higher education of the young: for, when education is controlled through compositional analysis, there is typically a steady rise in interest from the younger to the older strata.

For example, when all educational levels are considered together, the young are no less likely than the old to report awareness of current issues in the news (Table 4 · 2; Glenn, 1969, p. 27) to identify personalities and topics of political debate (Table 4 · 3; Glenn, 1969, p. 28), to express an opinion (rather than give "no opinion") (Glenn, 1969, pp. 25–26) or to avow interest in "politics" (which can, of course, have different meanings to different people).[12] Nevertheless, after education and sex are controlled, there is a typical increase by age on each of these dimensions. In other words, the slight differences among the age strata in political interest are largely explained by the differing educational composition of the strata. Thus the overall effect of the educational discrepancies between young and old is to minimize the age

[11] Glenn and Grimes (1968, pp. 565, 568–569), believe there may have been a decrease, though slight, in the propensity to vote between 1944 and 1964. Crittenden (1963, pp. 325–327), who also evaluates earlier trend data, notes a slight trend in the opposite direction; but, as compared with the Glenn and Grimes analysis, Crittenden uses less refined controls by education, no control on sex, and less recent data.
[12] Glenn and Grimes (1968, p. 570 footnote), report on a Gallup poll of March 1968.

TABLE 4 · 2 *Average percentage of "yes" responses to eleven "have-you-heard-or-read" questions*[a]

Years of school completed	Age		
	21–39	*40–59*	*60 and over*
Males			
7–8	56.2 (41)	57.8 (95)	61.4 (79)
1–3 of high school	61.5 (73)	70.2 (73)	70.8 (37)
4 of high school	70.5 (131)	72.8 (99)	77.3 (33)
All educational levels[b]	69.0 (380)	68.3 (379)	65.6 (250)
Females			
7–8	41.8 (37)	45.7 (92)	51.1 (68)
1–3 of high school	52.5 (94)	54.6 (78)	55.6 (34)
4 of high school	59.1 (194)	65.2 (121)	62.6 (42)
All educational levels[b]	57.9 (430)	57.8 (397)	53.0 (223)

[a] Examples of the questions are: "Have you heard or read anything about the trouble in the Formosa area?" (1955) and "Have you heard or read about the Black Muslims?" (1963). The ten surveys from which the questions come are Gallup Surveys 521, 524, 532, 543, 582, 588, 649, 673, 675, and 701.
[b] Includes respondents with less than 7 years of elementary school or more than 4 years of high school.
Note: Whites only. Numbers in parentheses are bases for the percentages (inflated by about 100 per cent by a weighting procedure).
Source: Glenn, 1969, p. 27.

variations in the several dimensions of political interest. It is the large proportions of well-educated persons among the young that enhances attention to public affairs within this stratum.

Given this substantial amount of avowed interest in political affairs, it seems clear that other factors must be operating to depress the rates of participation of young citizens.

b. Party identification A related aspect of the individual's motivation to participate in the political role is his sense of attachment to a party (quite apart from the question of which party—a topic to be discussed in Section 2). Partisanship, while it may not reflect interest in politics, is certainly a facilitating factor in the decision to vote. Here the age pattern is striking: partisanship, even more clearly than voting turnout, tends to increase with age. This finding is not attenuated by strata differences in educational composition, as in the case of political interest and awareness, but appears even when all educational categories are combined.

This association with age appears both in the cross-sectional differences among the strata (Sd) and in the life-course patterns (Ld) of selected cohorts of individuals. Cross-sectional analysis shows that the proportions of individuals who identify with one or the other major party go up consistently from age 21 to 24 to age 70 and over. As the complementary pattern, independent voters and voters who split their tickets tend to decline by age (Volume I, Chapter 19 · 2; Crittenden, 1963, pp. 326, 328). Moreover, a cohort analysis, based on shifts between two pairs of presidential elections (1946 to

TABLE 4 · 3 *Average percentage of correct responses to eleven public affairs questions*[a]

Years of school completed	Age		
	21–39	*40–59*	*60 and over*
Males			
7–8	28.2 (53)	38.3 (104)	43.2 (83)
1–3 of high school	41.9 (96)	49.8 (81)	47.6 (35)
4 of high school	55.1 (147)	59.6 (118)	62.6 (32)
All educational levels[b]	51.6 (462)	51.5 (452)	44.1 (262)
Females			
7–8	19.9 (57)	28.9 (105)	28.1 (72)
1–3 of high school	31.6 (112)	35.0 (86)	39.3 (34)
4 of high school	42.2 (226)	50.9 (138)	59.4 (39)
All educational levels[b]	39.5 (517)	40.6 (470)	36.5 (234)

[a] Nine of the questions asked for identification of personalities of recent prominence. The other two questions, from a 1948 survey, asked about the meaning of the term "cold war" and about the purpose of Voice of America broadcasts. The questions come from Gallup Surveys 432, 531, 532, 671, and 675.
[b] Includes respondents with less than 7 years of elementary school or more than 4 years of high school.
Note: Whites only. Numbers in parentheses are bases for the percentages (inflated by about 100 per cent by a weighting procedure).
Source: Glenn, 1969, p. 28.

1954 and 1950 to 1958) suggests that the probability of identifying with a party tends to increase over the life course.[13]

The mechanism connecting partisan loyalty with aging appears to be *duration* of party attachment, as Campbell and his associates (1960, pp. 161–163, 496–497) demonstrate in an ingenious critical test. Examining those (comparatively few) individuals in their sample who reported a shift in allegiance during adulthood, they showed that the longer a person thinks of himself as longing to a party, the stronger his attachment to it becomes, even when age is held constant. But when duration of party identification is held constant, age is no longer positively associated with strong attachment (indeed, it tends to become negatively associated). Thus the factor affecting partisanship is not membership in a particular age stratum at a particular time, but the fact that aging provides opportunity for longer-standing identification with a party. This is another instance of the general principle [*described in Chapter 10*] that aging allows the *accumulation of experience* in a role. And accumulated experience often results, in turn, in an increasing commitment to the role itself—a point to be further considered shortly.

Thus it seems clear that, even though education can enhance the political knowledge and interest of the young, persons entering adulthood tend to de-

[13] Crittenden (1963, pp. 327–328). The analysis, controlled on education but not on sex, compares the shift for each cohort with that for the total of all age categories, in order to eliminate the impact of particular periods.

lay, not only their voting participation, but also any channelling of their avowed interest through attachment to a political party.

c. *Legal barriers*   One obvious deterrent to voting by the young is the complex set of legal restrictions and regulations imposed at the local, state, and national levels in the United States as well as in other countries. Not only has the vote been widely denied to persons below a certain age, but it may have been discouraged also by the cumbersome machinery for registration or voting imposed upon first voters or upon persons who are geographically mobile.

First voters, who must make the decision for the first time and who may be deterred simply by lack of experience with the rules,[14] often face restrictions on voting that are not placed upon older voters. In the United States, first voters have often been required to show proof of citizenship, age, or literacy. Such legal preconditions for assumption of the voting role are not paralleled by required proofs of competency in the later years. Thus, the cost and effort involved in becoming a voter are often greater than those entailed in maintaining this activity.

The age pattern of *moving,* which peaks sharply among young people in their 20's [*see Chapter 6 by Starr, Section 3*], also militates against youthful voting through the various residence requirements (see also Volume I, Chapter 6 · C · 1). Many recent movers cannot meet these either in the new state or in the state left behind. Registration at place of legal residence can be difficult for those who are temporarily away at college or in military service; and once registered, these persons may still have to apply for absentee ballots in order to vote. A report issued by the Census Bureau on United States elections of November 1966 shows that young people are more likely than older people to cite residence requirements as a reason for not registering. Whereas, among all persons 21 and over who did not register to vote, only 19 per cent said they could not meet residence requirements, the comparable proportions for those aged 21–24 and 25–34 were 25 and 24 respectively (United States Bureau of the Census, 1968, p. 32). Thus a part, at least, of the difference in voter turnout by age is directly attributable to geographical mobility.[15]

---

[14] See Kelley, Ayres, and Bowen (1967). Note also that aging, as it represents enhanced opportunities to acquire requisite information, may be particularly important to *entry* into the political role. Unlike the occupational role, for example, where various counseling and employment services (often integral parts of the normal school curriculum) facilitate entry, information regarding various procedural aspects of political entry is often not made readily available. Thus learning how, when, and where to register, to vote, or to participate actively in party affairs depends heavily upon the initial motivation of the individual. Ignorance and misinformation in the population concerning such matters may be viewed as reflecting an absence of political socialization dealing with situational specification of the role. This lack may even contribute to "deviant" political behavior among the young, who may more easily learn from their peers how to protest, demonstrate, and picket than they may learn from their elders how to deal with more established political machinery.

[15] See also the estimates made by Glenn and Grimes (1968, pp. 569–570).

Legal obstacles appear, then, to hinder the entry of young people into the role of voter both *directly,* through stipulation of minimum age criteria, and *indirectly,* through residential requirements having their greatest impact on the young. However, it is not clear (because of the difficulty of controlling the many other factors entering into the decision to vote) how effective such deterrents are, or what the consequences may be of lowering the minimum voting age. One study of the few states in the United States that permitted those under 21 to vote prior to 1970 showed that only 30 per cent did so—a rate markedly lower than the approximately 50 per cent in the age category 21 to 24 (*New York Times,* June 23, 1970).

d. The demands of other roles   The mobility of young adults points to a more general characteristic of this age stratum: to the lack of full integration into the local community or into the other institutional structures of mature social life. [*See Chapter 6 · 2 by Starr.*] Just as young adults have special difficulties in adopting the political role, they may also meet greater problems than mature persons in organizing this role with other roles they must play. At the stage of transition from youth to adulthood, individuals must relinquish the roles of student, single person, and dependent offspring and must simultaneously assume the major new roles of worker, marital partner, and parent. Young adults may be diverted from political activity by these other roles, both by the unresolved differences among their new role-partners as to how they should think and act in the political role, and by the competing demands upon their time and energy imposed by the necessity for learning new roles.

The principle of *cross-pressures* or role conflicts, which arise from the incongruent demands of the groups to which an individual belongs,[16] has been widely applied in voting research as an explanation of the tendency for prospective voters to lose interest or to withdraw from the field (see Lazarsfeld, Berelson, and Gaudet, 1944, p. 62; Tingsten, 1937, pp. 230–231). As Lipset and his colleagues (1954, pp. 1146–1147) suggest, young people—because they are in the process of establishing new families and finding their way into new jobs, new neighborhoods, and new associations—frequently encounter conflicting expectations as to how they should vote; and they may often respond by not voting at all. As these individuals mature, they have time to resolve many of the conflicts that obstruct political action in their earlier years. That cross-pressures do tend to decrease with age is supported by some slight evidence. In the widely noted study of Elmira, New York, first voters are observed to be considerably more likely than persons over 35 years of age to disagree politically with their best friends (Berelson, Lazarsfeld, and Mc-

---

[16] Discontinuities within the individual's role sequence may also produce conflicts, though this matter has received little research attention.

Phee, 1954, pp. 96–97). And in a French study, husbands and wives are more likely to vote alike if they are over, rather than under, the age of 50 (Duverger, 1955, p. 48; cited by Lipset, 1963, pp. 220–221).

Quite apart from the probability of conflicting political expectations, these newly acquired major roles undoubtedly confront the young adult with *competing* demands of their own. This life stage is fraught with many problems that may seem more immediate than politics: problems of socialization, situational specification, and other kinds of learning; or problems of role incongruity in numerous areas outside politics. Among individuals who have reached maturity, much of this role learning may have been accomplished and many of the initial conflicts resolved. And people reaching the late 60's or 70's, typically having lost the major roles of middle life, have acquired the leisure time in which to keep up with public affairs and to participate politically.

In such ways, the salience of the political role may be negatively associated across the age strata with the unassimilated demands imposed by other, less volitional, roles. The systematic relationship of age to voting turnout finds its complement in the inverse relationship of age to the conflicting, competing, and unfamiliar expectations within the total role complex.

e. Societal commitment Conversely, it can be suggested that increases with age in overall commitment to the larger society[17] will heighten involvement in the conventional activities of the political role. That is, once the individual has "stakes" in a career, family, and community, he becomes aware of the political influences of strategic groups in society and alert to the direct relevance for him personally of political affairs generally. The concrete implications of many political decisions may have little meaning for the young person who has not yet developed his ties to a given community (with its school systems or its property taxes), or to the economy (with its job opportunities or its fluctuations in wages and prices).[18] In many periods of United States history, the young person has even shown slight commitment to the nation (with its domestic crises or its foreign entanglements). Perhaps it is only as the maturing individual organizes and becomes involved in his own system of adult roles that the polity ceases to be an abstraction, so that he recognizes a personal stake in the decisions by the nation or the local community that bind and obligate all members. And for old people, already engaged in the political role, voting is one way to maintain continuing ties to the larger society even after their major life roles have been relinquished.

This notion of societal commitment may well help to explain the parallel rise with age in voting turnout and in alignment with the party system. Correla-

---

[17] Compare the theories of Campbell et al. (1960, pp. 164, 496–498); Lipset et al. (1954, pp. 1128–1134). For a related notion of commitment, see Becker (1960); Smith (1969).

[18] See Volume I, Chapter 18 · B · 1 · c and 18 · B · 3 · a for relatively low commitment among young working people to present jobs.

tively, the absence of societal commitment may help account for the disposition of some young people, rather than voting, to utilize political channels outside regular electoral procedures.

Of all the age strata, it is the young who have had least time to make either a material or a psychological investment in existing societal institutions. Their lack of commitment to stabilized political structures undoubtedly makes it easier for them to envision new goals for the society and to accept new modes of political participation to achieve these goals, legitimating the use of extra-institutional or even extralegal means for pressing their political claims. They are in the age stratum with least to lose if, by taking nontraditional political actions, they should evoke negative responses and sanctions.[19] The lack of societal commitment seems especially relevant for understanding the student dissent of the late 1960's; it may have been particularly pronounced among the baby-boom cohort approaching adulthood in the 1960's because many of them were retained in the military or the educational systems[20] longer than was customary among earlier cohorts, thereby delaying assumption of the full range of adult roles [cf. *Chapter 7 by Parsons and Platt*].

RELATIONS AMONG STRATA

Whatever factors may impede conventional political participation by the young, this examination of voting shows that, under conditions in many modern countries, the electorate is open to domination by persons in their middle and later years. The numbers of people in the age strata over 35 or 40 years of age are large, and they constitute a substantial, if varying,[21] fraction of the population of voting age. Thus to the extent that voting is a key mechanism for exerting public influence on political leaders and representatives, the differential voting rates among age strata give disproportionate political influence to mature adults.

[19] Compare the exhortation of Marx and Engels to the workers: "You have nothing to lose but your chains."

[20] A comparison between college and noncollege youths, of similar age but unequal status as adults, might serve as a partial test of the cogency of this argument that lack of societal commitment disposes the young toward nonconventional forms of political participation. It must then be expected that youths not attending college should be the less motivated to seek nontraditional means of political expression because, as workers, they have already been "co-opted." By their assumption of adult roles and responsibilities, they have become part of the Establishment. While their acceptance of the associated norms and beliefs may be qualified, the costs of rebelling against these norms are already much higher for them than the costs for college youth. A United States survey (October 1968) of men and women aged 18 to 24 provides limited support for this hypothesis. The noncollege youth proved much less likely than the college contingent to assert that "draft resistance" or "civil disobedience" was "justified under any circumstances." And among the college youth, it was those least committed to traditional values who were most likely to advocate such extralegal political protests (*Fortune*, January 1969, p. 71).

[21] For example, the unusually large cohorts born in many Western countries following World War II produced sizable increases in the numbers turning 18 or 21 during the late 1960's (cf. Volume I, Chapter 19 · 6 · a).

This patterning of the age strata in the electorate is paralleled by the age stratification of leaders and officials within the political system. In general, leadership typically reaches its peak among people in their mature years. Numerous high-ranking positions (such as President, cabinet officer, ambassador, or United States Supreme Court Justice) are acquired and retained between the ages of 50 and 70. Hence, older people tend to be better represented than younger people among the elite who play strategic roles in national or local government (as well as in other decision-making structures outside the polity). (See Volume I, Chapter 19 · 5.) Thus a clear connection emerges between age and political position and power in modern societies.[22]

How does this age pattern affect the society generally? The maturity of leaders and of the average voter undoubtedly provides stability, since mature individuals can bring to bear both their commitment and their long experience. In some instances, however, this stability can rigidify, operating to retard political and social change. Thus the early experience of persons reared in rural areas or during a deep depression can sometimes impede the solution of current problems or becloud the understanding of emerging social system requirements.

When the established authorities do use their power to resist change, a reaction is sometimes provoked among key elements of the youngest age stratum who seek political expression for their discontent. Since voting (which is closed to many of them in any case) often has little rapid or visible influence on decision-making, the young may attempt to by-pass the traditional, or even the legal, channels. Seeking alternative modes of political participation, they may resort to demonstrations, sit-ins, social movements, or even to violence.

Of course, it is not only the young whose needs are thwarted by the established political leadership, and who may resort to various forms of nonelectoral activity. Among the aged in the United States, for example, there are various organizations of pensioners who maintain legislative lobbies; and during the Depression of the 1930's such pressure groups as the Townsend Movement gained broad followings by promising a financial panacea for older people. However, these political movements within the oldest stratum appear to center upon particular problems, to promote specific legislation for or by the old people, and even to fade away when these objectives are attained (see Volume I, Chapter 19 · 6 · b). By contrast, the young are open to social and political change of all kinds. It is easiest for them to be against what has been and to want something new. Not only are they least committed to the social order, they are also least committed to the conventional political ar-

---

[22] Compare the stereotypical view of the elite status of older people in many primitive tribes (Simmons, 1945, pp. 105–130).

rangements for maintaining this order. Hence it is this stratum whose unmet needs may press for change through nontraditional modes of political participation.[23]

However, the attempt to exert political influence by going outside the electoral machinery is tied to the content of political ideologies and attitudes —a topic to be discussed in the next section. The readiness of one age stratum to use extra institutional means can arise from attitudinal differences among the strata. And the potential for any open conflict between young and old—the topic of the final section—is heightened by the coexistence of sharp cleavages in political attitudes and the recourse by members of at least one age stratum to direct and militant modes of political participation.

2 Political ideologies and attitudes

Quite apart from the mode or the extent of political participation, there are also differences among the age strata in the content of political orientation. Yet these attitudinal differences, unlike the persistent age patterns in voting behavior, vary by time and by place, as well as by particular issues. Sometimes it is the young who stand alone in their views; sometimes it is the very old who differ from the other age strata. Sometimes the operation of the polity can be disrupted by sharp attitudinal cleavages between young and old in goals, ideologies, or attitudes toward social change.

DIFFERENCES AMONG STRATA

In the popular view, the old are generally believed to be more conservative than the young. And indeed there are considerable data to support this view. In the United States, surveys conducted in the 1950's show that the proportions of persons identifying themselves as Republicans increase by age. In Great Britain a similar pattern of affiliation with the Conservative party has also been observed (Volume I, Chapter 19 · 3 · a and b).

However, there are numerous exceptions. Older people are more likely than younger people to support various liberal economic measures from which they themselves might benefit, such as public housing, publicly owned electrical power, or government assistance in job placement (Volume I, Chapter 19 · 4 · b). By the same token, young people sometimes favor the extreme right. The Nazi (rightist) party in Germany was a truly young party, with almost 40 per cent of its members between the ages of 18 and 30, a percentage disproportionate to their numbers in the population as a whole (Gerth, 1940, pp. 529–530). Support for Castro following the (leftist) Cuban revolution was lowest among the youngest, those 21 to 27, out of a sample of Cuban

[23] Of course, it may be only the vocal segment of an age stratum that expresses dissent, disputes authority, or takes other political action on behalf of age-mates.

workers aged 21 to 59 (Zeitlin, 1967, p. 227). Similarly, in the United States the support for Wallace, the third-party right-wing presidential candidate in 1968, was somewhat stronger among the young people than among those over 30 (Erskine, n.d., p. 6).

That such age-related divergences in the views of the electorate on particular issues or occasions are so unpredictable leads us to an examination of the possible effects of aging (P2), cohort succession (P1), and the political climates or special events characterizing particular periods of history. Political orientations are, of course, linked especially closely to history, as new issues continually arise and old ones become resolved or are put aside only to re-emerge. Not only does the mood of the polity change over time, but so also does the meaning and content of political ideologies—witness the semantic changes in what constitutes liberalism or conservatism at particular historical periods. How, then, does age enter in?

CHANGES OVER THE LIFE COURSE (P2)

Only recently has it become feasible and useful to trace the relationships between aging and political attitudes within the welter of historical events. In the past, political theorists have sometimes simply assumed that aging has little or no effect: that individuals, having formed their opinions at an early age, simply maintain this stance throughout their lifetime.[24] And various psychological tests of attitudes and behavior in general show that older people tend to be more rigid than young people, less disposed to adapt to changing stimuli (Volume 1, Chapter 12 · 1 · a).

Some hypothetical patterns   Yet the existing evidence seems to cast doubt on any oversimplified assumption of rigidity in political attitudes. Scattered and tenuous as the available data are,[25] they afford one of the very few opportunities to study aging systematically as a social process. A reanalysis of such data drawn from the United States in recent decades (which illustrates the methods outlined in Chapter 2) begins to suggest how cohorts of individuals may change their political attitudes as they age. Two complementary hypotheses emerge:

Hypothesis 1: On *specific issues*, each cohort tends to change as it ages in line with the general trend in the society.

Hypothesis 2: On the *general* question of conservative versus liberal alle-

[24] Compare the discussion in Lipset, 1963, pp. 279–282. In Mannheim's formulation, the early impressions of a generation constitute the primary "stratum of experience" from which all later experiences take their meaning (Mannheim [1928], 1952, p. 298).

[25] Despite our good fortune in discovering relevant materials in a form suitable for cohort analysis, account must be taken of their limitations, as previously noted (cf. also Appendix). Apart from cultural and temporal restrictions, the data show only *net* shift in orientation; and the sampling procedures are not only inconsistent over time, but they are also potentially subject to serious, though unmeasurable age-related biases.

giance, each cohort tends to change as it ages toward a more conservative position.

Such hypotheses would be of considerable substantive interest, if further research covering other periods and other countries were to prove consistent with the empirical regularities so far observed in the present data.

One existing set of materials on specific issues (Hypothesis 1) is reported by Evan (1965), who compared opinion poll responses on ten items (two other items refer to our Hypothesis 2) that were repeated in approximately parallel versions about 20 years apart. The form of the analysis is illustrated in Table 4 · 4, which compares the proportions expressing a conservative attitude toward labor unions in 1938 and again in 1959. For example, in the cohort born about 1913, who moved from age 25 to age 46 (approximately) between these dates, the conservative proportion went down from 29 to 22. Similar declines also appear (at successively later stages of life) for each of the other three cohorts shown in the table. And, for comparison, the societal trend appears in the drop in conservatism from 32 to 20 in the total figures shown at the bottom of the table. Table 4 · 4 shows only one of the ten analyses, all of which approximate the same results: that is, regardless of whether the general trend moves in a conservative or in a liberal direction, aging follows the direction of this trend on a variety of specific topics chosen to reflect either a liberal-conservative or traditional-modern attitudinal dimension.

This indication that cohorts tend to shift as they age in line with societal

TABLE 4 · 4 *Cohort analysis of attitudes of disapproval toward labor unions*[a]

Per cent disapproving. (Approximate age in parentheses)

Date of birth (approximate)[b]	Period of observation	
	1938	1959
1913	(25) 29	(46) 22
1903	(35) 28	(56) 18
1893	(45) 27	(66) 26
1883	(55) 35	(76) 28
1873	(65) 40	—
1863	(75) 50	—
Total (all ages)	32	20

[a] The questions were: Are you in favor of labor unions? (1938); In general, do you approve or disapprove of labor unions? (1959)
[b] Data are for 10-year categories.
Source: Evan, 1965, Table 4. Adapted from *Computer Methods in the Analysis of Large-Scale Social Systems* edited by James M. Beshers by permission of the MIT Press, Cambridge, Massachusetts. Copyright © 1965, 1968 by The Massachusetts Institute of Technology and the President and Fellows of Harvard College.

TABLE 4 · 5 *Cohort analysis of self-identification as conservative rather than liberal in the United States*[a]

Per cent conservative. (Approximate age in parentheses)

Date of birth (approximate)[b]	Period of observation	
	1938	1957
1913	(25) 45	(44) 48
1903	(35) 40	(54) 50
1893	(45) 49	(64) 55
1883	(55) 50	(74) 58
1873	(65) 60	—
1863	(75) 61	—
Total (all ages)	48	48

[a] The questions were: In politics, do you regard yourself as a liberal or a conservative? (1938); Taking everything into account, would you say that you yourself are more of a liberal or more of a conservative in politics? (1957)
[b] Data are for 10-year categories.
Source: Evan, 1965, Table 6. Adapted from *Computer Methods in the Analysis of Large-Scale Social Systems* edited by James M. Beshers by permission of the MIT Press, Cambridge, Massachusetts. Copyright © 1965, 1968 by The Massachusetts Institute of Technology and the President and Fellows of Harvard College.

changes is of fundamental importance, should it be substantiated by further research and under varied conditions, for it rules out two alternative hypotheses about life-course processes. First, it contradicts the notion that cohorts show no change with aging. Thus it implies that individuals do not necessarily hold rigidly throughout life to opinions adopted when they first came of age as citizens. Second, it counters the stereotype that aging, if it results in change at all, results only in increasingly conservative or reactionary views, regardless of the issue.

When the data refer, not to attitudes or specific issues, but to the individual's *basic political position* (Hypothesis 2), the indications from cohort analysis do point to an apparently increasing conservatism with advancing age. For example, Table 4 · 5, also from the Evan data, shows a slight but consistent increase between 1938 and 1957 for each of four cohorts in their self-description as conservative rather than liberal in politics. These life-course changes, rather than following the position of the public as a whole, contrast with it; for, as the totals at the bottom of the table show, no parallel change took place.[26]

[26] Evan observed a similar set of cohort shifts between 1937 and 1961 on another question that asked for a hypothetical choice between a conservative and a liberal party; but here the total trend also was toward greater conservatism.

Clearer indications on this second hypothesis are provided by another analysis in which Crittenden (1962, pp. 651–654) finds a small but consistent drift of Democrats to the Republican party over the life course (see also Volume I, Chapter 19 · 3 · d). This finding applies to cohort shifts both in party identification and in voting between two pairs of presidential election polls in the United States—1946 versus 1954, and 1950 versus 1958. Crittenden's analysis includes several important refinements: it controls on two levels of education and excludes the South. It even attempts to offset the special effects of historical change and the powerful impact of particular elections, by correcting each cohort shift by the amount of partisan shift in the total electorate.[27]

There are various indications from other studies of the connection between Republicanism and a conservative stance. For example, Campbell et al., who asked a cross-sectional sample to recall their personal histories, found that the shift in party allegiance in the Republican direction was greatest among persons scoring especially high on a score of resistance to change.[28] Thus the drift toward Republicanism in the Crittenden data and toward avowed conservatism in the Evan data may both reflect the same underlying life-course pattern.

General versus specific orientations   What is the meaning of these empirically derived hypotheses? Although many precautions[29] ought to be taken in interpreting the sketchy materials at hand, let us nevertheless take the data at face value for the heuristic purposes of stimulating more extensive accumulations of data and of suggesting theories to explain how aging contributes to the operation of the polity. Let us ask: Why should aging bring about increasing conservatism in basic political position (Hypothesis 2) but not in attitudes on specific issues (Hypothesis 1)?

The distinction between basic political position and specific political attitudes is by no means unfamiliar in the sociological literature. Berelson and his associates (1954), in their analysis in *Voting*, distinguish between the numerous component decisions involved in any electoral campaign and the ultimate single decision between the two major parties. As they put it:

---

[27] The virtues of this analysis in controlling period effects (Pd) associated with national candidates and campaigns, as described in Chapter 2 · 4 · A, appear to be misunderstood by Cutler (1968, 1970).

[28] Campbell et al. (1960, pp. 148, 210, 213–215). Only a minority reported having changed their partisan orientation after they entered the electorate.

[29] Among these precautions is the consideration that the life-course shifts (Ld) on specific issues (Hypothesis 1), though following the direction of change for the total society, may differ from it in degree. For example, the Ld might be comparatively less pronounced than the total trend in either the liberal or the conservative direction, with the consequence that the older strata would always lag behind the younger. Or, if the societal change were controlled in the analysis, the Ld might all show a net shift toward increasing conservatism, with the consequence that Hypothesis 2 would have to be generalized to include specific issues as well as basic political position. Unfortunately, such possibilities must await further testing with data more complete than those presented by Evan.

. . . what starts as a relatively unstructured mass of diverse opinions with countless cleavages within the electorate is finally transformed into, or at least represented by, a single basic cleavage between the two sets of partisans. Out of many small disagreements emerges one big disagreement, and that is "settled" by the election (p. 183).

The distinction was picked up and amplified by Parsons (1959, pp. 84 ff.), who proposed that voters provide support to the polity at two levels: a lower level of advocacy of particular policies, and a higher level of generalized support for elected leaders who are to make the determinations that will be binding upon the collectivity. Parsons describes how each of these levels not only serves different functions in the operation of the political system but also requires the voter to make his decisions in different ways.

According to our interpretations, different criteria are employed at these two levels, and these criteria are, in turn, differentially related to the life course. At the lower level of specific policies, the decision-making process can be fairly simple and direct. The citizen is likely to have information, perhaps even experience, on single issues, so that he can weigh specific merits and demerits and can employ concrete standards of evaluation. At the higher level of his overall political position, however, the voter must focus less on the issues themselves than on individuals representing ideological positions. Here his decision involves some measure of generalized trust in the candidate or party, apart from particular issues. Trust is required because the voter cannot grasp the full complexity of many issues; he cannot find coherence in their diversity; and he knows that future issues, unforeseen at election time, are bound to arise. Moreover, it is unlikely that any one party can satisfy the voter's position on all issues. Thus he endorses the broad direction underlying the policies he prefers, hoping that this direction will accord with the greater part of his particular predilections and views.

SOURCES OF LIFE-COURSE CHANGE

How, then, does the distinction between basic and specific political attitudes apply to the dual findings on changes over the life course? At the lower level of advocacy of specific policies, it does not seem unreasonable that people, as they age, shift in either direction with the general trend (Hypothesis 1). Far from holding rigidly to fixed positions, they can be influenced by the climate of opinion, and can reassess particular attitudes in the light of recent information or their own experiences.

But what accounts for the apparent drift toward conservatism at the higher level of generalized support for programs and leaders (Hypothesis 2)? It should be emphasized in advance that, while individuals are aging, the society and the polity are also changing. Some issues (such as social security) are advocated at one time by one political party and at a later time by the opposing party (or they may disappear as issues).[30] Political parties, like aging individuals, can be influenced by the climate of opinion on specific topics. The labels "liberal" and "conservative"—or Republican and Democrat—fluctuate in their reference to many kinds of issues, as the content of ideologies and of party programs continually changes. Thus the individual's tendency with aging to adopt an increasingly conservative basic stance could be quite consistent with the flexibility of many of his opinions. This stance may sometimes merely mean increasing conservatism *relative* to the changing times, a striving to maintain personal stability in the face of societal change.

Socioeconomic status As one aspect of a person's vested interest in society, an increase in socioeconomic status over the life course is often postulated as an explanation for growing conservatism.[31] According to this argument, aging is accompanied by rising income, accumulating assets, increasing security and prestige, and by the associated desire to protect these advantages. Hence many older people turn to the Republican party as the preferred guardian of their own and their children's socioeconomic position.

Persuasive as this argument may seem, however, its explanatory power is limited on several counts. First, there is little evidence to connect improvement in socioeconomic status with a shift toward a more conservative pattern of voting or of political choice.[32] Indeed, Lipset (1963, pp. 272–273) adduces examples from several countries to show that social mobility in either direction —upward or downward—is likely to result in support for the more conservative parties. Moreover, income and economic well-being do not rise, on the average, over the entire life course, but tend to drop by the age of retirement (Volume I, Chapter 4 · A · 4)—a drop that is not paralleled in the data (slight though they are) on the shift toward conservatism shown in Table 4 · 5 (see also Volume I, Chapter 19 · 3 · d). And finally, even when people do improve their economic position with aging, the impact of this improvement on their political outlook requires still another unwarranted assumption: namely, that people use their own past lives as standards of comparison. If instead, older people were to make contemporaneous comparisons with members of the middle age strata, they would typically perceive themselves as relatively deprived in socioeconomic status; they might even (if this line of reasoning were correct) turn to a leftist, rather than to a conservative, position. But whether, in general, people use as reference groups other age strata of their own biographies is a question still unanswered.

[30] Cf. Berelson et al. (1954, pp. 208–212), on the life history of an issue.

[31] Cf. the discussion by Lipset (1963, pp. 283–284).

[32] Some negative evidence on this point may be adduced from the Crittenden finding that those with less than a high school education—who might be less likely to improve their position with aging—seem *no* less likely than better educated persons to switch to the Republican party (Crittenden, 1962, pp. 651–653).

Societal commitment   It is only when the status argument is broadened beyond the economic sphere that it becomes compelling as a possible explanation for life-course changes in political attitudes. For the longer a person has lived in the society, the greater his stake in it becomes: not only in the position he has achieved, but also in the relationships he has developed, in the social structures with which he has become familiar, and in the values associated with these structures. Thus the shift toward conservatism and toward those political leaders who can be expected to preserve the stability of the society, may represent the desire to safeguard these investments. In short, commitment—the key to many aspects of the aging process—seems as relevant here as it proved to be earlier in explaining voting participation (in Section 1).

For the political role, as for all other roles, growing commitment to society does not necessarily imply any blanket resistance to change in attitudes or values, but rather a resistance to changing those attitudes implicated in the fundamental structure of the person's environment or in the values associated with this structure. While basic values tend to be maintained over the life course, the implementation of these values may change in response to alterations in the social environment.[33] In a rapidly changing society, people may attempt to implement their basic values by continual reassessment of their attitudes toward specific policies, accepting particular policy changes perceived as nonthreatening to the shape of society, or reinterpreting their basic values to accommodate such changes. One means of maintaining both their cherished values and a stable social environment may be in the choice of a party or general political program that promises "to make haste slowly." Thus the shift to Republicanism would occur as people come to perceive this party as the one that preserves tradition, or as the party of stability in contrast to the Democratic party as the symbol of change. The person's tendency to shift toward political conservatism might then express, not a change at all, but an attempt to hold on to that structure to which he has worked out an adjustment, rather than risking the unknown consequences of change.

In sum, aging may operate to heighten the individual's commitment to society, by reinforcing both his involvement in social structures and his attachment to those social values he perceives to support these structures. Polit-

[33] Such a definition of resistance to change is consistent with various theories of social learning, which postulate that basic values are acquired in childhood and adolescence. Once learned, these basic orientations are likely to be maintained. They motivate the individual to perform the future roles he must assume. The changes made by the individual after he reaches adulthood are, according to this line of thought, mere implementation of these basic values, entailing specific norms, information, and behaviors. The potency and durability of fundamental, early-life values appear to be assured by the primacy and frequency of the learning situations in which they are inculcated, the intensity of rewards and punishments, and the partial reinforcement provided by the learning situation. See, e.g., Brim (1966, pp. 21, 26–27).

ically, this commitment can lead to a conservative stand among older people at the general level of support for leadership, though it need not result in a rigid traditionalism at the level of specific issues.

In addition to the possible effects of aging on the political orientations of the various age strata at a given time, particular cohorts are likely to differ from one another in ideology and in frame of reference because of the differing historical periods in which they were socialized.

The concept of "political generations" is a widely discussed special case of cohort differences as applied to the polity. Mannheim, in his early essay on "The Problem of Generations" ([1928], 1952, pp. 276–322), had noted that, since members of the same generation or age group share a common location in the social and historical process, they acquire a common *Weltanschauung*, adopting certain characteristic modes of thought and experience during the early years. Other scholars (such as Heberle [1951], Lipset et al. [1954], Lane [1965], Cain [1967]) have explicated the process by which the historical situation, in which each generation first forms its political ideas can also shape its future outlook and its reactions to subsequent events.

Without attempting to test this theory,[34] cross-sectional studies have used it widely to interpret differences observed among age strata. Thus studies made in the United States during the 1950's show that people who started to think seriously about politics or who first came to grips with political issues during the New Deal, are more likely to vote Democratic than those whose political views were formed during the earlier period of conservative dominance. In pre-Hitler Germany, the age compositions of the Nazi and Socialist parties were found to be, to an extent, predictable from the political climate of the first elections in which their members had participated (Lipset, 1963, p. 281). Or among American professors in the late 1960's, age differences in opposition to involvement in Vietnam were attributed to the varied outlook in international affairs current during their respective formative years (Downing and Salomone, 1969, p. 44).

Campbell and his collaborators (1960, pp. 153–155) have given some support to the emphasis on becoming a voter as the most crucial stage in the formation of political outlook. In their study of personal histories as recalled by a cross-sectional sample, it was the new voters who reacted more emphatically than the established voters in the general swing toward the Democratic party in the Roosevelt years.

The thorough understanding of cohort processes in the formation of political opinion still awaits types of analysis that are only now becoming feasible as

[34] [*For the types of information required to test this theory, see the discussion in Chapter 2.*]

stores of data from opinion polls accumulate [*see Chapter* 2]. Cohort differences at the *start* of the political career can be readily seen from any sequence of cross-sectional studies broken down by age. For example, Figure 4 · 1 compares the extent of support for racial integration in the schools between 1956 and 1963 in the United States (Hyman and Sheatsley, 1964, p. 23). Persons aged 21 to 24 at the earlier date show less support for integration than the more recent cohort reaching age 21 to 24 at the later date, a difference that can reasonably be attributed to the differing political climates encountered by the two cohorts. To be sure, the general trend toward increasing support appears to be reflected here in each of the older age strata also. But, since the graph does not show the start of the political career for any of those cohorts now at the older ages, it cannot take into account the possible effects of aging ($P2$) as these may confound the effects of cohort succession ($P1$).

For the purpose of disentangling cohort differences from life-course differences, *after* the cohorts have entered the political system, it is necessary to rearrange the data in the usual form for cohort analysis.[35] Table 4 · 4 from our reanalysis of the Evan data can be used again to illustrate this principle. In addition to the life-course patterns apparent from this table, described under Hypothesis 1, the cohort differences can now be explored by comparing along the diagonals of the table. It can be seen, for example, that when the 1893 cohort was aged 45 it was more likely to take a conservative view of labor unions (27 per cent) than the more recent 1913 cohort at approximately the same age (22 per cent). This same tendency for the earlier cohort to be more conservative than the recent cohort holds also for each of the other three available comparisons between groups of similar age. (Unfortunately, the Evan data are incomplete, omitting part of the information needed to examine the cohort differences at the crucial earlier ages around 25 and 35.)

In this instance, then, the cohort differences are consistent for all strata and reflect the general trend in the society—which is also away from the more conservative attitude (from 32 to 20 per cent). These data reveal the dynamic process whereby the successive cohorts can contribute to societal change. It is clear from Table 4 · 4 that the overall shift toward a less conservative view on this particular issue is due in part (though not entirely, as already indicated under Hypothesis 1 above) to the influx of new cohorts with a liberal attitude who replace the earlier, more conservative, cohorts, as they move on into the older age strata and eventually die out.

The data from this table, and on the nine other specific topics examined by Evan, can be generalized to add to our first two hypotheses (about life-course differences) the following hypothesis about cohort differences:

[35] The data in Figure 4 · 1 cannot be rearranged in this form simply because the age intervals fail to mesh with the date intervals.

FIGURE 4 · 1 *Support for racial integration of public schools, by age and region, United States, 1956 and 1963*

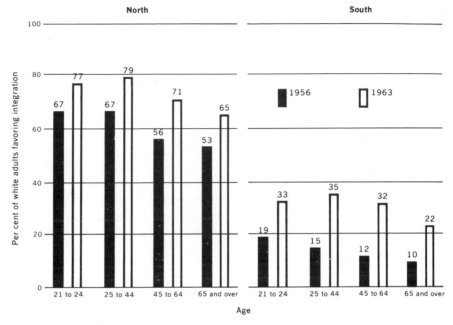

Source: Hyman and Sheatsley, 1964, p. 23; U.S. polls.

Hypothesis 3: When earlier cohorts are compared with more recent cohorts at similar ages, the differences follow the direction of the general trend in the society.

As it turns out, the Evan data (with only one exception) fit this hypothesis, regardless of the direction of the general trend on particular items.[36] The succession of cohorts can exert its influence either in the conservative or the liberal direction.[37]

CONSEQUENCES FOR THE AGE STRATA

It thus seems likely that trends of political opinion are affected by the dual processes of cohort succession and aging, and are in turn affected by history.

[36] Here again Evan's other two topics, those referring to the *general* question of conservative versus liberal allegiance, differ from the ten questions on specific issues: The general questions show no such consistent pattern of cohort differences—see Table 4 · 5 above and the following discussion of Table 4 · 6.

[37] Mannheim suggests a "dialectic" whereby each new generation, reacting to the conservative or the liberal content of its respective period, fights different opponents in the older generation. Mannheim ([1928], 1952, p. 229).

On specific issues, historical change alters political attitudes both through its impact on new cohorts as they enter the system and through influences on opinion throughout the life course. At the more general level of party allegiance or support for leadership, the relation between history and the age-related processes seems less pronounced. Each new generation of voters is undoubtedly somewhat influenced by the political climate at the time (mitigated in various ways to be discussed in Section 3 below). But with aging, most individuals seem to cling to early loyalties, while those who do change apparently tend toward conservatism regardless of the general trend.

How, then, do these dual processes operate with the forces of history to produce the patterns of political attitudes among age strata at particular periods? How do aging and cohort succession contribute jointly to the balance —or the imbalance and the strain—among the age strata, and to the shifts in this balance over time?

A fictitious example   The schematic illustration in Table 4 · 6 shows the age patterns of voting that would result over a series of election years provided certain assumptions are made about the underlying processes.

Over the *life course,* as each cohort ages it tends increasingly to vote for candidates of Party X (the resemblance to the Republican party is clear). This assumed tendency (consistent with Hypothesis 2) can be seen by reading across the rows of the table, with an exception in the 1964 election which will be explained shortly.

As for the *succession of cohorts,* adapting the assumption that seems reasonable in the light of existing knowledge, the table shows a general tendency for each new cohort to be less liberal in its position (to vote for Party X) than the preceding cohorts (as seen in the top diagonal for persons aged 21).

TABLE 4 · 6   *Fictitious cohort analysis of voting for candidate of Party X (conservative)*

Per cent voting. (Age in parentheses)

Date of coming of age	Election year (period of observation)					
	1932	1940	1948	1956	1964	1972
1972						(21) 60
1964					(21) 42	(29) 58
1956				(21) 45	(29) 40	(37) 53
1948			(21) 43	(29) 45	(37) 40	(45) 50
1940		(21) 36	(29) 39	(37) 43	(45) 39	(53) 46
1932	(21) 30	(29) 35	(37) 38	(45) 43	(53) 37	(61) 45

This cohort pattern, selected for purely heuristic purposes, was nevertheless implied by Lipset and his collaborators (1954, p. 1148), who noted that first voters in the 1952 election seemed more likely to vote Republican than the first voters in 1948. They speculated that voters who came of age during the Depression or the war decades of the 1930's and 1940's developed Democratic ties, whereas those who came of age during the subsequent years of prosperity and stability turned toward the Republican party.

A third source of variation in the data, *special period effects*, must of course also be taken into account in any set of constructs aimed to simulate reality. Voting in a given election is always affected, not only by broad social changes and ideological trends, but also by the particular personalities, events, and issues of the moment. Thus Table 4 · 6 is constructed to take account of certain known political situations: the swing toward the Democrats in the 1930's and early 1940's, the Republican victories of the 1950's, the special case of the Goldwater candidacy in 1964, and a putative conservative trend from 1968 to 1972. Such special situations account for certain exceptions in the two sets of general tendencies assumed to characterize the data in this table.

What is the composite of these underlying processes as they affect the age strata in the electorate for each election year? As can be seen by reading down each of the columns, the general pattern is for the younger age strata to be more conservative (more likely to vote for candidates of Party X) than the older strata. This outcome is obviously produced here by the flow of cohorts, with the conservative new cohorts successively displacing the older cohorts with their more liberal views. To be sure, the aging process is also at work, operating to counteract the cohort differences in the cross-sectional data through life-course shifts toward increasing conservatism. But the effects of aging are insufficient (in this example) to offset or reverse the direction of cross-sectional differences among the strata.

Other sets of assumptions about the strength or the direction of the underlying processes could, of course, yield entirely different age patterns in the electorate at a particular time, or could yield the same patterns via different routes. For example, liberal tendencies among older cohorts might be cancelled out by a pronounced increase in conservatism attendant upon aging. Or conservative origins of the older cohorts might reinforce the life-course tendency toward conservatism, resulting in a pronounced rise in Republican voters across the age strata in given elections.

As data become available for comparing cohorts over several time periods, the underlying processes need no longer remain largely speculative, but could be isolated and described by the methods illustrated in this fictitious analysis.

Possibilities of cleavage Of special concern are the conditions under which the joint effects of aging and cohort succession, rather than reducing the differences among age strata, can sharpen these differences and bring them into conflict. What circumstances affect the strength of the respective processes, heightening either the changes over the life course (Ld) or the differences among cohorts (Cd)? And what circumstances determine whether the two processes operate together in the same direction, or whether they tend to counteract each other by operating in divergent directions?

It seems clear that rapid social change or sudden crises, by impinging upon both processes, can often multiply the bases for political disagreement among age strata. Such events as famine, depression, epidemic disease, or the introduction of a new technology can produce differential interpretations and reactions among the strata. For example, new types of wars, with escalation of violence and attacks on civilian populations, may evoke fresh attitudes about war, especially among the young who may be called upon to wage war against civilians, whereas the old may misunderstand or even reject these attitudes. Conversely, the orientations of an older stratum have been shaped by earlier situations that may no longer be relevant for the young. In the 1960's, for instance many people in their 40's and 50's who as young adults had to worry about getting and holding jobs, were still concerned with economic security; while many young people, lacking early experience with a major depression, take jobs for granted and deprecate the older generation's preoccupation with security.

Such differences among age strata do not necessarily constitute political rifts, however. And although social change can provide the potential for sharp cleavage, such disagreements can either be modified or exacerbated by a variety of structural conditions and processual mechanisms. We turn now in Section 3 to a consideration of the sources of harmony or of sharp cleavage among age strata in the society.

3 *The potential for conflict*

Political rebellion of youth against age has erupted in many times and places. A comprehensive theory of age conflict in the polity should, therefore, explain why youth activism has arisen in such a variety of circumstances, why youth often initiates the conflict, why sharp political cleavages between age strata occur sporadically rather than continuously, and why the numbers and kinds of active protagonists tend to vary. In our analysis, we shall attempt merely to pinpoint a few age-related factors that may help explain tendencies toward age cleavage in political life, using as illustration the context of youth activism in the United States of the 1960's. The insights and clues suggested by this approach can lead perhaps, through critical tests of the data from other times and other societies, to the eventual formulation of a more general theory of political conflict as an aspect of age stratification.[38]

THE NATURE OF POLITICAL CONFLICT AMONG AGE STRATA

Conflict is the essence of political life in the sense that parties and candidates in democratic systems continually vie for political leadership. While young people and their elders have always disagreed about a host of political issues, the particular type of age-youth conflict that we shall discuss here—the syndrome dubbed the "generation gap"—has distinctive qualities. First, the *polarization* of differences among age strata in values, goals, and means for achieving goals, while affecting only certain segments of the population, is unusually pronounced. Second, and perhaps contributing to the development of polarization, the *issues* about which intergenerational disagreement centers are significant beyond the specific policies involved, holding profound implications for the total shape of the society [*compare Chapter 7 by Parsons and Platt*]. Third, the conflict is characterized by the acceptance by at least one age stratum of extrainstitutional or extralegal *means* of enforcement and resistance.

Certain circumstances that may set the stage for polarization have been noted in the previous sections of this essay. Under conditions of rapid change, youth and their elders are likely to diverge in political attitudes, with the more articulate young people seeking new goals and new solutions to political problems. The middle-aged and older strata, insofar as they differ from the younger strata both in goals and in commitment to existing political institutions, will lag behind the general thrust of social change. Since the older strata (by virtue of their sheer numbers, their greater electoral participation, and their already established power positions) have a disproportionate influence over political decisions, they can resist social change by actively opposing or refusing to respond to new situations, thus making for rigidity of the established system. Such a setting provides the structural conditions for a resort to noninstitutionalized modes of participation by the young—many of whom are blocked from voting and are only weakly tied to traditional politics.

Yet although such conditions have prevailed through much of the twentieth century, a period of rapid change in general, there was a so-called conformist generation of youth in the United States as recently as the 1950's. If the potential for sharp political cleavage among age strata has existed for so long, why does it become activated only sporadically?

---

[38] Sorokin discusses, at various points in his work (e.g., Sorokin, 1968), the historical fluctuations in the relative importance of age versus other bases of differentiation or inequality.

Several sets of age-related factors appear to operate in complex ways either to retard or to encourage sharp cleavages among age strata. As has often been observed, pronounced conflicts may be minimized in a pluralistic society by multiple solidary group affiliations. Thus deep rifts among age strata can, under certain conditions, be prevented by memberships in age-heterogeneous groups that cross-cut the lines separating the age strata. Divisive tendencies can also be affected by such processes as socialization in age-heterogeneous groups, or by age mobility; for, with individuals unable to remain long within the same age stratum, the forces making for cleavage have relatively little time to coalesce.

Age-heterogeneous group memberships   The notion that memberships in age-heterogeneous groups can act as a mechanism for reducing political conflict among age strata assumes that affiliation within a group (such as family, church, or work unit) tend to hold the members together—even though these affiliations (between parents and children, or between young members and old members) may cut across age lines. The ties that bind together members of different ages within these groups—common interests, shared sentiments, feelings of loyalty and affection—often transcend the purely political divergences among age strata. Thus, when the lines of political cleavage in a society tend to coincide with the lines between age strata, this cleavage can be muted by other social relationships that cross-cut these divisions [*see Chapter 10*].[39] For, if the political cleavage breaks out into open dissension, the intragroup ties are brought into play.

Memberships in groups that are not age-segregated can serve to unify the age strata both by influencing opinions in a common direction and by activating the bonds of loyalty or affection between persons with disparate views. Exposure to persons of differing ages—as in the family, at work, or in voluntary associations—entails exposure to the associated differences in political position. When persons of diverse ages interact with each other and share common goals, they not only have opportunity for mutual socialization on political matters, but their political decisions rest on a community of interests. Thus, in a work group, for example, the problems of the job may take precedence over many other problems; and, since people of different ages often work together, these common concerns may unify their political views (on unions, for example), which is especially likely where individuals of different ages occupy similar positions.

This sense of a common fate with others of different ages suggests how

---

[39] The same argument applies, of course, when political polarization coincides with other major societal divisions along lines of class, ethnic group, or religion, for example.

membership in age-heterogeneous groups may operate to forge unity among the age strata. Quite apart from age, association with others tends to produce mutual feelings of loyalty, even close emotional ties, so that the approval of these others "matters." When people who "matter" to one another are age-dissimilars, they are likely to avoid political activities threatening to disrupt those groups held together by affective or instrumental bonds. In this way the ties of common group membership among persons of differing age can foster agreement concerning both the content and form of political participation.

A lack of age heterogeneity in salient group memberships may perhaps account for the frequent involvement of young people, especially college students, in age conflicts.[40] Age-homogeneous groupings reduce the direct exposure of students to the political arguments of other age strata and insulate them from the sanctions of older people. Continuous association with other young people may thus foster a sense of age solidarity and a feeling of alienation from the adult world. Those societal conditions that intensify age-grading (such as a sudden increase in the size of one age stratum or the prolongation of education with a consequent delay in labor force entry) can thus contribute to potential polarization of the age strata.

Political socialization Political socialization in the family may be considered a special case of the reduction of age conflict through cross-cutting group affiliation. Since much political socialization takes place in the family, the process can serve to unite rather than separate the generations.

To be sure, some observers have looked upon the family as the source of age conflict rather than as a structure for the reduction of cleavage. Certain socialization practices have been cited as discouraging the young from adopting parental ideologies, so that entire cohorts can be exposed to early influences that loosen commitment to existing social structures. Both an authoritarian background and a permissive or egalitarian upbringing have been blamed for young people's rejection of established authority: the former because the young are presumably fighting an authoritarian father figure (cf. Altbach, 1967, p. 77); the latter because the young have been trained to expect immediate gratification and to question arbitrary authority (cf. Flacks, 1967, p. 61). Whatever the intrafamily relationships at fault, it is claimed that such attitudes toward parental authority, once engendered, are likely to be projected into the political arena.

However, it seems questionable that specific techniques of socialization can be blamed for student rebellion.[41] Both permissive and authoritarian up-

---

[40] Even though college students are members of several age-heterogeneous groups (the classroom, the family), direct association with adults is often limited either by geographical separation (as in the family) or by the low ratio of adults to young people (as in the classroom).

[41] Compare the discussion by Dawson and Prewitt (1969, pp. 117–120).

bringing are undoubtedly more pervasive than the incidence of student ac-tivism.[42] In the case of student activism in the United States in the 1960's, it appears that the content of political socialization was more crucial than the nature of parental relationships. Indeed, the success of parents in transmitting a given political content apparently contributed to youthful rebellion, not so much against parents themselves as against the commonly held views of the older age strata outside the family. Several scattered studies observe that parents of student radicals are more likely to hold radical or liberal views than are parents of other students (Flacks, 1967, pp. 66–68; Lipset and Altbach, 1967). Thus radical students, in questioning dominant ideologies, may be attempting to apply, rather than to reject, the political ideals learned at home.

Thus any theory that the political protests of youth constitute the rebellion of children against their own parents fails to provide a compelling or sufficient explanation of the available evidence for the 1960's, since this evidence sug-gests that many student activists, rather than having notably discordant rela-tions with their parents, often share radical ideologies with them. Even where young people are motivated to rebel against parents, their hostility need not be expressed in the political sphere.

On the contrary, many straws in the wind point to the likelihood that kin-ship ties influence the age strata more toward consensus than toward discord. The young person's partisan attachment, ideology, and motivation for political participation is to a great extent learned at home, at least in the United States. A high correlation has been noted between the political beliefs, especially the party preferences, of parents and their children.[43] Certain observers go so far as to suggest that individuals tend to be born into their political party much as they are born into probable future membership in the church of their par-ents (Hyman, 1959, p. 74). And, as with religious affiliation, to attack an individual's politics is often considered inappropriate, except in specifically political settings, so that there are only limited opportunities for other agencies to challenge the family as political socializer.

While most studies of political socialization refer to the indoctrination of the young, the reciprocal nature of the learning process should not be ignored. As parents teach their children various norms, they undoubtedly teach them-selves as well (Riley, Foner, Hess, and Toby, 1969), and children may in turn help their parents to accommodate to societal changes. In terms of political education, adult children may influence parents by reactivating attitudes and values initially inculcated by the parents when the offspring were younger. For

---

[42] It might be argued that since authoritarian family structures have characterized many so-cieties for extended periods of time (Germany is a ready example), this type of childrearing cannot adequately explain sporadic coniflct.

[43] For studies ranging from the 1930's to the 1950's, see Hyman (1959); Lipset et al. (1954, p. 1144). For a more recent study see Flacks (1967, pp. 66–67).

example, parents who taught their children to have sympathy for the under-dog or to believe in equality may have these values reawakened by their children's interest in putting such ideals into practice. Or, children who have more formal education than their parents may help to inform them about political issues. Reciprocal socialization between the young and their elders occurs outside the family as well, as between students and faculty in the university, for example. Insofar as young people successfully communicate new political ideas or values to parents, teachers, or other older people, or insofar as they reinforce long-held but latent views, then harmony rather than conflict between the generations is fostered.

Thus, on balance, the family appears to harmonize and integrate political commitments from generation to generation. Nevertheless, political socialization—like other aspects of social learning—is seldom completely effective.[44] And the lack of complete success can often contribute importantly to broad changes within the polity and the society as a whole, as the younger strata regard political issues from fresh points of view.

The inevitability of aging   A peculiar feature of the relationship among age strata, hence of the potential for conflict, is the fact that individuals ineluctably move up the age hierarchy. A comparison with sharp political cleavages along lines of social class is instructive. Political rifts between classes can appear when there is, first, a close and rigid identity of membership in a political party and in a particular class and where, second, the boundaries of various solidary groupings—rather than cross-cutting these merged lines of party-and-class—tend to fall within these lines and to exert political pressure in a common direction. This is similar to the fashion in which political cleavage can occur along the single axis of age (in the preceding sentences, the word "age" can simply be substituted for the word "class").

Beyond this parallelism, however, there is a major difference between class and age that stems from the *timing* of party affiliation. Partisan loyalty, as we have seen, develops slowly and tends to be maintained. Class status, on the one hand, tends to be consonant with this timing, because many people are not socially mobile, but retain their class identification (like their religious identification) over major portions of their lives. This persistence of class divisions tends to foster the institutionalization of cleavage along party lines. Age status, on the other hand, provides no such consonance with the timing of partisanship. Because aging requires mobility, there may not be time enough to consolidate the organization of an age stratum around a particular party or even a particular issue. Individuals, through their assumption of the new roles associated with the next higher age stratum, may literally outgrow certain

[44] There is somewhat more slippage between generations in attitudes toward specific issues than in party affiliation (Hyman, 1959, p. 74).

issues or may willy-nilly become members of the opposition. Such shifts are especially likely where isuues relate directly to the roles occupied at a particular age and for a relatively short portion of the lifetime, such as issues of the draft, legal voting age, or student power.

Under certain conditions, however, the mobility of individuals into older age categories may *stimulate* sharp cleavage among age groups. Because of its inevitability, aging can have the effect of creating a special urgency for quick solutions, since there is so little time for individuals to resolve the problems themselves. In this sense, there is good reason for calling the younger generation the "now" generation. And in periods of change, when organizational responses typically lag behind new situations, the use of nontraditional channels of political action may appear more likely to achieve quick results.

In such ways, the inevitability of the aging process seems capable of reducing age-youth cleavage through the movement of cohorts into new strata with new interests and new perspectives. Yet, aging can also encourage the divisive tendencies (perhaps over issues that are especially salient or emotionally charged) through the creation of a special sense of urgency in the age stratum that feels the imminence of the passing opportunities.

THE ISSUES OF AGE CLEAVAGE

We have been discussing various mechanisms that either reduce or enhance political disagreements among the age strata, the overt expression of these disagreements, or their emergence into sharp conflict. Among such mechanisms typically present in modern, rapidly changing societies, we have examined several (cross-cutting memberships in age-heterogeneous solidary groups, political socialization, and the rapid mobility from one age stratum to another) that serve often—but not always—to minimize disagreements among age strata or to prevent such disagreements from erupting into militant noninstitutionalized conflict.

Whether or not such mechanisms are effective in integrating age strata can depend, as our discussion of age mobility indicates, on the nature of the issues at the center of attention in the polity at particular times. In this regard, we find it helpful to refer to the well-known distinction between *class* politics and *status* politics. Different historical periods may be characterized by the relative stress in politics on issues that activate class interests, on the one hand, or status interests, on the other. And it is our contention that mechanisms that reduce age conflict are most likely to operate effectively when class politics are to the fore.

The distinction between class and status politics, implicit in the work of Max Weber (Gerth and Mills, 1958, p. 194), has since been part of political theory (see, e.g., Gusfield, 1966, pp. 13–24, 172–188; Hofstadter, 1964a, pp. 84–85, 88; and 1964b, pp. 98–100; and Lipset, 1964, pp. 308–309).

Concerning class issues (variously called material, interest, or position issues) there is a general agreement on definition. These are concerns that divide the polity in terms of material goals or the distribution and control of resources. No such consensus is discernible among the definitions of status politics,[45] which in practice appears to form a residual category. Status issues may represent claims to prestige, in the Weberian sense; but they may also involve a confrontation between opposed systems of moralities or styles of life, which are usually associated with particular groups and thus become a test of *their* status.[46]

Whatever the terminology (we shall speak of material versus ideal issues), we are persuaded that when material issues dominate the political scene, age cleavage is muted; conversely, when ideal issues come to the fore, the constraints on sharp age-youth conflicts become less effective and such conflicts are more likely to erupt.

Material (or class) issues as a basis for age-youth conflict Age is unlikely to be a major source of cleavage over material issues precisely because these issues are class-related. That is, material issues reflect and activate class interests, and these interests tend to cross-cut age lines, reducing the salience of age differences. When the interests of a class take precedence over age-specific interests, individuals of all ages within a class will tend to unite in pressing their claims.

Even in the special cases where the economic issues before the polity (such as taxation or special expenditures favoring a single age category) do tend to divide people along age lines, these issues are still unlikely to polarize age strata. For, in such instances, people from a particular socioeconomic class are likely to belong also to groups with common economic goals that cut across age lines, with consequent pressures against sharp conflict. For example, membership in an age-heterogeneous economic unit such as the family enables people of one age to benefit indirectly from programs directed at people of other ages. Specifically, pensions and Medicare relieve younger family members of the burden of caring for the old; or aid for the college education of the young eases the financial obligation of their middle-aged parents. In the shop, young people may be motivated to support liberal pensions for older workers as opening up jobs for themselves by easing older workers out of them.

[45] For example, Hofstadter broadened the terminology from "status" politics to "cultural" politics, which include such questions as those of faith and morals, tone and style, or freedom and coercion (Hofstadter, 1964b, p. 99). According to Gusfield, the term "status politics" has been used to refer to both status discontent and expressive elements. He reserves the term to refer to "political conflict over the allocation of prestige" and uses "expressive politics" to refer to "political action for the sake of expression [of frustration or feelings of hostility] rather than for the sake of influencing or controlling the distribution of valued objects" (Gusfield, 1966, pp. 18–19).

[46] This point is suggested by Gusfield (1966, p. 173).

Moreover, from the point of view of the younger strata, the inevitability of aging may reduce the salience of economic issues: for the incentive to initiate struggle over issues of this type is reduced when young people have hope (often quite realistic) for future improvement in their own material status, and when they also stand to benefit in the future from programs designed to help older people—a deferred gratification, as it were. Furthermore, economic issues appear to be generally more amenable to compromise than many other types of political questions. Often the former involve questions of "how much," and such quantitative controversies are subject to bargaining. It is exactly the politics of compromise around which traditional democratic procedures can best operate. Thus, even when old-young differences do emerge on these questions, the resort to militant tactics for their resolution is unlikely.

The potential for age cleavage concerning ideal (or status) issues By contrast, it is our contention that ideal issues (or status issues) are likely to evoke sharp rifts among age strata because the constraints that in other circumstances operate to reduce such cleavages are absent or relatively ineffective.

Two types of ideal issues appear to stimulate age-youth conflict. One type may be a literal claim for status. An age stratum perceives that it is not accorded the prestige it believes is due, and this perceived deprivation provokes a struggle to redress the wrong. The fight for "student power" or for autonomy may be interpreted as a claim to prestige and recognition that the youth group believes is wrongfully denied it. The fight to assure future jobs commensurate with their higher education is another such status claim. The second type of conflict-provoking issue operates apart from direct status concerns. Examples of such issues might be inequality in the face of stated ideals proclaiming equality, poverty in an affluent society, or a war that is considered unjust. These issues often refer to questions of a highly moral character, of what is right and wrong; they reflect a gap between the ideals to which young people were socialized and what is found in the real world.

Whatever the specific nature of these questions, they differ from material (class) issues in a number of ways. Ideal issues may be less likely to bring into play clear cross-cutting solidarities that can dull the sharpness of conflict. Moreover, these issues are not easily compromised. Since they tend to evoke moral fervor and emotional involvement,[47] they require "all or nothing" solutions. Finally, to the extent that these issues (or combinations of issues) kindle a feeling that only basic political changes can resolve the problems, older people are likely to oppose such changes. It is precisely the broad

[47] It is claimed by some observers that the loss of a sense of identity and belonging felt by some young people is projected into the political arena when more pressing economic issues are not prominent. If so, this may be one reason for the extreme emotional involvement displayed in these status struggles.

changes in direction of policy put forward by the young that older people regard as threats to their basic values and their way of life. It is these they are most likely to resist. For, as we have pointed out, as people age, they sometimes do shift toward a more liberal position on specific issues, but are likely to become more conservative in terms of their basic outlook concerning the overall structure of the society. The result is that a sharp clash between young and old on these more general issues is difficult to avoid and can be particularly bitter.

Although a mixture of ideal and material issues is undoubtedly always present, the relative significance of each type of issue varies from one time to another. It has often been noted that when material issues are less salient, status issues tend to emerge (Hofstadter, 1964a, p. 84; Lipset, 1964, p. 309). This does not mean that youth-age conflicts inevitably arise under circumstances of affluence or of relative economic peace. There are times when an event, such as a foreign policy crisis, perceived as a threat to the whole nation, unites all groups and strata. Conversely, conditions that threaten one particular age stratum (or significant portions of it) can induce strains or feelings of hostility toward the other strata, who may be held responsible. For example, the extraordinary numbers of people reaching young adulthood in the 1960's interfered with their inclusion in the labor force or their entry into the educational system. The Vietnam war, despite its ramifications throughout the whole society, is another event generating special strains and anxieties among youth, especially those subject to the draft. Thus the eruption of sharp age-youth conflicts depends not only on the degree to which class politics are muted, but also on whether or not specific events of the period produce a sense of relative deprivation in a particular age stratum.

The nature of the issues and the form of struggle   Status issues not only exacerbate youth-age conflict, but are likely also to cast this conflict into militant forms. Issues tinged with emotional overtones are especially apt to stir the latent propensity of the young to shun conventional politics. When young people feel particularly strongly about an issue, the knowledge that they remain young for so short a time can sometimes impart a special sense of urgency for quick resolution of the problem. This sense of urgency can be intensified because government machinery grinds slowly. For even if the mature strata who dominate the government are willing to change, it is not easy for them to do so.

In many ways this distinction between ideal and material issues is analogous to the distinction drawn in Section 2 between issues involving a general political outlook and those involving specific policies. Ideal issues, like the more general issues, do not lend themselves to piecemeal solution or to the type of gradual change to which older people often adapt through the process of resocialization. Rather, on ideal issues, fundamental changes are often called for, changes that appear to activate the resistance of older segments of the polity, in turn increasing the likelihood that militant tactics will be used by the young.

For these various related reasons, sharp age conflict in the polity is most likely to emerge when ideal (status) issues are predominant. The fact that these issues are often not manifest in political life helps to account for the sporadic rather than continuous occurrence of marked age-youth conflict. This type of issue is most likely to activate college youth who are not yet committed to major adult roles in the society and whose future status is thus anomalous. And it is around these issues that conflict-reducing mechanisms are least likely to operate effectively.

Yet, if such issues remain unresolved, this failure (except on age-restricted issues like the draft) gradually changes the age basis of cleavage around them. For a cohort, as it ages, carries its convictions about an unresolved issue into the older strata. And the many relationships in age-heterogeneous groups that come with full adult status provide channels for the diffusion of these dissident views throughout the society.

CONCLUSION

This exploration of the manner in which age is related to political performance and attitudes has reviewed much familiar ground. Nevertheless, examining the polity in terms of age can serve several functions. By showing the relevance of existing political theories to age-related behavior, this approach helps both to extend the generality of such theories and to apply them specifically. The focus on age patterns also reminds the political theorist of the complex way age differences in the polity may come about, thus shedding new light on some "old" problems. And the use of methodological approaches, developed for the study of age stratification, can yield new findings and new interpretations from existing data.

The explorations so far undertaken in this essay postulate certain *life-course* changes in political behavior and orientations. We have suggested that duration in a role (or complex of roles) has an important influence on role behavior, as aging is accompanied by increasing commitment to societal structures. This commitment can lead to heightened political participation after early adulthood, to the maintenance of voting well into old age. It can also lead to increasing support for leaders and policies perceived as stabilizing these structures. However, the analysis calls into question the inevitability of growing conservatism with age, proposing that people often do shift to more liberal positions as long as they perceive no associated threats to the basic structure of their relationships.

The familiar notion of "political generations" has been examined here along with other characteristics distinguishing *successive cohorts* within the polity. In an attempt to disentangle life-course shifts in political outlook from differences among cohorts, and to disentangle these in turn from the *period effects* of social change, some actual, but limited, data and a fictitious model were presented.

Our explorations have utilized several theoretical distinctions in the literature heretofore not directed to age and aging and has shown their relevance for understanding age and the polity. For example, the distinction made by Parsons between levels of issues has proved useful in understanding the variety of shifts in political ideas over the life course. The distinction between class and status politics was also productive of insights into the nature of conflicts, indicating that age may constitute one of the major bases on which status politics can emerge. Moreover, the distinction may be analogous in its essential outlines to the Parsonian distinction in that class politics often involves struggle over specific policies concerning allocation of resources, whereas status politics, conceived in the broadest sense, often focuses on the overall goals of the society. Thus the perspective of age has served to unite two strands of theory that have usually been treated separately. Finally, the notion that sharp conflict can be minimized through cross-cutting group memberships was found to be applicable to the age structure of the groups involved. Thus it was hypothesized that relationships across age lines in significant age-heterogeneous groups tend to reduce the possibility of sharp age conflicts in the polity. Such conceptual distinctions have been particularly helpful in dealing with age-youth conflict. When they are reformulated in terms of age they provide a somewhat different perspective for analysis of the "generation gap" than is found in many treatises on this subject.

Finally, the examination of the polity from the point of view of age stratification can yield new perspectives not only on the polity but also on the central topic of this book: age and aging. Thus the study of political attitudes can demonstrate ways in which the succession of cohorts diffuse change throughout the society. And the study of conflict in the arena of political life can specify the nature of the potential age conflicts that inhere in other sectors of the society also.

Works cited in Chapter 4

Altbach, Philip G., 1967. "Students and Politics," in Lipset, Seymour Martin, editor, *Student Politics*, New York: Basic Books, pp. 74–96.

Becker, Howard S., 1960. "Notes on the Concept of Commitment," *American Journal of Sociology*, 66, pp. 32–40.

Berelson, Bernard R., Paul F. Lazarsfeld, and William N. McPhee, 1954. *Voting*, Chicago: University of Chicago Press.

Brim, Orville G., Jr., 1966. "Socialization Through the Life Cycle," in Brim, Orville

G., Jr., and Stanton Wheeler, *Socialization After Childhood: Two Essays*, New York: Wiley, pp. 1–49.

Cain, Leonard D., Jr., 1967. "Age Status and Generational Phenomena: The New Old People in Contemporary America," *The Gerontologist*, 7, pp. 83–92.

Campbell, Angus, et al., 1960. *The American Voter*, New York: Wiley.

Cantril, Hadley, editor, 1951. *Public Opinion, 1935–1946*, Princeton, N.J.: Princeton University Press.

Crittenden, John, 1962. "Aging and Party Affiliation," *Public Opinion Quarterly*, 26, pp. 648–657.

————, 1963. "Aging and Political Participation," *Western Political Quarterly*, 16, pp. 323–331.

Cutler, Neal E., 1968. *The Alternative Effects of Generations and Aging Upon Political Behavior: A Cohort Analysis of American Attitudes Toward Foreign Policy, 1946–1966*. Oak Ridge, Tenn.: Oak Ridge National Laboratory.

————, 1970. "Generation, Maturation, and Party Affiliation: A Cohort Analysis," *Public Opinion Quarterly*, 33, pp. 583–588.

Dawson, Richard E., and Kenneth Prewitt, 1969. *Political Socialization*, Boston: Little, Brown.

Dickinson, Frank G., 1958. "The 'Younging' of Electorates," *Journal of the American Medical Association*, 166, pp. 1051–1057.

Downing, Lyle A., and Jerome J. Salomone, 1969. "Professors of the Silent Generation," *Trans-action*, 6, pp. 43–45.

Duverger, Maurice, 1955. "La Participation des Femmes a la vie Politique," Paris: UNESCO.

Erskine, Hazel Gaudet, n.d. *Public Opinion Quarterly* Summary of Gallup Polls: "Nixon-Humphrey-Wallace, April through September, 1968." Mimeographed.

Evan, William M., 1965. "Cohort Analysis of Attitude Data," in Beshers, James M., editor, *Computer Methods in the Analysis of Large-Scale Social Systems*, Cambridge, Mass.: Joint Center for Urban Studies of the M.I.T. and Harvard University, pp. 117–142.

Flacks, Richard, 1967. "The Liberated Generation: An Exploration of the Roots of Student Protest," *Journal of Social Issues*, 23, pp. 52–75.

Fortune-Yankelovich Survey, October 1968. As reported in *Fortune*, January 1969, pp. 70–71, 179–181.

Gerth, Hans, 1940. "The Nazi Party: Its Leadership and Composition," *American Journal of Sociology*, 45, pp. 517–541.

Gerth, H. H., and C. Wright Mills, editors, 1958. *From Max Weber*, New York: Oxford University Press.

Glenn, Norval D., 1969. "Aging, Disengagement, and Opinionation," *Public Opinion Quarterly*, 33, pp. 17–33.

————, and Michael Grimes, 1968. "Aging, Voting and Political Interest," *American Sociological Review*, 33, pp. 563–575.

Gusfield, Joseph R., 1966. *Symbolic Crusade*, Urbana, Ill.: University of Illinois Press.

Hacker, Andrew, 1961. "Sociology and Ideology," in Black, Max, editor, *The Social Theories of Talcott Parsons*, Englewood Cliffs, N.J.: Prentice-Hall, pp. 289–310.

Hauser, Philip M., and Raul Vargas, 1960. "Population Structure and Trends," in Burgess, Ernest W., editor, *Aging in Western Societies*, Chicago: University of Chicago Press, pp. 29–53.

Heberle, Rudolph, 1951. *Social Movements*, New York: Appleton-Century-Crofts.

Hofstadter, Richard, 1964a. "The Pseudo-Conservative Revolt (1955)," in Bell, Daniel, editor, *The Radical Right*, Garden City, N.Y.: Doubleday, Anchor Books, pp. 75–95.

————, 1964b. "Pseudo-Conservatism Revisited: A Postscript (1962)," in Bell, Daniel, editor, *The Radical Right*, Garden City, N.Y.: Doubleday, Anchor Books, pp. 97–103.

Hyman, Herbert H., 1959. *Political Socialization*, Glencoe, Ill.: Free Press.

————, and Paul B. Sheatsley, 1964. "Attitudes Toward Desegregation," *Scientific American*, 211, pp. 16–23.

Kelley, Stanley Jr., Richard E. Ayres, and William G. Bowen, 1967. "Registration and Voting: Putting First Things First," *American Political Science Review*, 61, pp. 359–377.

Lane, Robert E., 1965. *Political Life*, New York: Free Press.

Lazarsfeld, Paul F., Bernard Berelson, and Hazel Gaudet, 1944. *The People's Choice*, New York: Duell, Sloan & Pearce.

Lipset, Seymour Martin, 1963. *Political Man*, Garden City, N.Y.: Doubleday, Anchor Books.

————, 1964. "The Sources of the 'Radical Right': Coughlinites, McCarthyites, and Birchers (1962)," in Bell, Daniel, editor, *The Radical Right*, Garden City, N.Y.: Doubleday, Anchor Books, pp. 307–371.

————, and Philip G. Altbach, 1967. "Student Politics and Higher Education in the United States," in Lipset, Seymour Martin, editor, *Student Politics*, New York: Basic Books, pp. 216–217.

————, et al., 1954. "The Psychology of Voting: An Analysis of Political Behavior," in Lindzey, Gardner, editor, *Handbook of Social Psychology*, Volume II, Reading, Mass.: Addison-Wesley, pp. 1124–1175.

Mannheim, Karl (1928), 1952. "The Problem of Generations," in *Essays on the Sociology of Knowledge*, edited and translated by Paul Kecskemeti, London: Routledge and Kegan Paul, pp. 276–322.

Parsons, Talcott, 1959. " 'Voting' and the Equilibrium of the American Political System," in Burdick, Eugene, and Arthur Brodbeck, editors, *American Voting Behavior*, New York: Free Press, pp. 80–120.

Riley, Matilda White, Anne Foner, Beth Hess, and Marcia L. Toby, 1969. "Socialization for the Middle and Later Years," in Goslin, David A., editor, *Handbook of Socialization Theory and Research*, Chicago: Rand McNally, pp. 951–982.

Sheppard, Harold L., 1962. "Implications of an Aging Population for Political Sociology," in Donahue, Wilma, and Clark Tibbitts, editors, *Politics of Age*, Ann Arbor: University of Michigan Press, pp. 48–63.

Simmons, Leo, 1945. *Role of the Aged in Primtive Society*, New Haven: Yale University Press.

Smith, Thomas C., 1969. "Structural, Crystallization, Status Inconsistency and Political Partisanship," *American Sociological Review*, 34, pp. 907–921.

Sorokin, Pitirim, 1968. "Social Differentiation," in Sills, David L., editor, *International Encyclopedia of the Social Sciences*, 17 vols., New York: Macmillan and Free Press, 14, pp. 406–409.

Tingsten, Herbert, 1937. *Political Behavior: Studies in Election Statistics*, London: P. S. King & Son.

————, 1963. *Political Behavior: Studies in Election Statistics*, Totowa, N.J.: Bedminster Press.

United Nations Department of Economic and Social Affairs, 1956. "The Aging of Populations and the Economic and Social Implications," *Population Studies*, No. 26, New York.

United States Bureau of the Census. *Current Population Reports*, P-20, No. 143, 1965.

————, "Voting and Registration in the Election of November 1966," *Current Population Reports*, P-20, No 174, August 8, 1968.

Woodward, Julian L., and Elmo Roper, 1950. "Political Activity of American Citizens," *American Political Science Review*, 44, pp. 872–885.

Zeitlin, Maurice, 1967. *Revolutionary Politics and the Cuban Working Class*, Princeton, N.J.: Princeton University Press.

5

The work force

IN ASSOCIATION WITH **HARRIS SCHRANK**

The ways in which the revolutionary changes in education and retirement affect the work force are well known and have been extensively analyzed (like the accompanying retirement problems of older individuals and the problems of youth denied entry to the labor force). Not so well understood are the articulating processes that accommodate the constant succession of personnel within the occupational structure. For the work force is generally viewed as having a structure—one that undergoes orderly, or sometimes abrupt, change—despite the constant shifting of individuals in and out of work roles. How are the streams of individuals articulated with this structure?

For the express purpose of specifying the nature of such articulation, this chapter applies our conceptual model of age stratification (from Chapter 1) to the familiar example of the work force. While Foner's Chapter 4 on the polity focuses on processes of cohort succession and aging (P1 and P2 in our conceptual model), and Clausen's Chapter 11 on the life course takes special note of socialization for work (P4), the special emphasis of this present chapter is on that process, central to our model, which sociologists have come to call "allocation" (P3). As defined by Parsons and Shils (1951, p. 197), allocation refers to "the problem of who is to get what, who is to do what, and the manner and conditions under which it is to be done." Thus this essay aims to illustrate certain of the principles accorded more general treatment in Chapter 12 on allocation and on the related processes of socialization and the flow of cohorts.

This exploration of allocation as applied to the work force examines such topics as: selected aspects of the intricate societal arrangements that facilitate the entry of young people into work roles, and the transfer of older workers from work to retirement; the contributions made by older individuals through their own capacities, performances, and motivations, as they are allocated either to continued work or to retirement; and the ways in which socialization supplements the process of allocation to retirement by preparing people in anticipation and by aiding their learning of the new role once it has been entered. The essay is concerned throughout with the manner in which allocation and social-

ization are not merely forces for social conservation but may also con-
tribute to broad social change. Receiving special attention in the final
section are the potential consequences for social stability and change of
socialization and allocation as they operate to affect distribution of re-
wards and power among the various age strata. [See Chapter 10 for a
general treatment of the relations among the age strata.]

RELEVANCE OF VOLUMES I AND II

Much of the illustrative material in this essay is drawn from Volume I,
which gives extensive treatment to research on the nature and changes
of labor force participation (Chapter 3) and on the adjustments of in-
dividuals to the roles they play in work and in retirement (Chapter 18).
Related essays in Volume II are those by Sheppard (Chapter 6), who
interprets the human scene behind the statistics of labor force par-
ticipation, among older workers in particular; by Kreps (Chapter 7),
who describes the humps and valleys associated with differential eco-
nomic rewards among the several age strata; and by Eklund (Chapter
11), who extols the potential value for both work and retirement of
spreading education more widely over the life course.

In a recent year in the United States, an estimated combined total of 90 *mil-*
lion acts of labor force entry or exit took place (Parrella, 1970, p. 54). As
these millions of reciprocal arrangements are negotiated between employers
and employees, there are wide variations among individuals, occupations, and
industries. Yet both entry into the work force of a society and exit from it, and
to a lesser extent the expectations and sanctions for work performance, are
distinctly patterned by age, as revealed by massive statistical data on changes
in work force participation over recent decades in many countries. [*See Chap-*
ter 10 · 1 and Volume I, Chapter 3.] Our aim in this essay is not to explain
or describe in detail these striking age patterns—a task to which a vast literature has been devoted. We aim, rather, to investigate, against the background
of such patterns, the processes of articulation whereby people in the younger
age strata are brought together with work roles, while people in the older
strata are separated from them.

We shall illustrate these processes through selected examples. Such concrete illustration should amplify the brief notes sketched in Chapter 1 · 1 on
the linkages between people and roles. The familiar details, when exposed to
fresh scrutiny in terms of our model of age stratification, can begin to suggest
certain general principles. They indicate how allocation ($P3$ in our model),
typically supplemented by socialization ($P4$) operate—often in obscure ways
—both to produce differences among age strata in rates of economic activity,

and to generate pressure for many unanticipated changes throughout the society as a whole.

AGE STRATIFICATION OF THE WORK FORCE

In modern industrial societies (Volume I, Chapter 3 · A · 1), rates of labor force participation[1] for men (we shall deal only peripherally with women, whose age patterns are so different from men as to warrant entirely separate treatment) are low among adolescents, reach a peak approaching 100 per cent among persons in the middle years, and tend to decrease in the older age strata (see Figure 2 · 4). This pattern of strata differences, which seems to occur generally in industrialized nations, contrasts with that in agricultural countries today where the drops in rates of work force participation among both the young and the old are far less pronounced. Moreover, in those countries now classified as industrialized, there have been long-term tendencies for older people to leave the labor force at increasingly younger ages, while younger people enter it at increasingly older ages. In the United States, for example, the proportion of men 65 and over in the work force has declined sharply (with a notable reversal during World War II) from approximately two-thirds in 1900, to one-third in 1960, and to little more than one-fourth by 1968 (see Table 5 · 1).

At the other end of the age spectrum, one-fourth of the boys aged 10 to 15 were gainfully occupied in the United States in 1900, in contrast to 6 per cent in 1930 (Taeuber and Taeuber, 1958, p. 213). More recently (the Census Bureau no longer counts children under 14 in compiling labor force statistics) there was a sharp rise in economic activity of young people during World War II, followed by slight, but fairly consistent, declines for boys aged 16–17 and 18–19.[2]

Among women, whose labor force participation is at each age lower than that of their male counterparts, two separate peaks currently demarcate the age strata: first, at around age 20 and again—after a dip in the childbearing years—a new high between age 45 and 54 (see Figure 5 · 1). There has been a long history of cohort differences in the work-life patterns of women, with increases since World War II in the proportions of women, especially married

[1] In the United States, the labor force has been defined since 1930 to include persons employed or looking for work. These data are roughly comparable with those for other countries and for earlier years in the United States.

[2] United States Bureau of Labor Statistics (1969). Rates of labor force participation, which measure labor force status at a single point in time, supply only an inexact measure of actual patterns of entry or withdrawal from the labor force because individuals in an age stratum often move in and out of work between periods of measurement. This internal shifting is especially characteristic of the young, whose initial work experience is likely to consist of part-time and part-year employment. Thus, although in the United States today only a minority of teen-agers are counted in the labor force in a given week, a majority have been employed at some time during the preceding year. See Waldman (1969, pp. 23–31); also Parrella (1970, pp. 54–61).

TABLE 5 · 1   *Labor force participation rates, United States, 1900–1968*

Per cent in labor force

	Year							
Age	1900a	1920a	1940	1944	1950	1955	1960	1968
Males								
14–19	63.6	52.6	44.2	70.0	53.2	49.5	—	—
16–17	—	—	—	—	—	—	46.8	46.8
18–19	—	—	—	—	—	—	73.6	70.2
20–24	91.7	91.0	96.1	98.5	89.0	90.8	90.2	86.5
25–34	—	—	98.1	99.0	96.2	97.7	97.7	97.1
25–44	96.3	97.2	—	—	—	—	—	—
35–44	—	—	98.5	99.0	97.6	98.4	97.7	97.2
45–54	—	—	95.5	97.1	95.8	96.4	95.8	94.9
45–64	93.3	93.8	—	—	—	—	—	—
55–64	—	—	87.2	92.1	87.0	88.3	86.8	84.3
65+	68.3	60.1	45.0	52.2	45.8	40.6	33.1	27.3
Females								
14–19	26.8	28.4	23.3	42.0	31.5	29.9	—	—
16–17	—	—	—	—	—	—	29.1	31.7
18–19	—	—	—	—	—	—	51.1	52.5
20–24	32.1	38.1	49.5	55.0	46.1	46.0	46.2	54.6
25–34	—	—	35.2	39.0	34.0	34.9	36.0	42.6
25–44	18.1	22.4	—	—	—	—	—	—
35–44	—	—	28.8	40.5	39.1	41.6	43.5	48.9
45–54	—	—	24.3	35.8	38.0	43.8	49.8	52.3
45–64	14.1	17.1	—	—	—	—	—	—
55–64	—	—	18.7	25.4	27.0	32.5	37.2	42.4
65+	9.1	8.0	7.4	9.8	9.7	10.6	10.8	9.6

a Data prior to 1940, based on the notion of "gainful workers," are roughly comparable to labor force participation rates from 1940 on (Bogue, 1959, p. 421).
Note: Data from the *Current Population Reports* tend to indicate a slighly higher level of labor force participation than those from the decennial census (Sheldon, 1958, pp. 164–165).
Sources: Data for 1900–1955 from Bogue, 1959, p. 426. Sources cited by Bogue: Data for 1940–1955 from *Current Population Reports*, P–50, Nos. 61 and 72; data for 1920 from United States Census, 1940, Vol. III, *The Labor Force*, Part 1; United States Summary, Table 8, p. 26; Data for 1900 from United States Census, 1940, *Comparative Occupation Statistics for the United States*, 1870–1940. Data for 1960 and 1968, from United States Bureau of Labor Statistics, 1969, Bulletin No. 1630, p. 26.

women, entering the labor force during their middle years. [*See Chapter 2, Section 3 · A, and Figure 2 · 7.*] The age pattern of female labor force participation has not yet stabilized, however. Lately, the continuing increases in rates of female labor force participation have been relatively more pronounced for the younger women aged 20–34 years than for the middle-aged. The tendency for labor force participation among recent cohorts of young married women to increase regardless of the presence of young children may presage still further changes in the typical feminine patterns of labor force entry and exit (*Manpower Report of the President*, March 1970, pp. 46–48).

ASSOCIATED FACTORS

Few definitive explanations for the long-term decline in employment of the oldest and the youngest men have been demonstrated (see, e.g., Long, 1958,

FIGURE 5 · 1 *Female labor force participation rates, United States, 1920–1960*

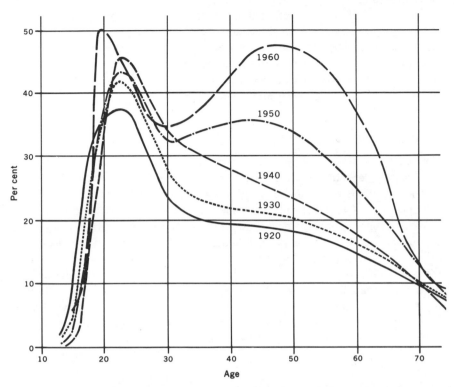

1960

1950

1940

1930

1920

Source: United Nations, 1962, *Manpower,* p. 35 (adapted); data for 1960 from 1960 Census of Population, Vol. I, Part 1, p. 487.

pp. 154–179; Durand, 1948, pp. 28–38; Bancroft, 1958). Nor shall we attempt to unravel this complex phenomenon. However, extensive research on a variety of factors associated with these trends, and with the differences among age strata today, points to many of the allocative mechanisms that concern us here. A central associated factor has been the decline in agricultural employment; activities that in 1820 engaged almost 85 per cent of all workers in the United States and more than half the workers by 1870, now attract only about one-twentieth (Taeuber and Taeuber, 1958, p. 203; Volume I, Chapter 3 · B · 2 · b). Along with this change, there has been a general decline in self-employment and an increasing concentration of many workers in large firms. With the establishment of organizational rules and practices of allocation, fewer and fewer people are free to make their own decisions about starting work, continuing it, tapering it off gradually, or employing others such as their own wives and young children.[3] There has been, instead, an expansion of public and private pension plans that afford alternative sources of income to increasing proportions of older workers, and that often specify the age for mandatory retirement. There has also been a steady rise in the educational level of the population. Extension of the period of formal schooling, while favoring younger workers because they are better educated and more recently trained,[4] also delays their entry into the full-time work force.

1 *Allocation to the work force*

The patterned differences among age strata in labor force participation are, to a degree, reflections of the nature of the occupational system and of the complex relations of occupations with other aspects of the social system. For example, age of entrance into professional and technical occupations tends to be postponed by educational requirements. And bureaucratically organized occupations tend to have upper age limits on participation. But the realization of these age patterns in the social and occupational systems depends upon the operation of articulating mechanisms that link people of particular ages to particular occupational roles. This essay will illustrate the nature of this linking process, starting with some of the formal and informal normative devices associated with initiation into work, and describing certain of the procedures and agencies for implementing such age-specific norms.

AGE CRITERIA

See Chapter 10 · 1 for age as a criterion of role incumbency

Age criteria for entering the work force, like the criteria for leaving it, are often manifested in various formal rules and informal norms. In most modern industrial societies, legislation establishes minimum ages at which children are permitted to work, and complementary legislation sets compulsory ages for school attendance. Other rules and laws affect the age structure of the work force by regulating, for example, minimum ages for automobile driving, military draft eligibility, rights to make contracts, or qualifications for political office.

There are also numerous attitudes, myths, and beliefs as to the appropriate age for entering the work force. Whether a person is regarded as "too old" or "too young" to start work may depend on many factors such as the sex, mari-

---

[3] Compare Max Weber's comments on the impersonality and universalism associated with bureaucracy. See, for example, Gerth and Mills (1958, pp. 196, 215–216).

[4] Note, for example, the impact of this trend on the scientific professions, as discussed by Zuckerman and Merton in Chapter 8.

tal status, or class background of the candidate (or of those making the evaluation); his physical or educational fitness for the particular job; the training or maturity required; or even the age of those who make determinations of the appropriate age for a particular job.

Such rules and norms do not determine the precise age of entry into the work force. They merely set certain constraints around it. For example, even at ages well above the legally permissible minimum, the labor force participation rates of young people are considerably below the rates for the middle age strata (see Figure 2 · 4 and also United States Bureau of Labor Statistics, 1969, pp. 26–27). To some extent, also, these rules and norms are a reflection[5] of the myriad specific decisions made by individual workers and employers as to who is to enter (or leave) particular jobs, and at what ages.

PROCEDURES AND AGENCIES

Rarely is entry into the labor force a matter of unaided self-allocation into jobs, or of simple negotiations between employers and applicants. Rather, the allocative process is facilitated, under today's conditions, by a variety of complex procedures, many of which operate through special agencies or organizations both inside and outside the economic sphere.

Procedures An important procedure for shifting human resources into the labor market is the *dissemination of general information* about the types of positions open to young people, and the qualifications required of applicants. As one recent national study of "career thresholds" among young males aged 14 to 24 illustrates, occupational information is not uniformly distributed (Parnes et al., 1969, pp. 119–138). Ability to identify the duties, educational qualifications, and relative income of various occupations is comparatively greater, for example, among persons receiving more formal education, living outside rural areas, having white-collar family backgrounds, coming from families who supply reading materials in the home, or having high school experience that is college preparatory or commercial rather than vocational or general. Thus age, independently of educational attainment, is associated with having occupational information, perhaps reflecting accumulation of exposure either to general sources of information or to specific labor force experience.

Young men seem to obtain information about specific job openings larely through informal channels (Parnes et al., 1969, pp. 100–101). When the employed youth in the study of career thresholds were asked how they found out about their current job, the greatest single source of information proved to

---

[5] For example, James Conant points out that the raising of the school-leaving age in many states followed the change in the pattern of school attendance of a majority of the youth (Conant, 1959, p. 95, as quoted by Trow, 1966, p. 439).

be friends and relatives (although older youth are less likely to rely on this source). A sizeable minority report checking directly with their employer, but relatively few cite an employment service or advertisement as their source of information.

Dissemination of information is but one procedure utilized by economic, governmental, familial, educational, and training agencies for allocation of young entrants to the work force. A complex apparatus facilitates (or impedes) *filing of applications* and access to job interviews. Applicants are *screened* through competitive examination (cf. Moore, 1969, pp. 873–874), personality inventory, informal interview, letter of recommendation, and other devices. Their credentials, such as age, level of education, or health are examined and *certified.* Once a candidate is judged qualified, still other procedures operate to negotiate admission and to *validate* role assumption by, for example, public announcement, record entry, or issuance of the facilities (such as tools or space) needed for job performance.

Agencies   Various allocative agencies, in implementing procedures over which they claim formal or customary jurisdiction, interact with one another to regulate the flow of new cohorts into the labor force. For many of these agencies, the regulation of this flow is far removed from their primary function, and their actual impact occurs in subtle and often unintended ways.

Within the economic sphere itself, the familiar structures[6] of the modern labor market operate directly to bring together, on the one hand, the prospective workers, with their particular abilities and needs and their personal estimates of the pros and cons of entering the work force now or at some later time; and, on the other hand, the individual employers, with their distinctive patterns of manpower needs and hiring practices, and with their particular beliefs and cost calculations, which influence their preference for new personnel at younger versus older ages. Thus the entry of new labor is mediated by, for example: the mass media as disseminators of employment information; the associations of employers, and the professional and occupational associations, as these may distribute information or set criteria for labor force entry; the employment agencies, which serve as intermediaries, often specializing in the problems of placing workers of a particular age; the personnel offices and recruiting agencies of the hiring firms. Moreover, some unions and other employee organizations can assure entry jobs through collective bargaining or political action, can provide specific job information, and can aid in screening and certification of candidates.

Of special relevance to the emerging theory of allocation is the fact that such agencies are not limited to those primarily concerned with the economic

[6] Compare, for example, the formulations by Alfred Marshall as discussed by Parsons (1937, pp. 141 ff.).

realm, but also include other agencies from institutional contexts that impinge with varying degrees of indirectness upon the work force. Thus the government (aside from its own role as a major employer) plays a prominent part in allocation through such activities as planning and manipulation of the economy, regulation of employment conditions, and—with direct and specific impact on the youthful work force—drafting young men into military service (See *Manpower Report of the President*, March, 1970, pp. 51–52; also see Waldman, 8/1969, p. 31). In addition, familial, educational, and training institutions not only socialize the young (thus generating the capacity and skill needed in the labor force, as Parsons and Smelser for example, have made clear; see Parsons, 1937; Parsons and Smelser, 1956; Smelser, 1963); such institutions often operate also as allocators. Technical schools, for example, set standards for performance in various occupations, certify levels of performance, and make referrals and recommendations. The role of the family in allocation, which we shall examine in some detail, illustrates not only the interrelatedness of allocative agencies, but also the diversity in procedures under differing sociotemporal conditions.

THE FAMILY AS ALLOCATOR

The changing functions of parents in allocating their children to the work force are closely associated with historical variations in age of starting to work.

Though young children commonly worked on farms in agrarian societies, or were apprenticed during their mid-teens under the medieval guild system, it is the Industrial Revolution, with its routinized tasks and its penurious wages, that typifies the economic exploitation of even the littlest children.[7] Not only did entire families enter the labor force in order to maintain the level of living formerly secured by the household head as a skilled workman, but also, as Smelser (1959, 1968) has shown, men were able to hire and supervise the work of their own children.

An examination of Smelser's study (1968) of changing family life among British textile workers under the impact of industrialization and urbanization proves highly instructive for understanding certain of the age-related allocative mechanisms that concern us in this essay. Smelser demonstrates that —contrary to accepted belief—there was no sudden transition from the preindustrial era, in which the father apprenticed his older sons to his trade, to the industrial era, in which economic aspects became differentiated from other facets of family life. In the early phases of the Industrial Revolution (from approximately 1770 to 1820), the entire family could continue to work together as a unit either in the factory or in the domestic putting-out system.

[7] Cf. Karl Marx (1936, Chapter 15). Among the various literary treatments, see *Germinal* by Emile Zola (1885); or *David Copperfield* by Charles Dickens (1850).

Thus in the early days of such innovations as the spinning jenny or the water frame, the workman could simply hire family members as his own assistants, a practice supported by the trade union regulations of the day, and could provide discipline and even some recreation on a job that lasted from sunrise to sunset.

It was not until technological developments broke down this family-apprentice system, requiring spinners to hire more assistants than they had children and forcing home weavers to send their children into the factories, that the father lost direct control over the economic activities of his offspring. Coinciding with this economic threat to family solidarity in England, the Factory Act of 1833 limited children's working hours to 8 (while the parents worked for 12), and also provided schools for children during several hours of the parents' working day. This splitting apart of parents and children, who could no longer work side by side, evoked considerable resistance, according to Smelser. Both masters and operatives clearly evaded the eight-hour regulation under the Factory Act. Moreover, the workers, after failing to secure a universal 8-hour day, agitated for a universal schedule of 10 or even 12 hours, schedules that would have restored the traditional link between parent and child on the working premises. It was the disruption of this link, paving the way toward separation of family and factory, that ultimately revolutionized the procedures for allocation to the work force.

Even today, however, parents still serve in various capacities as adjuncts to this allocative process. Though they may only occasionally assign their children to the work force directly (by taking them into family firms or setting them up in business, for example), they often supply information or advice, or serve as occupational role models (either positive or negative). In addition, parental support in the form of money or services (Sussman, 1965; Streib, 1958, p. 57; see also Volume I, Chapter 23 · B · 2) to young adult offspring may affect the age at which the young person enters the work force. Whether a child is given family support during the years necessary to prepare for an occupation, instead of being expected to work as soon as legally permissible, often depends on the size of the family income, the dependency load of the family, or the number of other earners in the family. (See, e.g., Blau and Duncan, 1967, Chapter 9; also Parnes et al., 1969, Chapters 2, 7, and passim.)

Such support is contingent also upon the values of parents in stressing future occupational success for their offspring as well as in advocating education as important to such success. Schoolwork as a means of advancing a young man's career, though widely espoused by American parents, has been generally less acceptable in the lower, than in the higher, socioeconomic strata. (As a classic example, see Hyman, 1953.) In families where current

TABLE 5 · 2 *School enrollment of young males, United States, 1920–1960*

Per cent enrolled

Year	Age				
	16	17	18	19	20
1960	87	76	55	38	28
1950	81	68	42	28	21
1940	76	61	38	23	14
1930	66	47	31	21	15
1920	48	32	21	14	9

Source: 1960 Census of Population, Vol. I, Part 1, pp. 372–373.

income requirements take precedence over future aspirations,[8] early-age work allocation of children is common. But when parents, whatever their own occupational status, do stress the importance of education for getting ahead, they can influence their sons' decisions to go to college rather than immediately to work (Kahl, 1953).

EDUCATION AND WORK

Predictably, youth who are enrolled in school, and who must therefore limit employment to vacation periods and hours when they are outside the classroom, are considerably less likely than nonstudents to be found in the labor force. Moreover, though students typically manage some employment during the school year, the proportion with work experience is lower than that of nonstudents of similar age (see Waldman, 1969, pp. 24–25). Thus student status tends both to delay labor force entry and to limit the extent of participation in the work force.

The impact of this relation between education and work is reflected macroscopically in the impressive complementarity between the historical increases in school enrollment in this country (see Table 5 · 2) and the rising age of labor force entry. Of course, the causal connections between the two are intricately involved with such other broad societal changes as those in the structure and productivity of industry, or in the general levels of consumption. As Long's (1958, pp. 156–157) analysis has shown, for example, the secular rise in incomes that allowed many parents to do without the wages of their children enabled them also to finance education through public school (by voting higher taxes) or even through college.

---

[8] An interesting analysis of working-class families in Newburyport, Massachusetts, however, during the latter half of the nineteenth century shows that it was often the more prosperous fathers, in contrast to the less prosperous, who consigned their children to unskilled occupations by withdrawing them from school and setting them to work at the age of 10 or 12 (Thernstrom, 1966, pp. 609–610).

But, if the industrial era has witnessed this striking coincidence between expanding education and the shifting age of labor force entry, we may well ask what will happen in the era Bell (1968) has termed "post-industrial." Already in the United States the service sector of the economy has displaced the manufacturing sector in relative importance (just as the latter had displaced the agricultural sector). Particularly dramatic has been the growing emphasis on the professional and technical occupations. If, in Bell's formulation (1968, p. 152), the further specialization of functions continues to shift "from the economic to the intellectual realm," we might expect the school to take on even greater importance as an allocator to the labor force,[9] resulting in heightened convergence between age patterns of education and of work force participation.

2 The transfer from work to retirement

The age patterns of separation from the labor force, showing striking declines in modernized countries and pronounced divergences between industrial and agricultural countries, challenge social inquiry of how exit from such a major social role as the occupational is effected, and of the social and individual consequences of the age patterns of relinquishment. Removing men from the work force, like admitting them to it, involves both normative age criteria and a set of facilitating procedures and agencies which, though commonly taken for granted, actively interweave and change in subtle and complex ways.

PROTECTIVE DEVICES

Up to retirement, many of the same age criteria and allocative devices that mediate the transfer out of the work force operate, in converse fashion, to hold men to it. There are numerous indications of a general increase by age in stability of labor force participation. In the United States, for example, various sets of data show that unemployment rates for persons (both men and women) 45 and over are generally below those for the younger strata, even when teen-agers are excluded from the analysis (Volume I, Chapter 3 · A · 3 · c); proportions of male workers changing jobs during a year decline steadily from age 20–24 to 65 and over; and workers in the middle strata, aged 45–64, are less likely than younger workers either to be discharged or to quit their jobs (Volume I, Chapter 18 · B · 1 · c).

These age patterns of labor force stability constitute another version of the principle so often stressed in these essays: duration in a role, which ac-

---

[9] An interesting example of an arrangement in which the school has a large measure of control over allocation to the labor force is reported by Granick (1961, p. 22), who observes that the American West Point system applies to Soviet students. Graduates choose from among available positions in order of their academic standing.

companies aging, tends to bind person and role together. Thus in regard to a man's work, quite apart from whatever commitment he as a person may develop, the allocative processes themselves are increasingly likely, the older he becomes, to protect his job. For example, numerous seniority or tenure provisions guard him, either formally or informally, against layoff and downgrading until he reaches the age of retirement. Such protections are widely provided, not only through trade union agreements, but among nonunion employers as well (Volume I, Chapter 3 · B · 4 · b).

To be sure, safeguards against the loss of work do not necessarily guarantee fulfillment of age-graded expectations or rewards for work performance [*as discussed in Chapter 11 by Clausen*], and failure to maintain these may contribute ultimately to the decision to retire. The upwardly mobile worker, such as a member of a profession or an employee in a corporate hierarchy, often reaches an apex in his career beyond which the remaining opportunities for advancement dwindle. Erwin Smigel (1964, pp. 44, 64) has said of the Wall Street lawyer entering a large firm, for instance, that he must be "up or out," usually within a ten-year period. One study of the occupational mobility of individual men over a ten-year period shows that the proportion shifting to higher occupational levels falls steadily by age strata from 25–29 up to 60–64, while the proportions experiencing no change in occupational level show a complementary rise (there was little age variation among the few downward shifters) (Reiss, 1953).

For some workers, especially those whose occupation does not follow a career line (Caplow, 1954, p. 108), the work role itself often deteriorates around the individual as he ages. As technical improvements and the advent of more recently trained workers exercise their impact in new standards of performance, in the creation of new occupations, and in the reorganization of work roles, older cohorts may not be able to meet emergent job expectations. Among automobile workers, for example, Barfield and Morgan (1969, pp. 89–93, 104, 121) report that difficulty in keeping up with the work and, less markedly, recent change in the nature of the job are associated with undertaking and with planning or actually undertaking early retirement. [*For another example, see the discussion by Zuckerman and Merton in Chapter 8.*]

The older worker's relative income position may, paradoxically, deteriorate as a consequence of economic growth (Volume I, pp. 82–84). Though the older worker's income tends to rise until the point of retirement, it often fails to keep pace with that of younger cohorts, who, because of economic growth, enter the labor force at successively higher levels of compensation. As a result, the older worker may perceive the relative lack of reward for his many years of accumulated experience, as younger workers surpass him in salary.

Thus workers at ages well below the point of retirement are likely to experience both relative and absolute diminution of rewards: they may be passed by for promotion or their services subtly undervalued; role inadequacy may be ascribed to them simply on the basis of age alone; or collective efforts through union negotiations, especially in periods of technical change, may fail to protect the older worker in achieving or maintaining improvements in wages, hours, or conditions.

AGE CRITERIA

The ages at which men finally leave the labor force are also connected with various formal and informal rules (See Volume I, Chapter 3 · B · 4 · b). A substantial minority of older workers in this country are required to leave their jobs when they reach an arbitrarily specified age.[10] In public employment, mandatory retirement is usual, with ages likely to be higher than 65 except for special categories (such as policemen, firemen, or soldiers) where the age is much lower. In private employment, where mandatory retirement is largely concentrated in firms also having private pension plans, the stipulated age is typically 65, though sometimes higher. Employers sometimes relax their maximum age rules under special conditions. Early retirement, at 60 or 55, for example, is permissible under most plans, usually, though not always, at reduced pension benefits (Wirtz, 1965, Volume II, pp. 33–35). Of course, some employees, after retiring from one job, move on into another.

Quite apart from any formal provisions, many employers—as well as the public at large—apparently do judge workers as "over-aged" or "too old" for a job, creating normative pressures for retirement. For them, age undoubtedly reflects some stereotypical view of performance capacities or some rough estimate of the comparative costs, business or social, of retaining older workers rather than pensioning them off. Thus a substantial minority of workers perceive employers and unions as putting pressures on employees to retire even before age 65, and a majority see younger people as feeling that older workers "should retire early and make room for others" (Barfield and Morgan, 1969, pp. 186, 205). Such attitudes and beliefs are not invariably unfavorable to the older worker, however (another instance of the general principle of wide individual variation within the older strata); for certain types of jobs, the older person may be valued exactly because he no longer has a self-interest in his own future career.[11]

The rules can operate to broaden, as well as limit, the range of acceptable ages or to increase the flexibility of age criteria. A case in point is the Age

[10] Barfield and Morgan (1969, p. 186) found in a national survey (1966) that, among non-retired family heads aged 35–59 years, 37 per cent face a compulsory retirement age.
[11] This point is suggested by Parsons (1960, pp. 171–172).

Discrimination in Employment Act of 1967, which, among other provisions with similar effect, sets penalties for employers who use phrases such as "age 25 to 35," "young," or "age over 50" in help-wanted notices. The intent of this Act is to eliminate age as a proscriptive criterion, substituting instead other criteria bearing more directly on job performance. Parsons (1960, p. 170) has pointed to the use of age as a practical criterion, during the period of rapid rise of large-scale organizations, for lessening the corporate burdens of carrying a superannuated staff and for opening the way for younger workers. As procedures for retiring develop, however, and as the retirement role becomes more widespread and more fully institutionalized, the rigidity of the age canon of 65 may become gradually mitigated and individuals may be judged more nearly on their merits.[12]

PROCEDURES AND AGENCIES

Though many workers, especially those in professional or technical fields and the self-employed, are free to make their own decisions about leaving the work force, various devices in intricate combinations and numerous social structures and agencies aid in the transfer of personnel in all occupational categories from work to retirement.

The constellation of agencies that contribute to these processes of role transfer include: families, friendship groups, voluntary associations, and other solidary groups who not only give emotional support to the retiree, but may also assign him to new types of duties and activities; economic agencies, including both the labor union and the employing firm that initially had major control over when, and under what conditions, a man is retired; and the government, which, through the introduction of social security in many countries, has assumed major responsibility for setting a floor under the incomes of retirees.

Among the most important of the devices utilized by these agencies in separating personnel from the work role is manipulation of the structure of rewards and opportunities available to the individual. Some of these, such as pensions or opportunities for leisure activities, have the effect of enhancing the attractiveness of leaving the work role by increasing opportunity to play rewarding alternative roles. Other devices, such as reduced pay or prestige, enforced retirement or prolonged unemployment, may lessen the desirability of the work role or close it entirely.

The family   While parents, as we have seen, often effect allocation *to* the work force by subsidizing the education or the early careers of their chil-

---

[12] In 1970, for example, a bill introduced into the United States House of Representatives regarding the employment of middle-aged and older workers calls for research "to explore and evaluate proposals for flexible or phased retirement," H.R. 18123, 302 (a) (2).

dren, the children, in their turn, participate much less directly to encourage their aged parents to *leave* the work force. In many agrarian societies, a familistic social organization provides security to the aged by sharing of food and by acts of deference that often enable them to remain in superordinate economic positions. In modern societies, statutory responsibility of adult children for their needy parents continues to exist in a number of countries and in many states of the United States (see Volume I, Chapter 4 · D · 2). In this country today, however, where the norms emphasize the independence and the dignity of the individual, opinion polls report a majority view that it is a person's own responsibility to save while he is young in order to help support himself after he stops working. Only a minority believe that children or relatives should take care of him, while the major emphasis is on government support through social security and other methods (Shanas, 1962, p. 169).

Under special conditions—notably when the parents are either sick or needy—young people do assume a degree of responsibility that assists parents in giving up, or tapering off, their economic activity. While there is some exchange of financial support between adult children and aged parents, with the children constituting a primary resource especially in case of illness or other emergency, the norms in the United States[13] stress a one-way flow from the older generation to the younger one; thus old people generally do not want help from their children, even though many children are willing to offer it (see Volume I, Chapter 23 · B · 2). Although children and grandchildren undoubtedly ease the transition to retirement—by providing companionship, emotional support, and a sense of usefulness—today's aged couple, with their increased years of joint survival and their tendency to live apart from their children, are likely to depend primarily upon each other, turning to children or relatives only under conditions of special need.[14] (See Volume I, Chapter 23 · A · 1 and 23 · A · 2 · b.)

The employing firm   Whatever efforts may be made by individuals to prepare for their future independence in old age, workers who lose or seek to change their jobs in the middle years—well before the nominal retirement age —often have difficulties in finding new ones. Although employing firms have made continual improvement over these decades in introducing pension plans (see, e.g., Livernash, 1968, p. 497) and protective devices for older workers, many workers are displaced because of relocation or shutdown of plants, cutbacks in staff, or temporary illnesses. And, for those workers who do become unemployed, the duration of unemployment increases sharply and steadily by age from those in their teens to those 65 and over (Wolfbein, 1963, p. 18).

[13] This may be less true in some other countries; see Stehouwer (1965, pp. 157–159).

[14] And, while the causal connections are complex, it is generally true that married men of all ages are more likely to be in the work force than men who are single, widowed, or divorced.

In an analysis of age discrimination in employment (1964),[15] Willard Wirtz, then Secretary of Labor, found only about one out of four employers stating a policy that imposed upper age limits for hiring. However, policy and practice are only loosely related. Of new workers actually hired in the surveyed firms, only 9 per cent were 45 or older, although men aged 45 and over made up 30 per cent of the unemployed. Explanations given by employers for hiring-age limits included incapability of meeting job requirements or company standards (although widely different standards were applied to essentially similar jobs), promotion from within, and reluctance of the older worker to accept reduced earnings; whereas the reasons *for* hiring older workers stressed stability, dependability, and knowledge and experience. Another obstacle may be private pension plans, which indirectly may tend to discourage employers from hiring older workers or older workers themselves from seeking to change jobs. As pension costs are commonly estimated, they tend to make older workers more expensive to the employer than younger workers. Moreover, in many plans, newly hired older workers cannot qualify for benefits; and some plans contain no means (such as vesting, early retirement, and portability) whereby workers can carry their pension rights to a new job.

The problems of older job seekers, though attributable in part to lower levels of education, cannot be explained away entirely in these terms; for even when education or level of skill are held constant, older workers are re-employed to a lesser extent than younger workers (see Volume II, Chapter 6 by Sheppard; see also Berkowitz and Burkhauser, 1969). A study of the job-seeking behavior of several hundred workers who had recently been unemployed, indicates some of the problems encountered by older workers (those 39 or over) in contrast with younger job applicants (Sheppard and Belitsky, 1966). For example, older workers reported differential treatment by the State Employment Service: compared with younger job seekers, smaller proportions were referred to employers for job interviews, given tests or counseled, or offered training in new occupations. When older workers were successful in finding new jobs (including skilled older workers) they received wage rates below those earned on the old job; while the opposite was true for younger workers. Moreover, older workers themselves are likely to use less vigorous and less effective tactics of job hunting than are younger workers; for example, they waited longer before starting their job hunt, visited fewer companies, and used less varied job seeking techniques.

Such scattered insights suggest how the allocative processes, whether by accident or design, operate to extrude from the work force many men well below the ages of 60 or 65.

Labor unions The complex web of rules typically specified in the labor

[15] Wirtz (1965, Volumes I and II); see also the further discussions of the Wirtz data in Axelbank (1969).

agreements of many industrialized societies today often include provisions as to seniority, retirement pensions, and age of retirement. Thus labor unions, through collective bargaining with employers, have been involved in agreements that have consequences for lowering the age of exit from the work force.

The principle of seniority, which assigns various preferences only on the basis of length of service with an employer, is a widespread manifestation of allocation according to age-related ascription rather than performance. Though seniority rules can benefit men at all ages, they are more likely to protect the jobs of workers growing old in the firm than to encourage the hiring of additional older workers.

Private pension plans, fostered by unions in recent years and highlighted in union-management negotiations,[16] typically also specify the age of retirement and can serve as inducements to retire. Thus, within two years after a union-negotiated liberalization of early retirement provisions was implemented among automobile workers, one-third of those eligible had promptly retired and another third were planning to retire before age 65 (Barfield and Morgan, 1969, pp. 71–75). Such response to the opportunity for optional early retirement indicates that the availability of pension income may strongly affect the decision to leave the work force.[17]

Government   Financial security for the retired person has become in modern society above all the responsibility of government. Public programs and governmental acts to meet the needs of the aged are, of course, not new. From the bread and circuses of ancient Rome to the modern welfare state, governmental programs have had varying histories in different countries throughout the world—depending upon particular social philosophies; upon the crises created by war, plague, or famine; or upon the maladjustments and dislocations created by basic changes in economic, religious, military, and other social institutions. But the feature of present-day systems of social security that distinguishes them from many earlier programs is their basis, not in need, but in impersonal norms of which a key criterion is age.[18] Social legislation avoiding the indignity of a means test was instituted in Germany as early as the 1880's; by 1925 in England; and by the mid-1960's, well over one hundred countries had social security programs.

The United States, slow to yield its philosophy of individualism, clung to vestiges of Elizabethan-type poor laws, not enacting an old-age pension pro-

---

[16] Private pension plans originally depended largely on the initiative of employers rather than of unions. For example, an analysis of United States private pension plans made in 1926 showed that the majority were noncontractual, dependent upon the employer's initiative (Epstein, 1926; cited by Donahue, Orbach, and Pollak, 1960, p. 342).

[17] However, the strength of this effect undoubtedly varies with the general state of the economy, the occupations of those affected, and various other factors.

[18] See the discussion by Donahue, Orbach, and Pollak (1960, p. 349).

gram until 1935 when, as a consequence of the Depression, the Social Security Act was signed. The basic plan has been supplemented in this country by other federal, state, and municipal programs, including Medicare, Medicaid, the Older Americans Act, income tax exemptions, subsidized housing and liberal financing of mortgages, and old age assistance as the last line of income defense.

Thus, by pooling their efforts, as Merton (1957, p. 566) had predicted in the 1940's, "big business," "big unions," and government have built a floor under the income of most of the retired aged. Perhaps ironically, much of the initial pressure in this country came less from the elderly workers themselves than from the younger workers and family heads who, by virtue of their unemployment during the Depression or their preponderant control over the expanding labor unions following World War II, made concessions to the old in order to secure jobs and improved working conditions for themselves.[19] The pension has become either a bribe or, in a more felicitous view, a formal reward for waiving the right to work.[20]

3 *The people involved*

The preceding examples we have been examining stress the nature of *societal* contributions to the processes of allocating people to the work force and, more especially, of withdrawing people from it. As we have indicated, these processes operate in complex and confusing ways, often quite apart from any clear intent or rational plan of the social agencies involved. The complexity of allocative processes is increased by the fact that the *individuals* being allocated act as partners—or opponents—of the societal agencies in making work force decisions. Their numbers determine the supplies of people of the appropriate age (element 1 in our conceptual model); their organic capacities and acquired skills (element 2) must be articulated with performance or nonperformance of the work role; their motivations (element 2), generated in the process of socialization, lead them to seek or to avoid various occupational activities and thus through self-selection to become active agents in their own allocation. In this section, we shall illustrate the nature of such individual contributions by focusing once more on the transfer from work to retirement.

NUMBERS AVAILABLE

The question has often been raised (for there is little agreement on the answer) whether historical declines in work force participation of the old and the

[19] See, for example, the accounts by Cottrell (1960, esp. pp. 627 ff. and 632 ff.); and by McConnell (1960, pp. 516 ff.).

[20] For an analysis of the disincentives to work built into United States Social Security legislation by reducing benefits in relation to income earned, see Jaffe (1970, pp. 10–11); see also Goffman (1962, p. 496).

very young reflect, as a society advances technologically, the sufficiency of a relatively smaller supply of manpower in meeting existing demands for goods and services. Despite technological advance, however, there have been no declines in the total supply of manpower in the economically developed nations to parallel the long term decline in employment of older men (see Volume I, Chapter 3 · B · 1). One reason the overall rates of labor force participation have not declined substantially is the increasing rate of participation by women. Moreover, the hypothetical estimates for the United States of work-life expectancy (Wolfbein, 1963, 1969) show that the average number of years that individuals spend in work during their lifetime have not decreased between 1900 and 1950 (even among males) but, because of increasing longevity, have increased substantially over this period. (However, the 1960 estimates did show a slight reversal of this trend, as a consequence of the steadily declining age of retirement.) Concomitantly, the increases in expectation of life have added notably since 1900 not only to the average number of years spent in growing up and going to school but also to the number of years spent in retirement (see Volume I, Chapter 18 · A · 1).

CAPACITIES AND PERFORMANCE

Is the older person, because of his age, a marginal worker to be displaced in the name of efficiency when other sources of manpower become available? There are two major respects in which his qualifications for competing with younger workers in holding his job or in getting a new one are comparatively inferior. He is likely to have certain handicaps, first, in health or psychophysical fitness, because of his advanced biological age; and second, in education, because he was trained when levels of educational attainment were generally lower. However, the standards of health or formal education set by employers sometimes appear too high or irrelevant for adequate performance of many jobs (see Volume I, Chapter 3 · B · 3).

Health As people grow older, they become subject to various organic changes and impairments that may affect their competence and restrict their activity. Thus the older a person is, the more likely he is to be outside the labor force because he is unable to work, presumably due to long-term physical or mental illness or disability. Poor health is the main reason given by workers themselves in explaining why they retired (Barfield and Morgan, 1969, p. 218); and those old people who do retire tend indeed to be less healthy than those who continue to work (see Volume I, Chapter 18 · C · 2 · b). Nevertheless, only a small proportion (some 15 per cent in the United States) of even those old people who are chronically ill are so severely handicapped that they cannot carry on their major work activity. And, as Long (1958, pp. 164–166) has pointed out, there is no evidence of any secular change in the health of older men that might explain their declining participation in the labor force.

Education In the face of the educational upgrading of the labor force, older people in general tend to have significantly lower educational attainment than young people. In addition, their less recent training takes on special importance in the light of recent technological changes. Among those in the labor force, the median years of school completed is notably lower for the age strata 65 and over and 55 to 64 than for the younger strata. Moreover, the discrepancy between old and young appears more marked today than in 1900, since educational advance was less rapid in the late nineteenth century than in the twentieth century (Long, 1958, pp. 179, 419–422); and, as more recently trained cohorts move into the younger strata, there is predictably a continued educational gap between older and younger members of the labor force.

In general, education is highly associated with occupational placement, for every age stratum.[21] However, the process by which educational attainment links the individual to the labor force and operates to the disadvantage of the older worker is often unclear. The extent to which general educational requirements set by employers bear a demonstrable relation to actual skills needed for competent job performance is still open to systematic investigation. Certainly technological change does not inevitably increase the complexity and technical requirements of affected occupations. For example, many of the specific jobs introduced by automation require minimal education and training, since the tasks demand simpler, if qualitatively different, skills.

Work performance Those men and women who remain in the labor force during their later years are not making generally inferior contributions, despite their age-related decrements in health and education and their frequently poor performance under laboratory conditions. Studies under actual working conditions show older workers performing as well as younger workers, if not better, on most, but not all, measures. On the whole, the productivity of older workers is steady and accurate, their attendance is regular, and their accident rates are no higher than those of younger workers (see Volume I, Chapter 18 · B). (Of course, such age patterns of actual performance are traceable in part to the labor market conditions and to selective processes that may retain in their jobs the more competent older workers.) That there is no necessary decline in creative productivity with aging is evidenced through analyses of the published biographies of contributors to numerous scholarly, scientific, and artistic fields (though widely quoted earlier studies had propounded somewhat misleading contrary findings).[22]

In addition to maintaining their productivity, many older people also take a generally positive view of their occupational role. As compared with the young,

---

[21] Taeuber and Taeuber (1958, pp. 219–220) show the high correlation in the year 1950 with both sex and color held constant. For a more recent analysis, see Jaffe (1970).

[22] Cf. Dennis (1956a, 1956b, and 1966). See also Volume I, p. 437, for cautionary note regarding interpretation of Lehman (1953).

older people still in the labor force tend to be more strongly committed to the kind of work they do, to adapt better to the job, and to express greater satisfaction with it. Moreover, despite their inferior education and the lowered aspirations attendant upon age, older workers do not fall very far short of the young in their sense of occupational adequacy or in the emphasis they place on the intrinsic satisfactions of the job itself. After all, they bring to their work levels of experience, commitment, and competence developed over a lifetime.

THE INDIVIDUAL'S DECISION

What course a particular individual takes as he approaches the conventional age of retirement is obviously not entirely determined for him by his continuing health and competence or by societal demands for the kinds of services he can perform. It is in part a matter of personal choice. In a sample of men aged 65 and over who had stopped working at their regular full-time job within the past five years, almost two-thirds of the wage and salary workers (and all the self-employed) said they had retired by their own volition (Palmore, August 1964, p. 5).

Reasons for retiring Nevertheless, about half the currently retired state that they retired unexpectedly, either earlier or later than planned (Barfield and Morgan, 1969, p. 219), a fact that may in part explain the somewhat different sets of variables associated with retirement plans and with the actual decision to retire (see Volume I, Chapter 18 · C · 2). Economic aspects of retirement—especially expected retirement income—figure most importantly in the planned age of retirement (Barfield and Morgan, 1969, p. 3 and passim). Interestingly enough, however, the level of preretirement earnings, though positively related to the individual's attitude toward retirement, is negatively related to his actual disposition to retire. Chief reasons given for actual retirement are poor health or inability to meet the physical and mental demands of the job. Less important but related to both planned and actual retirement age, are attitudes toward and degree of involvement in leisure activities, extent of satisfaction with the current job, and degree of general commitment to the value of work (Barfield and Morgan, 1969, passim; Streib and Thompson, 1957, p. 184). The unexpectedness of retirement for many individuals, however, suggests that predisposing attitudes and plans are mediated at the time of retirement by certain situational factors such as changes in health, in the nature of the job, or in the state of the economy.

Patterns of retirement The decisions made by many millions of individuals appear as a sifting process whereby particular categories of older people enter into retirement at different ages and with different degrees of finality.

Those older men most likely to remain in the labor force, while the majority of their fellows are retiring from it, are those with higher status occupations, such as professional and technical workers, managers, and proprietors.[23] Many of these are the same workers who are also comparatively likely to have attained a high educational level[24] and to be self-employed—categories showing a similarly high tendency toward continued labor force participation into old age.

Older men and women who do remain in the labor force often find ways of tapering off their work. They are, for example, less likely than younger people to work full time or all year. The proportions who work fewer than 35 hours a week rise steadily by age after a low point in the middle years. Among men with work experience in a given year (1964), these proportions include 2 per cent of those aged 35–44, 6 per cent of those 55–59, 10 per cent of those 60–65, 30 per cent of those 65–69, and 55 per cent of those 70 and over. The proportions who work fewer than 50 weeks of the year also increase by age beyond the middle years. Among men with work experience in the given year, these proportions include 17 per cent of those in the age stratum 35–54, 20 per cent of those 55–59, 25 per cent of those 60–64, in contrast to over 40 per cent of those 65 and over (Saben, 1966, p. A-5).

In addition to tapering off their work, many older people find other means of avoiding a sharp break with the work role even after retiring from a particular job or qualifying for social security benefits. Some shift to new jobs. A few leave and then re-enter the labor force, although such return to employment is rather uncommon once old people have stopped working entirely (see Volume I, Chapter 18 · C · 3).

Adaptation to retirement Once older people have retired, certain patterns of adaptation emerge (see Volume I, Chapter 18 · C · 4; Chapter 15 · 4 and 15 · 6; Chapter 17 · 3–5). Response to the new role of retired person seems on the whole to be fairly positive, although many retirees say they regret losing their work associates, the feeling of usefulness, the work itself, and (especially in the United States) the associated earnings. To be sure, adjustment to life is generally poorer among retired old people than among age peers who are still working, but this results in part from the selective process whereby the healthier and more advantaged oldsters tend to continue working.

Not surprisingly, satisfaction with retirement is associated with income and health (though there is no definitive evidence that retirement per se has a deleterious effect on health). Moreover, those who retire unexpectedly seem

---

[23] Sheppard suggests that the changing occupational structure of the labor force may tend, in the future, to reverse the trend toward declining participation among older people (see Volume II, pp. 190 ff.). Barfield and Morgan (1969), however, found no consistent relationship between occupation and plans for early retirement (p. 25). Emphasizing individual inclinations and increasing availability of adequate pension income, they predict even more widespread early retirement.

[24] However, Jaffe presents a cohort analysis of older men between 1950 and 1960 that shows remarkably *little* difference by educational level in rates of "retiring," though college graduates were still less likely to have retired than nongraduates, a finding that seems to merit further analysis (Jaffe, 1970, pp. 2–3).

considerably less likely than those who retired according to plan to feel positively toward retirement initially and to enjoy it subsequently. But the unexpected retirees also have fewer savings at the time of retirement and a lower postretirement income, factors that are highly related to satisfaction with retirement (Barfield and Morgan, 1969, pp. 61–67).

The generally positive acceptance of retirement has been attributed by some observers to a tendency on the part of some older people toward "disengagement," conceived (by Elaine Cumming and her collaborators) as a mutually satisfying process of withdrawal between the individual and society in preparation for the incapacitating diseases of old age and eventual death (see, e.g., Cumming and Henry, 1961). However, there is little evidence of any pronounced withdrawal from activity among any but a small minority of older people. Moreover, low levels of activity are likely to be associated with a low degree of satisfaction with life as a whole. Even voluntary retirement does not seem to represent motivated renunciation of all social participation, for activity in nonwork roles tend to be maintained or even increased. Scattered longitudinal studies suggest that the vast majority of older people maintain their prior levels of activity, so that many who do seem inactive in old age are merely persisting in an established life pattern (see Volume I, Chapter 17 · 5).

One interpretation that seems compatible with much of the available evidence is that acceptance of retirement depends strongly upon whether departure from work was perceived as voluntary or coerced. Psychological withdrawal is frequently a response to frustrations such as those imposed by ill health or social constraints. It has been shown, for example, that the withdrawal of old people in retirement is very similar to the response found among much younger men during the situation of general unemployment in the Great Depression (Riley, Foner, Hess, and Toby, 1969, pp. 972–974). Thus among young people, too, withdrawal is a not uncommon response when social structural barriers destroy the motivation to perform in accustomed roles or to learn new ones (Merton, 1957, Chapter 4; Parsons, 1951, Chapter 7).

For many who retire willingly, however—and regardless perhaps of previous attitudes toward the job—retirement can represent not a general withdrawal from social participation, but a welcome opportunity to engage in satisfying alternative activities. Given reasonably good health and adequate income, future cohorts are likely to experience retirement, not as preparation for the end of life, but as a continuation of an active existence in a new stage with its own goals and rewards.

4 Some problems of socialization

In our discussion of the processes articulating candidates with the roles available inside or outside the work force, we have paid little explicit attention to socialization—to the ways in which individuals in the several age strata have been prepared to play these roles. Yet without socialization, as Parsons and Shils (1951, p. 197) have put it, the allocation of claimants to scarce roles and to the associated rewards could result in a Hobbesian war of "every man against every man"; socialization prepares different individuals for different jobs by serving to focus aspirations, skills, competences, and tastes. We shall not deal here with learning to play new work roles or to adjust to alterations in careers, a topic developed in some detail by Clausen in Chapter 11,[25] but shall restrict ourselves to certain age-related dilemmas that stem from the content and from the timing of socialization. In regard to *content*, socialization (including formal education) imparts not only basic values and general knowledge but also specific information, skills, and motivations that are applicable to particular roles. In regard to *timing*, a striking feature of modern society is the concentration of formal education in the early years of life [*discussed in Chapter 12*], while comparatively little systematic attention is devoted during the middle or later years either to continuing general education or to practical retraining (see Chapter 11 by Eklund in Volume II). We shall illustrate various ways in which these aspects of content and timing can influence the preparation of mature individuals either for continued work or for retirement.

RETRAINING OF WORKERS

Many older workers face demands for new learning, as their earlier training becomes increasingly outdated or as they may shift to entirely new jobs and eventually to the new role of retirement. Yet, they are typically handicapped in ways that appear to discourage entry into adult training programs and that may actually reduce learning potential. For the older the worker, on the average, the lower the level of his formal schooling and his socioeconomic status, the less optimistic his occupational outlook, and the greater his personal constraints about attending classes or continuing his education generally (see Volume I, Chapter 18 · B · 4). Nevertheless, continued education, training, or retraining can be an important asset in helping the older worker to meet a widening variety of occupational demands or to satisfy the specific requirements of his particular job.

The value of occupational retraining both in educational institutions and in on-the-job situations has only recently begun to be tested here and abroad

---

[25] In the large and growing literature on occupational roles, the concept of "career" has been used to guide the analysis of the individual's relationship to his work role over his life course. (For an early volume in this field see Hughes 1958). Career patterns have been traced for a variety of occupations, and data are often given on the ages at which men reach various stages of progression within each occupational career line (e.g., research scientists: Glaser, 1964; top management: Warner and Abegglen, 1963; government workers: Warner, 1963; the military: Janowitz, 1964).

(see Volume I, Chapter 3 · B · 3 · c). According to an analysis by Somers (1966, pp. 119–123; 1967, p. 26), retraining appears to improve the employment opportunities of workers at all ages, even though older workers (45 and over) show somewhat less improvement than younger trainees in their 20's or early 30's.

Because older workers may be more difficult to retrain than are younger workers, the costs of retraining tend to increase by age.[26] Belbin (1965) has shown how many of the difficulties of retraining older workers can be overcome if suitable revisions are made in the existing methods of instruction, and he has actually spelled out principles for such revision.[27] Moreover, the amount of retraining required because of technological change is often slight—despite the early conjecture that automated jobs might be intrinsically unsuited to older workers. The evidence suggests that, for many older workers, successful socialization often requires, not so much the teaching of completely new technologies, as aiding the adjustment to changed work situations (involving, for example, smaller groups or greater emphasis on "minding" than on manipulating machines) (see Volume I, Chapter 3 · B · 2 · f; Foner, unpublished M.A. thesis).

Whatever the costs, retraining can make a difference not only to the performance and the morale of the worker, but also to the economy as a whole. Sheppard argues that the older worker, through retraining, becomes a more active consumer, a better taxpayer, and a lower dependency risk for the welfare programs of the community (Volume II, p. 178).

LOOSENING COMMITMENT TO WORK

See Chapter 12 · 2 for a fuller discussion of role relinquishment and role transfer

Whether or not occupational retraining may help to offset the educational gap between old and young, the great majority of workers follow a life-course pattern of either failure to rise further in the job after a period of early advancement, or of demotion after a peak in the middle years. Experiences with such patterns undoubtedly serve as a kind of anticipatory socialization for relinquishing work. Though formal retirement planning programs have been often introduced by companies or unions, much preparation for retirement at the place of work is likely to take more subtle, often unintended forms. Some insightful clues to the nature of rehearsal for retirement are afforded by a study of managers in a large corporation by Goldner (1965),[28] where demo-

---

[26] Moreover, employers may consider the costs of retraining to be relatively higher for older workers, who have a lower work-life expectancy than the young.

[27] See also the discussion in Volume II, Chapter 6 by Sheppard.

[28] The pattern of demotion found by Goldner is, of course, not necessarily typical.

tion had become a normal aspect of the subculture. Company superiors and coworkers communicate expectations of possible failure, and those already demoted serve as warnings to the others. While such mechanisms operate to prepare men for leveling off or for declining successes, other mechanisms hold the workers to their jobs until the time of retirement by cloaking these demotions in ambiguity or providing vague criteria for advancement.

This study indicates a variety of ways in which individual managers might adapt to changing work expectations of this kind (cf. Goffman, 1962, pp. 499–500). Some may counter threats of demotion by emphasizing the personal hardships suffered by those higher up or the price one must pay for moving up the career ladder. Some may shift their sphere of involvement—to community or family activities, for example—in order to compensate for defeats in work. Others may lose self-respect, evading encounters with former associates who may know of the demotion. Thus various defenses and preparations for occupational withdrawal may be set in motion far in advance of the retirement age.

PREPARATION FOR RETIREMENT

The extent to which future cohorts of older people can benefit from retirement will be markedly influenced both by anticipatory learning during their preretirement years and also by the content and the emphases retained from their initial phase of formal education. Studies of preretirement attitudes, reflecting current processes of socialization for eventual retirement, seem generally favorable, albeit vague. Not yet tempered by objective realities, however, such attitudes often differ sharply from the decisions finally made when the point of retirement is reached, and those individuals who are nearing retirement are somewhat less sanguine about it than are younger people (see Volume I, Chapter 18 · C · 1) (see also Barfield and Morgan, 1969, pp. 9, 196–205).

One study of high school students and their middle-aged parents (Foner, 1969) suggests how intergenerational relationships can affect the preparation for retirement. Consistent with the more general findings for adults in the country as a whole today (Volume I, Chapter 18 · C · 1 · e), these parents do little definite planning for retirement; and it appears that, especially among those whose offspring plan to go to college, parents set a higher priority on spending to help their children get started, than on spending for themselves or saving for retirement. At the same time, there is an interesting by-product of this involvement of the middle-aged parents with their offspring: in the process of socializing their children, the parents may in turn be socialized themselves. For example, in regard to attitudes related to the "good life" (the importance of developing one's own personality and interests or of devoting free time to family rather than to extra work), fathers' aspirations for themselves tend to match their aspirations for their sons more nearly than they match the standard by which these fathers were reared by their own (now aged) parents. In such ways aging individuals may transcend the confines of their own earlier training, thus keeping abreast of current trends even as they approach retirement.

Once retirement is reached, certain agents of influence are available to aid in learning which behaviors are "appropriate" to the new role. Here again offspring may influence their parents. Retired husbands and their wives can bring together their differing experiences in retirement, although older people do not generally serve as role models for one another (Rosow, 1967). Or the mass media can supply information about manners and customs. Perhaps more widely available than such sources of role learning are various sources of emotional support and permissiveness that can aid adjustment to retirement. Expert help may be furnished by ministers, social workers, doctors, or psychotherapists. Tension release, as well as a sense of participation with the environment, is offered through programs on television and radio. Expressive activity is fostered by old age centers and informal friendship groups. And above all, the solidarity of the family supports the attempts of the retired individual to reconcile discrepant or conflicting role expectations: the family permits a degree of childlike or idiosyncratic behavior in their elders (whom they at the same time isolate from outside sanctions).

To be sure, the family can often be a source of stress for a retiree—a long series of role realignments may be necessary before the retiree adjusts to his new status; and these adjustments may well be as great for the other family members as for the retiree himself.

EDUCATION FOR LEISURE

Whether the better educated and more affluent cohorts now young or in their middle years will have less difficulty and, therefore, less need of such expressions of emotional support and permissiveness from others in adjusting to retirement will depend upon the still emerging nature of retirement itself. Will it remain, to use Burgess' term, a "roleless role," with few clear or widely shared goals and expectations? Or will it become fully institutionalized as a new form of social life, as Donahue and her associates (1960, pp. 332 ff.) insist? Will it lead to occupational roles redefined to fit the older person who has left his regular work,[29] or to new emphases upon leisure and upon cultural or civic pursuits? Should retirement emerge as primarily a leisure role, will the noninstrumental aspects of formal education receive new value? For, if the "relevant" or "practical" aspects of socialization often stand the young job-

[29] Substantial increases in voluntary part-time work over the past decade are noted by Wolfbein (1969).

seeker in good stead, the retiree may well benefit most from the nontechnical, nonspecialized, nonvocational aspects of his socialization experiences.

All predictions are, of course, hazardous, and caution is required in predicting that, as the better educated cohorts reach retirement, they will focus upon leisure rather than new forms of work. Prior to World War II, housewives whose children were old enough for school were expected to engage in leisure activities (see Riley, Foner, Hess, and Toby, 1969, pp. 977–978). Yet in the intervening decades married women at this age have turned, not to greater leisure, but to a dramatic involvement in the labor force. Moreover, this marked trend, which appears to be associated with a changing definition of the woman's occupational role, is highly correlated with education. For, although in the United States the wife's labor force participation tends to *decrease* as her husband's income rises, when the husband's income is held constant, her participation tends to *increase* as her education rises (see Riley, Johnson, and Boocock, 1963; Mincer, 1968, pp. 479–480). Thus in the case of women expanding education seems to have led away from leisure toward enhanced occupational activity.

5 *Tensions and changes*

Whatever future changes might be effected in socialization for work or retirement—with education more evenly spread over the life course, for example, or with variations in the emphasis on general versus specific knowledge—the processes of socialization and allocation as they now operate are associated with, and can often cause, pronounced age differences within the labor force. Such differences make for particular types of relationships and strains among the age strata and can generate pressures for change, as we shall suggest by a few examples. In some instances, the consequent changes may affect social sectors outside the economy or even the society as a whole, as conflicts emerge, or as the failure of work or retirement to meet the needs of particular strata evokes deviant reactions that diffuse throughout the society (Riley, Foner, Hess, and Toby, 1969, pp. 974 ff.).

AGE HIERARCHY WITHIN THE WORK FORCE

Traditionally, the flow of cohorts through the work force has meant that, in some broad sense, older workers are continually hiring or evaluating younger workers and socializing them as replacements for themselves. Thus age has been correlated with higher status: with the greater knowledge and experience required for socialization and with the control over salary, promotion, and other rewards required for allocation.

Nowadays, however, this correlation between age and status in the work force may be more tenuous. Older women starting to work and older men embarking on a second career often find themselves being initiated by persons far younger than they. More generally, to the extent that educational institutions have taken over the apprenticeship function, young entrants bring to the work force a competence and an infusion of new knowledge that undermines the entrenched authority of the established workers. The hierarchical asymmetry of the work force was derived from a correlation between age and two types of competence—technical skill and experience; but to the extent that this duality breaks down, there is often a sharp break between the old who have the experience and the young who have the technical skill. Witness the problems of many corporate systems models or computerized operations, which, like the sorcerer's apprentice, run completely out of control. Built by the recently trained, they often fail to incorporate the accumulated wisdom of the past. And yet, when socialization is attempted by those who have come to understand the system through long knowledge of it, strains often arise because these older workers tend to resist innovations and changes espoused by the young.

Various practices both inside and outside the work organization offset certain of the strains generated by such inversions of the traditional age structure of socialization and allocation. For example, new recruits may be assigned to perform in new areas while older men assume general administrative roles that require prolonged experience rather than specialized or recent knowledge of the particular tasks. But there are limits to the usefulness of this mechanism: only a relatively few can be administrators, and new knowledge and techniques of administration are constantly evolving, which tend to undermine the expertise of administrators without educational recency. Moreover, lack of specialized knowledge may reduce the administrator to a position of formal authority without actual decision-making power (Moore, 1962).

Devices that have been developed for the retraining of older workers often avoid the tensions of age-incongruous relationships by separating socialization from other functions in the work organization. For example, socialization programs are widely undertaken outside of the work context. Summer conferences, professional sabbaticals, sensitivity or T-group training, meetings and various types of "back to school" programs have come to be commonly located "outside" the immediate work organization. This differentiation can relieve role strain since older workers, by leaving a company temporarily to be trained along with their age peers, avoid being taught within the company by young persons with higher, or potentially higher, positions than themselves. "Outside" socializers do not threaten the older socializee's status as would "internal" socializers.

Within the educational sphere, certain curricular emphases may tend to reduce strains and even to maintain hierarchical age grading within the work context. For example, a latent function of the type of education given in many of the "better" professional schools (e.g., the "national" law schools), where broad knowledge—not subject to obsolescence—rather than practical training is stressed, may be to preserve the domain of the older members of the profession.

Such practices, which either slow the erosion of age-based authority structures or ease the accompanying trauma, can have far-reaching consequences both inside and outside the occupational sphere. The general trend, while protecting the jobs of older workers through rights of tenure and of seniority, may at the same time be leading away from many of the normative expectations that age "should"—beyond childhood—serve as a basis for hierarchical ordering.

INEQUALITIES AMONG AGE STRATA

If the relationships among age strata are affected by the processes of allocation and socialization occurring within the occupational structure, these relationships are even more notably affected by age differences in the extent of participation in the work force at all.

Differing rates of involvement in the economic goal-directed activities of the society make for striking age-inequalities in financial status and in the time available for leisure pursuits. Just as age strata differ in political power [see Chapter 4], they differ also in economic rewards.

In regard to financial status (see Volume I, Chapter 4; and Volume II, Chapter 7, by Kreps), the median incomes of the several age categories in the population tend to form a bell-shaped curve with its peak in the middle years. The precise shape of the curve varies somewhat according to the measures used, but younger people in their 20's and older people over 60 or even in their 50's, have markedly lower median incomes than those in the middle years, even after various adjustments are made (for example, for family size). To be sure, there are enormous individual variations, especially among the aged, a few of whom have very high incomes indeed. Moreover, there are certain mitigating factors. Young people, who have a future against which to borrow (through mortgages or installment buying, for example), commonly spend more than they earn. Old people have had a lifetime to accumulate assets so that many of them, especially in the United States, own at least their own homes; and their incomes, often judged by economists as inadequate to meet their needs, are supplemented by public and private programs of financial security.

Yet the financial inequalities remain. For old and young alike, exclusion from the work force withholds from them the prestige accorded to occupational achievement and restricts both the standard of living and style of life. In addition, exclusion from the work force of increasingly large fractions of the young and the old places an ever-increasing burden of support (through taxation and various forms of transfer payments) upon those strata that do remain active in the economy.[30] As Mincer (1968, p. 476) contends, it is only those societies experiencing high per capita income that can afford to raise the age of entry into the labor force, lengthen the span of retirement, and permit only part-time work at the two extremes of age.

At both extremes, those individuals in a society of abundance who forego wages thereby acquire time that is free from work. Thus the inequalities among age strata apply to time as well as to money. To the extent that young and old are deprived of economic rewards they may have enlarged opportunities for noneconomic ones. While money, to be sure, is a necessary underpinning to the use of time (if the young are to benefit from education or the old are to enjoy the varieties of leisure), the comparative value of the rewards of time versus money is currently subject to keen debate. And the course of the future will in part be shaped by the uses made of the added increments of free time.

What will future cohorts of old people do with their retirement years? Leisure may remain primarily recreation, dominated by ad hoc goals, and the desire for immediate personal gratification. Or new instrumental activities may develop that substitute for former occupations.[31] Or achievement norms may become redefined to embrace disciplined leisure pursuits reminiscent of those of the leisure classes in ancient Athens, the Renaissance, or seventeenth-century England (Riley, Foner, Hess, and Toby, 1669, pp. 978 ff.).

And what of the young, as they now prepare for their entry into positions of influence in the economy? Many of them (if not conscripted for the military service) use their reprieve from the work force in labor of another kind—in extended education. Formal education can combine in itself, as we have noted, an "investment" in a future career together with a broad preparation for future leisure, including eventual retirement. But where will the predominant emphasis come to be placed? [*Compare the discussion in Chapter 7 by Parsons and Platt.*] A large segment of students today is still clearly imbued with the work-related postures of the Puritan ethic, as described by sociologists and intellectual historians from Max Weber to Talcott Parsons. Another segment of students or of young careerists, while accepting the importance of work, seems increasingly to insist that the job cannot have exclusive priority over compet-

---

[30] One could argue, however, that this exclusion permits higher earnings than would be possible if excluded strata were also a part of the work force.

[31] Of course, varying proportions of "free" time are now devoted to such "instrumental" activities as personal and household maintenance, political activity, and volunteer work in church and community. That these activities are often included in lists of leisure pursuits may simply reflect the fact that there is no money income attached; or it may reflect their valuation in the society relative to income-producing work. Interestingly enough, members of age catgeories most closely bound to occupational roles are sometimes also more likely than those with greater amounts of free time to engage in leisure pursuits of an instrumental nature. See, for example, United States Department of Labor, Manpower Administration (April 1969).

ing commitments to family, friends, or community. Still another segment (remarkably parallel to such literary romantics as Rousseau, Chateaubriand, Coleridge, Wordsworth, and their contemporaries[32]) strives for simpler societies, utopias, or a return to childhood, often seeking aid through such devices as cultism, hero worship, or drugs. Which of these segments will prevail? Can they coexist? What sets of values will pervade these younger cohorts? And, as these cohorts mature, confronting the realities and the conflicting commitments of full adulthood, what attitudes toward work and leisure will they carry with them?

The answers to many such questions will determine, not only the processes of socialization and allocation appropriate to the future, but the shape of the future society as well.

Works cited in Chapter 5

Axelbank, Rashelle G., 1969. "The Position of the Older Worker in the American Labor Force," in *Employment of the Middle-Aged Worker*, New York: National Council on the Aging, pp. 121–280.

Babbitt, Irving, 1919. *Rousseau and Romanticism*, Boston: Houghton Mifflin.

Bancroft, Gertrude, 1958. *The American Labor Force: Its Growth and Changing Composition*, New York: Wiley.

Barfield, Richard, and James Morgan, 1969. *Early Retirement: The Decision and the Experience*, Ann Arbor, Mich.: Braun-Brumfield.

Belbin, R. M., 1965. *Training Methods for Older Workers*, Paris: Organisation for Economic Co-operation and Development.

Bell, Daniel, 1968. "The Measurement of Knowledge and Technology," in Sheldon, Eleanor Bernert, and Wilbert E. Moore, editors, *Indicators of Social Change*, New York: Russell Sage Foundation, pp. 145–246.

Berkowitz, Monroe, and Richard Burkhauser, 1969. "Unemployment and the Middle-aged Worker," *Industrial Gerontology*, No. 3, New York: National Council on the Aging, pp. 9–19.

Blau, Peter M., and Otis Dudley Duncan, 1967. *The American Occupational Structure*, New York: Wiley.

Bogue, Donald J., 1969. *The Population of the United States*, Glencoe, Ill.: Free Press.

Caplow, Theodore, 1954. *The Sociology of Work*, Minneapolis: University of Minnesota Press.

Conant, James, 1959. *The Child, the Parent and the State*, Cambridge, Mass.: Harvard University Press.

Cottrell, Fred, 1960. "Governmental Functions and the Politics of Age," in Tibbitts, Clark, editor, *Handbook of Social Gerontology*, Chicago: University of Chicago Press, pp. 624–665.

---

[32] The striking similarity between the intellectual currents of the early nineteenth century and this aspect of youth culture today is apparent from Irving Babbitt's acerb analysis of the Romantic movement (Babbitt, 1919).

Cumming, Elaine, and William E. Henry, 1961. *Growing Old: The Process of Disengagement,* New York: Basic Books.

Dennis, Wayne, 1956a. "Age and Achievement: A Critique," *Journal of Gerontology,* 11, pp. 331–337.

———, 1956b. "Age and Productivity Among Scientists," *Science,* 123, pp. 724–725.

———, 1966. "Creative Productivity between the Ages of 20 and 80 Years," *Journal of Gerontology,* 21, pp. 1–8.

Donahue, Wilma, Harold L. Orbach, and Otto Pollak, 1960. "Retirement: The Emerging Social Pattern," in Tibbitts, Clark, editor, *Handbook of Social Gerontology,* Chicago: University of Chicago Press, pp. 330–406.

Durand, John D., 1948. *The Labor Force in the United States 1890–1960,* New York: Social Science Research Council.

Epstein, A., 1926. *The Problem of Old Age Pensions in Industry,* Harrisburg: Pennsylvania Commission on Old Age Pensions.

Foner, Anne, 1962. "Automation: Its Meaning for Sociology," M.A. Thesis, New York University.

———, 1969. "The Middle Years: Prelude to Retirement?" Ph.D. dissertation, New York University.

Gerth, H. H., and C. Wright Mills, editors, 1958. *From Max Weber,* New York: Oxford University Press.

Glaser, Barney G., 1964. *Organizational Scientists, Their Professional Careers,* New York: Bobbs-Merrill.

Goffman, Erving, 1962. "On Cooling the Mark Out: Some Aspects of Adaptation to Failure," in Rose, Arnold, editor, *Human Behavior and Social Processes,* Boston: Houghton Mifflin, pp. 482–505.

Goldner, Fred H., 1965. "Demotion in Industrial Management," *American Sociological Review,* 30, pp. 714–724.

Granick, David, 1961. *The Red Executive: A Study of the Organization Man in Russian Industry,* Garden City, N.Y.: Doubleday, Anchor Books.

Hughes, Everett C., 1958. *Men and Their Work,* Glencoe, Ill.: Free Press.

Hyman, Herbert H., 1953. "The Value Systems of Different Classes: A Social Psychological Contribution to the Analysis of Stratification," in Bendix, Reinhard, and Seymour Martin Lipset, editors, *Class, Status and Power: A Reader in Social Stratification,* Glencoe, Ill.: Free Press, pp. 426–442.

Jaffe, A. J., 1970. "Men Prefer Not to Retire," *Industrial Gerontology,* No. 5, New York: National Council on the Aging, pp. 1–11.

Janowitz, Morris, 1964. *The Professional Soldier,* New York: Free Press of Glencoe.

Kahl, Joseph A., 1953. "Educational and Occupational Aspirations of 'Common Man' Boys," *Harvard Educational Review,* 23, pp. 186–201.

Lehman, Harvey C., 1953. *Age and Achievement,* Princeton, N.J.: Princeton University Press.

Livernash, E. Robert, 1968. "Labor Relations, I. Collective Bargaining," in Sills, David L., editor, *International Encyclopedia of the Social Sciences,* 17 vols., New York: Macmillan and Free Press, 8, pp. 491–500.

Long, Clarence D., 1958. *The Labor Force Under Changing Income and Employment*, Princeton, N.J.: Princeton University Press.

McConnell, John W., 1960. "Aging and the Economy," in Tibbitts, Clark, editor, *Handbook of Social Gerontology*, Chicago: University of Chicago Press, pp. 489–520.

Manpower Report of the President, March 1970.

Marx, Karl (1867–1879), 1936. *Capital*, New York: Modern Library.

Merton, Robert K., 1957. *Social Theory and Social Structure*, rev. ed., Glencoe, Ill.: Free Press.

Mincer, Jacob, 1968. "Labor Force, II. Participation," in Sills, David L., editor, *International Encyclopedia of the Social Sciences*, 17 vols., New York: Macmillan and Free Press, 8, pp. 474–481.

Moore, Wilbert E., 1962. *The Conduct of the Corporation*, New York: Random House.

————, 1969. "Occupational Socialization," in Goslin, David A., editor, *Handbook of Socialization Theory and Research*, Chicago: Rand McNally, pp. 861–883.

Palmore, Erdman, August 1964. "Retirement Patterns Among Aged Man: Findings of the 1963 Survey of the Aged," *Social Security Bulletin*, 27, pp. 3–10.

Parnes, Herbert S., et al., 1969. *Career Thresholds:* A Longitudinal Study of the Educational and Labor Market Experience of Male Youth 14–24 Years of Age, Volume One, Columbus, Ohio: Center for Human Resource Research, Ohio State University.

Parrella, Vera C., February 1970. "Work Experience of the Population," *Monthly Labor Review*, pp. 54–61.

Parsons, Talcott, 1937. *The Structure of Social Action: A Study in Social Theory With Special Reference to a Group of Recent European Writers*, New York: McGraw-Hill.

————, 1951. *The Social System*, Glencoe, Ill.: Free Press.

————, 1960. "Toward a Healthy Maturity, " *Journal of Health and Human Behavior*, 1, pp. 163–173.

————, and Edward A. Shils, 1951. "Values, Motives and Systems of Action," in Parsons, Talcott, and Edward A. Shils, editors, *Toward A. General Theory of Action*, Cambridge, Mass.: Harvard University Press, pp. 45–275.

————, and Neil J. Smelser, 1956. *Economy and Society: A Study in the Integration of Economic and Social Theory*, Glencoe, Ill.: Free Press.

Reiss, A., 1953. "Patterns of Occupational Mobility for Workers in Cities," Chicago Community Inventory, University of Chicago (unpublished).

Riley, Matilda White, Anne Foner, Beth Hess, and Marcia L. Toby, 1969. "Socialization for the Middle and Later Years," in Goslin, David A., editor, *Handbook of Socialization Theory and Research*, Chicago: Rand McNally, pp. 951–982.

————, Marilyn E. Johnson, and Sarane S. Boocock, 1963. "Woman's Changing Occupational Role—A Research Report," *The American Behavioral Scientist*, 6, pp. 33–37.

Rosow, Irving, 1967. *Social Integration of the Aged*, New York: Free Press.

Saben, Samuel, 1966. "Work Experience of the Population in 1964," Special Labor

Force Report, No. 62, United States Bureau of Labor Statistics, Washington: Government Printing Office.

Shanas, Ethel, 1962. *The Health of Older People: A Social Survey*, Cambridge, Mass.: Harvard University Press.

Sheldon, Henry D., 1958. *The Older Population of the United States*, New York: J. Wiley.

Sheppard, Harold L., and A. Harvey Belitsky, 1966. *The Job Hunt*, Baltimore: Johns Hopkins Press.

Smelser, Neil J., 1959. *Social Change in the Industrial Revolution*, Chicago: University of Chicago Press.

————, 1963. *The Sociology of Economic Life*, Englewood Cliffs, N.J.: Prentice-Hall.

————, 1968. "Sociological History: The Industrial Revolution and the British Working-Class Family" in Smelser, Neil J., *Essays in Sociological Explanations*, Englewood Cliffs, N.J.: Prentice-Hall, pp. 76–91.

Smigel, Erwin O., 1964. *The Wall Street Lawyer: Professional Organization Man*, New York: Free Press of Glencoe.

Somers, Gerald G., 1966. "Retraining the Unemployed Older Worker," in Kreps, Juanita M., editor, *Technology, Manpower, and Retirement Policy*, New York: World, pp. 109–125.

————, 1967. "Evaluation of Work Experience and Training of Older Workers" (Report to the Naitonal Council on the Aging). Mimeographed.

Stehouwer, Jan., 1965. "Relations between Generations and the Three-Generation Household in Denmark," in Shanas, Ethel, and Gordon Streib, editors, *Social Structure and the Family: Generational Relations*, Englewood Cliffs, N.J.: Prentice-Hall, pp. 142–162.

Streib, Gordon F., 1958. "Family Patterns in Retirement," *Journal of Social Issues*, 14, pp. 46–60.

————, and W. E. Thompson, 1957. "Personal and Social Adjustment in Retirement," in Donahue, Wilma, and Clark Tibbitts, editors, *The New Frontiers of Aging*, Ann Arbor: University of Michigan Press, pp. 180–197.

Sussman, Marvin B., 1965. "Relationship of Adult Children With Their Parents in the United States," in Shanas, Ethel, and Gordon Streib, editors, *Social Structure and the Family: Generational Relations*, Englewood Cliffs, N.J.: Prentice-Hall, pp. 62–92.

Taeuber, Conrad, and Irene Taeuber, 1958. *The Changing Population of the United States*, New York: Wiley.

Thernstrom, Stephen, 1966. "Class and Mobility in a Nineteenth Century City," in Bendix, Reinhard, and Seymour Martin Lipset, editors, *Class, Status, and Power*, 2nd ed., New York: Free Press, pp. 602–623.

Trow, Martin, 1966. "The Second Transformation of American Secondary Education," in Bendix, Reinhard, and Seymour Martin Lipset, editors, *Class, Status, and Power*, 2nd ed., New York: Free Press, pp. 437–449.

United Nations Department of Economic and Social Affairs, 1962. "Demographic Aspects of Manpower," *Population Studies*, No. 33, New York.

United States Bureau of the Census, 1960 Census of Population, Vol. I, Part 1.

United States Bureau of Labor Statistics, 1969. "Handbook of Labor Statistics, 1969," Bulletin No. 1630.

United States Department of Labor, Manpower Administration, April 1969. *Americans Volunteer*, Manpower/Automation Research Monograph No. 10.

Waldman, Elizabeth, August 1969. "Employment Status of School Age Youth," *Monthly Labor Review*, pp. 23–31.

Warner, W. Lloyd, 1963. *The American Federal Executive*, New Haven: Yale University Press.

————, and James C. Abegglen, 1963. *Big Business Leaders in America*, New York: Atheneum.

Wirtz, W. Willard, 1965. *The Older American Worker: Age Discrimination in Employment*, I and II, (Report of the Secretary of Labor) Washington: Government Printing Office.

Wolfbein, Seymour L., 1963. *Changing Patterns of Working Life*, Office of Manpower and Automation Research, Department of Labor, Washington: Government Printing Office, pp. 6, 17–19.

————, 1969. "Work Force and Retirement Trends in the Older Population," Paper prepared for the 8th International Congress of Gerontology.

6

The community

BERNICE C. STARR

Analysts of the community have long been interested in articulating the relationship between the community as a social structure and the community as an ecological structure. To this twofold perspective, Bernice Starr, a member of the Rutgers Age Seminar, adds a third: the community as an age structure.

The introduction of age as a central element of community analysis sheds new light on the social and ecological aspects of equilibrium, disequilibrium, and change. Implicit in Starr's discussion is a fact of considerable significance: The equilibrium model of balance between needs and services in the social-ecological structure—a model that underlies much community analysis—can exist empirically only when the age composition of a community approximates a particular ideal type. First, the population must be widely distributed over the age strata, not restricted to a few homogeneous categories. Second, this age composition must remain fairly stable over time, with births balancing deaths and migration at a minimum. Such an ideal type bears little resemblance, of course, to the communities or neighborhoods of today's industrial societies. In fact, strain or disequilibrium often result from two age-related sources: (1) the aging of a population within a given community setting; and (2) the succession of population cohorts who, as bearers of social change, either adapt to or create changes in the nature of the community.

Much of Starr's discussion points to consequences of this central insight. Since, as she indicates in Section 1, many communities are created to serve specific age groups, the aging of the resident population creates a variety of questions concerning adaptive capacities of individuals, age-specific pressures for in- and out-migration, and pressures for change in the social and physical structure of the community.

The second section of the essay deals with the changing community needs and orientations of individuals as they age. Although much remains to be learned, both available data and reasoned speculation suggest that, as individuals live out their life course, they experience patterned changes in their residential needs, their use of community facilities and interaction within the community, as well as their orientations toward and definition of their residential environment.

Numerous other sources of disequilibrium impinge upon the community from the larger society and from the far-flung processes of cohort formation, migration, and dissolution. Thus the final section of the essay shows how the residential histories of successive cohorts reflect broad processes of social change, and result in spatial redistribution of the population and changes in the population characteristics of communities.

A great deal of the material in the Inventory (Volume I), though too often restricted to middle-aged and older people, provides relevant background for this essay. In particular, Chapter 6 describes the geographical concentration of older people in certain types of communities, the tendencies of the aged to be less mobile than the younger population and to own their homes, the characteristics of these homes, and the implications of housing for the range of human contacts, day-to-day activities, and available community facilities and services. More generally, Chapters 8 through 11 provide background on the physical limitations of older people as these affect their community requirements, Chapters 7 and 23 on family and household relationships, Chapter 24 on ties to neighbors and friends, Chapter 22 on leisure activities in retirement, and Chapter 25 on the roles of that fraction of the aged who live in institutions.

In Volume II, Chapter 8, John Madge deals with many practical possibilities and issues faced by architects and community planners who must determine the policies, develop the programs, and design the housing and other facilities appropriate to older age groups. He describes five stages or turning points at which older adults confront basic choices of how and where to live. The five stages are, briefly: (1) The departure of grown children *reduces the housing requirements of a family, but it is difficult at best to design homes which contract or expand. It is not unthinkable, however, for communities or neighborhoods to be so "balanced" as to permit a change of residence without major disturbances in established networks of friends and neighbors. (2) With all the problems and issues inherent in meeting the housing needs of* retired *people, one conclusion seems to emerge. Retirees want to keep in touch with everyday life, but at the same time they want to maintain their own sense of privacy. They want "intimacy, but at a distance." (3) Although* bereavement *is an almost universal experience of the married couple (save where both spouses die together), little if any systematic attention has been given to the consequent adjustments in housing needs and living arrangements. (4) In sharp contrast, much work has been done to develop housing criteria for* infirm or disabled *older people, largely centered on considerations of comfort, convenience, and safety. (5) Finally, if and when the time comes that an older person can* no longer care for himself, *new arrangements must be made either at home or in an institution. Despite much experimentation, the situation today is such that these arrangements typically reflect either outmoded medical practice, or inadequate understanding of the patient's needs, or both.*

It has, perhaps, been symptomatic of sociological myopia to devote little attention to those dimensions of human life that are not exclusively social. In this sense, the concepts of age and community share a peripheral position. Neither can be defined in purely social terms, since one is rooted in biological processes, the other in ecological patterns. Yet it is the very expansiveness of these concepts that permits fresh insights into social behavior and organization. Explicit recognition of biological and ecological processes, moreover, directs attention to dynamic as well as static dimensions, and thus compels the social scientist to confront important issues of equilibrium and change.

Within this framework, the community can be viewed as a locality-group[1] whose interaction patterns and social organization are conditioned both by the endless succession of new cohorts of residents, and the aging of each cohort over its own life course. Such a perspective suggests three analytical approaches. Focusing first on the *community* as a social and territorial unit, the primary concern is with the age structure. Does age composition vary with type of community? What social and physical phenomena account for variations? What are the patterns of spatial distribution and social interaction within age strata and among them? How do ecological, social, and demographic processes impinge on the balance between the "built environment,"[2] social organization, and age-specific needs of individuals?

Turning next to the *individual* as a member of the community at successive stages of the life course, we examine such questions as: How do persons at each stage adapt to distinctive characteristics of different types of communities? How do the social context and spatial arrangements of the community facilitate or constrain instrumental activities and expressive interaction throughout the life course? What is the subjective meaning of community for children, adolescents, adults, and older people; and what age-related characteristics or conditions color orientations to the community?

Finally, the flow of *cohorts* across communities calls attention to the impact of migration. What are the age patterns of mobility? How do cohort residence histories reflect social change? What are the consequences of intercohort differences in community experiences for individuals within cohorts, and for the sociocultural structure of communities?

---

[1] The concept of "community" has generated considerable controversy in sociological literature. See Popenoe (1968, pp. 82–90) for a summary of various analytic uses of the concept. Parsons' definition (1951, p. 91) provides the basis for this chapter: "A community is that collectivity the members of which share a common territorial area as their base of operations for daily activities."

[2] The "built environment" refers to the man-made structures that constitute the physical and spatial context of social life.

1 Age structure of the community

At a given moment in time, a community is a sociospatial unit consisting of persons who belong to various age strata. The relative sizes of the strata vary in different types of communities, and the pattern of these variations illustrates the interconnections among age, the physical environment, and social structure. Further, as the conjunction of ecological and biological processes alters the contours of the community's age pyramid[3] over a period of time, there are implications for both individuals and organizations within the community.

AGE COMPOSITION

In general, there appear to be three ecological axes of differentiation in the relative sizes of the age strata: (1) among rural, urban, and suburban places; (2) among communities with different bases of functional specialization; and (3) among ecological areas within cities. If the age distribution of the total population is used as the benchmark, patterned variations in community age structure become apparent.

Rural communities have higher proportions of children and older people than central cities, and fewer adults in the productive years. Small villages (under 1,000 population) outside urbanized areas have the highest proportion of persons over 65. In 1950, this age group constituted 13.5 per cent of the small village population in the United States; and in some regions, such as the North Central, almost 16 per cent of the village population was over 65 (Duncan and Reiss, 1956, pp. 48, 49; see also Sanderson, 1942). More striking is Conrad Taeuber's observation that "there must be a considerable number of small towns (in the Midwest and South) which have 25 per cent or more of their population in the 65 and over bracket" (personal communication). Arensberg and Kimball (1968, p. 155) note a similar pattern in Ireland, where rural counties have much higher proportions of older people than urban counties do. The suburban population is also characterized by a "substantial excess" of children, but typically has "relative deficiencies" of older people (Duncan and Reiss, 1956, p. 120). For example, in the early years of both Dagenham, England, and Levittown, New York, more than 40 per cent of the residents were under 13 years old, while less than 1 per cent were over 65 in Levittown as compared with 9 per cent in the United States as a whole (Dobriner, 1963, p. 93), and 2 per cent were over 60 in Dagenham as compared with 17 per cent in England and Wales (Willmott, 1963, p. 23).

Aside from urban, rural, or suburban variations, community age composi-

---

[3] A normal population not affected by migration assumes the shape of a pyramid in its age distribution. Natural increase, immigration, and emigration alter the contours of the pyramid. See, for example, Sorokin and Zimmerman (1929, p. 543), who describe the processes producing "spindle" and "top" shaped pyramids.

tion differs according to the economic base. Entertainment and recreation centers have higher proportions of persons over 21 than do other communities of comparable size and metropolitan status; military and public administration places, as well as "college towns," have younger populations (Duncan and Reiss, 1956, p. 304). There are a preponderance of adults between 18 and 30 in Berkeley, California, and in Madison, Wisconsin (Jones, 1966, p. 117), for instance, whereas 28 per cent of the population of St. Petersburg, Florida, is over 65 (Volume I, Chapter 6, p. 123).

Within the city, too, ecological zones have different proportions of young and old, as the differences among census tracts in Seattle attest (see Figure 6 · 1). In communities otherwise as disparate as Belfast and Harlem, demographers note that the inner zone, or commercial center, typically contains few children, and that the proportion of the very young increases with distance from the center (Jones, 1966, pp. 116–121; Frazier, 1961, p. 169). Patterns of urban age distribution are often associated with variations in fertility and mortality rates of religious or social class segments of the population. For example, the ecological areas of Belfast, Ireland, that have the highest proportion of children and adolescents are those that are predominantly Catholic (Jones, 1966, p. 119). In Newark, as in other northern cities, the low-income ghettos of the inner city are the zones with large numbers of children (Janson, 1968, pp. 158–162). The "slum belt" of San Juan, Puerto Rico, which is the zone with the lowest median income, also has the lowest median age: 17.7 years, compared with 23 years for the total city (Caplow, Stryker, and Wallace, 1964, pp. 48, 57–58).

AGE SEGREGATION

Of more interest than the mere size of the strata is their spatial arrangement and the opportunities for social interaction within and across various age lines. In certain communities sociospatial barriers tend to segregate the age strata. For example, if Dagenham in England or Levittown in New York is typical, many "new" suburbs are characterized by age homogeneity. Even in older suburbs or urban neighborhoods where the age mix may be more heterogeneous, the pattern of daily activities among children and young mothers, or older people, often precludes contacts with persons outside their own age group. Beyond the family and neighborhood, contacts are further limited by the tendency of organizations to be age-graded.[4] Churches, for example, have separate children's services, youth groups, and senior citizen clubs; PTA membership is confined to those in the same stage of the family cycle. For many children and young adults, then, the only contacts with older people are those within their own families. From the viewpoint of younger persons in such

[4] See, for example, Seeley, et al. (1963, pp. 86–117), who present a detailed description and analysis of age-grading in schools and recreational activities within a suburban community.

FIGURE 6 · 1   *Age and sex differentials, selected census tracts, Seattle, 1960**

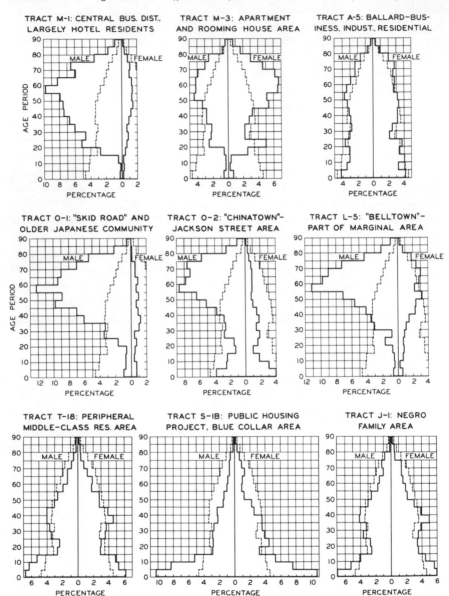

* The pyramid in each panel drawn in light dashed lines represents the total population of Seattle.

Source: Schmid, 1944; as reprinted in Schmid, 1968, p. 424.

communities, the old, like the poor, are invisible, even though both the number and proportion of older people in the society as a whole are increasing (Volume I, Chapter 1, p. 3; Chapter 2, pp. 16–18, 21).

There are also various special types of age-segregated residential settings. Retirement communities, both planned and unplanned, consist of a single age stratum. That is, some older people choose to live in "retirement villages" or in housing projects for the elderly. Others, trapped by poverty, bound by ethnicity, or attracted by the cosmopolitanism of the city, remain in inner city neighborhoods that contain disproportionate numbers of older people. In both cases, daily contacts with those of other ages are minimal. Similarly, college campuses and boarding schools constitute age-limited communities, in the sense that students interact neither with the very young nor the old. [*See Parsons and Platt, Chapter 7, on higher education.*] The Israeli children's villages represent another type of age-segregated settlement, in which the young from infancy on live in residential enclaves within the kibbutz, but have daily contact with parents and other adults at prescribed periods.

The *consequences* of spatial or social segregation extend in two directions. On the one hand, horizontal integration—or age-homophily (i.e., shared interests and values) among persons in the *same* stratum—is strengthened. According to some studies, for example, when older people are highly concentrated in the same neighborhood, they are more likely to have local friends and to visit with neighbors (Volume I, Chapter 6, p. 126; Chapter 24, pp. 567–570). To be in the minority in a largely age-homogeneous neighborhood can be tantamount to social isolation, as Gans (1967, p. 161) implies when he reports, "Although some elderly Levittowners were able to assume quasi-grandparental roles toward the street's children, others were lonely and uncomfortable among the young families. . . ." It is not only older people who find relations with age-similars rewarding. Mothers of young children express a preference for living near others in the same stage of the family cycle, so that they can share problems of childrearing, and exchange help or advice. And peer group solidarity among college students is undoubtedly enhanced by residential segregation. [*See Parsons and Platt, Chapter 7.*]

On the other hand, age segregation may be dysfunctional as it operates vertically to reduce community integration *across* age strata. Here the consequences for the community and society are complex and little documented by research. To what extent are discontinuities in youth culture and childrearing practices affected by situations of age homogeneity? If either community population distribution or social organization minimizes meaningful interaction between persons of different ages, what are the mechanisms (other than family interaction) of anticipatory socialization? That is, how do persons at each stage begin to learn values and behavior appropriate to subsequent age-related roles if contacts are primarily with age peers? How are communication and consensus between strata achieved? Can youth-generated innovations be diffused through the older strata under conditions of age-segregated residence? To what degree does geographic separation of older parents from their adult offspring loosen affective ties between generations? (See Volume I, Chapter 23.)

UNDERLYING PROCESSES

The size of the age strata within a community, and their spatial pattern at any given time, does not ordinarily remain static. Many processes are at work to change the size, composition, and location of the strata, and these changes in turn exert pressures on the physical and social environment. Ecological, social, and demographic processes are intertwined.

Age structure and the built environment Although buildings constitute an enabling rather than a determining influence on social organization, the man-made environment undoubtedly affects the age structure of the community (Gutman, unpublished). Perhaps the most important factor is the *housing supply.* New houses (especially moderately priced single-family dwellings) attract young families with children in both suburbs and cities. To a large extent the "newness" of Dagenham and Levittown, in conjunction with other housing characteristics, accounted for the youth of their initial population. Willmott (1963, pp. 22–23), noting the effect of time on the age distribution of a new community, comments: "One of the characteristic problems of any new settlement is that its population is 'unbalanced' in age; it is made up overwhelmingly of couples with young children, these being the kind of people most likely to need a home and most prepared to move to a new district to get one." After 10 years of settlement, the proportion of children under 10 in Levittown, New York, had decreased from more than 40 per cent to less than one third, and the percentage over 65 had tripled (although still far below the national proportion) (Dobriner, 1963, p. 93). The effect of community "aging" is even more clearly seen in Dagenham, where 27 years after it was built the proportion of children had decreased from 44 per cent to 20 per cent, and those over 60 constituted 16 per cent (as compared with 2 per cent in the beginning) (Willmott, 1963, p. 23).

Another aspect of the physical context of communities that affects age composition is the *type of housing* available. Small apartments in central cities discourage occupancy by families with children, at least those with sufficient income to exercise options. A study of the demographic characteristics of a Tokyo neighborhood explains certain peculiarities in the age structure by the large number of one-room apartments, which function to bar families with children (Dore, 1958, p. 23). By the same token, suburban zoning regulations prohibiting apartment construction in many American communities exclude older people.

To the degree that age and income are related, the *price of housing* also affects the age composition of a community. Comparing two census tracts in Etobicoke Township (outer Toronto), one in which the median value of housing was $19,355 and the other $34,573, Clark (1966, p. 87) found that 33.5 per cent of the homeowners in the first neighborhood were between 20 and 34 years old, while only 20.8 per cent in the more expensive area were in that age stratum.

The supply, location, and arrangement of *other structures* and facilities also influence the age composition of a community or neighborhood. Young families locate near schools and playgrounds; old people depend upon nearby shopping centers, churches, or public transportation (Volume I, Chapter 6, p. 128).

The built environment, then, not only takes shape as a response to age-related needs of community members, but also operates to influence the patterns of settlement and resettlement of the several age strata.

Changes in community role structure Age strata in a community expand or contract in response also to changes in the supply of age-related role opportunities. Thus urban centers in the United States received an influx of young adults from European countries and from rural areas when industrialization created job opportunities in the cities. Conversely, New England towns lost adults in the productive years as textile factories moved, just as the mechanization of agriculture reduced the size of the middle age stratum in farm communities. A further example of the consequences of an inadequate supply of work roles is cited in a study of the Jewish community in Providence, Rhode Island. There, a low sex ratio in the age group 25—44 of that ethnic segment has been attributed to "sex selective migration from the community to places of greater economic opportunity" for college-educated males (Goldstein and Goldscheider, 1968, p. 45).

A major domain of local responsibility within which age-specific roles can be manipulated is that of education. Desire for "better" education for their children motivates some parents to leave the city, shrinking the numbers in the youngest stratum. On the other hand, the inducement of state-supported higher education may account for increased proportions of young people in certain communities, as in California, for example.

The community, however, is more than a supplier of roles for the several age groups. As a political and social unit, the community may also assign individuals to specific age-related roles, establish age criteria for role entry or exit, and define age-appropriate behavior. The basic mechanism for age-grading throughout the early years is the educational structure of the community.

In the United States, localities make their own rules regarding age of entry into kindergarten. With the growth of nursery schools, moreover, an additional differentiation has been introduced in the early childhood stratum.

Some communities, in fact, develop such detailed and specific rules for each age segment that "one might say that terms for age grades—especially for children—are carried almost to the ultimate refinement. Not only is there . . . a sub-society of four-year-olds, as distinct from five-year-olds . . . but a system of expectations and a system of obligations as well" (Seeley, et al., 1963, p. 86). Twelve-year-olds may be defined as children if they are in the sixth grade of an elementary school, but are considered "pre-teens" with more privileges and responsibilities if they attend junior high school. Local custom also plays a role in dictating the "proper" age for adolescents to begin dating. In upper-middle-class communities, such as Crestwood Heights, youth is a time of "rushing at experience," as children are permitted or required to engage in growing-up activities at an early age (Seeley, et al., 1963, esp. pp. 69–73). Particularly for the young, then, whose major roles are enacted in the community, local norms define age-appropriate behavior.

Variations in community size and density can affect the bases for assignment to age statuses. In small towns, age and many related attributes of the individual are *known* by virtue of family membership, reputation, or long contact. Because of the transitory and segmental nature of social relationships in the city, however, characteristics such as age and class must often be *inferred* from appearance, dress, and mannerisms.[5] Thus the anonymity of urban transactions allows adolescents who are under the drinking age to purchase liquor, if they "appear" older.[6] Similarly, older persons may "pass" as younger in those social situations which are typically urban.

Aging within the community Change in both the social and the ecological structure of the community is inevitable. First, since communities are not closed systems, age-related role opportunities and definitions within the community are responsive to political, economic, and social trends in the larger society. Second, the built environment is also altered with the passage of time, by construction, renovation, decay, or demolition of buildings. A third element of change is the ineluctability of the aging process itself, which can disturb the balance between ecological and social structures.

The *housing* situation of the new suburb is a case in point. As the early experience of the British New Towns attests, architectural homogeneity is often coupled with age homogeneity at the time of settlement. That is, whatever the sequence of cause and effect, many new suburbs consist not only of

---

[5] Form and Stone (1957) found that "style symbolism" (manners, dress, conversational style) was the symbolism most frequently used by urban respondents in appraising social class status of others.

[6] See Wirth's classic description (1938) of urban modes of interaction.

persons in the same stage of the family cycle, but also of houses similar in size.[7] As the original residents age with the community and their families shrink in size, a dearth of small dwelling units presents them with two alternatives: they must maintain homes no longer suitable for their needs, or relinquish valued interpersonal ties by moving. Many elect to stay. As a consequence, the children of these families, having grown and formed their own nuclear families, find an insufficient supply of housing available, and so migrate to other communities. Thus a changing age distribution superimposed on a less flexible physical environment results in enforced geographic dispersion of kinship groups.

Similarly, the aging of a homogeneous young population can place severe strains on community *facilities*. At the outset, the preponderance of young families means a high birth rate. Rapid population growth, in turn, increases the demands on the educational system in particular, and on other child-oriented agencies as well.[8] When the relative proportion of youth and older people changes, however, community resources must be reallocated to permit the phasing out of youth-centered services, and the expansion of caretaking facilities for older residents. Organizations in a variety of institutional spheres —leisure, religion, education, health—may experience strain as personnel and programs adjust to, or fail to cope with, the needs of a different age stratum.

Nor are these trends and pressures confined to age-homogeneous suburbs. The density and diversity of the city create an even greater challenge for subsystems oriented to the needs of particular age groups. Within the central city, ecological processes of invasion, dispersion, and segregation alter the social configuration of neighborhoods. And the consequent changes in age distribution often compel the urban polity as well as voluntary organizations, economic establishments, and caretaking agencies in local areas to redefine goals or reformulate policies.

A TYPOLOGY OF COMMUNITY AGE STRUCTURE

This excursion into the dynamics of community age structure begins to suggest a typology that might prove useful in explaining the relationship between age and community. At one extreme is the "self-replenishing" community, with a heterogeneous and stationary age structure and little net migration over time. At another extreme is the community composed of a single cohort, whose children move away as they grow up, and whose members age and die out to-

[7] Willmott (1963, pp. 1–27, 38–39) notes that in Dagenham, with a population of over 90,000, and containing 27,000 houses, only 4 per cent of the dwelling units had one or two rooms. The overwhelming proportion of houses had two and three bedrooms.

[8] Willmott (1967, pp. 389–390) describes some of the consequences of an "unbalanced" age structure as it changes over time for public housing and social services in British New Towns.

gether. Intermediate types include the "fished out" rural community, whose young adults continually migrate to the city; or the "gold rush" community, built by an influx of adventuresome youths.[9] These and other types of community age structure are the result of complex combinations of age-specific fertility and mortality rates and age patterns of in- and out-migration in dynamic interplay. Thus, the "self-replenishing" community may exhibit an age structure quite similar to that of the "self-contained" community in traditional societies. However, it is *migration* that accounts for the first type, whereas *births and deaths* alone are the source of stabilty in the second. The intricate relation between process and structure is further illustrated in the case of communities with a bimodal age distribution. Such a distribution in the "fished out" type reflects a continuing *exodus* of young adults, but periodic peaks of *in-migration* can produce the same age structure.[10] Each type has its characteristic patterns, not only of age composition, migration, and vital processes, but also of social and ecological change.

2 *The community member over his life course*

Just as the age structure of the community changes over time, so do the adaptations of the individual to his community vary at successive life stages.

From infancy on, both the territorial boundaries and the social significance of community are relative to the fact and place of residence.[11] And, since residence is the locational referent of the family, the individual's relationship to the community varies with his age and, more specifically, with age defined in terms of family cycle stage. Thus, his community experiences in the early years are filtered through the perspectives of child-as-offspring; later it is adulthood linked with marital status that mediates his adaptation to the community.

At each age and stage of the family cycle, there are variations in the extent to which the individual obtains and transmits ideas, values, and rules of behavior in community interaction, in the intricacy of a network of relationships based on propinquity, and in the uses of and contributions to local services and facilities. The pattern of these variations suggests that the scope of the spatial system and the salience of the relational network surrounding the home may be linked to age-specific needs and capacities. Each stage of the

[9] These ideal types were suggested by Robert Merton and by John and Matilda Riley in a seminar on age stratification. Because several different dimensions are involved, a few selected types seem more useful than the full property space that underlies them.

[10] Jones (1966, p. 117), for example, notes that "many cities . . . show an old and young predominance because they have grown in two phases, after the first World War and after the second."

[11] Parsons (1960, p. 277) describes residence as "the main point of articulation between [biological and physical reference points] and some of the distinctively *social* structures."

life course, then, can be characterized (through a modification of the Merton (1957, pp. 393–406) typology) as a period of predominantly local or predominantly cosmopolitan adaptation to both territorial and social aspects of the community. Spatially, for example, the effective frame of reference at certain ages may be the neighborhood or local community, while at others the total metropolitan area or wider environment constitutes the relevant physical space (see Figure 6 · 2). With respect to the community as a social unit, differences stem from the nature of social networks in which the individual is likely to be involved during his early, middle, and later years. Just as his spatial field may be relatively circumscribed or extensive, so his interactional field may be concentrated or dispersed.[12] Age-related characteristics of the individual, and age-specific opportunities within the community, dictate the degree to which social and spatial adaptations are local or cosmopolitan.

What, then, are the conditions, at each stage of the life course, that affect the scope of territorial perspectives and social networks?

CHILDHOOD

Both the physical and social situation of the child make his orientation to community primarily local. Parsons' (1960, p. 276) description of community as the juncture of "locational reference" and ascriptive roles implies that, since childhood is the period, relative to subsequent stages, when ascriptive roles have primacy, a close-knit social network underlies local orientations. Role-partners often overlap, as each may be sibling and playmate, or neighbor and friend. Further, physical constraints on mobility, and the child's dependency status, limit territorial perspectives.

At this stage, moreover, the social functions of the local community are manifold. For the child, the community or neighborhood serves at once as the primary territorial unit, the supplier of role-partners, the major locus of activities, a pervasive cultural milieu, an intervening factor in his parents' socialization techniques, and a subjectively experienced phenomenon.

(1) *Community as territorial unit* In early infancy, of course, the child is largely confined to one room, and only gradually is his spatial field extended to wider areas of the home. During these early years even neighborhood is an "irrelevant concept," since the perceived physical environment does not go beyond crib, playpen, and carriage (Mann, 1965, p. 155).

With the child's increased mobility and autonomy, the block becomes the first effective community unit. As his social network is broadened to include peers as well as family members, the child's territorial range radiates from his home to a short distance on either side, and thence to the edges of the side-

---

[12] See Bott (1957) for a discussion of types of social networks.

FIGURE 6·2 *The spatial range of daily activities at different stages of the life course*

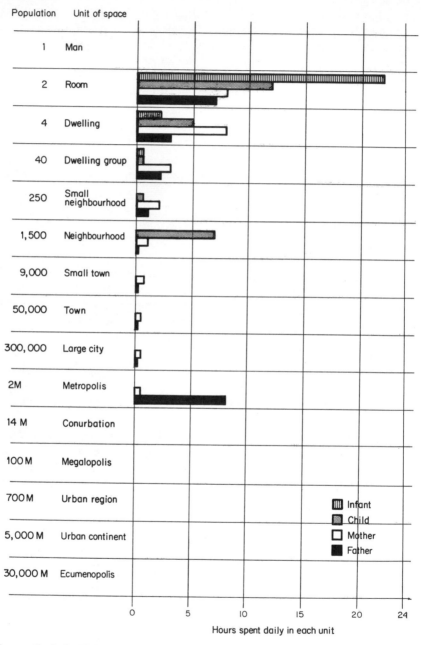

Source: Doxiadis, 1968, p. 381 (adapted).

walk.[13] In the suburbs, the familiar physical field may include the other side of the street, or it may be limited to contiguous backyards. Small children in the city may be barred by traffic from exploring beyond their own side of the street. At the same time, the density of urban design provides a varied, rather than extensive, physical imagery for toddlers. A study (Lukashok and Lynch, 1956) of the childhood memories of young adult Bostonians revealed that they perceived community in narrow dimensions, extending only as far as their own street. Some referred in their recollections to nearby streets as different neighborhoods. Most could recall with lucidity only the physical configurations of the area immediately surrounding home.

Although territorial perspectives are in the early years uniformly constricted by biological limitations, social class and place of residence introduce variations in localism as the child grows older. Middle-class children achieve some physical mobility with the bicycle, while urban children learn to use public transportation at an earlier age than their suburban counterparts. Although lower-class children may be granted greater freedom for independent exploration of the neighbohood, middle-class children of school age are exposed to wider geographical areas during shopping, visiting, and sightseeing trips with their parents.

(2) *Community as source of role-partners* The community, experienced by the child as a city block or neighborhood, is more than a comprehensible physical space. It constitutes the reservoir of peers from which playmates and friends are drawn, and for most American children, schoolmates as well. Propinquity plays a crucial role in determining friendship choices during latency, and tends to decline with adolescence. Gans (1967, p. 182) reports that the median distance of guests at children's birthday parties in Levittown increases with age (from 364 feet at age 3 to about 2,000 feet at age 12), and this appears to be the pattern for rural and suburban children in both the United States and England (although there is a dearth of empirical data on the relation between propinquity and friendship for children in urban ghettos).

Entry into school extends the territorial range, social networks become less concentrated, and new interests are acquired. Each of these contingencies contributes to a more ecumenical outlook; although relative to later stages of the life cycle, childhood is a time of local adaptations. Where the concept of neighborhood schools prevails, the school zone determines the geographical and social community of the child. At this period the size of the peer group is enlarged to include those attending the same school, so that friends may be either neighbors or schoolmates; and the child's spatial perspectives are expanded as he visits school friends who live beyond the area immediately adjacent to his own home. In this context it seems likely that upper-class children

[13] See Mann (1965, pp. 155–164) for a life-cycle approach to analysis of the neighborhood.

who attend boarding school are more cosmopolitan in spatial orientations (since they have cognitive familiarity with both school community and home community), while their interactional field continues to be concentrated—e.g., the same person is roommate, schoolmate, and friend. Similarly, if "open" schools supersede neighborhood schools in the ghetto, traveling or visiting patterns may provide the visual images necessary to convert "block dwellers" to "city dwellers."[14]

(3) *Community as locus of activities*   Just as the school setting supplies opportunities for more diverse role relationships and for familiarity with a wider geographical area, other social systems also become relevant with maturation, thus expanding the child's concept of community. Organized recreational and athletic activities, church groups, and clubs promote cosmopolitanism to a limited extent. Many of these organizations have links with regional or national associations, and by virtue of these the child is exposed to a broader frame of reference. However, the direct expression of organizational goals and the concrete pattern of activities remains in the physical space of the local community, in the social space of the local peer group, and within the cultural confines of local values and norms.

(4) *Community as culture area*   For the child, the community is more than a supplier of potential friends, an image of the physical world, and a resource for organized activities. As the social milieu within which his daily activities derive meaning, the neighborhood is a primary group, transmitting a system of values, beliefs, and rules of behavior specific to the locality. As a socializing agent, it reinforces or conflicts with prescriptions internalized in family relationships, so that "when [the] family and kinsfolk merge into it, its power as a defining and controlling force becomes particularly great" (Bossard, 1948, p. 526). In those ecological areas where spatial and ethnic boundaries coincide and function to strengthen community cohesiveness (as in the case of the Italo-Americans of Boston's West End [Gans, 1962a], or the Puerto Ricans of New York's Eastville [Padilla, 1958]), neighborhood social institutions present the child with an integrated culture, so that group identity and self identity are closely intertwined. Conversely, middle-class black families seek to escape the ghetto, not only because of the physical aspects of slums, but because of the incompatibility between family life style and neighborhood ethos.

(5) *Community and parental socialization*   The impact of the community on the socialization of the child lies not only in the pervasiveness and primacy of neighborhood culture. There is also an indirect effect in that the physical context and local norms influence childrearing practices. Recently

[14] Schorr (1963, Chapter 2) suggests that the block dweller's orientations, both cognitive and cathectic, focus on his neighborhood, while the city dweller conceives of the city as a territorial totality.

arrived Puerto Rican migrants in Eastville, for example, prohibit their children from playing in the streets in the belief that street contacts introduce their offspring to "bad company" (Padilla, 1958). An alternative course is taken by suburban parents, who specify as their reason for leaving the city the advantages for childrearing afforded by the safety of suburban streets and the privacy of single-family homes.[15] Yet there are urban planners (and presumably parents also) who feel that low density and homogeneity deprive children of those diverse though casual contacts available on the streets of the city that are necessary for development of cosmopolitan orientations among the young. According to this view, "semi-public surveillance" by shopkeepers, neighbors, and passers-by exposes children to optimum conditions of social control and easy sociability (Jacobs, 1961, pp. 29–88).

In addition to the implications of urban and suburban physical structure for supervision of children, parents are subject to the pressures of locally sanctioned childrearing methods. In an English housing "estate" (Mitchell and Lupton, 1954) and an American suburb (Gans, 1967), neighbors attempt to impose their standards of child behavior on others, and the costs of parental nonconformity are high. Among Levittowners who said that they had heard of quarrels among neighbors on their block, the largest proportion reported that these were in connection with issues of discipline and permissiveness. A single parental disagreement was generally amicably resolved, but repeated conflict over methods of childraising often resulted in open hostility, or occasionally in one of the families moving out of the community. One mother in the Liverpool estate, commenting on the difficulties of enforcing her own rules in the face of divergent techniques used by other parents, remarked, "You can't bring your children up as you would like to bring them up" (Mitchell and Lupton, 1954, p. 59). Similarly, Miller and Swanson (1960, p. 72) assert, "Any mother who deviates markedly from the childrearing practices of her neighbors is often subjected to social pressures." Describing one mother who did deviate, they conclude, "Had the family not moved from the neighborhood, they probably would have been forced to conform."

(6) *The meaning of community* Parental perception of the neighborhood as a socializing agent may focus on aspects that are quite different from those which are salient to the child. Age, as well as family status, greatly affects the subjective definition of the spatial and social environment, as Parsons (1960, pp. 251, 276) implies in discussing "the principal categories of *meaning* of territorial location to persons in roles." For the child, age-related capacities and dependency limit physical mobility and impose relatively narrow spatial boundaries. The neighborhood, encompassing over-

[15] Gans (1967, pp. 36–41, 236); Dobriner (1963, p. 58) refers to the "visibility principle"— i.e., ecological factors such as an open physical pattern and low density, which allow suburban mothers quick visual supervision of their children.

lapping and significant social relationships, represents to him the security of the visually familiar and the intimacy of primary bonds.

ADOLESCENCE

Individual maturation and societal role definitions extend the potential scope of community interactions and orientations at adolescence, while the physical and social structure of the community either encourages or inhibits this potential.

Having developed physical abilities and cognitive skills necessary for using technological modes of transportation, the adolescent is capable of greater *physical mobility*. While he is being "socialized out of" his family of orientation, relationships and activities no longer center exclusively on the home and neighborhood. At the same time, parents grant greater latitude with respect to time and space: he may be away from home for longer periods, he may travel further afield, and he is less accountable for his use of leisure time. At this period, the adolescent explores larger areas of town or city in conjunction with new leisure interests and in pursuit of more diverse social contacts (Bernard, 1939, p. 660)—or perhaps in response to the need for establishing symbolic distance between himself and home. The most important addition at this stage to his store of sociospatial experience is familiarity with the "center" of town or with the inner city. If parents provide the "right" amount of freedom, and the community or family supply either accessible public transportation or automobile, the spatial orientations of the adolescent become increasingly cosmopolitan. Transportation is, in fact, a major resource for the adolescent. It gives him access not only to places, but to peers —and when stimulating places and persons are not available, movement becomes an end in itself. For youth, "having a car" represents more than a mechanism for extending the territorial and social boundaries of the community. Merton suggests (personal communication) that one aspect of its symbolic importance lies in "the ever-present *potentiality* of moving freely and rapidly into broader areas—self-selected areas." Coleman (1962) and others emphasize the meaning of the car as a symbol of adult male status.

Within the local community, changes in psychosocial needs of individuals at this stage generate pressure for age-specific facilities. In comparison with his earlier years, the individual now seeks: (1) more frequent opportunities for peer group interaction; (2) an enlarged role repertoire; (3) alternative occupational role models; (4) greater diversity in contacts and activities; and (5) visual and spatial privacy, especially vis-à-vis adults. How do communities supply, or fail to supply, interaction opportunities, roles, activities, and physical space appropriate to the needs of adolescents?

Casual observation, as well as sociological study, shows that adolescents in "urban jungle" and "urban village,"[16] as well as in small towns, collectively pre-empt particular portions of community space. These areas are defined by them as both public and private——public in the sense that the space is outside the home and available to many; private because physical and social entry is selective (other age strata are excluded, as are nonclique members). Whether the physical form is sidewalk edge, street corner, or soda shop, the social function is to permit convenient, casual, and diverse contacts with peers. Adolescents differentiate public place from family place; the former is an area outside of parental jurisdiction. Thus, by extension, public behavior is not directly subject to parental sanction, as is behavior in the home. If the spatial definition of the "hangout" area contributes to the adolescent's sense of emancipation from the family, so the rules of interaction allow release from the tensions generated by the school. That is, rules for behavior while "hanging around" are relatively amorphous and peer-imposed (assuming a certain degree of tolerance by the community for this form of "nonactivity"), in contrast with the norms in a bureaucratic and authoritarian educational system. The costs of "hanging around" are low, both in money and in commitment, and the returns are high: peer contacts, observation of street life, and freedom from familial constraints. Central cities obviously offer a greater number and variety of places for such unstructured socializing than smaller communities do, and it may be for this reason that families with adolescents, in an English survey, chose to live in the city rather than in suburban New Towns (Morris and Mogey, 1965, pp. 24–25). Adolescents whose parents had relocated in a housing estate outside of London adjusted to the inadequacies of the suburban environment by spending their evenings in East London, often catching the last tube back (Young and Willmott, 1957, pp. 116–117). By the same token, teen-agers in Levittown complained of the failure of suburban design to meet their needs——shopping centers, which afford the anonymity and visibility necessary for street interaction, were too far from residential areas for easy access by nondrivers, and there were too few small stores for "hanging out."[17] Low-density areas also set limits on the potential size of age-similar peer groups, curtailing possibilities for forming new friendships.

In addition to space for casual contacts, the most frequent demand (whether articulated or not) adolescents make on their communities is for *recreational facilities*. The age-specific requirements are protection from adult intrusion, autonomy in planning, and separation of activities for each of the narrow age grades within the adolescent stratum. Again, new suburban

[16] Gans (1962a, p. 4) uses these terms to differentiate between those urban areas that "attract . . . the socially rejected," and those that are ethnic neighborhoods.
[17] Gans (1967, p. 206) titles one section of his study "Levittown is 'Endsville': The Adolescent View"; see also pp. 214–216.

communities, in comparison with central cities, often lack bowling alleys, skating rinks, and movies; but large cities, encumbered by size and bureaucratization, are less likely than smaller towns to provide *noncommercial* facilities for adolescents.

Despite increased mobility and emancipation from parental constraints, the adolescent is still dependent on and vulnerable to the cultural context of his community (albeit a wider physical community than during childhood). It has long been recognized (especially in the literature of delinquency) that some inner-city neighborhoods are less than adequate in facilitating the transition between childhood and adulthood. Relative to the suburb, of course, the social density is high enough to permit a large pool of potential friends, and anonymity allows a measure of privacy. But lack of consistency between the culture of these areas and the culture of the larger society means that the adolescent internalizes "community specific" occupational and familial role definitions, so that discontinuities between life cycle stages are exacerbated by discrepancies between community subculture and the wider society. In bedroom suburbs, the problem of culture integration has other sources; occupational role models and opportunities are often nonexistent, and the homogeneity of the local population insulates the adolescent from exposure to a variety of life styles and values.

Even when community inputs are less than optimum, adolescent adaptations are more cosmopolitan than those in earlier years, both in terms of spatial perspectives and social networks. Those with specialized interests or hobbies now have friends who are neither neighbors nor schoolmates; others enlarge their sphere of relationships and territorial familiarity through extra-community organizations; some discover new role-partners and new physical environments in the course of part-time work or voluntary activities.

That adolescents attach *symbolic connotations* to the immediate environs seems clear. Coleman (1962, p. 84), examining ascriptive criteria in the adolescent status system of ten midwestern high schools, found that students mentioned "coming from the right neighborhood" more frequently than family or religion. While middle-class youth impute social ranking significance to home and neighborhood, lower-class boys interpret territory in a different sense.[18] For some, a corner or street or specified neighborhood space is tacitly acknowledged to be the domain of a particular group, who then control access to their "turf" by other adolescents. Novels and drama, as well as sociological research (Jacobs, 1961, pp. 47–50; cf. Gans, 1962a, p.

---

[18] An anthropologist's definition of territory is most relevant at this stage: territory is "that section of space that is defended by the occupying individual or social unit . . . and that has a definite size . . . as well as a specific internal structure" (Hediger, 1961, p. 36). Hediger suggests that the functions of territoriality for animals are derived from propinquity—i.e., to facilitate communication within the group and to assure an adequate supply of mates by preventing geographic dispersion.

118; Whyte, 1955, p. 255), suggests the centrality of "turf" in some adolescent subcultures—at least for those boys who, lacking the resources necessary for extending spatial and social perspectives at adolescence, remain intensely local. Thus, one observer, noting the youth of those participating in the Watts riots, interprets their action as the assertion of "a claim to territoriality, an unorganized and rather inchoate attempt to gain control over their community, their 'turf' " (Blauner, 1968, p. 291).

As adolescence ends with the close of the high school career, ties to the family of orientation and to neighborhood diminish. For some young persons, heterosexual relationships or occupational roles expand the social network, and this together with ". . . the daily travel to work may well complete the break with the neighborhood" (Mann, 1965, p. 160). Middle-class youth transfer local orientations from the community of family residence to the college community [see Parsons and Platt, Chapter 7], while others at this period begin to develop a cosmopolitanism so broad as to transcend commitment to locality.

ADULTHOOD

In the span between adolescence and old age, occupation and family composition mediate the relation between individual and community. Residential mobility, for example, is closely related to these variables. It is young families with children, rather than older people or the unmarried who are most likely to be movers. Job opportunities, as well as family housing needs, are an important incentive for change in residence (see Volume I, Chapter 6 · C). It has been suggested, in fact, that migrations may be of two types: job-connected, and life-cycle, the latter occurring at the time of marriage or retirement (Shryock and Larmon, 1965, p. 591).

When one writer claims that "the attention which the individual gives to the territory is related to his age," he refers not to age per se, but to family cycle status (Shepard, 1967, p. 33). In Western society it is not adulthood, but parenthood, that shapes community orientations. A British sociologist comments, "At the stage of life where the young person is employed and unmarried the neighborhood may well have its fewest functions" (Mann, 1965, p. 160). Gans (1962b, p. 631) maintains that "the unmarried and the childless are detached from neighborhood life." Individuals and couples at this stage often live in rented housing, typically in areas of high transiency. At the same time, without family responsibilities and with greater resources of time and energy than at later periods, physical mobility is at its highest. Thus locational choice and evaluation of the community rest solely on instrumental considerations, such as accessible transportation, cultural and recreational facilities, and employment opportunities.

For many young couples, the birth of the first child precipitates a change in life style and a redefinition of residence requirements. When these needs are met by purchase of a house, the roles of parent and homeowner coalesce to form the basis of a new commitment to community. At this time also, the spatial mobility and the social networks of husbands and wives diverge (Mann, 1965, pp. 161–162). Diurnal migration of men away from home and neighborhood fosters cosmopolitan perspectives with respect to physical space (Beresford, seminar) and interaction in the occupational system extends the range of social relationships. Thus, Susser and Watson (1962, p. 125) observe, "Separation of home from place of work and multiplicity of roles tends to fractionalize community experience." Women, in contrast, tend to be confined by obligations of child care to the immediate neighborhood during the day (mobility in the evening varies with social class norms regarding use of babysitters and proximity of grandparents). For them also, children are catalysts in making local social contacts. Neighboring relationships and friendships may be initiated during the course of common carriage-pushing activities or joint supervision of child play. Testimony to the relation between propinquity and interaction for women at this stage is the expressed desire of housewives in Levittown to live near women with children of the same age, since childrearing problems vary with the age of the child. When offspring enter school, middle-class suburban mothers find themselves in an overlapping network linking family, neighborhood, and community organization. For the working-class woman, whether in British central city or American urban village, localism is reinforced by the tendency for kin or ethnic group to congregate in common residential areas. In Bethnal Green, a working-class area of East London, for example, 59 per cent of the married women lived in the same community as their parents (Young and Willmott, 1957, p. 21).

Where familism and home ownership constitute the basis of attachment to community for persons in the middle years, *social class connotations* seem likely to color the meaning of house and community (Beshers, 1962, Chapter 3). People oriented to achievement values and to mobility aspirations often define community in terms of socioeconomic status. Home and neighborhood then become visible manifestations of social position, and as such are maintained, valued, and defended from invasion by lower status racial and ethnic groups.

During the adult years as compared with earlier stages, *occupational statuses* assume new importance in influencing adaptations to the community. The pattern of limited residential mobility, combined with "social networks which are both close-knit and geographically contained," occurs most frequently among manual workers and entrepreneurs (Susser and Watson, 1962, pp. 136–146). Conversely bureaucrats, with varied residential experiences and segmental role relations, maintain more tenuous ties to the local community.

As developments in technology and social organization accelerate current *trends* in transportation, communication, and occupational systems, localism among adults will probably continue its long-term decline. Increasing scale of government, industry, and labor requires a highly mobile population, so that occupational roles entail residential moves or short-term traveling. Simultaneously, technological innovations reduce the space-time ratio involved in daily activities.[19] Men employed in higher bureaucratic positions often find that the locus of familial, occupational, and leisure roles, for example, may be suburb, satellite city, and inner city—all within the course of a single day. To the extent that such a situation curtails commitment to a particular community, cosmopolitan attitudes emerge. And for those adults whose major roles are occupational or intellectual rather than familial, community as a social and territorial unit may become irrelevant (Webber, 1963, 1964).

THE LATER YEARS

Generalizations about the community adaptations of older people are even more speculative than those about people at earlier stages—perhaps because the sheer length of the life span permits a larger number of permutations of experiences, roles, and relationships. Whereas children, for example, universally share the status of dependent offspring, and mature adults generally play the role of spouse and/or parent, the older person may be married or widowed, with or without children living in the home. Similarly, whereas children have no occupational status, and persons in the middle years are involved in occupational systems, older persons are variously employed or retired. Individual differences in health and in physical capacity are wider among older people. Each of these contingencies may affect community orientations in a different way.

Older people clearly value neighborhood relationships. Among the reasons most frequently cited for not wanting to move, despite housing inadequacies or economic problems, is the desire to maintain interpersonal ties in the neighborhood (see Volume I, Chapter 6 · C · 4). When friendship networks are local and the neighborhood also represents a cohesive sociocultural system, as in the case of older urban villagers, emotional investment in the community is particularly intense. Gans (1959, p. 19), referring to the effects of forced relocation on older residents of the West End, says, "The younger West Enders feel that they can adjust to a new neighborhood, but they expect that many of the older ones will not be able to do so and will die during the process." Less dramatic, but also indicative of attachments to the community, is the finding that older people in Dagenham, a British working-class suburb, were reluctant to move, although their homes were no longer functional. Long-

[19] Greer (1962, pp. 77–80) (space-time ratio is the cost in time and energy for traveling a given distance); see also Meier (1962).

established bonds involving home, family, and community were interwoven, and the tenacity of these ties transcended instrumental pressures (Willmott, 1963, pp. 39–40). For many older people, loss of a spouse or retirement reinforces these bonds, with the home becoming a surrogate for lost role-partners. In these situations, the continuity of community roles may compensate for the termination of marital or work relationships. Thus, a study of social isolation among older urban residents suggests that the role of neighbor may be a sequel to the role of breadwinner (Rosenberg, 1967, p. 146). For others, reduced physical capacity limits mobility, enhancing the value of a familiar environment and constricting the individual's spatial perspectives.

As in childhood, then, the subjective meaning of community for some older persons revolves about primary group relationships, especially when these are strengthened by the cumulative effect of years of stable residence. Yet the situation of the older person does not simply represent a return to the status of childhood with respect to the conditions that influence community orientations. There are several important differences. First, although mobility may be limited for some at this stage because of physical impairment, there are fewer social restrictions on movement—the oldster of 75 or 80 has finally escaped the obligation of obtaining parental permission (though, through an occasional reversal of roles he may need to get the permission of his grown children). Second, older people have had opportunities to accumulate spatial and social experiences, so that regardless of their current life style, visual images and reference groups are more diverse. Finally, local orientations at this stage rest on secondary as well as primary associations. Even if the older person has lost certain familial or occupational roles, he may retain civic, political, and religious affiliations. To the extent that these activities and interests are community-based they also create the climate for localism.

This reasoning suggests that there may be two kinds of locals among older people: in addition to those whose sociospatial perspectives focus on the neighborhood and on close-knit social networks, there are others whose localism is derived from contractual concerns (see Volume I, Chapter 6 · C · 3 · d and 6 · C · 3 · e). Certain older people discover that home ownership in itself constitutes a stake in the community (see Volume I, Chapter 6 · B · 6 · a), and that freedom from occupational and familial obligations allows greater participation in voluntary organizations.[20] Such circumstances at this stage of the life cycle may combine to deepen community commitment. Resources (time), investments (in property), and civic involvement—together with attachments to persons and place—promote parochial perspectives.

But, of course, not all older people are locals. For those with a measure of wealth, the later years may be the period when cosmopolitanism prevails—

[20] Mowrer (1958); however, some older people *reduce* their participation (Volume I, Chapter 21 · 1 · e).

again because of conditions unique to this stage of the life cycle. Release from occupational constraints or from family responsibilities (combined with adequate income) opens new options of residential location. For them, geographic space may be little more than an amenity. When age and retirement are defined as license to develop cultural or recreational interests, community becomes a matter of shared interests rather than shared space (Webber, 1963).

Still another type of older person finds community neither in propinquity nor in common interests. As he ages, the confluence of meager income, declining health, and loss of role partners attenuates his relationships in and with any community. Little is known, for example, about those individuals who reside in inner city areas characterized by single-room occupancy dwellings,[21] except that they appear to include disproportionate numbers of older people. Concepts of community may be meaningless to isolates who abrogate customary ties to persons or place.

Thus there are wide variations in community perspectives among older people. Moreover, for particular individuals, changes in family roles and in health and economic status may operate as cross-pressures. Advent of the empty nest period or of widowhood often is the occasion for reassessing housing needs (see Volume II, Chapter 8, by Madge). Living arrangements may require revision because of impaired health or physical disability. When reduced income and increased leisure accompany retirement, home and community assume different dimensions. Each of these exigencies may dictate changes in the residential nexus. Yet it is in just such situations that the older person is frequently caught in a bind. The advantages of moving, with potential gains in efficiency or economy of home management, must be balanced against the costs: loss of local friendships, of neighborhood bonds, or of secondary group affiliations. Questioned about their attitudes toward moving, older people cite reasons that reflect both instrumental values (housing and economic considerations) and expressive needs (ties to people and community) (Volume I, Chapter 6 · C · 4).

It appears, then, that the meaning of community for older people is an amalgam of the symbolism of earlier periods: security, familiarity, primary and secondary relationships. Yet there is an additional component. The typical older American, for example, has internalized societal values stressing achievement and individualism, and has developed attitudes and behavior reflecting these values (Volume I, Chapter 14). Accordingly, his community (whether wide or narrow in boundaries) is more than a social network and a spatial

---

[21] There have been studies of Skid Row residents (see, e.g., Bogue, 1963, p. 10, who estimates that the proportion of persons over 65 in Skid Row neighborhoods of forty-one American cities [1950] was about 35 per cent greater than the proportion of older persons in the total population of these cities), but these studies deal only with older male residents of particular areas. Similarly, there is a "hotel literature" (e.g., Hayner, 1964), but this does not focus on older persons who live in "single room occupancy" bulidings.

field. He evaluates it in the light of available transportation, suitable housing, health services, or leisure opportunities—those facilities that permit him to maintain independence and to retain as many roles as possible (Volume I, Chapter 23 · B · 1 · f and B · 2 · d). Instrumental as well as expressive needs color his concepts of community, so that it represents for him both an integrative social context and an enabling physical environment.

LIFE-COURSE AND COMMUNITY CHANGE

The individual whose community adaptations shift over his life course does not grow old in a static community. The age composition of the community is simultaneously changing. Thus many questions must be answered before the process of aging-in-a-community can be fully understood. What, for example, does it mean to be one of the old people who is left behind in a rural village? What does it mean to have moved into a suburban community as a young person, to have aged in that community while the community itself aged, and then to remain there as an older person during a large influx of young families? Questions such as these call attention to the crucial role of age in the life history of both individuals and communities; to the different, though interconnected, meanings of time for persons and for places; and to the dynamic interactions between changing community age structure and the aging community resident.

3 The impact of migration

The age composition of the community, and its implications for the individual, are affected not only by such intracommunity processes as those described in Section 1, but also by the broad movements of population across communities. Unlike immigration from foreign countries, which has fallen to a minimum in recent years, internal migration appears to be a persistent feature of our society. Such movements, combined with varying patterns of births and deaths, lead to the several types of community age structure suggested in the typology at the end of Section 1. They also bring into juxtaposition within the same community persons whose residence histories, as discussed in Section 2, can be widely divergent from one cohort to the next. [*Compare Chapters 2 and 11 in the present volume.*]

MOBILITY OVER THE LIFE COURSE

An important feature of migration is its age-relatedness. Full analysis of the residence histories of individuals, at least for the United States, still awaits compilation of the requisite data (see, e.g., Karl Taeuber, 1966, p. 417). But various estimates, based on partial residence histories or on net figures for population aggregates, indicate a remarkable stability in certain age patterns of migration from one cohort to the next.

First, there is a consistent tendency for migration to concentrate at the young adult ages. Among immigrants to the United States from foreign countries, the major waves over many decades have been drawn mainly from adults under age 45 (Conrad Taeuber and Irene Taeuber, 1958, pp. 67–68; Bogue, 1969, pp. 807–808). Similarly, internal migration comes to a sharp peak in early adulthood, as indicated by cross-sectional studies (see Volume I, Chapter 6 · C · 1) and by longitudinal information derived from census data. Thus Eldridge (1964), estimating net interstate migration for five-year cohorts, shows a propensity to migrate at ages 20–24 for a succession of cohorts born during the late nineteenth and early twentieth centuries (see also Shryock and Larmon, 1965, p. 580). Moreover, Eldridge notes a consistent tendency for each cohort reaching age 25 during a depression to respond in the same way: by a brief postponement of migration. Apparently neither changes in life style through historical periods, nor short-run economic conditions, appreciably alter the relation between life-cycle stage and migration. For recent cohorts as well as for earlier ones, assumption of work and family roles in young adulthood provides the impetus for high mobility.

Not only is the peak age of migration consistent, but within each cohort smaller proportions remain in the same size community as they grow older. Thus Karl Taeuber (1965, p. 455), reporting on partial residence histories for a sequence of cohorts, shows that, "within each cohort, the percentage residing in the same size category as [their] birthplace decreases with age. By age 18, the percentage in each case is down to 70–80, and it continues to drop sharply until at least age 34." Again, the pattern is similar for all cohorts, indicating that over the historical period studied, size-place redistribution levels off in the later years of the life cycle for every cohort.

Finally, as Taeuber shows in the same study, "persons tend to move to places not grossly dissimilar from those in which they previously lived [so that] redistribution up the urban hierarchy is [accomplished] . . . by a series of displacements, with farmers moving to villages and small towns, and residents of small cities moving to larger cities" (p. 460). This patterned sequence of size-place migration, called stage migration, appears in both the earliest and the most recent cohorts. Recent cohorts apparently share with those born in an earlier period a distaste for radical change in the size-density context of their environment.

COHORT DIFFERENCES IN INTERNAL MIGRATION

While such similarities among cohorts in the timing of migration suggest persistent patterns of adaptation to *life-cycle* exigencies, successive *cohorts* differ markedly from one another in several respects. As Bogue (1969, p. 797) notes, it is clear that "one cohort of persons may have a very different migration experience from another, depending on the economic, political, and social conditions that prevail during their lifetime." Within the United States, cohorts differ from one another, for example, in place of residence at birth and in direction of mobility.

(1) *The flow of cohorts*   The movement of cohorts from farm to village to city, and more recently to suburbs, affords dramatic illustration of the ways in which successive cohorts, which form the age strata of the society, can contribute differentially to broad social change. This movement is revealed in the study by Karl Taeuber (1965) of the residence histories of six cohorts in the period from before 1880 to 1958, a study that affords a unique opportunity to discern the extent and direction of population redistribution over the urban hierarchy (see Volume I, Chapter 6 · C · 2 · c).

The data (see Table 6 · 1) document the decline of a rural way of life in American society, with the accompanying trends toward urbanization and, more recently, suburbanization. For example, among the earliest cohort, about 39 per cent were born on farms, compared with about 21 per cent of the most recent. By age 24 the difference is even more striking: 29.5 per cent of the earliest cohort, 17.9 per cent of the middle cohort (born at the turn of the century), but only 10.2 per cent of the most recent (born in the 1930's) were still living on farms as young adults. Thus successive cohorts were increasingly likely to move away from the farm. Data compiled by the Department of Agriculture indicate that farm-to-city migration, which began slowly with the technological revolution in agriculture, and accelerated during the 1940's, may have passed its peak; and since the "overwhelming majority" of the smaller marginal farms are owned by middle-aged or older persons, who will give up their farming operations at retirement or death, the decline in farm-to-city migration seems likely to continue (*New York Times*, March 23, 1969).

In addition to differences in the rate of off-farm movement, the urban-suburban distribution of each cohort has changed over time. Earlier cohorts were more likely to settle in large central cities, while more recent cohorts migrated to the smaller cities and suburbs of metropolitan areas. At first, the proportion of each cohort living in large cities (over 500,000 population) at age 24 progressively increased (from 15 per cent of the earliest cohort to 20 per cent of those born thirty years later, but then declined (to 14 per cent of the most recent cohort). At the same age, 9 per cent of the earliest cohort and 20 per cent of the most recent were living in suburban communities (metropolitan places of less than 50,000 population).

A further indication of these trends in population redistribution appears in Table 6 · 2. The last column of the table shows the ratio of redistribution of larger to smaller places than the place of birth. Between birth and age 24, for

TABLE 6 · 1 *Size-of-place percentage distribution of cohorts at successive ages, United States*

Cohort: Age in 1958 and year of birth	Age	Total	Metropolitan			Nonmetropolitan			
			500,000 and over	50,000 to 499,999	2,500 to 49,999	Rural non-farm	2,500 to 49,999	Rural non-farm	Farm
18–24	Birth	100.0	15.5	16.6	6.4	6.7	16.7	16.7	21.4
(1933–40)	18	100.0	14.6	18.8	8.5	9.9	16.4	15.8	16.0
	24	100.0	13.9	21.0	9.2	11.3	19.0	15.4	10.2
25–34	Birth	100.0	17.5	17.5	6.4	6.5	16.1	16.6	19.4
(1923–33)	18	100.0	18.4	19.6	7.3	8.2	16.2	14.8	15.5
	24	100.0	18.0	20.5	9.7	11.5	15.4	14.5	10.4
	34	100.0	15.1	19.0	11.9	15.0	14.9	14.5	9.6
35–44	Birth	100.0	16.9	15.8	6.0	5.5	15.5	16.3	24.0
(1913–23)	18	100.0	18.6	18.4	6.7	6.4	16.2	14.2	19.5
	24	100.0	20.1	20.3	7.5	8.1	15.7	13.4	14.9
	34	100.0	16.8	19.3	10.4	12.9	15.0	13.9	11.7
	44	100.0	15.3	19.7	10.1	13.4	13.6	15.1	12.8
45–54	Birth	100.0	15.9	14.5	4.4	5.1	15.2	17.4	27.5
(1903–13)	18	100.0	17.8	17.9	5.4	5.9	15.8	15.0	22.2
	24	100.0	19.3	19.6	6.3	6.5	16.0	14.4	17.9
	34	100.0	18.7	20.2	7.8	8.5	15.8	13.9	15.1
	44	100.0	17.2	19.7	9.0	9.9	15.8	14.6	13.8
	45–54	100.0	15.7	19.3	9.9	11.2	16.0	15.3	12.6
55–64	Birth	100.0	14.8	12.5	4.1	4.6	15.1	17.2	31.7
(1893–1903)	18	100.0	15.9	16.0	4.7	5.0	15.4	15.7	27.3
	24	100.0	17.4	18.9	5.4	5.5	15.9	14.4	22.5
	34	100.0	17.9	19.6	6.2	7.3	16.2	14.3	18.5
	44	100.0	18.1	20.6	6.1	7.9	16.1	13.9	17.3
	55–64	100.0	15.6	20.2	7.7	10.7	16.4	15.2	14.2
65 and over	Birth	100.0	12.5	10.8	3.5	4.4	12.9	17.2	38.7
(to 1893)	18	100.0	13.7	13.3	3.9	4.5	14.4	16.4	33.8
	24	100.0	14.9	15.5	4.3	4.7	15.2	15.9	29.5
	34	100.0	15.3	17.6	5.2	5.7	16.5	16.3	23.4
	44	100.0	15.3	18.0	5.1	5.6	16.4	16.1	23.5
	65 and over	100.0	12.7	18.8	7.4	8.4	18.8	19.4	14.5

Source: Karl E. Taeuber, 1965, p. 452.

example, this ratio was 2.2 for those born before 1893, increased to 2.6 for the 1903–1913 cohort, and declined to 1.5 for the most recent cohort.[22] Karl Taeuber (1965, p. 457) notes the process of "changing balance between concentration in large metropolitan centers and dispersal within metropolitan areas. Older cohorts were redistributing up the urban hierarchy at a time when central cities were still growing rapidly, and suburbanization was not yet numerically dominant in metropolitan growth. Recent cohorts, with large proportions born and raised in large cities, are far more likely to participate in suburban movement at each stage in the life cycle."

(2) *Concomitants of urbanization* Much has been written about the

[22] The ratios in parentheses in Table 6 · 2 control for the problem that the high proportion of farm-born among the older cohorts can move only to larger places, whereas the high proportion born in large cities among the younger cohorts can move only to smaller places (Karl Taeuber, 1965, p. 457).

TABLE 6 · 2 *Comparison between size of birthplace and size of current place for cohorts at selected ages, United States (percentage distribution)*

Cohort: Age in 1958 and years of birth	Age	Same	Larger		Smaller		Ratio of larger to smaller	
			Size of place at specified age compared to size of birthplace					
18–24	18	69.4	19.0	(22.5)	11.6	(14.8)	1.6	(1.5)
(1933–40)	24	47.4	32.5	(38.3)	20.1	(25.3)	1.6	(1.5)
25–34	18	74.7	16.3	(19.8)	9.0	(11.2)	1.8	(1.8)
(1923–33)	24	56.0	29.0	(35.2)	15.0	(18.6)	1.9	(1.9)
	34	46.9	32.9	(39.6)	20.2	(25.5)	1.6	(1.6)
35–44	18	75.6	16.7	(20.1)	7.7	(10.2)	2.2	(2.0)
(1913–23)	24	62.0	27.5	(33.1)	10.5	(13.8)	2.6	(2.4)
	34	48.2	34.2	(41.2)	17.6	(23.2)	1.9	(1.8)
	44	45.7	36.8	(44.5)	17.5	(23.9)	2.1	(1.9)
45–54	18	74.6	18.1	(21.5)	7.3	(10.1)	2.5	(2.1)
(1903–13)	24	63.4	27.4	(32.6)	9.2	(12.7)	3.0	(2.6)
	34	52.5	34.2	(40.7)	13.3	(18.3)	2.6	(2.2)
	44	47.3	36.6	(43.6)	16.1	(22.3)	2.2	(2.0)
	45–54	43.3	38.6	(45.9)	18.1	(25.0)	2.1	(1.8)
55–64	18	79.2	14.8	(17.4)	6.0	(8.8)	2.5	(2.0)
(1893–1903)	24	66.8	25.1	(29.4)	8.1	(11.8)	3.1	(2.5)
	34	56.0	33.1	(38.9)	10.9	(15.9)	3.0	(2.4)
	44	52.9	35.7	(41.9)	11.4	(16.7)	3.1	(2.5)
	55–64	44.4	40.2	(47.1)	15.4	(22.6)	2.6	(2.1)
65 and over	18	80.9	13.8	(15.8)	5.3	(8.6)	2.6	(1.8)
(to 1893)	24	70.0	22.7	(26.0)	7.3	(11.9)	3.1	(2.2)
	34	58.0	32.5	(37.1)	9.5	(15.5)	3.4	(2.4)
	44	57.3	33.0	(37.6)	9.7	(15.9)	3.4	(2.4)
	65 and over	41.5	44.2	(50.5)	14.3	(23.3)	3.1	(2.2)

Note: Figures in parentheses are based on totals excluding those not exposed to the possibility of movement to a larger place (born in cities of 500,000 and over) or to a smaller place (born on farm).
Source: Karl E. Taeuber, 1965, p. 456.

concomitants of this flow of population to the cities. Among these concomitants are a shift in the occupational structure from an agricultural to an industrial base, a growing sense of national urgency about the "problems" of urban concentration and sprawl, and the disappearance from American culture of a pastoral mythology and a rural nostalgia. The literature describing urban life style and social organization is voluminous and needs no review here. But the theory of age stratification points to consequences of the juxtaposition within the same community of cohorts stemming from different phases of the urbanization process.

For example, intercohort differences in residence history can be conceptualized as intergenerational disparity between parents and children in the community context of early socialization, similar to the disparity between first- and second-generation immigrants of an earlier era (see Wirth, 1928, pp. 218–222, 241–243; Gans, 1962a, pp. 56–58, 204–209; Padilla, 1958). In this sense, interest focuses on three types of families:

	Type 1	*Type 2*	*Type 3*
Parent:	Rural	Urban	Urban
Child:	Urban	Urban	Suburban

Since the sociocultural environment of the community leaves its imprint on relationships and values internalized in the early years, it is likely that intergenerational dissimilarity in community context of childhood reduces the core of shared experiences and meanings between parent and child. Among black and Puerto Rican families, for example, where the Type 1 pattern is not uncommon, the parent who has himself been socialized to a rural way of life may have difficulty in transposing the childrearing methods of his own parents to his children. Furthermore, reciprocal socialization assumes new forms and new importance when the child, who has more easily adapted to the complexity and heterogeneity of the city, transmits the norms of an urban milieu to his parent.[23]

Strain is also endemic in Type 3 family situations as a result of the disjuncture between community experiences of parent and child. A father whose childhood roles were enacted against the backdrop of city streets, whose activities and friendships were colored by urban physical forms and social density, or whose socialization was linked to the ethnic culture of urban neighborhoods, has a different set of experiences and symbolic referents than his suburban son. The latter's play partners, in contrast, are likely to be a small number of peers aggregated in a backyard or quiet street; his neighborhood and school environment is stratified along class or religious lines rather than ethnic dimensions; and his "semi-public" street encounters are virtually nonexistent. Again, the parent who was himself an urban adolescent, accustomed to the easy access of public transportation, has no analogue in his earlier experience for his suburban offspring's "cult of the car."

Even in Type 2 families, identity of place of childhood residence does not assure a similar context of socialization for parent and child. Membership in different cohorts means that each confronts a time-specific urban situation in his early years. Certainly the city of the trolley car, machine politics, and ethnic heterogeneity constituted a different childhood environment than does the contemporary urban scene.

COHORT DIFFERENCES IN IMMIGRATION FROM OTHER COUNTRIES

Just as intercohort comparisons of internal migration can be interpreted to explain the growth of cities and suburbs, so cohort analysis of immigration calls attention to the changing culture of cities and to the differing residential histories of the several age strata at any given time. The census data in

[23] Wirth (1964, p. 235) points to an analogous process when he says, "The Americanization of the immigrant parents takes place, if at all, through the medium of the children."

Table 6 · 3, which are arranged to trace several cohorts over the adult years, show that, with age controlled, higher proportions of the earlier, as compared with the more recent cohorts, were foreign-born. At age 40–49, for example (read diagonally up from left to right), 22.3 per cent of the 1880's cohort were immigrants, but only 4.6 per cent of the cohort born in 1911–1920 were of foreign birth. At age 30–39, 16.5 per cent of the 1890's cohort were foreign-born, in contrast to 3.7 per cent of those born in 1911–1920. Certain implications of this sharply decreasing proportion of foreign-born from one cohort to the next, considered in conjunction with the increasing racial heterogeneity of the urban population, are suggested by one writer on old age who asserts "Replacement of a nationality-oriented group of aged with a racially-oriented group may have vast latent consequences for politics, housing, etc." (Cain, 1967, p. 90). Similarly, Glazer predicted that as these trends in the ethnic composition of cohorts continue, religion and race, rather than national origin, would be the basis of ideological divisiveness in New York.[24]

Recognition of the crucial link between a decline in the "immigrantness" of successive cohorts and far-reaching sociocultural change is, in fact, the theme of a study of the Jewish community in Providence, Rhode Island. Asserting that "the character and leadership of a community are generally determined by persons in the middle-aged segments of the population," the authors believe that there will be major changes in the attitudes and values of that community as leadership passes from cohorts that consist largely of the foreign born, to more recent cohorts with "a sizeable majority" of second-generation persons, and thence to age groups composed primarily of third-generation Jews (Goldstein and Goldscheider, 1968, pp. 42, 44).

CONCLUSION

In summary, differences in the residential histories of successive cohorts reflect social change: urbanization, suburbanization, declining ethnicity of urban culture. Further, since membership in a cohort assigns individuals to a given age stratum at a particular period, the implications of these processes for individuals and families is in terms of differences in community experiences and perspectives between age groups and generations.

Each successive cohort, then, as it is propelled by the historical currents of its era, is a carrier of and contributor to social change. Each enters the community and encounters a sociospatial setting shaped by earlier demographic, ecological, and social processes; each contributes to ongoing changes by virtue of its characteristic composition. Within the community itself, shifts in the age structure due to the flow of cohorts and the aging of each cohort

---

[24] Glazer and Moynihan (1963, p. 41); it has been suggested that these predictions have been borne out in such events as the New York teachers' strike of 1968.

TABLE 6 · 3 *Changing proportions of the United States (white) population that is foreign-born*

(Age in parentheses)

Birth date of cohort	Period of observation							
	1890	1900	1910	1920	1930	1940	1950	1960
1911–1920				(1–9) 0.9	(10–19) 2.4	(20–29) 2.8	(30–39) 3.7	(40–49) 4.6
1901–1910			(1–9) 2.0	(10–19) 4.3	(20–29) 9.0	(30–39) 8.9	(40–49) 9.6	(50–59) 10.0
1891–1900		(1–9) 1.1	(10–19) 5.7	(20–29) 13.0	(30–39) 16.5	(40–49) 16.2	(50–59) 16.4	(60+) 17.9
1881–1890	(1–9) 2.2	(10–19) 5.6	(20–29) 17.9	(30–39) 21.4	(40–49) 22.3	(50–59) 22.0	(60+) 21.9	

Source: Cain, Leonard D., 1967, p. 91 (adapted).

over its own life course create new conditions of equilibrium or disequilibrium in social organization. Nor is the physical environment impervious to the impress of time. Concomitantly, the broad outlines of societal trends and community changes derive detail and meaning in the lives of individuals, whose needs and capacities as community members differ at various stages of the life course. As these individuals adapt to age-related role opportunities, services, and facilities in the community, new elements of potential strain, stability, or innovation are introduced. Thus time, expressed in individual aging, in ecological and social processes, and in historical movements, is a subtle and complex current running through every aspect of the interrelationship between age and community.

Works cited in Chapter 6

Arensberg, Conrad M., and Solon T. Kimball, 1968. *Family and Community in Ireland*, 2nd ed., Cambridge, Mass.: Harvard University Press.

Beale, Calvin L., interview, reported by *New York Times*, March 23, 1969.

Bernard, J., 1939. "The Neighborhood Behavior of School Children in Relation to Age and Socio-Economic Status," *American Sociological Review*, 4, pp. 652–662.

Beshers, James M., 1962. *Urban Social Structure*, New York: Free Press of Glencoe.

Blauner, Robert, 1968. "Violence in the City," in Strauss, Anselm L., editor, *The American City: A Sourcebook of Urban Imagery*, Chicago: Aldine, pp. 287–292.

Bogue, Donald J., 1963. *Skid Row in American Cities*, Chicago: Community and Family Study Center, University of Chicago.

———, 1969. *Principles of Demography*, New York: Wiley.

Bossard, James H. S., 1948. *The Sociology of Child Development*, New York: Harper & Brothers.

Bott, Elizabeth, 1957. *Family and Social Network*, London: Tavistock Publications.

Cain, Leonard D., Jr., 1967. "Age Status and Generational Phenomena: The New Old People in Contemporary America," *The Gerontologist*, 7, pp. 83–92.

Caplow, Theodore, Sheldon Stryker, and Samuel E. Wallace, 1964. *The Urban Ambience*, Totowa, N.J.: Bedminster Press.

Clark, S. D., 1966. *The Suburban Society*, Toronto: University of Toronto Press.

Coleman, James S., 1962. *The Adolescent Society*, New York: Free Press of Glencoe.

Dobriner, William M., 1963. *Class in Suburbia*, Englewood Cliffs, N.J.: Prentice-Hall.

Dore, R. P., 1958. *City Life in Japan*, Berkeley and Los Angeles: University of California Press.

Doxiadis, C. A., 1968. "A City for Human Development," *Ekistics*, 25, pp. 374–394.

Duncan, Otis D., and Albert J. Reiss, Jr., 1956. *Social Characteristics of Urban and Rural Communities, 1950,* New York: Wiley.

Eldridge, Hope T., 1964. "A Cohort Approach to the Analysis of Migration Differentials," *Demography,* 1, pp. 212–219.

Form, William, and G. P. Stone, 1957. "Urbanism, Anonymity and Status Symbolism," *American Journal of Sociology,* 62, pp. 504–514.

Frazier, E. Franklin, 1961. "Negro Harlem: An Ecological Study," in Theodorson, George A., editor, *Studies in Human Ecology,* New York: Harper & Row, pp. 165–174.

Fried, Marc, 1963. "Grieving for a Lost Home," in Duhl, Leonard, editor, *The Urban Condition,* New York: Basic Books.

Gans, Herbert J., 1959. "The Human Implications of Current Redevelopment and Relocation Planning," *Journal of the American Institute of Planners,* 25, pp. 15–25.

———, 1962a. *The Urban Villagers,* New York: Free Press.

———, 1962b. "Urbanism and Suburbanism as Ways of Life: A Re-evaluation of Definitions," in Rose, Arnold M., editor, *Human Behavior and Social Processes,* Boston: Houghton Mifflin, pp. 625–648.

———, 1967. *The Levittowners,* New York: Random House.

Glazer, Nathan, and Daniel Patrick Moynihan, 1963. *Beyond the Melting Pot,* Cambridge, Mass.: M.I.T. Press.

Goldstein, Sidney, and Calvin Goldscheider, 1968. *Jewish Americans: Three Generations in a Jewish Community,* Englewood Cliffs, N.J.: Prentice-Hall.

Greer, Scott A., 1962. *The Emerging City: Myth and Reality,* New York: Free Press.

Gutman, Robert. "The Social Function of the Built-Environment" (unpublished).

Hayner, Norman S., 1964. "Hotel Life: Physical Proximity and Social Distance," in Burgess, Ernest W., and Donald J. Bogue, editors, *Contributions to Urban Sociology,* Chicago: University of Chicago Press.

Hediger, Heini P., 1961. "The Evolution of Territorial Behavior," in Washburn, Sherwood L., editor, *Social Life of Early Man,* New York: Wenner-Gren Foundation for Anthropological Research, pp. 34–57.

Jacobs, Jane, 1961. *The Life and Death of Great American Cities,* New York: Random House.

Janson, Carl-Gunnar, 1968. "The Spatial Structure of Newark, New Jersey, Part 1, The Central City," *Acta Sociologica,* 11, pp. 144–169.

Jones, Emrys, 1966. *Towns and Cities,* New York: Oxford University Press.

Lukashok, Alvin K., and Kevin Lynch, 1956. "Some Childhood Memories of the City," *Journal of the American Institute of Planners,* 22, pp. 142–152.

Mann, Peter H., 1965. *An Approach to Urban Sociology,* London: Routledge and Kegan Paul.

Meier, Richard L., 1962. *A Communications Theory of Urban Growth,* Cambridge, Mass.: M.I.T. Press.

Merton, Robert K., 1957. *Social Theory and Social Structure,* rev. ed., Glencoe, Ill.: Free Press.

Miller, Daniel R., and Guy Swanson, 1960. *Inner Conflict and Defense*, New York: Holt, Rinehart.

Mitchell, G. Duncan, and Thomas Lupton, 1954. "The Liverpool Estate," in *Neighborhood and Community*, Liverpool: University Press of Liverpool.

Morris, R. N., and John Mogey, 1965. *The Sociology of Housing*, London: Routledge and Kegan Paul.

Mowrer, Ernest R., 1958. "The Family in Suburbia," in Dobriner, William M., editor, *The Suburban Community*, New York: Putnam, pp. 147–164.

Padilla, Ellen, 1958. *Up from Puerto Rico*, New York: Columbia University Press.

Parsons, Talcott, 1951. *The Social System*, Glencoe, Ill.: Free Press.

———, 1960. "The Principle Structures of Community," in Parsons, Talcott, *Structure and Process in Modern Societies*, New York: Free Press, pp. 250–279.

Popenoe, David, 1968. "The Sociocultural Context of People, Groups, and Organizations," in Indik, Bernard P. and F. Kenneth Berrien, editors, *People, Groups, and Organizations*, Teachers College, Columbia University, New York: Teachers College Press, pp. 73–93.

Rosenberg, George S., 1967. "Poverty, Aging and Social Isolation," Washington: Bureau of Social Science Research. Mimeographed.

Sanderson, Dwight, 1942. *Rural Sociology and Rural Social Organization*, New York: Wiley.

Schmid, Calvin F., 1944. *Social Trends in Seattle*, Seattle: University of Washington Press, pp. 93–97.

———, 1968. "Age and Sex Composition of Urban Subareas," in Nam, Charles B., editor, *Population and Society*, Boston: Houghton Mifflin, pp. 423–426.

Schorr, Alvin L., 1963. *Slums and Social Insecurity*, Washington, D.C.: Government Printing Office.

Seeley, John R., et al., 1963. *Crestwood Heights*, New York: Wiley.

Shepard, Paul, 1967. *Man in the Landscape*, New York: Knopf.

Shryock, Henry S., and Elizabeth A. Larmon, 1965. "Some Longitudinal Data on Internal Migration," *Demography*, 2, pp. 579–592.

Sorokin, Pitirim, and Carle C. Zimmerman, 1929. *Principles of Rural Urban Sociology*, New York: Henry Holt.

Susser, M. W., and W. Watson, 1962. *Sociology in Medicine*, New York: Oxford University Press.

Taeuber, Conrad, and Irene B. Taeuber, 1958. *The Changing Population of the United States*, New York: Wiley.

Taeuber, Karl E., 1965. "Cohort Population Redistribution and the Urban Hierarchy," *Milbank Memorial Fund Quarterly*, 43, pp. 450–462.

———, 1966. "Cohort Migration," *Demography*, Vol. 3, No. 2, pp. 416–422.

Webber, Melvin M., 1963. "Order in Diversity: Community Without Propinquity," in Wingo, Lowdon, Jr., editor, *Cities and Space: The Future Use of Urban Land*, Baltimore: Johns Hopkins Press, pp. 23–54.

———, 1964. "The Urban Place and the Nonplace Urban Realm," in Webber, Melvin M., et al., editors, *Explorations into Urban Structure*, Philadelphia: University of Pennsylvania Press, pp. 79–132.

Whyte, William Foote, 1955. *Street Corner Society*, 2nd ed., Chicago: University of Chicago Press.

Willmott, Peter, 1963. *The Evolution of a Community*, London: Routledge and Kegan Paul.

————, 1967. "Social Research and New Communities," *Journal of the American Institute of Planners*, 33, pp. 387–397.

Wirth, Louis, 1928. *The Ghetto*, Chicago: University of Chicago Press.

————, 1938. "Urbanism as a Way of Life," *American Journal of Sociology*, 44, pp. 1–24.

————, 1964. "Culture Conflict and Misconduct," in Reiss, Albert J., Jr., editor, *Louis Wirth: On Cities and Social Life*, Chicago: University of Chicago Press, pp. 229–243.

Young, Michael, and Peter Willmott, 1957. *Family and Kinship in East London*, London: Routledge and Kegan Paul.

7

Higher education and changing socialization

TALCOTT PARSONS AND GERALD M. PLATT

The essay by Parsons and Platt attacks the fundamental question of the effect of historical change upon socialization and hence upon the very nature of the aging process. The authors, postulating that the increasing differentiation in the role structure of Western society requires parallel adjustments in the personality structure, describe changes in education that operate to meet this requirement. Thus the development of the individual's capacity for full social participation, possible in an earlier era through childhood socialization within the family, has been moving up the stages of the life course through a graded school system, until it has now come to rest upon mass education at the college level.

Any assessment of the argument set forth here requires a recognition of the underlying assumptions. Some of these are explicitly introduced by the authors for the express purpose of simplifying the discussion; others are basic to Parsonian theory in general. The particular direction and conclusions of the present analysis appear to rely upon such assumptions as the following: primary socialization as the acquisition of basic values, not as the mere acquisition of specific knowledge and skills; location of the major responsibility for socialization in family and education, rather than in peer groups; continuity between family and education as structures for socialization, articulation of these structures with the economy, and the simultaneous development of all three; historical processes of structural differentiation as positive contributions to the adaptive capacity of the society; persistence of the dominant American value pattern of "instrumental activism," with its emphasis on striving toward an ideal order; and, of special relevance to this essay, differentiation of the academic subsystem of the society, which is guided by "cognitive rationality" in much the same sense that an advanced economy is guided by economic rationality. Some of these assumptions may perhaps appear unrelated to a sociology of age. Upon closer scrutiny, however, many connections with the age-specific model proposed in Chapter 1 of this book do not lie far below the surface.

The paper constitutes a major addition to Parsons' earlier analyses of socialization through its focus on the new stage, called "studentry"; through its insistence upon the systematic linkage between the emergence of this new stage and evolutionary changes in the society; and through its interpretation of the student dissent of the 1960's in terms of the strains engendered by these linked developments. The central hypothesis is that, whenever the socialization process is significantly extended in response to a structural differentiation in the society, the affected age group experiences "disturbances" until the new norms and expectations have become fully institutionalized.

For a sociology of age, the implications of the piece are as significant as the contribution made by this major hypothesis. The analysis sheds new light, for example, on the age structure of the socialization context and, more generally, on the characteristics of the age strata in the society as a whole. Thus within a socializing system—whether university, school, or family—there is ordinarily an age difference between the socializer and the person being socialized; for, as the several cohorts progress through the system, it is the older ones who have already acquired the understanding that must be transmitted to the novices. There is also a difference between socializer and socializee in the portion of the life span committed to the system: faculty members, like parents in a family, usually have long-term stakes in their respective institutions, while the younger members are typically merely passing through. Socialization itself can be viewed, then, not only as individual development, but as an important aspect of the age relationships in the society.

Also implicit, though not fully explicated, in the Parsons-Platt discussion is the difference among age strata in the quality, as distinct from the quantity, of educational experience. In sheer numbers, 72 per cent of persons aged 75 and over have had only 8 years of schooling or less, compared with 17 per cent of those aged 25 to 29 (as described in Volume I, Chapter 4, data for the United States, 1960). Such cross-sectional differences among age strata are the direct result of social change over the past decades, reflecting the steadily increasing number of years spent in school by successive cohorts. But further cohort differences between young and old must accrue also from the changes described by Parsons and Platt in the structure of socialization systems, as education has become emancipated from its religious and ascriptive bases, and as the approach to knowledge has become increasingly rational and disciplined. Indeed, past changes in the character of educational experience may account for many of the age-related disparities observed today in sense of mastery over the environment or in political and economic views, as well as in occupational achievement or in interpersonal competence (see Volume I, Parts Three and Four).

If the Parsons and Platt essay is not in itself sufficient proof that an age-based inquiry can be sociologically provocative, then one need only start to list the additional questions it summons to mind. Item: Will some future period of further differentiation of American society add still another socialization system? If the stage now called "early maturity" is affected, will the age of entry into adulthood once again be postponed, or will some drastic change occur in the existing models of pre-adult socialization? Are consequent disturbances again predictable, before the norms and expectations of the new system become institutionalized? Item: Is there a possibility of extension of socialization over the life course (as suggested by Eklund in Chapter 11, Volume II) within the Parsonian definition of socialization as value acquisition, not as the mere implementation of previously acquired values? Item: What process is involved toward the end of life, when individuals must learn to adjust to retirement or to widowhood, at an age when socializee can *no longer be younger than socializer? Item: Under what conditions do the oncoming cohorts change the existing structures, instead of becoming socialized to them? Is it possible, for example, that the student dissent of the 1960's, which is described as pressing toward "dedifferentiation," might produce a reversal in the long-term trend toward increasing differentiation both in the educational establishment and in the society?*

If such questions seem worth asking, then a re-examination of education and socialization from the perspective of a sociology of age certainly holds promise of fresh insights and new understandings.

Differentiation of the economy from the family and the concomitant growth of the educational institution have had enormous effects on personality development, fostering an articulation with a changing social environment through a continuing differentiation of the personality structure.[1] However, each phase of the institutionalization of education at which participation has approached universal involvement has had disruptive consequences for that age stratum and for society in general. Accordingly, this paper will focus on mass higher education, which represents the most recent expansion of the educational system, and its implications for contemporary college student unrest.

Our institutional analysis, involving family, economy, and education, will stress the family as well as education because we assume continuity of the socialization process served by these institutions. Historically, three periods of societal change can be distinguished, each connected with different levels of personality differentiation and socialization. The first of these changes occurred in the family and was connected with educational innovations; the latter two were associated with mass participation in education. Each of these historical changes is related to particular stages of the life course of the individual (see Table 7 · 1).

In the first of these three historical periods, changes in the family produced alterations in the character of the pre-Oedipal and Oedipal phases of the life course. The Oedipal phase interweaves with the latency phase, in which children are extruded from the household to continue their socialization in the achievement-oriented and universalistically oriented school system

We would like to thank Jackson Toby and the authors of the volume for their untiring help in editing and reorganizing this paper.

[1] This is a theme taken up by Parsons and Bales (1955); by Parsons (1964); and by Weinstein and Platt (1969). Among these, Parsons has paid particular attention to the function of the educational system in this process. This paper carries some of these lines of thought further. The paper also relies heavily on the general framework developed in Weinstein and Platt (1969).

TABLE 7 · 1 *Stages of life course associated with societal changes*

Periods discussed in this chapter	Life-course stages	Level of mass participation in education	Family and college	Youth culture (or peer solidarity)
	1a Infancy			
1	1b Oedipal childhood		Father away	
	2a Latency	Grade school		
2	2b Adolescence	High school		Operative in various forms at stages 2a, 2b and 3a
3	3a Studentry	College	Teacher "away"	
	3b Early maturity			

(Parsons, 1959b and 1964). We attribute Freud's preoccupation with the Oedipal crisis in part to the differentiation of the firm (or other employing organization) from the family and the consequent diurnal absence of the father from the household and from the early socialization process.[2] Freud's recognition of the "latency period" following the Oedipal transition and Erikson's (1950) elaboration of this phase was related to the near universalization of grade school. In educational terms, the historical period associated with the strains of latency was not only one of mass development of grade school education, but also of the passage of laws prohibiting child labor and requiring minimal educational exposure. Latency can be conceived as a life stage of intensive instrumental learning in which erotic energy is directed toward the development of capacities suitable for participation in industrialized society. This stormy Oedipal-latency stage was reflected during the earlier phases of industrialization in personal histories involving preoccupations with authority, equality, autonomy, achievement, and esteem—preoccupations constituting major themes in the writings (but not in the theory) of psychoanalytic and literary figures at the turn of the century.[3]

The second period of change was connected with the near universalization of high school education, which occurred in the United States between 1920 and 1940. Coincident with this increase in the ratio completing high school, concern centered on the tumultuous character of the teen-age stage of life.[4] The disturbances accompanying adolescence tended to be explained during the 1930's and 1940's in terms of the biological transition to maturity. During the 1950's a preoccupation with adolescent youth culture emerged. The

[2] This is one of the main themes of Weinstein and Platt (1969, Chapters V and VI.)
[3] See Weinstein and Platt (1969, Chapter V and VI).
[4] Benedict (1938, pp. 161–167) was a typical attempt to understand the disturbing character of teen-age life from a cross-cultural point of view.

growth in the numbers attending and completing grade school and high school was gradual, perhaps contributing to a shading into each other of the effects of the Oedipal, latency, teen-age, and adolescent youth culture stages. Consequently the concerns with youth culture and student culture have tended to blend together.[5] Youth culture developed largely as a late effect of the mass participation in high school; and insofar as participation in higher education extends the period of "youth," such considerations are relevant to college cultures.

For analytic purposes, we distinguish college "student culture" from adolescent "youth culture" as related but independent phenomena. The emergence of student cultures in higher education reflects the third historical period of change, the growing numbers and proportions of persons now attending college.

We will not within this paper analyze all three phases, but focus on the last. We will point out analogous structural conditions underlying recent changes in the system of higher education and changes undergone earlier by the family, indicating the relevance of changes in these socialization systems for corresponding differentiations of life stages. For the contemporary period of change, as for the two earlier ones, the disturbances are seen as reactions to patterns not yet fully institutionalized; once these are stabilized, the resultant disturbances may be expected to subside. This does not imply that the Oedipal, latency, or adolescent phases are no longer stressful, only that the tension has decreased, so that passing through these stages is more routinely accomplished. Will contemporary student unrest follow the pattern of these earlier disturbances?

Although student revolts are characteristic of contemporary industrial societies, whether capitalist or communist, this paper will focus on Western society and in particular on the United States. One justification of this emphasis is that the United States has developed further along lines of differentiating and pluralizing its economic and social structures than other industrial societies. Starting with the Civil War, the United States witnessed two almost simultaneous changes: (1) the differentiation of the role of the father so that he engages in the occupational sphere as well as playing his role in the family; and (2) the departure of the post-Oedipal child from the family in order to participate in the educational system. This second change has led into an extension of the period of dependency and socialization. In quantitative terms, this extension has meant that the average amount of time spent in education has tended to increase for each new cohort of individuals over the past 60 or 70 years. Consequently, ever larger numbers are expected to engage in higher

[5] See, e.g., Erikson (1965). This work includes contributions by S. N. Eisenstadt, Talcott Parsons, Kenneth Keniston, and others.

levels of socialization in order to facilitate more successful participation in the differentiated and pluralizing environment.

1 *Background: the growth of higher education in America*

The evolution of the educational system has changed the relations among age strata, which are differentiated from one another because they have been socialized to a different extent for effective social participation. In addition, educational evolution produced a metamorphosis in the role sequences to be learned by successive cohorts and in the conditions for learning them.

Among the consequences is increased prestige and influence of the educational system, which can be gauged by a variety of indices. Some *qualitative indices* of the impact upon society are: (1) the widespread belief that many of society's ills can be alleviated, changed, and even cured through education; (2) the greater prestige enjoyed by the college-educated, and the importance attributed by the general population to the possession of a college education; (3) the emphasis placed on higher degrees as the basis for obtaining "better" occupational positions (i.e., for mobility) and as the basis for distinguishing the upper from the lower middle class (Jencks and Riesman, 1968, pp. 61–154); and (4) the influence in society enjoyed by the system of higher education, particularly in government and industry.

Such qualitative indicators of the heightened importance of education in America are matched by *quantitative measures* of growth, which are both causes and effects of the qualitative indices. Quantitative development can be measured along three dimensions: (1) by the rising number of institutions of higher education and related professional schools; (2) by the increasing number and variety of persons and groups involved in higher education at different levels; and (3) in the prolongation of the time that individuals are involved in the educational process. We will stress the latter two.

We wish to indicate here the differentiating patterns of values and the changes in educational structures associated with this educational growth. The main *value pattern* of the academic system (i.e., undergraduate and graduate faculties of arts and sciences) is *cognitive rationality* (Parsons and Platt, 1968a; Parsons, 1968b). This pattern obligates academic men to engage in the development, the manipulation, and the transference of bodies of knowledge judged in terms of empirical validity. Such activity is pursued on behalf of scholarly, academic, and disciplinary communities in order to develop knowledge and in order to train individuals at various levels in the necessary capacities and to commit them to this value pattern. Cognitive rationality may be viewed as a subvalue of the more general value of *instrumental activism*, which obligates the individual to incessant activity upon behalf of collective interests. In short, under instrumental activism, collective goals are the responsibility of the individual members (Parsons and White, 1961).

The period from the end of the Civil War to the turn of the century was critical for the institutionalization of cognitive rationality as a separate value pattern (Parsons and Platt, 1968a). During the period from 1876 to 1905, fifteen academic societies were established (Berelson, 1960, pp. 14–15), a development that symbolized (1) the establishment of national (or even international) universalistic standards for evaluating scholarly contribution—standards external to any particular academic institution; (2) the formation of a national community of scholars rather than local communities; and (3) institutionalization of the research obligation along with teaching as part of the academic man's role. Previously, scholarship, although a tradition of American academic men, had been mainly a private concern.

Once differentiated from other concerns and focused on cognitive matters, the American academic system began a process of expansion and upgrading. As the standards of evaluating faculty and students were cut loose from previous ascriptive bases, assessment came to be based on commitment to the newly differentiated academic value pattern. One of the outcomes of this process of educational development was the application of universalistic standards to the judgment of faculty and students according to acquired capacity to express the cognitive-rationality value pattern.

Along with the institutionalization of this value pattern, *structural changes* in education have occurred. *Mass* secondary education developed, as reflected in the rapid growth in the rate of high school completion—from 11.5 per cent of the cohort born in 1860–1864 to 65.1 per cent of the 1940–1944 cohort and about 70 per cent today (Jencks and Riesman, 1968). Moreover, over half of those graduating from high school now enter some higher educational institution.[6] Thus, approximately 40 per cent of persons 18 to 21 are enrolled for degree credit in an institution of higher learning (the figure was 36.4 per cent in 1961) (Simon and Grant, 1964, p. 76). The rates at which the 18 to 21 age group attended college increased rather slowly from 1870 until just prior to World War II and then accelerated following the war. In short, the major barriers to progression through the educational system have been moving up the life course; the age at which the majority of students leave the system has been continually deferred.[7] (See also Volume I, Chapter 6.)

There has also been increasing societal pressure to go on to achieve *higher degrees*, which is reflected in the increasing number of bachelor's

[6] This is considered a conservative estimate. See American Council on Education (1969, p. 93); data for 1963.
[7] Duncan (1968, pp. 620–622). See also the "selection points" for educational dichotomization of cohorts discussed in Parsons (1959a, pp. 29–36).

degrees conferred over the past century (*Historical Statistics of the United States, Colonial Times to 1957*, pp. 211–212). Furthermore, an upgrading has occurred toward degrees of higher quality. This is manifest in the extent to which training in the applied professions has been integrated with the university system and with the academic value pattern of cognitive rationality (though without entirely sacrificing the applied value orientations appropriate to these professions). Qualitative upgrading has also been evidenced by the even more rapid rates of growth in the numbers of *advanced* degrees conferred (both professional and academic) as compared with the baccalaureates. Implicit in these trends is the increased number of *years in the total life course* that individuals are involved in education.

Another aspect of educational change is the increased *socioeconomic* selectivity. While there has been a tendency for rising numbers of persons to reach and to complete college, there is some indication that the disparity in selection from high-status and low-status origins may be increasing—rather than decreasing—over time. In one study of United States males aged 25–64 years, the proportion of upper-status sons (as measured by father's educational background) who went to college increased for each successive ten-year age cohort. While mobility into the college-educated group by persons of lower status also increased, the increases have not been equal across the class structure (Spady, 1967).

These educational trends have produced three levels within the population. The first level consists of persons with terminal high school degrees (or less); this is still numerically the largest segment, but is a shrinking proportion of the age cohort. The second is a growing proportion of the population who have attended or completed college. The third is the smallest but the most rapidly growing segment—consisting of those who have gone on to postgraduate work for academic or professional degrees.[8] These three segments will continue to be identifiable for the foreseeable future.[9]

2 *Social structure and socialization in higher education*

What are the consequences of this rapid growth of the educated population? Our main theme concerns the implications of this growth for the socialization process. In *Family, Socialization and Interaction Process*, as well as in subsequent writing (Parsons and Bales, 1955; Parsons, 1964), the socializa-

[8] These groups correspond respectively to our "supporters" of, "appreciators" of, and "participators" in the academic value pattern as this is described in our Pilot Report. See Parsons and Platt (1968b, Chapter 1).

[9] Although the rate of increase in graduate student enrollment was lower in 1968–1969 than in previous years, the drop has been attributed by some observers to military draft inductions. See *New York Times*, May 20, 1969.

tion process was characterized as a progressive series of differentiations, each subsequent level numerically more inclusive and structurally more complex than the last. Socialization can be analyzed with respect to the differentiation of the personality and with respect to increasing complexity of the social structures and normative patterns in which the personality participates and to which it becomes committed. We will attempt to show that the separation of the college population from the noncollege population constitutes a further step in this differentiating process and that this step has features continuous with and analogous to the earlier phases of socialization.

The thrust of the analysis is in terms of analogous models at *different* social structural levels. Ontogenetic features are involved in relating the levels of socialization to one another, but these features are not the main point. In our analysis, each stage of socialization is viewed as having components which, though analogous to components of other stages, are analyzable at their own levels. The individual undergoing socialization must go through the process anew at each higher level. When we speak of student resistance to socialization pressures, we are *not*, like a number of popular and psychoanalytic writers, referring to baggage carried along from the infant and Oedipal stages. We are referring to the pressures at the student level and to resistances, reactions, and counter-pressures at that same level, not from earlier ones.

In any socialization context, structural asymmetries must exist between the agents of socialization and those being socialized in order for the oncoming generation to achieve maximal participation at the next level. In short, *age-graded domains of activity* are necessary as a structural feature of socializing agencies. There are negative consequences when such a structural arrangement does not obtain.

The rapid increase of higher education and its inclusiveness have exacerbated aspects of the strain inherent in socialization at the college level. Thus, a number of factors have coalesced upon this phase in the socialization process and have made its potential for strain more manifest than ever before. Among the factors contributing to this problem is the salient reference group for the individual student provided by the large proportion of young people now attending college. Second, mutual dependency has developed among college students because of their rapid increase in numbers and because they feel estranged from faculty and administration who, faced with expanded enrollment and preoccupied with research activities, are forced to dilute the performance of socialization functions. Third, despite changed faculty roles, demands for performance and standards of evaluation of students are higher than ever before and have increased the stresses to which students are exposed. Finally, students are confronted by social and political problems such as the draft, lack of suffrage, and the war in Vietnam that serve to intensify their sense of common plight.

The social science tradition has regarded adolescence (including the college years) as the final preadult stage of the socialization cycle. We depart from this tradition and conceive adolescence (including that phase of youth culture that accompanies it) as coinciding with secondary school; we conceive of higher education, both at the college and at the graduate and professional levels, as constituting a *post*adolescent phase. Five pairs of stages in the life course can be distinguished: (1) infancy (pre-Oedipal) and Oedipal child-hood; (2) latency and adolescence; (3) "studentry" and early maturity; (4) middle and late maturity; and (5) early and late old age.[10]

The early stages have been linked with the historical periods delineated at the beginning of this paper. More recently, development of full capacity for societal participation has been *moving up to later stages*, thereby length-ening the period in which childlike socialization occurs. For the bulk of the society, preadult status and a readiness for occupational participation has been occurring later—following extended education. Modern society is enter-ing a period when a college education is becoming a *requirement* for maxi-mal societal and occupational participation. Since a new stage is emerging, a new name for it may be appropriate; we have entitled it the "studentry" phase.

The emerging studentry phase   The term "studentry" is more likely to be used to refer to a collection of persons rather than to a stage of life. Popular language does not imply that being a student is a fully differentiated stage, although some university students remain in this status for ten years. That is, in the United States, studentry is not yet an institutionalized status fully differentiated from adolescence and from maturity, but it is developing in this direction.

Studentry is a new phase because of the growth of *mass* higher educa-tion since World War II, a phenomenon unparalleled in the history of human societies. Moreover, as the percentage of the age cohort completing high school approaches its upper limit, the college level is developing into a stage in the socialization series at which the cohort is broken into one portion that goes further in the socialization process and one that does not. Thus, the col-lege decision is part of the definition of the situation for members of each cohort (and for their parents) as they complete the adolescent phase.

To be sure, college attendance is still correlated with *status by birth*. The

[10] The first pair is primarily intrafamilial and universal. The second introduces the major extrafamilial factor of formal education. The first member of the second pair, latency, be-came universalized early, whereas for a long period a line was drawn between those who did and those who did not proceed farther to secondary education. Now completion of secondary education is approaching universalization; and a major portion of each cohort moves on to the college level. Studentry is the new status occupied by the more successful of the two main contingents in the cohort. This is one way to offer a schematic summary of the process of educational upgrading. Cf. Erikson (1950 and 1959).

change has been some increase in the proportion rather than massive inclusion of children from lower-status families (Spady, 1967). Yet college education has begun to penetrate into the lower middle class and into ethnic, racial, and other groups not previously exposed to higher education. Of most importance, the *expectation* of going to college has penetrated downward.[11] Because of competition for admission to college and the relative competitive disadvantage of lower-status groups who have developed expectations of college attendance, the relation between the college and the noncollege population may be developing into one of increasing tension.[12]

Another development in the American system of higher education helps define the structure of the student group once it reaches college, for studentry as a stage can best be understood in relation to later stages of the academic life course. While still in college, students prepare for later subdivision into the contingent destined for postgraduate studies and the "college only" contingent.[13] Postgraduate higher education has increased spectacularly. The main postgraduate division separates students training for the "applied" professions from "academic" students in graduate schools of arts and sciences training for the academic profession itself. Enrollment in the academic graduate schools has undergone more rapid growth than that in the traditional professional schools such as law or medicine and has been important in the professionalization of the academic faculty role itself. Once through graduate school, college teachers are those who were professionally trained in an academic field.

Socialization for early maturity The historical trend in the structure of Western society generally and of the academic system in particular has been toward greater differentiation, pluralization, and complexity. Simultaneously, change toward rationalization of social and personal life has occurred. The capacity of the individual to participate maximally in modern society ne-

---

[11] The Carnegie Commission on Higher Education (1968, p. 4) reports that "97 per cent of all parents questioned want their children to enter college."

[12] The evidence for this assertion is not strong. Obvious tension will be found among a subsector of those going on, that is, among those applying to the better schools. Although most high school graduates who apply to the better colleges and universities will probably get into an institution and even into a good institution, the competition among this segment to get into the "best" colleges is great because these colleges are heavily overapplied.

Tension can thus be described at two levels. At the most general level, it is the competition to go on at all: that is, the competition between those seekers for entrance to any college who are admitted and those who are not. The level of this tension depends upon the ratio of the number who apply to the number of places in colleges and universities and upon changes in this ratio over time. The second type of competition is that for admission to the "better" institutions. The level of this tension depends upon the ratio between aspirants to upper-level institutions and openings in upper-level institutions and upon the changes over time in this ratio and in the measurement of "upper-level" on these two dimensions. Since these data are not available, this line of thought must remain hypothetical.

[13] The postgraduate contingent has the closest relation to the research complex and the values of cognitive rationality embodied by the faculty.

cessitates attitudes and attributes compatible with this complex structure; these have been admirably described by Weber.[14] They include: (1) the conscious capacity to control one's activities, that is, to remain autonomous and to avoid dependency; (2) the ability to achieve and compete in an open market; (3) the control of impulse and affect, particularly in regard to ascriptive solidarities; and (4) the effort to govern behavior by criteria of rationality even when, for reasons of error or lack of knowledge, such standards cannot be perfectly achieved. The normative mandate is not that the individual withdraw all psychic energy from society in order to employ it for competitive ends, but rather that he commit himself to a multiplicity of collective activities and that he labor industriously in each of them. Such a formulation harks back to the Puritan doctrine of disciplined labor in a calling. In more contemporary terms, it means pluralistic involvement and activity. The network of involvement is difficult to integrate, on occasion placing great strain upon the individual. A problem for the individual today is that he cannot give any one or two of these collective affiliations absolute involvement without seriously jeopardizing the others. By engaging in one to the exclusion of the others, he jeopardizes potential involvement in other realms. A paradigmatic case is the relation of kinship ties to occupational mobility. Extended kinship ties inhibit occupational mobility; conversely, high rates of mobility, as normatively prescribed, loosen kinship ties.

The structural features of early maturity stand in contrast to those of adolescence and youth culture. In our society, mature relationships include elements (1) of *hierarchy* and (2) of marked *functional differentiation*. These elements are expressed in the family of procreation; the capacity to accept the roles of both parent and spouse shows personality maturity. Two other realms of expression are the *recognition of differential achievement* and the *acceptance of functionally necessary authority*. In both cases the individual must internalize the reciprocal role patterns involved. That is, he must recognize the achievements of others and become motivationally capable of high achievement himself, capable even of surpassing the levels of others (peers in particular) if this is legitimately done. Similarly, in authority situations, he must develop the capacity both to accept the legitimate authority of others and to exercise authority over others. The central obligation is to act *responsibly* in the interests of the value-based collective system.

The earlier stage of latency involved differentiation of the cohort on the axis of *achievement;* and achievement is also a basis of differentiation among adolescents between the college and the noncollege contingents (Parsons, 1959b). High school peer groups are stratified on a basis that empha-

---

[14] Although these characteristics are in Weber, the formulation offered here is taken from Weinstein and Platt (1969, Chapter VII).

sizes not only social class origin, but also the school performance of the individual. At the college level, there is a new system of peer solidarities, differentiated at the outset by the kinds of colleges different subgroups are admitted to and attend. A new striving for achievement rewards begins, intensely in institutions marked by strong competition for entrance and for records that will confer advantages in regard to future graduate training, occupations, or marriages.

What is new about the achievement emphasis in college compared with high school is the higher cognitive levels and the relative *specificity* of the tasks. As the cohort becomes a college class, it is differentiated both by levels of achievement and by fields (including many extracurricular fields of interest). The college curriculum comprises a wide range of intellectual disciplines with opportunity to specialize in almost any of them. The *same* group that as a college class has peer solidarity is also exposed to processes of differentiation by levels of achievement and by fields of specialization. This dual process of differentiation takes place in a setting where ascriptive criteria of status have been declining in significance, both relative to earlier stages of the individual student's life course and relative to previous historical periods of social development.

Such demands for hierarchical achievement and for specificity of application to selected fields of endeavor may stimulate counterpressures from the student peer group. A cohort of college students today may tend to emphasize, in their definition of peer solidarity, equality and functional diffuseness. With the suppression of age as a differentiating criterion in a college cohort and with the current pressures to coeducation, the ancient ascriptions of age and sex are weakened. Social status differences previously imported into the college situation and expressed in such forms as fraternities or clubs have also weakened. Hence student *gemeinschaft* is freer to call for an equality that runs counter to differential recognition of achievement and hierarchical authority. This egalitarianism finds expression, for example, in attacks on grading systems. The valuation of diffuseness finds expression in humanistic interest and in the demand for a philosophy of life rather than for technical training.

The egalitarian solidarity of the adolescent peer community involves a combination of two components, both of which are reflected in current usage of the term "commitment." The first is a diffuse common value-orientation resembling the one Piaget described as "moral realism."[15] The second component describes a diffuse emotional *attachment* of the members to the group

---

[15] Piaget (1965) writes: "We shall therefore call moral realism the tendency which the child has to regard duty and the value attaching to it as self-subsistent and independent of the mind, as imposing itself regardless of the circumstances in which the individual may find himself." See pp. 111 ff.

and to each other. These factors reinforce each other. Not only are the moral attitudes held with uncompromising commitment, but they are also associated with powerful affect, so that responses to challenge are passionate. Yet, if the transition to the orientation system of early maturity is to be accomplished, both components must undergo change. Both must be further differentiated, though the differentiated components must be built into a more generalized framework of orientation embracing specified value commitments[16] and more discriminating affective loyalties.

In terms of the *value-component,* the transition to be made in going from studentry to early maturity is from a *diffuse* moral commitment to one that is *both* highly generalized *and* more differentiated. In the studentry phase, there tends to be a unified set of collective goals. Since diffuse collectivities have little division of labor, they can achieve only limited goals; the participant's commitment is tested by the intensity of his devotion to these goals. After the transition to early maturity, there is a plurality of different, equally legitimate subgoals among which the participant must allocate commitments and loyalties. He cannot personally contribute effectively to the implementation of all these legitimate but *specific* value-patterns. However, he can subscribe to the common legitimacy of the values governing the manifold of subvalues. This manifold implies a generalized value-pattern within which the subvalues are held together. The distinction between *undifferentiated* diffuseness of the value component and *generality* admitting of differentiation *at lower levels* of specification is frequently overlooked.

Regarding *affective attachments,* the transition to maturity involves a parallel distinction between general and specific levels. Adolescent peer loyalty tends to be diffuse and undifferentiated, a total identification with one's own group. One of the consequences may be an unrealistic idealization of one's own group and an unrealistic derogation of other groups, in short, ethnocentrism. With socialization into a more differentiated and pluralistic collective system, this identification tends to give way to an allocation of loyalties among several collectivities within a multiplicity of groups, albeit with special loyalty accorded to two or three. Yet, if such a system is to be stabilized, it must have participants who not only allocate their own loyalties among two or more subcollectivities at given lower levels of differentiation, but who can do this without sacrificing their loyalty to the overall collective system. Thus, a mature man must be loyal *both* to his family and to his employing organization, and these loyalties must be compatible with loyalty to other, more inclusive, community groups. Pluralistic loyalties involve both identification and

[16] The use of the term commitment in common parlance is different from the technical way it is being employed here. On the conceptual formulation of value commitment specification, see Parsons (1968c).

affective attachment. Indeed, this pluralization of attachments and the necessity for balances and adjustments among them make affect as a generalized medium important (See Parsons, 1970). A man should at the same time love his wife and children; he should "love" his job, his community of residence, his community of coworkers, and his country; but he cannot love any one of them absolutely and to the exclusion of the others.

The noncollege population   The import of this section will be clarified by considering the situation of that segment of the population not exposed to college-university socialization. Of course, the noncollege population achieves maturity in the biological and sociological sense. But by virtue of early termination of education, the noncollege segment fails to *maximize* its participation in the society. This limitation is reflected in occupational and financial ceilings prevalent for most individuals in this category. As the economy and the society change, maximum participation for the individual is linked to higher levels of education and socialization.

The limitations of the noncollege population can be attributed to lack of technical and cognitive capacities normally acquired as a result of attending college. In addition, since the college experience constitutes socialization, missing this experience means more limited value transformations and commitments. That is to say, the college population develops further while the noncollege population remains embedded at less differentiated value levels. Although the high school experience is not a miniature of the college experience, the college and noncollege populations do not constitute discontinuous categories of persons committed to discrete value orientations. Continuity of value orientations exists along with a degree of shared academic values between the high school and college systems. If this were not the case, it would be very difficult for high school students to go on to college. There is value overlap between the two systems, and there is also continuity between the populations that pass through them. The continuities are as noteworthy as the differences. However, in a discussion of degrees of difference, quantity tends to turn into quality; there are qualitative differences between the college and the noncollege populations.

What are the specific socializing effects of college? First, the adolescent culture is transformed during the college experience by the development of the capacity to accept higher levels of achievement for self and for others. To achieve these higher levels requires the acceptance of authority rationally required by coordinated effort. The second change is the development of the capacity to participate in and to accept a more differentiated environment together with extensively pluralized courses of action. College populations, through exposure to the value of cognitive rationality, change farther along these two dimensions than noncollege populations, although this development is not without stress, tension, and reaction. By contrasting college and noncollege populations along these two lines of socialization, we can isolate the effects of the transformation resulting from the college experience.

With regard to authority, the structure of the high school organization remains more *hierarchical* than the college organization. Authority stems more from position (office) than from expertise. Compatible with this greater role for bureaucratic authority, rote learning of facts persists in the high school to a greater extent than at college, despite the pragmatic influence of John Dewey. Such organizational contrasts are complex and problematic. There is also great variation among high schools, based on such factors as the quality of the particular high school, the community in which it is situated, the grade level to which the analysis is addressed, the orientation of the school (e.g., vocational or college-preparatory), the educational experience of the staff, and the degree to which the school organization has changed as a result of the infusion of college value orientations. Yet, with all these sources of variation and in spite of the complaints of some college students that the university is too "authoritarian," the high school is, even in the context of the learning situation, more bureaucratic in its organization than the college.

There is tension between hierarchical authority and the value pattern of cognitive rationality.[17] Cognitive rationality fosters evaluation on universalistic grounds, that is, an evaluation of contribution without regard to the source of authority. Cognitive rationality also fosters institutionalized conditions for autonomous behavior. Students who do not go beyond high school are *more* likely than the college-educated to be more responsive to hierarchical authority and readier to base evaluations on ascribed positions. They are *less* likely to have developed the tools of rational manipulation with which to direct their own lives. Respect for authority and the capacity to challenge it is class-related (Adorno et al., 1950; Christie and Jahoda, 1954; Rokeach, 1960). The issue is whether compliance with authority is based upon universalistic standards of evaluation or upon standards tied to hierarchy. Over and above the differences in the organizational settings of the college and the noncollege populations, the college population tends toward the former set of standards, the noncollege population toward the latter.

The second dimension of college socialization is the extent of *differentiation*. The organizational environment and the permissible courses of action are narrower on the average in high school than in college. Thus socialization in the high school does not develop the same toleration of a spectrum of differentiation and pluralization that grows out of the college experience. This difference is not merely the product of the larger number of areas of study available in college, although this factor is influential; the difference is due mainly to the differing degrees to which the two systems are embedded in the

[17] Erich Fromm (1944) contrasts "rational" and "irrational" authority.

values of the larger society. The high school is less free of social value orientation, while the college is differentiated from both religious and applied concerns.[18] Respect for "God, country, mother" are central concerns of the high school education. These symbols imply undifferentiated commitment to religious, political, and kinship values.

There is a popular suspicion that the college experience results in an irreverent and secular graduate. The contrary argument is tenable: The college student learns to locate a multiplicity of collective affiliations within a differentiated network, giving relevance to each affiliation, and attributing to none an absolute commitment (although some hierarchy may exist among them). A transformation that occurs in the college phase of socialization is the acceptance of complexes of solidarities for self and the acceptance of the legitimacy of still other complexes beyond one's own interests and pursuits. By contrast, the high school student is more committed to a circumscribed environment grounded in the values of the larger society. He is more affectively bound to a limited number of ascriptive solidarities, such as his family and his religious organizations. His standards of evaluation and potential courses of legitimate action are also circumscribed by these affiliations (Chinoy, 1955; Iwanska, 1958; Rosenberg, 1957; Whyte, 1955).

The higher educational system, with its emphasis on cognitive rationality as a value pattern, has institutionalized and extended those orientations and patterns of action described by Weber in his analysis of Western history. The college experience extends the socialization process, developing the individual so that his personality can articulate with the rapidly differentiating, rationalizing, and changing society. Flexibility, autonomy, and ego-strength are related features of this extended socialization.

COLLEGE VERSUS THE FAMILY SYSTEM OF SOCIALIZATION: BASES OF SOLIDARITY AND STRAIN

Studentry, as a stage of socialization, can be understood through analogy between family and college as socializing agencies. The family and the college have undergone parallel types of differentiation in achieving their modern forms. In the family, differentiation was in the form of extrusion of the economic functions from the household to the factory and the office. The end product of this differentiation internal to the family was a sharper division of labor between the two parental roles than existed before. The father became the wage earner, i.e., the incumbent of an occupational role structurally differentiated from his familial roles (Smelser, 1959; 1968). From the point of view of the previous kinship system, he became the *pater absconditus* who deserted his family. Among the repercussions of this change in paternal roles

---

[18] A case in point is the return to Bible reading in the schools, contrary to the decision of the Supreme Court.

has been a redefinition of sex roles for children, beginning with the Oedipal phase. Prior to the Industrial Revolution, Freud's work would have been incomprehensible (Weinstein and Platt, 1969).

Within the *faculty* also, structural changes have been taking place. For a large segment of the best-trained academic men, undergraduate teaching is only one of several functions in their academic role-set. Research and graduate teaching constitute the two other major functions. Additional functions include participation in academic self-government as an administrative duty and various services outside the academic system proper.

A significant effect of institutionalizing cognitive rationality in American colleges and universities has been the reordering of the three major role obligations in relative importance. Research, the purest embodiment of the value of cognitive rationality, has become the primary obligation, with graduate teaching ranking next, and undergraduate teaching third in the value hierarchy.[19] Service and administration are lower on this hierarchy, while professional training in applied fields (undergraduate and graduate) is off on another branch interwoven with other value patterns.[20] Research is no longer the work of amateurs, a function performed by someone who is a gentleman as well as a scholar. Research and the values supporting it set the tone for the academic system. This tendency is the more pronounced the higher the prestige of the institution within the academic scale of stratification.

The college teacher, qua faculty member, is also *pater absconditus*. The teacher absconds, not primarily to the "fleshpots" of monetary gain, but to the "irrelevancies" of esoteric intellectual interests, which are neither immediately practical nor do they solve the ultimate problems of the human condition. Like the worker of the Industrial Revolution, however, the professor has typically not left the college but has kept one foot in graduate and undergraduate teaching and one foot in research, the ideal obligational arrangement for the majority of American academic men.[21]

[19] This is a ranking of the salience of functions for the *system*, not for any individual participant in it.

[20] The institution of higher education need not be termed a "university" or be large. What is important is the value of cognitive rationality in setting the standards for evaluating faculty and students, for recruiting, and so on. In this context, Jencks and Riesman (1968) are partially correct in categorizing Yale, Michigan, Amherst, and Oberlin as being "university colleges" using essentially university standards toward their faculty and undergraduates. Although the situation is more complex than this, Jencks and Riesman have captured one dimension: the high level of *differentiated* standards of cognitive rationality for evaluation of students and faculty, irrespective of the size of the institution in which that value pattern is institutionalized. For a multiple orientational portrayal of the American academic system and its relation to the cognitive rationality value pattern, see Parsons and Platt (1968a) and Parsons (1968b).

[21] Our analysis of a national sample of academic men (not yet published) indicates that this arrangement is the preferred one. See Parsons and Platt (1968a, p. 321, footnote). This research has been conducted under the support of a National Science Foundation grant

Another analogy between the early stages of socialization and the college arises out of the organization and patterning of affect. For the family, a caveat in the socialization process is the *incest taboo,* which forces the child to renounce his erotic attachment to his parents so that he eventually (ideally) becomes motivationally capable of forming an attachment to an age-peer of the opposite sex. After this Oedipal transition, solidarity in the family shifts from an erotic to an affectional basis. The child enters the period of latency, emerging in adolescence with preadult heterosexual interests and desires. At the same time, starting in the latency period and culminating in adolescence, there is a transfer of affective solidarity from the family to the same-age peer group. This transfer defines the patterns of adolescent youth culture and carries with it a sense of independence from the older generation described in familiar ways in the literature (Parsons, Keniston, and others in Erikson, 1965).

The later stage of studentry is parallel to latency because again there is instrumental learning and also because during the studentry period an *affective taboo* develops against the diffuse expression that characterizes adolescent peer groups. From a functional point of view, the period of studentry is directed at breaking up the peer group as the youthful archetype of diffuse, affective, undifferentiated solidarity.[22] Studentry prepares the way for new valuations of achievement and responsibility. Typically, the process involves repressing the need for diffuse affective solidarity and simultaneously undergoing a transformation comparable to the transformation of childhood eroticism to versions characteristic of latency and then of adolescence.

The attachments which have to be transformed in this process are not the familiar cross-generational ones of pre-Oedipal and Oedipal childhood, but are *same*-generational;[23] in relation to the age strata, they are not vertical but horizontal. Like erotic ties to parents, they do not simply disappear, but are transformed, to reappear in restructured form in "early maturity" as an element of cohesion among the multiple groups to which the adult belongs. Hence, for individual motivation, this functional problem is different from that

(#GS-2524). We acknowledge this support, although the material in this paper is not part of that study.

[22] To a degree, the young adolescent also belongs to religious, ethnic, geographic, and other solidarities that are relatively undifferentiated and affectively bound. During the studentry phase, the character of these ascriptive solidarities and degrees of identification with them undergo transition also, later being "fitted into" a more comprehensive scheme of adult participation. We single out the adolescent peer group because, unlike the others, it must not only be transformed, but it must also be "passed through" and, for the normally functioning adult, "left behind."

[23] There is also an incest taboo against too strong an affective tie between faculty (as "parents") and students, as indicated below.

in the Oedipal erotic transformation. It becomes necessary to free the individual from the affective ties of a powerful group within his own generation in order for him to accept and enter into early maturity.

Faculty roles in socialization   There are several bases of tensions between faculty and students. Such tensions are comparable to the tensions between parents and children, but at the studentry stage peer solidarity exacerbates the strains. Both equality and diffuseness are emphasized by the peer group through social-structural and personal-emotional pressures; and these emphases have become sources of tension within the socialization system of the college. Although children in a family may on occasion coalesce and offer resistance to the authority and the socialization efforts of their parents, their activity is scarcely as systematic as that of the student peer group; it is restricted by the age differences among the children.

In discussing the incest taboo in the family, we have stressed the significance of two conditions: first, that the typical father has through his occupational role been a link between the family and the larger community; and second, that a role and status differentiation exists between the generations. The combination of the two is basic to the socialization function of the family, especially in the Oedipal phase. Through the father role as a symbolic model, the values of the larger community are given leverage. Moreover, the security of affectively based solidarity in the family makes it motivationally possible for the child to accept the discipline required by the socialization process.

For the studentry phase, counterparts of these familial conditions are necessary for performance of the dual functions of research and teaching. The *same* groups of people typically perform *both* the function of teaching undergraduates and the research and other functions dissociated from undergraduates. If our interpretation of the nature and importance of the studentry phase of the socialization cycle is valid, the involvement of the academic profession in functions outside undergraduate teaching does not constitute neglect of teaching responsibilities. This view would be tantamount to saying that a father's involvement in the occupational world, both as income earner and as conferrer of status on the family, constitutes neglect of his responsibility to his children. It would be equivalent to idealizing the preindustrial ascriptive fusion of kinship with the productive functions defined by occupational roles.

Nevertheless, one of the sources of strain in the university today, similar to the strain in the family in the earlier period of its differentiation, is that faculty may have become too involved with research. The family parallel is the situation where parents are involved in their occupational and other commitments to the point of neglecting the socialization of their children. One measure is the reduced time spent by faculty in teaching. However, according to our data, faculty members would not choose to rid themselves of *all* teaching.[24] Nevertheless, students complain about the "absence" of faculty from their classrooms just as early twentieth-century literary figures complained about the absence of fathers from the household (see Kafka, 1954).

Though less frequently mentioned, another respect in which paternal absence is felt justifies our analogy between the family and higher education: the withdrawal of expressive and nurturant relationships between faculty and students. The socialization process in the family, particularly the acceptance of severe discipline and the circumscription of erotic expression, is buffered by affective solidarity between parents and children. A condition similar to this should exist in higher education, especially in the teacher-student relationship. Involvement with research and other external activities has minimized this aspect of the exchange between students and faculty. The relative downgrading of the expressive component has had negative repercussions for the socialization process.[25] Indeed, this decline may be a source of tension today and may magnify the unwillingness of today's students to accept the discipline involved in higher educational socialization.[26]

Hierarchical asymmetry Faculty members manifest hierarchical superiority over students on three bases, all of which are challenged today by the equalitarian tendencies of the student peer structure. The first basis of hierarchy is *age status*. Thus, any residual antagonism toward parents or adults generally can be applied to faculty. The second is superior *competence* in the subject matters involved in the educational process. The third is the exercise of *authority* through grading or recommendations.

The incidence of these asymmetries bears on the student through his instructors in particular courses. A tendency of the student peer solidarity, however, is to treat the entire faculty or the combined faculty and administration, as counter-solidarities or opposing collective entities.[27]

[24] See Hacker (1965, pp. 25 ff.) for the position that faculty would give up all teaching if they could. Also see Gross (1968) for the low priority given to teaching. With regard to actual and preferred distribution of graduate and undergraduate teaching, see Parsons and Platt (1968b and 1968a).

[25] An important question for the future concerns the possible bifurcation of the academic roles of researcher and teacher, analogous to the earlier differentiation between the roles of mother and father within the family [*Editors' note*].

[26] As suggested to the authors by Harvey Brooks, nurturant functions have shifted to psychiatrists, counsellors, assistant deans, tutors, teaching fellows, and junior faculty. But the effect of this shift may be that of reinforcing the student view of senior faculty as absconders. Junior faculty and teaching fellows have been placed in ambiguous and ambivalent roles *vis-à-vis* students and senior faculty. This uncertain status, together with responsibility for nurturance of students, may be a source of identification with student activists. [*See footnote 28.*]

[27] Compare the parallelism with the Marxian conception of class consciousness. Socialist activism was directed to the mobilization of proletarian consciousness, assuming the solidarity of the bourgeoisie. Student activism seems to take student solidarity for granted and to project the necessity for a faculty-administration solidarity punitively directed against them. The sharpening of issues does create a solidarity which either did not exist before or was rather tenuous to start with.

One target of student movements has been the two-class structure (faculty as the "upper" class and students as the "lower" class) of the college community.[28] The student challenge has been expressed with varying degrees of radicalism, including at the extreme a demand for the "free university," that is, for total abolition of status distinctions between students and faculty. This demand represents an attempt to mitigate socializing pressures that threaten the egalitarian structure of solidarity in the student peer group. Given the general values of American society, the most obvious alternative to the two-class model is that of the democratic association. Student participation is interpreted to mean that those exercising the authority of leadership should be regarded as responsible to a democratic constituency, the majority of whom are students.

In spite of the moral appeal of this arrangement, such a model fails to take account of the socialization function of the academic community. *Socialization* means that the academic community exists not only to satisfy the current needs or wishes of the majority of its student members, but *to develop and transform* the structure of those needs and wishes. The socialization function of the family requires a status difference between the parental group and that of the children, a difference that in the academic case is based on age, competence, and authority.

Characteristics of family solidarity A further condition of family socialization, pointed out in numerous studies,[29] is the necessity for maintaining solidarity of the *parental coalition* as a collective socializing agency in which the members perform differentiated roles. In the family case, this solidarity is

[28] An interstitial case pointed out to us by Matilda Riley and Marilyn Johnson is teaching fellows and teaching assistants, who are in the middle between faculty and undergraduates. At Columbia in 1968 and in Berkeley in 1964 during the periods of crisis, they tended to align themselves with the undergraduate students and to become the radical leadership. According to the Cox Commission report, it was the junior faculty who felt in the middle and aligned themselves with the students.

During the Harvard crisis of 1969, the teaching fellows maintained their middle ground and assumed a leadership role. This was evidenced in the first mass student meeting at Soldiers' Field where the proposals of the teaching fellows were overwhelmingly supported. The teaching fellows privately admitted that they took this position in order to prevent a power vacuum and a deterioration of the strike to the extreme Left. How long the moderate teaching fellows could have sustained this position and their newly assumed leadership had the faculty not moved quickly to ameliorate radical and black student demands, remains problematic.

Thus, teaching fellows and assistants may contribute to undergraduate student opposition by providing radical leadership and legitimacy through their somewhat superior status. On the other hand, these interstitial members may be in a position to play an integrative role in the academic community. Which of these courses is likely to be taken by teaching fellows and assistants in a situation of student-faculty strain is influenced by the nature of socialization and its attendant strains at this level of "studentry." It is apparent, therefore, that the role of teaching fellow or assistant and the role of junior faculty require special analysis if student-faculty relations are to be understood.

With regard to these issues, see Avorn et al. (1968); Cohen and Hale (1966); Cox (1968); Katope and Zolbrod (1966).

[29] A particularly illuminating discussion is in Lidz, Fleck, and Cornelison (1965).

promoted by the erotic relations of the parental couple. These relations go beyond an organic significance; they are culturally constitutive of marriage and the family as a basic symbol of the diffuse enduring solidarity of the couple (Schneider, 1968). Following the Oedipal transition, the children are excluded from *any* erotic relationship to the parents or to each other; this is the incest taboo. Parents not only gratify each other sexually; they also love each other affectively. The children are included in the family solidarity at the *affective*, but not the *erotic* level.

Parents also cooperate with each other in the *management* of their own lives, the development of their children's lives, the organization of household and extrahousehold concerns, and so on. With respect to these practical affairs of the family, children in the modern family have been consulted extensively (Weinstein and Platt, 1969). But limits remain on the extent to which children can be included in the management and decision-making functions of the family unit.

Two other conditions affect the balance between integrative and disintegrative tendencies in the modern family. First, the family's *relative isolation* from kinship, ethnic, community, and other ascriptive ties make it an independent managerial unit concerning its own affairs; second, this isolation places members in a special affective *dependency relationship* with respect to each other. This special relationship is even more pronounced for the parents than for the children. Not only is the parents' affective dependency grounded in the exclusiveness of their erotic relationship; the parents are ideally joined for life, whereas the children will develop new familial affective relationships of their own. The isolation of the family unit and the mutual dependency of members work in opposing directions. Solidarity is enhanced because the family confronts the internal and external managerial tasks as a single unit and because the affective exchanges are intensified by the limited number of family members. On the other hand, this enhanced solidarity is achieved at the cost of tensions engendered by functioning without much help from the outside and by the ambivalence engendered by the increased affective dependencies (Freud [1911], 1958, Vol. 12, pp. 218–226).

Thus, the modern family exists in a delicate balance between integrative and disintegrative forces. For the parents, the integrative forces are nourished by eroticism, and in most cases the parents do stay together. In contrast, the family of orientation breaks up for the children. Upon reaching adulthood, the children leave to create their own families, reducing their affective relationship with their parents. Inclusion of the children in the erotic complex after the Oedipal transition would inhibit the child from breaking with his parents and establishing a family of his own and would also disrupt the parental bond.

Characteristics of university solidarity   Such points, obvious in the family setting, have parallel implications for the university. To pursue the analogy requires identification of considerations in the academic system *analogous to the erotic complex* in the family. We suggest two analogous components in pursuit of the value pattern of cognitive rationality. The first relates to commitments to the value pattern and to opportunities for its expression. The second relates to solidarities within which the oncoming generation is socialized into the value pattern.

With regard to commitments, a population divides into a center and a periphery in terms of its commitment to a value pattern (Shils, 1961). Although the population of faculty and students is arrayed on a continuum manifesting no sharp breaks, the faculty is closer than the students to the center of the cognitive rationality pattern, both in commitment and in expression. There are three bases for this difference. First, the value pattern is grounded in the faculty occupational roles and obligations. Second, faculty members have undergone long careers, educational and often occupational, in developing these commitments and the related technical capacities and experience. Finally, there is a difference in levels of competence, with faculty members generally superior in academic capacities to undergraduate and even graduate students.

Being at the center of the value pattern puts the faculty into a position analogous to parents. The students, although sharing with the faculty a commitment to cognitive rationality, stand lower on the scale. Like parents, faculty members must have an autonomous opportunity to implement their value pattern in ways they think best.

As the second analogue of the erotic complex, the faculty also requires opportunities to reaffirm *solidarities*. The main reference groups for academic men are (1) their immediate colleagues and scholarly associates beyond the specific institution and (2) their students, graduate and undergraduate. Within these contexts academic men orient their behavior so as to reinforce these solidarities.

The differentiation of cognitive rationality from other value patterns gives academicians the opportunity to pursue scholarly contribution unhampered by external impingements and immediate demands. At the same time, specific patterns (like academic freedom) have developed to ensure insulation and to guarantee autonomy. So protected, the scholar can make his contribution to knowledge and its transmission free from external demands or surveillance.

The scholarly expression of value commitment safeguarded by academic freedom parallels parental exclusiveness in the erotic complex. In the marital relationship, the sexual act is an expression of the partners' commitment to the mutually valued state of their marriage and to the solidarity of this marriage above other shared involvements (their children, parents, friends, jobs, and so on). The act of scholarly contribution is an expression of commitment to the shared academic value pattern and of solidarity with the scholarly community, both local and national. A publication is more than another listing on the vita; it also means that academic values and solidarity with the scholarly community have centrality for the faculty member (Parsons and Platt, 1968b).

In line with this reasoning, academic men need the opportunity to manage their value commitments free from undue interference and from direct evaluation by those at the periphery of the value pattern. Outside supervision would reduce the viability of academic freedom and would reduce the autonomy required for self-directed contribution. It might also prevent reassertion of commitment to the shared value patterns and weaken the solidarity of the community that shares these patterns. To insist that academic men must always contribute in terms of social, political, practical, or religious concerns would have a deflationary effect on their commitments to cognitive rationality. Such insistence would have regressive consequences for the 60-year trend toward rising levels of achievement in the academic system. Evaluation of scholarship could no longer be based on the quality of contribution to knowledge but on criteria external to the values of cognitive rationality.

Faculties strive for independent management of their cultural commitments to the community of scholars to which they affirm their solidarity. In this area, academic men are concerned with maintaining their identity vis-à-vis external units as parents are concerned with maintaining a special relationship vis-à-vis both children and extrafamilial obligations.

Faculties also strive for control over the local academic community and its *internal* concerns. On a particular campus, the issues revolve about the socialization of students and about the reaffirmation of the solidarity of the faculty as a collective unit for achieving this end and for articulating local conditions with the demands of the wider scholarly community.

In this internal area, as in the family situation, sources of integration and of strain develop within faculties. The development of a clearer definition of the academic man's situation has contributed to integration. Institutionalization of cognitive rationality, differentiated from religious and applied societal value patterns, delimited academic men's role obligations and defined the bases of evaluation transcending particular academic fields. Faculties, like the family, have become more functionally specific in their concerns. Such problems as financing, evaluating undergraduate applications, or managing the social and moral lives of undergraduates have been given over to the administration and, the last increasingly, to students. Faculties became absorbed in the contribution to, and the transmission of, knowledge. They have drawn together as operative units involved more exclusively in academic areas and dedicated to a unified standard for evaluating performance. This unified standard acts as the integrative basis cutting across the diversity of academic fields.

Although the institutionalization of cognitive rationality produced greater solidarity, it also created *disintegrative* tendencies. By legitimating a range of intellectual pursuits, any one of which accords with its prescriptions, the value pattern has fostered proliferation of differentiated fields and subfields. Each of these fields has its theoretical concerns and its objects of empirical study. Many have been incorporated as separate departments within a single university. The consequences of high degrees of differentiation tend to reduce faculty cohesion.

A faculty, like a family, must manage problems connected with achievement of its primary goals—in the first instance contribution to and transmission of knowledge, but also the maintenance of its collegial solidarity and its solidarity with students. It cannot overlook the needs of its various student and faculty subsections or even certain of the demands of the larger society. Faculty members, in order to perform their functions, must confront the problem of solidarity. Like the parents in a family, faculty members as socializers must form a stable coalition in the face of their students if they are to perform their teaching and socializing functions successfully.

To be sure, students also require a degree of solidarity with their faculty as a condition for acceptance of the necessary disciplines, for socialization, and for growth. But most students, like children in a family, pass through the system; their solidarity—their affective ties with the faculty—becomes attenuated. Too great an identification with the faculty would inhibit students from making the break with their colleges and universities and accepting less affective ties when they reach the status of alumni.[30] The eventual dissolution of this solidarity across age lines has been less problematic than the loosening of student solidarity with their peers.

Faculty solidarity, like parental solidarity, is achieved largely through selection procedures. Men are appointed to faculties because they tend to have values and abilities in common with those already on the faculty. They have exhibited commitments to scholarship, and they have achieved, or will potentially achieve, levels of prestige and reputation similar to the achievements and attitudes of persons already on the faculty.

If the selection of faculty is based on standards that have primacy for scholarly, academic, and faculty concerns, the analogy between family and faculty must be modified. A new faculty member appointed or promoted from junior to senior rank is like a second rather than a first marriage. Insofar as the

[30] The regressive behavior of some alumni at reunions is a standing joke on college campuses.

parallel between the family and the college community holds, children from the first marriage, if old enough, are usually consulted. The final decision, however, remains with the adults; children exercise advisory, not directly determinative power, when parents contemplate remarriage. Students have not typically been involved in faculty appointments, but this practice may well change.

Even prior to changed procedures of selection, faculty solidarity is problematical. Communality of attitudes toward the academic endeavor alone is insufficient (as it is insufficient in a marriage) to sustain the solidarity of faculty in the face of changing circumstances and exigencies. Structural arrangements must be propitious if the faculty is to maintain its solidarity and to accomplish its scholarly and socializing functions.

One means of symbolically reaffirming commitment and solidarity (at both the national and the local levels) is the act of scholarly contribution. Certain asymmetries between faculty and students and conditions of privacy for the faculty also seem required if the faculty is to avoid the strains that have often characterized the family context. Such strains include the following: (1) reduced faculty solidarity if students are too fully included in faculty decisions; (2) disturbances analogous to those between marital partners should children beyond the Oedipal phase be included in the erotic complex; (3) barriers and inhibitions to the students' full transition to early maturity if studentry were to be included at all faculty levels; and (4) incapacities analogous to those of the child who fails to achieve heterosexual interests and desires following the latency period, that is, full differentiation between those who do and do not become academic professionals.

The structural arrangements necessary to avoid potential strains must be predicated on the location of the faculty at the center of the value pattern of cognitive rationality. Faculty have the moral obligation and the technical capacity to implement this pattern in both the socialization and the scholarly contexts. In the socialization context, this means the exposure of students to the logical patterns of this value and to the range of knowledge available in academic discourse. While the patterns and knowledge to be communicated are on the cognitive level, they are connected with affective components of the socialization process: with the *acceptance* of achievement, competence, and specific forms of hierarchical authority associated with commitments to this value pattern and of the legitimacy of each field of knowledge in a differentiated and pluralized intellectual environment. At the affective level, both components are symbolically representative of these dimensions in the larger society. As in the family with children, students need not come into direct contact with societal values or be directly involved in political or occupational achievement in order that they internalize such patterns; they can learn through socializing contact with their teachers. The internalization of achievement, hierarchy, and differentiation depends on the acceptance of the legitimacy of these mandates for self as well as others.

In the managerial realm, the faculty requires the development and maintenance of organizational arrangements that maximize opportunities for the expression of their value commitments in research and teaching and for the transfer of value patterns to the students (socialization). These organizational arrangements take the form of decision-making as to conditions for research, for teaching, and for the relation of research and teaching to each other. A delicate balance exists between the obligations to the two areas, a balance difficult to achieve.

In the family, management of concerns directly relevant to the parents cannot be fully shared by children. In the academic system, the parallel concerns reside especially in the research function. Insofar as organizational arrangements for research do not negatively affect the socialization of students, the specifics of the research properly remain in the control of the faculty and its members. In the family, the children cannot decide what their father's occupational role should be or the specific manner of his engagement in it. Such a role for children would be impossible because fathers (like faculty) have committed themselves to their occupations prior to the arrival of their children and because the organization of work occurs in institutions external to the family. Similar conditions with regard to research obtain for faculty in their relation to students.

The other major managerial function of the faculty is the socialization of students. While living conditions, coeducational arrangements, or extracurricular activities are relevant to socialization, curriculum is fundamental. This area is the main context for socialization to the value pattern in both cognitive and affective respects. Curriculum is also an area in which there is tension between students and faculty. Two different questions about curriculum are of managerial concern. The first is: *Who* should teach, that is, what should be the process of selection of faculty? (These questions are raised most sharply in the blacks' demands for selecting their own faculty [Bunzel, 1968]). The second set of questions ask: *What* should be taught? *How* should it be taught? What should be the nature of student-faculty relations in the teaching context? and how should what is taught relate to other societal problems (e.g., the relevance problem)? For both problems, similar solutions have been suggested: greater democratization. For example, it has been suggested that curriculum, because it impinges upon students, should be organized in a democratic way through negotiations between faculty and students. The experience of the modern family teaches that democratization is no panacea. The inclusion of children has gone a long way in matters influencing internal family organization, decision-making, and even the socialization process. However, perfect political democracy between children and parents is impractical; ultimate precedence must remain with parents. For similar reasons, the university cannot develop into a democracy constituted by an undifferentiated constituency of faculty and students.

Proposals for student participation in the corporate decision-making processes of the academic system usually involve some representative scheme, though some advocate (more often in Europe than in the United States) "full" democracy with every member of the community having one vote (Crozier, 1968; Maynatz, 1968). Our analysis indicates that account must be taken of the managerial problems that are the province of the faculty, problems such as curriculum content, evaluation and grading procedures, or appointments to faculty posts. Inclusion of students in many areas is feasible. However, as in the case of the family, authority, competence, and responsibility probably have to be disproportionately wielded by the older, trained, and experienced group.[31]

Privacy as a condition for the expression of solidarity   Another aspect of the problem of student participation has not been adequately considered. In faculties and in subgroups such as departments or committees, a component of solidarity appears to be the functional equivalent of the rela-

---

[31] In spite of the fact that we have offered general rules (ideal) for the total academic system, especially if it is to continue to be guided by its own values and to serve its own ends, we set no specific formulas of organization for particular institutions. Institutions of higher education, like families, can manifest a great deal of organizational variation, dependent upon their size, more specific goals, faculty orientations and training and their position in the total academic system. We can briefly make explicit only a few sources of variation.

The type of institution is one major source of variation. What can be accomplished and what mechanisms of integration and involvement can be developed between faculty and students at a small residential college may not be possible at a large urban university or college. Also, solutions of these problems for private and public institutions will probably vary.

Second, the domain or dimension of concern will be another source of institutional variation. Those issues more directly articulated with the academic value system will remain more exclusively faculty concerns. Those problems and issues more distant from the value pattern will fall more fully under the student jurisdiction. However, with regard to all dimensions of the academic system, student involvement will be increased.

Closely connected to this second source of variation is the mechanism of integration that will be employed in restructuring the university. On some issues the solution will go in the direction of consultation with students. On other issues the students will have partial or equal voting power with faculty. There will be a rough correlation between consultation and degree of centrality to the value system of the academic matter under concern and between voting and its distance from the cognitive rationality pattern. But this will not always be the case and, with regard to particular institutions, it need not be so at all.

A good number of today's students are engaged in gaining more control over their lives and more inclusion in the college and university environments in which they spend a considerable portion of their academic and social lives, for which they expend a great deal of energy and effort, and of which they expect to become a part. A goodly number of faculty are concerned with the autonomy that departments, faculties and universities and the academic system have achieved. They are thus engaged in fending off student encroachment, as in the past they struggled against religious, practical, and political encroachments. Recent surveys indicate that student and faculty opinion on these issues is far apart (see, e.g., Wilson and Gaff, 1969; *Gallup Opinion Index*, June 1969). Some meeting ground for the system as a whole will have to be achieved, but very few institutions will resolve these differences in exactly the same way.

tions between the parents in the family. This analogy relies heavily on the privilege and exclusiveness of the parental partners in the erotic complex in marriage. We employ here a metaphor that should be taken only in the symbolic sense. The critical issue, closer to a Durkheimian than a Freudian formulation, is that of the existence of conditions for the ritual reaffirmation of solidarity and the accomplishment of managerial functions, which are primary concerns for parents and faculty and which would have disruptive consequences for these functions and for children and students if conducted under public scrutiny. If the analogous logic applies here, there should be aspects of the internal corporate relationship of colleagues from which students *ought* to be excluded. Their inclusion would interfere with their socialization and with faculty solidarity and managerial functions.

For the adolescent, concern with diffuse peer solidarity tends to dominate the personality. Thus, for components of adult personality to develop, this adolescent need system should be repressed. Such repression is one of the socialization tasks of the studentry phase, and it is for this reason that studentry may be thought of as "second latency." The adolescent need for diffuse solidarity, after being repressed, may reappear later, in the stage of early maturity; it reappears in restructured form, constituting an element of cohesion among the multiple groups to which the adult belongs.

Just as inclusion of the latency-to-adolescent child in parental erotic relationships would prevent both erotic and other aspects of maturing,[32] so inclusion of students in the affective solidarities of their teachers may interfere with processes of student maturation. Students could interpret their roles in the faculty groupings in terms of adolescent solidarity patterns and therefore as more diffuse and undifferentiated than such roles at the faculty level are. Consequently, students would be integrated into the academic community at an immature level of personality differentiation. They would not have developed to the point where they could treat solidarity with the faculty as one of a manifold of possibilities among which they choose, making responsible selective commitments. Put in more familiar psychological language, inclusion of students would probably encourage dependency rather than the requisite responsible autonomy.

The marital erotic relation is, as Schneider points out, a symbolic focus of solidarity with components both of affect and of commitments. In its fully legitimate form, parenthood is implicit. Sexual intercourse is the physiological means of procreating children and also the cultural symbol of the right and duty to procreate and to rear children in the setting of the family. The affective solidarity and the instrumental economy of the family includes the children; but this inclusion does not apply to participation in the erotic relation of

[32] Especially cogently argued by Lidz, Fleck, and Cornelison (1965).

the parents. Their sexual relation is a symbolic ritual, not only of privileges, but of their collective responsibility as a socializing agency in the family. Interpreted in the context of the Durkheimian theory of ritual, sexual intercourse, in which the partners act out their solidary commitments, reinforces their capacity to function *together* as an effective socializing agency.

There are also nonerotic concerns of the parents from which even relatively mature children are legitimately excluded. Problems in the maintenance of solidary relations between parents are often so subtle and complex that they must be handled in private or with the help of professional therapists. Moreover, parents have special responsibility for the welfare of the family and for the relationships among the partners, the children, and the family as a whole. Frequently, disruption of family functioning is prevented if parents clarify their thinking about such problems between themselves without involving the children at every step. Parental privacy does not contradict the rights of children to participate and be consulted in the process of familial decision-making, only of their right to participate in *all* stages, phases, and levels of the process (Cottle, 1969). Children can be included in these decision-making processes as concerned parties who can influence outcomes rather than as power-holders who can decide outcomes. In short, children cannot direct their own socialization; in the end they must, unlike the parents, pass through the family.

To carry these considerations over to the college setting, members of a faculty and its primary subunits (departments or committees) need opportunities for the ritual expression of their solidarity and for the reaffirmation of value-commitments essential to effective scholarship and student socialization. A faculty, even more than the parents within the family, is a differentiated collectivity including representatives of a range of disciplines, subdisciplines, and cross-cutting academic interests linked to interests outside the college community, both academic and applied. Such a collectivity has centrifugal tendencies. Yet effective performance in scholarly realms and in the socialization of undergraduate students depends on maintaining faculty solidarity (see Stanton and Schwartz, 1954).

Students have rights of participation in the affairs of the academic community of which they are a part. These rights imply student functioning beyond that of being passive receptacles into which knowledge or values are poured. But these rights are compatible with the exclusion of students from participation in some academic collective responsibilities and in the personal affairs of faculty members.[33]

[33] See Parsons (1969), and the entire issue of *Daedalus* (Spring 1969). An aspect of the doctrine of "privileged communication" important for the professions is the protection of the privacy of the relationship. Confidential information given by a client to his attorney or by a patient to his physician may not be divulged outside that relationship. Another aspect

Privacy, "the voluntary withholding of information," is the appropriate concept under which to formulate the points of interest here. Protection of privacy is grounded in the Western value system; it has recently been reaffirmed in connection with the rights of human beings as subjects in research. Privacy is not, however, a simple value. It is balanced against opposing obligations, as in the contrast between the relation between the privileged communication of attorney and client, and the obligatory disclosure of information under oath on the witness stand. Similarly, where the products of faculty autonomy and decisions impinge directly on student concerns, a delicate balance between privacy and publicity must be sought (Shils, 1956). Thus privacy implies distinctions between participation and exclusion from participation, including a range of barriers to different types of participation.

Privacy is not secrecy. Secrecy is clandestine, and is on occasion a necessary evil that societies must tolerate. When a system such as the academic is under pressure, and trust among the parties involved breaks down, privacy is misconstrued as secrecy. Shils (1956) has correctly suggested that "the demand for extreme solidarity is the product of the fear of betrayal. The passion for publicity is the passion for a homogeneous society, a passion which emerges from the conception of politics as the relation between friend and foe." And further, "the obsessive fear of secrets culminates in the denial of the right of private difference, which is the denial of the right of others to possess a sphere of privacy" (pp. 34–35). Nothing more adequately characterizes the desires and fears of the more extreme radical students regarding academic faculties and the governance of universities.

We have asserted that the collectivities of the academic system are primarily associational and integrated by influence. Pressures toward total publicity, however, are those toward greater control, more emphasis on power and toward the homogeneous dedifferentiation of which Shils speaks.

The exclusion of children (and of nonmembers of the family) from the parental erotic relation is an instance of the couple's right to privacy. The idea that faculties or departments have parallel rights of privacy is less familiar. Yet the logic of the analogy points to this conclusion. Faculty membership can

---

concerns the privacy of the professional practitioner. A client of an attorney may not legitimately be inquisitive about whatever legal problems the attorney may have himself or in his relations to other clients. Also, a patient may not legitimately inquire about his physician's personal health problems or about those of other patients.

Similar considerations concern the grounds on which the professional practitioner reaches many of his decisions with respect to his advice or treatment of the client or patient. The practitioner is obligated to communicate his conclusions, to explain the situation and the alternatives, etc. He cannot, however, escape the responsibility for staking his *professional* status in counselling action, and this responsibility cannot be shared by nonprofessionals.

We interpret the academic role, including the teaching aspect of it, to be a professional role. The privacy of the professional component of the teaching institution stands on the same basis as does the privacy of other kinds of professional roles.

be defined to imply legitimate areas of privacy. Protection of privacy should apply to occasions where members need not be as much on their guard as they normally are in relations with noncolleagues who might easily misinterpret what they say or do. Information properly regarded as confidential is protected by the concept of privacy, but processes of evaluation for which the deciding group must take collective responsibility should also be protected. There are also subtleties of what is said and how, such as the expression of emotion, both positive and negative.

Within the context of the performance of their socialization and managerial functions, faculty privacy is necessary if policy decisions—regarding, e.g., research programs, new faculty, new students, and evaluations of extant faculty and students—are to be achieved without the jeopardy of premature disclosure of decisions or actions, without exposure of personal or confidential matters, with the right to pursue exploratory discussions without invoking misunderstandings or premature criticisms and without alienating persons or groups as a result of what is discussed in private.

Thus, areas of privacy parallel to those of the family occur in the faculty: (1) ritual aspects of the expression of solidarity, including the equivalent of a "kiss-and-make-up" resolution of conflicts; (2) relationships internal to the collectivity itself—to the faculty, department, or committee; and (3) exercise of collective responsibility for the welfare of the institution as such, including its student component. The conception of the college as a socializing agency implies that the faculty and its subunits have responsibilities not shared with students. Privacy may be necessary to facilitate the exercise of such responsibilities, particularly when matters under discussion relate to effective implementation of academic value patterns in teaching and research, the areas of central faculty concern.

3 Dissenting student movements

We shall apply our analysis in a review of themes of student dissent during the late 1960's, relating these themes to the foci of the system of higher education and to the potentially disruptive and constructive consequences of student activism.

THEMES OF DISSENT

The themes of contemporary student movements can be categorized in terms of their critiques of the Establishment, their assertions as to how it should be changed, and their ideas of what should be substituted in its place. These themes are not clearly organized by those who enunciate them. Nevertheless, four clusters can be distinguished.

Theme 1   The first cluster contains a *moral* emphasis that attributes grave shortcomings to the social order, shortcomings symbolized by the Vietnam war and by "racism." The academic community is implicated through "complicity," either as actively perpetuating the war and racism or as refusing to get involved—that is, remaining neutral. The critics suggest that the university admit its share of the general responsibility for these moral evils and reform.

More broadly, there is the tendency to conceive society as a seamless moral web in which each of its elements is measured by an *absolutistic* set of moral imperatives and is judged either to measure up or to fail. Wherever society fails, the critics wish it to be actively combated. They conceive of a polarity between those in the population who are morally pure (the dissenters and protesters) and those who are guilty (i.e., the nondissenting elements of the society, excepting the poor and the powerless).

Theme 2   The second cluster of themes concerns the idea of *community*. The critics charge that the established system is one of isolation, competitiveness, and ruthless pursuit of self-interest regardless of the interests of others. In its stead, a new community of genuine love and solidarity should grow up to replace anomic relationships. The feeling that only younger people have a genuine capacity for community justifies the slogan, "Don't trust anyone over 30."

The community theme is related to the solidarity of the youthful peer group, as described in Section 2. Peer-group solidarity is also related to the egalitarianism permeating student and New Left movements. Egalitarianism implies concern with the disparity of rights between disadvantaged and privileged groups. In the academic context, the status distinctions between students and faculty members are questioned. Objections are also focused on the grading system, which highlights the inequalities between faculty and students.

Theme 3   A third set of themes complains of *depersonalization and bureaucratization*, symbolized in the phrase of being treated like "just another number" or "an IBM card." A related slogan is the desire to "control the decisions which affect one's life," which is one motivation for the interest in participatory democracy. The bureaucratization theme suggests hostility toward as well as an ideological interest in egalitarianism. (Here, egalitarianism refers to political power rather than to influence or privilege in the community.) In the academic setting, egalitarian attack is directed more against the administration than against the faculty. Critics invoke the principle that collective decision-making should occur in the framework of the voluntary democratic association, a model carried over to the academic community. In its extreme form, more common in Europe than in the United States, the demand is made for academic government on the basis of one member, one vote. The subtheme that such democracy should be "participatory" implies suspicion and distrust of authority, even of elective officers, leaders, or representatives. Thus, the bureaucratization theme is one source of the anarchistic strain in the radical student movements.

Theme 4 Finally, a fourth cluster of themes attacks the cognitive preoccupation of the academic system, even with regard to technical subjectmatters. The demand is for greater *expressiveness* and self-fulfillment in contrast with the desirability of cognitive mastery of subject matter for its own sake. The theme is connected with enhancement of interests in the arts as contrasted with the sciences. Expressiveness invokes a bohemian way of life, long connected with the arts and recently related to the pressure for extension of coeducation.

These four clusters are not independent of each other. For example, the expressive emphasis of the fourth and the participatory element of the third shade off into each other. While these two have much in common, they discriminate between the more politically activistic tendencies associated with the third cluster and the more expressive withdrawing, hippielike tendencies emphasized in the fourth.

The significance of these theme-clusters can best be understood in relation to the main structural trends of modern society and of its academic subsystem. Such an examination at the level of values should take into account the larger society, the general system of action, and the cultural system.[34]

The dominant American value pattern, already depicted, is that of *instrumental activism* (Parsons and White, 1961). The first component, "instrumental," has a universalistic emphasis; the second, "activism," emphasizes performance. The universalistic component precludes stress on a single collective goal-orientation for society as a whole; rather a multiplicity of goal orientations is legitimately possible. The achievement component emphasizes contribution of the individual or subcollectivity to the successful functioning of the system as a whole. Normative pressure is toward specific achievements and toward a multiplicity of units and subcollectivities within a division of labor. Moreover, instrumental activism necessarily implies affective neutrality rather than expressiveness and affectivity.

Instrumental activism is institutionalized in the main structure of American society. The society is pluralistic with elaborate division of labor. Its solidarity is primarily "organic" in Durkheim's sense. Societies of this type

---

[34] For readers interested in the technical analytical bases of such an examination, we are selecting, as central to the structure of American society and its academic subsystem, those components involved in two functions, the adaptive (A) and the integrative (I). We deal with those functions at three different levels of system reference: the cultural level, the general action level, and the societal level. Our emphasis is on the stability of patterning on the I-A axis of the Parsonian four-function paradigm. At the societal level, this axis is the focus of Durkheim's conceptualization of organic solidarity. The tendencies to deviation incorporated in the themes we have reviewed have in common the pressure to move away from this I-A focus to a focus on mechanical solidarity centering on the other pair of functions, that is, the L-G axis. See Parsons (1960).

can be characterized by: (1) decentralization of the governmental system; (2) extensive legal rights of individuals and subcollectivities; (3) widespread development of markets and economic exchange; and (4) proliferation of voluntary associations.

These features of the society are reflected and even enhanced in the academic subsystem (Parsons and Platt, 1968a; Parsons, 1968b). The American academic system is pluralistic and decentralized. Though differentiated from other structures in the society, it is bound to them in relations of organic solidarity. A distinctive feature of the academic system (when compared, for instance, to markets, mass communication systems, democratic government, and voluntary associations) is commitment to the value of cognitive rationality at the cultural level. This value commitment is congruent with instrumental activism at the societal level. Such congruence implies close interdependence between the stabilities and disturbances of the society as a whole and those of the academic subsystem. Societal strains and conflicts ramify throughout the system and affect the educational system because the societal system is at higher cybernetic and integrative levels of the institutional structure.

In the course of the present century, the academic system has developed into a position of immense societal importance.[35] This growth in importance has occurred not only organizationally with respect to *wealth* and *power*, but also with respect to *commitments* to its subvalues and with respect to its *influence* on society in areas relevant to these commitments. The maintenance and implementation of academic values have consequently become necessary for the stability and development of the society.

Cognitive rationality is symbolically associated at the cultural level with the moral values of tolerance, openness to opportunity for achievement, and solidarity of membership in a community of intellectual equals. (For the group at the center of the academic value pattern, we speak of the "community of scholars.") This value-anchorage, apart from the intrinsic merit of intellectual endeavors, is superordinate to the *adaptive* commitments of Western society. To provide this value-anchorage effectively, cognitive rationality must be supported by noncognitive components. Such components include the morality underlying cognitive disciplines,[36] an adequate *affective* basis for the necessary commitments and solidarities, and the institutionalization of the more liberal and pluralistic components of the social order.[37]

---

[35] See Parsons and Platt (1968a). The academic system's growth in size and influence is discussed in Section 1 of this paper.

[36] Compare the analyses of values of the intellectual disciplines developed in: Merton (1957); Barber (1952); Storer (1966).

[37] The focus on phenomena Durkheim called organic solidarity, which we have sometimes called "institutionalized individualism." See footnote 34.

The ideology of student dissent, inchoate as it appears to be, shows coherence within the value framework of American society. The four themes isolated from the varied protests and criticisms of the Establishment are similar in direction. Their common feature is the pressure toward *dedifferentiation*. In familiar, though inexact, sociological terminology, the plea of all four is for the restoration of *gemeinschaft*.

This formula is oversimplified. We shall undertake to specify the principal components of dedifferentiation and the relation of these components to the corresponding sources of tension in the situation. The four clusters of themes have two main foci of tension—a "dual stress"—which stem from adaptive and integrative subsystems of the familiar four-function paradigm, as shown in Table 7 · 2. Underlying the themes of student dissent is a repudiation of the adaptive-integrative emphasis of American society generally and of the academic subsystem in particular.

Adaptation　We can begin this analysis with the adaptive function, which relates the value complex of cognitive rationality to intelligence. Student dissent places the academic system under strain by derogating the rational basis of the modern cultural system. Yet this basis underlies not only cognitive rationality and its setting in the larger society, but also legal formalization and institutionalization and the framework of institutionalized individualism.

TABLE 7 · 2　*The functional subsystems of a society*

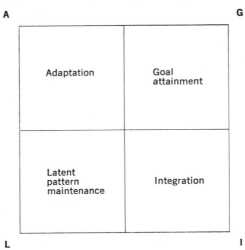

Source: Parsons, Bales and Shils, 1953, p. 182 (adapted).

In opposition to this basic rationalization, students attribute virtue to spontaneity without regard to rational controls. Psychologically, spontaneity exalts irrationality and, on the social level, embraces anarchism. This is the context of the famous doctrine, associated with Marcuse, of the "repressive tolerance" of liberal society. The radical movement seeks freedom from the cultural restraints of the modern heritage, or, as Durkheim would put it, promotes *anomie*.

The cognitive (adaptive) function of the academic context is also challenged by student anti-intellectualism, which seeks to replace impersonality with expressiveness and aestheticism. One slogan substitutes self-fulfillment as the goal of education in place of the acquisition of knowledge for its instrumental use. Paradoxically, an individualistic stress, related to anarchistic strains stemming from distrust of authority, is affirmed concomitantly with approval of collective action that can subordinate the individual and subject him to group discipline. This is a recent version of the dilemma of the socialist movement caught between libertarian individualism and Leninism.

Within an orderly individualistic society, however, self-fulfillment is less disruptive of adaptation than is the anarchistic-irrational emphasis. Self-fulfillment as a slogan allows room for *both* cognitive-rational and expressive-aesthetic values and activities rather than forcing an either-or choice between them.

Integration   Turning to the integrative focus, we have stressed the differentiation of the academic complex in two respects: first, specification of value-commitment and, second, pluralization of subgroups within collective organization. The radical-student challenge to the integration of the academic system presses toward *dedifferentiation* in both these respects.

Relevant to value commitments, moral absolutism means that any collectivity or type of activity is evaluated, not in terms of its contribution to the outcome of processes in a complex and differentiated system, but by an undiscriminating standard arbitrarily applied to *all* system units. Are they "good" or "bad"? The effect is refusal to accept a differentiation of system levels relative to functional differences. Such promiscuity in evaluation symbolically parallels the doctrine, "What is good for General Motors is good for the country."

Since political functions are necessarily included within the good-bad judgment, there is a temptation to judge the university in terms of its political relations. For instance, given the obvious urgency of the problems of the ghetto, the question addressed to a professor, regardless of his discipline and his lack of expertise in ghetto problems, becomes: "What have *you* been doing to alleviate distress and injustice in the ghetto?" If the reply is, "Not much," the professor thereby stands morally condemned; at best, he is callous. Thus, failure to recognize differentiation in the application of value commitments tends to politicize the university.

Differentiation of the academic system in its second aspect, pluralization, occurs at the level of social organization. The processes cognate with those of value-commitment concern the differentiated autonomy of subcollectivities and the rights of these subgroups (1) to give priorities to their own standards in internal problems of organization and (2) to implement their own specified and differentiated subvalues.

While moral absolutism is directed to the aspect of dedifferentiation on the level of value commitments, the theme of community challenges the autonomy of differentiated collective interests. A derivative of this theme is pressure toward depluralization, that is, pressure to restrict autonomy in the name of allegedly "higher" collective interests and obligations. The issue, however, is that of subcollective autonomy. Autonomy is ordinarily justified on the presumption that contributions to collective goals will have positive outcomes that cannot immediately be accounted for. The dedifferentiation tendency restricts such autonomy and asserts the imperative necessity of giving priority to the "top" collective interest, whatever that interest may be at a particular time. Furthermore, it is urged that involvement with this interest should be immediate and direct; it should push all subcollective interests aside.

A link exists between individual expressiveness and this urge to immediate collective action in a politicized context. Urgency of action and hence of results generates pressure to take drastic action and to be impatient with institutionalized procedures. This impatience can lead to direct action and to confrontation tactics. The individualistic component, now given an expressive emphasis, underlies the demand for participatory patterns of organization, minimizing not only bureaucratic rationalization but also authority on a representative basis to elected leadership. Hence the themes of immediacy, direct action, confrontation, and "maximum feasible participation" are combined. The outcome is the enlistment of individualistic and expressive needs in the service of strenuously advocated collective goals—goals that usually transcend the academic community and often, as in the case of ROTC, tie into national politics.

Pattern maintenance and goal attainment   The main thrust of these four themes of protest challenge structures in the academic world that institutionalize the primacy of cognitive rationality, of associational collegiality, and of procedural decorum. At the same time, the protest themes attempt to redefine the *cultural value* bases and the *goal-orientations* of the system.

On the whole, student pressure on the pattern-maintenance function is toward a community of peace, harmony, and spontaneity where love prevails over materialistic, worldly concerns. This sometimes leads in an overtly religious direction (as in the case of the late Pitirim Sorokin or, on a different level, of Timothy Leary). On the goal-orientation side, the symbolic slogan is "student power," accompanied by an urge toward militancy, confrontation, and exacerbation of conflict. The apparent contradiction between love and power can be rationalized by a combination of two assertions. The first assertion is that, by the tenet of moral absolutism, the opponents are "bad" so that it would be immoral not to combat them with every available resource. The second is that this conflict is temporary and that, as soon as victory ("revolution") is won, the era of peace and harmony will begin. Such combinations of overtly incompatible assertions can be traced from the eschatological expectations of early Christianity, through many millenarian sects, to the Communist movement with its advocacy of violent "class struggle" and its expectation of an ultimate state of perfect harmony. The resemblances point to a utopian strain in the New Left ideology.

SOME CONSTRUCTIVE POTENTIALITIES OF STUDENT ACTIVISM

The history of social movements shows that utopian ideologies fail to provide blueprints of actual societal development. These ideologies are never merely put into practice by social engineers. Though destined for a complex series of transformations, certain parts of the ideology eventually come into favor and are built into subsequent social structures. This is true of Christianity taken as a whole (see Parsons, 1968a). No society has, even after 2,000 years, become a literal institutionalization of the Sermon on the Mount; and the utopian strain persists. As another example, the democratic revolution produced utopian thought in both its earlier and later phases. While no democratic society has become a Jacobin paradise, where the general will prevails without opposition or internal division, who can deny the seminal importance of the line of thought from Rousseau to Robespierre (Weinstein and Platt, 1969, Chapters II–V)? Similar examples can be found in the socialist and the communist movements. The student protest movement, like other utopian movements, contains a mixture of impracticality, paranoia, and of idealism that may ultimately improve our societies.

We conceive of student protest and of reactions to it in a double context. The first is that of developmental changes in the structure of modern society, centering on mass higher education. The second is that of the socialization of the individual. In our analysis, the two are linked with each other; our success in connecting the two aspects systematically is a measure of the contribution of this paper to sociological knowledge. Part of the linkage is the theoretical expectation that major social change should evoke ideological reactions—*in part* irrational—from those involved; at the same time, that the corresponding pressures of socialization should produce analogous ideas or fantasies in individuals under stress. These ideational outputs of the process of change are connected with each other on the level of their meanings as symbolic expressions of both societal and personal strains (Weinstein and Platt, 1969, Chapter I).

Such fantasy-ideologies have *destructive* aspects. To take the Oedipal complex, no one argues that sons should kill their fathers and marry their mothers in order to resolve their tensions. On the level of social structure, it is similarly unrealistic for all relatively deprived groups to destroy the power structures that they identify as the source of their frustrations and to take over the community structures that the previously powerful "controlled." Where the acting-out of such fantasies has occurred, the subsequent course of events has been far from smooth, as in the fifty-year history of Soviet Russia or, more recently, in China and the new nations of Africa.

Nevertheless, such ideological reactions also have *positive* aspects. With respect to the present student protests, themselves in part a revolutionary movement, we should mention these potentially constructive implications. The best starting point is the realization that, in contexts of tension, attitudes are basically *ambivalent*. Indeed, hostility toward a given structure (either pattern or socializing agency) may reflect attachment to that structure. The antithesis of cathexis is not hostility but indifference. The parallel to the rebellious Oedipal son preparing himself for fatherhood on the social level are the Jacobins, who were not indifferent to the state created by the wicked Bourbons and who wanted to establish a reformed version of this *same* political entity. Similarly, for Marx and his followers, the capitalism that they regarded as an absolute evil created the enhanced "forces of production," which socialism was expected to take over and adapt to its own use. The present student radicals are for the most part deeply identified with the academic system. They want, along with its transformation, to be included in it. In a poignant way, they seem to be saying, "We don't trust you (the faculties and administrators), because we know how immoral you are. But *why* won't *you* trust *us* and accept us a little more?" This positive attachment evokes constructive rather than disruptive symbolic themes inherent in contemporary student movements. These constructive themes can potentially be built into a positive developmental process of structural change in the society. Four such constructive themes are apparent in the current American setting and fit our paradigmatic analysis (see Section 4).

Equality of the sexes An old theme in the American setting—equality of the sexes—has revived recently in academic communities and elsewhere. In academia, coeducation involves overtones of promoting social justice through improving the position of a discriminated-against group, thus strengthening the inclusiveness of mass higher education. Long established in some colleges, it is now part of traditionally one-sex institutions such as Yale and

Vassar. The new element is the assault on the conception of the sex-segregated college in favor of total coeducation, including dormitory and eating arrangements.

Coeducation may seem a regressive step diminishing the pure attachment of college education to career prospects and to instrumental values generally. Relative to men, women tend to be more expressive than instrumental in orientation. Hence, for men, the extension of coeducation constitutes dilution of the instrumentalism of the academic system. By somewhat de-emphasizing the instrumental orientation, the extension of coeducation gratifies the need to emphasize the expressive side. At the same time, integration of the feminine contingent more fully into the academic community upgrades the feminine level of cognitively oriented achievement and instrumental responsibility. Thus, coeducation need not lead toward anti-intellectualism, but rather, for both sexes, toward a differentiation between intellectual aspects of the college experience and more expressive aspects.[38]

Thus extension of coeducation can serve both to mitigate the major foci of strain in the current situation, and to strengthen the general component of inclusiveness, which is essential to *mass* higher education. It is the latest phase in the long history of the movement toward "emancipation of women," so that it builds on foundations that are deeply grounded in social and cultural tradition. That the outcome of coeducation today will be the total eradication of relevant social role differences between the sexes is, however, doubtful.

Concern with blacks The second constructive component in student protest, especially in America, centers around the racial issue. As a problem of public policy and integrity, racial justice is the most salient internal problem for American society. This is partially so because of our earlier successes in integrating other excluded groups, notably the "new immigration" waves of a half-century ago (Glazer and Moynihan, 1963).

What is distinctive about student concern with the racial issue is not who the students side with (they agree with large sectors of the liberal community, including most of the Establishment; Glazer, 1968), but their sympathy with militancy. The militant stance on the part of some white students is matched by the wave of black militancy that has erupted in the colleges, centering in demands for the establishment of "black studies" programs and a variety of issues concerning black student control. The student blacks and the militant white student groups, especially Students for a Democratic Society

[38] In general, this issue, at the levels of role and personality, relates to the capacity for men and women to be *both* instrumental and expressive (and thus to become more alike in behavioral style). Currently, women's "liberation" movements, highly politicized and allied with the Left, are demanding legitimacy for women of instrumental behavior and its consequences for political and occupational inclusion. But just as important, though less organizationally codified, is the marked trend on the part of men toward more expressive behavior in terms of feelings, mannerisms, and styles of dress.

(SDS), are not harmonious despite common causes (*Ramparts,* June 15, 1968). To the extent that the blacks, more than the militant whites, are making claims legitimated by institutionalized societal values, they are thereby gaining a broader white constituency and making a stronger bid for success in attaining their goals.

Various factors point to solidarity of interest in the cause of racial integration between the academic and the societal communities. At present blacks have an opportunity to achieve full inclusion by pushing their cause with just enough militancy to permit the academic establishment to fulfill its usual obligations and interests while cooperating with the black studentry to institute the required changes.

In sum, both the extension of coeducation and the enhanced concern for black students constitute processes of increasing *inclusion* (Parsons, 1966). The two differ in their approach to inclusion in that coeducation is a process of differentiation in the personalities of the sex groups and in their cultural orientations, whereas concern with blacks is a process of upgrading. With the increasing impingement of higher education on the society as a whole, upgrading of the black subsector depends on increase in the proportion of blacks who will join the company of educated men.

War versus peace A preoccupation outside the academic fold is the problem of war and peace, a general problem in the world since World War I, but particularly in the United States because of the Vietnam war. This issue gives student radicals, with their disposition toward moral indictment of the society generally, an opportunity to condemn the United States. While presenting moral and political issues, the war has also had a realistic impact on student interests through the draft. The draft is a morally complicated issue because the policy of student deferments has aroused guilt in those occupying a privileged position and has added doubts about internal justice to sentiments against war and imperialism. Not surprisingly, the charge of complicity on the part of the academic community has come to the fore, fed by circumstances such as university involvement in war-related research or with training programs for the military in Vietnam.

The Vietnam issue has led to militant tactics involving obstructionism, confrontation, and violence. But student antiwar protest, as in the field of civil rights, has also had a positive impact. With respect to policy toward the war, the support of Senator McCarthy's presidential candidacy in the 1968 primaries helped to raise policy issues. Similarly, the raising of the complicity issue by student dissidents has brought university administrations and faculty members to heightened concern and self-examination. The wave of actions concerning ROTC constitutes one outcome; questioning of the status of war-associated research constitutes another.

On the two issues of war and of racism (in society and in academia) the more extreme militants have sought to politicize the academic community, attempting to enforce fulfillment of academic "moral" obligations as these are defined by the radicals. By giving priority to these obligations over all others, their effort is to have academia forego the obligations associated with cognitive rationality and with the professional complex per se. In both instances, student activism has stimulated the mobilization of wider forces by appeal to more general values of the American community. In particular, the pressure from students has mobilized supporting sentiment on the part of the faculty, who generally hold a left-of-center orientation.

The problems of war and racism, one of them outside of academia and the other on its boundary, are evanescent and in that sense symbolic of broader concerns. Even if and when the racial problem in the United States is solved through full inclusion of Negroes into first-class social and political citizenship, other problems of social injustice and discrimination in the societal community will remain. Similarly, settlement of the war in Vietnam, or even the stabilization of political relations with respect to organized force in the world as a whole, does not imply that the problems of the world community will have been solved for all time. Issues other than war and peace or imperialism—and equally acute and distressing—will arise.

For American students, the racial issue symbolizes the problem of the moral quality of the societal community in which the academic community is embedded. Toward this societal community young people must, during the stage of studentry, work out evaluative orientations; and these orientations must include a definition of their own obligations as active participants. The issue of war and peace, on the other hand, symbolizes the problem of the role our *nation* should play in the world community and by inference the problem of the nature of that world community itself.

Extreme forms of politicization are incompatible with a differentiated academic system and with the special function of socialization with which we are concerned in this essay. Nevertheless, student involvement with these two political issues has had a significantly positive impact on value-implementation in the society as a whole; this involvement has promoted the internalization of the values of social responsibility during the studentry stage of the aging process.[39]

Student participation   The fourth context in which student activism has operated constructively is in the drive for student participation in the decision-making processes of the academic community. Student participation in deci-

[39] This role may be compared with that of the labor and trade union movements in the history of the Industrial Revolution. These movements played a part in bringing about the institutionalization of the welfare state, thereby counteracting many of the more exploitative forces of the industrial system. They did not, however, in the main industrial countries lead to the proletarianization of the organization of the industrial system.

sion-making presents problems at least as complicated as those in the other three contexts. The drive to participation contains a regressive component as a continuation of the adolescent phase of peer solidarity. Since it is partly motivated by student resistance to the socialization they need if they are to emerge from the undergraduate academic confines into the wider world, the motivation to participate in the decision-making process may conceal an "incestuous" component: a desire to become too firmly a part of the academic system.

Conversely, the faculty role is parallel to that of the parents in familial socialization. Faculty are in a position to exert pressure to direct student motivation and interest outside the *local* academic unit. Capacity to exert such pressure rests on the faculty's maintaining status superiority as a collectivity within the relevant differentiated context. This status superiority rests upon three components: (1) technical competence, (2) differentiated commitment to the central academic value of cognitive rationality, and (3) higher levels of responsibility for those social systems grounded in professional career-commitment.

Since collective decision-making inherently relates to authority and power, students are predisposed to interpret the frustrations of their position in terms of their inferior power and status and to feel that they need and deserve enhanced power and position. Despite this frequently erroneous inference, students should and can assume considerably more power than they have had.

The student power issue is symbolically committed to the notion that the appropriate model for the government of the academic community is the democratic association. Such a model treats students as the majority in a constituency to which both faculties and administration should be held responsible. Carried to an extreme, this doctrine asserts that ultimate power should rest in the total membership with "one member, one vote." This ideologically congenial model is incompatible with the faculty's professional expertise and socializing responsibilities. Faculties, like other professional groups, should not be responsible *to* any particular constituency in the democratic sense. They are responsible *for* the implementation of the values of the academic system. These values require support from many other segments of the society beside the academic segment within which the students are one part.

From this perspective, student activism is constructive to the extent that it results in students taking appropriate kinds of *responsibility*. A shift from serving as passive objects of the teaching process to active participants in the process implies that students should be participants in the defining of the educational function and in collective decision-making. In what ways and within what limits this participation should be implemented constitute unsettled questions whose solutions will permit a great deal of variation (see footnote 31).

If increased participation is to be constructive, however, the orientation of the relevant student groups must be differentiated in two ways through socialization. The first way involves student internalization of the status differentiation between faculties and students with respect to competence, commitment to academic values, and the attendant responsibilities in collective decision-making—a combination that precludes total equality. The second way involves student internalization of the differentiation between the functions of the academic system and the functions of other sectors of the society. This differentiation is necessary to avoid a student demand for immediate relevance and the resulting politicization of the academic system.

The demand for relevance is constructive insofar as it prevents exclusive preoccupation with the internal academic community. After all, an outcome of student socialization should be emancipation from undue attachment to alma mater. But the student should become motivated to graduate as an educated man, not simply as a passionate participant in *non*academic concerns.[40] His student participation in the academic community and his internalization of its values should make him intellectually critical of the political causes in which he participates (Parsons and Platt, 1968b, Chapter I, pp. 15 ff.).

The student participation issue seems to us potentially the most important of the four constructive outcomes of student activism. On this issue hinges the integration of the academic community in relation to its stratification. Student participation in the academic community presents a parallel problem to that of integration of the adolescent in the family for the earlier phase of socialization. The post-Oedipal child has renounced erotic ties to his parents and looks toward acceptance as a full member of the family. At the studentry stage, the parallel problem is renunciation of the adolescent peer solidarity in favor of membership in the more differentiated, achievement-oriented, academic community.[41] The student role implies such membership—with the condition that the student be oriented to completing his studies and to leaving both the status of student and the college community of his studentship.

The four main themes of student dissent have in common a deviant desire on the student's part to "eat his cake and have it too"—to have the privileges and immunities of student status, but at the same time to be treated as the equal of the members of the faculty; to exercise to the full the functions of militant political activism with respect to the wider society, but at the same

[40] The theme of the complicity of academia in the evils of the larger society may be symbolically related to this status of "alma mater"—we think the mother-symbolism is significant. Like the Oedipal son, the student likes to feel that "mother" is really "pure." Discovery of her involvement outside the academic "home" may then be taken as evidence that she is "really" no better than a "whore."

[41] A shift from primacy of affect to primacy of recognition.

time to be protected by academic sanctuary and academic freedom; to enjoy the gratifications of expressive individualism, but at the same time to benefit from the prestige and moral respect of an institution grounded in the disciplines of cognitive values and instrumental contributions.

Indeed, we may sum up our discussion of student dissent by noting two clusters of deviant pressure. One, centering in the structure of the academic community, is a tendency to advocate an egalitarian solidarity, including all elements in the utopian tradition. The second is the tendency to push individualistic needs for impulse gratification beyond institutional controls and definitions, including bounds imposed by cognitive orientations. This pressure is manifested in anti-intellectualism, in the self-fulfillment syndrome, and in extreme forms of irrationalism and anarchism.

The normative institutional framework central to the modern academic system is individualistic. However, its individualism rewards disciplined cognitive achievement within the framework of a life of expressive satisfactions and, on the organizational side, rests on a pluralistically differentiated social structure. This structure is integrated in an organic solidarity. "Student power," in the dedifferentiated version of full democracy, presses for mechanical rather than organic solidarity.

The points developed in this paper do not fully explain current student disturbances. However, an ingredient in a comprehensive explanation of student behavior is a view of the interconnections among the mass growth of the student population, its structural changes, and its socialization. This ingredient has been neglected, leading to widespread puzzlement even among sophisticated social scientists over apparently bizarre student behavior.

4 Concluding remarks

In the first section of this paper, we analyzed the broad historical perspective underlying the formulations offered here. We suggested that currently a new and very important stage of socialization is emerging, which we refer to as "studentry." This new stage, not yet fully institutionalized, has contributed to increased pressures on students, thus exacerbating student discontent as reflected in contemporary student movements. Our analysis takes this form, not because we wish to "rob" the student activists of their realistic concerns, but because we believe that the student movement, like any social movement, is motivated by both conscious and unconscious forces. We have focused on the more basic forces underlying broad student movements, rather than only on the radicals' explicitly stated bases for action.

The second section was an analysis of the structure of the situation in which students, especially undergraduates, are placed in the current system of higher education, and of the strains to which, consequently, many groups of students are exposed. Structured situations for groups of individuals, which may also be seen as subsystems of a society, often do impose strains on participants, but the nature and significance of these strains may vary, potentially having positive functions in the larger social system, rather than, for example, simply denoting malintegration.

The problems of students in the system of higher education can be examined within the more general context of the social organization of learning. Learning, in this sense, includes two basic processes: the process of assimilating the cognitive content of subject matter and methods of dealing with cognitive problems; and the process of internalizing the values and norms of the social systems of reference as part of the noncognitive, if not nonrational, structure of personalities. The latter process is what is ordinarily called *socialization*, and it has been our primary concern. Though the two processes are so intimately intertwined as to be only analytically distinct, their separation is theoretically productive.

The most intensive analysis of socialization as internalization of values carried out by social scientists has concerned the years of early childhood, culminating in the Oedipal transition, which is fraught with strains that are by no means simply a function of the Western middle-class family (Anne Parsons, 1969). During these years, the primary social environment is the family. We have long had the conviction that the socialization process was continuous from the phases impinging on the preschool child in the family through those in which he is involved in the system of formal education. This theme was previously developed for the phase of "latency" following the Oedipal transition, and for adolescence (Dreeben, 1968; Parsons, 1959b). What is new about our present analysis is not the assertion of continuity in socialization, but the attempt to support that assertion with a detailed analysis and empirical materials regarding a new phase. The advent of *mass* higher education has created a social situation in which the educational system is the primary vehicle of a phase of the socialization process that did not previously exist for most individuals. A symptom of the newness of the phase of studentry is the disposition of sociologists and psychologists still to treat adolescence as the "final" phase before "full" maturity (Friedenberg, 1959).

Putting aside the interesting question of whether the *whole* life course until old age may fruitfully be regarded as a process of socialization, clearly the phase of studentry is distinctive. Compared with the preceding phases it represents a maximal dissociation from the family of orientation. Moreover, the social systems in which the student is placed are characterized by types of social structure that, in sociological tradition, present drastic contrasts to that of the family. Many readers will hence quite legitimately wonder how we bridge the gap between socialization in the family and in the system of higher education.

It is with respect to this problem that our use of the term "analogy" requires elucidation. For some reason, analogy has come to be a pejorative term in social sciences, while in two other disciplines, namely biology and law, quite the contrary is true. We use it to describe a complex and subtle *combination* of similarities and differences. As Eisenstadt (1956) has pointed out, the social structures of kinship and of the major macroscopically significant subsystems differ sharply in modern societies, but the child in such societies is required to move from one to the other. The former may be summarily described as particularistic and functionally diffuse, the latter as universalistic and functionally specific. We maintain, however that, insofar as both types of social system have socialization functions, they also have *similarities* of structure that cross-cut their centrally important differences. It is with respect to these similarities that the systems may be said to be analogous. And it is on this fundamental analogous function in the family and in higher education that our analysis hinges. Refutation of our analysis of significance must demonstrate theoretically and/or empirically that socialization is not a primary function of both these systems.

The first and primary structural similarity is that both the family and the system of higher education—and, we suggest, all other socialization systems —are differentiated on an hierarchical axis, of parents and children in the one case, faculty and students in the other. In both, the learning process is not fully symmetrical; both parents and faculty members are more "teachers" than "learners," though there is a learning process the other way, and in some respects a very important one (Parsons and Bales, 1955).

As it happens, both cases of hierarchical differentiation involve, not only relative superiority, but a difference of stage in the life course. Faculty members, on the average, approximate the age of the parents of their students. This age relation, however, is related to another basic similarity between the family and higher education: faculty members, like parents, have a long-term "career" commitment to their roles, whereas both children and students occupy roles requiring a transient commitment from which they not only expect, but are "pressured," to graduate.

Another common feature related to Erikson's (1950) conception of adolescence as providing a "moratorium" on the way to full adulthood, is a certain insulation of both systems from the interaction system of the environing society. In this respect studentry is a substantially *modified* extension of adolescence, in that the student is still in part protected against environing pressures, at the price of certain elements of dependence, of which inability to earn a full financial living is prototypical. There is also a notable inhibition of marriage, at least among undergraduates.

As a function of the combination of hierarchical difference and dependency we have argued that those who are the senior in the socialization process enjoy certain privileges of privacy vis-à-vis the junior, and that in some form this privacy has important positive functions. For the family, the erotic relation between the parents is the *locus classicus* of privacy, but the privilege of privacy extends also to "managerial" functions on behalf of the family. The fundamental relevance of privacy, however, is to the maintenance of conditions for the solidarity of the coalition among socializing agents.

Though the similarities described above may not constitute an exhaustive list, they are sufficient to establish an analogy, in the theoretically fruitful sense, between the family and the university or college as socializing agencies in the society. We are also fully aware that, because of the recency of the relative crystallization of the modern phase of mass higher education, many phenomena currently occurring are occasioned by rapid change as such rather than the inherent strains of a socialization process; but that the latter component of strain should be present and important, however, is an essential thesis of our analysis.

The task of disentangling the more or less general manifestation of strains reflecting the disorganizing effects of social change from those attendant on the socialization functions of higher education is highly complex, and we do not claim to have made more than a beginning in this respect. The main contribution of Section 3 of our essay has been to suggest and to attempt an approach to such an analysis at an empirical level. The thrust of this exposition is the contention that the primary themes of the current student protest movement show a striking "fit" with what one would expect if the strains of a socialization process do in fact constitute a major factor in the underlying social psychology. Moreover, here our analogy is helpful in suggesting that many of these themes can be interpreted as variants of the classical Oedipal themes, "translated" into an idiom appropriate to a much later phase of the life course. Thus the strictures on the oppressiveness of faculty-administration authority have a close resemblance to the corresponding resentment against paternal authority. Similarly, the "impersonality" of the academic institutional system is contrasted with the intimate affectivity that would be associated with the maternal component of the family. Indeed, there may be a tendency to define this maternal component (e.g., the symbol *alma mater*) as the "real" essence of the college and the "hard" tasks of cognitive learning as an unwarranted intrusion, unless confronted "spontaneously" rather than externally imposed.

Our exploratory analysis of current protest is *not* intended to suggest that the student revolt is "essentially Oedipal," a revolt against actual fathers (Feuer, 1968). Quite the contrary, we interpret it as a phenomenon grounded in much more general features of modern society—the need for and partial institutionalization of a complex and time-extended process of socialization that has now entered a new phase. This phase *resembles* the Oedipal in that it also imposes seemingly harsh demands and severe psychological strains on the individual, but the specific demands, the individuals on whom they impinge, and the specific strains, are very different in the two phases. Resolution of the conflicts manifest in the new phase will surely not derive from "reform" of the family with special reference to the early childhood years, but will have to involve more general structures of the society, including, of course, the system of higher education itself on which the present essay is focused.

When we speak of an analogy, specifically that between the Oedipal family and higher education, we do not intend *only* an extraction of similarities between socialization systems at discrete stages of the life course. Though we have not had space to develop the full approach, we have throughout assumed the importance of *continuities* through the succession of phases. Such continuities characterize the shift of the child's primary interests from the family into the system of higher education and the associated structures of peer associations. A more complete analysis would be devoted to detailed examination, not only of the character of each separate stage, but also of the nature of the transitions from one to the next. Once the evidence for continuity is mobilized, our analogy would then describe a set of phenomena that are diverse in certain respects but understandable in terms of common theoretical propositions.

One of the fundamental differences between the family as a socializing system and the university lies in the fact that parents are socializing their children to be, in their turn and among other things, themselves parents, whereas college teachers are socializing only a minority of their students to become college teachers and academic professionals. This difference is indeed critical. The critical point is contained in the phrase "and other things" in the first clause of the preceding sentence. The typical modern adult—with, to be sure, very important exceptions—is a parent, but decreasingly, even in the case of women, only a parent. Family socialization is clearly, at the appropriate levels, not only socialization for future familial roles, but at the same time, that of a personality equipped to participate in a variety of other, structurally different roles. Occupation looms large in this category of "other" but is by no means the only extrafamilial case.

Studentry socialization differs in that typically, since academic professionals constitute a small minority of the "educated" adult population, only a contingent will in fact go on to that type of career. If, however, the system of higher education is to be viable in the wider society, the values and norms internalized in this contingent must be part of the same system as those entering into quite different careers in the wider society, serving nonacademic functions. There is perhaps here an interesting parallel to an earlier situation in the family. Girls were being socialized above all for the roles of wife and mother, whereas boys were to be husbands and fathers, to be sure, but *also* to compete in the larger world of occupation, politics, and the like.

In a curious sense, perhaps, the academics of today are comparable to the women of yesterday. They are to be anchored in the partially segregated socialization system that is higher education, which of course is the primary source of genesis not only of new personalities, but of new knowledge. They are perhaps, in a curious sense of reversal, the symbolic "mothers" of the coming adult generations, whereas the men and women of practical matters are the symbolic fathers. This, at least, is *one* way to characterize the special status of the adult component of the current academic system, which in a broader sense is unquestionably adult but perhaps enjoys, and should, a partial insulation from other aspects of the macrosocial world.

Works cited in Chapter 7

Adorno, T. W., et al., 1950. *The Authoritarian Personality*, New York: Harper & Brothers.

American Council on Education, 1969. "Ratio of First-Time Student Residents to High School Graduates, by Region and State, 1963," in *A Fact Book on Higher Education*, First Issue 1969, Washington, D.C.

Avorn, J. L., et al., 1968. *Up Against the Ivy Wall*, New York: Atheneum.

Barber, Bernard, 1952. *Science and the Social Order*, Glencoe, Ill.: Free Press.

Benedict, Ruth, 1938. "Continuities and Discontinuities in Cultural Conditioning," *Psychiatry*, 1, pp. 161–167.

Berelson, Bernard, 1960. *Graduate Education in the United States*, New York: McGraw-Hill.

Bunzel, John H., 1968. "Black Studies at San Francisco State," *The Public Interest*, No. 13 (special issue), pp. 22–38.

Carnegie Commission on Higher Education, 1968. "Quality and Equality: New Levels of Federal Responsibility for Higher Education," New York: McGraw-Hill.

Chinoy, Eli, 1955. *Automobile Workers and the American Dream*, Garden City, N.Y.: Doubleday.

Christie, Richard, and Marie Jahoda, editors, 1954. *Studies in the Scope and Method of "The Authoritarian Personality,"* Glencoe, Ill.: Free Press.

Cohen, Mitchell, and Dennis Hale, editors, 1966. *The New Student Left*, Boston: Beacon Press.

Cottle, Thomas J., 1969. "Parent and Child—The Hazards of Equality," *Saturday Review*, February 1, 1969, pp. 16 ff.

Cox, Archibald, 1968. *Crisis at Columbia: Report of The Fact Finding Commission Appointed to Investigate the Disturbances at Columbia University*, New York: Random House.

Crozier, Michel, 1968. "French Students, a Letter from Nanterre-LaFolie," *The Public Interest*, No. 13 (special issue), pp. 151–159.

Daedalus, Spring 1969. Vol. 98, No. 2.

Dreeben, Robert, 1968. *On What is Learned in School,* Reading, Mass.: Addison-Wesley.

Duncan, Beverly, 1968. "Trends in Output and Distribution of Schooling," in Sheldon, Eleanor Bernert, and Wilbert E. Moore, editors, *Indicators of Social Change,* New York: Russell Sage Foundation, pp. 601–672.

Eisenstadt, S. N., 1956. *From Generation to Generation,* New York: Free Press of Glencoe.

Erikson, Erik H., 1950. *Childhood and Society,* New York: Norton.

————, 1959. "Identity and the Life Cycle," in Klein, George S., editor, *Psychological Issues,* New York: International Universities.

————, editor, 1965. *The Challenge of Youth,* Garden City, N.Y.: Doubleday, Anchor Books.

Feuer, Lewis, 1968. *The Conflict of Generations,* New York: Basic Books.

Freud, Sigmund, (1911), 1958. "Formulations on Two Principles of Mental Functioning (1911)" in *The Standard Edition of the Complete Psychological Works of Sigmund Freud,* edited and translated by J. Strachey, London: Hogarth Press.

Friedenberg, Edgar Z., 1959. *The Vanishing Adolescent,* Boston: Beacon Press.

Fromm, Erich, 1944. "Origins of Neurosis," *American Sociological Review,* 9, pp. 380–384.

Gallup Opinion Index, June 1969. "Results of Survey of College Students," pp. 6–7.

Glazer, Nathan, 1968. "Student Power in Berkeley," *The Public Interest,* No. 13 (special issue), Fall 1968, pp. 3–21.

Glazer, Nathan, and Daniel Patrick Moynihan, 1963. *Beyond the Melting Pot,* Cambridge, Mass.: M.I.T. Press.

Gross, Edward, 1968. "Universities as Organizations: A Research Approach," *American Sociological Review,* 33, pp. 518–544.

Hacker, Andrew, 1965. "The College Grad Has Been Shortchanged," *The New York Times Magazine,* June 6, pp. 25 ff.

Historical Statistics of the United States, Colonial Times to 1957, Series H327–338, "Institutions of Higher Education—Degrees Confered by Sex: 1870–1957," Washington: Government Printing Office, 1960.

Iwanska, Alicja, 1958. "Good Fortune: Second Chance Community," Pullman, Washington: Washington Agricultural Experiment Stations, Institute of Agricultural Sciences, State College of Washington, Bulletin 589.

Jencks, Christopher, and David Riesman, 1968. *The Academic Revolution,* Garden City, N.Y.: Doubleday.

Kafka, Franz, 1954. "Letter to His Father," in Kafka, Franz, *Dearest Father: Stories and Other Writings,* New York: Schocken, pp. 138–196.

Katope, Christopher, and Paul G. Zolbrod, editors, 1966. *Beyond Berkeley: A Sourcebook in Student Values,* New York: World.

Lidz, Theodore, Stephen Fleck, and Alice R. Cornelison, 1965. *Schizophrenia and the Family,* New York: International University Press.

Maynatz, Renate, 1968. "Germany, Radicals and Reformers," *The Public Interest*, No. 13 (special issue), pp. 160–172.

Merton, Robert K., 1957. *Social Theory and Social Structure*, rev. ed., Glencoe, Ill.: Free Press.

Parsons, Anne, 1969. *Belief, Magic and Anomie: Essays in Psychosocial Anthropology*, Chapter One, "Is the Oedipus Complex Universal? The Hones-Malinowski Debate Revisited," New York: Free Press.

Parsons, Talcott, 1959a. "General Theory in Sociology," in Merton, Robert K., Leonard Broom, and Leonard S. Cottrell, Jr., editors, *Sociology Today*, New York: Basic Books, pp. 29–36.

————, 1959b. "The School Class as a Social System: Some of Its Functions in American Society," *Harvard Educational Review*, 20, pp. 297–318. [Reprinted in Halsey, A. H., Jean Floud, and Arnold C. Anderson, editors, *Education, Economy and Society*, New York: Free Press, 1961.]

————, 1960. "Durkheim's Contribution to the Theory of Integration of Social Systems," in Wolff, Kurt H., editor, *Emile Durkheim, 1858–1917: A Collection of Essays*, Columbus, Ohio: Ohio State University Press.

————, 1964. *Social Structure and Personality*, New York: Free Press.

————, 1966. "Full Citizenship for the Negro American? A Sociological Problem," *The Negro American*, Boston: Houghton Mifflin, pp. 709–754.

————, 1968. "Christianity," in Sills, David L., editor, *International Encyclopedia of the Social Sciences*, 17 vols., New York: Macmillan and Free Press, 2, pp. 425–446.

————, 1968b. "The Academic System: A Sociologist's View," *The Public Interest*, No. 13 (special issue), pp. 173–197.

————, 1968c. "On the Concept of Value-Commitments," *Sociological Inquiry*, 38, pp. 135–159.

————, 1969. "Human Experimentation and the Professional Complex," *Daedalus*, 98, pp. 325–360.

————, 1970. "Some Problems of General Theory in Sociology," in McKinney, John C., and Edward A. Tiryakian, editors, *Theoretical Sociology: Perspectives and Developments*, New York: Appleton-Century-Crofts.

————, and Robert F. Bales, 1955. *Family, Socialization and Interaction Process*, Glencoe, Ill.: Free Press.

————, Robert F. Bales, and Edward A, Shils, 1953. *Working Papers in the Theory of Action*, New York: Free Press.

————, and Gerald M. Platt, 1968a. "Considerations on the American Academic System," *Minerva*, 6 pp. 497–523.

————, and Gerald M. Platt, 1968b. *The American Academic Profession: A Pilot Study*, Cambridge, Mass. Multilith.

————, and Winston White, 1961. "The Link Between Character and Society," in Lipset, Seymour Martin, and Leo Lowenthal, editors, *Culture and Social Character*, New York: Free Press of Glencoe, pp. 89–135.

Piaget, Jean, 1965. *The Moral Judgment of the Child*, trans. Marjorie Gabain, New York: Free Press.

Ramparts, June 15, 1968. "The Siege of Columbia," pp. 24–39.

Rokeach, Milton, 1960. *The Open and Closed Mind*, New York: Basic Books.

Rosenberg, Morris, 1957. *Occupations and Values*, Glencoe, Ill.: Free Press.

Schneider, David M., 1968. *American Kinship: A Cultural Account*, Englewood Cliffs, N.J.: Prentice-Hall.

Shils, Edward, 1956. *The Torment of Secrecy: The Background and Consequences of American Security Policies*, Glencoe, Ill.: Free Press.

————, 1961. "Centre and Periphery," in *The Logic of Personal Knowledge: Essays Presented to Michael Polanyi*, London: Routledge and Kegan Paul, pp. 117–131.

Simon, Kenneth A., and W. Vance Grant, 1964. *Digest of Educational Statistics*, Washington: U.S. Office of Education, Bulletin # 18.

Smelser, Neil J., 1959. *Social Change in the Industrial Revolution*, Chicago: University of Chicago Press

————, 1968. "Sociological History: The Industrial Revolution and the British Working-Class Family," in Smelser, Neil J., *Essays in Sociological Explanation*, Englewood Cliffs, N.J.: Prentice-Hall, pp. 76–91.

Spady, William G., 1967. "Educational Mobility and Access; Growth and Paradoxes," *American Journal of Sociology*, 73, pp. 273–286.

Stanton, Alfred H., and Morris S. Schwartz, 1954. *The Mental Hospital: A Study of Institutional Participation in Psychiatric Illness and Treatment*, New York: Basic Books.

Storer, Norman W., 1966. *The Social System of Science*, New York: Holt, Rinehart and Winston.

Weinstein, Fred, and Gerald M. Platt, 1969. *The Wish to be Free: Society, Psyche and Value Change*, Berkeley: University of California Press.

Whyte, William Foote, 1955. *Street Corner Society*, 2nd ed., Chicago: University of Chicago Press.

Wilson, Robert C., and Gerry G. Gaff, 1969. "Student Voice—Faculty Response," in *The Research Reporter* (The Center for Research and Development in Higher Education) University of California, Berkeley, Vol. IV, No. 2, pp. 1–4.

8

Age, aging, and age structure in science

HARRIET ZUCKERMAN AND ROBERT K. MERTON

Scientists, and social scientists in particular, have come to recognize that increments of understanding are yielded by a conception of science that goes beyond cognitive structure and technological apparatus to include the social system *of science. In this essay, Harriet Zuckerman and Robert K. Merton utilize this conception to broaden understanding in two major directions: the sociology of science and the sociology of age stratification.*

By introducing relevant concepts of age stratification into the sociology of science, they develop new theoretical statements and fresh evaluations of available evidence on such subjects as the relation between the growth of science and the age structure of the scientific population, or the influence of scientific codification on age patterns of scientific behavior. They show how both historical trends and the socially patterned process of aging enter into the allocation of teaching, research, and administrative roles in science. In examining the extent of gerontocracy in science, they advance the basic idea that such inquiry must deal not only with the age hierarchy in distribution of powerful positions, but also with the consequences of this age structuring of power for younger scientists, for the accumulation of scientific knowledge, and for the relation of science to social policy. Through their discussions of collaboration in authorship and of shifts in scientific concerns, they illustrate the diverse ways in which the process of socialization intermeshes with processes of aging and cohort succession to affect the structure and culture of science.

The innovative treatment by Zuckerman and Merton of these central problems in the sociology of science is in itself enough to mark their essay as a notable contribution. But the importance of this contribution extends farther, for they have also expanded the potential of a sociology of age stratification, rather than simply drawing upon it. The authors have added to our still meager stock of finely honed conceptual tools. The happy choices of "juvenocracy" and "juvenescent population" and of "role-attrition" and "role-retention" are concepts and terms that will, no doubt, find permanent residence in the literature on age. More profoundly, Zuckerman and Merton also add concrete illustration of the relation of age to social process, structure, and change. Their analysis of the growth of science, for example, points to ways in which the environing social system sets limits upon a changing age structure. Their discussion of codification in science reminds us that socialization (in this case the rapidity with which new roles are learned) can influence the allocative processes and press for a reordering of the age structure of power. Not least, their lucid examination of scientific roles, including collaborative roles, emphasizes the fundamental point that we must not allow unchanging role labels—parent, child, friend as well as scientist— to obscure the changes in role performances that actually take place historically and over the life course. In such manner does the theory of age stratification develop as it is applied.

Critical overviews of a particular subject are ordinarily occasioned by the need to consolidate rapid advance in knowledge about it and to identify new directions of research. That is surely not so here. The best case that can be made for a chapter dealing with age stratification in science is that so little is known about it. In point of fact, systematic research over the years has been devoted to only one problem in this field: the patterns and sources of changes in the productivity of scientists during their life course. Beyond that, just about any methodical research on age, age cohorts, and age structure in science would qualify, through prior default, as a "new" direction.

The character of this chapter is therefore practically dictated by the twin circumstance that few theoretical questions have been addressed to the phenomena of age stratification in science and that only scattered investigations have dealt with these questions. Since the field is so short on facts, we must here be long on conjectures. Still the path of acknowledged conjecture, leading from mere guess and surmise to the neighborhood of grounded hypothesis, has its uses too. It can take us to a problematics[1] of our subject: the formulation of principal questions that should be investigated together with the rationale for considering these as questions worth investigating. For this purpose, we draw upon both the scattered evidence in hand and the model of age stratification developed by Matilda White Riley, Marilyn Johnson and Anne Foner.[2]

Put in utterly plain language, the aim of this chapter is to set out the little

We are indebted to Ian Maitland for his assistance. The writing of this paper was supported in part by a grant from the National Science Foundation to the Program in the Sociology of Science, Columbia University.
[1] On the concept of problematics and of problem-finding, see Merton (1959, pp. v, ix–xxxiv).
[2] We refer in the main to Chapter 1 of this volume.

that we know and the much that we do not know but could know about the sociology of age differentiation in science and to explain why we should want to know it.

The paucity of materials on age differentiation in science appears to be the product of two distinct kinds of neglect in sociology. The first is the strangely slight attention given to age stratification generally even though age is recognized as one of the universal components of social structure. The second is the perhaps greater and now equally strange neglect of the entire sociology of science which, until the last decade or so, had enlisted the sustained interest of a remarkably small number of investigators. Neglect of this subject is odd if only because both advocates and critics of science are agreed that science is one of the major dynamic forces in the modern world. The convergence of the two kinds of neglect has meant that it was most improbable that sociologists would methodically investigate age differentiation in science. Nevertheless, enough work has been done to furnish a basis for formulating the problematics of the subject.

In this chapter, we deal with only a limited range of those problems. The first section is concerned with the connections between the growth and age structure of science; the second, with the relations between one aspect of the cognitive structure of science, here called "codification," and age-patterned behavior in science; the third, with age-related allocations of roles and with role-sequences in science; the fourth, with the operation of age-stratified structures of authority, principally in the form of gerontocracy; the fifth, with age- and prestige-stratified patterns of collaboration in science; and the sixth, final section dealing with age-patterned foci of problems selected for scientific investigation.

1 *Growth and age structure of science*

By all the rough-and-ready measures now available, science, with its various interacting components, has been growing more rapidly than most other fields of human activity. For example, the population of scientists, with a doubling time of about 15 years, is far outrunning the accelerating rate of increase in the general population. The science population of the United States, comprised of scientists, engineers, and technicians, grew from just under half a million in 1940 to 1.8 million in 1967. (About 300,000 of these in the latter period are estimated to be scientists [United States Bureau of the Census, 1970, p. 525].) The number of doctorates annually awarded in science has increased from about 60 in 1885 to some 16,000 in 1969, a growth rate of some 7 per cent per annum through this long period (National Academy of Sciences—National Research Council, 1970). And as Price (1963, Chapter 1; 1961, Chapter 5) has observed, the number of scientists and of scientific journals, articles and abstracts, and, more recently, the funds available for research have all been increasing exponentially at varying rates.

Of immediate interest to us is that this growth results from the recruitment into science of youthful cohorts, principally in their 20's, and practically not at all from the migration into it of older persons drawn from other occupations. And once in science, they tend to stay there. One now hears much about the so-called flight from science, but the historical pattern still remains. Scientists continue to be a tenacious lot, seldom leaving science for an entirely different occupation,[3] although there is an appreciable amount of transfer between fields of science at various phases in the life course. This raises a significant sociological problem in its own right, one that has been little explored in the sociology of occupations.

> *Query:* How are occupations arrayed in terms of rates of growth in personnel, and how do these rates and their components of entries and exits compare at different phases in the life course? What structural properties of occupations and characteristics of people recruited by them make for observed patterns of turnover?

Such detailed and systematic comparisons between age-stratified rates of turnover in various occupations are in short supply.[4] All the same, we suppose that classes of occupation have their exits and their entrances, distinctively patterned by age. In the case of science, transfers of personnel to other fields have been so conspicuously small that we take it to be in this respect near one extreme in the family of occupations. Once in the profession, scientists generally exit only through death or reluctant retirement.[5]

The patterns of growth and turnover in science are probably affected in at least three ways by the long period of socialization required to qualify for scientific work. Even in recent years, with the substantial funding of scientific education through fellowships and training grants in the United States, it takes an average period of 11 years after entry into college to obtain the doctorate in science (National Science Foundation, 1971, p. iii). First, the prolonged period devoted to acquiring the knowledge, skills, attitudes, values, and behavior patterns of the scientist means, as we have noted, that few enter the profession in later years after they have been at work in some other occupation. Second, this entails a considerable investment in the prospects of a career in science. The investment is not merely economic, with its financial

---

[3] This statement refers to those who have actually begun to work in science, not to those who have taken an undergraduate degree in science. In the United States, about half of all college graduates majoring in science and engineering go on into other occupational fields. See Brode (1971, p. 207).

[4] In the absence of suitable comparative investigations, Super (1957, Chapter 4) touches the periphery of this problem by impressionistically examining "occupational life spans."

[5] There is, however, a fair amount of mobility through the statuses and roles *within* the social system of science, as we shall see in a later section.

costs of education and its foregone income during the period of preparation, but is affective as well. It is investment in a preferred way of life and commitment to it. Third, the high rate of attrition before entering the profession probably reflects a stringent process of social selection. Some 40 per cent of candidates for the doctorate fail to complete their program of graduate study (Berelson, 1960, p. 154), possibly leaving a more deeply committed and intellectually apt residue to go on into science.

Such modal patterns of entry and exit, coupled with the exponential increase in numbers of scientists, leave their stamp upon the age structure of the profession; and, as we shall indicate, this structure in turn affects both the normative system of science and its intellectual development. Figure 8 · 1, which compares the age distribution of scientific personnel with that of all employed personnel in the United States, suggests the ways in which the life-course processes of entry and exit combine with growth through cohort succession to yield the current age structure of science. On the one hand, the impact of delayed entry of scientific personnel into the labor force, necessitated by long years of prior training, is apparent from comparison of the age categories under 24 and 25–34. The relative size of the older strata, on the other hand, reflects the *juvenescent effect* of rapid growth on the age structure, as the size of entry cohorts expands. Despite the tendency of scientists to delay their retirement, the proportion of the scientific population in the older age strata is relatively small. Thus the age structure reflects the counteracting patterns of life-course and cohort flow.

The rate of increase in the population of scientists far outruns that of the American population at large, which results in an increasingly youthful population of scientists, both absolutely and comparatively. Their higher rate of increase means that scientists in the aggregate are also more youthful than the other professions. For example, more than half of those listed in the 1968 National Register of Scientific and Technical Personnel are under the age of 40 and 81 per cent of them under 50, compared with 63 per cent for lawyers and physicians (United States Bureau of the Census, 1970, pp. 65, 155, 525).

EDUCATION, AGE STRUCTURE, AND ALLOCATION

As with all social statuses and group memberships,[6] the status of "scientist" is not merely a matter of self-definition and ascription but also, and more significantly, of social definition and ascription. It is not enough to declare oneself to be a chemist or psychologist or space scientist; in order for the given status to have social reality it must be validated by "status judges," those institutions and agents charged with authenticating claims. Licensing boards for

---

[6] For a theoretical analysis of group membership and nonmembership, see Merton (1968b, pp. 338–351); the concepts of status-judges and status-imputation are treated in Merton (1958).

FIGURE 8 · 1 *Comparative age structures: scientific personnel and total employed personnel, United States*

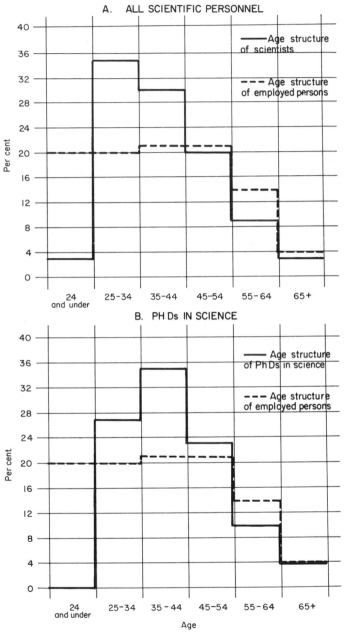

Source: National Science Foundation, 1969, p. 50; U.S. Department of Labor, 1968, p. 30.

many professions and specialty boards in medicine are only the more visible and firmly institutionalized specimens of status judges. The criteria for the status of scientists are typically educational attainment ("earned academic degrees") and role-performance ("experience").

Since formal education is typically confined to the early years in life, the changing age structure of science is closely related to a concurrent educational upgrading of the scientific population. As Harvey Brooks (1971, p. 319) has highlighted this trend:

> A striking fact is that in 1968 the percentage of the age cohort receiving Ph.D.'s in science and engineering and medical or dental degrees was higher than the percentage of the corresponding age cohort that received bachelor's degrees in science and engineering in 1920.

This rapid change in the educational composition of the science population is a special and illuminating case of the general rise in the level of education. As Riley and Foner have noted (1968, Volume I, Chapter 5), the long-range rise in formal education for the population at large has meant that, at any given time, older people are educationally disadvantaged in comparison with younger ones. In the special case of science, we deal of course with the uppermost reaches of the educational distribution, and this introduces distinctive complexities. It may not be so much the social change in the level of attained education but the cultural change in the extent and character of scientific knowledge that presents the age cohorts of scientists with distinctive ranges of difficulties and opportunities. All this may lead to problems of career obsolescence and kindred difficulties for scientists in their life course. It also introduces various problems for the social organization of science; for example:

> Query: How do the social and cultural changes in the education of scientists and in the growth of scientific knowledge affect the working relations between cohorts of scientists? Do they make for social cleavage and discontinuity between them? What social mechanisms, if any, bind the cohorts together and make for continuity in scientific development?

Thus the changing age and educational structure of science is congruent with the self-image, prevalent among scientists, that pictures "science as a young man's game." But this expression, repeated on every side by scientists young and old, does not refer primarily to the age (or sex) distribution of scientists. Rather, it only announces a widespread belief that the best work in science is done at a comparatively early age. This posited linkage between age and significant productivity is still the focus of the little research that has been done on age stratification in science and we shall be examining that research in detail. But here, the imagery of science as the prerogative of the young gener-

TABLE 8 · 1   *Median age of Ph.D's* ᵃ *in selected science fields*

Field	Median age[b]
All scientific fields	41.2
Mathematics	38.2
Physics	38.3
Chemistry	41.0
Biological sciences	41.8
Psychology	42.2
Sociology	44.1

[a] When medians are computed for all personnel, with or without the Ph.D., the rank order is roughly similar except that sociology rises to third place.
[b] Computed from grouped data by straight line interpolation.
Source: National Science Foundation (1969, pp. 50 ff.) (adapted).

ates another kind of sociological question, this one dealing with the linkages between age structure, prevalent values, and social organization.

> *Query:* How do the age structures of occupations and their component specialties relate to age-connected values (e.g., youth as asset or liability)? How do they relate also to other forms of stratification within the occupation (e.g., allocation of authority-statuses and roles, of rewards, etc.)?

AGE AND EDUCATION IN THE COMPONENT SCIENCES

Turning from science in the large to the constituent sciences, we find that the median age of their personnel varies considerably, as appears in Table 8 · 1. These divergences reflect sociologically interesting differences in the social definitions of boundaries of disciplines and of criteria for admission into them. In part, the age differences in the various science populations merely reflect a differing mix of scientists, who often hold doctorates; engineers, who rarely do, and technicians who almost never do.[7] As can be seen from Table 8 · 2, some 37 per cent of American scientists held doctorates in 1968, but the figures ranged widely from 95 per cent (anthropology) to 7 per cent (computer sciences) among the disciplines. Thus the social science populations, with comparatively fewer technicians, have far higher proportions holding doctorates. Still, as we have seen in Table 8 · 1, when comparisons are confined to those holding doctorates, substantial differences remain in the median ages of workers in the various sciences.

Very likely, the differing age distributions of component sciences result largely from differing rates of recruitment of new scientists and interchanges of personnel between the sciences at various stages in their educational and

---

[7] The Committee on Utilization of Scientific and Engineering Manpower of the National Academy of Sciences reported in 1964 that fewer than 2 per cent of engineers had a Ph.D. No comparable counts have been published for technicians, no doubt because it would be a waste of funds, public or private, to search for what is known not to be there.

TABLE 8 · 2 *Percentages of scientists holding doctorates, according to fields of science, United States, 1968*

Field	Percentage holding doctorate
Anthropology	95
Psychology	64
Linguistics	62
Political science	59
Economics	53
Sociology	51
Biological sciences	48
Physics	44
Statistics	35
Chemistry	31
Mathematics	28
Earth and Marine Sciences	21
Agricultural sciences	18
Atmospheric and space sciences	9
Computer sciences	7
All fields	37

Source: National Register of Scientific and Technical Personnel (1968), adapted from Table, p. 23.

occupational careers. Although we assume that age-specific death and retirement rates are much the same for the various sciences, rates of transfer, which vary among age-strata, affect their age structures (National Science Foundation, 1971, pp. 16, 30). Substantial transfers from one science to others have been found in the course of undergraduate education (Reitz, 1972) and longitudinal studies have identified streams of interchange among practicing scientists (Harmon, 1965, Chapter 5). Yet, despite some strands of evidence, the sources of age differences among the sciences remain almost as much unexplored territory as the range of their consequences for the character and rate of development in the various sciences.

SLOWING GROWTH RATES OF SCIENCE

It has long been recognized in principle that the exponential growth of science at a rate greater than that of society could not continue indefinitely. Manifestly, the rate of expansion in the numbers of scientists, the amount of resources allocated to science and in the volume of scientific publication would have to slow down. Otherwise, as Derek Price (1963, p. 19) is fond of writing and as many others are fond of quoting, "We should have two scientists for every man, woman, child and dog in the population, and we should spend on them twice as much money as we had."

There are signs that, at least in societies with a substantial science base, the rate of expansion has tapered off. In the United States, for example, the resources expended for research and development have remained at about 3 per cent of GNP since 1964 (Martino, 1969, p. 769). There are indications, also, that the proportion of college graduates going into science has reached a ceiling (Brode, 1971, pp. 206–208).

Such equilibrium growth rates have direct consequences for the age and opportunity structures of science, as Martino has indicated (1969, p. 772). A direct consequence, of course, is an increase in the median age of scientists. Slackened increase in resources will mean fewer new research installations and new departments in new universities. In due course, the age structure of research groups will probably change with possible consequences for their productivity.[8] The rate of increase in the volume of scientific publication will tend to diminish. But if Weiss and Ziman are correct in suggesting that the proliferation of scientists and the big expansion in funds for research have resulted in an even more rapid proliferation of trivial research and trivial publications,[9] this decline in volume of publication need not mean a corresponding decline in the growth of knowledge. Finally, since the various changes do not occur uniformly in the individual sciences, the relative rates of development of long established and newly emerging disciplines will probably continue to differ (Rose and Rose, 1969, pp. 250–251).

2 Age stratification and the codification of scientific knowledge

In principle, the sociology of knowledge and, more narrowly, the sociology of science are concerned with the *reciprocal* relations between social structure and cognitive structure. In practice, however, sociologists of knowledge have dealt almost exclusively with the influences of the social structure upon the formation and development of ideas. And when sociologists of science have investigated the "impact of science upon society," this has been principally in the form of examining the, chiefly unanticipated, social consequences of science-based technology. In neither case is the effort made to trace the consequences of the cognitive structure of the various sciences for their distinctive social structures.

Yet the problem of the significance of cognitive structure for social structure is with us still. We propose to touch upon a limited case in point by examining one aspect of the cognitive structures of the sciences—what we call "codification"—in its relations to their distinctive age structures. Since so

---

[8] Vlachý (1970, pp. 132–134) and Thiemann (1970, pp. 1428–1429) maintain that the age structure of research groups affects their productivity, but little is yet known about this question. Available data reflect differences in the productivity of age strata rather than in various distributions of these strata.

[9] Weiss (1971, p. 135); Ziman (1969, p. 361) puts the thesis vigorously: ". . . the consequences of flabbiness [in science policy] are all too sadly evident in all quarters of the globe —the proliferation of third-rate research which is just as expensive of money and materials as the best, but does not really satisfy those who carry it out, and adds nothing at all to the world's stock of useful or useless knowledge."

little preparatory work has been done on this problem, our observations are altogether tentative, designed to raise questions rather than to answer them.

Codification refers to the consolidation of empirical knowledge into succinct and interdependent theoretical formulations. The various sciences and specialties within them differ in the extent to which they are codified. It has often been remarked, for example, that the intellectual organization of much of physics and chemistry differs from that of botany and zoology in the extent to which particulars are knit together by general ideas. The extent of codification of a science should affect the modes of gaining competence in it. Experience should count more heavily in the less codified fields. In these, scientists must get command of a mass of descriptive facts and of low-level theories whose implications are not well understood. The comprehensive and more precise theoretical structures of the more codified field not only allow empirical particulars to be derived from them but also provide more clearly defined criteria for assessing the importance of new problems, new data, and newly proposed solutions. All this should make for greater consensus among investigators at work in highly codified fields on the significance of new knowledge and the continuing relevance of old.

The notion that the sciences and specialties differ in the extent of their codification is not, of course, new. Some 20 years ago, James Conant introduced the counterpart idea that the various branches of science differ in "degree of empiricism." As he put it, "Where wide generalizations and theory enable one to calculate in advance the results of an experiment or to design a machine (a microscope or a telescope, for example), we may say that the degree of empiricism is low" (1950, p. 9). In our terms, the more codified a science or scientific specialty, the lower its degree of empiricism.[10]

By consolidating both data and ideas in theoretical formulations, the more highly codified fields tend to obliterate the original versions of past contributions by incorporating their essentials in the newer formulations. As Paul Weiss noted in his influential paper, "Knowledge: A Growth Process" (1960, p. 247), "Each field of knowledge must be accorded its own merit ratio between generalization and particularization, taking for granted that assimilation will be driven to the utmost limits compatible with the nature of the field." In this sense, the more highly codified the field, the higher the rate of "obsolescence" of publications in it. Weiss measured differentials in obsolescence by the age distributions of references appearing in publications in various

---

[10] The recent distinction between "hard" and "soft" science also bears a family resemblance to the concept of codification. Storer (1967) uses that pair of terms to characterize sciences given more, or less, to quantification and to rigor. Price (1970) has suggested various features which are distinctive of the literatures of hard science, soft science, technology, and other fields of learning.

sciences, a procedure which has since been described as "citation analysis."[11] Weiss found that references to recent work were much more frequent in "analytical physiology than in its more descriptive biological sister sciences" of zoology and entomology.

The general pattern has since been confirmed for a wider variety of disciplines.[12] The journals in fields we intuitively identify as more highly codified —physics, biophysics, and chemistry—show a larger share of reference to recent work; they exhibit a greater "immediacy," as Derek Price calls it.[13] By way of illustration,

> 72% of the references in *The Physical Review** are to papers published within the preceding five years, as are
> 63% in the *Cold Spring Harbor Symposium* on quantitative biology;
> 58% in *Analytical Chemistry;*
> 50% in the *Anatomical Record;* and
> 47% in the *American Zoologist.**[14]

Similar citation data suggest that the social sciences are intermediate to the physical sciences and the humanities in degree of codification. The findings are notably consistent. As we have just seen, in the more analytical physical sciences, about 60 per cent or more of the citations refer to publications appearing within the preceding five years. In the humanities—represented by such journals as the *American Historical Review, Art Bulletin,* and the *Journal of Aesthetics and Art Criticism*—the corresponding figures range from 10 to 20 per cent. In between are the social sciences—represented by such journals as the *American Sociological Review* and the *Journal of Abnormal and Social Psychology*—where from 30 to 50 per cent of the citations refer to equally recent publications.

[11] In his monumental *Introduction to the History of Science,* (1927–1948), George Sarton often quantified the citations of a major scientific work to previous works as one way of establishing its intellectual heritage. Eugene Garfield suggested the use of systematic citation indexing for historical research in 1955 and developed the computerized Science Citation Index in 1964 (see Garfield, 1955; Garfield, Sher, and Torpie, 1964). With its more than 20 million bibliographic citations, the SCI data base has greatly advanced citation analysis in historical and sociological investigations of science.

[12] Derek Price has done most to extend the use of "citation-and-reference-analysis" to distinguish modes of development in the various fields of learning. For early work, see Price (1963, pp. 78 ff. and 1965); for recent work, Price (1970). The abundance of citation studies includes Broadus (1952 and 1967); Burton and Keebler (1960); MacRae (1969).

[13] "Immediacy is much increased use of the last few years of papers over and above the natural growth of the literature and its normal slow aging." "A literature growing at the rate of 5 per cent per annum," Price goes on to calculate, "doubles in size every 13.9 years and contains about 22 per cent of all that has been published in its last five years of publication." This means, of course, that the extent to which a field focuses on new work and so makes for obsolescence of earlier work is measured by the excess of recent citations beyond what would be expected on the basis of growth in the literature (Price, 1970, pp. 9–10).

[14] The data identified by an * are from Price (1970); we have compiled the rest.

It appears, moreover, that the citation pattern of a science transcends national and cultural boundaries. At any rate, American, European, and Soviet journals of physics have been found to exhibit almost identical age distributions of citations (Dedijer, 1964, p. 461).

One limited aspect of the cognitive structure of the various sciences, then, is the extent of their codification. We want now to explore possible relations between codification and age-patterned behavior and processes in the sciences, along the following lines:

1. The extent to which codification affects opportunities for scientific discovery by different age strata;
2. age differentials in responsiveness to new scientific ideas in fields that are variously codified;
3. the effects of codification upon the visibility of scientific contributions; and
4. the linkages between codification, changing foci of research and opportunities for discovery.

CODIFICATION AND AGE DIFFERENTIALS IN DISCOVERY

We begin with the premise that up to a given age, older and more experienced scientists have an edge on their much younger colleagues in the opportunities for discovery. After all, they know the field as the novice does not. What needs to be explained, in our view, is not so much discovery by experienced and knowledgeable elders as discovery by newly trained youth. In this connection, we need to ask whether discovery by young scientists is more frequent in some sciences and, if so, how this comes to be.

Codification facilitates mastery of a field by linking basic ideas in a theoretical framework and by reducing the volume of factual information that is required in order to do significant research. This should lead scientists in the more codified fields to qualify earlier[15] for work at the research front—at least, as collaborators of more mature investigators. And early achievement in science may give an enduring advantage, by providing both increasingly abundant facilities for research and early access to the social networks of scientists at the research front where information and criticism are exchanged and motivation for getting on with one's work is maintained.[16] The best known because heavily publicized specimen of this process is that of the 25-year-old James

[15] This early start may also reflect early recruitment to the more codified sciences. We know of no data on the matter but share the widespread impression that decisions to go into mathematics and physics are made much earlier than decisions to enter the soft sciences. The significance of age at time of the decision to enter the field of medicine is examined by Rogoff (1957) and by Thielens (1957, pp. 109–129 and pp. 131–152).

[16] See the informed and astute account of how young scientists achieve entry into the "Invisible College" of their specialty by the physicist and sociologist of science, Ziman (1968, pp. 130–134).

D. Watson[17] soon finding his way into the center of work on the structure of DNA once he was sponsored by his intellectually influential teachers, Salvador Luria and Max Delbrück. In this process, intellectual mobility and social mobility (of a jointly sponsored and contest variety) are mutually reinforcing.

The organization of scientific inquiry and of training in science also promote early entrance into the research role. In a sense, young scientists are more apt than their expert teachers to be abreast of the range of knowledge in their field. Since advanced research in science demands concentration on a narrow range of problems at hand, the established specialist experts, intent on moving ahead with their own research, tend to fall behind on what others are doing outside their own special fields. But, at least in the best departments, students are trained by an *aggregate* of specialists at work on the research front of their specialties. This brings them up to date, if only for a time, in a wider variety of fields than their older and temporarily more specialized teachers.

This pattern we believe to hold in all the sciences but we suspect that it is more marked and efficacious in the more highly codified sciences, those that provide more powerful means for acquiring competence in consolidated current knowledge. The opportunity structure confers two advantages on the young in the more codified fields: the chance to begin research early as qualified junior colleagues and the chance to have training that is both up-to-date *and* relatively diversified. Both should advance their opportunities for making significant research contributions early in their careers.

It is from this standpoint that we come upon the one problem that has almost monopolized discussions of the, in fact, multiform connections between age and scientific activity: the time of life at which scientists do their most important work or, as it is sometimes put, the relations between age and scientific productivity. The data bearing on this subject are faulty or severely limited but, on first inspection, they seem to confirm our expectations. Various investigators report lower median ages for discoverers in physics and chemistry than in the more descriptive biological sciences, with these being lower in turn than in the behavioral sciences (Lehman, 1936, p. 162; 1953, p. 20; Adams, 1946, p. 168). Nobel laureates in physics, for example, were on the average 36 at the time of doing their prize-winning work; laureates in chemistry, 38 and those in medicine and physiology, 41.[18] This does not mean, of course, that a higher rate of discovery in youth is the norm in the more codified sciences, much less for them all. Apparently, we sometimes need to be

---

[17] Watson's detailed account (1958) of how all this worked out for him is one of the many features of *The Double Helix* that make it an unexampled personal document in the sociology of science.

[18] Data for 1901–1950 are drawn from Manniche and Falk (1957, pp. 302 ff.), and for the period 1951–1969 from Zuckerman (1972).

reminded that median ages at time of discovery tell us that half of the discoveries were made after the median age as well as before. In contrast to the usual emphasis, Lehman's findings could be reported, for example, as indicating that "fully half" of the discoveries listed in Magie's *Source Book of Physics* were made by scientists *over* the age of 38 or that "fully half" of the discoveries listed in genetics were by scientists *over* 40.

Beyond this, we need only mention other caveats in the use of these data on age and scientific achievements. They are faulty in two basic respects. First, they do not take into account the age structure of the scientific population. As we know from the exponential growth in the numbers of scientists, the young ones make up a hefty percentage at any given time and so they will produce a large aggregate of contributions. But of course this does not provide the needed evidence on comparative rates of scientific contributions at various ages. What is required are data not on the proportion of contributors in each age stratum but on the proportion of each age stratum making contributions. This requirement holds even in comparing age-linked rates of productivity among the various sciences since, as we have seen, the age composition of the sciences does differ appreciably.

Second, Lehman's studies do not take into account, as Wayne Dennis has emphatically demonstrated, the biasing effects of differing life spans on the distribution of achievements at various ages.[19] The fact that short-lived scientists are cut off from making any contributions in later years factitiously enlarges the proportions assigned to young scientists in data on age and achievement that do not take longevity into account. The essential issue is caught up in the lament of Newton over the premature death at age 34 of his protégé, the mathematician, Roger Cotes: "If he had lived, we might have known something." Or the similar observation by John Maynard Keynes about the brilliant young logician and mathematician, Frank Ramsey, robbed of his future at the age of 27.

We suggest, moreover, that the statistical bias in apparent age-specific productivity differs among the variously codified sciences. In doing so, we depart a bit from the ancient adage that the good die young. We propose a less crisp but more germane version: *comparatively*[20] more good mathematicians and physicists than good historians and sociologists die young. In saying this, we do not propose the improbable hypothesis that rates of premature mortal-

[19] Dennis (1956a, 1956b, 1956c, 1966). For a discussion of the fallacies in the interpretations drawn from the Lehman data and the implications of the Dennis data, see Section 3 of the Appendix; See also Riley and Foner (1968, Chapter 18 · B · 2).

[20] The emphasis on "comparatively" is intended to signal that we are not dealing here with the question of differences between the various fields in the talent of their recruits. That is an interesting question in its own right and in other connections; it is not a relevant question here.

ity are in fact higher in the more codified fields than in the less codified ones. We assume the same rates of age-specific mortality but an earlier age of prime achievement. Mathematicians of genius who died prematurely, such as a Galois dead at 21 or a Niels Abel dead at 26, have been enduringly identified by their early work as being of the first rank. But by hypothesis, sociologists or botanists of genius who die young will have fulfilled less of their potential in their early years and so do not even appear in the standard histories of their fields. This reconstruction is consistent with the Dennis data, which suggest that a far larger share of the total life output of long-lived mathematicians and chemists than of equally long-lived historians, botanists, and geologists is completed during their first decade of work. This sort of thing can thus foster the illusion that good mathematicians die young but that, say, good sociologists linger on forever.

To this point, we have centered on differentials in rates of scientific contributions by age-strata in sciences codified in varying degree. We have now to touch upon the further question whether the truly transforming ideas in science, the fundamental reconceptualizations, are more apt to be the work of youthful minds rather than older ones. T. S. Kuhn, in his vastly influential book on scientific revolutions, suggests that creators of fundamental new paradigms are almost always young or very new to the field (1962, pp. 89–90). A long and familiar roster of cases illustrates his suggestion. Newton wrote of himself that at 24, when he had begun his work on universal gravitation, the calculus and the theory of colors: "I was in the prime of my age for invention, and minded Mathematics and Philosophy more than at any time since." Darwin was 22 at the time of the Beagle voyage and 29 when he formulated the essentials of natural selection. Einstein was 26 in the year of three of his great contributions, among them the special theory of relativity, and finally, eight of the ten physicists generally regarded as having produced quantum physics were under the age of 30 when they made their contributions to that scientific revolution (Gamow, 1966).

Arresting illustrations of this kind are of course not enough to show that young scientists are especially apt to revolutionize scientific thought. But in the absence of systematic data on the age composition of scientists in various historical periods, they remain the basis for the generalization being widely accepted as commonplace. Yet, as Kuhn himself goes on to say, it is a generalization that "badly needs systematic investigation."

CODIFICATION AND AGE DIFFERENTIALS IN RECEPTIVITY TO NEW IDEAS

As we have suggested, new developments in the more codified sciences are closely linked to work done just before. These sciences grow, as Price puts it, "from the skin." As a result, awareness of new ideas and critical acceptance of them is especially important in the codified sciences. If certain age strata are more responsive to them, this increases their chances for making further discoveries.

It has often been said that aging leads to growing resistance to novelty and specifically, that older scientists tend to resist new ideas.[21] As Planck, who did not develop the idea of the quantum until he was 42, remarked: ". . . a new scientific truth does not triumph by convincing its opponents and making them see the light, but rather because its opponents eventually die, and a new generation grows up that is familiar with it."[22]

Observations of this sort, based on lore rather than systematic evidence, raise the perennial questions: is it really so? and if so, how does it come to be?

If there are these age-stratified differences in receptivity to new (and sound) ideas, this should be reflected in various behaviors. For one example, younger scientists should rely more on recently published research and cite it more frequently than older scientists in the same fields. For another, the age strata of scientists should differ on what they take to be the most significant contributions to their field. Some limited data in hand lend credence to these inferences.

We find (Zuckerman, unpublished data) for a small sample of scientists that those under 30 are more given to citing recent work (papers published in the five years preceding their own) than men in the same fields who were on the average 30 years older: 71 per cent of the references in the work of the younger investigators and 58 per cent by the older ones being to the recent literature.[23] But the pattern does not hold for all older scientists. Nobel laureates do not exhibit the same citation behavior as their less distinguished age peers. They appear to be just as responsive to new research as men 30 years their junior, with 73 per cent of their references being to the most recent literature. This finding bears only tangentially on the Planck doctrine but it does suggest that attentiveness to new developments in science is stratified by both age *and* scientific achievement.

Substantive differences in judgments of what constitutes important work may crystallize, as Hagstrom has noted, into "generational disputes." But, as

[21] [*But see the changes over the life course in political attitudes reported in Chapter 4 · 2 by Foner.*]

[22] Planck (1949, pp. 33–34). This must surely be one of the most frequently quoted observations of its kind in recent years. It was put to good use by Bernard Barber in his paper on resistance to scientific discovery (1961), and, among others, by Kuhn (1962, p. 150); Hagstrom (1965, p. 283), and Greenberg (1967, p. 45).

[23] Stephen Cole (1969) found the same pattern for a variety of scientific fields. Since the process of refereeing and editing scientific papers before publication probably tends to homogenize initial age differences in citations, even small differences between age strata in the published papers represent an *a fortiori* case.

he goes on to say, "even if some disputes are generational, they need not be simply 'innovative youth' versus 'conservative age.' Rather, the outlook of a generation is strongly influenced by events occurring when its members embark upon their careers. Age may be more radical than youth" (Hagstrom, 1965, pp. 284–285).

The evidence on age differentials in receptivity to new ideas in science remains thin and uncertain. But should further investigation find, as the widespread belief has it, that older scientists are indeed more resistant to new ideas, that would only raise a series of questions of how that comes to be. It would not follow, for example, that it results from physiological aging or senescence.[24] As Barber has noted in this context, *aging* "is an omnibus term which actually covers a variety of social and cultural sources of resistance." He goes on to suggest several possible social and cultural components in such resistance:

> As a scientist gets older he is more likely to be restricted in his response to innovation by his substantive and methodological preconceptions and by his other cultural accumulations; he is more likely to have high professional standing, to have specialized interests, to be a member or official of an established organization, and to be associated with a "school." The likelihood of all these things increases with the passage of time, and so the older scientist, just by living longer, is more likely to acquire a cultural and social incubus. But this is not always so, and the older workers in science are often the most ardent champions of innovation.[25]

This provides in effect, a formidable agenda for investigation of age-associated differences in receptivity and resistance to new conceptions in science.

CODIFICATION AND VISIBILITY OF SCIENTIFIC CONTRIBUTIONS

We turn now from considering possible age-patterned responses to new ideas, irrespective of their source, to consider possible differences in the responses to new ideas advanced by scientists of differing age. The visibility of new ideas in a discipline may be affected by the sheer volume of its literature, which may, in turn, be related to its degree of codification. That is not of interest here. However that may be, our interest lies instead in the direct implications of codification itself for the visibility of ideas introduced by scientists of differing age.

It would seem that new ideas are more difficult to identify as important in disciplines that are largely descriptive and only spottily and loosely organized

---

[24] For systematic review of the evidence on the multiple interpretations of such types of data, see Riley and Foner (1968).

[25] Barber (1961, p. 602). On much the same point, see also Hagstrom (1965, pp. 283–284).

by theory. In these less codified disciplines, the personal and social attributes of scientists are more likely to influence the visibility of their ideas and the reception accorded them. As a result, work by younger scientists who, on the average, are less widely known in the field, will have less chance of being noticed in the less codified sciences. Put another way, the Matthew Effect (Merton, 1968a, pp. 56–63)—the tendency for greater recognition to be accorded contributions by scientists of great repute—is apt to operate with special force in the less codified fields.

Correlatively, in the more codified sciences, new ideas, whatever their source, can better carry their own credentials. Important contributions by young scientists or older ones, for that matter, are not only more visible in the codified fields; they are taken more seriously since their theoretical importance can be more readily assessed. This tends to put the young on a par with eminent seniors in communicating ideas and in having them noticed.

Although Stephen Cole's studies of the Matthew Effect have been confined to physics, his findings are suggestive in this regard. In this highly codified science, the work of eminent investigators is incorporated into ongoing research only a little more quickly than contributions of comparable quality by less distinguished investigators. The age of physicists also has little effect on the speed with which their ideas diffuse (Stephen Cole, 1970, pp. 297, 299). In physics, then, the merits of the investigation seem to govern its reception with the attributes of the investigator playing only a small part. Comparative study is now needed to find out whether the strength of the Matthew Effect does in fact vary inversely with the extent to which sciences are codified.

CODIFICATION, INTER-SCIENCE TRANSFERS, AND DISCOVERY

Although, as we have seen, scientists seldom leave the occupation of science altogether, a considerable number transfer from one field to another. About a quarter of American scientists have made shifts of this kind, the rates of transfer differing among the various sciences of origin and, of course, among age cohorts (Harmon, 1965, pp. 50–52; National Research Council, 1968, pp. 59–62).

Scientists who have left the field in which they were trained, to work in another where they were not, constitute a special class of newcomers. In certain respects, these older neophytes are functionally like the younger novices in that field. Both are being rapidly introduced to the research front of the field although the older newcomers differ from the younger indigenous recruits in having been less comprehensively trained in the new field. Both include people bringing new perspectives on old problems to the degree that they have not acquired commitments to the definitions of problems or to the form of their probable solutions that are conventionally adopted in that field.

The transfers, unlike their young colleagues just beginning to work in science, also bring with them styles of research new to their adopted field, as was dramatically the case when physicists turned their attention to biology and created the field of molecular biology.[26] In part, the contributions of newcomers derive from their tranferring to the new field standards and modes of investigation customary in their field of origin.

Some of the attributes of the more codified sciences that facilitate the fairly rapid learning of essentials by the incoming student thus facilitate as well effective transfer into the field by older, experienced scientists. Historical and statistical data (Harmon, 1965, p. 51) suggest that transfers tend to occur among sciences codified to about the same extent with a subsidiary pattern of movement toward less codified fields. There is little interchange between the extremes of codification: between physics and, say, botany or zoology.

The general pattern of such transfers has been connected by Joseph Ben-David to what he describes as "role-hybridization": applying the means usual to Role A in trying to achieve the goals of Role B. As he sums it up:

> Scientific disciplines differ in the degree of their theoretical closure and methodological precision. The phenomena most similar to role hybridization would be shifts from a theoretically and methodologically more advanced discipline to one less advanced. These must be distinguished from shifts between two disciplines of the same level and from less to more advanced disciplines (Ben-David, 1960, pp. 566–567; see also Ben-David and Collins, 1966).

The processes and consequences of patterns of transfer among variously codified sciences have only begun to be investigated. But something of the process can be pieced together for the eminent men who have changed fields. They often exhibit an almost playful arrogance about the time required for retooling. Symbolic stories abound. Leo Szilard is said to have taken all of three weeks at Cold Spring Harbor in order to effect his transformation from physicist to biologist, this at the age of 47.[27] Francis Crick's leap from physics into biology has been twice chronicled (Watson, 1968; Olby, 1970). The same theme of the rapid acquisition of fundamentals appears in Wadding-

[26] The *Festschrift* for Max Delbrück, one of the founders of molecular biology, consists largely of a remarkable series of lively and informative personal accounts of the beginnings of the field. See Cairns, Stent and Watson (1966). *What is Life?*, a short book by the physicist Erwin Schrödinger, proved decisive in transforming physicists into biologists. For a further account of the emergence of molecular biology, see Fleming (1969, pp. 152–189).

[27] Some 14 years earlier, Szilard had been told by the physiologist A. V. Hill that he could pick up the essentials of physiology by simply setting himself the task of teaching it (Szilard, 1969, p. 98).

ton's account of the European origins of molecular biology. He writes of the journey to the first conference of geneticists and crystallographers:

> Most of us tried to sleep on the benches in the general saloon, but Darlington and [the crystallographer] Bernal kept sea-sickness at bay by the former teaching the latter "all the genetics and cytology anyone needs to know" throughout the course of the night. Before dawn, Bernal had already decided that the mitotic spindle must be a positive tactoid. . . . (Waddington, 1969, p. 318).

This suggests not only that much can be learned in short order but also that knowledgeable newcomers accustomed to being in command of their field, even if they are not quite of Bernal's caliber, can achieve enough understanding of fundamentals to introduce new ideas at the outset.

These topflight migrants from one science to another seem unworried by their ignorance of the problematics prevailing in the new field. This keeps them from some stale preconceptions. Maria Goeppert Mayer, the Nobel laureate, provides an apt example. Her work on "the magic numbers problem" (a problem of such profound interest that it had been given a name) and her subsequent development of the shell model of the nucleus, she reports, depended on a specific kind of ignorance. Trained as a physicist but working mainly in physical chemistry, she was not brought up on the "Bethe Bible"[28] and so was unhampered by knowing "what everyone knew" about spin-coupling.[29] Focused naivete and focused ignorance evidently have their functions in science—especially for anything but naive and otherwise immensely informed scientists.[30]

Like geographic migration, intellectual migration in the form of transfers from one science to another should lend itself to cohort analysis. Are there certain times in the careers of scientists at which they tend to make the change? Do these patterns persist among successive cohorts or are they fairly constant? Have there been historical changes in the frequency and patterns of transfers? Are the migrants in science representative of the field, more able on the whole, less so, or bimodal in their distribution of capacity and achievement?

Whatever the patterns of transfer they need to be examined within the con-

[28] In a series of papers published in the late 1930's in *Reviews of Modern Physics*, Hans Bethe attempted to consolidate what was known then about the atomic nucleus. That these papers had unparalleled impact on physics is registered in the fondly respectful title by which they are known.

[29] J. H. D. Jensen, who independently solved the same problems, interestingly enough, was also unaware of prevailing ideas of spin-coupling.

[30] On the general idea of the uses of ignorance under certain conditions, see Moore and Tumin (1949, pp. 787–795). On the "outsider" in science and technology, see Gilfillan (1935, pp. 88–91); Ben-David (1960, pp. 557–59); Merton (1970b).

text of the intellectual organization of the sciences of origin and sciences of destination.

3 Scientific roles

INVENTORY OF ROLES IN SCIENCE

Like other domains of social life, the social structure of science has its distinctive array of statuses and roles, allocated to members through complex processes of social selection. We focus here on the status of scientist. But we should note in passing that the social structure of science, especially as we know it today after centuries of institutionalization and social differentiation, contains a variety of other statuses and roles. Often indispensable to the effective advancing of scientific inquiry, these parascientific roles include technicians of every stripe, the builders of experimental apparatus and instruments and the broad spectrum of assistants engaged in facilitating scientific work (for example, by preparing and taking care of experimental materials).[31]

Like other statuses, the status of scientist involves not a single role but, in varying mixture, a complement of roles. These are of four principal kinds: research, teaching, administrative, and gatekeeper roles.[32] Each of these is differentiated into subroles, which we only note here but do not consider in detail.

The research role, which provides for the growth of scientific knowledge, is central, with the others being functionally ancillary to it. For plainly, if there were no scientific investigation, there would be no new knowledge to be transmitted through the teaching role, no need to allocate resources for investigation, no research organization to administer, and no new flow of knowledge for gatekeepers to regulate. Possibly because of its functional centrality, scientists apparently place greater value on the research role than any of the others. As is generally the case in maintaining a complex of mutually sustaining roles, ideology does not fully reflect this differential evaluation of roles in the role-set: scientists will often insist on the "indispensability" and consequently equal importance of the ancillary roles. Yet, almost in a pattern of revealed preference, the working of the reward system in science testifies that the research role is the most highly valued. The heroes of science are acclaimed in their capacity as scientific investigators, seldom as teachers, administrators or referees and editors.

The research role divides into subroles, distinguished to varying degree in the different sciences. In research, scientists define themselves and are defined by others as experimentalists (or, more generally, empirical investi-

[31] For a short inventory of roles in science, see Weiss (1971, pp. 29–30).
[32] For the general conception that each status has its distinctive complement of roles, or its role-set, see Merton (1968b, pp. 422–438).

gators) or as theorists, with occasional high-yield hybrids such as Enrico Fermi or Linus Pauling embodying both subroles effectively. This differentiation seems more marked in the more codified sciences. Little is known about the processes leading scientists to adopt one or another of these subroles. In the lore of science, this is not even problematic. Scientists are assumed to become either experimentalists or theorists as their highly specific capacities dictate. But it seems that the process is more complex than the simple matching of roles to self-evaluated capacities. It presumably involves, at the least, interaction between developing self-images of aspirants to scientific investigation, socialization by peers and mentors, and continuing evaluation of their role performance by peers, superiors, and themselves.

To the extent that the research role in science involves interaction between scientists, it also makes for some, often reciprocal, teaching and learning. The teaching role, particularly in the sciences, calls not only for explicit didactics but, probably much more in the sciences than in the humanities, for tacit instruction through observed example. The master-apprentice relation is central to socialization in the sciences, particularly in laboratories which provide for mutual observability by master and apprentice. This structural difference between the sciences and the humanities is reflected in the fact that the status of postdoctoral student is widespread in the sciences and rare in the humanities.

There is, in the normative system of science, an ambivalence toward the preferred relations between the research and teaching roles. For some, the norm requires the scientist to recognize his prime obligation to train up new generations of scientists, *but* he must not allow teaching to pre-empt his energies at the expense of advancing knowledge. For others, the norm reads just as persuasively in reverse. We have only to remember the complaints about Faraday that he had never trained a successor as Davy had trained him, yet consider the frequent criticism of scientists who give up research for teaching. There are indications, as we shall see, that the time scientists allocate to the roles of teaching and research changes during the life course.

A third major role of scientists is ordinarily (and not very instructively) caught up in the term "administration." The term often covers a wide gamut of quite distinct structural conditions, ranging from occasional service on advisory or policy-making committees, through direction of a small-scale research inquiry to full specialization in the one role as with full-time "science administrators" or "R & D administrators." What is described as the increasing bureaucratization of science often refers to the growing number of full-time administrative roles and their growing power to affect the course of scientific development. And such bureaucratization, precisely because it involves allocation of resources to the various sciences and to groups and individuals within them, also tends to engage more of the "non-administrator" scientists in administrative activities: the preparation of prospectuses on work planned and of reports on work done, this in addition to the dissemination of the actual results of scientific investigation.

Although it is often (and loosely) included under "administration," a fourth role of the scientist needs to be distinguished from the others since it is basic to the systems of evaluation and the allocation of roles and resources in science. This is the gatekeeping role.[33] Variously distributed within the organizations and institutions of science, it involves continuing or intermittent assessment of the performance of scientists at every stage of their career, from the phase of youthful novice to that of ancient veteran and providing or denying access to opportunities.

The operation of the gatekeeper role affects contemporary science in its every aspect. First, with regard to the input and distribution of personnel, these scientists are asked to evaluate the promise and limitations of aspirants to new positions, thus affecting both the mobility of individual scientists and, in the aggregate, the distribution of personnel throughout the system. In American science, at least, and probably in other national communities of science, this gatekeeping function seems to involve a mixture of Turner's types of mobility: contest mobility based on role performance and reinforced by the norm of universalism and sponsored mobility in which elites or their agents help recruit their successors fairly early.[34]

Second, with regard to the allocation of facilities and rewards, the gatekeeper role, at least in the American social structure of science, operates largely through broad- or narrow-spectrum "panels of peers." These panels recommend and, in the usual event, determine the distribution of fellowships, research grants, and honorific awards. The term "panels of peers" refers to the fellow-scientists of assumed competence in the fields in question and not, of course, to age peers, as we shall see in examining the age structures of groups of gatekeepers.

Third, with regard to the outputs of the variously allocated resources, the gatekeeper role is organized principally in the subroles of referees, charged with gauging the validity and worth of manuscripts submitted for publication, and of editors and editorial staff who make the final determination of what shall enter this or that archive of science.[35] Here again, we shall want to identify phases of their careers in which scientists tend to be most involved in

[33] As is well known, the notion of the gatekeeper role was introduced into social science by Kurt Lewin (1943). Alfred de Grazia (1963) and Diana Crane (1967) refer to editors of journals as "the" gatekeepers of science. This usage is too restrictive; gatekeepers also regulate scientific manpower and the allocation of resources for research.

[34] For the general concepts, see Turner (1960); for their pertinence to the case of science, see Hargens and Hagstrom (1967); also Zuckerman (1970, pp. 243–247).

[35] Research on the operation of this role has lately burgeoned; for example, see Crane (1967); Whitley (1970); Zuckerman and Merton (1971).

these roles that help shape the permanent record of scientific work, and to find out whether there are distinctive age-related patterns in their performance of these roles.

ROLE-SEQUENCE AND ROLE-ALLOCATION IN SCIENCE

As we have noted, individual scientists have their own mixtures of these four roles, according different amounts of time and energy to each of them. At the extremes of specialization, scientists are engaged in one of these roles to the full exclusion of the others; more commonly, they will perform all of them in varying mix. For individual scientists, the question arises whether there are patterned sequences in preponderating roles during the life course. And for successive cohorts of scientists, the correlative question arises whether there are historical changes in the distribution of scientific roles.

In considering these questions, we should note that what is *role-sequence*[36] from the standpoint of the individual moving along the phases of his life course is *role-allocation* from the standpoint of the social system of science. Role-sequences, that is, the succession of roles or role-configurations through which appreciable proportions of people move in the course of their lives, are presumably affected by role-allocation, that is, patterned access to the structure of opportunity to engage in the various roles. The first deals with patterned career-lines, the other with (historically changing) processes and structures of role distribution. Concretely, individual preferences and social system pressures interact to produce the observed historical patterns of role-sequences.

Systematic data on role-sequences are in short supply generally and all the more so in the sociology of science. An approximation to investigation of role-sequences is provided by studies of "occupational careers,"[37] which, however, tend to deal with patterns of mobility from one occupation to another rather than with patterned sequences of role-configurations for individuals remaining within the same occupation. For the field of science, there is a unique set of data assembled by Lindsey Harmon (1965), which traces the succession of role-complements for six cohorts of American scientists receiving their doctorates in ten major fields of science at five-year intervals from 1935 to 1960. Substantively, the Harmon Report provides incomparable clues to the patterned sequences of roles for American scientists in the last generation or so; procedurally, the Harmon data exemplify the great difficulties of disentangling from such cohort analysis the components of role-sequences in life course and of historical shifts in role-allocations, difficulties to which we have

---

[36] For the general conception of status- and role-sequences, see Merton (1968b, pp. 434–438).

[37] For instructive examples of the difficult art of "career analysis," see Wilensky (1960 and 1961); Miller and Form (1964).

been alerted by the Riley-Johnson-Foner model of age stratification [*see also Chapter 2 and the Appendix*].[38]

Table 8 · 3, drawn from the Harmon Report, summarizes the average proportions of time which six cohorts estimate[39] they have assigned to various role-activities at successive periods in their careers. The evidence bears upon both role-sequences in individual life courses and upon social changes in the role structure of science.

First of all, for each cohort, the figures across the rows show a steady decline during the *life course* in the proportion of time assigned to research and a steady increase in the time assigned to administration.[40] Teaching, like research, also tends to decline over the life course, with the interesting exception of 1950, when each cohort increased the relative time devoted to teaching. This deviation from the general life course pattern apparently reflects, as Chapter 2 alerts us to note, the impact of unique historical events upon the age strata. For the observed historical bump in role-sequence probably represents the additional teaching that came with the rapid expansion in "GI" programs of education just after World War II.

Second, Table 8 · 3 also reflects *historically changing* patterns in the distribution of time American scientists assign to their several roles at each stage of their careers. This can be seen by inspecting the left-to-right diagonals in the first two parts (a and b) of Table 8 · 3. Consider, for example, the top diagonal of those having just received the doctorate. Each more recent cohort tends to devote less of its aggregate time to teaching and more to research. The historical trend at each of the other stages of the scientists' careers also approximates this decrease in aggregate cohort time assigned to teaching and the increase in that assigned to research, except for the dramatic departure of the 1945 cohort (note that the 1945 row tends to fall out of line with each of the diagonals in parts a and b of the table). The experience of the great influx of World War II veterans into colleges and universities seems to have left an enduring imprint upon the 1945 cohort which, just entering upon their careers at the time, continue at each succeeding time period to interrupt the general cohort trend of less teaching and more research.

Interestingly enough, the cohort trends in teaching and research are not accompanied by complementary trends in administrative activity (shown in

---

[38] The cohorts of scientists in this study are thus of one kind identified in Chapter 1 · 1 · D: aggregates of people who share not a common date of birth but a common date of entry into the field.

[39] Grateful for these incomparable data, we do not here discuss the question of possible response error deriving from the fact that these retrospective estimates of the allocation of time cover periods ranging up to 25 years. Harmon is thoroughly aware of the problem and internal evidence suggests that errors in reporting are random rather than systematic.

[40] We report the full table from Harmon but attach no significance to the category of "all other" activities. At best, this is a catchall with unidentified ingredients. Moreover, it does not appear to be patterned by age in any systematic fashion.

TABLE 8 · 3 *Distribution of time assigned to their various roles by selected cohorts of American scientists*

(Years since Ph.D. shown in parentheses)

Date of Ph.D.	Work period					
	1935	1940	1945	1950	1955	1960
a. Percentage of time devoted to teaching						
1960						(0) 33
1955					(0) 34	(5) 33
1950				(0) 40	(5) 34	(10) 31
1945			(0) 41	(5) 42	(10) 36	(15) 34
1940		(0) 42	(5) 30	(10) 33	(15) 28	(20) 28
1935	(0) 47	(5) 44	(10) 35	(15) 36	(20) 33	(25) 32
b. Percentage of time devoted to research						
1960						(0) 48
1955					(0) 48	(5) 43
1950				(0) 45	(5) 41	(10) 37
1945			(0) 42	(5) 36	(10) 34	(15) 32
1940		(0) 42	(5) 40	(10) 36	(15) 33	(20) 28
1935	(0) 36	(5) 33	(10) 32	(15) 29	(20) 28	(25) 26
c. Percentage of time devoted to administration						
1960						(0) 10
1955					(0) 8	(5) 15
1950				(0) 7	(5) 16	(10) 24
1945			(0) 11	(5) 16	(10) 22	(15) 26
1940		(0) 8	(5) 18	(10) 22	(15) 30	(20) 34
1935	(0) 8	(5) 14	(10) 23	(15) 28	(20) 30	(25) 32
d. Percentage of time devoted to other functions						
1960						(0) 8
1955					(0) 9	(5) 8
1950				(0) 7	(5) 8	(10) 9
1945			(0) 6	(5) 7	(10) 8	(15) 8
1940		(0) 8	(5) 12	(10) 9	(15) 9	(20) 10
1935	(0) 9	(5) 8	(10) 10	(15) 8	(20) 9	(25) 10

Source: Harmon (1965, p. 65) (adapted).

the diagonals of Table 8 · 3, part c). The absence of any consistent trend here raises some question about the nature of the historically increasing bureaucratization of science. To be sure, each cohort of scientists devotes relatively more of their aggregate time to administration as they age. But, age for age, contemporary scientists devote no larger proportion of their aggregate time to administration than did scientists in past years.[41]

A third type of comparison of the figures in Table 8 · 3, comparison down the columns, reveals for each time period the combined effects of the life-course patterns, cohort trends, and unique historical events we have described. Thus the column for a particular year represents the structuring of scientific roles among the *age strata*. Here we find that, although the age strata do not differ substantially in time devoted to teaching, they do show striking differences in research and administration.

At any given time in the past quarter-century, the younger the stratum of scientists, the more of their aggregate time they devote to research and the less to administration. In 1960, for example, this ranges in linear progression from 26 per cent of all work time being assigned to research by the 1935 cohort (then 25 years past the Ph.D. and presumably in their early 50's) to 48 per cent by the most recent cohort of 1960 (then having just received the doctorate and presumably in their late 20's). Put more generally, these results suggest that the social system of science provides more time for the research role to younger than to older scientists. Like the youthful age structure of science generally, this distribution of roles accords with the widespread ideology[42] that holds that "science is a young man's game."

These data, representing aggregate averages for cohorts, of course provide only a rough approximation of individually patterned role sequences among scientists. They do not indicate the *composite* patterns of time that scientists allocate to their various roles at each phase in their careers. Nor, unlike panel data, do they indicate changes in these patterns for individual scientists during the course of their careers.

Partial but suggestive evidence on the individual patterning of roles can be found in the Harmon data (1965, Tables 9–11, pp. 19–21; Appendix 6, Tables A, B, C, and D). Of particular interest are the age patterns of specialization that can be identified. While there are no notable age differences in the pro-

---

[41] Aggregate data of this kind do not allow us to distinguish between role-specialization in the form of full-time administrators and other changes in the distribution of time among the several role-activities by individual scientists. As noted earlier in this section, both types of change are often and indiscriminately caught up in the phrase "the bureaucratization of science." It should be noted also that changes in the proportions of scientists employed by universities, government, and industry affect the observed historical patterns.

[42] We describe this as ideology since it includes both idea and norm, both what is assumed to be and what should be. It is of course only one component in the ideology about the roles of young and old in science.

portion spending full time on some one activity in their current jobs[43]—
on teaching or research or administration—there are striking differences
among the age strata in the *type* of specialization that does tend to occur.
These differences parallel those found in the cohort analysis of Table 8 · 3
above. Thus the young are far more likely than the old to give the major portion of their time to research; conversely, the older strata are more likely to
specialize in administrative roles (while age differences in teaching are not
pronounced). For example, Harmon finds that

> The proportion of scientists devoting no time at all to research on their present
> job is twice as large in the oldest age category as in the youngest; the propor-
> tion devoting full time to research is half as large.
>
> Among the oldest, the percentage spending full time in administration is four
> times aś large as in the youngest stratum.

The same general patterns emerge in examining the *composites* of roles performed by scientists in the several age strata. For example:

> In the oldest age category, about half who do no teaching also do no research,
> most of these specializing in administration.
>
> In the youngest category, of those who do no teaching, 70 per cent spend their
> time predominantly in research.

The Harmon data contain additional clues that the greater emphasis on
research among younger scientists reflects some attrition over the life course
of the research role within the composite of roles performed by individuals.
Comparing allocations of time on the first job held by scientists with allocations on the current job, Harmon emphasizes the modal tendency toward
persistence of role-patterning by individuals over the life course.[44] His data
also show, however, that among those who do shift, those decreasing the proportion of time devoted to research far outnumber those enhancing their
research roles.[45]

Data such as these identify major patterns of role-specialization. But they
tell us nothing, of course, about the kinetics of role-sequences and role-
retention, the social and psychological mechanisms through which and the

---

[43] As can be observed by adding the relevant percentages in Harmon's Table 9 (p. 19), 31
per cent of the youngest age category, 27 per cent of the middle stratum, and 30 per cent of
the oldest category devote full time to either teaching or research or administration.

[44] Harmon (1965, pp. 19–22). Note that all cohorts are combined in this portion of the
analysis.

[45] Derived by comparison of the summated frequencies in the upper-right diagonal (in-
creasers) with the lower left diagonal (decreasers) of Harmon's Table 11 (p. 21). A similar,
though less pronounced, tendency to attrition is apparent through parallel analysis of individual shifts in the teaching role (Table 10, p. 20), clearly pointing to administration as
the activity compensating for declines in research.

structural contexts within which the observed patterns come about. These largely remain matters for speculation.

MECHANISMS OF ROLE-ATTRITION AND ROLE-RETENTION

The ideological accent on youth in science provides part of the context for shifts in roles. In its extreme form, the doctrine holds that the best scientific work is done early in the career with nothing of consequence to be expected after that. P. A. M. Dirac, one of the more powerful minds in theoretical physics, found occasion to express this gloomy version, partly in parody, partly in sadness:

> Age is, of course, a fever chill
> that every physicist must fear.
> He's better dead than living still
> when once he's past his thirtieth year.[46]

On this view, the scientists who have made significant contributions early in their careers burn out soon afterwards. And the many more who have done little in their early years can count on doing even less later on. For both, continuing to do research with advancing age is at best an act of self-deception. This extreme form of the ideology typically includes the premise that each scientist has within him a fixed quantum of contributions to make and that this is soon exhausted.[47]

A less severe version of the ideology, reinforced perhaps by Lehman's widely publicized and somewhat misleading data, holds that creative work peaks early in the scientist's life and diminishes more or less rapidly both in extent and consequence. The edge is sometimes taken off this version by noting that what age loses in creative powers, it can gain in mature experience. This provides a rationale for continuing in the research role with a degree of restrained optimism. John von Neumann, known for contributions of the first order to several branches of mathematics, took this to be the case for his own field:

> When a young man, he [von Neumann] mentioned to me several times that the primary mathematical powers decline after the age of about twenty-six, but that a certain more prosaic shrewdness developed by experience manages to compensate for this gradual loss, at least for a time. Later the limiting age was slowly raised (Ulam, 1969, p. 239).

---

[46] It is appropriate that Dirac should have formulated his mathematical theory describing the relativistic electron when he was 26 and that he became a Fellow of the Royal Society at 28 and a Nobel laureate just over the watershed age, at 31.

[47] The idiom puts it that scientists have no more than a paper or book "in them." Without at all subscribing to the total ideology of youth, Price and Beaver (1966) press the idiom further by referring to coauthors who manage to "squeeze out" of themselves the fraction of a paper that is in them.

Without assuming that ideology determines behavior, we should note that the extreme version of the ideology of youth in science thoroughly undermines the case for continuing in the research role, while the moderate version provides it with no great support. All apart from other considerations, this is the sort of ideological climate that we would expect to make for attrition of the research role, just as the Harmon data indicate.

There is reason to believe that the general pattern of shifts from research to other roles holds more for journeymen scientists than for the more accomplished scientists. Sociological theory leads us to expect and scattered evidence leads us to believe that the more productive scientists, recognized as such by the reward system of science, tend to persist in their research roles, forcing death rather than retirement to spell the end to their research careers. One piece of evidence deals with the scientific ultra-elite, the Nobel laureates. Compared with less distinguished scientists matched with them in age, specialty, and type of organizational affiliation, the laureates begin publishing research earlier in their career and continue to publish longer (Zuckerman, 1967, pp. 392–393). On the average, the laureates were not quite 25 years old at the time of their first papers, while scientists in the matched sample were past 28. What is more in point in the matter of role-retention is the publishing record toward the other end of the career. Of the nine laurates and their matches who had passed the age of 70, all the laureates but only three of the paired scientists continued to publish, indicating that they have more staying power in the research role. In part, this may result from their being subject to consistently greater expectations, both from others in the immediate and extended environment, to remain productive in research and in part, from their having established routines of work, also supported by the environment. One laureate, then past 80, reports that he feels no obligation to continue doing research—as he puts it, "After all, enough is enough"; nevertheless, his papers continue to appear in the scientific journals.[48] The oldest laureate, F. P. Rous, was described as "still hard at work" at the michelangelical age of 87.

Retention of the research role, or its attrition, among scientists ranked high in accomplishment seems to be affected also by their selection of reference individuals and reference groups for self-appraisal. Some take their own prior achievements as a benchmark and conclude that the prospects are slight for their maintaining that standard. They become more receptive to the opportunities for taking up other roles: administering research organizations, serving as elder statesmen to provide liaison between science and other institutional spheres or, occasionally, leaving the field of science altogether for

---

[48] In her restudy of 54 eminent scientists, 17 of them over the age of 65 at the time of her revisit, Anne Roe (1965) also found that they tended to persist in their research, even when taking up administrative roles.

ranking positions in university administration or international diplomacy. Other eminent scientists take the run of scientists as their reference group. They conclude that even if youthful peaking has occurred for them, they will continue to be far more productive, even on the assumed down slope of their careers, than most other scientists at the peak of their careers.

> *Query:* The generic problem of the determinants of selection of reference groups remains unsolved. Taking the matter of role-retention by scientists as a strategic case in point, we ask: What leads some scientists, highly productive in their youth, to take this as a reference mark and to anticipate *relative unproductivity* in the future while other scientists, equally productive in their youth, anticipate *relative productivity* as they compare their work with that of most scientists even in their most productive years.

The value system of science can make for a retention of the research role in spite of the ideology of research as essentially a young man's game. Of the various roles in the institution of science, greatest value is attached to research, theoretical and experiential. As a result, the self-esteem of scientists once effectively engaged in research depends greatly upon their continuing to do research, even though they may be plagued by doubts stemming from the ideology of youth. Beyond that, many scientists, precisely because they are minds trained in scientific inference, realize that even if scientific productivity or creativity does decline with aging for most scientists, it of course remains unsound to assume that this must hold for any particular scientist.

Conducing to retention of the research role is the comparative ambiguity about the kind and number of contributions to knowledge that would justify one's continuing in research. Since few make pathbreaking contributions, even an occasional craftsmanlike piece of work may be enough to maintain the self-conception of being engaged in research. This is particularly the case for academic scientists who, in the aggregate, appear to devote much the same proportion of their time—about one-fifth—to research during the greater part of their active career. It is the scientists in nonacademic employment, whose research productivity is presumably gauged in more utilitarian terms, that successively devote less of their time to research and more to administration.[49] This pattern suggests that the criteria of what constitutes "satisfactory research" differ within the social subsystems of science in academia and industry with consequent differences in rates of role-retention.[50]

Patterns of role-retention and attrition probably differ also among the various levels in the social stratification of science. For there are socially stratified differences in opportunity-structure and in socially patterned pressures in

[49] The data on these patterns are set out in the second career patterns report following up the Harmon Report (National Research Council, 1968, p. 53).
[50] For apposite observations, see Marcson (1960) and Glaser (1964).

science as in other departments of social life. Eminent research scientists are often subject to cross-pressures. On the one hand, in accord with the principle of cumulative advantage, their earlier achievements in research ordinarily provide them with enlarged facilities for research. On the other, the prestige they have gained in the research role often leads them to be sought out for alternative roles as advisors, sages, and statesmen, both within the domain of science and in the larger society.

In the main, however, the socially reinforced commitment to research seems to prevail in the upper reaches of the stratification system. This occurs even though there appears to be a ratchet effect operating in the careers of scientists such that, once having achieved substantial eminence, they do not later fall much below that level (although they may be outdistanced by newcomers and so suffer a *relative* decline in prestige). Once a Nobel laureate, always a Nobel laureate. But the reward system of science makes it difficult for laureates, if we may put it so, to rest on their laurels. What appears from below to be the summit of accomplishment becomes, in the experience of those who have reached it, only another way station. Each contribution is defined only as a prelude to other contributions. Emphatic recognition for work accomplished, in this context, tends to induce continued effort, serving both to validate the judgment that the eminent scientist has unusual capacities and to testify that these capacities have continuing potential. Such patterned expectations make it difficult for those who have climbed the rugged mountains of scientific achievement to call a halt. It is not necessarily their own escalating Faustian aspirations that keep the more accomplished scientists at work. They are subject to the enlarged expectations of their peers and reference groups. More is expected of them, at least for the time, and this environment of expectation creates its own measure of motivation and stress. Less often than might be imagined is there repose at the top.[51]

Although socially reinforced motivation for continuing in research may be greater for high-ranking scientists, they are far from absent for the rest of us who know ourselves to be, at best, journeymen of science. For one thing, our own more modest contributions can be compared with those of even less distinction, as we select reference groups and individuals that sustain our self-esteem. For another, the prevailing imagery of science as a vast collectivity in which each contributes his bit to build the cathedral of knowledge also helps to maintain the ordinary scientist in his research role.[52] Nevertheless, this would not seem to provide the same degree of social reinforcement that accrues to outstanding scientists.

[51] This account of the process of socially reinforced aspirations and of consequent role-retention draws largely upon Merton (1968a, p. 57).
[52] On this imagery of science and for evidence bearing on its validity, see Jonathan Cole (1970).

All these observations suggest the hypothesis that attrition of the research role and enlargement of teaching, administrative, and other roles will tend to occur earlier and relatively more frequently among scientists lower in the stratification system of science. So far as we know, there has been no systematic investigation of this conjecture, although Harmon's cohort data for 10,000 scientists could be adapted to the purpose by incorporating indicators of standing in the field in the body of data already in hand. However, some evidence does bear tangentially upon the conjecture. Zuckerman (1972, Chapter 6) provides qualitative evidence for the reinforcing character of recognition in the early years of research for Nobel laureates and Stephen Cole and Jonathan Cole (1967, pp. 388–389; also J. Cole and S. Cole, 1972, Chapter 5) have found for a sample of American university physicists that the more recognition for their early work received in the form of citations by variously productive physicists, the more often they continued to be productive in research. Since degrees of recognition by the community of scientists make for location in the stratification system, this evidence is at least consistent with the hypothesis.

The patterns of shifting from research to other roles are not all of a kind. They differ phenomenologically and in their social and psychological mechanisms. In one pattern, the shift expresses a change in the values of the scientist or an enlarged access to alternative roles, which, in some sense, are more highly rewarding to him than research. In either case, the change represents a pull of the new role rather than a push from the old. The scientist searches out the shift rather than having it imposed upon him. He does not doubt his contining competence to do research. He simply prefers another role that seems more significant to him. He may be responding to rapidly changing values in the larger society or modifying his values in more idiosyncratic fashion or simply finding an administrative post, with its better pay and greater power, more attractive to him. He perceives the change as one of extending his scope, perhaps by helping to shape the changing place of science in the society or by helping strategic publics to understand the risks, costs, and benefits of science and science-based technology.

In other cases, the scientist finds that his research no longer measures up to his standards and so takes little satisfaction in continuing with it.[53] He turns to an alternative role. This class of changing roles is sociologically unproblematical, requiring little interpretation.

[53] We should perhaps remind ourselves that to note the faults in the Lehman kind of data on age and scientific productivity does not mean that there is no relation between the two. The quantity and quality of scientific output may in fact decline for the aggregate of scientists in the later years and, in any case, such declines are known to occur for individual scientists (just as for occasional others, research continues unabated or occasionally expands). We refer here to those scientists who experience a declining research output and so are motivated to take up other roles in science.

A superficially similar but actually quite different pattern of shift in roles is that of the private self-fulfilling prophecy. In these cases, the scientist would prefer to go on with research. But he has become persuaded that he is approaching an age at which his creative potential, great or small, is bound to decay. Rather than continue in a role in which he believes himself destined to fall increasingly short, he makes a pre-emptive shift. He assumes new administrative responsibilities, turns more of his attention to teaching, becomes active in the public business of science. Once the premise of his prospective diminishing capacity for research is accepted, the pre-emptive adaptation becomes entirely sensible. But as with every kind of self-fulfilling prophecy, the question is, of course, whether the original premise leading to the behavior which seemingly validates that premise was sound in the first place.

Another pattern of shift from the research role also involves a self-fulfilling prophecy but in its more consequential public form. Here the shifts in role are system-induced, not personally induced. The process is set in motion not by the individual scientist's own definition of his capacity to continue doing research but by the institutionalized belief that the amount and quality of scientific output generally deteriorate badly after a certain age. To the extent that this belief is incorporated in policy, some older research scientists reluctantly find themselves elevated into administrative posts and others find their facilities for research limited. Subsequent declines in research output with age seem only to confirm the soundness of the policy and are taken as fresh evidence for the general validity of the belief in declining productivity with age.[54]

Both kinds of self-fulfilling prophecy, the self-generated and the socially generated, interact and reinforce each other. Social assessments of role-performance come to be reflected in self-images, and behavior in accord with those self-images tends to make for the patterned social assessments. What interests us here is the possibility that appraisals of the research may turn out to be stratified by age, with younger scientists being especially critical of older scientists. Consider as a case in point the psychological and sociological bases for the ambivalence of apprentices to their masters.[55] In the psychological analysis of the pattern, the apprentice esteems the master and takes him as a role-model while also aiming to replace the master who, after a time, stands in his way. Without assuming that such ambivalence is typical, we can readily identify many instances in the history of science: Kepler's strong ambivalence toward Tycho Brahe; Sir Ronald Ross's toward his master Manson in the quest for the malarial parasite, his devotion to his teacher pushing him

[54] For a statement of the social costs involved in policies of "premature retirement" from research in socialist countries, see Szafer (1968, pp. 33–34).

[55] The following passage on ambivalence draws almost verbatim on Merton and Barber (1963, pp. 92–93).

to extravagant praise, his need for autonomy pushing him to excessive criticism. Or consider, appropriately enough, the checkered history of psychoanalysis itself with the secessionists Jung and Adler displaying their ambivalence toward Freud; in sociology (to come no closer home to our own day), the mixed feelings of the young Comte toward Saint-Simon; in psychiatry, the mixed feelings of Bouchard toward Charcot; and in medicine, of Sir Everard Home toward John Hunter; and so on through an indefinitely long list of apprentice-master ambivalence in science.

The probabilities of such ambivalence of apprentices toward masters—or, to put the matter more generally, of younger toward older scientists—presumably differ according to the context provided by the social structure of science. For example, ambivalence may be more apt to develop when, owing to the paucity of major chairs in a field, the talented apprentice finds that he "has no (appropriate) place to go" after he has made his mark other than the place occupied by the master (or others like him). But if the social system of his science provides an abundance of other places, some as highly esteemed as that currently occupied by the stratum of masters, there is less structurally induced motivation for ambivalence. And by the same token, the masters, in the reciprocity of relations, may be less motivated to develop ambivalence toward the apprentices who, in more restricted circumstances, might be competing with them as "premature" successors.

> *Query:* Do age-stratified cohorts cf scientists tend to adopt criteria differing in stringency if not kind in assessing the research of others or does a commonality of criteria transcend age differences? To what extent do cohorts agree in judging the research accomplishments and continuing potential of leading scientists in their field? Do these patterns differ according to the "market situation" in the various sciences and within the same science in various social systems that differ in the opportunity-structure for young scientists?

The various patterns of role-change in the life course involve an interplay between the individual's own expectations and those prevailing in the relevant social environment. This means, of course, that role-changes are affected both by developments distinctive to individuals and by trends in their environment. Individuals experience the social correlates of their own aging in particular social contexts. The contexts affect the meaning they attach to those changes and their adaptations to them. Early retirement from the research role should thus have different consequences for successive cohorts of scientists who come upon this experience at differing points in the historically evolving social structure of science. For scientific investigators to turn to the role of science administrator or science educator at a time in which such changes are relatively infrequent is quite another kind of experience than doing so when it has become common. In complementary fashion, both the probability and consequences of such shifts from research to other roles differ according to the changing degree of support—economic, technical, and social—available for research. The rapid growth in such resources has meant, for example, that the advanced graduate student or newfledged Ph.D. can now obtain technical help and services not available to seasoned investigators a generation ago (cf. Kusch, 1966, p. 12). This change may directly affect the age of entry into consequential research and indirectly affect the competitive positions of the various age cohorts of research scientists.

The Riley-Johnson-Foner model and Pinder's striking formulation of "the noncontemporaneity of the contemporaneous"[56] both suggest to us that the various age cohorts of scientists will tend to perceive the allocation of resources and the role structure of science from differing perspectives. For the newest cohorts, coming into science at a time of abundance, the availability of resources is largely a matter of ordinary expectation. After all, this is all they know from their own direct experience. The older cohorts tend to see this as drastic change, and not necessarily all for the better, as they nostalgically and sometimes invidiously contrast the current affluence to their own difficult days as novice investigators when outside resources were meager and inner resources all-important.

Other age-connected differences in perspective may derive from the allocation of roles within the changing status-structure of science. Younger scientists often come to see the positions of power practically monopolized by older scientists. For although the professionalization and institutionalization of science and the great growth in the resources of science have multiplied the number of policy-making roles, it may be that the exponential increase in numbers of scientists, all apart from other processes, has tended actually to decrease the proportions of the newer cohorts in these positions and to raise the age at which they enter them.

These few observations on the differing perspectives of younger and older scientists might seem to imply that the relations between these cohorts are dominated by stress, strain, and conflict. But to focus on the structure and

[56] *"Die 'Ungleichzeitigkeit' des Gleichzeitigen"* is the seemingly paradoxical phrasing adopted by the art historian, Wilhelm Pinder, to introduce his distinction between *Gleichzeitigkeit* (contemporaneity or temporal coexistence) and *Gleichaltrigkeit* (coevality, coetaneity or the condition of age cohorts). Consider this germane passage: *"Jeder lebt mit Gleichaltrigen und Verschiedenaltrigen in einer Fülle gleichzeitiger Möglichkeiten. Für jeden ist die gleiche Zeit eine andere Zeit, nämlich ein anderes Zeitalter seiner selbst, das er nur mit Gleichaltrigen teilt. Jeder Zeitpunkt hat für Jeden nicht nur dadurch einen anderen Sinn, dass er selbstverständlich von Jedem in individueller Färbung erlebt wird, sondern—als wirklicher 'Zeitpunkt,' unterhalb alles individuellen—schon dadurch, dass das gleiche Jahr für einen Fünfzigjährigen ein anderer Zeitpunkt seines Lebens ist, als für einen Zwanzigjährigen—und so fort in zahllosen Varianten"* (Pinder, 1928, Chapter 1 and p. 11). This sort of observation on contemporaneous age-cohorts and their perspectives is fully caught up in the Riley-Johnson-Foner model.

processes making for tension and conflict is not, of course, to say that these are all. We have noted the integrative aspects of complementary age-connected roles in the process of socialization in science where, perhaps more often than in other disciplines, the roles of teacher and student soon become transformed into those of research colleagues. The differentiated age structure of research groups provide bases for cooperation as well as conflict. It is probably in the politics of science that conflict between the age strata of scientists runs deep (Greenberg, 1967, Book One).

4 Gerontocracy in science

The claim that the organization of science is controlled by gerontocracy is anything but new. Complaints to this effect appeared as early as the seventeenth century and perhaps before. But the vast historical changes in the scale and power of science greatly intensify and complicate the problems of social control.

DYSFUNCTIONS OF GERONTOCRACY

Neither empirical evidence nor theoretical reason leads us to suppose that rule by elders is more characteristic of science than of other institutional spheres. Gerontocracy may turn out, in fact, to be less marked in science. But it can be argued that rule by elders is apt to be more dysfunctional for science than for other institutions. For although the Ogburnian notion that science and technology develop and change more rapidly than other parts of civilization and culture has yet to be empirically demonstrated,[57] we do know that the values of science call for maximizing the rate of developing knowledge and the procedures and equipments required to advance that knowledge. And with the great expansion of the personnel and resources of science, scientific knowledge has for some time been growing at an accelerating rate. Now it is an old and plausible sociological maxim, though one more often announced than confirmed by actual investigation, that the higher the rate of social and cultural change, the less the advantage of age, with its obsolescent experience.[58]

[57] Ogburn advanced this idea in his classic *Social Change* and developed it further in several monographs. Its validity has been questioned, principally by Sorokin; see Ogburn (1922); Sorokin (1937, Volume 4).

[58] The observation has been made in one form or another through the centuries. Here is how Roberto Michels put it in 1911: "The ancient Greeks said that white hairs were the first crown which must decorate the leaders' foreheads. Today, however, we live in an epoch in which there is less need for accumulated personal experience of life, for science puts at every one's disposal [such] efficient means of instruction that even the youngest may speedily become well instructed. Today everything is quickly acquired, even that experience in which formerly consisted the sole and genuine superiority of the old over the young. Thus, not in consequence of democracy, but simply owing to the technical type of modern civilization, age has lost much of its value, and therefore has lost, in addition, the respect which it inspired and the influence which it exercised" (Michels, 1949, p. 76).

It has been further argued, most emphatically by the distinguished physicist J. D. Bernal, whose own major contributions to crystallography have continued in his seventh decade, that "the advances in basic conceptions have become so rapid that the majority of older scientists are incapable of understanding, much less of advancing, their own subjects. But nearly the whole of what organization of science exists, and the vital administration of funds, is in the hands of old men"(Bernal, 1939, p. 116 and also pp. 290–291). Bernal suggests, moreover, that as science expands in numbers, complexity, and influence, and as it becomes more closely linked with government, industry, and finance, its control is increasingly exercised by older scientists.

Plausible as these observations are, they have yet to be systematically investigated. The fact is that we do not know the comparative extent of gerontocracy in science and in other principal institutional spheres. Nor do we know whether the vast expansion of science has brought with it enlarged control by gerontocrats. Nor, finally, do we know whether gerontocracy is more dysfunctional[59] for the development of science and for the society than alternative forms of age-patterned control, such as proportional age representation or, at the other extreme, juvenocracy.[60] Since comprehensive evidence on these complicated questions is absent, here are a few straws in the wind.

EVIDENCE OF GERONTOCRACY: THE NATIONAL ACADEMY OF SCIENCES

Consider the age composition of the National Academy of Sciences, the influential organization of scientists established during the Civil War and designated by Congressional charter to advise the federal government on matters of science. Apart from its own membership of some 900, the Academy draws upon thousands of other scientists through its operating adjunct, the National Research Council. Designed as an honorary society as well as an advisory body, the Academy is not likely to have a membership numerically representative of the entire national population of scientists: in regional distribution, university affiliation, age, or anything else.

The average age of Academy members is 62, with about a quarter of them being 70 or older. In 1969, three-quarters of the members of advisory committees and panels of the National Research Council were over 45; a third over 55. This contrasts with the median age of 41 for all scientists (holding doctorates) in the United States in 1968, with a quarter of these being under

---

[50] It has sometimes been said in wry or acerb mood that gerontocracy may even be a good thing in science; it leaves the young productive scientists free to get on with their research and helps to occupy the time of those who are no longer creative.

[60] To the extent that existing social structures tend to be reflected in language, there is perhaps a certain interest in noting that while the word "gerontocracy" has been around for at least two centuries, the word "juvenocracy" appears here, so far as we know, for the first time. It is, unfortunately, a hybrid. But a language which has absorbed such inelegant hybrids as "electrocution" and even "sociology" can surely make room for a much-needed another, such as "juvenocracy."

TABLE 8 · 4 *Mean age at election to National Academy of Sciences according to organizational affiliation of scientists, 1863–1967*

Affiliation	Mean age	Number
Major universities.	48.9	843
Government	51.5	141
Other universities and colleges	51.8	285
Industry	53.3	70
No affiliation	53.7	54
Retired	66.8	12
		1405
	No information	8
	Total	1413

Source: Zuckerman (1972, Chapter 6).

the age of 35. Contrasting age distributions such as these give high visibility to the pattern of gerontocracy.[61]

The elite character of the National Academy plainly affects its age composition. Scientists are seldom elected to membership on the basis of a single contribution to science, however outstanding; a continued record of contributions is ordinarily required. Young talented scientists are left to ripen on the vine before they are picked for membership. Moreover, scientists drawn from the various sectors of employment are evidently judged to meet the Academy's criteria for membership at different ages, as can be seen from figures in Table 8 · 4.

The scanty data we have assembled on the National Academy indicate no continuing historical trend toward recruiting older scientists. As early as the turn of the century, when the astronomer George Ellery Hale was elected to the Academy at the very early age of 35, he described it, in the words of a friend, "as more interested in keeping young men out of its membership than in acting as a vital force in the scientific development of the United States."[62] The mean age at time of election continued to rise until 1940 but has since remained fairly constant at a somewhat lower level as we see in Table 8 · 5.

Contrary to first impression, historical patterns of this sort may help account for the belief that positions of prestige and power in science are increasingly held by older people. For even in cases when the age at which they acquire these positions has stabilized or declined somewhat, this has been occurring in a period when exponential growth has been producing an increasingly youthful population of scientists. This results in widened discrepancies of age between the governing and the governed and might be enough to pro-

[61] Concerned with this and kindred problems, the National Research Council has established a panel to examine the composition of advisory committees. These figures are drawn from the preliminary report of that panel.

[62] True (1913, p. 73). We are indebted for this reference to the preliminary report of the NRC panel on advisory committees.

TABLE 8 · 5 *Mean age at election to National Academy of Sciences, 1863–1967*

Time of election	Mean age	Number
Before 1900	47.0	195
1900–1919	49.2	158
1920–1939	51.7	252
1940–1959	50.5	522
1960–1967	50.7	286
		1413

Source: Zuckerman (unpublished analysis).

duce a sense of increasing gerontocracy. Moreover, when, as in the case of the National Academy, the status, once acquired, is retained for life,[63] the aging of the group is encouraged by the increasing longevity of its members.[64]

The age-distribution of those occupying the positions of power in science does not tell us, of course, how that power is exercised. Systematic inquiry, rather than swift assumption, is needed to find out whether there are age-patterned differences in policies and the exercise of power. Such studies have yet largely to be made.

EXERCISE OF POWER: THE REFEREE SYSTEM

One recent study of the referee system in science (Zuckerman and Merton, 1971, pp. 92–94) touches upon the question. Drawing upon the archives for the nine years 1948–1956 of *The Physical Review*, the outstanding journal in physics, the study examines the behavior of scientists of differing rank and age in the gatekeeper's role. The referee system calls for evaluation of manuscripts by experts on their subject. It comes as no surprise, therefore, that referees for *The Physical Review* were drawn disproportionately from physicists of high rank.[65] Compared with the 5 per cent of the 1,056 authors (themselves in some measure a selected aggregate),[66] almost 12 per cent of

[63] Members of the Academy recently rejected the proposal that they should become emeriti after the age of 75.

[64] The longevity of college graduates has been increasing in the United States for at least the past century.

[65] In the first rank are those physicists submitting manuscripts who, by the end of the period (1956), had received at least one of the ten most respected awards in physics (such as the Nobel prize, or membership in the Royal Society or the National Academy of Sciences). Physicists of the second rank, although they had not been accorded any of the highest forms of recognition, had been judged important enough by the American Institute of Physics to be included in its archives of contemporary physicists. The remaining contributors comprise the third rank in this hierarchy. Referees are ranked by the same criteria.

[66] The special nature of this sample of authors must be understood as (a) resulting from considerable preselection through decisions to produce and submit manuscripts; (b) consisting only of sole authors of manuscripts, with joint authors excluded; (c) consisting of a 20 per cent sample of third-ranked contributors, but of *all* first- and second-ranked physicists submitting singly authored manuscripts during the study period. Had the sample included all single authors of every rank, fewer than 2 per cent would be included among the first rank.

the 354 referees assessing their papers were in the highest rank. Moreover, these 12 per cent contributed one-third of all referee judgments. They refereed an average of 8.5 papers compared with 3.8 for the referees of intermediate rank and 1.4 for the rank-and-file. And although 45 per cent of the referees were under the age of 40, thus giving major responsibility to the relatively young, we know that physicists are altogether a youthful aggregate and research physicists particularly so.[67] Fully 74 per cent of the papers submitted to *The Physical Review* came from physicists under the age of 40.

The referees, then, are older and higher in prestige and rank than the authors or the general population of physicists. But, as we have noted, such a skewed age distribution among those holding power is simply a static indicator of structure; it provides no information about the functioning and consequences of that structure. Age-distribution does not in itself represent gerontocracy. For even when used descriptively rather than invidiously, the word "gerontocracy" ordinarily carries with it the notion that power disproportionately placed in the hands of the elder comes to be used to their own advantage or, in more moderate version, that it results in policies and decisions that differ drastically from those that are or would be adopted by younger power-holders. In the case of the gatekeeper role, we want to know, then, whether the behavior of referees is systematically affected by their own age and rank as well as by the age and rank of authors.

One piece of evidence takes us a certain distance toward gauging the extent to which the rejection and acceptance of manuscripts for publication was affected by the standing of referees and authors. In examining this evidence, we should note again that eminence in science derives largely from the assessed quality of past and not necessarily continuing scientific accomplishments. And we have found that, in science, as in other institutional spheres, positions of power and authority tend to be occupied by older men. From these joint patterns, it would seem that if sheer power and eminence greatly affect the decisions of referees, then manuscripts submitted by older eminent scientists should have the highest rate of acceptance.[68]

But at least in physics, the distinctively young man's science, this is not what we find. As we see in Table 8 · 6, it is not the oldest scientists whose papers were most often accepted but the youngest ones. And the age-graded rates of acceptance hold within each rank in the hierarchy of prestige. Both eminence and youth contribute to the probability of having manuscripts ac-

[67] It will be remembered from the first part of this paper that physics has the lowest median age among the several major fields of science and from our discussion of role-sequence that the physicists engaged substantially in research are the youngest of the lot.

[68] On the general hypothesis, see Storer (1966, pp. 132–134). This hypothesis assumes that the identity of the authors of manuscripts is known to the referees; this is the case for *The Physical Review*, which does not try to provide for anonymity of authors, since, it is maintained, this cannot be achieved in most cases. Referees, however, are generally anonymous.

TABLE 8 · 6 *Rates of acceptance of manuscripts, by age and rank of authors* (The Physical Review, *1948–1956*)

	Prestige rank of authors							
	Higher rank physicists		Intermediate physicists		Third rank physicists		All ranks	
	%	No.	%	No.	%	No.	%	No.
Age of authors	Ac-cepted	Pa-pers	Ac-cepted	Pa-pers	Ac-cepted	Pa-pers	Ac-cepted	Pa-pers
20–29	—	—	91	287	83	385	87	672
30–39	96	80	89	519	77	440	85	1039
40–49	95	58	83	236	73	79	83	373
50+	80	87	71	126	50	14	73	227
No information on age							61	423
Total papers							80	2734

cepted; youth to such a degree that the youngest stratum of physicists in the third rank had as high an acceptance rate as the oldest stratum of eminent ones[69] whose work, we must suppose, was no longer of the same high quality it once was.

This is a first indication that the "gerontocratic" body of gatekeepers does not exercise its power by denying or restricting access of younger physicists to publication in the most widely read and most influential journal in the field. This still leaves open the possibility that it is not the age of the author as such but his age *relative* to that of his referees which systematically influences appraisals of his manuscripts. Such biases in judgment might take various forms, depending upon the pattern of relative age.[70]

When referees and authors are age-peers, an hypothesis of *age-stratum-solidarity* would have it that referees typically give preferential treatment to manuscripts just as a counterhypothesis of *age-stratum-competition* would have it that, under the safeguard of anonymity, referees tend to undercut their rivals by unjustifiably severe judgments.

When authors are older than referees, an hypothesis of *age-status-deference* would hold that the referees give preferential treatment to the work of the older established scientists just as a counterhypothesis of *age-status-envy* would have them downgrade the work of older scientists.

And when referees are older than authors, an hypothesis of *sponsorship*

[69] Some caution must be exercised in this comparison, however, since most of the scientists for whom no information on age was available are in the third rank. These scientists have a relatively low acceptance rate and, should they also be disproportionately young, could depress the acceptance figure for the younger third-ranking scientists below that for the oldest first-ranking.

[70] On the concept of relative age, see the Riley-Johnson-Foner model [*Chapters 1 · 1 · D; 10 · 1; also 9 · 2 by Hess*] and the theoretical analysis by Eisenstadt (1956, Chapter 1, *passim*).

or patronage would maintain that referees are unduly kind and undemanding while a counterhypothesis of *age-oppression* would have them overly demanding of the young.

Differing in other respects, these six hypotheses are alike in one: they all assume that the relative age of referee and author significantly biases the role-performance of the gatekeepers, either in favor of the author or at his expense. More concretely, all the hypotheses assume that the rates of acceptance of manuscripts submitted by each age stratum of authors will differ according to the age of the referees passing judgment on them.

The data assembled in Table 8 · 7 seem to run counter to most of these hypotheses.[71] For the most part, the relative age of author and referee has no perceptible influence on patterns of evaluation. With one exception, both younger and older referees are more likely to accept the work of younger authors, a finding that parallels the age pattern of Table 8 · 6. And each age stratum of authors, again with one exception, has the same proportion of papers accepted by referees of differing age. Interestingly enough, the pattern of evenhanded treatment by older and younger referees holds even for that class of physicists who were not well enough known to have their ages listed in any of the standard registries of scientists.

The one exception to the general pattern appears in the youngest stratum of authors who have more of their papers accepted by older referees than younger ones. This tentatively identified exception is consistent with the hypothesis of acute competition within the age-cohort in the earliest phase of their careers and with the hypothesis that older scientists are less demanding in assessing the work done by progressively younger scientists. The data allow no unequivocal choice between the hypotheses. Either or both may obtain. In any case, neither the general pattern nor the limited departure from it exhibits distinctively gerontocratic patterns of evaluation among the gatekeepers of this major scientific journal.

This particular case is enough to suggest the general point: a skewed age distribution of scientists assigned authoritative roles is one thing; what they do in exercising their authority can be quite another. But, of course, we cannot conclude from this one inquiry that there are no patterns of age-graded evaluations or policy-decisions in science. Much more research will be needed to examine and develop this major question. For example, just as the several sciences differ in age-structure, so they may differ both in the age distribution of authoritative roles and in age-patterned performance of those roles. We hazard the conjecture that the more theoretically codified the science the greater the consensus among the age strata in their patterns of evaluation.

[71] The separate effects of each of these hypothetical processes cannot, of course, be weighed by examination of a single set of cross-sectional data, since several tendencies may operate in tandem or in opposition to produce observed proportions.

TABLE 8 · 7 *Referees' decisions[a] to accept manuscripts, by age of authors and referees* (The Physical Review, *1948–1956*)

Age of authors	Age of referees				Total judgments by referees	
	Under 40		40 and over			
	% Accept-ances	No. Judg-ments	% Accept-ances	No. Judg-ments	% Accept-ances	No. Judg-ments
20–29	59	106	76	136	68	242
30–39	63	193	63	189	63	382
40–49	63	65	58	71	60	136
50+	43	42	43	61	43	103
No information	53	106	52	96	52	202
All ages	58	512	61	553	60	1065

[a] The data refer to the number of judgments, not papers, made by 344 external referees and do not include judgments by the two editors. The table omits 18 cases in which there is no information on the age of the 10 referees judging them. Since papers judged exclusively by the editors are omitted, the analysis is based on judgments of fewer than half the total papers reported in Table 8 · 6.

The more codified disciplines such as physics should exhibit less disparity between age cohorts than less codified disciplines such as sociology on all manner of evaluations: the comparative significance of problems requiring investigation and of contributions to the field as well as such questions of science policy as the allocation of resources to various kinds of research.

It should be noted also that the question of gerontocracy in the formation of broad science policy remains as much a matter of conjecture as the question of gerontocracy within scientific disciplines. We know, for example, that the mean age of members of PSAC (President's Science Advisory Committee) has been about 50, with the Eisenhower advisors being somewhat older and the Kennedy advisors somewhat younger.[72] But we do not know how far the age composition of this and of other advisory and policy-making groups affects the substance of science policy.[73] In exploring this question, we need to distinguish the age composition and the rates of turnover of these influential groups, recognizing that each may have its independent effect. It would come as no surprise to find that optimum science policy is apt to be developed neither by gerontocracy nor by juvenocracy but, like the community of scientists itself, by age-diversified meritocracy.

[72]

Year	Mean ages of members of PSAC		No. of advisors
1958	Eisenhower	53.8	(18)
1962	Kennedy	49.0	(17)
1965	Johnson	50.3	(15)
1969	Nixon	50.5	(11)

[73] On the general issue, see Rose and Rose (1969, pp. 266–268).

5 Age, social stratification, and collaboration in science

The extent to which significant interaction takes place within age strata and between them, together with the consequences of such patterns, are no better known for the domain of science than for most other institutional spheres. Although there has been no investigation to determine which activities in science tend to be age-segregated or age-integrated, it is evident that some basic functions of science are served through institutional arrangements involving interaction between age strata rather than separation of them. First among these is, of course, education and training both in the narrow sense of transmission of knowledge and skills and in the broader sense of socialization involving the transmission of values, attitudes, interests, and role-defined behavior. Since he has himself been variously engaged in the process of professional socialization, just about every scientist has his own opinion about how that process actually works. Yet the plain fact is that there has been little methodical investigation of that process in science.[74]

> *Queries:* Which components in the culture of science are principally transmitted by older to younger scientists? And which are largely acquired from age peers? Do these age-channeled streams of socialization merge or diverge? Which of the values, interests, and patterns of behavior derived from differing age strata are mutually supporting, complementary, or at odds? Do the observed patterns of socialization tend to persist so as to be much the same for successive age cohorts or are they subject to change, among other things, in response to the changing boundaries, technology, problematics, and substance of the sciences? How does the age-patterned process of socialization differ among the various sciences and these, in turn, from socialization in other fields of learning (such as the humanities and technology)?

GROWTH OF RESEARCH COLLABORATION IN SCIENCE

Just as the early years of education in science generally provide in varying degree for interaction between age strata, so in particular with that advanced form of socialization that takes place through collaboration in research.[75] This form of socialization takes on growing importance as the social organization of scientific inquiry has greatly changed, with collaboration and research teams becoming more and more the order of the day. One pale reflection of this change is the sustained growth in the proportion of scientific articles published by two or more authors. Table 8 · 8 shows each successive

---

[74] But see Becker and Carper (1956) for the case of physiologists; Underhill (1966) for physical, biological, and social scientists; and Aran and Ben-David (1968) for medical researchers.

[75] This discussion of age and collaboration in research draws extensively on Zuckerman (1965b, pp. 394–396).

TABLE 8 · 8 *Percentage of multiauthored papers in the physical and biological sciences, social sciences, and humanities,[a] 1900–1959*

Date of publication	Physical and biological sciences	Social sciences	Humanities
1900–1909	25 (928)	—	—
1910–1919	31 (1,686)	—	—
1920–1929	49 (2,148)	6 (2,643)	1 (1,822)
1930–1939	56 (3,964)	11 (3,905)	2 (2,088)
1940–1949	66 (4,918)	16 (4,328)	2 (1,972)
1950–1959	83 (9,995)	32 (6,605)	1 (2,304)
Total	66 (23,639)	20 (17,481)	1 (8,186)

[a] The figures were compiled by counting the number of authors of articles appearing in a sample of journals for two of every ten years. The physical and biological sciences include the fields of physics, chemistry, biology; the social sciences include anthropology, economics, political science, psychology, and sociology; the humanities, history, language and literature, and philosophy.
Source: Zuckerman (1965, pp. 55–104) (adapted).

decade of this century registering a higher percentage of multiauthored papers in the physical and biological sciences.[76] The social sciences begin this practice later and sparingly but then rapidly increase the rate of collaboration. Both contrast with the humanities, which have practically no place for collaborative research reported in scholarly articles.

RANK-STRATIFIED RATES OF COLLABORATION

Imperfect indicators of the actual organization of research as they are, the data on multiple authorship nevertheless raise some questions and suggest some conjectures. Does the practice of collaborative research obtain to the same extent on all levels in the social stratification system of science? More concretely, how does this stand with an institutionally identified elite, such as Nobel laureates, compared with the collaborative practices found in a sample of scientists matched with them in terms of age, field of specialization, and type of organizational affiliation? And how do the rates of collaboration compare at various ages and phases in the scientific career?

As a crude approximation to an answer—crude since the data do not allow us to compare age cohorts throughout their life course—Table 8 · 9 presents age-specific rates of collaboration for the laureates and their less elevated counterparts. Laureates are somewhat more given to collaboration, with 62

[76] For data based on other samples showing similar results, see Clarke (1964, pp. 822–824). We do not examine here the relation between actual patterns of research (individual, with and without assistants; collaboration of varying numbers of peers; small-team research and large-scale research) and the number of authors of papers published by these types of research formations. There is evidence that research patterns and size of author-sets are correlated, though not as closely as is sometimes assumed by the many investigators who have used authorship data as indicators of research practices. The question is considered in some detail in Zuckerman (1965, Chapter 5).

per cent of their papers being multiauthored compared with 51 per cent of those by the age-matched sample. The difference holds, moreover, at every age. Table 8 · 9 also exhibits a slight curvilinear relationship between age at publication and multiauthorship for both laureates and the matched sample. We cannot explain these patterns, but other evidence enables us to speculate on their sources.

Consider first the seeming curvilinear pattern in which collaboration appears to be more frequent in the middle years. We say "seeming" pattern not because we really doubt this set of data but only because we know that more extensive data on age cohorts are required to *establish* the authenticity and to discover the generality of the pattern. It must be admitted also that we give credence to the numerical data in hand for the worst of reasons: they tally with our conjectures about age-connected processes making for collaboration.

These processes can be reconstructed in terms of age-patterned opportunities and age-patterned motivations for collaboration. As novices being inducted into the mysteries of the craft, young scientists who collaborate at all with mentors will typically do so with only one of them at any given time. Beyond that, the young scientists, sometimes at the urging of their sponsors, are motivated to do their own work and to establish a public identity within the field by publishing papers of their own. Not quite paradoxically, the motivation of beginning scientists to publish single-authored papers may only be strengthened by the great historical increase in papers with several, sometimes many, "authors." For the distinctive contributions of the individual get lost in the crowd of scientists putting their names to the paper and this, as they know, is especially damaging for young scientists who have not published independent work that testifies to their abilities. On this view, the smaller proportion of collaborative papers published in the early years of the career results in part from the often stressful operation of the reward-system that has developed in science.

Toward the other end of the career, the dropoff in published research,

TABLE 8 · 9   *Percentage of multiauthored papers by age at publication, for Nobel laureates and a matched sample of scientists*

Age at publication	Laureates	Matched sample
20–29	58 (523)	40 (288)
30–39	65 (1,382)	55 (756)
40–49	66 (1,641)	53 (590)
50–59	60 (1,198)	51 (622)
60 or over	55 (768)	46 (264)
Total	62 (5,512)	51 (2,520)

Source: Zuckerman (1967, p. 395).

which we have noted in the data put together by Wayne Dennis (1956a, 1956b, 1956c, 1966) may mean that collaborators are no longer as available as before. It is in this phase also that scientists often turn to broader "philosophical" or "sociological" subjects of a kind that have no place for collaboration.

It is the middle years, then, that presumably provide both the greatest opportunity and deepest role-induced motivation for collaborative work. Should the curvilinear pattern of collaboration turn out to be fairly general, it need not be counteracted by the historical trend toward more and more collaboration in the sciences; for the reasons we have indicated, it may even become more marked in successive age cohorts.

Consider now the consistently higher rates of collaboration among laureates at each phase of their life course. Throughout our interpretation, we make the rather undemanding assumption that, *on the average*, laureates exhibited evidence of greater talent for research than a random assortment of other scientists of their age in the same field. This perceptible difference would have set certain consequential processes in motion—processes such as self-selection and selective recruitment. In their 20's, as their capacities became identified, laureate-to-be were more often selected as apprentices by scientists of assured standing. (Although it would be too much to say that laureates are bred by laureates, it is the case that 42 of the 83 American prizewinners worked, as younger men, under a total of 54 older laureates.) There is reason to assume that these masters were more willing to grant coauthorship to their apprentices than were those of less elevated and secure standing.[77] This would make for the higher rate of published collaboration by laureates-to-be in their youth.

The life chances of scientists are greatly improved by having their substantial abilities identified early.[78] By the time they were in their 30's, every laureate had a position in a major university or research laboratory providing a micro-environment of other scientists in his specialty. By that time, many of the future laureates were making the status transition from junior to senior collaborator. They had acquired resources for research enabling them to sur-

[77] Only one laureate complained that he had been deprived of authorship by his senior collaborator when, in his judgment, it was deserved. Far more often, the laureates reported what they perceived as generous treatment in the matter of coauthorship with their typically eminent sponsors.

[78] On the bias in favor of precocity built into current institutions for detecting and rewarding talent, see Gregg (1957). The crucial point, which holds in the domain of science as well as in the field of medical practice of which Gregg writes, is this: ". . . *once you have most of your students of the same age*, the academic rewards—from scholarships to internships and residencies—go to those who are uncommonly bright for their age. In other words, you have rewarded precocity which may or may not be the precursor of later ability. So, in effect, you have unwittingly belittled man's cardinal educational capital—time to mature." For further sociological implications of this institutionalized bias, see Merton (1960, pp. 310–313).

round themselves with younger scientists wanting to work with them on the problems in hand.

RE-ENACTED ROLES IN AGE COHORTS

As they move into the role of senior collaborators, the laureates seem to reproduce the same patterns of collaborative work with youngsters that they themselves experienced when they were young. This may turn out to be one of several kinds of *re-enactment of role-defined patterns of behavior* at successive stages in the careers of scientists, especially those who occupy statuses comparable to those of their masters in the past. They are in a position to attract promising young scientists whose contributions are sufficient to merit coauthorship, much as the laureates, when they were young, were also included among the authors of papers. They are also in a position, even before receiving the Nobel prize (since most of them were eminent before being accorded that ultimate symbol of accomplishment), to exercise cost-free *noblesse oblige*, the generosity expected of those occupying undisputed rank, by granting authorship even to junior collaborators who, in the given case, may not have contributed much.

We cannot demonstrate that the laureates are more apt than less distinguished scientists to acknowledge the contributions of junior associates since we do not know how much the younger men had actually contributed. We can, however, compare the *degree* of recognition given to collaborators on jointly authored papers. We can approximate a check on this model of the laureates' re-enactment of collaborative roles as they move through their career by comparing the variously *visible name-orders* of authors of joint papers published by the laureates and by scientists in the matched sample (who, we now report, were matched not only for age, specialty, and organizational affiliation but also for the initial letter of their last name).[79] A prevalent type of name-ordering gives prime visibility to the first author.[80]

The evidence is consistent with our model of complementary roles being re-enacted in the course of the life-work-cycle.[81] The laureates-to-be, when they were in their 20's, were first authors on nearly half of all their collaborative papers at the same time that scientists in the matched sample were first

[79] This is designed, of course, to control for variations that would otherwise occur in cases of alphabetical ordering of authors.

[80] On the social symbolism of name-ordering among authors of scientific papers, see Zuckerman (1968).

[81] It should be emphasized that the samples consist of scientists working within a particular historical and institutional context: one sample comprises 41 of the 55 laureates at work in the United States (in 1963); the matched sample was drawn from *American Men of Science*. Obviously the attribution of authorship would be quite different in institutional frameworks where all or much of the research done in a laboratory or department is regularly ascribed to their chiefs. This is just another instance of institutional contexts serving to pattern interpersonal relations.

only a third of the time. In papers coauthored with their laureate masters, the pattern is even more marked, with the young scientists being first authors in 60 per cent of the papers and the laureates in only 16 per cent.[82] Moving into the role of senior collaborator, the laureates, by the time they are in their 40's, reduplicate the pattern taking first authorship on only 26 per cent of their collaborative papers at the same time that the scientists in the matched sample do so in 56 per cent of their collaborative papers. The negligible cost of this kind of *noblesse oblige* for scientists who have made their mark is put in so many words by a laureate in biochemistry:

> It helps a young man to be senior author, first author, and doesn't detract from the credit I get if my name is farther down on the list.

Substantial qualitative evidence obtained in interviews with laureates confirms that this kind of re-enactment of complementary roles often occurs when they have attained a status like that of their own masters. But this fact does not rule out other, not necessarily incompatible, interpretations of the numerical evidence on first-authorship. The dual pattern of authorship might also reflect age-associated changes and rank-stratified differences in the extent of contributions to collaborative papers. In their youth, the laureates-to-be might in fact have contributed more to jointly published papers than their age-peers in the matched sample and so appear as first author more of the time. And, in their maturity, the laureates, having attracted talented youngsters, might simply be re-experiencing the same phenomenon, this time from the perspective of the senior role, with their young collaborators making prime contributions and so being accorded first place. Correlatively, the age-matched scientists of less distinction, in their youth, will have contributed less and received first authorship less often in their collaborative papers with their less distinguished mentors just as, in their maturity, they re-enact the pattern by attracting, on the average, less talented youthful collaborators than those coming to the laureates and so would themselves turn up more often as first authors. It is the processes of self-selection and selective recruitment operating within the context of the reward-system of science, rather than any autarchic scientist playwright, which recreate this drama in many times and places with the plot and roles remaining intact, and the only change being that the inevitably aging members of the cast now play, in the style of their mentors, roles complementary to the ones they played in their youth.

---

[83] Neither laureates-to-be nor their laureate masters were first authors in the remaining 24 per cent of papers. This situation is in marked contrast to papers coauthored by scientist peers, both of whom later became laureates. For these papers, one future laureate is just as apt as the other to be first author in papers having at least three authors.

The observed patterns of authorship might therefore involve the re-enactment of complementary roles at different phases in the career in an apparently different way than we had at first supposed. They might reflect the objective situation of differing extent of contribution rather than the exercise of *noblesse oblige* that came with established standing. In broader theoretical perspective, however, these hypotheses turn out to be much the same. They bring us back to the general idea, much emphasized in our discussion of gerontocracy, that the age distribution of power and authority in science as elsewhere is only a static structural fact and does not, in itself, tell us much about how that power and authority are actually exercised.

In the matter of deciding on authorship and name-order as symbolic of contribution, it is generally the senior investigator who has the authority. The exercise of that authority is hedged in by norms and by constraints of maintaining a degree of cooperation in the research group. As the laureates and the matched sample of scientists take over control of these decisions, they apparently do not exercise raw power by putting themselves uniformly in the forefront. At the least, the data suggest, they tend to accede to the norms governing authority; at most, and especially when secure in high rank, they engage in cost-free supererogation.

This much can be said then about our specimen of interplay between social stratification and age stratification in science. Having moved early into the higher reaches of the opportunity structure, the laureates are more apt to collaborate at every age than other investigators of less eminence. Their tendency toward collaboration we take to be reinforced by their ability to contribute enough to merit association and coauthorship with masters in the field when they are young and by status-supported dispositions to share authorship with the young when they are mature or old. And, to repeat, these patterns obtain within an institutional framework that calls for ascribing credit for research on the basis of contribution rather than having it uniformly assigned, as in an authoritarian framework, to the head of a department or laboratory.

But, as we have suggested earlier in this section, the change toward Big Science, partly reflected in the growth of multiauthorship, makes for a change in the structure of power and authority in science where, goodwill, *noblesse oblige*, and normative constraints notwithstanding, it becomes increasingly difficult and sometimes impossible to gauge the contributions of individual scientists to the collective product of ever larger groups of investigators. The possible consequences of this structural change on the information- and reward-system of science have been strongly formulated by Ziman:

> It is obvious, in the first place, that there is a grave threat to the convention of awarding promotion, or other forms of recognition, on the strength of pub-

lished work. The mere fact that a candidate for a lectureship in elementary particle physics has his name amongst the dozens of 'authors' of some significant discovery says little about his scientific skill. In the long run, the leader of such a team gets the credit for its contributions to knowledge, but he must be already the selected and tested boss of a big group. Evidence of ability at a more junior level can only be assessed within the framework of the project itself, just as it would be in an army, a civil service or other bureaucracy. This . . . puts direct power into the hands of the seniors, and opens the way to careerism, personal autocracy, and other evils, as well as giving the advantage to the 'other-directed' personality, at the expense of those protestant virtues of being 'inner-directed' which have contributed so much, in the past, to the scientific attitude. . . . [O]ne of the primary functions of the conventional communication system is losing weight. The necessity of maintaining an open market for the creations of the individual scholar, as objective evidence of achievement and promise, is no longer evident (Ziman, 1970, pp. 191–192).

Without going into the matter further, it becomes evident that the apparently bland subject of age patterns of collaboration opens up into a large array of basic questions about the operation of contemporary science. Here, as elsewhere in the field, we are still long on demonstrable questions and short on demonstrated answers. But we have seen enough, in this section of our chapter and in the section touching upon gerontocracy, to identify a variety of related problems.

> *Queries:* How much and in which respects do the structures of authority in Big Science and in Smaller Science actually differ? To the extent that they do, how does this affect the operation of the communication system and reward system? What are the consequences of varicus authority-structures for scientists of differing age and at different phases in their careers? To what degree are power and authority correlated with age in different sciences and in various national scientific establishments? Which decision points, at every level in the social organization of science, are most consequential for the advance of scientific knowledge? How can more headway be made in investigating the process of decision-making in science at the several levels of its organization?

6 *Age strata and foci of scientific interest*

Historical changes in the foci of scientific work are a matter of experience familiar to sufficiently long-lived scientists and a commonplace among historians and sociologists of science. But how these changes come about and how they are distributed through the community of scientists remains a long-standing and knotty problem,[83] which has lately attracted a renewed interest. As much else in the history, philosophy, and sociology of science, this recent development is a *self-exemplifying pattern* in which workers in these fields are registering a sort of shift in research interests much like that of scientists whose comparable behavior they are trying to interpret or explain.

Both reflecting and deepening the renewed interest in this problem is Thomas S. Kuhn's book, *The Structure of Scientific Revolutions,* which in less than a decade has given rise to a library of criticism and appreciative applications.[84] To judge from the assorted use of this book in just about every branch of learning, it has become something of a complex projective test, meaning all things to all men and women. We do not propose to add still another interpretation of the book in referring to its at least symptomatic relevance here. For our purposes, it is enough to note that Kuhn puts forward three relevant points in his book and supplementary papers. One, he joins Popper in a major concern with "the dynamic process by which scientific knowledge is acquired rather than . . . the logical structure of the products of scientific research." Two, central to this kind of inquiry is an understanding of "what problems [scientists] will undertake." And three, it "should be clear that the explanation must, in the final analysis, be psychological or sociological. It must, that is, be a description of a value system, an ideology, together with an analysis of the institutions through which that system is transmitted and enforced" (Kuhn, 1970, pp. 1, 21).

Kuhn thus reinstitutes as a concern central to the history and sociology of science an understanding of the changing foci of attention among scientists; more specifically, the question of how it is that scientists seize upon some problems as important enough to engage their sustained attention while others are regarded as uninteresting. But Kuhn seems to us too restrictive in saying that the sociological form of the answer to questions of this kind must ultimately be in terms of a value system and the institutions that transmit and enforce it. Sociological interpretations of extratheoretical influences upon the selection of problems for investigation in a science include more than its norms and institutional structure. They also include exogenous influences upon the foci of research adopted by scientists that come from the environing society, culture, economy, and polity, influences of a kind put so

---

[83] Among philosophers of science, Karl Popper has been concerned with the problem in a long series of books and papers at least since his *Logik der Forschung* (1935). See the translation in its second edition (Popper, 1960). For an early sociological effort to investigate what are described as the "foci and shifts of interest in the sciences and technology," see Merton (1970a, Chapters 2 and 3).

[84] Kuhn (1962). For a recent and, in some of its essays, penetrating examination of Kuhn's ideas, see Lakatos and Musgrave (1970). For an energetic attack on both Kuhn and Lakatos, see Agassi (1971, pp. 152–164).

much in evidence these days in the heavily publicized form of changing priorities in the allocation of resources to the various sciences and to problem-areas within them as to become apparent even to the most cloistered of scientists. All apart from such exogenous influences, there is the question, of immediate concern to us here, of (the largely unintended) influences upon the foci of research that derive from the social structure as distinct from the normative structure of science, that is, that derive from the social composition of scientists at work in the various disciplines.

In this paper, we happen to deal with the problematics of the age structure of the sciences and specialties within them as one part of their respective social structures just as others might deal with the problematics of their religious, ethnic, or political composition. We have noted in Section 1 that the age structures of the several sciences vary. This at least suggests that the age cohorts entering science at different times may have tended to find different sciences of prime interest to them. The further question whether the age strata *within* a science tend to focus on different problems and to approach the same problems in different ways remains, of course, moot. It is an exemplary question for the sociology of science directing us to one form of interaction between the social structure and the cognitive structure of science and inviting the thought that, in some of its aspects, the cognitive structure of a field may appreciably differ for subgroups of scientists within it.

Scraps of evidence as well as speculation suggest that there are age-patterned foci of research interest and theoretical orientations in the sciences. That this is the case is so fully implied as almost to be expressed in Kuhn's own observation, which we have encountered earlier, that "Almost always the men who achieve [the] fundamental inventions of a new paradigm have been either very young or very new to the field whose paradigm they change" (Kuhn, 1962, pp. 89–90). But Kuhn turns out to be instructively ambivalent about this statement. At one moment, he considers it common enough a generalization to qualify as a cliché and a point so obvious that he should hardly have made it explicit, while at the next moment, he thinks it a generalization much in need of systematic inquiry. In the conspicuous absence of methodical evidence as distinct from much anecdotage bearing on the matter, we are inlined to dissolve the ambivalence by plumping for further investigation.

The question of there being age-patterned foci of attention and theoretical perspectives in science need not be limited to the rare cases of fundamental changes in the structure of prevailing theory. There is reason to suppose that such age-stratified differences obtain more generally. Although the modal pattern is probably one in which the several age cohorts of investigators in a field center on much the same problems, we should not be surprised to find a subsidiary pattern in which young and older scientists tend to focus their work on different problems and so to attend to somewhat different segments of the work going on in the field. It should not be difficult to find out whether such subsidiary age-stratified patterns do occur. A systematic content-analysis[85] of papers published by scientists of differing age would yield the information needed on the foci of research just as systematic citation analyses[86] would yield the correlative information needed on the range of work to which they are paying attention.

Consider briefly how patterns of citation might reflect age-stratified differences in the foci of scientific attention. Our conjectural model of the sources and consequences of such differences involves a re-enactment of complementary role-behavior by successive age cohorts much like that which we have provisionally identified for patterns of scientific collaboration. We begin with one well-worn assumption and one familiar fact. The assumption (which is also adopted by Kuhn) holds that the time in their career at which scientists encounter ideas will significantly affect their responses to them. The familiar fact is the strong, and perhaps increasing, emphasis in science on keeping up with work on the frontiers of the field, i.e., with new work.

Whether the intensity of concern with keeping abreast of new work is age-stratified or not—we know of no evidence bearing on this—it should have somewhat different consequences among the age cohorts. Plainly, the work that scientists come to know as new when they enter the field ages along with them. As incoming cohorts move toward what in science is a swiftly approaching middle age, the work they had focused on in their youth has grown "old," as age of publications is judged in much of contemporary science.[87] The problems, new or old, which members of the older cohorts are investigating will often reactivate memories of pertinent work in the literature which they had encountered as new in years gone by. Meanwhile, the younger cohort working at the same time turn their attention primarily to new work (just as

[85] For rather primitive instances of such content-analyses of scientific work, which did not, however, go on to examine possible differences among scientists of differing age or rank, see the classification of papers in the *Philosophical Transactions* 1665–1702 and the research recorded in the minutes of the Royal Society in the seventeenth century (Merton, 1970a, Chapters 3, 10, and Appendix).

[86] Ever since the invention of the Science Citation Index, citation studies have been increasing at such a rapid rate that they threaten to get out of hand. Many methodological problems are being neglected in their frequently uncritical use. Moreover, the very existence of the SCI and the growing abundance of citation analyses (even for such matters as aids in deciding upon the appointment and promotion of scientists) may lead to changes in citation practices that will in due course contaminate or altogether invalidate them as measures of the quality of research. This would not be the first case where the introduction of statistical records of role performance has led to a *displacement of goals* in which the once-reliable statistical indicator rather than the actual performance becomes the center of manipulative concern. On the early use of citation analyses, see Garfield, Sher, and Torpie (1964); for a critical overview of methodological problems in citation-analysis, see J. Cole and S. Cole (1972, Chapter 2); S. Cole and J. Cole (1971); and Whitley and Frost (1971); on displacement of goals, see Merton (1968b, pp. 253–255); on displacement of goals in statistical measures of performance, see Blau (1955, Chapter 3).

[87] It will be remembered from Section 2 of this Chapter that the half-life of references in many of the sciences is 5 years or less.

their middle-aged colleagues did in their youth). But not having the same immediate knowledge about work which had been done in the, for them, remote past of 15 or 20 years before, they are less apt to be put in mind of earlier germane investigations.

In this model, scientists in each successive cohort re-enact much the same citation behavior at the same phases of their career. By doing so, younger and older scientists *to a degree* contribute differently to the development of science: the older scientists providing somewhat more for intellectual continuity by linking current work with work done some time before; the younger scientists pushing ahead somewhat more on their own, less "encumbered" by past formulations. We suggest that although the norms governing the communication of scientific knowledge are much the same for all, leeway in their observance is enough to allow for the occurrence of such unplanned, and often unnoticed, variation in the age-patterned reporting of scientific work.

If these conjectured differences do in fact obtain, they should be reflected in various ways. For one thing, younger scientists should be given more than older ones to making rediscoveries: findings and ideas, independently arrived at, that are substantively identical with earlier ones or functionally equivalent to them.[88] The Santayana dictum that those who fail to remember history are destined to repeat it should hold with special force in the domain of science— subject more than other spheres of culture to the objective constraints of finding authentic solutions to designated problems.[89] And if the conjectured differences obtain, we should also find age-connected patterns of references and citations along the lines suggested by the preliminary and tentative investigations by Stephen Cole and by Zuckerman,[90] which, it will be remembered from Section 2 of this chapter, found that older scientists are more likely than younger ones to cite older publications.

When scientists themselves do not understand this reiterative pattern of age-related foci of attention, they are ready to pass invidious judgments upon the behavior of those in "the other" age stratum. Older scientists then describe younger ones as parochial if not downright barbarian in outlook, little concerned to read and ponder the classical work of some years back and even less concerned to learn about the historical evolution of their field (the judges forgetting all the while that the new youth in science are only reproducing the

---

[88] On patterns of rediscovery, see Merton (1968a, Chapter 1).

[89] In suggesting this, we do not subscribe to positivistic or Whig doctrine.

[90] Stephen Cole (unpublished); Zuckerman (unpublished data). We should also note again that age-patterned differences in references and citations represent a finding *a fortiori* (i.e., under conditions tilted against the hypothesis). For any such differences observed in print are there in spite of countervailing suggestions by referees and colleagues (often differing in age from the author). Further investigation would compare the age-distributions of references in collaborative papers written by age-peers (old or young) and by authors of substantially differing age.

attitudes and behavior they had exhibited in their own youth). In turn, younger scientists deride the orientation of older ones to the past as mere antiquarianism, as a sign that they are unable to "keep up" and so are condemned to repeat the obsolete if not downright archaic stuff they learned long ago (the judges being all the while unable to anticipate their own future behavior that they will then likely perceive as providing needed lines of continuity in scientific development).

Historical changes in patterns of citation may provide context for these sequential patterns of citation during the life course. The exponential growth in the numbers of scientists and of scientific publication may result in changed norms and practices with respect to linking up work on the research front with that which has been done some time before. More specifically, this raises the question whether it is the case that, as science becomes bigger in every aspect, a not altogether functional adaptation develops in which successive cohorts of scientists give less and less attention to pertinent work of the past while scientific publications provide less and less space for it. This may be still another instance in which historical changes in the social and cognitive parameters of science interact with sequential patterns in the life course to produce both similarities and differences in the behavior of successive cohorts of scientists.

Concluding remarks

An exploratory paper like this one has no place for "conclusions" but it does call for a few afterthoughts.

Plainly we have only touched upon the problematics of our subject, not having discussed a variety of questions which even now could be examined to good purpose. Here is a scattering of examples:

—How is the *age of research groups* related to their scientific productivity?[91]

—What is the age distribution of the "founders" of new formations in the various sciences: e.g., new specialties, new forms of investigation (laboratories), new journals, scientific societies, etc.?

—What is the relation between the quantity and quality of scientific output at various phases in the scientific career?

—How is age variously associated with intellectual authority[92] and with bu-

---

[91] For a critical examination of the question since the first studies by H. A. Shepard, W. P. Wells, D. C. Pelz, and F. M. Andrews, see Smith (1970); also Vlachy (1970).

[92] Most emphatically, peers in science need not be age peers. A century ago, William Perkins was, at 23, the world authority on dyes just as a Joshua Lederberg or a Murray Gell-Mann were authorities in their subjects at a comparable age today. This sort of thing should lead us to abandon the practice, common in the jargon of sociology and psychology, of having the word "peers" refer elliptically only to "age peers." As everyone else seems to know, "peer" refers to one who is of equal standing with another, in whatever terms that standing is gauged: political rank, esteem, authority, *and* age.

reaucratic authority in science, and what are the consequences of such differences for the development of scientific disciplines?

—What historical changes have occurred in the span of research careers and how do these relate to the durability of the intellectual influence of scientists?

—To what extent do age cohorts in science develop into age-sets with their continued interaction and solidarity to produce old-boy networks (not unlike new-boy networks)?

Perhaps enough has been said to indicate what we take to be the principal aim of investigating questions of this sort. That aim is to find out how age and age structure variously interact with the cognitive structure and development of science.

Works cited in Chapter 8

Adams, C. W., 1946. "The Age at which Scientists do their Best Work," *Isis*, 36, pp. 116–169.

Agassi, Joseph, 1971. "Tristram Shandy, Pierre Menard and All That: Comments on *Criticism and the Growth of Knowledge*," *Inquiry*, 14, pp. 152–164.

Aran, Lydia, and Joseph Ben-David, 1968. "Socialization and Career Patterns as Determinants of Productivity of Medical Researchers," *Journal of Health and Social Behavior*, 9, pp. 3–15.

Barber, Bernard, 1961. "Resistance by Scientists to Scientific Discovery," *Science*, 134, pp. 592–602.

Becker, Howard S., and James Carper, 1956. "The Elements of Identification with an Occupation," *American Journal of Sociology*, 21, pp. 341–348.

Ben-David, Joseph, 1960. "Roles and Innovations in Medicine," *American Journal of Sociology*, 65, pp. 557–568.

————, and Randall Collins, 1966. "Social Factors in the Origins of a New Science: The Case for Psychology," *American Sociological Review*, 31, pp. 451–465.

Berelson, Bernard, 1960. *Graduate Education in the United States*. New York: McGraw-Hill.

Bernal, J. D., 1939. *The Social Function of Science*. New York: Macmillan.

Blau, Peter M., 1955. *The Dynamics of Bureaucracy*. Chicago. University of Chicago Press.

Broadus, R. N., 1952. "An Analysis of Literature Cited in the *American Sociological Review*," *American Sociological Review*, 17, pp. 355–357.

————, 1967. "A Citation Study for Sociology," *American Sociologist*, 2, pp. 19–20.

Brode, Wallace R., 1971. "Manpower in Science and Engineering Based on a Saturation Model," *Science*, 173, pp. 206–213.

Brooks, Harvey, 1971. "Thoughts on Graduate Education," *Graduate Journal*, 8, no. 2, pp. 319–336.

Brozek, Josef, 1951. "The Age Problem in Research Workers: Psychological Viewpoint," *Scientific Monthly*, 72, pp. 355–359.

Burton, P. E., and R. W. Keebler, 1960. " 'Half-life' of Some Scientific and Technical Literatures," *American Documentation*, 11, pp. 18–22.

Cairns, John, Gunther S. Stent, and James D. Watson, editors, 1966. *Phage and the Origins of Molecular Biology*. Cold Spring Harbor: Laboratory of Quantitative Biology.

Clarke, E. L., 1964. "Multiple Authorship: Trends in Scientific Papers," *Science*, 143, pp. 822–824.

Cole, Jonathan R., 1970. "Patterns of Intellectual Influence in Scientific Research," *Sociology of Education*, 43, pp. 377–403.

———, 1969. *The Social Structure of Science*. Columbia University, Department of Sociology, unpublished dissertation.

———, and Stephen Cole, 1972. *Social Stratification in Science*. Chicago: University of Chicago Press.

Cole, Stephen, unpublished. "Age and Scientific Behavior."

———, 1970. "Professional Standing and the Reception of Scientific Discoveries," *American Journal of Sociology*, 76, pp. 287–306.

———, and Jonathan R. Cole, 1967. "Scientific Output and Recognition: A Study in the Operation of the Reward System in Science," *American Sociological Review*, 32, pp. 377–390.

———, and Jonathan R. Cole, 1971. "Measuring the Quality of Sociological Research: Problems in the Use of the Science Citation Index," *American Sociologist*, 6, pp. 23–29.

Conant, James B., 1950. Foreword. *Harvard Case Studies in Experimental Science*. Cambridge, Mass.: Harvard University Press, pp. 1–10.

Crane, Diana, 1967. "The Gatekeepers of Science: Some Factors Affecting the Selection of Articles for Scientific Journals," *American Sociologist*, 2, pp. 195–201.

Dedijer, Stevan, 1964. "International Comparisons of Science," *New Scientist*, 379 (February), pp. 461–464.

de Grazia, Alfred, 1963. "The Scientific Reception System and Dr. Velikovsky," *American Behavioral Scientist*, 7, pp. 38–56.

Dennis, Wayne, 1956a. "Age and Productivity among Scientists," *Science*, 123, pp. 724–725.

———, 1956b. "Age and Achievement: A Critique," *Journal of Gerontology*, 11, pp. 331–337.

———, 1956c. "The Age Decrement in Outstanding Scientific Contributions," *American Psychologist*, 13, pp. 457–460.

———, 1966. "Creative Productivity between the Ages of 20 and 80," *Journal of Gerontology*, 21, pp. 1–8.

Eisenstadt, S. N., 1956. *From Generation to Generation: Age Groups and Social Structure*. New York: Free Press.

Fleming, Donald, 1969. "Emigré Physicists and the Biological Revolution," in Fleming, Donald, and Bernard Bailyn, editors, *The Intellectual Migration*. Cambridge, Mass.: Harvard University Press, pp. 152–189.

Gamow, George, 1966. *Thirty Years that Shook Physics*. Garden City, N.Y.: Doubleday.

Garfield, Eugene, 1955. "Citation Indexes for Science," *Science*, 122, pp. 108–111.

———, 1970. "Citation Indexing for Studying Science," *Nature*, 227, pp. 669–671.

———, L. H. Sher, and R. J. Torpie, 1964. *The Use of Citation Data in Writing the History of Science*. Philadelphia: Institute for Scientific Information.

Gilfillan, S. Colum, 1935. *The Sociology of Invention*. Chicago: Follett.

Glaser, Barney G., 1964. *Organizational Scientists: Their Professional Careers*. Indianapolis: Bobbs-Merrill.

Greenberg, Daniel S., 1967. *The Politics of Pure Science*. New York: New American Library.

Gregg, Alan, 1957. *For Future Doctors*. Chicago: University of Chicago Press.

Hagstrom, Warren, 1965. *The Scientific Community*. New York: Basic Books.

Hargens, Lowell, and Warren Hagstrom, 1967. "Sponsored and Contest Mobility of American Academic Scientists," *Sociology of Education*, 40, pp. 24–38.

Harmon, Lindsey R., 1965. *Profiles of Ph.D.'s in the Sciences: Summary Report on Follow-Up of Doctorate Cohorts, 1935–60*. Washington: National Academy of Sciences–National Research Council, Publication 1293.

Kuhn, Thomas S., 1962. *The Structure of Scientific Revolutions*. Chicago: University of Chicago Press.

———, 1970. "Logic of Discovery or Psychology of Research?" in Lakatos, Imre, and Alan Musgrave, editors, *Criticism and the Growth of Knowledge*. Cambridge: Cambridge University Press.

Kusch, Polykarp, 1966. "Style and Styles in Research," *The Robert A. Welch Foundation Research Bulletin*, 20.

Lakatos, Imre, and Alan Musgrave, 1970. *Criticism and the Growth of Knowledge*. Cambridge: Cambridge University Press.

Lehman, H. C., 1936. "The Creative Years in Science and Literature," *Scientific Monthly*, 43, pp. 151–162.

———, 1953. *Age and Achievement*. Princeton, N.J.: Princeton University Press.

Lewin, Kurt, 1943. "Forces Behind Food Habits and Methods of Change," *Bulletin of the National Research Council*, 108, pp. 35–65.

MacRae, Duncan Jr., 1969. "Growth and Decay Curves in Scientific Citations," *American Sociological Review*, 34, pp. 631–635.

Manniche, E., and G. Falk, 1957. "Age and the Nobel Prize," *Behavioral Science*, 2, pp. 301–307.

Marcson, Simon, 1960. *The Scientist in American Industry*. New York: Harper & Row.

Martino, Joseph P., 1969. "Science and Society in Equilibrium," *Science*, 165, pp. 769–772.

Merton, Robert K., 1958. *Status-Sets and Role-Sets: Structural Analysis in Sociology*. Unpublished manuscript.

———, 1959. *Sociology Today: Problems and Prospects* (with L. Broom and L. S. Cottrell, editors). New York: Basic Books.

———, 1960. "Recognition and Excellence: Instructive Ambiguities," in Yarmolinsky, Adam, editor, *Recognition of Excellence*. New York: The Free Press.

————, 1968a. "The Matthew Effect in Science," *Science*, 159, pp. 56–63.

————, 1968b. *Social Theory and Social Structure*, enlarged edition. New York: Free Press.

————, 1970a. *Science, Technology and Society in Seventeenth Century England*. New York: Howard Fertig; Harper & Row [first published in 1938].

————, 1970b. "Insiders and Outsiders: An Essay in the Sociology of Knowledge," in R. N. Saxena, editor, *Conspectus of Indian Society*. Agra, India: Satish Book Enterprise.

————, and Elinor Barber, 1963. "Sociological Ambivalence," in Tiryakian, Edward A., editor, *Sociological Theory, Values and Sociological Change: Essays in Honor of Pitirim Sorokin*. New York: Free Press, pp. 91–120.

Michels, Roberto, 1949. *Political Parties*. New York: Free Press [first German edition, 1911].

Miller, Delbert C., and William H. Form, 1964. *Industrial Sociology*, revised edition. New York: Harper & Row.

Moore, Wilbert E. and Melvin M. Tumin, 1949. "Some Social Functions of Ignorance," *American Sociological Review*, 14, pp. 787–795.

National Academy of Sciences–National Research Council, 1970. *Doctorate Recipients from United States Universities 1958–66* and *Summary Reports for 1967, 1968, 1969 and 1970*. Washington: Government Printing Office.

National Research Council, Office of Scientific Personnel, 1968. *Careers of PhD's: Academic versus Nonacademic. A Second Report on Follow-up of Doctorate Cohorts 1935–60*. Washington: National Academy of Sciences Publication 1577.

National Science Foundation, 1969. *American Science Manpower 1968: A Report of the National Register of Scientific and Technical Personnel*. Washington: National Science Foundation 69–38.

————, 1971. *Science & Engineering Doctorate Supply & Utilization*, May 1971. Washington: National Science Foundation 71–20.

Ogburn, William F., 1922. *Social Change*. New York: Viking Press.

Olby, Robert, 1970. "Francis Crick, DNA and the Central Dogma," *Daedalus*, 99 (Fall), pp. 938–987.

Pinder, Wilhelm, 1928. *Das Problem der Generation in der Kunstgeschichte Europas*, 2nd edition. Berlin: Frankfurter Verlags-Anstalt.

Planck, Max, 1949. *Scientific Autobiography and Other Papers*. New York: Philosophical Library.

Popper, Sir Karl, 1960 [1935]. *The Logic of Scientific Discovery*. New York: Basic Books; London: Hutchinson.

Price, Derek deSolla, 1961. *Science Since Babylon*. New Haven: Yale University Press.

————, 1963. *Little Science, Big Science*. New York: Columbia University Press.

————, 1965. "Networks of Scientific Papers," *Science*, 149, pp. 510–515.

————, 1970. "Citation Measures of Hard Science and Soft Science, Technology and Non-Science," in Nelson, Carnot E., and Donald K. Pollack, editors, *Communication Among Scientists and Engineers*. Lexington, Mass.: Heath Lexington Books, pp. 3–22.

————, and Donald deB. Beaver, 1966. "Collaboration in an Invisible College," *American Psychologist*, pp. 1011–1018.

Reitz, Jeffrey G., 1972. *The Flight From Science*. Columbia University, Department of Sociology, unpublished dissertation.

Riley, Matilda White, and Anne Foner, 1968. *Aging and Society*, Volume I. New York: Russell Sage Foundation.

Roe, Anne, 1965. "Changes in Scientific Activities with Age," *Science*, 150, pp. 313–318.

Rogoff, Natalie, 1957. "The Decision to Study Medicine," in Merton, Robert K., George G. Reader, and Patricia Kendall, editors, *The Student-Physician*. Cambridge, Mass.: Harvard University Press, pp. 109–129.

Rose, Hilary, and Steven Rose, 1969. *Science and Society*. London: Allen Lane, The Penguin Press.

Sarton, George, 1927–1948. *Introduction to the History of Science*, 3 volumes in 5 parts. Baltimore: Williams and Wilkins.

Smith, Clagett G., 1970. "Age of R and D Groups: A Reconsideration," *Human Relations*, 23, pp. 81–96.

Sorokin, Pitirim A., 1937. *Social and Cultural Dynamics*, 4 volumes. New York: American Book Co.

Storer, Norman W., 1966. *The Social System of Science*. New York: Holt, Rinehart and Winston.

————, 1967. "The Hard Sciences and the Soft: Some Sociological Observations," *Bulletin of the Medical Library Association*, 55, pp. 75–84.

Super, Donald E., 1957. *The Psychology of Careers*. New York: Harper & Row.

Szafer, Władysław, 1968. "Creativity in a Scientist's Life: An Attempt of Analysis from the Standpoint of the Science of Science," *Organon*, 5, pp. 3–39.

Szilard, Leo, 1969. "Reminiscences," in Fleming, Donald, and Bernard Bailyn, editors, *The Intellectual Migration*. Cambridge, Mass.: Harvard University Press, pp. 94–151.

Thielens, Wagner Jr., 1957. "Some Comparisons of Entrants to Medical and Law School," in Merton, Robert K., George G. Reader and Patricia Kendall, editors, *The Student-Physician*. Cambridge, Mass.: Harvard University Press, pp. 131–152.

Thiemann, Hugo, 1970. "Changing Dynamics in Research and Development," *Science*, 168, pp. 1427–1431.

True, Frederick W., 1913. *A History of the First Half-Century of the National Academy of Sciences*. Washington: National Academy of Sciences.

Turner, Ralph, 1960. "Sponsored and Contest Mobility and the School System," *American Sociological Review*, 25, pp. 855–867.

Ulam, Stanislaw, 1969. "John von Neumann, 1903–57," in Fleming, Donald, and Bernard Bailyn, editors, *The Intellectual Migration*. Cambridge, Mass.: Harvard University Press, pp. 235–243.

Underhill, Ralph, 1966. "Values and Post-College Career Change," *American Journal of Sociology*, 72, pp. 163–172.

United States Bureau of the Census, Department of Commerce, 1970. *Statistical Abstract of the United States for 1970*. Washington: United States Government Printing Office.

United States Department of Labor, 1968. *Employment and Earnings for June 1968*. Washington: Government Printing Office.

Vlachý, Jan, 1970. "Remarks on the Productive Age," *Teorie A Metoda* [Czechoslovakia] II, pp. 121–150.

Waddington, C. H., 1969. "Some European Contributions to the Prehistory of Molecular Biology," *Nature*, 221, 5178, pp. 318–321.

Watson, James D., 1968. *The Double Helix*. New York: Atheneum Press.

Weiss, Paul A., 1960. "Knowledge: A Growth Process," *Proceedings*, American Philosophical Society, 104, pp. 242–247 [reprinted in Weiss, 1971, pp. 124–133].

———, 1971. *Within the Gates of Science and Beyond: Science in its Cultural Commitments*. New York: Hafner.

Whitley, Richard D., 1970. "The Operation of Science Journals: Two Case Studies in British Social Science," *Sociological Review* (new series), 18, pp. 241–258.

———, and Penelope A. Frost, 1971. "The Measurement of Performance in Research," *Human Relations*, 24, pp. 161–178.

Wilensky, Harold L., 1960. "Work, Careers and Social Integration," *International Social Science Journal*, 12, 543–560.

———, 1961. "Orderly Careers and Social Participation," *American Sociological Review*, 26, pp. 521–539.

Ziman, John, 1968. *Public Knowledge: The Social Dimension of Science*. Cambridge: Cambridge University Press.

———, 1969. "Some Problems of the Growth and Spread of Science into Developing Countries," The Rutherford Memorial Lecture, *Proceedings of the Royal Society*, A. 311, pp. 349–369.

———, 1970. "The Light of Knowledge: New Lamps for Old," The Fourth Aslib Annual Lecture. *Aslib Proceedings*, May, pp. 186–200.

Zuckerman, Harriet, 1965. "Nobel Laureates in the United States: A Sociological Study of Scientific Collaboration." Columbia University, Ph.D. dissertation (unpublished).

———, 1967. "Noble Laureates in Science: Patterns of Productivity, Collaboration and Authorship," *American Sociological Review*, 32, pp. 391–403.

———, 1968. "Patterns of Name Ordering among Authors of Scientific Papers: A Study of Social Symbolism and Its Ambiguity," *American Journal of Sociology*, 74, pp. 276–291.

———, 1970. "Stratification in American Science," *Sociological Inquiry*, 40, pp. 235–257.

———, 1972. *Scientific Elite: Studies of Nobel Laureates in the United States*. Chicago: University of Chicago Press (in press).

———, and Robert K. Merton, 1971. "Patterns of Evaluation in Science: Institutionalisation, Structure and Functions of the Referee System," *Minerva*, 9, 1 (January), pp. 66–100.

9

Friendship

BETH HESS

Friendship, a topic to which sociologists have devoted only fragmentary attention, is brought into new perspective by Beth Hess through the wide-ranging application of the literature on aging and society. Her essay illustrates the theoretical clarification to be gained from an analysis of the ways in which age enters into a given sphere of social relations. A volitional relationship, frequently enduring but sometimes transitory, friendship has often been judged of only minor interest to social scientists—as depending more upon idiosyncrasies of personality than upon regularities of culture and social structure, and as providing only a secondary and potentially tenuous source of social solidarity and integration.

This essay questions both these assumptions. Hess points to ways in which friendship, at varying life stages of the participants, is subject to diverse sets of structural constraints reflected in the other roles that individuals play, the presence (or absence) of normative expectations and conditions of age homophily, and the availability of age peers in the immediate environment. As a relationship heavily dependent upon the individual's total cluster of roles at various stages of life, friendship contributes through a variety of connections to the integration of these roles. Moreover, during life stages in which individuals may be excluded from major social roles, friendships may serve both as sources of emotional support and stability of self-image, and as anchorages for integration of the individual with the larger society. Similar functions are operative during periods of transition in role sequence when, subjected to intensive socialization and role change, peers share a common deprivation of customary role-playing opportunities in the face of demands for new behavior. Thus age, as a singularly important variable defining the past, present, and future location in society of the individual and his friends, enters fundamentally into an understanding of the structure and functions of friendship relations.

RELEVANCE OF VOLUMES I AND II

While the practicing professions discussed in Volume II have paid little heed to the potentials of friendship, Chapter 24 of Volume I is devoted to the relation of the older person to his friends and neighbors. Falling between the plethora of material on certain aspects of youthful friendship and the dearth of material on friendship in the middle years, old-age friendship has received a moderate amount of research and theorizing. Thus it is clear, for example, that friendships and neighborly relations tend to be maintained well into later life, especially in the higher socioeconomic strata; that long-time residents in a neighborhood are most likely to have acquired extensive ties to neighborhood friends; and that older people, like people at all stages of life, tend, though by no means exclusively, to have friends who are similar in age to themselves.

However, the available materials on old people, even when supplemented by current understandings of friendships in other age strata, are sufficient only to raise a wide variety of questions:

Does the character of a particular friendship change over the life course of the participants? As the situation and needs of the aging individual change, to what extent does he add new friends to meet new needs, exchange old friends for new ones, adjust the character of existing friendships, or renew old friendships that had been allowed to lapse?

Under what conditions do age dissimilars become friends? How do the functions (and the character) of these friendships differ from those of age similars? How does the relative age of the participants affect the reciprocity of friendship choice? Are age-heterogeneous friendships, like class-heterogeneous friendships, less likely to be marked by reciprocal choice, with the friend of "superior status"—the older person —less likely to reciprocate? Would the aged, who have relatively fewer age mates available, tend to show a reversal of this hierarchical tendency?

What is the relation between age and sex in friendship networks? Between age and education, occupation, and other potentially intervening variables?

Has social change affected the conception of friendship or the nature of friendship relations in such ways that age differences may reflect cohort differences as well as differences in life stage?

If sociological attention is redirected to such questions as these, the aims of this essay will be amply met.

Friendship, a dyadic relationship that involves the sharing of affect, concerns, interests, and information, has certain distinctive characteristics relevant to an understanding of how the age of role partners affects their social relations. First, of course, a particular friendship involves two people, a self and an other. Thus age enters into friendship at two levels. At one level, age is a characteristic of the individual participant; at the other, age is a relational attribute of the friendship dyad, as characterized by participants of similar or differing ages. At both these levels, age influences the process of friendship formation, maintenance, and termination.

Second, friendship is a highly volitional relationship and may be terminated by a single defection. Therefore the friendship dyad is particularly vulnerable, as Simmel notes (1950, pp. 122–125, 137–138, 324–326). Unlike the marital dyad, it has no legal protection against dissolution and no formally and specifically prescribed rights and obligations. Friendships, then, are essentially fragile, requiring continuing reaffirmation by both participants.

Finally, friendship, at least in American society, carries powerful connotations of "peership," of both similarity and equality in status. Thus the potential for friendship and the nature of the friendship relation must be affected by the extent to which age serves the social system as a basis for symmetry.

Little is known about the age patterns of friendship, either at a given time or over the life course. Although scattered studies[1] suggest only slight differences among age strata in the number or intensity of their friendships, to evaluate the relevance of age for friendship from available researches involves many difficulties. At the least, such evaluation requires considerable secondary analysis to control for socioeconomic status, education, available free time, and other major variables that may mediate the association between age and friendship. An additional difficulty is that existing studies do not grapple in comparable ways with the inherent difficulties of distinguishing between friends and neighbors, or of encompassing the wide array of friendships accumulated by individuals of different ages. Moreover, commonly employed measures of the extent of friendship—which may include such dimensions as the number of friends or the time spent in interaction—obscure important differences in the composition of the friendship network and in the activities and functions of friendships through the life course.

In the absence both of adequate data and of a satisfactory overarching theoretical model, this essay focuses on only a few selected aspects of friendship that appear to be related to age, and that merit further conceptual formulation and research. Since the essay is intended only to suggest the advantages to be gained by such treatment of the subject, the reader will find notable omissions. The principal focus is on how one socially patterned source of variation, the life-course stage of the individual, affects the nature of his friendship relations. Still to be investigated is the extent to which variations in friendship among the several age strata may reflect not only life-course differences but also the impact on particular cohorts of historical events and trends. Friendship is examined largely as a dyadic relation, with relatively little consideration given to possible age variations in the character of the larger friendship network in which the dyad may be located. Moreover, many of the potentially age-related psychological aspects of friendship are not explored here, as these might shed light, for example, on subjective meanings to

---

[1] Phillips (1967, pp. 485–486) shows no differences by age between 21 and 50+ among 600 persons in New Hampshire, on a score that includes taking an active part in organizations. Several small studies cited in Volume I, Chapter 24 · 1 · b, show little difference between middle-aged and old people in association with friends and neighbors—up to advanced old age. Tomeh (1964) does show a decline with age in a score that includes relatives and coworkers as well as friends and neighbors; this is based on a Detroit sample, with place of residence controlled.

the participants or on personality factors in capacity to form and maintain friendships of varying degrees of intimacy.

Within the boundaries of such limitations, we turn, now, to the main body of our discussion. Section 1 examines the operation of age in the acquisition or loss of friends (element 3 in the conceptual model set forth in Chapter 1) through the connections between friendship and other major roles. Section 2 considers how age enters into the formation of friendship, and affects the processes of friendship maintenance and dissolution. Finally, Section 3 explores the ways in which the association between friendship and age is tied to processes of socialization and social control (P4 in our conceptual model).

1 *Friendship and other roles*

A central theme of this essay is that the number and type of friendships open to an individual at particular stages of his life course depend less upon explicit age criteria for the friendship role itself than upon the *other* roles that he plays. As his total cluster of roles changes over his lifetime, so do his friendship relations undergo change.

This focus upon the embeddedness of friendship in other social structures does not imply that friendship itself may not be an independent basis for the patterning of important relationships at certain life stages.[2] However, the extent to which friendships are independent of other social roles remains a moot question, depending in part upon a person's age and in part upon the particular nature of his familial and other relationships. Notably, Parsons (1951, p. 189) does not refer to friendships among the major diffuse solidarities involving adults (especially male adults) in an achievement-oriented society, although he does recognize the salience of peer group relationships in preadulthood, when the obligations of friendship do not seriously compete with the responsibilities of occupation and family. Slater (1963) regards societal constraints upon dyadic intimacy, especially in the male-female love relationship, as operating to prevent withdrawal of cathexis from larger social systems. The friendship dyad too, we suggest, will evoke similar restraints if it threatens to divert emotional energy from family relationships as well as from work and community attachments. The more approved same-sex relationships, notably for males, would thus be those that also imply integration into more inclusive social systems, as with relatives or work-mates. However, since the opportunity to participate in these more inclusive systems varies with age, we might expect constraints upon exclusive dyadic intimacy to vary in parallel manner.

At the empirical level, there have been various attempts to test the as-

---

[2] Note, for example, Eisenstadt's observations (1956, pp. 101–107) on nationalist youth groups.

sumption, often implicit in such formulations of the place of friendship in the social structure, that sociability is a finite quantity. What is not used up in one realm of activity, such as the family (e.g., Bott, 1957, pp. 60–69, 180; Nelson, 1966; Udry and Hall, 1965), or the most intimate friendships (Caplow and Forman, 1950, p. 362), is free to be dispersed among less intense relationships. Such studies, still largely inconclusive, are based on samples of diverse ages and give little indication that this zero-sum theory of sociability may be appropriate at all stages of life.

TYPES OF CONNECTIONS

The connections between friendship and other roles in the individual's repertory can take differing forms, which receive varying degrees of emphasis over his life course. Commonly observed forms include fusion, substitution, complementarity, and competition.

These types of connections are not mutually exclusive; indeed, they may on occasion be found to coexist in a single friendship dyad. In brief outline, we single out four major kinds. [*Compare Chapter 10 · 1.*] Certain friendships may (1) be viewed as *fused* to other, more central, roles in the sense that performance of the friendship role is contingent upon performance of that other role, and both must be played (or not played) at the same life stage. Fusion may reflect either normative expectations inhering in the role structure or situational limitations created by the nature of the role cluster. Friendship may also (2) *substitute* for major roles, at periods when the individual is deprived of opportunity to perform certain functions in major roles and seeks to actualize these functions through friendship relations. Or friendships may (3) be *complementary* to major roles, encompassing different and noncompetitive functions that may enhance overall role performances. Finally, friendships may (4) be *competitive* with other roles, competing either for the individual's time or for his value allegiances. Competition between roles differs from the first three types of role connections, however, in that it produces an essentially unstable situation. It not only creates strain in the individual and threatens the integration of his role cluster, but it also contains the seeds of an active opposition between membership groups.

FUSION

The most striking examples of fused friendships attach to the principal spheres of adult activity: family, work, community. As characteristics of the *role structure*, opportunities for fused friendships may be more prominent in middle age than at other stages, if only because the widest variety of marital, parental, occupational, and community roles are open to persons in the middle years. Such a description of the role structure of middle age does not necessarily imply, however, that the middle-aged individual actually forms more fused relationships than persons in other age groups. Regardless of his age, any given individual may have many friendships, which may be variously connected to his roles; indeed, they might all be fused to a single role.

Family roles   In the United States, the unit of participation in many friendships is the married couple (or, earlier, the boy-girl dyad of late adolescence when many friendship groups may be open only to couples). Such friendships become available, of course, only when the participants reach ages at which couple-dating and marriage are permitted, and are generally closed off when the cross-sex relationship is dissolved through disaffection, divorce, or death. In a sample of middle-aged, middle-class friendship dyads, for example, there is evidence that married couples constitute the visiting units on weekends and evenings, even though this does not necessarily imply identity in friendship choice among marriage partners.[3] Thus, visiting friends may be an activity of the married pair, but an individual's choice of "best friend" need not be dependent upon his spouse's choice. Rather, it seems most fruitful to view the married state as a condition under which certain other persons are available as friends; whether or not these become "close" friends depends upon other sets of variables, social and psychological. Quite often, researchers have blurred this distinction between availability and the formation of friendships on the one hand, and the maintenance of intimate friendships on the other.

That the married state provides a pool of potential friendship choice is illustrated by what little data there are on the friendship patterns of the unmarried. Widows (even relatively younger ones) see friends less often than they did when their husbands were alive, they take less interest in new people they meet, and their companions are more likely to be other husbandless women than males (Evans, 1966, pp. 146–148). And in old age, married persons generally associate with friends more than widowed or single persons do (Volume I, Chapter 24 · 3 · a). The loss of marital status, then, may close off certain friendships, or at least make these more difficult to maintain at some previous level of interaction.

Another age-related family role with implications for fused friendship is that of parent. Parents are brought into contact with other parents through the friendships of their offspring, or through the parents' mutual association in youth-oriented activities, such as Parent-Teacher Association, scouting, or car-pooling. Having children of the same age may be a magnet for friendship formation when shared concerns and interests on behalf of their offspring lead to exchange of information and mutual support of their attitudes, feelings,

---

[3] Hess (1971). In a selective sample of 152 couples queried about their two best friends, well over three-fourths of the amicable visits took place as couples, while only 54 per cent of the couples' friend choices showed similarity between husband and wife. See also Babchuk and Bates (1963); Babchuk (1965); Adams and Butler (1967).

and behavior.[4] When, however, the relation of their offspring to one another supplies the principal basis of friendship among the parents, the friendship is less likely to survive the period of active parenthood.

Sex roles   During much of an individual's life, a cross-sex friendship is potentially a sexual relationship, and thus in many societies, friendships between men and women are subject to negative sanctions ranging from suspicion to outright taboo. In preadolescent childhood, when sexuality is presumed to be absent or latent, there may be a relaxation of constraints upon cross-sex friendships. However, even at this stage, children show a marked preference for friends of the same sex. Whether this preference is more the result of normative control than of the stage of biological or social maturation is open to question. In adolescence, the distinction between same-sex and cross-sex relations comes to the fore. Friends of the opposite sex are not simply "friends"; they are "girl friends" or "boy friends" or—defensively and implying no erotic involvement—"just friends." Adult cross-sex friendships typically occur through fusion with marriage, as discussed above. But in these friendships, the unit is the *couple*, not the individual, thus presenting a barrier to cross-sex extramarital intimacy. In old age, sexuality is thought to wane and, as in early childhood, friendships with the opposite sex may no longer carry sexual connotations. However, the differential mortality of males and females sets limits to the formation of cross-sex friendships in old age, reinforcing whatever general barriers to friendship formation are posed by age itself. Thus the fusion of friendship with the sex role is so nearly complete through most of the life course that "friend" in popular usage, as well as in this essay, generally refers to another of the same sex (see Maisonneuve, 1966, pp. 113–131; Merton, West, and Jahoda, 1948, Chapter 7).

Work roles   The daily contacts and common frame of reference of the work place form a clearly important basis for friendships in adulthood, although there is great variation in the extent to which these friendships carry over to nonwork times and places. While work roles afford opportunities for friendship formation, there are also powerful constraints upon work-based friendships: competition between colleagues, demands for higher loyalty to the organization, conflict with obligations to family and community. In one sample of geographically mobile, upper-income, middle-aged employees of large national corporations, less than half of "best" friend choices were business-based.[5]

---

[4] See Merton, West, and Jahoda (1948). In two communities studied, residents with children more often had local friendships than childless couples.

[5] Hess (1971). This represents 46 per cent of first choices and 29 per cent second choices of 152 men. Only 5 to 11 per cent of their wives' choices were accorded to "the wife of a business colleague of (my) husband." Compare Maisonneuve (1966, p. 214) in whose sample of males the workplace is the single most important source of friendships initiated in adulthood.

That work friendships nevertheless have important functions in performance of the occupational role is well-documented by the many researches on informal work cliques, beginning with the reports of Roethlisberger and Dickson (1940). Such studies show, for example, that the threat of withdrawal of sociability is a powerful lever in securing conformity to informal work norms. Moreover, occupationally based friendships can also operate to integrate the members within the formal organization, or within the environing social system, thus enhancing efficiency or allowing the organization to extend its sphere of control. Studies of combat behavior during World War II made clear that achievement of the goal of the military establishment was dependent upon informal organization of friends, who were largely motivated to fight through mutual support and approval under the common threat of war (Williams and Smith, 1949, p. 2; Shils, 1950). Widespread recognition today of the importance of primary group solidarity for corporate functioning means that work-based friendships are often explicitly encouraged by the major role system, as in use of military "buddy" arrangement, or in the encouragement of a company's employees to live in the same residential areas, associate after work, and participate in favored community activities.

When the work role is relinquished at retirement, daily interactions with friends at one's place of work are, of course, effectively closed off. Moreover, the shared interests and concerns that support the friendship receive less reinforcement, especially when the friend remains at work and continues to accumulate experiences that the retiree cannot share. Whether work-based friendships survive retirement may depend heavily upon whether alternative bases for shared experience exist or can be developed. Residing in the same community, for example, or having friends face the new role of retirees simultaneously may supply needed common foci of concern. Unfortunately, we do not yet have adequate data to judge the extent or effects of loss of workplace friends in retirement (Volume I, Chapter 24 · 3 · c). Moreover, it seems likely that limiting of friends in retirement is mediated by such intervening conditions as lessened physical and financial resources.

Community roles   The integrative functions of friendships previously noted assume major importance in the case of community-based friendships, where there is no essential conflict between investment of self in friendship and in the larger system to which friends belong. [*See Section 2 of Chapter 6 by Starr.*]

The *voluntary associations* one joins as resident of a given community, whether these are devoted to purely local goals or are regional branches of national associations, obviously open up contacts with others sharing some important concern or characteristic. To the extent that these groups are themselves age-based ("Golden Age" or youth clubs, for example, or Junior Chambers of Commerce, Young Democrats and Republicans), or founded as a consequence of some historical event affecting members at roughly the same life stage (veteran groups, or certain radical political clubs), friendships will be channeled toward age-mates.

In general, membership rates tend to rise slowly to a peak in mature middle age and remain at plateau until 60 (Volume I, Chapter 21 · 1 · a). It has been suggested that membership in voluntary associations is a means of introducing oneself into a new community, an entering wedge into more stable friendship relations in the new neighborhood.[6] If so, then we might expect—since the young are more likely to move, while voluntary association membership continues to rise through middle age—that membership rates are generated in differing ways in younger and older age groups. For the young, joining community organizations may be primarily a means of finding new friends. For the middle-aged, already established friendships (as well as other investments in the community) may be the impetus for voluntary association membership.

Neighborhood friendships are those fused to the role of resident in a particular community. The prominence of such friendships within the individual's network is affected by age in at least two ways. First, age strata vary in their ability to move about freely. Clearly, the very young and very old are severely restricted in the distances they can cover to recruit or maintain friendships. In this sense, then, age strata differ in their dependence upon the immediate environment.[7] Second, since change of residence is closely tied to young adulthood (Volume I, Chapter 6 · C · 1 · a), today's cohorts who are in their middle or later years have had greater opportunity to establish friendships, especially "old" and close friendships, in their current community.

Length of residence, which is often a function of age, is directly associated with the likelihood of knowing and visiting neighbors, and of having evolved close relationships with some of these. In one sample of high-income middle-aged couples, the number and closeness of neighborhood friends increased with years of residence.[8] Similarly, Langford has shown in a United States study of social security beneficiaries that the proportions of older people

---

[6] See, for example, Litwak (1961). However, Hess (1971) finds voluntary associations rarely mentioned as a source of "best friends" among members of an upper-income suburban community. Yet Merton and his colleagues have pointed out that the import of voluntary associations for friendship patterns in a particular community undoubtedly depends on the particular environment and social structure. In the studies conducted by these researchers, voluntary associations were found to have considerable influence on friendship. Where common local concerns involved residents in voluntary associations, friendships within the community were stimulated, and community roles became the basis of status-homophily.

[7] Lawton and Simon (1968), who have dubbed this the "environmental docility hypothesis," found that those older persons somehow deprived in the means of moving about—physically, financially, or emotionally—tended to form friendships more dependent upon proximity than did less deprived old people.

[8] Hess (1971). However, see Merton, West, and Jahoda (1948), who find that the impact of length of residence depends upon the type of community under study.

knowing a large number of neighbors well enough to visit or having most of their friends in the neighborhood, rise sharply with duration of residence (Volume I, Chapter 24 · 2 · a and b, p. 565). Altogether, among people aged 65 and over, nearly half say that most of their friends live nearby as neighbors, a finding that may reflect not only the dependence of the aged on the immediate environment but also length of residence.

However, friendships originally established as neighborhood relationships are not necessarily contingent on neighboring—on continued visiting and exchange of services. Such friendships often endure even after persons move away from the community, though the character of the friendship may change in the absence of immediate help and services. We might hypothesize that these spatially dispersed relationships become rewarding on altogether different grounds—perhaps some prior investment of the self is periodically reinforced or vindicated through their retention. We might further speculate that friendships that survive geographical separation may become increasingly frequent as younger cohorts come to regard jet travel as a normal mode of transport, residential mobility as a way of corporate life, and the long-distance telephone as a substitute for face-to-face interaction.

SUBSTITUTION

Just as, at some life stages, friendships tend to be fused to other roles, so also do friendships often serve on occasion as substitutes, or functional equivalents, for these major roles.

For family roles Friendship groups may be fostered among individuals at periods when they do not live in kinship units or are prevented from performing customary aspects of kinship roles. For example, there are age-associated risks for most kinds of displacement to institutional living, such as college dormitories, military barracks (Parsons, 1951, pp. 170–171), prisons, mental hospitals, or homes for the aged (Volume I, Chapter 25 · 4 · d). In such cases, the presence of peers may compensate for the enforced absence of family and other kin.[9]

A distinctly age-related form of removal from a given family context occurs in middle age when one's children leave home to complete their education or to form families of their own. Both subunits—the parents and the offspring—are left without certain customary opportunities for role playing. In the case of parents there is only scattered evidence of any enhancement of friendship interaction after the period of active childrearing; but the obvious fact that more time is available at roughly the same level of energy previously expended in family roles points to this possibility. At yet a later life stage, when one of

[9] For example, the conditions under which friendship solidarities may be functional among prisoners are discussed by Sykes (1958, p. 82); among inmates of mental institutions by Goffman (1961, pp. 56–60).

the parents dies, the survivor typically fails to fill the void with increased contact with friends (but this phenomenon, as we shall remark later, depends somewhat upon the social composition of the widow's environment).

Among the very old, nearby friends may help in certain ways to replace distant kin. Neighbors are commonly cited by old people as providing immediate instrumental services such as checking in periodically, help in shopping, and general availability in emergencies (Volume I, Chapter 24 · 5 · a and b). Friends may also serve in place of relatives to fill expressive functions, as companions in spare time activity (as suggested, for example, in Cowgill and Baulch, 1962, p. 48). But it is still moot whether or not there is a tendency among old people for the level of interaction in friendship networks to compensate for decrements in kinship networks. Two studies (one in Cleveland by Rosow, 1967, and another among working-class elderly men in Philadelphia by Rosenberg, 1967) fail to find any consistent relationship between frequency of contact with neighbors and with relatives. However, Rosow does find that among those notably disadvantaged (in respect to marital status, employment, income, or health), contact with neighbors is inversely related to contact with children who live nearby (Volume I, Chapter 24 · 3 · b; see also Rosenberg, 1967).

For major roles of adult life   The failure of the adult world to offer effective roles to young people may maintain them in the youthful peer group beyond the usual limits. Lack of employment, for example, may help keep "corner boys" hanging around, and hanging together, well into manhood (see, for example, Whyte, 1955; Liebow, 1967). Today, while work opportunities for the relatively young and for the untrained are restricted, large numbers of young people have been absorbed into the system of higher education so that postadolescents are also retained in the peer groups of "studentry" as well as in the gangs of the unemployed noncollege youth. [*See Parsons and Platt, Chapter 7 in this volume.*] Thus many who have the trained capacities to perform in adult roles are relegated to a limbo in which they are denied opportunities to exercise these abilities. As this limbo becomes a socially structured phase of life, increased reliance on the support of status-similars may be expected, indeed unwittingly reinforced by others. That such peer solidarities are less in evidence among working noncollege youth lends support to these speculations (CBS Reports, 1969, p. 32).

COMPLEMENTARITY

Complementarity between friendship and another role implies a kind of symbiosis, in which the adequacy of performance and rewards in one role depends upon opportunity to perform in the other. The complementary nature of friendship must, then, depend upon the functional consequences—for both individual and social system—of another role (or roles) open to the individual at a particular age.

The complementary functions of friendship are perhaps most often discussed as the sources of expressive support and tension management—counterparts to the filial role or the student role as the source of rewards and punishment—in the learning or performance of instrumental roles. Thus the diffuse solidarities of adolescent peer groups are viewed as adjuncts of socialization to achievement-oriented adult roles. Or the leisure activities of adult friends are viewed as adjuncts to the maintenance of performance in occupational roles, as described in Section 3.

However, complementarity of friendship relations to other roles need not be limited to these expressive, supportive functions. It is likely, for example, that play groups of early childhood are important auxiliaries to the family as much for the opportunities for instrumental learning and reinforcement they provide as for their expressive contributions. At the other end of the age spectrum, the help and services offered old people by neighborhood friends may be complementary to the expressive solidarity that even distant kin may be able to supply.

COMPETITION

Friendship is not a role with definite boundaries and specifications for performance. The obligations of friendship are generally diffuse, and so may compete with the demands of other roles. This competitive tendency may be contained by a countervailing tendency to treat friendship as a residual status, activated only after other institutional role expectations have been fulfilled. However, friendship seems to be one relationship, especially in American society, without any clear normative consensus regarding its place in a hierarchy of role obligations. Thus there is continuing risk that assertion by the individual of any particular hierarchical ordering of friendship relative to other roles will be viewed as deviance by those role partners not accorded precedence.

Attempts to prevent competition between friendship and other roles have implications for the nature of the individual's friendships, for the number of friends he can manage, and for his tendencies toward deviance. Each of the other three types of friendship relation described above may become competitive in terms of demands on the individual's time. Among mature adults, for example, the sheer number of relationships that must be juggled appears to subject this age stratum to special risks of competition in friendship relations.[10] Perhaps, as a result, friendships of the middle years are most

---

[10] See Maisonneuve (1966, pp. 242–243) on potential conflict between friendship and business, political, or family roles. For the most part his respondents expressed strong unwillingness to sacrifice friends, except for family reasons.

likely to be specifically differentiated and compartmentalized. Thus relationships between bridge friends, bowling friends, neighbors, or business friends, may be bounded by narrowly defined sets of activities. In this way the potential demands of diffuse, intimate relationships are avoided; by the same token, however, the rewards and functions of friendship as traditionally defined may be lost.[11]

Preadults, who have a relative abundance of free time, might be expected to be protected against competition in friendship relations. However, the complementarity that seems to characterize adolescent peer groups (Section 4) can subject this age stratum to competition of another kind. Complementary roles, since they mutually supply each other's lack, are differentiated, organized around divergent sets of normative expectations. For example, although the formal system of education tends to stress individualistic achievement, the peer group is more likely to emphasize diffuse loyalty and mutual support. If conditions arise in which either or both the relevant membership groups demand the individual's exclusive allegiance, then previously complementary roles may become opposed. Thus the theoretical differences between sociologists who view the adolescent peer group as complementary to adult society, and those who view it as antipathetical, may not be so great as is sometimes supposed. Each may be viewing essentially the same phenomenon in differing circumstances. [*Compare the related discussion by Parsons and Platt in Chapter 7.*]

Older people appear least likely to be exposed to competitive demands between friendships and other roles. Since they are comparatively less involved in major role obligations, elderly persons have much free time. Moreover, in contrast to age groups that must continually form new friendships, they tend to rely on established friendships, whose very duration implies greater opportunity for resolution of conflicts over time-allocation or value-allegiance.

2 *Formation, duration, and disruption of friendship*

While a given individual tends to make certain kinds of friends or to lose them as his total cluster of roles changes over his life course (Section 1), a friendship is affected by the age, not of one person alone, but of at least two people. Thus the joint ages of the role partners enter in special ways into the forma-

---

[11] Parsons (1951, p. 189) suggests that friendship relations, while diffuse among adolescents and possibly among old men, tend to be specific among mature males so as to allow expressive gratification without incurring the obligations of diffuse attachments.

Cf. Hess (1971), which shows that fewer than one-fourth of the *best* friendships of the men, and fewer than half those of their wives, are characterized by "high diffuseness" in communication. In general, business-based friendships tend to be less intimate than those based upon neighboring, either from a previous residence or long current residence.

tion, maintenance, and disruption of particular friendships (an aspect of element 3 in the model outlined in Chapter 1). Moreover, the ages of the friends undoubtedly affect the character of the friendship (element 4), although this topic is not discussed in this essay.[12]

Accordingly, one important property of friendship is *relational age*. That is, a person (himself of a given age) may choose a friend who is *defined as* older, younger, or the same age as himself. The boundaries for describing pairs of friends as of "similar" or "differing" age probably vary over the life course and must, therefore, be carefully specified in particular investigations. Thus during childhood, when socializing agents commonly attempt careful regulation and definition of stages of development, a difference of a year or two may distinguish age similarity from age difference; whereas in the adult years, friends born as much as half a decade apart may describe themselves as of the same age.

Of course, age as a relational criterion [*as discussed in Chapter 10 · 1*] operates in allocating role-partners in many spheres. In marriage, for example, a man typically chooses a wife a few years younger than himself, and certain subtle social controls work against large age discrepancies, most notably in the case of a woman marrying a man considerably younger. But relational age has a special pertinence to friendship because of the multiplicity of friendships in which a given individual participates, and because the volitional character of the relationship enables either partner with comparative ease either to form new friendships (even in old age, many people report making new friends —Volume I, Chapter 24 · 1 · c and 2 · b), or to allow old friendships to lapse.

FRIENDSHIP FORMATION

Many friendships are formed between persons of similar age. This tendency, which may be more or less pronounced at different stages of life, can be variously explained. On the one hand, age is undoubtedly an important constituent of homophily. That is, people are likely to choose one another as friends because their similarity in age, like their similarity in other characteristics, signals mutuality of experience, tastes, or activities. On the other hand, age similarity in friendships may arise less from reciprocal choice than from constraints imposed by cultural expectations, or by the age-homogeneity of many environments within which interaction occurs and mutual attachments develop.

Age and friendship choice   Status similarity (including age similarity)

---

[12] As yet there is little analysis that fits together the subjective viewpoints of both partners in the friendship dyad. However, such analysis is undoubtedly essential for an understanding of the age structure of friendship choice. Moreover, it may be expected that age, like social class, will prove to be a powerful factor affecting the probability of reciprocal friendship choices.

and value similarity are well-recognized relational bases for friendship *generally*, a phenomenon for which Merton coined the term "homophily," in contrast to "heterophily" or attraction between those who differ in status or values (Lazarsfeld and Merton, 1954, p. 23). Homophily is presumed to affect who chooses whom as a friend at all stages of the life course (and also, who might cease being friends with whom). The nature of the postulated process has been described and illustrated in two different papers: one by Lazarsfeld and Merton (1954), based on an analysis of two housing communities; and another by Newcomb (1961), based on intensive observation of students in a residence hall, and utilizing the balance theory of Heider (1946, 1958) and its further modification by Festinger (1957). As Merton puts it, common statuses, and the common values with which these are associated, "make social interaction a rewarding experience, and the gratifying experience promotes formation of common values" (Lazarsfeld and Merton, 1954, p. 36). If common values fail to emerge, however, the imbalance between liking another person and disagreeing with him is a punishing experience.[13] In such a case, the individual can attempt to redress the balance, either by bringing the values into alignment by changing his own, converting his friend, or by disliking the other person rather than liking him. This process affects, of course, not only the initial stage of friendship formation, but also the duration and possible disruption of the friendship (to be discussed later in Section 2), although the stages at which homophily operates can rarely be disentangled in the empirical studies.

Our present concern is not with homophily generally, but with age as a basis upon which status-similars may be chosen. There are two important respects in which age similarity among friends can index common values and interests. First, age similarity signifies mutuality of life-course stage, the sharing of major role experiences—encountering similar role sequences and similarly structured strains, past, present, and future. Second, age similarity means belonging to the same cohort—that is, having experienced the same historical era, having shared similar socialization and educational contexts, and having met the impact of many common historical events and changes. Therefore, certain values, norms, and attitudes are likely to be held in common, and particular life styles are likely to be familiar and comfortable to members of the same cohort—"speaking the same language" saves the costs of working out a new common vocabulary.

It is not known whether or not age homophily operates equally at all stages of life. School children, adolescents, and college students appear to choose

---

[13] However, perception is in the first instance apt to be balance-promoting, so that any discrepancies between age peers might not be immediately apparent, but only become known through continued interaction.

friends who are in their same school grade.[14] And in old age, friendships oc-cur most often, though not exclusively, among age peers (Volume I, Chapter 24 · 4 · a). But what happens during the middle periods of life? Is age homophily more important, relative to other bases of friendship, at the two extremes of the life course than in the middle? For adults generally, it may be that other status distinctions are overriding, so that friendships tend to form between persons who, regardless of their age, have in common such characteristics as parenthood, marital status, occupation, or socioeconomic class. But among preadults, or among old people in retirement or after mov-ing from a former community, such status distinctions may be blurred and age as a criterion may predominate.

Such discussion begins to suggest the *conditions* under which age (like other readily apparent status characteristics) may be an overarching con-sideration in friendship formation. Stated most broadly, our hypothesis is that age, as an ascriptive base for friendship selection, is most salient at those life stages where the individual's role cluster is least differentiated. Thus in American society, age homophily should be most pronounced where differentiations by universalistic performance and achievement criteria are either absent or disrupted from some prior equilibrium.

In youth, the common condition of not participating in the differentiated roles of productive adulthood (so valued in an achievement-oriented society) seems to enhance the effect of age per se upon diffuse solidarity. Toward the end of the life course, where the role cluster again becomes dedifferentiated, there seems to emerge an "all in the same boat" perception of self and age peers that increases the importance of age homophily—the importance of solidarity generated by the shared experiences of retirement and widowhood, of historical era, of inculcation into a generational value pattern that may no longer be the dominant one of the society. Another common bond of the elderly may derive via the "looking-glass self" from the tendency of others to lump old people together, divesting them of the individuality, which in our society is attached to occupancy of productive roles. Once retired, people are no longer clearly distinguishable by what they *do*, and the new age-related status overrides former attributes. In sum, being an adolescent or a widow or a retiree, by loosening the individual's ties to the more instrumental societal matrices, thereby enhances, we suggest, the significance of age as a ready indicant of common conditions. But in middle age, the multiplicity and variety of roles played, the linking of friendships to these, the focusing and segmentation of interests among work, family, and community, often operate

[14] For example, Hollingshead (1961, p. 210); Priest and Sawyer (1967, pp. 641–643). For techniques of handling homophily in research, see, for example, Riley (1963, Volume I, pp. 182–183); and Coleman (1958, pp. 34–36).

to compartmentalize friendships, to make their bases more specific than diffuse, and thus to reduce the extent of age homogeneity in friendships.

A few scattered clues in the literature on friendship further specify the conditions under which age might become more or less important in friendship formation. Merton (Lazarsfeld and Merton, 1954, p. 22) points to the connection between community context and the operation of homophily: friend selection based on age and other ascribed characteristics was more widespread in the less cohesive of the two communities studied. And, in their study of college residences Priest and Sawyer (1967, p. 643) noted a decrease in floormate friendships based on the approximate age peership of college class (as well as on proximity) from autumn to spring and from one academic year to the next. One inference from these tenuous clues might be that, as groupings become more integrated so that common purposes emerge and personality differences become more apparent, age becomes less likely to provide the basis of friendship selection. While the pool of age-mates may be a handy source of friends in newly formed aggregates, the selection of friends ultimately depends upon canons of taste, personality inclinations, or salient common interest that are not necessarily related to age.

Thus exceptions to the principle of age homophily are to be expected under certain conditions. Some friendships certainly form across age strata, and these are not necessarily anomalies. A general principle enunciated by Homans (1961, pp. 317, 334–335; 1950, pp. 215–216, 251) for example, allows the inference that pairs of friends, if not from the same stratum, might be drawn from markedly different rather than adjacent strata. That is, the costs of interacting with superiors (or inferiors) can be reduced by choosing either status-equals or persons who are so clearly superior or inferior that relative statuses are not in doubt, and therefore not tension-producing. Applying this principle in the family context, Homans cites the close affection observed in certain primitive tribes between alternate generations (e.g., grandfathers and grandsons), in contrast to the more strained relations between consecutive generations (e.g., fathers and sons) where the nearness in age *still admits potentials* for rivalry.

Age and cultural prescriptions   While age similarity in friendship may result in part from homophilous choices by individuals, these choices are not entirely unconstrained. For age similarity tends also to be a normative component of the friendship role, implicit when not explicit. This normative emphasis becomes apparent as we realize that age similarity is seldom seen as a fact to be accounted for, whereas dissimilarity in age between friends may arouse suspicion, require explanation from the participants, or evoke societal control reactions ranging from ridicule to attempts to enforce separation. Age heterogeneity in friendship may be suspect because it appears to threaten deep-rooted assumptions about the very nature of the friendship bond: that people are held together by what they have in common. When members of the society are confronted by marked age differences in a friendship pair, they often feel compelled to ask what such disparate individuals can have in common. The mere asking of such a question carries the implication that they may have nothing legitimate or desirable in common, that instead the basis of the friendship may be pathological, immoral, or otherwise aberrant, signifying regression of one of the participants, precocity of the other, or instrumental manipulation rather than expressive cathexis. Thus, though age similars are unlikely to be asked to indicate that they share common concerns, friends who differ in age may be expected to account for their relationship.

Age homogeneity appears to be most explicitly endorsed in the preadult years, when parents and adult socializing agents widely recognize the peer group as an important auxiliary in the socialization process. Orderly progression in training for adult roles requires, on the one hand, that the child be prevented from remaining in, or regressing to, some earlier stage. On the other hand, such training requires that the child be shielded from assuming or rehearsing roles for which he is inadequately equipped, in which he cannot be rewarded, or in which failures of performance may jeopardize eventual conformity to adult role expectations.

The child's social behavior, of which interaction with friends is one important aspect, supplies a measure of the adequacy of the child's development. Thus the older child who persists in associating with younger children is often seen as either refusing to acquire behaviors appropriate to the "normal" child of his age or as engaging in excessively dominant, nurturant, or other deviant behavior. Though the younger child with older companions is perhaps less frequently an object of concern, he too may be subjected to negative sanctions as unduly precocious, as compensating for some deprivation, as failing to learn what his age-mates are learning at a particular time, or as acquiring habits and orientations forbidden to his age. Thus the tendency toward age homogeneity in preadult friendship appears to arise not merely from the unguided preferences of the participants themselves, but also from the conscious and deliberate efforts of socializing agents to control the age structure of children's friendships.

Whether or not age homogeneity maintains its normative power into the years of maturity and old age is open to question, and might prove a profitable topic of research. There is some indication that, with the onset of adulthood, age as a basis of solidarity may subside in importance, while other bases of friendship formation become more prominent. To the extent that adults play a variety of roles, any one of which may offer a focus of common interest in friendship, age heterogeneity between friends may well be regarded as permissible because of the sharing of statuses that cut across age lines. Yet, as in childhood, age-heterogeneous friendships may remain outside cultural definitions of "normal" whenever they are associated with differences in hierarchical status, values, or life styles.

Age and propinquity Another constraint upon the operation of age homophily is the age composition of the environing population. If it can be assumed that most persons prefer, and that the norms prescribe, the choice of age-similars as friends, the further question arises: Does having friends depend upon the close availability of age similars? Proximity is recognized, in general, as aiding the formation of friendship[15]—especially perhaps among the very young and the very old who are most affected by geographical restrictions. [*See Section 2 in Chapter 6 by Starr.*] But how does age affect the operation of proximity as a selective factor? If peership acts as a social screen, can it be assumed that proximity necessarily operates within age lines as a physical screen (Priest and Sawyer, 1967, pp. 646, 648)?

A number of studies conducted in *age-homogeneous settings* have established the importance of propinquity—at least among students, both married and unmarried, and among the very old. One such study, which has influenced much subsequent research, was conducted by Festinger, Schachter, and Back (1950) during the 1940's in a residential complex for married students at Massachusetts Institute of Technology. The effects of physical and functional distance upon friendship were striking: the closer the neighbor, the more likely to be friend; and the more advantageously located the apartment in terms of traffic flow within the complex, the more likely its occupants to have extensive friendship networks. Similar findings in a student village have been reported by Caplow and Forman (1950). That is, when those in the given area are already status-similars in age, interests, and occupation, sheer closeness and availability may become determining factors in the choice of friends.[16] This phenomenon is not restricted to students, since at least two studies of old people in age-segregated congregate residences also demonstrate the power of proximity as a basis for friendship choice (Friedman, 1966, pp. 567, 569; Lawton and Simon, 1968, p. 110).

An interesting question concerns the *relative* importance of age similarity and propinquity as the basis for forming friendships: Do people choose age similars if age dissimilars are more readily available? Among the few relevant attempts is the exploration by Priest and Sawyer (1967, pp. 638–643, 648) of all friendship choices in one student residential hall over a four-year period. While proximity and liking were found to be consistently related, so also

[15] Merton and his colleagues, in their widely influential housing studies, early recognized the importance of proximity in friendship formation and investigated the operation of propinquity in considerable detail. See Merton, West, and Jahoda (1948); Merton (1948).

[16] A critique of such studies objects to generalizations about friendship based on student housing communities, arguing that students are so bound up in their academic world that they have little time, energy, or money for socializing outside the housing complex (Gross and Martin, 1952, pp. 562–563).

were age similarity and liking—that is, friends tended to be drawn from class-mates, and the degree of liking was highest for students in the same college class. As for which was the better predictor, age peership or proximity, it appeared that, among floormates, peership was more closely correlated with attraction than was proximity. Proximity, the authors conclude, reduces the "cost" of friendship interaction, but it is peership that increases the reward. Evidently, where all are residentially close, the shared interests and status of peership may become crucial to choice of friends, just as, where all are of the same age, more distinctive criteria may predominate.[17]

Age-heterogeneous settings offer far better opportunity, of course, to test the operation of homophily than do such aggregates of persons of nearly uniform age. While the available evidence is here again limited, several studies of old people living in the community suggest two relevant principles. First, older people's friendships occur often, though by no means exclusively, among age peers (Volume I, Chapter 24 · 4 · a). And second, having age similars nearby tends to foster local friendships. For example, Rosow (1967, pp. 70–71, 79–81) found in Cleveland that older people living in the same apartment building with more rather than fewer elderly neighbors are more likely to visit or associate with neighbors often and to have large numbers of local friends. And Messer (1966, p. 6) found in Chicago that old people in age-homogeneous housing are more closely associated with friends and neighbors than are those in age-heterogeneous housing. Of additional interest is the comparison made between age and income by Rosenberg (1967, p. 561) in his study of a working-class sample in Philadelphia. While both the age and the income of the surrounding residents appear to be independently related to the friendship patterns of older people, the relationship to age is clearly the more pronounced of the two. Thus the age structure of the neighborhood may be a key factor affecting the friendships of the aged. (For further details, see Volume I, Chapter 24 · 2 · d.)

Such tentative indications of the importance for friendship development of the availability of age-mates offer considerable challenge to further research. Scrutiny of friendship networks of varying ages and under varying conditions are required to insure that certain of the current findings are not mere artifacts of the research procedure. Some researchers, after examining a relatively closed, age-homogeneous community, marvel at the extent of interaction and friendship formation within it. Other researchers ask questions that limit friendship choices to others within an age-homogeneous community, precluding discovery of any existing age differences between friends

---

[17] As, for example, in Gans' Levittown study (1967) in which location or "functional distance" did operate to restrict neighboring to an area of three to four houses on all sides, but among adjacent groups of houses, neighboring took place between the most "compatible" rather than physically nearest neighbors (Gans, 1967, pp. 156, 159).

outside. Moreover, the pervasive cultural assumption of age homophily may in itself influence both researchers and respondents in such a way as to exclude investigation of age heterogeneous relationships. Research designs may be such that neither the old widow nor the neighborhood child who stops by after school for cookies and milk are led to label one another valued friends, which they may nevertheless be.

DURATION AND DISRUPTION OF FRIENDSHIP

Friendship is not only related at its inception to the ages of the partners; it also has a life course of its own. Since many pairs of friends are of similar age to start with, the friendship proceeds *pari passu* with the aging of the individuals involved. Moreover, the duration of a friendship tends to be bounded, if only roughly, by the age of the participants. Very young people cannot have "old" friendships. Nor can very old people look ahead to long extensions of friendship into the future.

Persistence of homophily   To what extent, then, is age related to the duration, or the disruption, of friendships originally formed because age-mates were attracted to one another? How does age enter into the postulated mechanisms whereby common status can either hold friends together through shared values and attitudes, or alternatively can encourage friends to part once their values and attitudes diverge? At least one study of college students (Newcomb, 1961, pp. 254–255) supports the proposition that value positions are more stable than attractions to friends—that, in this age stratum at least, people are quite ready to shift their personal preferences in favor of individuals with whom they are more closely in agreement. Yet, even if shared values were to prove the overriding consideration in enduring friendship, common age status is at best a crude index of such sharing. Thus continuing communication between age-similar friends may often reveal value differences that were initially obscured by the status similarity, and age alone may be an insufficient bond between the partners.

However, there is one special feature of age (in contrast to socioeconomic status, for example) that may turn out to support the continuance of age-based homophily: namely, the fact that the members of a friendship pair necessarily age together. Thus both those sets of age-related factors are likely to persist that may have fostered the formation of the friendship at the outset: friends who were alike in age to start with continue to share, not only (1) the same sequence of life-course stages, but also (2) the same historical and environmental events.

Friendship duration   There are many indications that "old friends" may be the "best" friends. Not only have old friends shared the passage of time, as marked by external history and the progression of life stages. They have also accumulated joint experiences in their long relationship together. To the extent that a person is what he has been, those who have been there with him have a special claim on affection which may survive numerous vicissitudes. As Priest and Sawyer (1967, p. 648) put it, "When old friends are best, then, part of the reason may lie just in their oldness."

This theme recalls a general principle of our conceptual model (Chapter 10 · 2): that commitment to a role is a function of the years of a person's life that he has spent in that role. Acting in a given role implies a certain investment of self, and the longer the performance the greater the stake one has in having his presentation accepted. The individual's very sense of identity is made up, in part, of acquired social ties. Since self-acceptance often depends on being accepted by others, friendship, because of its volitional character, provides an important test of this principle of commitment.

In maintaining commitment, the past may be idealized as one ages, or a "nicer, simpler" self may be embodied in the memory of past friendships. Diffidence, the emotional cost of potential rebuff, or fear of failure in establishing friendships may all operate to inhibit the making of new friendships and favor the retention of those no longer representing trials of self. It would seem that these potential costs of new friendships would rise with age, since with each year an individual has that much more added to his own idea of who and what he is, to his "presenting self."[18]

The tendency of friendships to persist is illustrated in situations where friends are separated by *moving*. Since young adults are more likely to move, persons in their middle and later years are less likely to encounter geographical separation from friends. Yet, even in such situations, it appears that the maintenance of friendship is not necessarily contingent upon proximity or continuous interaction, but may endure under conditions of infrequent contact and separation in time and space. Childhood and college friends,[19] military service buddies, even friends from a previous residence may still be considered one's "best" friend even though rarely seen. At some time in the past,[20] then, sustained and intense interaction may have obtained to create the enduring bond. Possibly, distance between them serves a positive function in insulating these friends against the knowledge of changes in those characteristics upon which the relationship was originally based.

Whatever the sustaining mechanisms, there is a tendency for certain

---

[18] Goffman (1959, p. 222) suggests that ". . . we may expect individuals to relax the strict maintenance of front when they are with those they have known for a long time, and to tighten their front when among persons who are new to them."

[19] For example, proximity becomes less important as a basis for college student friendships as the school year advances, suggesting that friendships once established, gather their own momentum (Priest and Sawyer, 1967, p. 648).

[20] Association of frequency of contact between friends with duration of the friendship appears to be but a special case of a principle often elucidated by learning theorists: The establishment of a response may initially require frequent reinforcement but, once established, only occasional reinforcement will ensure maintenance of the activity.

kinds of friendships to persist even when friends are no longer in close proximity. Such a tendency, noticed by Babchuk and Bates (1963, p. 384) and labeled "suspended primary groups," has been substantiated by Hess (1971) in a sample that is homogeneous in respect to many factors that might confound the relationship between duration and friendship: age, socioeconomic status, and recency of moving. Data from this study of 150 middle-aged, middle-class couples who had moved within 5 years into a new community brought the unexpected finding that the first-choice "best" friend was most likely to come from a previous residence, for both husbands and wives, whereas the second "best" choice was likely to be a "new" neighbor. That a basically mobile sample should retain "old" friends presents an interesting paradox: The conditions for disruption of these relationships also work to enhance the value of old friendships, which possibly serve as anchors, at least until the newcomers have had time to sink roots in the new location.[21]

With regard to the closeness of the friendships in this particular sample, intimacy (defined as "talking about personal problems and feelings") is more characteristic of the long-term friendships. Interestingly, intimacy is not associated with frequency of visiting in the case of "old" friends, though it is with the "new" ones. There is, it seems, something so compelling about friends one has been able to keep across time and space that intimacy can be re-established on the infrequent occasions of meeting.

Though having lived a certain length of time determines the possibility of having "old" friendships, with age also setting limits to the potential for extension of an existing friendship into the future, the tendency to sustain friendships may be more characteristic of *certain life stages* than of others. Thus the sharing of concerns and interests, or the mutuality of need-dispositions, may be relatively short-lived in childhood, adolescence, or in specific friendships tied to the early years of marriage or of childrearing. For example, the adolescent peer group, while it performs a unique and necessary function for its members, must itself be left behind if the youngster is to make the final step into adulthood.

Orientations toward enduring friendships may also vary with stage in the life course. In later life, enduring friendships may be as valued for the few years remaining as for the many years before which have gone into developing the relationship. Age here becomes important in both of its extensions—past and future (cf. Maisonneuve, 1966, p. 479). At earlier periods in life, when the future seems unbounded, the value attached to an "old" friendship can be diluted by the many possibilities of choices ahead; but, as these possibilities

[21] The number of best friends who are current neighbors did tend to increase with length of residence; that is, new neighbors were mentioned, generally as second choice, only after respondents had been settled for at least 2 years.

are gradually reduced, an "old" friend becomes "dearer" in both senses of the word.

When the past is a longer span for contemplation than the future, then what has already happened tends to assume enlarged importance. If human perception is affected by this perspective, we might expect restructuring of past experience. In this fashion, persons who had known one another only slightly at some earlier period, might, upon remeeting, conjure up together the memory of diffuse attachment, a tendency that might well increase in the comparative role-lessness of the later years. Such retrospective friendships could be considered as *substitutes* for more concrete enduring relationships, with memory replacing interaction during the intervening years.

Disruption of friendship While some friendships are maintained over the passage of years or cultivated more intensely through shifts and expansion of common concerns, other friendships are lost (see, e.g., Maisonneuve, 1966, pp. 217–223). Whether or not a friendship survives can depend upon exigencies affecting, not both, but just one of the partners. And many of the age-related exigencies producing the dissolution of friendship are not matters of personal decision, but are outside the control of the persons involved.

The limiting case is that of *death* of one of the partners, a likelihood that increases with age, as does *disability* or illness that can interfere with the homophilous character of the friendship. Homophily can also be disturbed, though less abruptly, when roles to which the friendships are *fused* are themselves relinquished as, for example, when parental, work, and marital roles are progressively given up with age (see Section 1). Consequent status discrepancies tend to increase the cost of interaction, and the current inequality of the friends will threaten their relationship unless the shared satisfactions of contact can compensate. Even though geographical separation does not necessarily affect diffuse, solidary attachments, it can nonetheless interfere with the "neighboring" character of many friendships, with the spontaneous visiting, or the instrumental exchange of services.

Certain kinds of *substitutive* and *complementary* friendships may also be subject to disruption, as the role clusters of the individuals change. Friendships may be viewed by other social system members as inappropriate substitutes for particular major roles, for example, if this major role is itself defined by the larger society as properly relinquished. Thus the adolescent who seeks parent figures in his peer relations may be under considerable social pressure to relinquish the substitute familial roles he has established. Or a friendship that functions as a substitute for a major role not yet assumed may be vulnerable to disruption once the individual enters this major role. It has been argued, for instance, that adolescents withdraw from delinquent friendships as they find jobs and girls they wish to marry (see Toby and Liebman, unpublished). Moreover, friendships that have functions complementary to another role may be endangered by loss or alteration of this role, thus placing new burdens on the friendship to assume lost functions or to redefine foci of interest. For example, certain of the specific "shared-leisure" friendships that characterize middle age may endure into the later years, when complementary occupational and marital roles are lost, only if these friendships expand to include more diffuse interests and solidarities.

3 Friendship and socialization

Against this background of the ways in which friendships develop and relate to other roles over the life course, numerous further questions arise as to the functions of friendship at successive life stages. On the one hand, these functions can be variously affected *by* those age-related processes that govern occupancy and performance in social system roles (P3 and P4 in our conceptual model), as described in Chapter 12. On the other hand, friendship groups can make various contributions *to* these processes. In particular, as this last section will indicate, friendship can contribute, both directly and indirectly, to the process of socialization. Despite the restriction of most available research to the earlier years, such contributions undoubtedly continue throughout life, as the increasing sociological awareness of later-life socialization attests (see, e.g., Brim, 1966; Riley, Foner, Hess, and Toby, 1969).

DIRECT CONTRIBUTIONS

There are many indications that friends can aid directly—though perhaps to a limited degree—in the learning of new and altered roles and in the relinquishment of old ones. At certain life stages, friends can impart instrumental knowledge to one another, they can provide mutual opportunities for role rehearsal, or they can set controls upon one another's behavior.

In childhood, for example, Piaget (1948) claims that play groups are essential for the development of moral realism that comes from the experience of cooperation, of getting along with coevals, of agreeing together on the rules of the game.

A large literature specifies the functions of play groups and peer groups in the gradual weaning of the preadult away from his family of orientation and in preparing him for future roles in his own family of procreation. For instance, Dunphy (1963) in Australia and Smith (1962) in the United States, though working independently, similarly arrived at a developmental schema, a "natural history" of the peer group: from a one-cell, one-sex mass; through group dating, to a many-celled formation of cross-sex pairs, which finally dissolves as these unique pairs split off and severally go through the sequences of steady dating, pinning, engagement, and ultimately marriage. The beauty of this arrangement is that each structural change in the peer group initiates the socializee to a new phase in age-sex relationships, from monosexual clique to married pair; or conversely, as new age-sex relationships necessarily develop along the road to maturity, the peer group structure evolves and changes to provide the necessary support and guidance for role learning, experimentation, or possible failure.

Nor is the friendship network of young people as unstructured as commonly thought. Internal arrangements of roles within the group often facilitate the functions of both socialization and social control. Even in the case of Whyte's "corner boys" (1955, pp. 255–268) a clear set of reciprocal obligations bound the members to certain positions vis-à-vis one another. Thus to act in a manner different from that expected brought immediate regulatory reactions from the other boys, while not being able to act in the accustomed manner created psychological disturbances in several instances.

In another example, the mechanisms by which social control is exerted within the adolescent peer group have been explicated by Riley and Cohn (1958). This study shows how the networks of friends and enemies within a high school class tend to channel the motivations of some individuals in conformist, others in deviant, directions.

A full picture of preadult peer groups, then, must take into account the internal arrangements for social control as well as the progressive changes in form that permit socialization through these years of intensive role-learning and unlearning.

Adulthood, too, appears to provide opportunities for socialization among friends. Initiation into the marital role or the parental role may enhance the position of friends as imparters of information, especially where (as in respect to contraception or childrearing) social change may have rendered out-of-date the advice of one's parents.

Because of social change, however, the impact of friends as socializers can shift markedly over the individual's life course. Since friends are typically members of the same cohort who share the same life experiences,[22] peer group influence is likely to be supportive of tradition in the later years, in marked contrast to peer support of innovation during youth. In this respect, we might postulate that peer socialization is sharply differentiated from the intergenerational model of socialization within the family, where the life-course pattern of influence is directly reversed. For, within the family, the socializee is taught established norms by his parents while he is young, whereas in his old age his children, in their turn, attempt to inform him about the new norms

---

[22] To be sure, there are also instances in which friends may exert influence across adjacent cohorts. Thus the changes in dating behavior wrought by the automobile were worked out by one generation of youth and then transmitted to the next.

of their changing world. Thus, at either end of the life course, peers and kin-folk appear to exert countervailing influences. Whether or not these influences are actually in conflict is an important question, to be considered shortly.

Before examining friendship as an adjunct to the family or other socializing agency, what can we say in summary about the direct contributions to socialization by friendship itself? Here a comparison with the conceptual model set forth by Parsons and Platt [*Chapter 7*] is illuminating. According to this model, age asymmetry is typically inherent in structures principally devoted to primary socialization—that is, to the acquisition of basic values. Since the oncoming generation must be continually socialized to roles open at successive life stages, it is the older members of the society, those who have already experienced these major life roles, who are ordinarily designated as qualified to teach the younger members. In order to accomplish this task, certain inequalities of competence and of authority to evaluate performances must be maintained—inequalities that are not entirely compatible with the modal type of status similarity in friendship.

Such incompatibility sets certain interesting restrictions upon the connection between friendship and socialization (to the extent that friendship constitutes homophily rather than heterophily and socialization does approach the Parsons and Platt model). First, friends cannot be socializers in the full Parsonian sense. While friends can aid in instrumental learning or in the implementation of values, the status inequality required for teaching the values themselves creates barriers to a friendship relation between socializer and socializee. And second, where primary socialization is required, friends may be less effective agents than others who are status superiors.

Thus, in the socialization of the young at key points of role transition, friends probably contribute only indirectly, serving as supplements to the major agents of socialization. However, in the socialization of the older person, who must also confront drastic role changes, there can be no socializers who are broadly superior in age. The old person must often rely for guidance, then—if not entirely upon previous anticipatory socialization—upon age-mates such as spouse, friend, or sibling; or upon younger people such as adult offspring. To be sure, these socializers may often be status superiors in certain respects; they may have more recent knowledge, higher income, or greater vigor. But they cannot be superior in age. And this means that they cannot have experienced in advance the old person's current stage of life. To whom, then, does the old person have recourse? Does he turn to religion? To the mass media? To professional counsellors? Or does he define in new ways his relation to his friends, as well as to his surving kin?[23]

[23] The function of a "confidante" (either friend or relative) for the preservation of mental health in old age has been demonstrated by Lowenthal and Haven (1968).

A situation parallel to that of old age, in which age superiors cannot function as socializers, may arise in periods of revolutionary change—periods in which the basic social values undergo transformation. As representatives of the *ancien régime*, older members of society are not competent to implement the new order. Surrogates for the traditional agents of socialization may then develop through stratification of the peer grooup and a more rigid differentiation of the leadership. Such differentiation, however, by weakening the age homophily may thereby weaken the solidarity of the peer group.

INDIRECT CONTRIBUTIONS

A key proposal of this essay is that friendship serves as an important supplement to other roles at life stages characterized by intense socialization. Such stages require radical redirecton of pattern variable orientation (to use Parsonian terms) or the establishment of new relationships when new roles must be learned, former roles relinquished, or transfers made from one role to another, as from student to worker, or from spouse to widow (see Riley, Foner, Hess, and Toby, 1969, especially pp. 956, 970–973). These are those moments that some societies have emphasized in rites of passage in which the primary group of peers assume great importance: where the transfer from one age-category to another involves greatest change in the individual's mode of participation in his culture, or where the changes are most abrupt (Linton, 1942).

While the several ways of relating friendship to other roles (described in Section 1) undoubtedly all have implications for socialization, the focus of this discussion is on friendship as a complementary role (or as a potentially competitive role) that combines with other roles to perform the required functions at such critical stages.

Transition points in preadulthood Two such transition points at early life stages figure prominently in Parsons' analyses of American society: preadolescence or "latency," and adolescence.[24] The play group of latency supports the child's first steps outside the world of family into a social system of power equals judged on universalistic bases of status. A second major step into social systems outside the effective controls of kinship occurs with the young person's first ventures into cross-sex relationships, within the protective milieu of "youth culture" norms and practices, and under the aegis of the adolescent peer group. In both instances, the peer group combines with two other socializing agencies, family and school, to perform the functions requisite for the development of the individual's personality and for his eventual integration into larger social systems (including the expansion of cathexes, the internalization of nonfamily interactive systems, and the learning of new

[24] Parsons and Bales (1955, pp. 113–131); Parsons (1942). See also various related discussions in more recent writings of Parsons.

pattern-variable orientations). And in both instances, the anxiety attendant upon learning is so great that the youngster falls back on his own-sex peer group for permissiveness and emotional support. Thus the friendship groups of childhood and adolescence, rather than being anomalous constructions of misguided youth, are seen to have functions for the individual and for the social systems within which he must operate as an adult.

A more general formulation is presented by Eisenstadt,[25] who draws upon cross-cultural and cross-temporal data for his monumental study of age groups and the social system. Building upon Parsons' pattern-variable alternatives, Eisenstadt demonstrates the rise of age-homogeneous groups in those societies where family and kinship units cannot confer full adult status on their young; namely, where the orientations to role relationships in adult activities are quite the opposite of those that characterize family and kinship interaction. There comes a time, Eisenstadt says, when ". . . youth must forsake reliance on ascription and collectivity orientation and acquire the attitudes and values appropriate to universalistic criteria of achievement in modern society. . . ." And it is at this point that a need-disposition for the company of peers throws the youngster into the protective environment of age-mates. Here he attempts to suppress inappropriate behaviors, he tries out new roles, and he internalizes nonfamily interaction systems. The peer group is a protective envelope and sympathetic sounding board during this transitional phase with its obvious potential for personal strain. Eisenstadt stresses the point, however, that, like the family, the age-homogeneous group of adolescents cannot confer full social status: to become a member of the adult society, the individual must eventually break away from the solidarities of youth —a break that may become increasingly difficult with the rising number of years spent by the young person in this situation (as Parsons and Platt suggest in Chapter 7).

The peer group of adolescence can also serve the interests of agents of socialization other than the family. It can provide expressive outlets for tensions generated in the instrumental, competitive atmosphere of the school. Or, as in the case of Elmtown's youth (Hollingshead, 1961, pp. 204–242), it can reinforce the social class structure of the adult world. While Hollingshead's adolescents were deeply involved in informal clique life, these groups also served to contain and control, channeling "friendships within limits permitted by the social system of both the adult and the adolescent social worlds." In other

---

[25] Eisenstadt (1956, Chapter 1, esp. pp. 21–55). Interaction with kinship units, says Eisenstadt, require judgments based upon affectivity, particularism, diffuseness and emphasis on quality. If these judgments are also sufficient for performance in the larger society, the age-heterogeneous kinship group can do the job of preparing its young for adulthood. However, where the converse pattern alternatives characterize the larger society (requiring judgments based upon performance, affective-neutrality, universalistic and specific criteria), then the youngster needs experience in interactive systems outside the kinship framework.

words, the clique was able to do what youngsters often resist when done by parents, to keep friendships within approved social class limits. Clique ties among Elmtown's youth were strongly associated with social class, school class, and prestige equals within the school class; and dating patterns similarly "are a reflection in large part of the adult social structure." It is important to note, however, that one of the more powerful factors inhibiting solidarity among age peers of differing social class may be that transitions into adulthood occur at differing ages for college and noncollege students. Their life courses are "out of phase," compounding the differing substance of their experiences.

Transition points in adulthood While little is known about the processes of socialization in later life, it seems likely that here too friends may afford a source of support or permissiveness during the trauma of transitional stages, even when primary agencies for socialization are missing. At entry into the marital and work roles of young adulthood, the frequent interaction with peers (noted in Section 2) may provide opportunity, not only for mutual learning, but also for problem-sharing, role experimentation, and escape into the sheer fun of sociability. At the stage where grown children leave the home, the mother (if she does not transfer to an occupational role) may seek support in interaction with peers through bridge or golf clubs, voluntary associations, or just visiting.

In old age, the major transitions require the relinquishing of familiar roles and the learning of new roles that, unlike the situation of preadulthood, promise little reward (see Riley, Foner, Hess, and Toby, 1969). However, if our model of the socializing functions performed by preadult friends is valid, we might expect to find special *types* of friendship activity at the points demarcating movement into retirement, widowhood, or disability. These are the occasions when a person looks to others, not only for direct aid in socialization (for behavior cues for the information required, and for the sanctions that tell one whether the role performance is correct), but also for indirect aids—for support and permissiveness in trial-and-error learning, for validation of self, or for ritual observance (as of birthdays or anniversaries).

Here we might speculate that family and friends may be complementary groupings, agents of socialization to different aspects of growing old. The family may serve to socialize the aged member into new intergenerational relationships, while the peer group provides a frame of reference for confronting the wider society, the former shoring up intergenerational ties, the latter to some extent providing a protective isolation. These need not be conflicting tendencies. Indeed, the evidence does not indicate that widowhood or retirement necessarily intensify the amount of activity with nonkin (Volume I, Chapter 24 · 3). And, while old-age friends serve both expressive and instrumental functions of many kinds, friendship ties tend to be less significant and close than ties to children (Volume I, Chapter 24 · 5 and 6). Yet, friends may offer a strong second line of defense to the old person as he attempts to preserve both the attachment and detachment required for what Erikson (1959, pp. 98–99) has described as the developmental task of old age: placing one's life in full perspective, knitting the strands together to achieve a sense of wholeness or integrity rather than of despair or disgust.

Complementarity versus competition   To what extent may peer groups at any age, as they serve functions differentiated from those of other socializers, thereby confront the person with conflicting expectations? Since peer groups, as we have suggested, may differ markedly from family groups on the dimension of traditionalism-innovation, for example, do the expectations of these two groups create role conflicts for the individual, especially for the very young or the very old?

For old people, there are as yet few answers to this question, except for the previously indicated fact that, in general, friends and neighbors are regarded as less important than children and other relatives and serve more as a complement than as a substitute for kinship association.

For the young, however, there are numerous indications that friendship relations cannot be fully understood in terms of opposition to family and school, or as replacing functions which the family is unwilling to assume, but, rather, as an agent complementary to both family and school. The nature of this complementarity, suggested by several studies already cited (such as those by Eisenstadt, Dunphy, or Smith), has been specified in a series of researches by Riley and collaborators.[26] (While the concrete results of research on youth conducted prior to 1969 may no longer be applicable to the contemporary scene in the United States, the underlying mechanisms are of interest. In this instance, it is noteworthy that replication in the early 1960's of findings obtained a decade earlier produced almost identical results.) A comparison of parents with peers as reference groups for high school students showed that, both in value sharing and in communication, peers are important in youth culture affairs, but parents tend to be even more important as the adolescent looks ahead to his future as an adult. The conflict perceived, on the average, between peer expectations and parent expectations is not sharp, focusing largely upon a difference in the respective emphases of peers and parents upon youth culture norms versus adult norms.[27] Meanwhile the adolescent himself can, in the typical instance, handle this conflict by personally

---

[26] Although most of this research is still to be published, see Riley, Riley, and Moore (1961). For further comments on this material, see Parsons and White (1961).

[27] Nonetheless, as Parsons and Platt point out in Chapter 7 of the present volume, strong peer solidarity may exacerbate whatever value differences do exist through its emphasis on age similarity as a basis for affective attachment.

regarding the norms of youth culture as ephemeral, having little bearing upon adult life.

Such illustrations suggest how friendship groups, acting as supplementary socializers, can serve both adaptive functions for the individual and integrative functions for the society. Friends can provide the permissiveness and emotional support required for socialization during key stages of role transition, thus aiding the processes of personality development and integration. During these stages also, friendship groups, by providing an escape, can frequently insulate the larger society from the deviant tendencies of the socializee—from the rebellion of the adolescent, for example, or the escapism of the recently bereaved elderly widow.[28]

CONCLUSION

In this necessarily speculative essay, we have described how the ages of people can have important bearing on their friendships, affecting whom one has as a friend, the kinds of relationships likely to develop between friends at various ages, and the conditions under which friendships are formed, maintained, or dissolved.

Since age refers to life stage (the differing set of major roles the individual has experienced, currently occupies, or is expected to enter in the future), it refers also to a complex of social positions that shape and constrain friendship relations, and with which friendship is interdependent. The sequence of entry and exit through these role clusters implies changing socialization requirements throughout the life course—and hence the periodically heightened value of friends for learning appropriate behaviors and for the expression of emotional support. These aspects of friendship may assume varying importance over the life course of individuals. Thus the middle span of adulthood, as the period of greatest social activity, may be characterized by a relatively greater prominence of narrowly *specific* friendship relations, many of which may be fused to major roles. The importance of having friends and the *diffuse quality* of these relationships may be more closely related to the life-course periods before and after, when friendships may substitute for more central roles or be complementary to the efforts of socializing agents. At periods of intensive role learning and role loss, friends function not only as a valued resource for the individual, but also as a more important mechanism of societal integration than is commonly recognized.

Age is also a cohort attribute, signifying a common history, a moving together through the important events of the era, the opportunity to evolve familiar, comfortable life styles and attitudes. To the degree that another in-

[28] Compare the "institutionalized deviance" described by Parsons (1951, p. 305), and elsewhere in his works.

dividual is similar in these respects, the conditions of status and value homophily exist; friendship between these persons is less costly in terms of understanding and image management than is interaction with status- and value-dissimilars.

Further, age indicates ability to "master," or at least to avoid, physical restraints of one's environment. At the same time, the availability of age-mates affects the extent to which age homophily can operate.

From the limited choices of childhood, through the intensive peer group activity of adolescence, the individual moves into the productive roles of adulthood and interaction with a variety of other people. Many of those whom one meets at work, or church, as neighbors, or through one's spouse will become one's own friends. The friendship process requires varying amounts of time for the participants to exchange information so that the full set of personality and attitudinal data needed for assessment of one other can be produced and evaluated. Yet any close friendship is an investment of self, so that having enjoyed a "best" friendship at some life stage permits the relationship to endure through time and space—indeed, not being in continual contact may serve to insulate the friendship from disturbing information. To have an "old" friend, moreover, implies an investment built up over a long period, which may be costly to repudiate, making it easier to gloss over tensions which might disrupt "younger" friendships, rather than to admit that one was mistaken all along. Thus, we suggest that while proximity and homophily are of greatest importance in the formation and possible dissolution of friendships, a crucial additional factor in the *duration* of friendship is simply the passage of time, as it indexes the accumulation of previous *investments of the self*.

These then are some of the themes which may serve to explicate the relationship between age and friendship. The success of such explication is an important test of principles proposed in the conceptual chapters of this volume.

Works cited in Chapter 9

Adams, Bert N., and James E. Butler, 1967. "Occupational Status and Husband-Wife Social Participation," *Social Forces*, 45, pp. 501–507.

Babchuk, Nicholas, 1965. "Primary Friends and Kin: A Study of the Associations of Middle-Class Couples," *Social Forces*, 43, pp. 483–493.

———, and Alan P. Bates, 1963. "The Primary Relations of Middle-Class Couples: A Study in Male Dominance," *American Sociological Review*, 28, pp. 377–384.

Bott, Elizabeth, 1957. *Family and Social Network*, London: Tavistock Publications.

Brim, Orville G., Jr., 1966. "Socialization Through the Life Cycle," in Brim, Orville G., Jr., and Stanton Wheeler, *Socialization After Childhood: Two Essays*, New York: Wiley, pp. 1–49.

Caplow, Theodore, and Robert Forman, 1950. "Neighborhood Interaction in a Homogeneous Community," *American Sociological Review*, 15, pp. 357–366.

CBS Reports, 1969. "Generations Apart," A Study of the Generation Gap Conducted for CBS News by Daniel Yankelovich, Inc., New York: Columbia Broadcasting System.

Coleman, James S., 1958. "Relational Analysis: The Study of Social Organizations With Survey Methods," *Human Organization*, 17, pp. 28–36.

Cowgill, Donald O., and Norma Baulch, 1962. "The Use of Leisure Time by Older People, *The Gerontologist*, 2, pp. 47–50.

Dunphy, Dexter C., 1963. "The Social Structure of Urban Adolescent Peer Groups," *Sociometry*, 26, pp. 230–246.

Eisenstadt, S. N., 1956. *From Generation to Generation*, New York: Free Press of Glencoe.

Erikson, Erik H., 1959. "Identity and the Life Cycle," in Klein, George S., editor, *Psychological Issues*, New York: International Universities Press, Part 1.

Evans, Franklin B., 1966. "When Death Do Us Part: The Problems and Adjustments of Middle Class American Widows" (unpublished).

Festinger, Leon, 1957. *A Theory of Cognitive Dissonance*, New York: Row, Peterson.

————, Stanley Schachter, and Kurt Back, 1950. *Social Pressures in Informal Groups: A Study of Human Factors in Housing*, New York: Harper & Brothers.

Friedman, Edward P., 1966. "Spatial Proximity and Social Interaction in a Home for the Aged," *Journal of Gerontology*, 21, pp. 566–571.

Gans, Herbert J., 1967. *The Levittowners*, New York: Random House.

Goffman, Erving, 1959. *The Presentation of Self in Everyday Life*, Garden City, N.Y.: Doubleday, Anchor Books.

————, 1961. *Asylums: Essays on the Social Situation of Mental Patients and Other Inmates*, Garden City, N.Y.: Doubleday, Anchor Books.

Gross, Neal, and William E. Martin, 1952. "On Group Cohesiveness," *American Journal of Sociology*, 57, pp. 546–564.

Heider, Fritz, 1946. "Attitudes and Cognitive Organization," *Journal of Psychology*, 21, pp. 107–112.

————, 1958. *The Psychology of Interpersonal Relations*, New York: Wiley.

Hess, Beth, 1971. "Amicability," Ph.D. dissertation, Rutgers University.

Hollingshead, August B., 1961. *Elmtown's Youth*, New York: Science Editions.

Homans, George C., 1950. *The Human Group*, New York: Harcourt, Brace.

————, 1961. *Social Behavior: Its Elementary Forms*, New York: Harcourt, Brace & World.

Lawton, M. Powell, and Bonnie Simon, 1968. "The Ecology of Social Relationships in Housing for the Elderly," *The Gerontologist*, 8, pp. 108–115.

Lazarsfeld, Paul F., and Robert K. Merton, 1954. "Friendship as a Social Process: A Substantive and Methodological Analysis," in Berger, M., T. Abel, and C. H.

Page, editors, *Freedom and Control in Modern Society*, Princeton, N.J.: Van Nostrand, pp. 18–66.

Liebow, Elliot, 1967. *Tally's Corner*, Boston: Little, Brown.

Linton, Ralph, 1942. "Age and Sex Categories," *American Sociological Review*, 7, pp. 589–603.

Litwak, Eugene, 1961. "Voluntary Association and Neighborhood Cohesion," *American Sociological Review*, 26, pp. 258–271.

Lowenthal, Marjorie Fiske, and Clayton Haven, 1968. "Interaction and Adaptation: Intimacy as a Critical Variable," *American Sociological Review*, 33, pp. 20–30.

Maisonneuve, Jean, 1966. *Psycho-Sociologie des Affinities*, Paris: Presses Universitaires de France.

Merton, Robert K., 1948. "The Social Psychology of Housing," in Dennis, Wayne, editor, *Current Trends in Social Psychology*, Pittsburgh: University of Pittsburgh Press, pp. 163–217.

———, Patricia S. West, and Marie Jahoda, 1948. *Patterns of Social Life*, New York: Bureau of Applied Social Research, Columbia University. Mimeographed.

Messer, Mark, 1966. "Engagement with Disengagement: The Effects of Age Concentration" (unpublished).

Nelson, Joel I., 1966. "Clique Contacts and Family Orientations," *American Sociological Review*, 31, pp. 663–672.

Newcomb, Theodore M., 1961. *The Acquaintance Process*, New York: Holt, Rinehart & Winston.

Parsons, Talcott, 1942. "Age and Sex in the Social Structure of the United States," *American Sociological Review*, 7, pp. 604–616.

———, 1951. *The Social System*, Glencoe, Ill.: Free Press.

———, and Robert F. Bales, 1955. *Family, Socialization and Interaction Process*, Glencoe, Ill.: Free Press.

———, and Winston White, 1961. "The Link Between Character and Society," in Lipset, Seymour Martin, and Leo Lowenthal, editors, *Culture and Social Character*, New York: Free Press of Glencoe, pp. 89–135.

Phillips, Derek L., 1967. "Social Participation and Happiness," *American Journal of Sociology*, 72, pp. 479–488.

Piaget, Jean, 1948. *The Moral Judgment of the Child*, Glencoe, Ill.: Free Press.

Priest, Robert F., and Jack Sawyer, 1967. "Proximity and Peership: Bases of Balance in Interpersonal Attraction," *American Journal of Sociology*, 72, pp. 633–649.

Riley, Matilda White, 1963. *Sociological Research, Volume I. A Case Approach*, New York: Harcourt, Brace & World.

———, and Richard Cohn, 1958. "Control Networks in Informal Groups," *Sociometry*, 21, pp. 30–49.

———, Anne Foner, Beth Hess, and Marcia L. Toby, 1969. "Socialization for the Middle and Later Years," in Goslin, David A., editor, *Handbook of Socialization Theory and Research*, Chicago: Rand McNally, pp. 951–982.

———, John W. Riley, Jr., and Mary E. Moore, 1961. "Adolescent Values and the Riesman Typology: An Empirical Analysis," in Lipset, Seymour Martin, and

Leo Lowenthal, editors, *Culture and Social Character*, Glencoe, Ill.: Free Press, pp. 370–386.

Roethlisberger, F. J., and William J. Dickson, 1940. *Management and the Worker*, Cambridge, Mass.: Harvard University Press.

Rosenberg, George S., 1967. "Poverty, Aging and Social Isolation," Washington: Bureau of Social Science Research. Mimeographed.

Rosow, Irving, 1967. *Social Integration of the Aged*, New York: Free Press.

Shils, Edward A., 1950. "Primary Groups in the American Army," in Merton, Robert K., and Paul F. Lazarsfeld, editors, *Studies in the Scope and Method of "The American Soldier,"* Glencoe, Ill.: Free Press, pp. 16–39.

Simmel, Georg, 1950. *The Sociology of Georg Simmel.* Translated by Kurt H. Wolff. Glencoe, Ill.: Free Press.

Slater, Philip E., 1963. "On Social Regression," *American Sociological Review*, 28, pp. 339–364.

Smith, Ernest A., 1962. *American Youth Culture*, Glencoe, Ill.: Free Press.

Sykes, Gresham M., 1958. *The Society of Captives*, New York: Atheneum.

Toby, Jackson, and Edna Liebman. "The Integration of Adolescent Delinquents into Conventional Society: The Impact of Girlfriends and Wives as Agents of Further Socialization" (unpublished).

Tomeh, Aida K., 1964. "Informal Group Participation and Residential Patterns," *American Journal of Sociology*, 70, pp. 28–35.

Udry, Richard, and Mary Hall, 1965. "Marital Role Segregation and Social Networks in Middle-Class, Middle-Aged Couples," *Journal of Marriage and the Family*, 27, pp. 392–395.

Whyte, William Foote, 1955. *Street Corner Society*, 2nd ed., Chicago: University of Chicago Press, p. 100.

Williams, Robin M., Jr., and M. Brewster Smith, 1949. "General Characteristics of Ground Combat," in Stouffer, Samuel A., et al., editors, *The American Soldier, Studies in Social Psychology in World War II*, Vol. II, Princeton, N.J.: Princeton University Press.

PART 3

THE NATURE OF AGE STRATIFICATION

Whereas the essays in Part 2 have illustrated various aspects of age in relation to selected spheres of society, Part 3 deals with age stratification as it intersects these spheres. The three chapters in this part, using ideas and examples drawn mainly from these essays and from Volumes I and II of Aging and Society, *will specify in further detail the conceptual model outlined in Chapter 1 of this book, stressing two essential themes: first, the inevitable and irreversible processes of aging and cohort flow that produce age strata; and, second, the strains toward change arising from the arhythmic relationship of these age processes to other societal dynamics.*

Chapter 10 will consider, at the macroscopic level, the division of every society into age strata, the interrelationships among these strata, and their synchronic changes and variations across time and space—quite apart from the participant individuals. At a microscopic level, the chapter will also regard these strata from the viewpoint of the individual, showing the ways in which the particular stratum to which he belongs at a given time affects the complex of roles he is expected to play, the rights and privileges accorded to him in each role, the manner in which individuals at varying ages differ in their capacity to perform these roles and in their reactions and adaptations.

Chapter 11 by John A. Clausen will explicate the dynamic processes whereby individuals, passing through the biological and social stages of the life course, also enter, perform, and finally relinquish the roles and role complexes afforded by the social structure. It describes the strains encountered by the person as he progresses through the age strata, showing how, as Eisenstadt (1956, p. 28) puts it, "the awareness of his own age becomes an important integrative element, through its influence on his self-identification."

Finally, Chapter 12 will point to continuities and disruptions experienced at the societal level because new participants are continuously being born, living out their lives, and dying. It will describe how the flow of cohorts fits individuals together so as to stratify the society by age; and how two special processes—allocation and socialization—operate to articulate the succession of cohorts with the social structure as each cohort requires continuous reassignment and retraining to perform essential tasks. The chapter will attempt to show how—through this sequence of many cohorts, each marked by the imprint of history and in turn leaving its own imprint—human beings of different ages become inextricably involved in, and contribute to, societal currents of stability and change.

The objective of this volume is to stimulate the development of a theory, not to enunciate one. For age is fundamental both to social structure and to social change. And, as age stratification emerges as a special field for sociological inquiry—supplementing and helping to locate such current concepts as socialization, social class, or social mobility—it must at the same time be integrated with other substantive fields of sociology.

10

Age strata in the society

Beguiled by the fact that age and aging are characteristics of individuals, sociologists often overlook the crucial influence of age structure as a societal characteristic. Yet both the roles and the population in any society are stratified by age, much as they may be stratified by sex, social class, or race. Age, in Mannheim's insightful formulation, "locates" individuals in the social structure. There is much evidence that, for example, a person's activities, his attitudes toward life, his relationships to his family or to his work—as well as his biological capacities and his physical fitness—are all conditioned by his position in the age structure of the particular society in which he lives. Thus, as the total society changes, the age strata, which tend to persist quite apart from particular people, are among those bases of social organization that, as Sorokin (1968) put it, can shape sociocultural life and the historical course of mankind.

As a means of exploring the power of age stratification for explaining many aspects of social structure and social change, this chapter considers the age strata of society in cross section. While much previous discussion of age, here and elsewhere in the literature generally, has been restricted to discrete strata or to discrete institutional spheres, it is only by cutting through the total society at particular periods of history that we can inquire into the ways in which strata fit together within the macrocosm. Thus our review in this chapter, which pulls together numerous strands from the foregoing essays, rests on the construct of the full set of strata that coexist in the overall society and that move together synchronically across time, adding a dynamic dimension often lacking in cross-sectional analyses.

AGE STRATA AND OTHER SOCIETAL DIVISIONS

Full development of the implications of age stratification requires understanding not only how people and roles are differentiated by age within a society, but also how the age strata intersect with other societal divisions. For age stratification can occur in varying forms in subpopulations[1] (among blacks, for example), in institutional spheres (such as the polity or the economy), or in corporate groups.[2]

[1] Sorokin (1947, p. 281) discusses "intra-group stratification" in this sense.
[2] There is also a stratification based, not on chronological age, but on the duration of incumbency by individuals in particular roles. People who were initiated into a system together or during the same period (like inmates of a mental institution or employees of a firm)

When the population of a country is arranged by chronological age, from newly born infants to the oldest people alive, age is a continuum. Thus, like certain other criteria of stratification—income or occupational prestige, for example—age in itself is a continuous measure,[3] so that clear-cut boundaries between strata acquire sociological meaning only as they *index* socially significant aspects of people and roles. *People* in different age strata are differently situated in society, constrained not only by their biologically related capacities and potentials, but also by the sequences of social roles they have already experienced, currently occupy, and may expect to move into. Partitions between strata are further differentiated by the social *roles* that are normatively prescribed, proscribed, or permitted to members of these strata.

Since age is only one of the bases for locating individuals within the society, age stratification must be apprehended in its relation to other social groupings and categories. If, as in Figure 10 · 1, one visualizes the people and the roles in the society as divided by horizontal lines into age strata (however delineated), then these age divisions cut across, or sometimes tend to parallel, the other divisions of the society: the divisions into lower-level structures or solidary groups (like families, work organizations, or communities); and also the broader divisions into such categories as labor force status, political party identification, or sex.

Group membership   People located in the several age strata are simultaneously members of other groups—a fact of immediate concern throughout this book. Thus every individual—depending partly on his age—plays a role in one or more groups or institutional spheres, as schematized in Figure 10 · 1. Each of these roles affects the behaviors and attitudes typically expected of him, as well as the rights and privileges accorded to him.

Within any one group, a person's role and his relations to the other group members depend in part upon the age distribution of the group itself. Some groups are contained within a single stratum (they are age-homogeneous). Other groups cut across lines dividing the strata (they are age-heterogeneous); and even an age-heterogeneous group may itself be stratified by age, so that, within a church or a school, for example, the significant members of an individual's role-set (to use Merton's term [1957, p. 369]) may be similar in age to himself. Thus age as an element in human relationships—of love or hate, conflict or solidarity, dominance or submission—can refer to individuals

---

share, and often acknowledge, a similar status, even though they may differ in age. New insights can be gained when organizations, too (although we do not develop the point here), are stratified according to the length of time that the organization has existed. As one example, see Stinchcombe (1965, pp. 153–159).

[3] Parallel to the perennial question of whether social class is a continuous or discrete phenomenon, we are concerned with the extent to which phenomena indexed by age do exhibit discrete boundaries, and with the extent to which the various socially meaningful partitions coincide in delineating similar age boundaries.

FIGURE 10 · 1   *Relation of groups to age strata (a schematic view)*

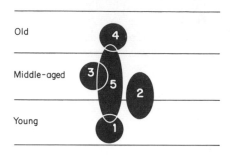

1 – High school peer group
2 – University
3 – Work group
4 – Senior center
5 – Family

of the same age or of different ages in one or in several different groups. Moreover, age-based relationships in one group context can sometimes affect those in another, as cleavage between students and faculty in a university may disturb the attachments between parents and offspring within the family. [*See the related discussions in Chapter 4 by Foner and Chapter 7 by Parsons and Platt.*]

Subpopulations   Members of the several age strata belong not only in particular groups, but also in particular subpopulations affecting social life, such as social classes, sex categories, or races. Sorokin has raised a series of questions about the interrelationships of the main types of stratification (or differentiation) as they merge or cross-cut one another in diverse parts of the population and at different periods of history (Sorokin, 1968, p. 409; see also Sorokin, 1947, pp. 181 ff.). Neugarten (1963; see also Cumming, 1963, pp. 385–391) regards sex as so crucial a division that special theories of aging are required for men and for women. The relation between social class and age status as alternative bases for politics (in the tradition of Weber, Hofstadter, and Lipset) has been discussed in the last section of Chapter 4 by Foner. There are numerous tendencies in our own society for age lines to correspond with other divisions. Thus educational level declines with age, the foreign-born are highly concentrated in the oldest strata, or sex ratios tend to be correlated with age. Yet few of these lines converge completely in any highly differentiated, pluralistic society, and individuals who are alike in age may be widely separated in other subpopulations of a matrix criss-crossed by myriad societal divisions.

Any rounded view of age stratification, then, cannot focus on the roles in single groups or institutional spheres, but must examine the age-related intersections of these roles.

AGE STRATA AND CHANGE

Age stratification, despite its interrelationships with many other types of stratification or differentiation, is uniquely distinguished from them in one crucial respect: its ineluctable connection with the dynamics of society, with societal stability and change. For age stratification rests upon the inexorable processes of cohort flow through the society and of individual aging within these cohorts. These processes and their interpenetration with the changing society, will be discussed in subsequent chapters. Here our focus is on the changing society itself, as it comprises the fully stratified structure of old and young.[4] Of primary relevance to social dynamics are those changes in the age strata occurring over the course of history in a single society, as industrialization or urbanization advance, for example, or as wars or other crises occur.[5] Of additional interest, simply as demonstration that the particular arrangements imposed on social life by age itself are far from universal, are the wide variations observed through comparison of age strata in different social structures and under differing social and environmental conditions.

The aim of this chapter, then, is to illustrate the utility of a synchronic view of the age strata, as these strata are composed of roles and role players and as they can contribute to the nature of society, its cultural and subcultural variability, and its changes. We shall devote considerable attention to the structural elements in our conceptual model [see *Chapter 1*], in the belief that amplification and clarification of such concepts can evoke significant questions and can begin to suggest some answers. The first section of this chapter will describe the age structure of roles, outlining both the nature of this structure and the inequalities of opportunities, rewards, or power that the structure can impose. Section 2 deals with the people who are located in the several age strata and whose individual differences and similarities are channeled, on the one hand, by the age-specific roles they encounter and, on the other hand, by basic demographic and organic constraints. Section 3 points to the utility of exploring relationships—the way people feel and act toward one another—both within and between age strata. It speculates about such questions as: How prevalent within a given stratum is solidarity or consciousness of kind? What meaning do similarities or differences among the strata have for relationships of consensus or cleavage? What kinds of relationships are associated with harmony or conflict, with stability or change? Finally, Section 4 outlines some of the potential pressures for change that are gen-

---

[4] For the purposes of understanding the underlying processes of aging and cohort flow, of course, cross-sectional views can often lead to fallacious interpretations. [See *Chapter 2 · 3*.]

[5] These are the period differences (Pd) discussed in Chapter 2.

erated through elements of our conceptual model. What strains are entailed by age-specific imbalances between role expectations, and trained capacities, or between supplies of people and of roles? How do such strains, if left unresolved, engender deviance, innovation, or various forms of social change?

1 *The age structure of roles*

The influence of age on diverse social phenomena rests not only upon the people who are characterized by age but also upon the role structure mediating human behavior and attitudes. Parents and their young children, for example, relate to each other across age lines in ways that can shift over time. Thus marked variations in childrearing practices have been observed for many decades (Miller and Swanson, 1958, pp. 3–29; Bronfenbrenner, 1958). Yet such historical changes in age-relationships cannot be attributed to aging, and explained as shifts over the life course of particular individuals; because of the obvious fact that infants, and the young adults who are their parents, are not the same people from one decade to the next. Rather, these changes can be understood only as they are socially structured; they require examination, not of the people themselves, but of the social roles of parent and of infant.

Since age, like sex, is a universal basis for role assignment (cf. Gulliver, 1968, p. 157), all societies are characterized by differences among age strata both in the numbers and kinds of roles available and in the expectations, facilities, and sanctions associated with these roles (elements 3 and 4 in our conceptual model). Yet the place of age in the role structure is by no means fixed, but operates in notably divergent fashion in differing sociotemporal situations (although most of our examples come from a single time and place—and even occasionally, for clarity's sake, from a single institutional sphere).

In this section, then, we shall consider four lines of inquiry into the age structure of roles that may lead to enhanced comprehension of the structure of society as a whole: the number and kinds of roles available in the age strata; age as a criterion for role incumbency; the scope and boundaries of the age strata; and the inequalities among age strata in role opportunities and rewards.

NUMBERS AND KINDS OF ROLES

Before examining some of the principles by which age enters into the numbers and kinds of roles in the social structure (element 1 in our conceptual model), we touch upon enough of the familiar and immediate examples to clarify the nature of the differences among strata. Consider a few of the roles played by typical men at three different ages (45, 25, and 65) in the United States today.

At age 45, we might think of the modal male as a full-time member of the labor force, as a husband and father, and as often active in his church and in community organizations. As a consequence of his work, he may well be a member of an occupational association. Through his job, his community, and his church membership he has acquired many and diverse friendships. He maintains such roles in his family of orientation as son, sibling, nephew; in addition, he plays the major roles of husband and father in his own family of procreation; and through marriage he has acquired new relationships to in-laws. At age 25, a young man has already entered many of the same major roles as those performed by the 45-year old. Yet, as compared with the middle-aged man, he may have lower-level jobs in the occupational structure (may indeed still be moving around from job to job); he is less likely to be married, to vote, to be a member of a voluntary association, or to attend church. At age 65, by contrast, the typical male no longer works. He is less likely than the younger man to have a living spouse. And, compared to the 45-year old, he is less likely to play certain minor roles, such as member of a voluntary association.

Some dimensions of difference Such sketches (although they refer to actual role occupancy rather than to abstract concepts of the roles available) begin to suggest some of the ways in which roles can differ by age strata. We shall illustrate such dimensions of difference by continuing our contemporary American example. One major dimension is the totality of age-appropriate roles: both the *repertoire*—that is, the number of different kinds —of roles, and the number of *openings* or positions of each kind. While it is difficult to generalize about numbers of openings, it appears in general that the repertoire is more limited in childhood, early adulthood, and old age than in the middle years.

Another dimension on which roles differ by age concerns the kinds of groups involved. Certain age strata play roles that are principally embedded in primary groups, thus tending in modern society to stress the expressive, rather than the instrumental functions. In childhood, a good many roles belong to primary groups; in adulthood, both primary and secondary relationships are important; while in extreme old age, primary group affiliations again tend to predominate. Clearly, instrumental activities are stressed in middle age.

Age strata differ also in the priority given to particular roles. Individuals do not invest their time or effort equally among the roles they play, and those roles requiring the greatest investments vary according to age. In childhood and adolescence, precedence tends to be accorded to the role of student; in maturity, to the work role for the man and to the roles of wife and mother for the woman; in old age, to leisure and to family roles.

Furthermore, roles appear to be more closely constrained by biological stage in early childhood and in old age than at other life stages. At these extremes, limitations in locomotion and other physical shortcomings affect both numbers and kinds of roles that can be performed.

Above all, there are important differences among age strata in the general social evaluation of the roles to be played. For example, valuation of work as a "calling" may lead to a denigration of retirement, or the preparatory aspects of the student role may lead to its devaluation as a subordinate status. Such differences in the social valuation of roles result in age-related inequalities of opportunities and rewards, a topic to which we shall return in later sections.

Role complexes   The roles open in the several strata vary not only in number and in kind but also in the complex ways in which they are interconnected. Certain types of connections [*as described in the discussion of friendship in Chapter 9 by Hess*] provide useful tools for analyzing many interesting questions about the age structure of roles (and also about the individuals of varying age who must cope with such role complexes, as discussed in the following section).

Certain roles are *fused* in the sense that one is contingent upon the other, so that both must be played (or not played) at the same time or life stage; and the nature and bases for fusion often differ among the role strata. Friendship roles are fused to such other age-related roles as worker or student. Roles in voluntary associations are often contingent upon other roles, as membership in occupational associations depends on being a worker, in the Parent Teacher Association depends on being a parent or teacher, or in school clubs depends on being a student. In the United States, the role of parent is normatively contingent upon having entered the marital role (an example of fusion based on norms rather than on purely situational factors). Whenever minor roles are contingent upon major ones, loss of these major roles—as among old people—can drastically reduce the total store of roles available. Roles can also affect one another by being *mutually exclusive.* Age-related examples are the roles of worker and retiree, spouse and widow, soldier and civilian. Or roles may be *complementary* to one another, each encompassing related, but different and noncompetitive, functions. Thus roles in peer groups complement family roles where the latter—as in adolescence or in the postparental stage—are under strain or in transition. Or, at appropriate life stages, roles in the polity and community may complement work roles, as the prestige or social contacts of the one may enhance performance of the other; or as one may compensate for activities and rewards not permitted by the other.

Changes and variabilities   The numbers and kinds of roles available at varying ages, and the complex interrelationships among them, change as society changes—just as they also vary under differing conditions when different societies or subpopulations are compared. Despite an abundance of specific illustrations, little systematic knowledge exists regarding historic trends in the age structure of roles. We might speculate, however, about the broad direction of such changes.

The process of functional differentiation characterizing social structure over several centuries has, through its interrelated consequences, profoundly altered the nature of age-specific roles along at least three lines. First, the mere proliferation of roles has undoubtedly increased the total repertoire available to all age strata. Second, transfers of functions among the various institutional spheres have transformed both the numbers and kinds of roles within each sphere, to which the age strata relate in diverse ways. And third, the elaboration—first, of childhood (Ariès [1960], 1962) and currently, of old age—as separate and lengthy stages of the life course suggests that the roles available in the social structure may be increasingly organized around age as an axis.

Some of the ways in which roles open to the several age strata can reflect historical change are exemplified by the occupational shifts accompanying economic and technological development. These trends have led to increases in the number of occupational roles in the whole society and also to changes in the types of roles and in the numbers of openings of each type. For example, in recent years both new occupations and many openings within these occupations have resulted from the introduction of computer technology, while in other occupations (glassblower, blacksmith, or railroad fireman) the number of openings has become miniscule. Such changes have had a differential impact on the age strata. The appearance of new occupations, often requiring new kinds of training, are likely to be initially more available to younger than to older workers. Declines in the number of openings per type of job, however, may affect younger and older workers equally, unless the older are given preference through seniority provisions. These changes are also likely to have an impact on other institutional spheres. For example, as job training is removed from the occupational system, it becomes concentrated in educational institutions, which are especially geared to the young.

Indeed, the complex interrelationships among the occupational, educational, kinship, and many other structures in modern society mean that changes in any one sphere tend to have repercussions in the others. Thus, the "professionalization" of former leisure activities such as science or social welfare has tended to deny these roles to the older age strata, despite the disproportionate amounts of leisure time at the disposal of the elderly. As another example, a new occupational role of "baby sitter," available primarily to adolescents and the old, may be viewed as emerging out of several trends including: redefinition of women's roles in the family, concomitant admission of large numbers of adult women to the labor force, separation of residence and place of work, and extension of childhood as a period of dependency requiring supervision and control.

Not only the numbers and kinds of roles but also the role complexes available to the several age strata (which tend to vary by sex, socioeconomic status, or cultural background) have changed markedly throughout history. For example, as recently as 1940 in the United States, the overlap in occupancy among major roles—marriage, work, or school—among young men aged 20–24 was considerably less pronounced than it was two decades later, as Table 10 · 1 suggests (Beresford and Rivlin, 1966). That it has been possible for male students to combine their student role with the roles of worker (at least part-time), husband, and father has undoubtedly been aided by such situational factors as increased availability of financial aids and by changes in the norms concerning the appropriateness of young wives' supporting their husbands. Normative pressures as well as situational constraints have so changed that certain roles are no longer mutually exclusive.[6] Three or four decades ago it was difficult for a woman to arrange her life so that she could perform effectively both in the labor force and as wife and mother; in many circles, such an undertaking was frowned upon, even when children were of school age (Parnes et al., 1969, pp. 56, 61, 64). Indeed, it might even be suggested that not only are the roles of wife, mother, and worker no longer mutually exclusive but that their combination is tending to become normatively prescribed. That is, rather than merely permitting young mothers to combine the roles of mother and worker, once their children have reached school age, it may be expected of them.

Thus many historical changes in the society (which we assume to be "given" within our model, as in Figure 1 · 2), have imposed differing constraints upon the age strata through their impact on the structure of roles.

AGE AS A CRITERION OF ROLE INCUMBENCY

Compare Chapter 12 · 3 regarding allocative processes

If age—a characteristic exhibited by individuals—is built into the structure of roles as a criterion governing occupancy or exclusion, in what manner does this come about? Through the allocative processes whereby individuals of the appropriate ages are assigned to roles, age criteria operate to affect *who*, and *how many* people, shall perform which roles and activities and shall receive the associated facilities and sanctions. The nature and effectiveness of the allocative mechanisms [*to be discussed in Chapter 12*] depend in part upon whether the age criteria are explicit or implicit.

Age, or some range of ages, may be employed directly as a standard for

---

[6] By contrast, other roles (as with the stricter division between work and leisure) have come to preclude one another.

TABLE 10 · 1 *Roles of young men and women, United States, 1940 and 1960*

Sex, age, year	Per cent enrolled in school or college	Per cent in labor force	Per cent married, spouse present[a]	Per cent head or wife of head of household
Males				
16–19				
1940	49.4	41.4	1.6	1.2
1960	65.8	50.0	3.6	3.4
20–21				
1940	12.4	83.5	13.8	10.3
1960	25.8	81.4	26.1	25.9
20–24				
1940	5.3	91.1	33.6	28.5
1960	15.1	89.4	52.0	51.9
25–34				
1940	NA	95,2	66.5	62.1
1960	6.5	94.9	77.4	80.1
Females				
16–19				
1940	47.7	24.6	12.9	9.2
1960	60.8	32.6	16.3	14.8
20–21				
1940	8.7	47.4	38.0	30.0
1960	16.6	48.3	52.1	52.3
22–24				
1940	2.4	43.5	55.5	47.3
1960	5.3	42.6	71.5	73.9
25–34				
1940	NA	32.9	73.3	67.3
1960	2.7	35.3	82.5	87.9

[a] Ratio of spouse present to total married estimated from broader age-groups, 1940, for ages under 25.
Source: Beresford and Rivlin, 1966, p. 252; adapted from U.S. Bureau of the Census: *Sixteenth Census of the United States; 1940, Population,* Vol. IV, Part 1, Tables 9, 11, 14, 24; *Census of Population 1960,* PC(2)-5A, Table 8, 9.

role entry and exit, or may operate indirectly through linkage with other criteria for role incumbency or with the aging or the cohort succession of the people involved.

Indirect age criteria   Criteria of role incumbency may be indirectly related to age in a number of ways. Some of these are tied to the *life course* and reflect differences among age strata due to social, psychological, or biological aging (as discussed in Section 2). For example, there are relatively few athletes in the older strata, not so much because criteria for exit are directly set, as because certain physical abilities are concentrated in the young. Widowhood is also indirectly related to the life course, because mortality of the spouse is higher at older ages. Or age differences in voter registration may reflect, in part, social differences by age in geographical mobility [*see Chapter 6 by Starr*]. In another instance, relatively few mothers with young children enter the labor force. Here the age boundaries for participation arise because childbearing is biologically bounded by age, and this indirect biological criterion becomes normatively defined: mothers of young children should not work.

Also tied to aging and indirectly creating differences among strata in role entrance or exit are those criteria that define some *interval of time* that must have elapsed prior to assumption of the role. Experience or duration of occupancy in some prior role is not infrequently a standard for assignment. Thus many school systems require twelve years of attendance before granting a high school diploma, effectively controlling age of entry into college. Pension agreements sometimes permit retirement, not at a specified age, but after a specified number of years of employment [*see Chapter* 5]. Customs of seniority in the United States Congress (established in 1910 in order to take away from the Speaker of the House the power of direct appointment) have ensured that committees are chaired by older Congressmen. Or, seniority provisions in union contracts can contribute to exclusion from the labor force, hence to unemployment, of workers in the youngest strata.

Frequently, indirect age criteria exercise their effect, not through aging, but through *cohort* processes. Cohort differences in size, composition, socialization, or experience may sometimes, by affecting the balance between supplies of roles and of role players, affect the opportunities for the various age strata in particular roles. The higher education of younger strata today, for example, appears to affect the modal ages for occupying various related roles.

Direct age criteria   Like the criteria that indirectly link age to the structure of roles, the direct imposition of chronological age or age boundaries in role assignment takes a variety of forms. Age standards for role incumbency are most evident when they are embodied in *formal* rules or explicit policies. Compulsory school attendance laws, the stipulation of minimum voting age in election laws, the age regulations of administrative bodies such as draft boards, the age of legal liability for various misdemeanors, the age policies of social work agencies in defining eligible clientele such as adoptive parents or narcotic addicts, the retirement age specified in contracts are all examples of formally established age criteria. By contrast, age standards may represent *informal* norms and beliefs about the kinds of roles or activities appropriate for people of various ages, or the expected age gap (relational age) between role-partners. Informal norms tend to be less specific than formal rules in setting age criteria, for people may have only vague notions of "too young," "too old," or the "right" age for certain activities, and the boundaries distinguishing these categories are not easily identifiable. Thus it is not clear at just what age an individual is "too old" to enter college, or to be sexually active, or to dance—though causal experience persuades that many such norms are operative and have strong influence on behavior.

Age standards for role incumbency, as with other social norms, imply varying degrees of obligation and may operate as *prescription* (or proscription) or merely as preference or *permission* for entering or relinquishing a role.[7] Thus some roles are characterized by a good deal of latitude in the application of age standards. Where such latitude exists, informal criteria may play an important part in shaping the scope of the age strata and the sharpness of the boundaries, even where precise minimum or maximum age boundaries have been legally established. Thus in the United States, most states have set minimum ages for marriage without parental consent. Yet the actual mean age of first marriage is higher than the established minimums. Among other factors,[8] informal beliefs about the appropriate age for marriage and about prior performance in other age-related roles, such as education or occupation, influence the actual age of entry into marital roles. Entry into some roles may also be delayed beyond the legal minimum age because of formal requirements or prior roles. For example, formal educational and training requirements for entry into specific occupations effectively increase age at first assuming the work role beyond the minimum at which an individual may leave school and obtain working papers.

Certain roles may involve prescribed ages for entry but permissive ages for exit, or the reverse. Persons may enter the labor force by a given age in most states but in many occupations they must leave by age 65. In contrast, children must go to school by a certain age (usually about 6) but they may leave at almost any age beyond the prescribed minimum (usually 16).

Normative versus factual criteria   These examples point to the further principle (suggested by Robert Merton) that not all age criteria, whether direct or indirect, are based on norms that specify appropriate or prescribed ages for role entry or exit. Some criteria may, instead, be factual. Factual criteria can arise from various situations and processes (including biological and demographic processes) that—without immediate reference to socially defined standards—result empirically in particular age patterns of role occupancy. Unlike normative criteria, which are aspects of the role structure, purely factual patterns refer to people in the age strata and constitute criteria only in the sense that a mode or average may be treated as a standard. However, many patterns that are initially factual often become embodied in the mores. For example, if in fact large numbers of young people marry at an early age, this situation may be translated into the "proper" age for marriage; or if in fact large proportions of older workers retire from the labor force,[9] the

[7] The reader will recognize that the "4 P's" employed here to classify age norms are those formulated by Robert Merton (1957, p. 133).

[8] One of these other factors appears to be the availability of role-partners.

[9] [*Compare the use of age criteria in the work force, Chapter 5 · 1 and 5 · 2.*]

modal retirement age may become the normatively expected age. Moreover, factual changes can produce changes in the normative criteria, as trends toward earlier ages of marriage or of retirement can mean a progressive lowering of the ages considered appropriate.

Criteria for exclusion It is important to note that an age criterion for role incumbency works in two ways: by defining the admission of certain age strata to specified roles, other strata are excluded, having been defined as *not* possessing the requisite characteristics for role performance. (Depending upon the reward values associated with the role in question, exclusion may be experienced as either deprivation or as fortunate escape.) Age criteria for socially desirable roles operate, then (if not as direct taboos) as residual definitions of incompetence and dependence.

Such invidious definitions may be reinforced by protective laws or special benefits. Note the many regulations and provisions associated with the status of the very young and very old in our society, apparently designed to minimize mistreatment or neglect: school lunch programs, reduced admission or transportation prices, guardianship laws, social security, or juvenile court procedures. Such provisions may in themselves call to public attention the relative deprivation of these strata.

Exclusion from one role through age limits may sometimes operate to ensure the competing claims of some other role. Thus children may be legally excluded from the labor market, not because they are incompetent to perform certain occupational activities, but because they are defined as needing a lengthy period of education instead.

Relational age Finally, age is also a relational criterion, affecting the relative ages deemed appropriate for the role-partners of people in particular age strata (see the interface between age strata and membership groups suggested in Figure 10 · 1 above). In this country, some typical expectations are that friends will be of the same age, that wives will be a few years younger than their husbands, or that siblings will be spaced two or three years apart.

There are thought-provoking differences among institutional spheres in the definitions of relational ages. In certain spheres, it appears that the age criteria (either normative or factual) for ego's role-partners vary with the age stratum to which ego himself belongs. In the educational system, for example, the youngest students have teachers who are older than they and peers who are of their own age; but older students, those in college and beyond, are likely to have fellow students whose ages range widely and to have many teachers who are close to themselves in age.[10] And to the extent that adult education becomes more pervasive, a situation similar to that in the work force [*see Chapter* 5 · 5] may arise, where older students face teachers younger than

[10] [*See Chapter* 12 · 2 *for discussion of the implications of this situation.*]

they. In other spheres, such as the family, no such reversals can occur; although the age gap between parents and offspring is by no means fixed (except for a given parent-child dyad), the offspring cannot be biologically older than his natural parents.[11]

Changes and variability   No mere list of examples can begin to suggest the variability in such age criteria through history, across societies, and among subpopulations within societies. For example, periods of war or revolution can extend the age-scope of both the military and the economic arms of a society, so that young children and aged men and women serve as soldiers or as workers.

Even roles seemingly linked to biology show wide variation. Contraceptive techniques can terminate the childbearing years long before the age of menopause. Entry into marriage often bears little relationship to the biological age of puberty. In the United States, women typically marry younger than men, and there was a tendency over several decades (up to the 1960's) for the age of marriage to decline (Glick and Parke, 1965, pp. 188–196; United States Bureau of the Census, March 25, 1970). The norms of many different cultures range from those permitting child marriage to those requiring delay until the man has, for example, become an independent owner of his own farm. Relational age criteria also vary. If, in the contemporary United States, "May-December" marriages are frowned upon, as are marriages where the husband is more than a few years younger than his wife, many other societies held quite different views on the appropriate ages of husband and wife. Especially where there are plural marriages, husbands may be far older than wives. And Goode (1963, p. 287) cites certain regions in pre-Communist China where the typical pattern was for the wife to be as much as 8 or 9 years older than her husband.

Apart from the differences in relational age criteria among strata at a given time, there are many changes and variations over time. During the twentieth century in the United States, for example, we note a trend toward "age polarization" within the nuclear family: the constriction in the period of childbearing coupled with the smaller number of children counterposes a set of similar-aged children against the older generation of father and mother whose ages have come increasingly closer together over the same period of time.[12] Such changes have far flung implications for the traditional patterns of socialization of younger by older siblings, or for the potential coalition of children against parents.

---

[11] While the chronological differences in age between a parent and his child remain constant over the life course, the power relations may shift.

[12] Conversely, the constriction of the childbearing years means that the parents of a particular cohort of children may now be more nearly similar in age than in an earlier period.

The way age operates as a criterion for entering or leaving a role affects both the scope of the age strata and the boundaries between any two strata. When the role structure is viewed in cross section, as in Figure 10 · 1, each age stratum can be imagined as a band that is more or less broad in scope (from age 10 to 20, for example, or from age 10 to 11). Also the boundaries separating strata can encompass either a brief or a protracted span of time.

Age scope of strata   At any given time and place, the number of years contained in an age stratum varies greatly by roles and by institutional spheres. Thus most men currently in the occupational role are in a broad stratum roughly between age 17 and age 65 (or less), in contrast to the far narrower age-scope of the student role or the military role. *Within* particular roles, too, there are strata of differing scope, as the student role is age-graded by single years; or the marital role is stratified into age-related categories (such as preparental, parental, postparental) of unequal extent.[13]

Not only are there variations among institutional spheres, but the age-scope of the strata changes at different times and under different conditions. For example, the student role has increased in scope over the past century and, according to Parsons and Platt in Chapter 7, we are now witnessing the emergence of a new stratum, that of "studentry." And within the modern family, if the stratum of jointly surviving husbands and wives has been widening, the scope of the childrearing stage appears to have been narrowing.

Why the scope of life stages in various spheres changes can again be explained only by the full complexity of history. The changes within the family life have been associated with such factors as greater longevity, independent housing, or the contraction of the childbearing phase. The extension of student years is undoubtedly related both to upgrading of the roles to be learned and the productivity of an economy that can operate without the labor of the young. But the changes in scope of the age strata have important implications for the structure of society and for the particular kinds and durations of experience to which people are exposed.

Strata boundaries   The transfer from one stratum to the next can be either *sharp* or *gradual,* sometimes taking place by stages. Exit from work can occur through tapering off [*see Chapter 5*], or it can consist of a complete break between the last full day of work and the first full day of complete retirement. Marital rites can be performed in a few moments or they can extend over long periods—perhaps decided while the spouses-to-be are still children, negotiated over a period of years, and finally consummated many years later through some official feast or marriage ceremony (Van Gennep [1908], 1960).

[13] [*For further examples, compare Chapter 12 · 3.*]

Quite apart from the span of time involved, boundaries at different stages and under different sociotemporal conditions can be *flexible* or *rigid*, depending upon how the age criteria define them. Flexibility in age criteria can, for example, provide organizations with maneuverability in adapting to changing needs or supplies of manpower at particular ages; or it can give individuals greater freedom of choice than permitted under rigid standards.

Consistency of boundaries   A compelling problem is presented by the fact that, in modern societies, complexes of roles that are largely inhabited by persons of like age are often defined at the boundaries by inconsistent age criteria. For example, the legal age requirements denoting entrance into adulthood may vary by several years for criminal liability, drinking, driving, marriage, school-leaving, voting, draft eligibility (or liability, as the case may be), residence outside the parental household, or welfare eligibility. Such age status inconsistency (parallel in some respects to "class-status inconsistency") affects both the structure of roles and the role-incumbents (who will be discussed in Section 2).

By contrast, the paradigmatic case (reportedly approximated by a few preliterate tribes) is the society in which the age boundaries of all the major roles within an age stratum coincide. Eisenstadt (1956, pp. 63 ff.) has described the example of the Nandi, a relatively undifferentiated tribe in Kenya with a societal-wide system of age sets. Among the Nandi, each male belongs to one of the seven age sets: two groups of boys, one of warriors, and four of elders. Membership in an age set is a key indicator of a person's status, and most of the important roles are allocated and regulated through these sets.

Within modern differentiated societies, there are certainly no "age grades" strictly analogous to this simple model, where the stratum involves the total range of age-graded roles and there are no boundary inconsistencies (see, e.g., Gulliver, 1968, p. 157). To what extent, then, can an age stratum today be thought of as an *age status*? Social structure is ordinarily not so tightly elaborated and differentiated that it consists entirely of roles. For example, some activities and normative expectations are age-allocated but are not tied to specific roles, such as permission to wear cosmetics at age 13, to drive a car at 17, or attend "adult" movies at 18, to drink alcoholic beverages at 21. Various consumer products (furniture, toys, or clothing) are specifically designed for people of particular ages, attesting to the notion that such terms as "young," "middle-aged," "old," "adult," or "adolescent" have some intrinsic meaning in themselves. Moreover, the notion of age as a generalized status is supported by the fact that various behaviors are popularly viewed as age-*in*appropriate (such as first marriage or working at an entry-level job at the age of 50 or 60). Such situations suggest an additional concept, which we call *"age incongruity."* This concept, referring to violation of age-related expectations or of age criteria for role incumbency, will be useful for examining several types of strain in role relationships or for considering inconsistencies between age-related expectations and capacities for performance (to be discussed in Sections 3 and 4). For, apart from specific roles, people are called upon to "act their age," a colloquial reminder that norms governing a general age status may be invoked to constrain behavior.

Such generalized age expectations, though not limited to particular roles, often seem to derive from specific roles that are prepotent within a role complex. Thus the emergence of adolescence as a distinct status in most industrialized countries is apparently tied to prolonged schooling and delay of entry into the work force; in an earlier period, childhood was followed directly by adulthood. Similarly the fact that among south Irish peasants the term "boy" is often used for males who would be considered adults in other countries is related to the relatively late age at which they become landowners or get married (see Arensberg [1937], 1950). Or women with grown children may be marked as middle-aged, and be expected to conduct themselves accordingly, regardless of their chronological age.

Age and other bases of stratification   Since age is rarely the only basis for stratification or differentiation in the social structure, two questions arise that might greatly broaden the scope of conventional sociological inquiry.

First, how is age related, in any given society, with other bases of stratification? Age and sex, according to Gulliver (1968, p. 157), appear to be the only two reference points that are universally used for ascription in all societies. Parsons (1961) describes several societies, including some in Western Europe in the eighteenth and nineteenth centuries, where age-based superiority in kinship tended to coincide with superiority on three other major bases of social structure (political power, religion-based values, and control of economic resources). In the United States today, however, there may be no such unitary elite and correlations between age divisions and other divisions may be changing. In the United States, for example, where education is highly correlated with age, and education itself is achieving pre-eminence among the distinguishing criteria of social class (Parsons, 1961, p. 262), we may expect increasing convergence of age stratification with class stratification. In this country, too, entry into marital status is increasingly based upon age rather than upon economic considerations or intrafamily dependency. On ideological grounds, age (or seniority) as a direct, normative criterion may be used for a wider variety of roles than social class, which is often proscribed as a basis for allocation. However, the incipient tendencies against using age as a discriminatory factor in hiring suggests that age, like other ascriptive characteristics, may be in the process of becoming included among proscribed criteria.

A second question concerns the conditions under which age may predominate over other role criteria as a basis of stratification. The outstanding importance of age emerges clearly in kinship-regulated societies since age is built into the structure of generations. For example, Eisenstadt (1956, pp. 51 and passim) develops an elaborate theory showing how the significance of age, as an ascriptive phenomenon organizing diffuse role relations, increases to the degree that these characteristics accord with the general value system of the particular society. In other types of societies, as where the predominant norms stress achievement, Eisenstadt shows how age is a key criterion for a particular stratum—that of adolescence—where individuals must move from the diffuse, ascriptive context of the family to the universalistic adult world.

Such theories, which merit wider testing over time and place, might provide clues to still a third question: Under what circumstances does one age stratum hold sway over other age strata? In agrarian societies, the old are reported to have held the greatest power and influence; in today's society, hegemony seems to inhere in late middle age; for the future, it may be that the young will effectively assert themselves. But this question leads to our next topic, that of inequalities among age strata.

INEQUALITIES AMONG STRATA

So far the discussion has focused on the numbers and kinds of roles in the age structure (element 1 in our conceptual model), indicating—but not stressing—the fact that the opportunities associated with many roles produce inequalities by age. We have noted that roles, with varied goals and norms, are differentially valued by society. And it is the interlocking between the normative expectations of particular roles and the dominant values of the society that influences the nature and the amount of rewards conferred upon role players—either in money, approval, or prestige. If, for example, the roles open to people in their middle years in the United States today seem more consonant than old-age roles with the achievement values of contemporary society (McClelland, 1961), these roles are thereby more highly rewarded than those allocated to either the young or old.

Age affects not only who may have opportunities to play certain roles, but also how the activities associated with these roles are to be performed and with what rewards. Let us, then, turn to the ways in which age can enter into the role *expectations,* into the *facilities* for performance, and into the *sanctions* (rewards and punishments) for meeting these expectations—element 4 in our conceptual model. The meaning we shall attach to these terms is exemplified in the role of student in school, a role which in American society is explicitly age-related. In each school grade, comprising students who are approximately similar in age, expectations for performance specify the knowledge and skills to be mastered, and conformity to these expectations is regularly tested and evaluated. Facilities are provided in the form of educational materials like textbooks, laboratory exercises, or lectures; and these materials are explained and interpreted by teachers whose experience and knowledge are presumably superior to the student's. The training materials themselves and the complexity of the subject matter are ordered according to grade level. Finally, contingent upon meeting the stated expectations, rewards are bestowed in terms of evaluative "marks" and promotion to the next higher grade.

Age-related expectations   Beyond this student example, the normative expectations attached to various roles differ markedly among the age strata. Not all roles are like that of student in requiring increasingly higher levels of achievement in the successively older age strata. Indeed, in certain roles the expectations may be less stringent for successively older strata, as where the standards for work performance of older workers in some occupations are subtly defined as inferior to standards set for younger workers. In still other institutional spheres the age-related expectations differ only in kind, with no necessary age-ranking of performance standards. For example, the obligations of marriage partners change with the advent of children, with the number and the ages of the children, and with the departure of the last child from home;[14] or heterosexual friendships tend to be normatively proscribed among young children, but not among adolescents. Other roles have few age-specific differences in expectations, or none at all, once eligibility for the role has been established. Beyond the stipulated voting age, for example, the norms for citizens of all ages tend to be alike. Similarly, many blue-collar jobs involve no graded expectations among mature workers; and even occupations considered to be "careers" rarely prescribe set numbers of age divisions or precise ages for particular norms of performance [*see Chapter 5*]. There are other instances in which errors or deviance may be tolerated at early stages in a role but not at later stages, as the poor performance of a housewife may be accepted as long as she is young, or the pranks of students may be more permissible than similar behavior among adults.[15]

Roles vary too in the clarity with which age expectations for role performance are stated. In contrast to the student role, where the performance criteria at each age are openly embodied in tests and other formal requirements, expectations for many other roles are indirectly and obscurely communicated (hence not always fully understood). Often the only clues to the different kinds of behavior expected at different ages come from variations in the attendant facilities or rewards—as when the same performances that receive positive sanctions at one life stage receive negative sanctions at another. In the occupational role, for example, an older worker may lack approbation—not because

[14] The relationship of age to situational role-specification is discussed by Parsons (1951, pp. 236–242).

[15] Compare Parsons' discussion (1951, pp. 305 ff.) of youth culture as institutionalized deviance.

his performance is any less adequate than that for which he was previously rewarded—but because, although he is still doing the "same old thing," he is threatened with replacement by younger workers. Or parents may be approved for nurturant treatment of their very young childen, but disapproved if they fail to teach independence to these same children at the stage of adolescence.

Relational age, or the relative ages of an individual and his role-partners, can also affect the norms (as well as the rewards) governing the relationship. For example, as pointed out in Chapter 9 by Hess, the age-similarity on which many friendships are based is closely associated with the anticipation that friends have interests or qualities in common.[16]

Age-related facilities and rewards Pronounced as the age differences are in expectations, it is the differences in facilities and rewards that can produce inequalities among the strata. In various respects, certain strata are comparatively deprived of those positive sanctions that can give a sense of purpose and accomplishment, of the resources for learning and performing, or of the socializing agents who can act on behalf of society to transmit its expectations and its rewards. Such deprivations are especially likely to seem illegitimate when they are incompatible with institutionalized expectations.

In the political role, for example, although the voting expectations as embodied in written statutes may be the same for all strata beyond the minimum age of voting eligibility, the facilities for performing as a voter are far from equally distributed by age, as Chapter 4 by Foner has made clear. Young people confront many obstacles to voting: stiff residency requirements in the face of high residential mobility, inconveniences of absentee ballots for those in the army or away at school, or literacy tests. Such impediments to voter participation are imposed especially upon the young, while older adults face fewer such obstacles.

In the occupational realm, to take another instance, a person over 65 not only has comparatively small chance of retaining his job or acquiring a new one [as described in Chapter 5], but is also afforded few societal supports in the not-yet-crystallized role of retiree. Here he may suffer from lack of positively valued and clearly defined goals, from a societal indifference that offers little incentive for performance, and from a paucity of facilities for anticipatory learning or of aids to role performance. Such inadequacies can have their negative consequences for some individuals: for example, retired older people, as compared with those of the same age who are still working, seem more likely to feel old or to have low morale (even among people with similar levels of health and socioeconomic status). (See Volume I, Chapters 13 · 10 and 15 · 4; but see also Volume I, Chapter 18 · C · 4.)

[16] For age-homophily in friendship, see Volume I, Chapter 24 · 4 · a; compare the discussion of homophily in Lazarsfeld and Merton (1954, pp. 23–24).

Marital roles too exhibit instances of age-related deficiencies. Little incentive is provided young women in the United States today for prior learning of the role of housewife, and few facilities have been available in past decades for learning the role of sexual partner. Such lacks may be related to a greater sense of housewifely inadequacy among younger than among older women, or (to the extent that inhibitions of premarital sexual activity persist) to a long and difficult period of sexual adjustment among young married couples. And even the student role displays certain age inequalities. Older students in college or in graduate school, unlike younger students in high school, often have less than the full attention of their teachers, because teachers in college divide their time between instruction and research.

Changes and variability Such examples of age inequalities in role-expectations and rewards, while drawn largely from the United States today, appear in diverse forms in other cultures as well. Moreover, in any one society, such inequalities shift over time as concomitants of social change. Indeed, the process of social change can be so rapid that, as Parsons once put it (1951, p. 242), "even over the span of active adult life . . . the [role] expectations of an early period must be considerably readjusted to meet the requirements of a later one." Indeed, many of the examples of age inequality we have just cited may be attributable to societal failures to adapt to changing conditions. The vague expectations and deficient rewards for retirees, for example, accrue in part from the lag between social norms and the massive displacement of men from the labor force. Possibly, the statutory constraints on youthful participation in voting may also be regarded as vestiges of laws that were initially fashioned to meet the needs of an earlier era.

In general, then, no society simply provides individuals of different ages with an equal array of roles, defining these roles clearly, and providing adequate facilities and rewards to motivate the expected performances. Instead, while the nature of the differences vary from time to time and from place to place, the age strata are unequal both in the roles available and in the facilities and rewards for role performance.

2 Age strata in the population

How does this changing age structure of roles within a given society influence the social behavior and attitudes of the people who perform these roles?[17] Our conceptual model points to a clear correspondence between the role structure and the age strata within the population. We think of the members of any given society (as "actors" engaged in social activities) as divided into strata according to their age. These strata comprise varying num-

[17] Compare Mannheim ([1928], 1952) who addresses this question.

bers and kinds of people (element 1 in the model), who as individuals differ in their capacities, motivations, and strategies for performance in social roles (element 2). At any given period of time, people in different age strata must live as members of the society, finding their place in relation to others who may be similar or different in age, and making choices among whatever opportunities are available to them. And over time, as we have seen, the age strata of young, middle-aged, and old persons persist within the macrocosm of the changing population and the changing structure of roles, although the particular individuals in any stratum are continuously moving on and being replaced.

But how does it come about that, within a given society at any given time, individuals display diverse capacities, motivations, and performance patterns *by virtue of being located in different age strata?*

DIMENSIONS OF TIME

The answer to this question involves the two distinct dimensions of time outlined in Chapter 1 · 3: a life-course dimension and an historical dimension. These two dimensions can be thought of as the special coordinates for locating individuals in the age structure of society. On the first dimension, individuals at the *same* stage of the *life course* have much in common. They tend to be alike in biological development, in the kinds of roles they have experienced (such as worker, spouse, parent of dependent child), and in the sheer number of years behind and potential years ahead. People at *different* life-course stages tend to differ in these very respects. The rough index of this life-course dimension is years of chronological age, which is of interest to us, not intrinsically, but only because it can serve as an approximate indicant of personal (that is biological, psychological, and social) experience—and this experience carries with it varying probabilities of behavior and attitudes. This life-course dimension is the familiar one, which includes the age-related organic changes affecting physical and mental functioning, and which links the biological and the social sciences.

But a second time dimension for locating an individual in the age strata also affects his probability of behaving or thinking in particular ways. This dimension refers to the *period of history* in which he lives. People who were born at the *same* time (a cohort) share a common historical and environmental past, present, and future. People who were born at *different* times (different cohorts) have lived through different intervals of history. Thus any individual —just as he might be ethnocentric—is almost certainly (to coin a much-needed new term) *"cohort-centric."* That is, he views his own stage of life from the unique point of historical time at which he himself is standing. The rough index of this historical (or environmental) dimension is the date, or the calendar year; although here again our concern is not with dates themselves, but with the particular sociocultural and environmental events, conditions, and changes to which the individual is exposed at particular periods.

It comes as no surprise, then, that each of the age strata has its own *distinctive subculture*. Thus a cross-sectional view of society shows, for myriad characteristics, patterns that are closely related to age. In our own society today, we are well aware of the differences among young, middle-aged, and old in labor force participation, consumer behavior, leisure-time activities, marital status, religious behavior, education, nativity, fertility, childrearing practices, political attitudes—to name only a few. Such age-related subcultures differ from time to time and from place to place, as all the age strata in a society display differences (or similarities) in behavior and attitudes on these two dimensions of life course and history.

This section will examine some of the questions posed by the existence of these age-related subcultures. It will describe the linkages between these subcultures and the demographic and organic aspects of the people involved, note the importance of experience as a critical aspect of the life-course dimension, indicate certain problems encountered by individuals as they confront the role structure, and illustrate the strata differences in individual response to such problems.

DEMOGRAPHIC AND ORGANIC BASES

Fundamental to an understanding of the age strata of the population are the underlying demographic and organic bases. On the one hand, these bases set limits, respectively, to the changing numbers and kinds of people available to play roles, and to the individual capacities for role performance. On the other hand, both the demographic character of the population and the physical state of its members have societal antecedents as well as consequences. Procreation is subject to diverse social controls, ranging from infanticide and abortion to regulation of the age of marriage, restrictions on sexuality, and modern methods of contraception (see, e.g., Davis and Blake, 1956). And both health and mortality are conditioned by such social factors as standard of living, education, and advances in medicine and public health.

The demographic base[18] The demographic changes that characterize Western civilization, apparently unparalleled in human history, have profound societal implications. In the United States (see Figure 10 · 2), as in most Western nations, there have been dramatic alterations in the *size* of the population, affecting the *distribution* of people among age strata and, as mortality rates decline, the *expectation of life*. The current age structure (the product of birth, death, and migration rates in the past) in economically advanced

[18] See Volume I, Chapter 2. [*Compare Chapter 2 · 1 and Figure 2 · 2 in the present volume.*]

FIGURE 10 · 2   *Distribution of United States population by age strata,*
1880–1970

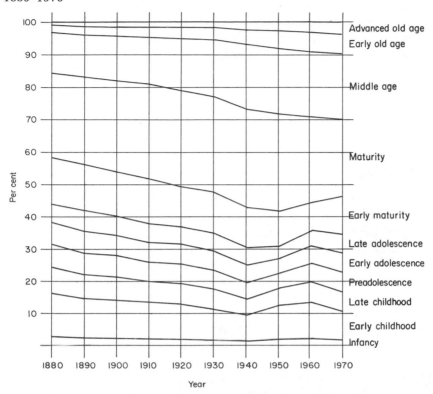

Source: Data for **1880 to 1950** from **Bogue, 1959, pp. 96–97;** compiled from 1950 Census of Population, Vol. II, Part 1, Table 98. Data for 1960 from 1960 Census of Population, Vol. I, Part 1, p. 148. Data for 1970 from Current Population Reports, Population Estimates and Projections, Series P-25, No. 448, Aug. 6, 1970, p. 19 (Series C projection).

countries, as compared with the less advanced, comprises comparatively low proportions of children under 15 (about one-fifth to one-fourth of the total population), about two-thirds in the 15–64 year age range, and comparatively large proportions (from 8 to 12 per cent) in the stratum aged 65 and over (Mayer, 1968, p. 365). By contrast, the less industrially advanced countries have far larger proportions of children, while only 3 or 4 per cent of the population are old people 65 and over.

The long-term tendency for a population to "age," characteristic of industrialized societies generally, has resulted (apart from the baby boom following World War II) from major declines in fertility. These declines, by markedly reducing the percentage of children, initially raise the percentage of persons of working age and later the percentage of the elderly.[19] Eventually declining fertility reduces the broad base of mature individuals that have been available in the middle strata as potential parents or workers.

Not only have there been changes in the West in the numbers and proportions of people in the several age strata, but the *composition* has also been changing. Mortality rates generally, save for underdeveloped areas where maternal deaths are common, are higher at all ages for males than for females.[20] Although at birth there are more males than females, by old age there is typically an excess of females over males. In the United States this discrepancy has been widening over the past several decades, as life expectancy has increased more rapidly for females than for males, so that there are now only about 73 men for every 100 women in the category of people 75 and over.

Other important compositional differences among the age strata reflect changing patterns of migration. In the United States, the proportion of foreign-born is highest among older people (19 per cent of those 65 and over in 1960 compared with 5 per cent for the country as a whole). Because of the restrictive immigration laws after 1920, the proportion of foreign-born is decreasing rapidly as the early immigrants die. Internal migration, since it is confined largely to young adults, tends to deplete their numbers in the place of origin, especially the rural areas, while increasing their numbers in the new destinations, especially in the suburbs [*see Chapter 6 by Starr*].

The secular declines in mortality (and the consequent increase in the expectation of life), have benefited the young primarily, but have also improved the chances for many people of surviving into old age. The change is not in the *span* of human life (the ultimate length of life attainable by a member of the human species), but in the proportion of people who outlive the ills of infancy, who escape maternal deaths and the other risks of young adulthood, and who thus reach the higher limits of the life span. The average lifetime in ancient Rome or medieval Europe is esimated at 20 to 30 years. In the United States, as in several Western countries, a man born in the middle of the last century could look forward to four decades of life; today a man can expect to live well into his 60's, a woman into her 70's. Death is no longer

[19] In the United States, the proportions of the population who are 65 and over, according to several series of projections that use differing assumptions as to fertility, will continue to rise over the next several decades. However, there will be a temporary hiatus in this rise near the turn of the twenty-first century, as the small cohort born during the Depression reaches old age. United States Bureau of the Census (August 6, 1970).

[20] The persistent tendency for females to outlive males suggests a biological (in addition to a social and environmental) relationship between sex and longevity. Lower mortality rates for females than for males have been observed under controlled sociocultural conditions (as in religious orders removed from the strains of ordinary living), in fetal life (where male stillbirths outnumber female), and even among certain animal species. See Volume I, Chapter 9 · 1 · c.

an adventitious, but a normal, event (Parsons and Lidz, 1967; John Riley, 1968). And individuals can prepare to play the full succession of roles throughout the age strata.

The organic base   While the size and composition of the population circumscribe the supply of personnel available to perform social roles, physiological processes set certain constraints on the performance capacities that distinguish old people from young people (see Volume I, Part Two). The age structure of the society is fundamentally affected by biology not only through the succession of births and deaths but also because individuals at different stages of life show important differences in physical structure and function. Of course, it would be utterly fallacious to assume that all age-specific physical characteristics are necessarily reflective of a biological, or even a social, process of aging. Nevertheless, individuals[21] in the several age strata at a given time display distinct differences in health and physical functioning that affect their social adjustment and the contributions they can make to society.

Cross-sectional views of the age strata show that older people are generally in poorer health than the young. Public health experts assert that age is more highly associated than other factors with the variations in most diseases (MacMahon et al., 1960, p. 86). To be sure, the incidence of acute illnesses declines from infancy to old age; but there are increases in chronic conditions (in such impairments as failing vision or hearing and—beyond age 50—in such diseases as rheumatism and arthritis, heart disease and high blood pressure).[22] By age 65 in the United States, for example, some four out of five persons have at least one chronic condition. Thus, except for a peak in childhood, there are increases by age in the number of days spent in restricted activity or in bed.

Physical conditions that demarcate the age strata are related not only to health but also to behavior—though the causal linkages are by no means clear. For example, older people, when compared with younger people, are more likely to show deficits in sensory and perceptual skills, in muscular strength, in the ability to react quickly, in complex sensorimotor coordination (such as that required in driving a car), and, among persons over 60, in memory, learning, and various aspects of intellectual functioning. There are also declines from adolescence to old age for both men and women in sexual activity, though this capacity persists at least into the 70's or 80's.

Unfortunately, there is little information about trends over time in health, physical functioning, or the associated changes in behavior. For the population as a whole, to be sure, the rising proportions of older people point to the likelihood of increasing prevalence of the chronic conditions associated with

[21] There are, of course, wide variations among particular individuals within each stratum.
[22] The increase with age of chronic conditions, particularly those that are irreversible, is another instance of our general principle of accumulation. [*Compare Chapter 2 · 2 · B.*]

middle and later life; indeed, there have been increases over the century in death rates resulting from heart disease or cancer. But it is uncertain whether individuals of a given age today are healthier than individuals of the same age in the past. Medical advance may have improved their physical condition, or it may, by interfering with the principle of survival of the fittest, have yielded a larger but less hardy population.

One example of probable historical changes in age-related behavior can be gleaned from two sets of psychological studies of performance on intelligence tests. First, when age strata are compared at a single time (through cross-sectional studies), intelligence reaches a peak among people in their late teens or early 20's and then declines with age in the older strata—a finding of considerable significance for macroscopic understanding of the society.[23] A second set of studies, which trace individuals longitudinally over the life course, have begun to suggest quite a different pattern, which does not show the rapid decline after the early 20's. Why the difference in the two sets of results? A likely interpretation is in terms of the long-term upward trend in education that has been associated with historical change. Intelligence test performance is highly correlated with educational level, and education sets older cohorts sharply below younger cohorts.

This example points to the difficulties, as well as to the importance, of studying the social and historical conditions under which organic properties of individuals may indeed set limits to their performance.

Societal implications   However indeterminate the constraints set by demographic and organic processes, the differences among age strata associated with these processes can have major societal consequences. As one example, consider a change in the age distribution of the population alone (even if there were no change in physically based capacities). A society with a rising proportion of young people may be expected to change in its overall outlook, its style of life, or its crime rate—in ways quite different from another society marked primarily by rising proportions of old people (compare Kiser, 1962, p. 18; see also Chapter 2 · 4).

Or consider just a few of the social repercussions of our previously noted point: that the rising numbers of proportions of old people in the population mean that more and more persons each year are subject to the chronic ills and disabilities associated with old age (see especially Volume II, Chapter 8 by Madge; and Volume I, Chapter 6). In terms of medical care, for example, not only are more physicians and nurses required, but the character of their practice is shifting to a greater focus on the chronic ailments and disabilities associated with senescence. In terms of housing, there is a patent need for design of dwellings that will provide for the comfort, safety, and convenience

[23] To presume that such differences are due to the process of aging would, in this instance, constitute a "life-course fallacy," as described in Chapter 2.

of the elderly and infirm. In terms of community facilities, old people failing in health and vigor are especially dependent upon nearby facilities like stores, buses, out-patient medical services, churches, or recreational activities. In terms of institutional care, appropriate hospitals, nursing homes, or homes for the aged must be provided for those older people no longer able to manage in their own homes. Without regard to such further concomitants as the financial burdens or the demands on relatives and neighbors, the example is sufficient to stress the crucial connections between the age strata in society and their demographic and organic bases.

EXPERIENCE: PAST AND FUTURE

Apart from these demographic and biological linkages—difficult as they are to delimit and to evaluate—how does the changing social structure operate to shape capacities and to motivate performances? In the society as a whole, as Robert Merton, for example, puts it, "Structure constrains individuals variously situated within it to develop cultural emphases, social behavior patterns, and psychological bents" (1957, p. 123). But how does age, as a social phenomenon, enter into these constraints? Let us start by outlining the life-course aspects of this question, before examining the role structure as a whole. Let us inquire into the effects on the age strata of the differing sequences of social roles to which individuals in the respective strata must accommodate. For the age patterns of many characteristics derive from similarities or dissimilarities among strata in actual past experience and potential for experience in the future.

Types of experience Even when experience in a single type of role, such as work, is considered, age strata differ in the extent to which members employed have been farmers, are white-collar workers, or are in large-scale bureaucratic organizations as compared to small independent businesses. Such divergent experiences can engender age-related work attitudes, like willingness to take risks or to bear responsibility (see, e.g., Miller and Swanson, 1958; Merton, 1957, pp. 195–296). Moreover, different work experiences emphasize distinctive skills, such as the ability to get along with people rather than to manipulate things.

Age strata differ also in past socialization. The divergent norms and attitudes underlying this socialization have dissimilar consequences for how—or even whether—they perform certain roles. For example, people of different ages often evaluate rewards differently, so that some seek in their work a sense of personal fulfillment, while others are seeking financial return. Or, when personal problems arise, age can influence the source of help they choose—whether family, clergy, or professional services, for example. Moreover, the importance of formal education, which cannot be too often recapitulated, distinguishes age strata through its impact on knowledge, skills, and attitudes. In terms of formal schooling, only 17 per cent of those now aged 25–29 in the United States have had as little as 8 years compared with 72 per cent among older people 75 and over. There are strata differences also in the recency of this education, and in its quality as reflected in the number and content of subjects taught and in the teaching methods. The "new math" is an example of a teaching method to which age strata have been selectively exposed. But even if the duration and the content of education had been substantially the same for all the age strata, the recency of education among the young serves to differentiate them from older people who had more time in which to forget.

Duration of experience   Individuals in the several age strata tend also to differ in the length of time in which they have been exposed to various events and have filled various roles. Thus the concept of *duration* or *accumulation of experience* is a central principle of the sociology of age. The older a person is, the longer he has had to store up acquired knowledge and a repertoire of internalized role relationships. In some instances, he may have learned to abstract from his many specific experiences; to develop a consistent, general orientation to his world; and to incorporate an extensive inner forum (to use Mead's term) for assessing the expectations of others. He may have learned how to use his wider experience to reconcile specific norms with larger value systems and to resolve role conflicts. Indeed, insofar as the personal ambitions of the eldest members are no longer at stake and they can afford to take the larger view, they may be especially equipped to approach problems in terms of long-run implications for society.[24]

Duration in particular roles can have numerous implications for the way a person performs a role or even whether he is permitted to occupy certain roles at all. Why is it that employers so often seek experienced workers to fill job vacancies?[25] Here experience is viewed as enhancing the caliber of role performance. In other roles, as in marriage according to some reports (Blood and Wolfe, 1960, p. 264), too long an experience together may sometimes impair the capacities of role-partners to bring freshness and excitement to the relationship. Duration in one role can also influence opportunities to perform in related roles; for example, the longer the duration of residence in a community, the greater the number of neighborhood friends older people are likely to have [*see Chapter 6 by Starr*].

Finally, there may be a tendency for duration in a socially valued role to increase *commitment*[26] to it. Since duration gives opportunity for repeated or extended performances, it can increase emotional investment in such perform-

---

[24] This idea has been suggested in Parsons (1960, pp. 171 ff.).

[25] See the discussion, for example, in *The Wall Street Journal* (November 2, 1970).

[26] Becker (1960); Kanter (1968). This tendency does not apply, of course, to roles in which the individual is not motivated to invest himself, such as a hated job or being an "inmate."

ances as long as these are rewarded, thereby adding to the likelihood that the associated attitudes will become set. At work, duration may militate against innovation. In politics, the longer a person thinks of himself as belonging to a political party, the stronger his attachment to it becomes [see *Chapter 4 by Foner*]. Thus, relatively long duration in a role can have both negative and positive consequences for the individual and society.

The future potential Age strata differ not only in past experience but in future time remaining. A few in the oldest stratum can succeed to such roles as chairman of the board. In general, however, the number of years to which a man can realistically look forward influences the risks he is willing to take and the further investment he is likely to make. For example, older men are less likely than younger ones to feel they can go farther in their present line of work, and they evince less interest in continuing occupational training (cf. Volume I, Chapter 5 · 4). To be sure, such attitudes (often sober assessments of situations controlled by the "Peter principle" that each man rises only to the level of his incompetence) might change if older men's chances of actually going farther were improved (see Peter and Hull, 1969).

In sum, many characteristics of the age strata are socially structured via the role sequences along the life-course dimension. Life-course patterns themselves, and cohort differences in these patterns, will be treated in detail in Chapters 11 and 12. However, it is only by viewing these differing cohort patterns in cross section that we can understand the societal age strata at particular periods of time.

SOCIAL-STRUCTURAL BASES

If the role structure and its changes can influence the characteristics of each age stratum on the life-course dimension, they can also affect all the age strata simultaneously on the dimension of historical time. Society as a whole, and its shifting roles, can be imagined as a web through which individuals of various ages are passing. And at any historic moment, this web traverses the entire population, regardless of age.[27] Thus many aspects of the role structure —differences among strata in the number and complexity of roles, problems posed by inconsistency of boundaries between strata, or discontinuities between roles in contiguous strata—all help to shape the capacities, motivations, and performances of individuals who though differing in age, all coexist within the same society.[28]

Number and complexity of roles As the roles open to the several strata vary in number and in the complexity of their interconnections, how does the

[27] [*Compare the discussion of cohort effects versus period effects in Chapter 2, Section 4.*]

[28] [*Many of the topics outlined here are discussed in greater detail in Chapter 11 by Clausen.*]

individual who has reached a given age accommodate? If the base of his role choices is broad, how does he make his decision?[29] Is there an optimum number of roles an individual can handle adequately with a minimum of strain? Theoretically, at least, negative effects may ensue either from holding too many or too few roles. The individual with many major roles to "manage"—in the contemporary United States most likely among middle-age people—may be overwhelmed by his multitudinous obligations. And in middle age, he not only has many roles to play but is also expected to perform at high levels in each of them. Clearly there is a great potential for role pressure in this age stratum.[30] At the same time, the person with relatively few roles open to him may suffer because he has a superfluity of time or because he has been deprived of roles involuntarily (cf. Bredemeier and Stephenson, 1962, pp. 131 ff.).

While noting the obvious problems associated with having "too many" or "too few" roles, we may still speculate that once adulthood has been reached, the person with few roles may derive fewer satisfactions from this limited repertoire than does the person with a wider variety of roles. Among middle-aged couples in the working class, for example, where husbands seem generally not to belong to voluntary associations or to engage in varied activities with relatives or friends, marriages may be lusterless by contrast to middle-class couples of the same age, who report both a greater variety of activities and a greater satisfaction with marriage (cf. Komarovsky, 1964, pp. 330–334). Among old people, many of whom spend much of their time in idleness, those with low rather than high levels of activity seem more likely to feel lonely, neglected, and unneeded (Volume I, Chapter 15 · 6 and Chapter 22 · 2).

Thus, to pose the problem of the number of roles at a given age in zero-sum terms seems fruitless. While time is finite, it is not clear what limits control the number of roles that can effectively be played at the same stage of life. The great number of roles men in their middle years are able to juggle, and their relatively high-level performance in each role, combined with their apparent sense of gratification, suggests (as a reverse of Parkinson's law!) that individuals are capable of expanding the use of their time to encompass a great many activities.

Nevertheless, the individual who elects to play a multiplicity of roles is likely to encounter difficulties as well as rewards. Brim (1966), in his discussion of later life socialization, stresses the necessity of learning how to mediate the conflicting demands imposed upon the individual—not only between roles but also within roles—by virtue of his multiple group memberships.

---

[29] Simmel ([1908], 1964, p. 140) points out that each new group with which an individual becomes affiliated circumscribes him more exactly and more unambiguously. White (1961) discusses this issue under modern conditions.

[30] Goode (1960) describes this problem as "role strain." See also Wilensky (1961).

Boundary inconsistencies When the complex of roles open to a given stratum involve different ages as the entry criteria, serious identity problems for the individual can ensue. Such problems, though noted in particular instances,[31] deserve fuller exploration. The inconsistencies represent structural sources of strain for the individual, in some ways analogous to the strains imposed by class status inconsistency (cf. Lenski, 1954). For example, varying age definitions of adulthoood can evoke ambivalent reactions from persons expected to perform as adults in some situations but not in others. However, the alternative possibility should not be ignored: that inconsistencies in age boundaries may have certain positive consequences.[32] For example, they can permit the individual to become accustomed, first, to one role and later, to another. Entering marriage, the labor force, and parenthood at approximately the same time may be more stressful than assuming these roles at intervals. Similarly, the simultaneous adjustment to both widowhood and job loss may be more difficult than adjustment to each one separately.

Discontinuities between strata[33] The impact of the role structure on individuals depends further on the degree of compatibility or continuity between the role complexes in contiguous strata. Individuals making the transfer from one stratum to the next must not only prepare in advance to cross the threshold, but they must also adjust to the new sets of roles at the next higher age level. The new set may either provide direct substitutes for former roles, compatible with the values and attitudes of the previous complex; or alternatively, it may present entirely different norms that require restructuring of orientations or activate defense mechanisms leading to potentially deviant adjustments.[34] Thus much depends upon the degree of normative consonance between roles available in adjacent strata. [*See the discussion of Benedict in Chapter 11 by Clausen and of role transfers in Chapter 12 · 2.*]

Special problems and potentials for resolving them are associated with major transition points in the life course of individuals. In our society, for instance, the transition from youth to adulthood appears to be an especially stressful time, since youths must assume, not one, but many new roles simultaneously; and the ways in which they function in these major roles affects their whole future. There are potential conflicts among these many new roles and discontinuities with the old roles just relinquished. That youth are aware of these conflicts is indicated by the reports of the youngest adults themselves. Yet it is also these young adults who among all age strata in one

---

[31] Davis (1944) shows how the social development of adolescents in American society lags behind physical development, placing contradictory and confusing demands upon adolescents.

[32] [*See the discussion in Chapter 11 by Clausen.*]

[33] [*Again see Chapter 11 by Clausen, where major treatment is given to this topic.*]

[34] Riley, Foner, Hess, and Toby (1969, pp. 971 ff.) discuss this point at length.

study (Gurin et al., 1960, pp. 19–20) were most likely to say they are "very happy." Perhaps the problems perceived in particular roles interfere with optimum performance (consider the relatively low levels of performance among young adults in the polity [*Chapter 4 by Foner*] on many measures of productivity and at work [Volume I, Chapter 18 · B · 1 and B · 2 and see Section 4 of this chapter]), although such problems do not determine their general outlook. After all, the young have the future! For them, it may well be realistic to assume that these initial difficulties will be resolved and that in the long period ahead, high rewards will be forthcoming.[35]

For people in the middle age strata, a major transitional problem is learning how to cope with failure, with the fact that they may not have achieved their major goals. Yet people in this age category play a multiplicity of roles, and may have accumulated successes in some though not in others. Moreover, their financial situation and health are likely to be relatively good. Thus failure to achieve in certain roles may be compensated by a heightened salience of performance in gratifying roles. For example, the man in his 50's who has been by-passed for promotion may find compensation in intensified activity in the community or in the family. Here positive rewards can compensate for the negative aspects of work roles.

For people in the oldest strata, transitions often mean giving up major valued roles with few substitutes that can compensate. Yet the accumulated experience of a lifetime has taught old people how to "cope." On the whole, old age is the life stage in which net rewards are lowest. Yet the relatively high level of acceptance of this stage poses a still-to-be answered question as to the resources with which older people handle the deficiencies of their remaining roles.

INDIVIDUAL RESPONSES

What, then, are the subjective responses of individuals in the various strata who contribute their capacities and skills to role performance and encounter various difficulties and inequalities in the role structure, but are nevertheless provided with certain societal opportunities and rewards? What life views are held in different strata? What are the satisfactions? How do these subjective experiences vary with the social context in which individuals find themselves?

Reactions to inequalities   We have paid considerable heed to the age-related inequalities or differences in rewards in contemporary society. Yet little is known about whether such inequalities are perceived as *inequities* by the role incumbents themselves. Social deprivation does not depend simply upon evaluations placed by others on the roles people play. People are likely

---

[35] Back and Bourque (1970) find that individuals tend to rate their lives more highly in anticipation than in retrospect.

to judge their own situation, not merely according to inequalities, but in part according to what they feel they "deserve." And the sense of relative deprivation,[36] as subjectively experienced, implies a standard or reference group for comparison. Thus persons of a given age may, for example, use age peers rather than other age strata as their reference group; or they may use for comparison earlier or anticipated stages of their own life course.

Certain clues to current reactions (which, we must remember, reflect the current state of society) inhere in the manifold data on the views and life satisfactions of old people, who, in contrast with the young, are in many respects objectively deprived. The evidence points to a situation in which older people seem typically to have come to terms with themselves to a greater extent than many younger people have. Older adults display an acceptance of their lot and an unconcern about many problems that may help to compensate for deficits in capacity or even in societal opportunities for role performance.

There are sharp differences among age strata in many opinions, feelings, and dispositions toward such central aspects of life as health, personal problems, or death. Certain recurrent themes are discernible beneath the myriad specific differences, as old and young define and assess their life situations differently, and hence are inclined toward varying courses of action. Older people tend to have less sense of mastery over the conditions of their lives than do younger people, considering the world potentially less changeable. They tend (paradoxically) to stress the responsibility of the individual for his own destiny; whereas younger people are more likely to stress environmental influences. In line with such differences in definitions of the situation, old and young tend to favor different types of approaches to life situations. Thus older people, defining many of life's ills as inevitable, may be more disposed to seek palliative rather than corrective or preventive treatment. However, when older people do become committed to a particular course of action, they may be typically as willing and able as the young to implement it. Thus much of the often-noted passive acceptance of the aged may perhaps be explained through their differing definitions and evaluations of the situation rather than through any age-related tendency toward generalized withdrawal.

Adjustment to life also shows characteristic age patterns in our own society. Here there are various indications that the young may be the happiest. Yet, if age is associated with a general diminution of the opportunities for happiness, there are many specific areas in which old people's reactions and gratifications compare favorably with those of young people. The typical oldster not only expresses a sense of adequacy and self-worth, but is also as

---

[36] This concept, employed by Samuel A. Stouffer and his collaborators in their studies of the American soldier (1949), has been clarified and elaborated in Merton (1957, pp. 234 ff.).

likely as the younger person to seem content with his occupational and familial roles and to encounter no greater problems in them. And despite the objective difficulties confronting him, he appears even less likely to worry about his health, for example, or his finances. Thus—contravening the putative wretchedness of old age—the older the age stratum to which a person belongs in today's society, the more nearly he seems to have become reconciled to many of the specific conditions of his life.

The impact of societal conditions　Such differences in the attitudes and satisfactions of old and young, while partly traceable to differences in education and to the life-course dimension, also illustrate the importance of the historical dimension. Long-term social and cultural changes have meant that each new cohort (generation) has been socialized to new understandings, norms, and habit patterns—in Mannheim's terms, to new ranges of "experiential, intellectual, and emotional data" ([1928], 1952, p. 291). Such ranges differ radically from time to time and from place to place, so that the divergences among age strata in views of life are variously patterned. People currently old enough to have lived through a major depression and a major war have quite another *Weltanschauung* from children too young for such exposure. The Great Depression produced feelings of extreme concern over financial security, which undoubtedly still affect the political views and the attitudes toward work of the cohorts involved. Wars tend to influence the age at which individuals enter the roles of spouse or parent and, for some, whether they marry at all.

Even when all the age strata experience the same event simultaneously, they may, because of their respective life stages, respond differently. Thus wars, while impinging on the entire population, have a special effect on the young; or certain diseases (such as German measles) have more serious effects if contracted at one life stage than at another.

As an example of the effect of societal conditions upon the age strata, let us consider how (as noted in Chapter 5) older people respond to retirement. While many welcome the new role and increase their interest in various activities, many others evidence low morale or find it difficult to keep occupied. Their time budgets take conspicuous note of just sitting, standing, looking out the window, or napping.[37] Now let us ask whether such responses are peculiar to the state of being old, or whether they can be traced to the particular social context of older people in today's society. For example, would a situation in which jobs are generally unavailable evoke from the young responses similar to those noted among retired older people?

[37] Whether or not the predominant pattern for given individuals is to increase or decrease their activity levels over their later years remains a moot point (see, e.g., Maddox, 1963). The difficulties of interpreting panel observations on older people are noted in Volume I, Chapter 17 · 5 · a.

Some answers to this question are available from studies that probed into just such a situation—into the general unemployment in several countries during the Great Depression.[38] Among these unemployed, a few found functional equivalents for their lost jobs (such as home repair or gardening). Others became resigned to unemployment, renouncing their earlier expectations of success and redefining the virtues of their roles as homemakers or parents. And still others were defensive or deviant in their reactions, blaming their misfortunes on scapegoats, losing self-esteem, resorting to excessive drinking or to criminality. But of all the responses to the severity of this unemployment crisis, *withdrawal* was by far the most common, often giving way to complete apathy and indolence, sometimes erupting into physical or mental illness. And for many, deterioration of skills and gradual acceptance of the unemployed status tended to result in complete unemployability. In short, the responses of younger workers are strikingly parallel to those of older workers if the circumstances are similar—if, as in the case of retirement at early ages today, loss of the work role is widespread, of long duration, and often imposed upon the individual quite apart from his own choice. In all age strata, social structural barriers can destroy the motivation to perform in accustomed roles.

We have chosen this example, then, in which it is not age alone that elicits particular responses, to demonstrate our central point: that many of the attitudes, satisfactions, and performances that constitute subcultures among the age strata are evoked by societal conditions and changes rather than simply by processes inherent in biological or social aging.

3 Age strata and social relationships

The division of people and roles into age strata, characterized by the distinctive subcultures we have been observing, poses additional questions as to the nature of social *relations* both between and within strata. For not only the behavior and attitudes of discrete individuals, but also social relationships—people's actions, judgments, and positive or negative feelings toward each other—are channeled through the age structure of the particular society. Such relations may be characterized in many ways: as solidary or conflictful, as equalitarian or authoritarian, as formally or informally organized, as functionally interdependent or functionally autonomous, as integrated or segregated, as diffuse or specific, and so on through the list of myriad properties by which, taken together, the core of sociology may be defined. Though we shall deal only with selected and often speculative illustrations, it must become clear that the structure of social relations cannot be understood without reference to age relations.

[38] For a full analysis of this parallelism, see Riley, Foner, Hess and Toby (1969, pp. 972–974).

Concern with relationships *between* strata is immemorial. Many aspects of the cleavages or the bonds between old and young, dramatized by philosophers and poets of the ancient past,[39] are still widely discussed today. Is there an inevitable gap between generations? Is youth culture inevitably oppositional vis-à-vis the adult society? Do the elderly constitute a disadvantaged minority group, regarded with prejudice by the majority? Or do they control important centers of power, refusing to yield to the young? And, if many conditions foster intergenerational conflict or exploitation, what other conditions foster relationships of harmony or reciprocity?

Of less interest, perhaps, are relationships *within* strata. Yet many studies have noted that, where age lines are pronounced, there are tendencies for members of the same stratum to form attachments, whereas strain or outright conflict (often mediated by seniors) tend to develop between strata. Eisenstadt (1956, esp. pp. 66, 87–89) has compiled an extensive summary of such studies. And among his many examples, such tribes as the Nandi give evidence of equality and loyalty between age-mates, contrasted with competition and animosity between adjacent age-sets; or among Irish peasants, similar, though less overt, age patterns can be discerned from the groupings in which people sit, or walk, or go to church, and from the particular intergenerational expressions of annoyance, boredom, or chafing against restraint. The drama and consistency of these many accounts can easily lead to an oversimplification that disregards the countertendencies toward competition among age peers or toward integration across age divisions. Thus we shall discuss here a variety of considerations necessary for understanding age relationships, first, within given strata and second, between strata.

RELATIONS WITHIN STRATA

Parsons once wrote that age, like sex, constitutes:

> . . . one of the main links of structural continuity in terms of which structures which are differentiated in other respects are articulated with each other ([1942], 1949, p. 218).

Let us speculate about the implications of this provocative remark.

To be sure, individuals who are similarly located within the social structure need not develop awareness of their common lot; nor do they necessarily form stable systems of interaction. Moreover, even when an age stratum is organized—formally or informally—in a system of age-homogeneous groups, such groups may be highly differentiated, either internally or in relation to one another, according to other bases of stratification such as sex, class, or

---

[39] Reinhold (1970) gives many examples of the generation gap in antiquity.

ethnic affiliation (as suggested in Figure 10 · 1). Thus age-based solidarity may be problematic and only intermittently activated.

Forms of intrastratum relationships   Nevertheless, both age-consciousness and age groups of interacting individuals are found in most societies, simple or complex, though in widely varied forms and with diverse functions (see, e.g., Eisenstadt, 1956; Gulliver, 1968). Societies vary, for example: in the prevalence of such groups, in the total number of age strata involved, in the proportion of all members in a given stratum likely to be included in the group, in the scope of activities, in the extent to which such groups regulate their members' behavior or are organized and regulated by other age strata, in transitoriness or permanence through the life course of successive cohorts, and in the degree to which they are explicitly institutionalized.

Consider, as just one instance of such diverse forms and functions, the *inclusiveness* of an age group—the extent to which everybody in the relevant age stratum shares membership. In some primitive tribes, age groups are reported to be universal, cutting across the entire society. In antiquity, there were numerous groups to which most male citizens (or their sons) belonged, such as the elders (men over 60) in Sparta from whom the Senate was elected, the formally organized groups of young Spartans who performed educational and military tasks, or the Athenian *epheboi* who received military training between the ages of 18 and 20.[40] Contemporary age groups also differ markedly in inclusiveness. For example, in the educational system of the United States today, the lower grades include practically all children in the age stratum; whereas colleges and universities are far less inclusive, dividing that stratum into distinctly different substrata of college versus noncollege youth.

How inclusive an age group is holds possible implications for the relationships among its members, affecting, for example, the group's potential as a base for societal power or influence. The subdivision between college and noncollege youth, as discussed by Parsons and Platt in Chapter 7, may well inhibit the solidarity of the age stratum. By contrast, widely shared age consciousness can often produce a sense of unity, as Sorokin points out (1947, pp. 181–183), even when only a minority are actually organized to symbolize and intensify this unification. However, the relationships among members of an age stratum depend not merely upon inclusiveness and other formal aspects, but also upon the conditions fostering varying degrees of solidarity or antagonism.

Dimensions of intrastratum solidarity   The degree of solidarity within age strata can be classified along such dimensions as shared orientations,

[40] Compare the reports by Eisenstadt (1956, pp. 141–146).

consciousness of kind, interaction toward common goals, or the development of organized groups—dimensions that often cumulate to enhance capacity for common action.[41] And such common action can then be directed toward cooperation or conflict with other age strata, thus shaping the forms of solidarity or antagonism within the society as a whole.

Eisenstadt, though restricting much of his analysis to adolescent age groups, identifies two general conditions facilitating within-stratum integration. He asserts that age-homogeneous groups:

> . . . have an inherent tendency towards solidarity because of (a) the common definitions of life-space and destiny; and (b) the common sharing of emotional strains and experiences during the period of transition . . . (1956, p. 46).

Thus age can be an integrative force because of the shared experiences and the common position in society of persons occupying similar role complexes at the same period in history. Nor is such communality of interest limited to youth. In the United States, for example, outside of family groups, people in all age strata tend (though by no means exclusively) to have friends who are similar to themselves in status characteristics—notably age—that signal mutuality of experiences, tastes, or values.[42] As the sociological literature shows [*see Chapter 9 on friendship by Hess*], such choice of age-mates is only a special case of the widespread phenomenon of homophily (or similarity among friends in status or in values).[43]

Strata differences in conditions of solidarity   A brief review of the situation in our society in three strata (adolescence, old age, and middle age) will suggest in more detail the manner in which age is a central element in homophily.

First, of all age strata, *adolescents* seem particularly likely to have a community of interests and common life experiences. Harmony of interests derives in part from the similarity in their role complexes. Because they fill relatively few major roles, divergence among their role complexes is likely to be slight, since the number of combinations into which these few roles may be organized is limited.[44] In addition, adolescents often share common tasks—such as ritual duties, or even fighting—but more especially preparation for adult roles. These preparatory periods tend to be marked by tension and anxiety, for they represent points of transition to adult roles that differ impor-

---

[41] Note that our definition of an "age group" utilizes such sociological dimensions, rather than adhering strictly to anthropological distinctions among "age group," "age grade," or "age class." For a summary of anthropological usages, see Gulliver (1968).

[42] But compare the point made by Clausen, in Chapter 11 · 5, that individuals making a smooth transition to middle or later life tend to have younger friends with whom they identify.

[43] Merton defines this concept in Lazarsfeld and Merton (1954).

[44] Compare Simmel's comments ([1908], 1964, p. 140) on the probability that individuals will participate in overlapping role complexes.

tantly from the roles in family or in school that must be relinquished (Eisenstadt, 1956, pp. 44–55; Benedict, 1938).

In addition to mutual problems attendant on the transitional nature of this life stage, adolescents are likely to feel deprived or even isolated because of the denial of adult rights and privileges. In familistic societies the structure of the family or descent group often blocks attainment of maturity by younger members, either because authority is vested in the older people or because the extension of the incest taboo or other norms act to restrict sexual relations. In modern nonkinship societies, young people also are wont to perceive that they are denied their "just" prerogatives, as they clamor for participation in decisions that affect their lives. [*See Chapter 4 by Foner.*]

Finally, the knowledge that they share a common lot is promoted because adolescents are in a position to interact and communicate with one another outside the family. It is in adolescence that individuals may leave the physical boundaries of their family. [*See Chapter 6 by Starr on age-related physical limitations of the social world.*] And, in modern societies, adolescents leave the family for school and youth groups often sponsored by the adult society. Thus, as they are literally thrown together, and can readily communicate about their common problems or tasks, stable ties to one another are developed.[45]

Second, the situation of *old people* affords many striking parallels to that of adolescents. The transition to old age, accompanied as it is by the relinquishment of major life roles, is also fraught with tensions and frustrations. Here, however, discontinuities stem from making the transition from the larger society to the family or some other primary group. Further, old people may perceive themselves as relatively deprived as they must give up valued positions of authority or of prestige and as, in modern societies, they experience reduction of income. Perceived deprivation is not confined to modern societies where, for example, retirement is institutionalized. Nadel (1952, pp. 22–25), for example, has noted the reluctance of older people in certain primitive societies to cede privileges to younger persons—even to the point of open resistance to societal norms requiring that they yield. Yet prior to the modern period, when relatively few people lived to old age, cohesion within the old age stratum was problematic. Even in the present day, because many old people suffer from such limitations as physical disabilities or financial deprivations, their ability to interact with one another beyond the immediate confines of their residence is restricted, perhaps restricting also devel-

[45] Much of this discussion leans on Eisenstadt's (1956) survey of age groups in primitive, historical, and modern societies, which tends to focus on youth. It is of interest that relatively little mention is made of female age groups—possibly because of gaps in ethnographers' reports or because there are indeed fewer female age groups. Whether the same pattern would be found today is questionable. Rutgers studies of high school students, for example, show peer interaction more pronounced among girls than boys.

opment of a sense of community. This may be one reason why old age clubs attract only small proportions of old people (Volume I, Chapter 21 · 4).

These examples among adolescents and old people, then, suggest certain factors that may encourage cohesion and solidarity within age strata. Individuals of the same age are drawn together by common tasks, common needs, and similar problems, problems that are exacerbated by having to make major life transitions. Consciousness of their mutuality of interests is promoted by physical proximity and ease of communication. Of course, in the modern period of mass communication, knowledge of mutual interests can be obtained through the mass media, evoking similar feelings and reactions without face-to-face interaction. Thus discrete persons of similar age, through parallel responses to public events, often act "as if organized."[46] Even so, age consciousness, and cohesion of age similars, are likely to be intensified by actual physical proximity, a necessary condition for the formation of interacting groups.[47]

Third, these examples of adolescence and old age suggest that in modern societies, the *middle strata* may be less likely to have close ties, since in some respects they have fewer common interests and problems. Unlike the young, who share impediments to achieving adult status, and unlike the old, who share relinquishment of full social status, the middle-aged do enjoy full status in the society. And because the repertoire of different socially valued roles they play is greater than the number available to either younger or older strata, their individual interests seem likely to diverge or be competitive. In fact, while certain segments of the middle-aged may achieve a degree of solidarity, inclusive age groups appear to be less prevalent in this stratum than among younger and older strata.

Changes in intrastratum relationships Yet it may be that a number of factors are converging to produce solidarity within age lines among all strata in the contemporary United States. The rapidity of social change alone, for example, can sharpen the differences among strata, and can thereby contribute to a sense of uniqueness among members of each single stratum. The expansion of education has extended the social (and often physical) segregation of age-similars from children in the lower schools to older adolescents and even to young adults in colleges and universities. [*See Chapter 7 by Parsons and Platt.*] Even many of today's middle-aged, those who have left the

---

[46] Sorokin (1947, p. 182) uses this term for persons who, even though not members of organized age groups, behave as if they were interacting members of a group because of similarity in age (or other status).

[47] The importance of propinquity in promoting interaction and group ties was stressed by both Marx and Simmel. Marx attributed the lack of class consciousness among the French peasants in part to their physical isolation from one another. Simmel suggested that the first associations of workers depended largely on the fact that they were neighbors (Marx, [1852], 1964, p. 109; Simmel [1908], 1964, p. 129).

city to rear their children in suburbs, have experienced long years of age-homogeneous neighborhood settings. [See Chapter 6 by Starr.] And old people, despite their problems, merely because of increasing longevity retain larger numbers of their age peers as associates (as noted by Spengler, 1969, pp. 375–376). In many respects the society is an age-graded one, with a high potential for strong ties to develop within each age stratum.

The possible long-term consequences of such heightened conditions of within-stratum solidarity may be double-edged. On the one hand, it may be beneficial to the individuals involved. Age peers have long been recognized as easing the transition from childhood to adulthood (cf. Eisenstadt, 1956); and they may perhaps aid adjustment in old age and at other points of transition in the life course as well. On the other hand, if age peers increasingly turn to each other for aid and comfort, or if they band together to seek benefits for their age group, detriments to relationships between strata may ensue, as ties between generations become attenuated or the potential for cleavage or conflict are increased.

RELATIONS OF INTERDEPENDENCE AND EXCHANGE AMONG STRATA

Of perennial concern, as we have noted, are the ties between, rather than within, strata. The questions of age relations that preoccupy us today, as they have engrossed observers over the centuries, are primarily those concerned with cohesion versus cleavage between generations. Yet many other aspects of the linkages among age strata deserve attention also. As a preliminary, then, to addressing the more emotionally laden problems of solidarity and conflict, we shall first examine certain other types of interstratum relationships, starting with interdependence and exchange, and then discussing authority and deference.

Two illustrations from different institutional spheres will point out the interconnectedness of the age strata. They will also suggest how the nature of this interconnectedness is not necessarily predictable from the structuring of age relations, but may depend upon the particular values and role organization involved.

In family relations A first example deals with the interdependence and exchanges between generations within the family, revealing a pattern that we term *"sequential relationships."* If we begin with the elderly generation of parents and their adult offspring, well-known findings (Volume I, Chapter 23 · B · 2) report widespread exchanges of material support. This support varies in amount and kind, ranging from financial contributions and care in illness to baby-sitting and help with housework and home repairs. Contrary to previous notions of an upward flow of contributions *to* older people, these findings indicate that the flow of support between aged parents and their adult offspring is two-directional, either from parent to child or from child to parent as need and opportunity dictate. Indeed, among older people (in the United States, at least), the proportions who *give* help to their offspring appear to exceed the proportions who *receive* help from their offspring.[48]

Let us now, however, include in the example still a third generation of the family, for it is our contention that many a commonplace observation about relations between selected age strata can take on new significance through extension to other strata as well. Let us move from the flow of material assistance between aged parents and their middle-aged children to the flow between this middle generation and *their* young children. The point can be illustrated by one small study[49] in which middle-aged parents were asked what they would do with money unexpectedly received. Only 2 per cent said they would use it to help their aged parents. But this was not because they would spend it on themselves or save it for their retirement; it was rather because, in the main, they would reserve it to help their children get started in life. Furthermore, the aged generation concurs; they do not expect repayment. The middle generation, then, does not neglect the old because of preoccupation with their own needs (in fact, they are far readier to offer help than are their aged parents to want it or to accept it), but because of their preoccupation with the needs of their young children. In short, the flow of material support tends to be not reciprocal but sequential—with each generation (regardless of its means) attempting to aid the next younger generation.

As such a finding intimates, many middle-aged parents, by investing their resources in the future of their young children, are not only restricting any potential help they might give to the older generation; they are also restricting the accumulation of assets for their own later life. Moreover, any lack of family support for aged parents by adult offspring now appears in a new light. Against the full backdrop of all the interacting strata, the relationship of the middle to the older generation cannot be dismissed as willful indifference or neglect—hence as a source of blame or guilt, but rather as an expression of normative agreement among all the generations about the direction in which aid should flow.

In economic relations As another example, illustrative of social changes in the interconnectedness of the age strata, consider the differing circumstances of employment of older and younger men at various periods of history (as discussed in Chapter 5). In the early days of the Industrial Revolution in England, the father (or grandfather), as a skilled workman in his own right, could take his children with him into the factory, training the adult sons himself and supervising the little children throughout the long workday (cf.

---

[48] See, for example, Shanas (1966); Streib (1965); see also the more general discussion by Streib and Thompson (1960).

[49] Foner, unpublished Ph.D. dissertation (1969); based on data from a Rutgers study of the sets of parents of 400 students in two New Jersey high schools, 1964.

Smelser, 1968). Thus his authority within the family could penetrate into the work place, preserving traditional ties among the generations. If such an arrangement encouraged bewteen-strata solidarity, then the subsequent changes marking the relative positions of older men and boys in the work force may have undermined this basis in many Western countries. As both the youngest and the oldest workers have been gradually winnowed from the labor force over the twentieth century, today's society presents a complex web of economic dependency of nonparticipants upon the productivity of workers in their middle years (cf. Kalish, 1969).

RELATIONS OF AUTHORITY AND DEFERENCE

In addition to relations of interdependence or exchange among age strata, the superiority or domination of certain strata over others is a central feature of social life. Relations of authority and deference can serve to integrate the age strata, but they can also foster latent or overt hostilities of subordinates toward superordinates (cf. Lenski, 1966, pp. 426–428).

Hierarchical ordering The extent to which relations of authority and deference are hierarchically ordered by age varies by cultures and by roles within particular cultures. Historically, the predominant direction of deference seems to have been from the youngest strata toward the mature, or even to the oldest, strata.

Traditional China provides one of the more extreme examples of a structure where old people were generally respected and even venerated. Not only absolute age, but also relative age, served to define obligations, privileges, and relations of difference. The Chinese even had distinct kinship terms for older and younger siblings, and the younger owed respect and honor to the older (Leslie, 1967, p. 101). Older role-partners in general had greater authority and received deference from younger role-partners *because* of their age.

Such hierarchical ordering by age is neither universal nor inevitable, however, but depends upon certain conditions that can vary over time and space. Maintenance of the ordering means that the dominant older strata actually succeed in monopolizing the roles and performing the activities that are valued by the society. Thus traditional relations of deference can be threatened whenever the legitimacy of age-based role hierarchies is challenged (as we shall discuss) or whenever the competence of role incumbents to perform the requisite activities is undermined. In most primitive and agrarian societies, old age (at least up to senility) seems to have been generally associated with some special competence or characteristic regarded as an asset in the respective culture, such as usefulness in the performance of chores, skill in dancing or story-telling, control of property rights, power in the family, seasoned experience, or (especially in preliterate societies) extensive knowledge

(Simmons, 1960, pp. 85–87). By contrast, in the United States today, though the norms still require respect for those who are considerably older, the general applicability of this norm appears to be in the process of modification. For example, in the occupational sphere, a number of trends may disturb the traditional aspects of age relations. The experience of older workers no longer provides them with a necessary basis for authority, as the superior and more recent knowledge and skills of younger people become a more salient criterion for superordinate status. The labor force entry of many middle-aged women has meant that not all occupational neophytes are young. And if, as widely surmised, "second careers" are becoming a noticeably frequent phenomenon, they too may increase the divergence between traditional age relations of deference and the actual hierarchical positions of old and young. Similarly, in the educational sphere, movements for adult education, retraining, training for second careers, or deferment of advanced education by women all contribute to administrative superiority of the young over the old. Some observers suggest that the aged are increasingly taking on the coloration of a minority group (see, e.g., Palmore, 1969, pp. 47–57; Rose and Peterson, 1965).

Age-incongruous relationships To the extent that, despite such changes, some generalized respect for seniors still persists as a norm in contemporary society, behavior that fails to conform to this norm can produce stressful relationships. Age-inappropriate behavior can result from many of the ongoing changes that disturb the traditional hierarchy. Thus older workers may resent having to take orders from young supervisors. Or young teachers may not know how to cope with older students. Moreover, traditional norms governing relations of deference are difficult to maintain when any one of the role partners fails to conform to age-related expectations. Parents who mimic the young in their life style make it difficult for children to respond to parental authority, for example.

Strains resulting from relational age incongruities, like those arising from the breakdown of traditional age hierarchies, can affect the basic conditions of solidarity or cleavage among strata, the topic to which we now turn.

THE POTENTIAL FOR CONFLICT AMONG STRATA

If the scattered evidence points to diverse forms of interdependence or deference that can integrate the age strata, divisive tendencies also, though often latent, are apparently universal. As potential sources of conflict, age inequalities in power, prestige, or access to material resources seem omnipresent. The centuries-old ideological differences between old and young have been exemplified during the 1960's by political divergences over the goals of society, foreign policy commitments, or priorities in domestic expenditures. [*Compare Chapter 4 by Foner.*] Thus Sorokin (1947, p. 193) speaks of the struggle between generations as "a continuously flowing river" that "constantly undermines and reconstructs the social institutions."

Nevertheless, divisive tendencies do not necessarily become manifest in antagonism nor erupt into organized conflict. The mere fact of inequality among age strata (as is true of other types of stratification also) is not a sufficient condition for age cleavage.[50] And our examples of interconnectedness across age lines have shown that differences—and even lack of reciprocity—are not inevitably accompanied by frustration or aggression.

Conflict-reducing mechanisms A number of mechanisms operate, either by reducing discord or enhancing solidarity, to mitigate or prevent age conflicts.[51] We shall take note of four such mechanisms. First, the likelihood of cleavage is diminished when there is value consensus in a society over what is desirable and over the legitimacy of existing distributions of these desiderata according to age. Second, linkages across age strata may be strengthened, and contentions minimized, by the facts of aging and cohort succession themselves. Third, where clashes do break out, they may often be contained through institutionalization of rivalry or through segregation of the conflict within narrow boundaries. Finally, affiliations with solidarities that cut across age lines can create salient age-heterogeneous interests that impede united action of one age stratum against another.

Legitimation of inequalities Inequalities of opportunities and rewards are often legitimated through societal definitions of age-related needs, or through societal evaluation of the past, present, or potential future contributions of the respective age strata. For example, a concentration of power in the hands of the old may be regarded as commensurate with contributions based on their accumulated experience; disproportionate expenditures on education of the young may be judged appropriate as an investment in their future contributions; or large outlays for medical care of the aged may be justified both as rewards for their past contributions and in terms of their special needs. Whatever the rationale for legitimation of inequality, this legitimation depends not only upon a consensus in basic value positions, but also upon a system for allotting facilities and rewards, to which all the age strata subscribe.

Linkages through aging and cohort succession Another conflict-reducing mechanism rests on the inevitability of aging and the flow of cohorts. Though individuals vary in age, they can, at each stage of life, experience all past stages in retrospect and all future stages in anticipation. This experien-

---

[50] Nor is it even a necessary condition, since simple conquest may be the aim of age strata in conflict.

[51] *[For a discussion of such mechanisms in relation to the polity, see Chapter 4 by Foner.]*

tial time dimension opens the way for a subjective and empathic sharing of the life course by all the age strata. When this occurs, the old may sympathize with the difficulties of youth insofar as they can remember not too different adolescent problems of their own. (However, lest anyone forget that there are cohort differences as well as similarities in adolescent problems, let him take note of Margaret Mead's (1970, pp. 80–81) stricture that "as long as any adult thinks that he can . . . invoke his own youth to understand the youth before him, he is lost." And the young, though not yet confronting the rewards or disappointments of middle and old age, can extend their own lives in imagination, taking the roles of their elders. Moreover, the inevitable succession of generations may serve to reassure the young that their chance will come, and to assure the old of the continuity of their own existences where the young may yet achieve what they have left undone.

Even where underlying hostilities exist, these may be deflected or contained by the assurance of age mobility. Thus the deviance of youth may be tolerated by adults as a "passing phase," as long as the young adhere to central societal values of success.[52] And young people themselves may limit the degree[53] to which they will risk their future by alienating those older people who control the gateways to positions of security, prestige, or wealth.[54] Moreover, the fact that adolescence passes quickly makes certain deprivations so temporary that they may not provide sufficient motivation for expressing hostility.

Institutionalization or segregation of conflict   Where the potential for age conflict exists, there are ways in which it may be diverted. In many societies, there are institutionalized rivalries (competitive sports between students and alumni, fights between older and younger boys) that serve as symbolic expression of hostilities. To cite the Nandi again, there is often real animosity between adjacent age-sets, with the set holding power reluctant to hand it over. One means of avoiding real battles is the tribal ceremony in which there is a symbolic show of force between the retiring and the new warrior age-set (Eisenstadt, 1956, p. 64).

Alternatively, age-related aggression and hostility are often channeled into limited, and sometimes peripheral, areas of social life. For example, among Irish peasants, potentially hostile behavior of young against old is minimized by segregating the deviant behavior in informal groups of the young (Eisen-

---

[53] Compare the discussion of youth culture as institutionalized deviance by Parsons (1951, pp. 305–306).

[53] Compare, for example, Matza's comment (1964) that, as boys get girl friends and jobs, they define delinquency as "kid stuff." See also Toby and Liebman (unpublished).

[54] By the same token, it might be argued that aging may have the opposite effect among older people. Among the Mesakin, for example, Nadel notes that deviant behavior is displayed by older men who must make some kind of symbolic gift which tokens their impending death. The older men always refuse making the gift and it often has to be taken by force. See Nadel (1952, p. 23).

stadt, 1956, pp. 88–89), as youthful deviance has often been segregated in the United States. There are numerous instances in which the struggle between age strata is contained, as Sorokin (1947, p. 193) puts it, within "many small detachments." Many conflicts, rather than spreading through the whole society, are limited to relations between young and old in particular institutional spheres. There are, for example, dissensions in a particular family (as between first- and second-generation immigrant members); in a work organization (as over higher present wage increases versus improved pension funds); or in a religious association (as over the primacy of a social welfare orientation versus a strictly devotional emphasis). Discord within the boundaries of a restricted sphere can sometimes serve not only to divert hostility but also, through counteropposing struggles, to mute tendencies toward more general conflict in the total society.[55]

Cross-cutting group affiliations Whereas age conflicts in diverse institutional spheres can sometimes offset each other, solidarities that cut across age lines (as in Figure 10 · 1 above), can affect relationships between age strata. Theorists have suggested that in complex societies, multiple group affiliations serve generally to minimize conflict. One of the early formulations of this principle stated:

> Every species of social conflict interferes with every other species in society . . . save only when lines of cleavage coincide; in which case they reinforce one another. . . . These different oppositions in society are like different wave series set upon opposite sides of a lake, which neutralize each other if the crest of one meets the trough of the other, but which reinforce each other if crest meets crest while trough meets trough. . . . A society, therefore, which is ridden by a dozen oppositions along lines running in every direction may actually be in less danger of being torn with violence or falling to pieces than one split just along one line. For each new cleavage contributes to narrow the cross clefts, so that one might say that *society is sewn together* by its inner conflicts (Ross, 1920, pp. 164–165, quoted by Coser [1956], 1964, pp. 76, 170).

How might this principle operate in terms of age? Since, in a pluralistic society, persons belong to many age-heterogeneous groups, they are thereby exposed to the distinctive viewpoints of the various age strata, as we have seen. In such a situation, the firmly held views peculiar to one's own stratum are difficult to maintain. Further, even if divergent views between persons of different ages do emerge, the affective ties and common interests they share can act to suppress the open expression of hostility. Indeed, at times

[55] According to Coser ([1956], 1964, p. 77) even within a single organization, a multiplicity of conflicts can reduce sharp cleavages. For example, in bureaucracies conflicts between various bureaus and offices and between officeholders along many divergent lines may prevent formation of a united front.

the salience of the common goals of these other groups may take precedence over those of an age stratum. Thus, as these affiliations cross-cut age strata, unity within an age stratum is reduced and solidarity between age strata may be enhanced.

OPEN CONFLICT AND SOCIAL CHANGE

Yet, despite the numerous possibilities for preventing or reducing conflict and building solidarity across age lines, sharp age cleavages do occur. Under what conditions are such conflicts likely to emerge? Under what conditions are conflict-reducing mechanisms likely to break down?

Problems of legitimation Conflict over previously legitimated inequalities among age strata tends to develop only when certain ages enjoy seemingly unjustified superiority or domination over other ages. The sources of such challenges to the distributive features of the society are many and must, in each instance, be traced historically. At times, events conspire to make inequalities so severe that they can no longer be tolerated. Thus extreme poverty among many old people not only flouts accepted standards of justice in the United States, but also deprives this stratum of the resources to enjoy the leisure roles now allotted. Or, the monopolization of power by the mature stratum may actually undermine the traditionally accepted modes of distributing resources; as, for example, when the old effectively block the expansion of education required to make room for all qualified applicants. In some instances, the relation of age to the basis for legitimation of inequality may shift over time as, for example, superior knowledge may no longer be concentrated among the old.

Since legitimation of inequalities rests, as we pointed out earlier, on dual bases, its collapse can take two forms: either as an attack upon the modes of distribution of socially valued facilities and rewards among age strata, or as a rejection of the underlying social evaluations. The first form of age conflict, then, is over the relative share of social rewards claimed by each stratum (or, perhaps less often, over the relative share of social contributions each stratum is permitted or forced to make). In such a cleavage, there may still be basic agreement among the strata over the underlying values and ends. There may be no differences of definition as to what constitutes a reward, or what kinds of actions contribute positively to the larger society, or what goals should be accomplished. In the second form of conflict, however, there are divisions along age lines over basic values, over the purposes of social life, over what constitutes the "good" life for the individual. For example, in the 1960's ideological differences emerged between young and old about the over-all goals of the society—differences so sharp that Reich (1970) speaks of a "revolution of consciousness" comparable in scope to that accompanying the Protestant Reformation and Industrial Revolution.

Breakdown of other conflict-reducing mechanisms   Given such pos-sibilities for conflict, the cleavage between age strata may become more spectacular, open, or organized to the extent that the solidarity-building mechanisms are absent or fail to operate. For example, the promise of future improvements in status as a result of *aging* is not always perceived as inev-itable by the young, or even desirable, and so may not operate to reduce their hostility toward the more privileged strata. Either the young have doubts re-garding their own survival in a militaristic world, or they challenge the value of the promised rewards, preferring personal fulfillment to monetary success, for example.

Conflicts along age lines can also be encouraged when these lines, rather than intersecting with other group affiliations, *coincide* with other lines of cleavage. This appears to be the case where revolutionary movements aimed at changing the basic social structure are able to enlist disproportionate num-bers of an age stratum, often becoming part and parcel of a more general revolt (cf., e.g., Sorokin, 1947, pp. 181–183, 193; or Eisenstadt, 1956, p. 312).

In many instances, too, *segregation* of rebellious groups may promote, rather than deter, conflict. Thus the isolation of deviant youth groups in age-homogeneous settings may serve only to insulate them from the corrective sanctions of other age strata or from the cross-cutting pressures of age-heterogeneous solidarities. Or age conflicts that were initially restricted within major social organizations or institutional spheres have a potential for spreading to the whole society. For example, conflicts between age strata in educational institutions can, because of the strategic importance of schools in contemporary culture, ramify throughout other institutional spheres and evoke cleavages not specifically related to educational issues.

Clearly, then, age conflicts may become a vehicle for social change   On the surface, conflicts among the strata that take the form of outright rejection of central societal values and goals may seem more serious in their implications for change than conflicts over inequalities. A moment's reflection should persuade, however, that both types of conflict, just as they may emerge from broad social changes, can also contribute to subsequent states of society. On the one hand, conflicts over the distributive arrangements in the role struc-ture may *reflect* strain-producing relative deprivations of differential life-stage locations of the age strata. Such conflicts, like those over the ideal shape of society, may also reflect the continuing entry of new cohorts reared in social, economic, and physical environments that differ from their prede-cessors. And, on the other hand, both distributive and ideational conflicts could ultimately *result in* profound social changes. For the distribution of social goods is inextricably tied to the organization of societal roles. Hence, to alter the inequalities among age strata—tantamount to altering the nature of relationships among these strata—is to alter the structure of the entire society.

4 Pressures for change

See Chapter 1, Sections 1 · 1 · C, 1 · 2 · A, and 1 · 2 · B; Chapter 12, Section 4

Implicit in much of our discussion of the age strata have been indications of possible strain and tensions that can exert pressure toward change. In particular, we have emphasized the widespread connections between age and two major sources of potential change inherent in any society: inequalities in distribution of facilities and rewards that become defined as inequities, and malintegration of values. Thus we have shown, first, how socially valued roles, while open to certain age strata, may be denied to others. And strains can be produced by denying to some members of society what they think they are entitled to. In the words of Parsons and Shils (1951, p. 232), "any society in which the allocations create or maintain dissatisfaction will be open to change." Second, we have also shown how values, ideologies, and attitudes can differ among age strata, as reflections of both the life-course dimension and the historical dimension of time, or as conflicting or contradictory role demands can vary by age. And divergences in values can lead to change through conflict, through deviance from institutionalized patterns, or through shifts in balance between two established patterns.

IMBALANCES BETWEEN PEOPLE AND ROLES

Still another source of potential change, to which we have not yet given explicit attention, is inherent in our conceptual model of an age-stratified society. According to the model, the strata are composed both of roles and of role players. Let us now consider the possibility that roles and role players are poorly matched. Clearly, there can be imbalances at both the societal and the individual levels: societal discrepancies in the numbers or the kinds of people and roles available in particular strata, and gaps between role expectations and individual motivation or capacity for performance at particular ages. While the processes of allocation and socialization [*see Chapter 12*] operate continuously to bridge such discrepancies and gaps by articulating people and roles, many imbalances in the age structure are beyond the reach of such processes.

Supply and demand for personnel   If we think of the numbers of roles and the supply of age-appropriate role-players in terms of "supply" and "demand," the two may often, at least in theory, be compatible. Some roles, as defined in a particular society, are limited in quantity only by the size of the population of the appropriate age. The supply of friendship roles, for example, is in principle limited only by the capacities and willingness of individuals at particular ages to form and maintain friendship relations and by the supply of role players available in particular age strata [*see Chapter 9 by Hess*]. Or—again in principle—in situations of universal and compulsory age-allocation such as school attendance, the number of available roles is determined by the sizes of the affected strata. In order for the balance to be maintained here, the structural facilities, including the complementary roles of teachers, must expand or contract in response to demographic patterns of fertility, mortality, and migration.

In practice, of course, this principle often fails to apply. By 1970, for example, after many years of a shortage of public school teachers, a surplus suddenly appeared (*New York Times*, July 19, 1970)—traceable in part to the slower rates of increase in the numbers of children reaching school age that followed the previously spiraling demand for teachers occasioned by the postwar baby boom. Many other instances of imbalance come to mind. Thus the sex mortality ratio among old people, by limiting the numbers of available men, forecloses to many elderly widows the possibility of remarriage. Or the hierarchical structure of corporate enterprise restricts the number of top management roles relative to the supply of ambitious older men. Or the low fertility rates during the Depression may result by the 1980's in a shortage— or perhaps in a supply more nearly approximating the demand—of experienced men in the mature strata equipped to fill administrative slots in government or business.

Manifestly, the question is not simply one of balancing the quantity of people and roles, for quality is also involved. Even when the numbers of people and of roles within an age stratum are roughly commensurate, certain individuals can be overdemanded and others underdemanded as the available kinds of roles (or of role complexes) restrict the kinds of people capable of meeting specifications. For example, in a situation of sufficient numbers of jobs to absorb all young entrants to the labor force, the general level of these jobs may be too low to match the needs or the capabilities of the aspirants. And the inadequacy of roles open to certain types of young adults can foster youth groups socially regarded as deviant.

Thus, as numbers and kinds of roles in the age structure of a society continually change, these changes may fail to synchronize with contemporaneous changes in numbers and kinds of role players at the requisite ages. Structured imbalances in the age strata can arise from many sources, including: emergence of new roles, disappearance of others, or alterations in role expectations, facilities, or rewards; societal changes in the way roles are organized; changes in fertility, migration, or mortality, or in the social controls over any of these processes. As imbalances develop, they often tend to persist because of rigidities or slow rates of change in the role structure or in the population.

Aspects of the role structure may be resistant to change, for example, because of ties to institutionalized basic values, or because of the opposition of powerful vested interests. And even in those instances where birth rates (also influenced by basic social values) may change in response to shifts in demands for personnel, any effects of changes in fertility necessarily lag behind these demands.

Role expectations and performance   What are the parallel imbalances at the individual level? Theoretically again, the trained capacities, needs, and motivations of individuals in the several strata constitute a set of limits on role performance and role expectations for particular incumbents are at least roughly geared to these limits. In practice, however, there are many failures of correspondence between role performance by the age strata and role expectations.

Consider just a few of the performances, styles, or behaviors that distinguish particular age strata, but seem to have no clear counterpart in the age structure of role expectations. Item: Rates of voting participation are highest among people in the middle strata (aged 35 to 65) and lowest among those under age 24 [*see Chapter 4 by Foner*], raising questions about the political role performance of the young who, despite their superior education, are least likely to meet the general normative expectation that citizens should vote. Item: Social norms dictate maintenance of independence in old age, but many old people lack the facilities of income, health, or education needed for independence. Item: The tendency for husbands and wives in the middle strata to engage in social visiting as couples only can prevent the single, widowed and divorced from meeting expected patterns of behavior in friendship roles (Hess, 1971, unpublished Ph.D. dissertation). Item: In many types of routine jobs, the youngest workers display the lowest levels of actual performance (in consistency of work, regularity of attendance, or even in some instances of productive output) (Volume I, Chapter 18 · B · 1).

These examples hint at some of the ways in which individuals may be unqualified—or sometimes overqualified—for the roles they play. In work performance, the comparatively high levels attained by older workers, despite their frequent handicaps in physical functioning or in educational background, may represent "overachievement," while the relatively poor records of younger workers in jobs demanding neither wisdom nor long experience may represent "underachievement." In work, as in voting and in various other activities, the roles open to the young may fail to offer the desired rewards, or to provide opportunities for enactment that are commensurate with their capacities and training. Thus if young workers slack off on the job and are often tardy or absent, they may still feel they can match the output of older workers, or they may recognize little connection between achievement and the age-related opportunities for advancement. If, as has been frequently suggested, many roles utilize only a small fraction of the input of which individuals are capable, the modal discrepancy may perhaps be greatest among the young. Among the old, by contrast, a distinctive feature appears to be the remarkable extent of individual variability in many behaviors and characteristics. The oldest stratum in this country contains both the richest and the poorest, both the most powerful and the utterly powerless, both the senescent and those with no noticeable organic decrements.

The most pronounced gaps between role expectations and performance may occur, then, in the youngest, and (for certain individuals) in the oldest, age strata.

SOME CONSEQUENCES OF IMBALANCE

When roles and role players are poorly matched, as in such examples, the resultant tensions and strains can lead to various forms either of adjustment or of change [*as discussed in detail in Chapters 11 and 12*].

Adjustments Many processes, apart from those of allocation and socialization, operate within the population or the role structure to redress age-related imbalances. Supplies of *people* are modulated through environmental conditions (famines, earthquakes, for example) or through social intervention (contraception, control of pollution or of disease, for example). Modifications in the age structure of *roles* are made—either by special design or as aspects of broader changes—through alterations (1) in the numbers and kinds of roles available; (2) in the requirements of these roles; or (3) in the age criteria for role incumbency.

The multiple possibilities for adjusting roles in all three of these respects —either to increase or decrease their claims on personnel—is suggested by the detailed discussion of the age structure of roles in Section 1. Thus, in the first place, the available roles may be restructured by providing new or additional substitute roles such as roles of foster grandparent, volunteer, or consultant, available to old people (cf. Riley, Foner, Hess, and Toby, 1969) or paramedical specialties for young veterans trained in the medical corps. Or existing roles can be contracted as, for example, the suitability of motherhood as a full-time role for young women may be challenged (see, e.g., Rossi, 1964). As a second form of role modification, the role itself is often adapted so that more (or fewer) people in the age stratum desire its rewards or can meet its standards. More people can be accommodated, for example, if role expectations permit satisfactory performance by age strata previously defined as lacking the requisite ability; facilities and opportunities to learn are enhanced; or sanctions are changed to increase perceptions of the role as "right," "proper," or "gratifying." Thus more young people can become college students if admission requirements are made less stringent, or young mothers can occupy work roles if maternity leaves are provided, or leisure in old age can be more enjoyable if socially approved. And third, in roles where the correlation between age and performance ability is not great, the age criteria for role assignment may be revised—as airline pilots, for example, may no longer be required to retire at a young age.

Change Where adjustments fail to re-equilibrate roles and people, however, unresolved strains can produce frustration, potential deviance, or demands for adjustment on the part of individuals; and, for society, contradictions, discord, and other internal pressures for change. And resultant changes can take any one of the usual forms, from evolutionary development or innovation to revolutionary alteration or chaotic disruption.

CONCLUSION

This chapter has focused on the current interplay among all the strata at given periods of history. It has emphasized an approach to age stratification that is structural and synchronic, not in any static sense, but in its embracement of the entire society. That is, while its design for analysis is cross-sectional, it utilizes not a single cross section but a sequence of cross sections as these can be traced over time.[56]

The import of our discussion here centers in the parallels between age stratification and other forms of stratification. We have stated our conviction that age stratification, like divisions based on class or sex or race, for example, is essential for understanding important aspects of social structure and social change. Beyond that, we have raised many questions answerable only through further investigation or through following past trends into the future. Is it true, for example, as Banton (1965, pp. 34–39) among others contends, that age, like sex, becomes decreasingly likely to predetermine human behavior as societies advance in political and technical sophistication? Will the kinds of rewards defining class stratification retain their power in a "post-industrial society" (Bell, 1968, pp. 152–153), or in a world pervaded by a new "consciousness" (Reich, 1970). Implicit in such questions is the need to broaden the sociologist's conception of stratification beyond notions like social class to a view that encompasses all the major divisions of society and their changing interrelationships (see, e.g., the *International Encyclopedia of the Social Sciences*, 15, pp. 228–337; Svalastoga, 1964).

This chapter, then, stresses the similarity of age to other bases of stratification, and the subsequent chapters will stress its uniqueness: the inevitability of the processes underlying age stratification. These final chapters, by examining the interface between the changing age structure of society and the changing life-course sequences of individuals, will demonstrate the integral connection between age stratification and social stability and change.

[56] [*Compare the discussion of period (or current) analysis in Chapter 2.*] See also Riley and Nelson (1971); Riley (1963, Volume I, Unit 12).

Works cited in Chapter 10

Arensberg, Conrad M. (1937), 1950. *The Irish Countryman*, Gloucester, Mass.: Peter Smith.

Ariès, Philippe (1960), 1962. *Centuries of Childhood: A Social History of Family Life*, New York: Knopf and Random House, Vintage Books.

Back, Kurt W., and Linda Brookover Bourque, 1970. "Life Graphs: Aging and Cohort Effect," *Journal of Gerontology*, 25, pp. 249–255.

Banton, Michael, 1965. *Roles: An Introduction to the Study of Social Relations*, New York: Basic Books.

Becker, Howard S., 1960. "Notes on the Concept of Commitment," *American Journal of Sociology*, 66, pp. 32–40.

Bell, Daniel, 1968. "The Measurement of Knowledge and Technology," in Sheldon, Eleanor Bernert, and Wilbert E. Moore, editors, *Indicators of Social Change*, New York: Russell Sage Foundation, pp. 145–246.

Benedict, Ruth, 1938. "Continuities and Discontinuities in Cultural Conditioning," *Psychiatry*, 1, pp. 161–167.

Beresford, John C., and Alice M. Rivlin, 1966. "Privacy, Poverty, and Old Age," *Demography*, 3, No. 1, pp. 247–258.

Blood, Robert O., Jr., and Donald M. Wolfe, 1960. *Husbands and Wives: The Dynamics of Married Living*, New York: Free Press.

Bogue, Donald J., 1959. *The Population of the United States*, Glencoe, Ill.: Free Press.

Bredemeier, Harry C., and Richard M. Stephenson, 1962. *The Analysis of Social Systems*, New York: Holt, Rinehart & Winston.

Brim, Orville G., Jr., 1966. "Socialization Through the Life Cycle," in Brim, Orville G., Jr., and Stanton Wheeler, *Socialization After Childhood: Two Essays*, New York: Wiley, pp. 1–49.

Bronfenbrenner, Urie, 1958. "Socialization and Social Class Through Time and Space," in Maccoby, Eleanor E., Theodore M. Newcomb, and Eugene L. Hartley, editors, *Readings in Social Psychology*, 3rd ed., New York: Henry Holt, pp. 400–425.

Coser, Lewis A. (1956), 1964. *The Functions of Social Conflict*, New York: Free Press.

Cumming, Elaine, 1963. "Further Thoughts on the Theory of Disengagement," UNESCO *International Social Science Journal*, 15, pp. 377–393.

Davis, Kingsley, 1944. "Adolescence and the Social Structure," *Annals of the American Academy of Political and Social Science*, pp. 8–16.

————, and Judith Blake, 1956. "Social Structure and Fertility: An Analytical Framework," *Economic Development and Cultural Change*, 16, pp. 211–235.

Eisenstadt, S. N., 1956. *From Generation to Generation; Age Groups and Social Structure*, Glencoe, Ill.: Free Press.

Foner, Anne, 1969. "The Middle Years: Prelude to Retirement?" Ph.D. dissertation, New York University.

Glick, Paul C., and Robert Parke, Jr., 1965. "New Approaches in Studying the Life Cycle of the Family," *Demography*, 2, pp. 187–202.

Goode, William J., 1960. "A Theory of Role Strain," *American Sociological Review*, 25, pp. 483–496.

————, 1963. *World Revolution and Family Patterns*, New York: Free Press.

Gulliver, P. H., 1968. "Age Differentiation," in Sills, David L., editor, *International Encyclopedia of the Social Sciences*, 17 vols., New York: Macmillan and Free Press, 1, pp. 157–161.

Gurin, Gerald, Joseph Veroff, and Sheila Feld, 1960. *Americans View Their Mental Health, A Nationwide Interview Study*, New York: Basic Books.

Hess, Beth, 1971. "Amicability," Ph.D. dissertation, Rutgers University.

International Encyclopedia of the Social Sciences, 1968. 17 vols. Sills, David L., editor, New York: Macmillan and Free Press.

Kalish, Richard A., 1969. "The Old and the New as Generation Gap Allies," *The Gerontologist*, Vol. 9, No. 2, Part I, pp. 83–89.

Kanter, Rosabeth Moss, 1968. "Commitment and Social Organization: A Study of Commitment Mechanisms in Utopian Communities," *American Sociological Review*, 33, pp. 499–517.

Kiser, Clyde V., 1962. "The Aging of Human Populations: Mechanisms of Change," in Tibbitts, Clark, and Wilma Donahue, editors, *Social and Psychological Aspects of Aging*, New York: Columbia University Press, pp. 18–35.

Komarovsky, Mirra, 1964. *Blue-Collar Marriage*, New York: Random House.

Lazarsfeld, Paul F., and Robert K. Merton, 1954. "Friendship as Social Process: A Substantive and Methodological Analysis," in Berger, M., T. Abel, and C. H. Page, editors, *Freedom and Control in Modern Society*, Princeton, N.J.: Van Nostrand, pp. 18–66.

Lenski, Gerhard E., 1954. "Status Crystallization: A Non-vertical Dimension of Social Status," *American Sociological Review*, 19, pp. 405–413.

————, 1966. *Power and Privilege: A Theory of Social Stratification*, New York: Mc-Graw-Hill.

Leslie, Gerald R., 1967. *The Family in Social Context*, New York: Oxford University Press.

McClelland, David C., 1961. *The Achieving Society*, Princeton, N.J.: Van Nostrand.

MacMahon, Brian, Thomas F. Pugh, and Johannes Ipsen, 1960. *Epidemiologic Methods*, Boston: Little, Brown.

Maddox, George L., 1963. "Activity and Morale: A Longitudinal Study of Selected Elderly Subjects," *Social Forces*, 42, pp. 195–204.

Mannheim, Karl (1928), 1952. "The Problem of Generations," in *Essays on the Sociology of Knowledge*. Edited and translated by Paul Kecskemeti, London: Routledge and Kegan Paul, pp. 276–322.

Marx, Karl (1852), 1964. *The Eighteenth Brumaire of Louis Bonaparte*, New York: International Publishers.

Matza, David, 1964. *Delinquency and Drift*, New York: Wiley.

Mayer, Kurt B., 1968. "Population, IV. Population Composition," in Sills, David L., editor, *International Encyclopedia of the Social Sciences*, 17 vols., New York: Macmillan and Free Press, 12, pp. 362–370.

Mead, Margaret, 1970. *Culture and Commitment: A Study of the Generation Gap*, New York: Doubleday, Natural History Press.

Merton, Robert K., 1957. *Social Theory and Social Structure*, rev. ed., Glencoe, Ill.: Free Press.

Miller, D. R., and G. E. Swanson, 1958. *The Changing American Parent*, New York: Wiley.

Nadel, S. F., 1952. "Witchcraft in Four African Societies: An Essay in Comparison," *American Anthropologist*, 54, pp. 18–29.

Neugarten, Bernice L., 1963. "Personality Changes During the Adult Years," in Kuhlen, Raymond G., editor, *Psychological Backgrounds of Adult Education*, Chicago: Center for the Study of Liberal Education for Adults, pp. 43–76.

Palmore, Erdman, 1969. "Sociological Aspects of Aging," in Busse, Ewald, and Eric Pfeiffer, editors, *Behavior and Adaptation in Late Life*, Boston: Little, Brown, pp. 33–69.

Parnes, Herbert S., Robert C. Miljus, Ruth S. Spitz and Associates, 1969. *Career Thresholds:* A longitudinal study of the educational and labor market experience of male youth 14–24 years of age, Volume One (February, 1969), Columbus, Ohio: Center for Human Resource Research, Ohio State University.

Parsons, Talcott (1942), 1949. *Essays in Sociological Theory, Pure and Applied*, Glencoe, Ill.: Free Press.

———, 1951. *The Social System*, Glencoe, Ill.: Free Press.

———, 1960. "Toward a Healthy Maturity," *Journal of Health and Human Behavior*, 1, pp. 163–173.

———, 1961. "Introduction to Part 2: Differentiation and Variation in Social Structures," in Parsons, Talcott et al., editors, *Theories of Society*, 2 vols., New York: Free Press, pp. 256–264.

———, and Victor Lidz, 1967. "Death in American Society," in Schneidman, E. S., editor, *Essays in Self-destruction*, New York: Science House.

———, and Edward A. Shils, 1951. "Values, Motives and Systems of Action," in Parsons, Talcott, and Edward A. Shils, editors, *Toward a General Theory of Action*, Cambridge, Mass.: Harvard University Press, pp. 45–275.

Peter, Laurence J., and Raymond Hull, 1969. *The Peter Principle*, New York: William Morrow.

Reich, Charles A., 1970. *The Greening of America*, New York: Random House.

Reinhold, Meyer, 1970. "The Generation Gap in Antiquity," in *Proceedings of The American Philosophical Society*, Vol. 114, No. 5 (October 1970) pp. 347–365.

Riley, John W., Jr., 1968. "Death and Bereavement," in Sills, David L., editor, *International Encyclopedia of the Social Sciences*, 17 vols., New York: Macmillan and Free Press, 4, pp. 19–26.

Riley, Matilda White, 1963. *Sociological Research, Volume I, A Case Approach*, New York: Harcourt, Brace & World.

———, Anne Foner, Beth Hess, and Marcia L. Toby, 1969. "Socialization for the Middle and Later Years," in Goslin, David A., editor, *Handbook of Socialization Theory and Research*, Chicago: Rand McNally, pp. 951–982.

———, and Edward E. Nelson, 1971. "Research on Stability and Change in Social Systems," in Barber, Bernard, and Alex Inkeles, editors, *Stability and Social Change: A Volume in Honor of Talcott Parsons*, Boston: Little, Brown, pp. 407–449.

Rose, Arnold M. and Warren A. Peterson, 1965. *Older People and their Social World*, Philadelphia: F. A. Davis.

Ross, Edward Alsworth, 1920. *The Principles of Sociology*, New York: Century.

Rossi, Alice S., 1964. "Equality between the Sexes: An Immodest Proposal," *Daedalus* (Spring 1964), pp. 607–652.

Shanas, Ethel, 1966. "Family Help Patterns and Social Class in Three Countries," Presented at the Meetings of the American Sociological Association, Miami.

Simmel, Georg (1908), 1964. *Conflict and The Web of Group-Affiliations*, Translated by Kurt H. Wolff and Reinhard Bendix. New York: Free Press.

Simmons, Leo W., 1960. "Aging in Preindustrial Societies," In Tibbitts, Clark, editor, *Handbook of Social Gerontology*, Chicago: University of Chicago Press, pp. 62–91.

Smelser, Neil J., 1968. "Sociological History: The Industrial Revolution and the British Working-Class Family," in Smelser, Neil J., *Essays in Sociological Explanation*, Englewood Cliffs, N.J.: Prentice-Hall, pp. 76–91.

Sorokin, Pitirim A., 1947. *Society, Culture and Personality*, New York: Harper & Brothers.

————, 1968. "Social Differentiation," in Sills, David L., editor, *International Encyclopedia of the Social Sciences*, 17 vols., New York: Macmillan and Free Press, 14, pp. 406–409.

Spengler, Joseph J., 1969. "The Aged and Public Policy," in Busse, Ewald W., and Eric Pfeiffer, *Behavior and Adaptation in Late Life*, Boston: Little, Brown, pp. 367–384.

Stinchcombe, Arthur L., 1965. "Social Structure and Organizations," in March, James G., editor, *Handbook of Organizations*, Chicago: Rand McNally, pp. 142–193.

Stouffer, Samuel A. et al., 1949. *The American Soldier*, 2 vols., Princeton, N.J.: Princeton University Press.

Streib, Gordon, 1965. "Intergenerational Relations: Perspectives of the Two Generations on the Older Parent," *Journal of Marriage and the Family*, 27, pp. 469–476.

————, and Wayne E. Thompson, 1960. "The Older Person in a Family Context," in Tibbitts, Clark, editor, *Handbook of Social Gerontology*, Chicago: Chicago University Press, pp. 447–488.

Svalastoga, Kaare, 1964. "Social Differentiation," in Faris, Robert E. L., editor, *Handbook of Modern Sociology*, Chicago: Rand McNally, pp. 530–575.

Toby, Jackson, and Edna Liebman. "The Integration of Adolescent Delinquents into Conventional Society: The Impact of Girl Friends and Wives as Agents of Further Socialization" (unpublished).

United States Bureau of the Census, 1960. 1960 Census of Population, Vol. I, Part 1.

————, March 25, 1970. *Current Population Reports*, P-20, No. 198.

————, August 6, 1970. *Current Population Reports*, P-25, No. 448.

Van Gennep, Arnold (1908), 1960. *The Rites of Passage*. Translated by Monika B. Vizedom and Gabrielle L. Caffee. Chicago: University of Chicago Press, Phoenix Books.

White, Winston, 1961. *Beyond Conformity*, New York: Free Press.

Wilensky, Harold, 1961. "Life Cycle, Work Situation, and Participation in Formal Associations," in Kleemeier, Robert W., editor, *Aging and Leisure*, New York: Oxford University Press, pp. 213–242.

11

The life course of individuals

JOHN A. CLAUSEN

Whatever the age structure of a society and however sharp the boundaries between age levels, individuals move more or less smoothly from each stratum to the next highest, somehow integrating their experiences into a coherent whole, which may be viewed from a variety of perspectives. From the perspective of the Bible's "dust to dust, ashes to ashes," the process is but one cycle in an infinite series. The early growth and late decline of strength and power over the course of a life also evokes the image of the "life cycle." Another related image is that of successive generations coming into being and then dying out.

Yet few individuals seem to experience their lives as cyclical in nature. The decline of physical strength and sexual power that accompanies aging is by no means comparable to the tremendous thrust of early development. In many respects, in fact, an individual may show continued development until extreme old age. There is not only continuity but also a continual unfolding of new possibilities almost to the very end. For most of the life history, then, the term "life cycle" seems to be somewhat inappropriate.

However, the course of a human life does entail many events that from a generational perspective may be viewed as cyclical. The sequence of events that has been called the "family cycle," in which one moves from dependent family member to independent individual, spouse, and parent and then (potentially) back to "empty nest," to widowhood and possibly dependency is certainly the prime subsidiary cycle. But other social roles and role sequences may entail similar ebbs and flows of involvement and vital investment. Thus, how one labels the whole of the life history depends upon particular images, though in the pages that follow, we shall use the terms "life course" and "life cycle" interchangeably.

The life course is, most simply put, the course of aging, but, as is evident from previous chapters, the passage of years has several facets and many implications. Biological aging involves a number of interrelated processes of growth and maturation, of differentials in the attainment of maturity and in the decline of optimum performance. The individual must adapt recurrently to the facts of his own development and aging. Inevitably, aging also brings a continual accretion of experiences, which the individual draws upon in formulating who he is and where he is going. Beyond this, almost from the very start, aging brings the development of interests and goals that will influence an individual's choice among alternative paths or even lead him to cut out a path through heavy underbrush that deters most of his peers from leaving the beaten paths.

Parallel to biological aging, and largely setting the frame of reference within which the individual defines and redefines his goals and self-image, is the structure of expectations and relationships through which he sequentially passes. Certain possibilities exist for him as positions to be occupied, roles to be played. One role may link to another: college graduation makes possible admission to law school, and law school graduation makes possible a legal career. Conversely, failure in a given role may preclude the assumption of others. A life is made up of several subcycles of interlinked roles: student roles, family roles, career roles, community roles. Within a subcycle, role sequences may be closely linked; between cycles—family and career, for example—the linkages are likely to be lesser. Nevertheless, a marked change in one sequence is likely to mean some change in the others and in their relative saliences.

The general aim of the present chapter, then, is to examine the life course for the light it throws on the nature and meaning of age for the individual member of a given cohort. Attention will be focused on the role sequences experienced by individuals in contemporary society and the selection and socialization processes that influence the life course. We shall also examine a number of issues concerning personality development, identity, and the psychological dynamics entailed in role transitions and the process of aging.

1 The analysis of the life course

Consideration of the life course almost immediately leads to an effort to break down that course into constituent phases or stages. Shakespeare's seven ages of man (*As You Like It*, II, vii) and Erikson's eight stages of psychosocial development (1950, 1968) are the best known such formulations. Of Shakespeare's seven ages, the first two and the last two are specifically age-linked: "At first the infant, muling and puking in the nurse's arms; then the whining schoolboy" and, at the other end, "the sixth age shifts into the lean and slippered pantaloon, with spectacles on nose and pouch on side

. . ." and finally, "last scene of all, . . . is second childishness and mere oblivion." The other three "ages" are really social roles—lover, soldier, justice—that have a strong age reference, especially if one considers each as a kind of ideal type. Romeo, the lover, is strictly an adolescent; the soldier, "full of strange oaths," is *par excellence* the young adult male; and the lawyer does not often become a justice until he has acquired the wisdom and the round belly of middle age. Shakespeare's seven ages are a dramatic statement of the fact that persons change markedly from one age level to the next in the images they evoke and in the selves they present to the world. One is a different person by virtue of changing physique, changing major social roles, and changing participation in society.

If Shakespeare's seven ages are most widely known by the general population, Erikson's eight stages are certainly the most widely quoted in social science and psychiatric literature. Erikson's formulation of the life cycle is psychoanalytically based and seeks "to make explicit those psycho-social insights that often remain implicit in clinical practice and theory" (1968, p. 286). Erikson's concern is with the development of personality, especially of identity. He postulates a series of crises or critical problems that must be resolved in the course of development, each defining a stage and (potentially) resulting in the attainment of a more mature level of functioning for the individual. Each such attainment is said to depend on the proper sequence of prior attainments, though precursors of each level of maturity exist prior to the critical time for its emergence. In infancy, the critical task is attainment of trust; in early childhood (age 2 or 3) the child must achieve autonomy or be faced with shame and doubt; at the "play age" (3 to 4) the child achieves initiative and conscience by resolving his Oedipal guilt; at the school age he develops a sense of industry and competence or comes to see himself as inadequate. Adolescence is the time for achieving an integrated sense of identity. Young adulthood brings true intimacy in relationships, according to Erikson, while maturity brings concern with establishing and guiding the next generation. Old age is seen as the period for achieving and maintaining full integrity and wisdom or falling into despair.

Erikson has addressed his attention to aspects of personality development and life experience that are almost universally salient in social functioning. They are problematic in that they must be achieved through socialization and adaptation. It is this fact, I believe, and not the sequence of stages in which Erikson has embedded his clinical insights, that has made his formulation so popular. Individual and group departures from Erikson's postulated sequence are frequent, and there is little evidence to support the thesis that autonomy, initiative, and intimacy—or even identity—tend to be definitively achieved *at* any given stage or *by* any given time. Each of these attributes has different meanings at different age levels, as Erikson himself notes, and some degree of each may be demanded at more or less clearly specified times in any given social milieu, but phase movements differ sharply. Erikson's stages, then, are valuable principally as a medium for his insightful analysis of developmental aspects of identity. Neither the stages nor the concepts they illuminate are precisely enough defined to permit systematic research, though they give rise to many hypotheses worth formulating with sufficient precision to make testing possible.

PROBLEMS OF DELINEATING LIFE-COURSE STAGES

When stages can be linked to the maturational level of the organism, as in childhood and early adolescence, it is not difficult to delineate specific tasks and developmental phases that are particularly salient in a given period. One can evaluate the individual's performance of these tasks or, perhaps more important, note how persons in his social set evaluate his performance. It then becomes a problem for empirical research to ascertain the consequences for the individual's later development of success or failure in resolution of the tasks of any particular stage.

In addition to accomplishment of specific developmental tasks, the effects of possession of certain characteristics can also be examined within the framework of life stages. Physical attributes, for example, may have greater importance at certain ages than at others. How does possession of valued attributes at the critical phases influence the life course? Do athletic ability in a young man or early glamour and beauty in a young woman—attributes that lead (in the United States, at least) to popularity in the adolescent peer group—give lasting advantages to their possessors? Or, to take another example, how does the age-structure of one's closest friends and associates influence or vary with the life course?

The decision to analyze the life course as a sequence of stages forces evaluation of the constancy of the points dividing the stages. The life course consists of many sequences, and some developmental accomplishments and status transitions are more closely linked with age than others. During the early years of life, maturational stages tend to occur within fairly narrow ranges. Still, even these narrow ranges may shift historically. We know, for example, that sexual maturity comes earlier now than in Shakespeare's time, though perhaps not much earlier than for the precocious Romeo and Juliet. And individual differences do exist. Almost all children start the first grade at 5 or 6 in the United States, but some move ahead more rapidly than others. As the spread increases, cumulative achievement in relation to grade level becomes a criterion for evaluation. Indeed, distinctions are noted much earlier, as a child is termed a "late talker," or an "early walker." Thus, as Bernice Neugarten and her associates (1965) have noted, we have personal timetables that reflect social norms as to when various events and role changes should take place. An important question to examine, then, is the extent to which being early or late in some sequences affects one's timing in others. For example, do girls and boys who mature early—who are "old for their years"—have an advantage over late maturers? How much difference does such acceleration make for the life course?

Once full physical maturity has been achieved, age as such becomes a basis for stage definitions primarily to the degree that there are clear age norms for status transitions. In simpler societies, where there is less role differentiation, nearly all persons of the same sex may be expected to make a given transition at a particular time, and such transitions may be highly ritualized. We emphasize, they *may* be expected to make the transition together, but only to the degree that age-grading is an important basis for social organization. For example, among the Nyakyusa, a West African society in which the villages themselves are organized on the basis of age level (beginning as new settlements of boys aged 10 to 13 or 14), power and influence are passed along from one age cohort to another in rituals that constitute a rededication of the social structure (Wilson, 1951). One's life course is to a large extent dependent on the composition of his age-village and the family status of the highest ranking male in that village.

In the contemporary United States, role transitions within the adult years are differently patterned within the social structure, especially according to one's social class, ethnic background, and occupation. This is most obvious for such transitions as college attendance, entry into first job, military service, and age of marriage. Age-linked expectations impinge differently on later careers as well. Because of these variations, stage analyses of the adult years are likely to be fruitful primarily as we deal with sequences within particular roles. Even here, the postulation of definable stages may be less fruitful than the analysis of how roles come to be ordered for a particular individual. This will be a major concern of the present essay.

DETERMINANTS OF THE LIFE COURSE

The trajectory of a human life is the product of many forces—genetic, physiological, ecological, social, and cultural. Physical and social-psychological development interact in a social matrix made up of group memberships and of shared or conflicting expectations that bind men to each other or divide them and that contribute crucially to the individual's own identity. What an individual is at any given time—what goals he pursues, what meanings events have for him, how he relates to others, and how others view him—depends upon the complex sequence of interactions among the influences upon him and the patterns that he himself has evolved for coping with his world.

There appear to be four major components underlying the development of the life course and the individual's performance of the major social roles that make up so large a part of that course: (1) the personal resources that the individual can command—his intelligence, appearance, strength, health, temperament; (2) the sources of support and guidance that help to orient him to his world and assist him to cope with it; (3) the opportunities available to him or the obstacles he encounters as these are influenced by his social class, ethnic membership, age, sex, and personal contacts, as well as the effects of war, depression, and major social changes that impinge differentially upon particular birth cohorts; and (4) investments of effort that the individual makes in his own behalf (his commitments) and his mobilization of effort toward these ends. There is, then, an enormous range of influences to be considered. Only the most gross sequences and interactions have been studied.

A BRIEF NOTE ON METHOD

Research on the human life course requires either that one study individuals over long periods of time or that one attempt to reconstruct the course of individual lives retrospectively. Except when records of the individual's past acts, attitudes, and affiliations exist, the reconstruction of the past is fraught with difficulty. It is the nature of man to reinterpret his world and its events in the light of his own immediate needs. If the child is father to the man, the events of later years nonetheless rewrite the remembrance of things past. One need not undergo psychoanalysis to realize that the events of the past have been rewoven into personal myths. We need only be confronted by our own letters, by photographs, or by reports of other participants presenting quite a different record than that which has been enshrined in our own memories.[1] But if retrospective reinterpretation creates problems in reconstructing life histories, it is nevertheless the sustenance on which our identities thrive, and, as analysts, we shall have to rely heavily on individual reconstructions.

Longitudinal studies afford the possibility of systematically examining linkages between early and later life experience, but only if the experiences that are of theoretical interest have been conceptualized, categorized, and assessed at appropriate times. Intensive longitudinal research is inevitably costly and limited to relatively small groups of subjects who are drawn from a single locality. If mature investigators start research with a cohort of infants, the investigators are likely to be retired or dead before their subjects reach middle life. Systematic data collection over the years becomes tremendously complex; there are always gaps caused by inability to reach subjects at designated times or to monitor transitional stages as closely as would be desirable. Nevertheless, where longitudinal data do exist for several decades of life, they yield a sounder basis for constructing the actual sequence of events and

[1] See the systematic analysis of problems of retrospection in the monograph by Yarrow et al. (1970).

orientations during the life course than does any reconstruction from retrospective reports.

Adequate understanding of a given person's life history requires that one know both how that person viewed influential events at the time of their occurrence and how he subsequently interprets them. Ideally, one would like to know the nature of the "objective realities" that were encountered at any given time, the individual's perceptions of them at the time (as perhaps indicated in letters, diaries, or other contemporary records) and his later reconstructions of what occurred and the consequences for him of both objective and subjective pasts. A turning point may not be recognized as such until well after it has passed. It may be recognized by associates or by research staff but not by the person who has shifted his course. Perhaps more often, it is registered subjectively, at least to some degree, before it is apparent to others. Even with longitudinal data, then, subjective reconstructions are of great importance.

Cross-sectional data on age differences—which also, of course, reflect cohort differences [*see Chapter* 2]—often constitute our major basis for making inferences about probable life-course changes. To the extent that such cross-sectional data do not merely report age differences in performance or in personal attributes but inquire about the individual's past performance and his perceptions of change, they will be more likely to permit valid inferences about the life course. If, for example, many older persons not only report less visiting outside their neighborhoods but also comment that they had done much more visiting when they were still driving their own cars, we shall have some confidence that the observed age differences reflect a change in visiting patterns with aging and are not primarily due to cohort differences (though, of course, cohort differences may also exist).

From these preliminary considerations of conceptual and methodological issues, we turn now to a closer look at the nature of the life course and its determinants. It would be desirable to consider major cultural and historical variations in the salience of features and influences upon the life course, for clearly they are enormous. This is unfortunately beyond our scope and ability, so that we shall confine attention almost entirely to the life course in contemporary America.

Our commentary will be largely chronological, beginning with the start of life, but we shall make a number of excursions as we consider the interrelationships of the components. From time to time, we shall draw upon data from the Oakland Growth Study, a longitudinal investigation of a cohort of individuals followed since the early 1930's, when they were entering junior high school. Such longitudinal data give us some basis for inferring linkages between early attributes and experiences and later phases of the life course. One never knows whether such linkages are peculiar to a local population, a single cohort, or a historical era.

Thus our description of the life course in the contemporary United States is largely a description of an imaginary cohort, derived principally from cross-sectional studies, our own longitudinal study of a cohort now distinctly middle-aged, and scattered other longitudinal studies. As stressed throughout this book, only in the absence of social change are such data likely to yield valid information about the typical life course, even for a single society. Perhaps it is inevitable, then, that any particular image of the life course will be tinged with the writer's own cohort-centrism. Against the danger that we draw generalizations that are not sufficiently qualified, let the reader constantly ask himself: Are such relationships as have been noted plausible for the entire set of cohorts in the society in the light of changes in norms and social structure that have occurred over time? Toward the end of this essay, we shall return to this general issue.

2 *The developmental years: infancy through adolescence*

By far the most rapid growth and the most extensive learning experiences of the entire life course occur in the early years. Whether or not particular kinds of learning are critically linked to particular maturational stages, so that failure to learn at the appropriate stage results in a lasting deficit, there is substantial evidence that later cognitive, emotional, and social development are at least markedly influenced by the events of early years. Experiences of infancy and early childhood are regarded as especially crucial by psychoanalytic theory, which holds that the organization of personality and its basic orientations are laid down during this period. Three of Erikson's eight stages of the life cycle come before the child has begun school, and fully one-third of Lidz's detailed analysis of the life cycle is devoted to the preschool years.[2] In the present chapter, however, with its focus upon the dynamics of passage through the age strata, the early years will receive less attention than would be warranted if we were dealing primarily with personality or cognitive development. Moreover, despite the weight of clinical and common sense evidence for the strong influence of early experience, it is remarkably difficult to document systematically any specific influences of early experience upon the later course of development.[3]

Paucity of evidence on the effects of particular socialization practices or

[2] Lidz (1968) has produced the first full-length book on the life course viewed in psychoanalytic perspective.
[3] See, for example, Caldwell (1964) for a careful review of the evidence on the effects of infant care.

experiences in the early years is paralleled by the dearth of evidence as to the influences of constitutional differences, differences that, could they be measured precisely, would supply a reference for evaluating the effect of subsequent experiences. It seems quite probable that differences in temperament and energy level influence the course of life, but measures of such attributes show marked instability or unreliability in the early weeks and months. Some differences are manifest at birth, but maturational differentials during the early years can apparently change the relative ranking of children on a large number of biological attributes. In addition, assessments of the effects of socialization practices on the one hand, or of constitutional differences on the other, are enormously complicated because the two sets of influences are in interaction from birth. Parental response to children seems from the very first to be determined not merely by the parents' personalities and earlier socialization experience but by the child's own characteristics and actions. As a consequence, the child's capacities and potentials cannot be assessed during the early months of life, nor can one assume that socialization experiences under which one child thrives will be equally appropriate to another.

INFANCY AND EARLY CHILDHOOD

At birth the child carries a bundle of ascribed statuses (race, sex, kinship position) and a bundle of potentials profoundly affected by his genetic and social heritages. The potentials carried by his physical constitution will facilitate or impede particular performances that will be expected of him at various stages of development.[4] Maturation plays a major role in setting the time for early life achievements, such as grasping, walking, talking, and the development of other motor skills. Training will achieve little unless the child has reached the requisite maturational level, but once at that level he moves ahead quickly. Cognitive and linguistic skills also develop sequentially and appear to have their maturational thresholds, though here theorists are not in complete agreement. Piaget views individual development as proceeding through a series of more or less invariant stages in which certain schemas

---

[4] Major defects, such as congenital deafness, blindness, or serious malformations tend in themselves to set the individual on a life course distinct from that of normal peers. They do so not only because they preclude participation in certain scheduled activities and experiences that are standard expectations for a given group, but perhaps even to a greater extent because the basis of exclusion serves as a stigma. It sets the individual apart as different, imperfect, deficient, and therefore presumably not capable of achieving full participation in adult society. Such persons are not expected to maintain normal timetables. Consideration of the life course of persons who possess major constitutional defects is beyond the scope of our treatment, but we may note that they are but one instance of persons "counted out" at some point in the life course. They must cope with a situation that many eventually encounter, in which they are expected to opt for somehing less than a full adult career. Often they will be treated as if they belonged to a much younger age group and will be presumed to exhibit the degree of dependency and other signs of immaturity that are expected of members of that younger group.

or modes of experiencing and organizing experiences are successfully dominant.[5] Though cultural experience may influence such development, he holds that in the last analysis it is the nature of the organism and its maturation that accounts for such sequences.

In the beginning, the infant has no sense of his own boundaries. He must acquire the sense of where he as a physical object ends and where the environment begins. More important, of course, he comes to have a sense of self as he interacts with others. He comes to respond less immediately to internal bodily states and more to social objects. Initially helpless, yet in a sense omnipotent in a world of nurturing adults, he is faced with performance demands as soon as he begins to show a measure of developmental progress. Erikson has proposed that the sense of basic trust is the first crucial component of personal orientation to develop in life. A sense of trust (or of distrust) of others will later become entwined with the child's emerging sense of self, for "self" and "other" are, as Baldwin (1913, p. 15) noted, "born together."

Early childhood is the period of primary socialization, in which the child must learn a wide variety of physical, perceptual, cognitive, and social skills. He moves from complete dependency toward autonomy, from amorality to absolutistic values to conventional morality, from being a total stranger to knowing his way around people, places, and things. The scheduling of the tasks that are to be accomplished in the course of primary socialization varies with the task. Norms for learning to sit, walk, and talk are closely linked with maturational stage, and parents are very much aware of them. Norms as to when the child is regarded as old enough to feed himself or dress himself are less clearly defined and depend on parental personalities as well as on cultural orientations. Societies differ quite radically in this regard. Bronfenbrenner (1970, pp. 17–18) has noted that in Russian nursery schools very small toddlers are expected to learn to dress themselves and tie their own shoes, something most American teachers and parents would regard as quite beyond the children's capacities.

It is commonly assumed that all children follow a more or less standard course of socialization during the early years, just as all children in elementary school follow the same curriculum. True, there is likely to be high redundancy in the socializing messages that the average child receives. Moreover, general cultural expectations are sufficiently below the potentials of talented children so that it may seem that all but defective or markedly deprived children should be able to meet them. However, the assumption of standard early experience is not a valid one for highly differentiated societies such as our own. Linguistic usage, food preferences, and social attitudes—to take three quite different kinds of early social learning—vary according to

[5] See Flavell (1963) for a description and assessment of Piaget's formulations.

social class, ethnic background, and region of residence. They are taken in by the child as naturally as is the air he breathes. They become a part of his cognitive apparatus and symbols of his social origins. They identify him as he moves outside the home. And they may affect his life chances in other settings even more than do his physical constitution and his inherent intellectual capacity. Above all, differences in social status and in subcultural norms mean that children from one background will experience discontinuity and difficulty in transitions that are nonproblematic for those from a different social background.

One of the most powerful motivating forces in socialization is identification based on affection and mutual involvement. Strong positive identification of the child with his parents leads him to adopt their values and their perspectives. In part this is unwitting; in part it entails choosing among available alternative values. Less obvious is the identification of parents with their children and its influence on the parents' own perspectives. In times of rapid social change, close parent-child ties probably tend to constrain the child from taking over drastically new values and life patterns. In the face of massive changes in moral values and norms, however, such close ties may actually help induct some parents into new ways of viewing the social order.

THE SCHOOL YEARS

Entrance into school is the first major transition common to all life histories in our society. It is a transition for which children are variously prepared. Some can hardly be said to be prepared at all, though almost all will have heard about school and know that going to school is a sign of growing up. Some will be eager to learn reading and writing, some apprehensive about leaving home, some fearful because they have heard from older siblings or peers about the discipline they will receive.

In school the child has a new role and a greatly enlarged group of peers. He is explicitly defined as a learner, expected to acquire new skills and knowledge at a pace set by his teacher, who also imposes general standards of performance that have nothing to do with the child's particular relationship to the teacher. If the child's behavior is markedly immature and he is unable to meet the demands of the classroom, he may be taken out and given another year to mature or he may get special attention. If the behavior patterns he has learned at home are too much at variance with those of the classroom, he will in all probability be disciplined and be singled out as a "problem." To be thus singled out is likely to create a lasting reputation. School personnel will in general expect the child to continue to be a problem; the child, in turn, will feel that there is something wrong with him, but he may be quite unable to understand what that something is or what he can do about it.

Once he starts school, the child is subject to a kind of evaluation, relative to his age-mates, that is quite different from any that has taken place hitherto. His ability to handle himself with his peers, his performance of school tasks, his comportment and his self-assurance are all subject to scrutiny by persons who may be affectively neutral in their judgments. The teacher's responses to him are likely to be much influenced by his cooperativeness, his behavior, and his ability to do school work well. The responses of his peers are likely to depend on his initiative and daring in peer activities, his ability to handle himself well in the games children play.

EARLY INFLUENCES OF APPEARANCE AND PHYSIQUE

Appearance and physical skills probably have a greater effect on life chances than most of us like to admit. The "attractive" child gets more attention and more positive feedback from peers and adults. In the preadolescent years, moreover, it appears that body build exerts a powerful influence on peer ratings, especially in the working class. To a high degree, those boys and girls who are perceived by their peers as leaders tend to be muscular and strong. The thin, frail boy or girl is rarely so rated; he tends to be devalued, especially in the working class (unpublished data from the Oakland Growth Study). Measured intelligence, on the other hand, does not seem to have any appreciable effect on peer ratings until much later.

Peer evaluations certainly affect the child's own identity. The athletic child who is a poor student and the good student who is a poor athlete modify their activities as they develop awareness of their own strengths and weaknesses. They formulate somewhat different images of what they want and are, and build up different patterns of association with others.

Organisms mature and age at different rates. A few girls reach menarche by 10; late maturers may be 15. Boys mature a bit later but with a comparable spread. Whether the index of maturity is the proportion of ultimate height achieved by a given age or the developmental stage of primary and secondary sex characteristics, there is great variation among individuals. In a sense, the early maturers are comparable in their physical development to late maturers who are several years older. The various aspects of maturing are highly intercorrelated, but age of attaining maturity is not at all related to intelligence, or to other attributes that determine one's grade placement in school. Therefore, once the early maturers begin the adolescent growth spurt, they pull away from their later-maturing peers in height, strength, and potential sexuality. Differences are maximum in the early senior high school years. The implications for the individual's sense of identity and for his subsequent career line are not negligible.

Early-maturing boys excel their late-maturing peers in athletic performance. They appear to develop a greater sense of competence and self-confidence. Data from a longitudinal study by Jones (1965) show that at age 16 early maturers were seen as more relaxed, matter-of-fact, and poised. At 33, they scored significantly higher than later maturers on scales of the California Psychological Inventory (CPI) labeled "socialization," "good impression," "responsibility" and on other scales suggesting conventional adjustment or conformity to dominant cultural norms. Late-maturing boys, on the other hand, appeared to be more expressive and at the same time more tense during the high school years and at age 33 they scored higher in "psychological mindedness" (sensitivity to others) but also higher in psychoneurotic tendencies.

Whereas early attainment of physical maturity tends to have largely positive social and psychological consequences for boys, the picture is quite different for girls. Early maturing of girls appears to have the primary consequence of providing a sign of changed status for the opposite sex. The early-maturing girl tends to catch the eye of older boys. She is under pressure to date and participate in a new social world at a much earlier age than is the early-maturing boy. Particularly in the working class, she is likely to be caught up in activities and relationships that may impair her performance as a student and lessen the attractions of remaining a student.

Few studies have attempted to relate physique or other aspects of physical development to adult career lines aside from documenting the importance of physical attractiveness for the upward mobility of women through marriage, a topic to which we shall turn later. It appears that the maximum effects of body build and physical development occur in the preadolescent and adolescent periods. Moreover, such effects are most sharply manifest in peer society. Teachers ratings, for example, show far less relationship to somatotype than do peer ratings, and personality assessments in adulthood show generally lower correlations with body build components than do comparable assessments in adolescence. Nevertheless, some physical attributes continue to influence significantly the individual's social stimulus value. Extremes of height, weight, and facial attractiveness lead often to stereotypic responses from others. Thus, a recent follow-up study of male graduates from an engineering school found a significant positive correlation between height and salary earned five years after graduation. There is no reason to assume that tall engineers are more competent than short ones, but they are undoubtedly more imposing in a job interview and quite possibly have somewhat more obvious self-assurance.

Whether or not the psychological correlates of body build reflect underlying constitutional differences, these attributes are less salient in adult performances than in childhood and adolescence. Insofar as the psychological correlates may be the resultant of stereotypic classification ("hot-tempered redheads," "strong silent" types, etc.), the stereotypes are likely to be less compelling as the child grows older, when they tend to be superseded by criteria of actual performance. Nevertheless, there are some evidences of continuing operation of stereotypes, and "life reviews" in the middle years suggest that prestige or devaluation relating to one's physical development in the preadolescent and adolescent years can have lasting effects upon the self-image and on role commitments.[6]

ALTERNATIVE TRACKS IN ADOLESCENCE

Childhood and adolescence are full of discoveries of things one can or cannot do well, things that are exciting or dull, things that involve one in groups of like-minded others or that insulate one from having to be involved with others who are threatening. In general, the adolescent's political orientations, his social attitudes, and his values are closely similar to those of his parents. Usually, his choice of friends will initially be based on residential propinquity, then on common school experience, and then on similar values and interests. Parental suggestion, the stimulus of teachers or classmates, or simple discovery through reading or casual involvements may lead to the formulation of goals and commitments early in adolescence or at any later period. Even if clear-cut interests having implications for occupational choice do not emerge, the adolescent may form an image of the general style of life he wishes or the general realm of his intellectual concerns. Personality aspects —conventionality, conservatism, social confidence—along with intellectual skills and the largely fortuitous impact of particular teachers in particular subjects in high school and college lead to further narrowing of interests. At every step, there is a potential for identity formation, but by no means a necessary latching onto the identities waiting to be claimed.

Well before adolescence, the average child is spending far more time with

[6] A brief comment on the special case of the outstanding athlete may be in order. A physique that gives one special capacities, like any other unusual talent, will shape the life course most when it leads to high social visibility and a career or role opportunity for a person whose alternatives would otherwise be limited. To be 6 feet 10 inches tall is to be marked for a basketball team, even if one has not shown great ability to handle his body. The tall youth of middle-class origins who has high intellectual skills and opportunities to pursue any career that he wants is far less likely to become a professional basketball player than is the comparably endowed youth whose initial occupational horizons are markedly constricted. Professional sports and entertainment have long been roads to upward mobility for persons from groups disadvantaged in competition for other occupational opportunities. The particular sports in vogue at a given time do, of course, change like any other occupational specialties.

From the standpoint of age-group analysis, the career of the professional athlete presents some interesting features. It seems likely that relatively few individuals plan to become professional athletes before they have demonstrated very superior performance as amateurs. Emerging evidence of superiority thus opens up a new career possibility, and increased concentration on becoming outstanding tends to close off, for most aspirants, intensive preparation for some other career.

Once they have established themselves as professionals, however, most athletes can anticipate only a decade or two of competition. At this point they either become candidates for coaching or team management jobs, or they must move into wholly new career lines. The superstars will early form business affiliations that capitalize on their names or will have this option readily available, but there must be many less well-known athletes who suddenly find themselves forced to compete with job candidates many years their junior.

his peers than with his parents. Obviously, there are great variations in the course of parent-child relations in adolescence, and close emotional ties and consonance of his basic values with those of his parents are in no way precluded by his involvement in the peer society. But the immediate interests of the average adolescent are in many respects different from those of his father and mother. Pressures for peer group conformity make it important to demonstrate a high measure of autonomy from control by parental standards, but this does not necessarily negate those standards.[7]

Adolescence as an age-grade entails marked shifts from the loci of control and initiative that characterized infancy and childhood. The activity patterns of infancy and childhood were closely related to maturational level and closely monitored by older socialization agents. The physical and mental capabilities of the adolescent are not appreciably less than those of the adult, and close monitoring is out of the question. Parents and teachers continue to exercise great influence in many spheres, but peer influence and self-directed activity increase enormously.

We know relatively little about the ways in which particular interests and personal commitments develop and change in these years. Parental personalities and relationships have an impact on the child's interests and performance as they do on his conception of himself. Domination of the child by his parents, particularly by an authoritarian father, appears to discourage achievement motivation in the child (Elder, 1963). Devaluation of the child by his parents engenders anxiety that may immobilize him or lead to fiercely competitive efforts to win approval outside the home. Ann Roe's studies (1951) of eminent physical and biological scientists found that they came from homes characterized by detached, unemotional relationships. She suggests that the future scientists early abandoned efforts at human involvement and turned their attention to understanding the world of ideas and impersonal things.

In adolescence the sorting and selecting of individuals into alternative tracks becomes much more evident and increasingly less reversible. Goals become crystallized for some, while others drift. Here one's social class may markedly modify the consequences. The higher-status youth whose plans are uncertain but who views college attendance as a matter of course has plenty of time to find himself. The lower-status youth who is not strongly motivated toward achievement is much less likely to attend college. He will drift into the labor market, and his life course will thereafter tend to be quite different from that of his college-bound class peer.

The processes of choice and sorting that take place in the adolescent period relate to friendship and to the establishment of intimate ties with the

---

[7] Thus Riley et al. (1961) note that adolescents are more likely to share future-oriented norms with their parents but current youth-culture norms with their peers.

opposite sex as well as to academic and intellectual interests. If we emphasize academic sorting processes here, and especially those that lead to or preclude graduation from college, it is because they have unparalleled consequences for the life course in mid-twentieth-century America. A substantial body of research supports the proposition that college attendance and subsequent graduation are markedly influenced by ability and by parental social status (Sewell and Shah, 1967). The better educated one's parents, the more likely one is to perceive them as favoring college and the more likely one is actually to go to college. Parents who have themselves attended college can guide their offspring toward academic sequences that are appropriate to the children's interests. They can help enrich their children's school experience through discussion of topics under study in school. Some fathers whose own career aspirations have been thwarted by lack of education may strongly urge their sons to get as much education as possible, but they are usually not able to offer as much guidance and supportive involvement as ᴗetter-educated fathers.

The adolescent's ability to do well in high school, which is dependent on his intelligence, his orientation to school, and his motivation toward academic achievement, is also a strong predictor of college attendance. Motivation is particularly important in the working class, where most parents may not really be committed to college for their children; the working-class youngster who wants to go to college must be sufficiently determined to overcome financial and informational deficits. For such lower-status youth, teachers tend to be very important influences on college aspirations and plans.

Once in college, both parental social status and ability again make a difference in predicting graduation. Among Wisconsin high school graduates of the class of 1957, for example, Sewell and Shah (1968, p. 200) found that 22 per cent of the males and 15 per cent of the females subsequently graduated from college. The effects of ability (primarily intelligence) were striking: 42 per cent of the high school boys and 29 per cent of the girls in the top third on a junior year test of ability subsequently graduated from college compared to 4 per cent of the boys and less than 3 per cent of the girls who had scored in the bottom third of ability. But with ability held constant, the effects of parental status remain substantial. Considering the brightest third, 65 per cent of the males and 62 per cent of the females graduated among those whose parents had both attended at least a year of college; while only 28 per cent of the males and 15 per cent of the females graduated among those equally bright high school graduates whose parents had not themselves graduated from high school.

Half a century ago one might have placed the critical level of education at high school graduation (and it would have been far less "critical"), but recent research strongly suggests that college graduation is for most men almost a condition of high occupational status (Eckland, 1965; Elder, 1968). Only a relatively small proportion of nongraduates are likely to achieve high occupational status unless they can step into a family business or have exceptional talents that are much in demand. For the average male, then, future prospects are to a considerable degree shaped by academic accomplishment in the high school and college years.

For girls, too, college attendance shapes future statuses, though perhaps in ways that differ from males. Alternatives to college for a female are likely to be almost immediate marriage or a short-term job, then marriage. For women maturing in the period 1930—1960, at least, it appears that their style of life, the timing of their having children, the way in which they raise their children, and the nature of the marital relation itself have depended to a significant degree on the ultimate social status achieved by their husbands. Girls who go to college not only have opportunity to prepare themselves for careers but also have a wide range of continuing contacts with men who will occupy high occupational statuses. Girls who aim for upward mobility through marriage, but who do not go to college, must depend on other settings for opportunities to meet men with comparable prospects.

3 Career development[8]

Full adult status for the male entails economic self-sufficiency (and hence, for the great bulk of Americans, a regular occupation), stable relationships with the opposite sex (leading to the establishment of a new family of procreation) and social-political participation as a citizen and community member. Entrance into these new statuses is closely age-patterned, if not age-determined, and the role sequences they entail tend to be somewhat interdependent. This poses problems of presentation, since it is difficult to deal adequately with any one of these sequences without invoking the others to some degree. Therefore, as we examine particular role sequences in some detail we shall also take note of the nature of interdependencies among sequences.

For the average male, no other social role approaches the occupational role in the salience and pervasiveness of its influence on other aspects of the life course. In general, in contemporary America, the later a man completes his education and enters an occupation for which he has been preparing, the

[8] This section is devoted solely to the work careers of males, an exclusiveness that reflects in part the literature on work careers, in part the cultural tradition that the occupational activities of women are typically sporadic and secondary to marital and parental roles, lacking characteristics of a career line. Yet, a comparable analysis might be made of female work-life careers, especially since career concerns are of increasing salience to women and may, among the younger cohorts, be approaching those of males. By contrast, there are some clues that the younger cohorts of males may be rejecting the pre-eminence of work and career development in determining their life styles.

more fully will that occupation engage him for the rest of his active days. Conversely, the earlier he starts work, the less likely is his occupation to become his consuming life activity, largely, of course, because his work setting is less likely to offer the scope and opportunity for expression of interests and for advancement that is afforded the more highly educated and therefore later entrant into the labor force.

It would be a mistake, however, to assume that most people move in an orderly fashion from their academic training or initial work experience into a continuous career line. Less than half experience "orderly careers," in the sense of moving through several related steps, and fewer still move in an orderly progression from their first jobs (Wilensky, 1961a).

EARLY OCCUPATIONAL INTERESTS AND CHOICE

From the time that he first becomes aware of the existence of occupations the child undergoes some measure of anticipatory socialization into an occupational role. Initially, of course, occupations are represented for him by individuals who bear the occupational label and its symbolic trappings. The child's first verbalization of occupational preferences has little to do either with his social situation or with his personal qualifications but rather with the fantasies he has built up around images relating to certain occupations. The research of Ginsberg and his associates (1951) indicates that unrealistic fantasies tend to dominate the thinking of children up to about age 11. For some individuals fantasies continue to be important into adulthood. Prior to adolescence, however, most children begin to become aware of the general qualifications that are required for particular occupations and some of the potentialities that the occupations afford. How realistically they think about their occupational possibilities seems to depend in large part on the kind of guidance they are given by parents and school personnel and by the economic conditions of the time.

For children growing up in a period of depression, preoccupation with getting some kind of job may begin a great deal earlier than with children growing up in a time of affluence. This hypothesis is supported by Elder's analysis (forthcoming) of longitudinal data on a cohort of subjects who were adolescent during the depression of the 1930's. Boys whose families experienced much deprivation were more preoccupied with occupational choice and formulated specific occupational plans earlier than did their nondeprived peers. Subsequently, more of those from deprived families pursued stable and orderly careers and more achieved their earlier avowed occupational goals.

For youth who go to college, firm occupational choice may be deferred until well beyond adolescence, while for those who do not go beyond high school, some kind of choice has to be made at an earlier time. For those most disadvantaged in the labor market, one can hardly speak of occupational choice but only of the search for a job. At the other extreme are those who prepare for a profession like medicine where the choice must be made relatively early in one's college career but formal entry into the occupation lies six to ten years ahead. Between these extremes, for most persons there is a narrowing of occupational interests as the time of job seeking approaches. The less preparation one has for any particular type of work, the more likely one is to try out several possibilities, if the job market is good.

COMMITMENT TO THE JOB

How many jobs make a work life? The answer is hard to come by for any cohort of workers, and there are obviously great differences within and among cohorts, especially between the various occupational levels in any given cohort. At lower occupational levels, it appears that job shifts tend to be very frequent in the first decade of working, as the individual seeks better opportunities in pay, advancement, or working conditions, or as he seeks a more congenial kind of work. Many individuals do not find a suitable kind of work until well into the second decade of their work lives. For example, among subjects in the Oakland Growth Study, fully a third of the men did not find the kind of work they wanted until after they were 30 years old. At age 40, a fifth reported that they definitely expected to change jobs within the next five years, and only one-third reported themselves fairly certain that they would *not* change jobs. Most often, of course, they planned to stay in the same general field, but a few planned shifts of fields as well as of employers. Yet this was an upwardly mobile group, most of whose members had achieved middle-class or even upper-middle-class status. Clearly, job changes in themselves may provide important avenues of upward mobility for many career lines.

At some point in the work life of most individuals, however, the accumulation of interest, experience, skill, or seniority in a given line of work will have created a commitment to that occupation. It may be an enthusiastic commitment with anticipation of increasing psychological and economic rewards, or it may be a grudging acknowledgement that one is not likely to do better in some other field. The man who is still searching for the right occupation beyond 40 is likely to recognize that his career is in deep trouble. Indeed, our longitudinal data suggest that he is likely to characterize himself as verging on being a failure, no matter how many excuses he can offer for not yet having established himself in a stable line of work.

Those who have early committed themselves to a profession or other occupation for which they have trained are most likely to remain in that occupation, even if its intrinsic satisfactions prove to be less than originally anticipated. Most often, of course, intrinsic satisfactions are found to be proportional to the amount of preparation, since the jobs occupied offer greater opportunity for initiative, less close supervision, and the kind of activities that interest the worker. Moreover, it would seem that the longer the period of preparation (during which many gratifications must be deferred) and the more intrinsically rewarding the job, the more salient the job becomes as a core element in one's identity. Even less rewarding jobs, however, put their imprint on identity. Hughes and his students (1958) have documented the ways in which the members of occupations develop rationalizations about the less satisfying or less prestigious aspects of their work in order to give it greater value in their own eyes and in those of outsiders.

A man's job is to a considerable degree an index of his social standing in the community. Jobs are obviously ranked and serve to rank their incumbents. Highest prestige is accorded to members of occupations that require superior intelligence or judgment, permit the worker much autonomy, and entail challenging and satisfying activities. The most devalued jobs, however, have aspects that, if more fully appreciated by others, might raise the status of the occupation. Conversely, high professional status may be maintained by keeping dirty linen well locked in the closet. But status is only one aspect of an occupation, and the particular compensations that might offset this aspect for one man will differ from those another would take into consideration. Good pay, convenient hours, lack of tension, contact with congenial others may make up for lack of intrinsic satisfactions. Eventually, in the course of a career, all are likely to enter into occupational evaluation to some degree.

AGE AND ASPIRATIONS

Age is, of course, a major frame of reference—through comparison either with age-mates or with some earlier period of one's own life—for assessing one's standing in his occupation. Has one kept up with or surpassed most of one's age-mates, or are younger competitors moving ahead? During the early years of his career, a man's aspirations may be his primary referent, but his aspirations must often be adjusted once he has gone some distance on a particular track. If he has moved faster and further than he expected, his dreams may soar. If he has not managed to achieve as much as he had counted on, he must either lower his aspirations or redouble his efforts, perhaps shifting fields or jobs as well. Despite emphasis on achievement in the United States, even in management positions most men do not expect to go all the way to the top, and as they advance in years their self-evaluations are more frequently anchored in the progress made from the beginning of their careers than in the determination to reach the top. By age 45, they tend to be strongly "anchored downward."[9]

The man who works with his hands knows what his ceiling is likely to be. He is likely to reach that ceiling by his 40's, though his pay may continue to

[9] See Tausky and Dubin (1965) for data on management personnel in five northwestern business firms.

rise because of seniority. In managerial and professional jobs, by contrast, one may just be getting well established by his early 40's. Major supervisory responsibilities are likely to be just beginning. At the same time, however, the costs of striving are to be weighed against the possibility of having a more leisurely yet quite comfortable life as a success without being a "world-beater." The businessman who is passed over for a crucial promotion may be relieved even though his ego has been somewhat deflated. In a highly competitive segment of a highly competitive society, nearly everyone must accept that all can't be big winners, and, in fact, once one has achieved a certain rank he can most often count on being treated with consideration even when demoted.[10] In periods of depression, of course, the consequences of not holding one's own may be much more devastating.

Intermeshed with the influence of motivations to get to the top is the influence of signs, beginning in the middle years, that one is no longer getting better at most aspects of his job but may indeed be doing some things less well or less easily. Though the older worker may have a larger store of knowledge and experience than his younger colleagues, in some situations his knowledge will be outmoded. Especially in technical jobs, the older worker is much less likely to keep up with new developments. Moreover, the pre-retiree who disparages a younger coworker with the announcement that "I've forgotten more than you'll ever know" may be unwittingly revealing his own anxiety; he simply cannot mobilize his past experience with sufficient speed and accuracy to capitalize on it. Many men approaching 50 voice some anxieties of this sort.

There are obviously many different kinds of career patterns, with different consequences for other aspects of the life course. Careers in the armed forces and in civil service permit one to retire after 30 or sometimes even fewer years. Second careers are then quite possible, permitting a much higher level of income maintenance before and after the final retirement. We know little about the adaptational problems posed for those who enter a new field and often a new kind of community life at 50 or 55. Such transitions are undoubtedly eased by the existence of a pension that makes it possible to consider job interest above income. One need not take an unappealing job if he can manage to get along with no job at all; something better is bound to turn up.

Typical career sequences are most readily apparent in bureaucratic organizations. The man whose career is locked in a single organization tends to make its norms and rules his own. The reformer tends not to last, while the man with "staying quality" tends to build up an investment in getting as far as possible and not jeopardizing his job by antagonizing superiors. The

[10] See, for example, Goldner (1965) for a discussion of personal adaptations to demotion among executives in a large corporation.

"bureaucratic personality" as an ideal type or stereotype has been well characterized by Merton (1957, pp. 195–206) and graphically depicted by Balzac and other writers, but most workers in bureaucracies approximate the ideal type to only a limited degree. If they are modestly successful, their lives are stabilized in a network of relationships and expectations that change slowly and present few surprises but nevertheless afford some scope for ingenuity and personal style. The men who are most successful will at times face substantial jumps in responsibility, in their job locations, and even in the type of role played in the organization. Moreover, such men are probably more likely to change organizations once they achieve visibility as "comers."

Some professions offer career development almost as orderly as that possible in a career spent in a single large bureaucracy. Most, nevertheless, offer choice points and alternative lines of development that pose very different kinds of challenges. The practical considerations that enter into decision processes, the pushes and pulls, vary by personality of worker and spouse, by phase of family life, by developments in occupational specialization and economic conditions.

It would be a serious mistake to assume, as some writers seem to, that occupational careers are primarily a matter of learning a role and then performing it. When one examines occupational histories and the rationales given for them, it becomes evident that one's like or dislike of associates, the attitudes of one's wife and children, and the attractions of a particular community, as well as intrinsic job satisfactions, opportunities for advancement, level of income, and conditions of work all influence decisions to leave (or not to leave) one employer for another. Some men seek more responsibility and higher status, while others are content at some point to ease their striving.

JOB, FAMILY, AND COMMUNITY

For most men, entrance into the world of work is separated from marriage by only a few years. Norms regarding the economic prerequisites to marriage have markedly changed during the twentieth century. Not many girls today bring to marriage "hope chests" in which they have accumulated the linens and other items once expected of a proper bride. Nor do most men feel that they must have substantial savings before they can consider marriage. If one has confidence in his future prospects, temporary expedients for getting along may be quite enough to permit launching a marriage. A settled job for the prospective bridegroom is all the economic security that most parents of today's brides are likely to expect. Persons who married during the Depression years, or who long postponed marriage because of economic insecurity, may not be less concerned than their parents were in the early 1900's about economic security, but, in the middle class at least, their concerns take a very different form in the affluence of the 1960's. Moreover, their children are far less concerned about economic prerequisites of marriage. Many will marry while still students.

Nevertheless, the attainment of a degree of economic independence on the part of a young man permits him a far more diverse range of social activities with the opposite sex than would otherwise be feasible. Courtship and marriage pose no serious problems for the man already economically established. On the other hand, the man who knows he must undertake many years of intensive study and training prior to his entry into an occupation is likely to engage in more casual relationships with the opposite sex and to avoid commitment. If a person faced with long years of education establishes a strong emotional tie with a member of the opposite sex and contemplates marriage, he must either attenuate his own investment in study or rely upon a prospective spouse to help support him during the training period. Not infrequently, it appears, long-range educational and occupational goals may be sacrificed in order to marry and perhaps have children at an earlier age.

More generally, the concordance of certain phases of the occupational career and phases of the family cycle maximize economic concerns at certain age periods. Setting up a household entails substantial expense for furniture and equipment. If there are no savings, installment purchases quickly put a demand on future income. If neither member of the couple has a car, they tend to purchase one very quickly (Lansing and Morgan, 1955). The pressures on liquid assets are high at the start of a new family, but in the period before children arrive both husband and wife are likely to work and thus keep on top of their commitments. With the arrival of children, however, the demand for income and job security is markedly increased. A somewhat larger salary than the one on which the young single worker enjoyed easy living now seems quite inadequate for the sole support of a family.

The interlocking of work, family, and consumer cycles has consequences for each. For the worker who can only hope to move slowly up the income ladder while continuing to do essentially the same job—as is true of a great many production workers, salesmen, and clerical workers—job morale tends to drop as salary comes under more and more pressure.[11] For the young man on the rise in a profession, or the businessman determined to move well up the ladder, the demands upon income lead to increased drive for advancement and may take him out of the home for longer and longer work hours just at a point when his wife feels the greatest need to escape the drudgery and unremitting pressure of her homemaking and maternal chores. How one responds to such pressures depends, then, both on the nature of one's occupation and on one's prospects of marked success in that occupation.

[11] For a more detailed discussion and documentation, see the excellent treatment by Wilensky (1961b); see also Herzberg et al. (1957).

Wilensky (1963) has characterized the contrasting patterns of the man who works long hours in one job, anticipating substantial future return, and the "moonlighter," who takes on a second job to provide additional income when it is most needed. Moonlighting can occur at any occupational level, from unskilled labor to the professions. Wilensky notes that the moonlighter, above all, *is a man caught in a life-cycle squeeze*—he has many dependents and family resources below what his modest aspirations require" (p. 110). Further, men who take a second job to deal with the squeeze tend to have had somewhat disorderly careers, frequently because they have entered a different line of work after having been blocked in their efforts to get ahead in their earlier line of work. These, then, are men with a strong drive who did not get "on the track" early. Their careers have not been orderly, but they are not downwardly mobile and they are certainly not down and out. At a later stage in the life course they may indeed achieve comfortable circumstances and a degree of upward mobility.

A contrasting career pattern is that of the man who likes his job and sees the prospect of considerable advancement in it. He may spend as much time on his one job as the moonlighter invests in two. His family sees no more of him, but we may assume that his wife shares satisfaction in the success of his more orderly career. From Warner and Abegglen's (1963) study of successful executives and Elder's (1969a and b) analysis of the satisfactions and family patterns of upwardly mobile members of the Oakland Growth Study cohort, we know that the men who are upwardly mobile tend to select (and be selected by) women who have high aspirations and social skills. Upwardly mobile men generally achieve a higher level of education, delay marriage and parenthood and, by virtue of their superior preparation, start work at higher salaries and move more rapidly ahead than their nonmobile peers.

With increasing success in a job that a man enjoys, we find increasingly great investment not only in the job but in community affairs. Often, of course, the contacts made in charitable or community-improvement activities serve to facilitate the achievement of occupational goals. But for many participants it would seem that the sense of being successful and effective involves a feeling of obligation to be active in community affairs. This is, of course, especially true of the wives of successful men, many of whom find at least a partial sense of fulfillment by their activities as volunteers. Men whose careers demand wide contact tend to belong to a larger number both of work-related and of community-oriented organizations and at the same time to invest themselves much more heavily in the job. This leaves less time for family and for leisure, and indeed, upwardly mobile men assign relatively greater value to work than to family and leisure as sources of satisfaction.[12]

[12] Based on analyses of Oakland Growth Study data in Elder (1969b, p. 314). See also Wilensky (1961a; 1961b).

On the other hand, men who have not achieved as much as they had hoped to achieve, and those whose jobs are not intrinsically rewarding, spend less time on the job and invest themselves hardly at all in the community. By their mid-40s they shift more of their time toward family and leisure activities. As Wilensky notes, if these men belong to any organizations beyond church and union, they do so casually, and give them little time. Their pattern is to do the job in a reliable way but to check job-concerns at the workplace door and "retire into the heart-warming circle of kin and friend" (1961b, p. 235). We may assume that many will approach retirement with pleasant anticipations, since they have in effect begun to move toward the tempo and activities of retirement a decade or two before the event.

4 Marriage and the family cycle

Almost everybody grows up in a family setting and the great majority of individuals seem to take for granted, from an early age, that they too will marry and have children.

The family cycle or family life cycle, as it is frequently called, is defined in terms of stages of family development. Most families, except those founded in consensual or common law marriage, undergo a period of initial childlessness during which the newly married couple establishes a household and works out mutual adaptations. Some couples remain childless; for them the family life cycle is essentially defined by age and the nature of their relationship. Most couples have children, and for them the patterning of daily life tends to be most affected by the age of the youngest child. The number of stages delineated in the family cycle will vary according to one's purpose; the current discussion will touch briefly on the following:

Newly married couple
Children in the home ("nesting stage")
    Youngest child under 6 (preschool)
    Youngest child 6–12 (preadolescent)
    Youngest child 13–17 (adolescent)
    Youngest child 18 or over (unlaunched)
Older married couples with no children at home ("empty nest")
Widowed

As we shall see, the usefulness of the concept of the family cycle and the data generated by its application in research derive from the expectations and requirements that are imposed upon husband and wife as their children appear and progress along their own life courses. Families may be broken at any stage of the cycle, of course, but the constraints upon parents posed by the ages of their children continue to operate. The stages of different occupational careers are so diverse as to defy systematic analysis except within narrowly defined occupations; age predicts increased stability, seniority, and satisfaction, and, to a degree, increased responsibility, but not much more. The stages of the family cycle, on the other hand, permit us to say a good deal about pervasively important developments in the lives of most individuals.

CORRELATES OF MARRIAGE

One's conception of married life is, of course, initially derived from observation of one's own parents or parent surrogates and subsequently from observing the families of one's friends and acquaintances, from the mass media, and from contemporary folklore.[13] Most men and women tend to contemplate marriage only casually and vaguely before they start to date seriously.

The decline in age of marriage for both men and women is reflected in the normative expectations as to when a man or woman should marry.[14] These expectations result in both external and internal pressures. Once a girl reaches sexual maturity, she is of interest to older males as a potential sex partner or wife. Unless she has very strong career commitments, she is likely to view the men she knows well, and who express a romantic interest in her, as potential husbands. To the extent that they are interested in marriage and that she is attracted to them, marriage will be weighed against alternative courses or considered more and more seriously as affording a role consonant with her other planned roles.

Early marriage is likely to take place when other roles are unsatisfying and tension-laden. Among subjects of the Oakland Growth Study, for example, girls who married early—before the age of 20—reported greater emotional upset while in high school, more often had strained relationships with their fathers, and were rated considerably lower in academic achievement than their later-marrying peers.[15] Moreover, the early-marrying girls had shown themselves more oriented to domestic interests while in school, had begun to date at an early age and had early formed stable relationships with boys. These girls more often had sexual relationships while still in high school— most often with the man they married soon thereafter. Girls who married relatively late (at 23 or later), by contrast, had been more closely supervised by their mothers early in adolescence, and they had reported less independent activity with peers during the high school years.

Women who attend college are likely to marry relatively late, and those who have definite career expectations tend to marry later still. Available data suggest that late marriers were more academically oriented in high school

[13] The various sources of socialization for marriage and parenthood are discussed in detail by Hill and Aldous (1969).
[14] Neugarten et al. (1965) note a high degree of consensus that a woman should marry before she is 25 years old, and a man a year or two later.
[15] Here again, I am indebted to Glen Elder for the findings. See Elder (1970).

and viewed themselves as superior students (but they did not have higher IQ's). Late marriers among Oakland Growth Study subjects dated less and were much less likely than young marriers to go steady during the high school years.

Thus a variety of antecedent characteristics and experiences—physical, social, and psychological—influence the age at which a girl marries and the kind of man she selects or accepts. Moreover, a woman's status in life is much more likely to depend on her husband's occupation than on her own career. It is of interest, then, to consider what characteristics are associated with upward mobility through marriage.

In a society in which physical attractiveness is perhaps more highly valued in women than intellectual ability or generalized competence, a woman's attractiveness tends markedly to influence the exchange process that characterizes marital selection. Women who are attractive and well-groomed are more likely to marry men who have, or will ultimately attain, higher social status than that of the girl's family. Attractive girls tend to be more popular with boys throughout the adolescent years and tend to spend more time with boys on dates, at parties, and in other peer activities. The positive feedback the attractive girl receives from adults and peers undoubtedly bolsters her self-assurance and encourages her to develop social skills to a greater extent than most of her less attractive peers. At the same time, such girls may learn modes of response and develop personality characteristics that have decidedly negative connotations; girls who are very feminine and pretty not infrequently learn to use their physical attractiveness to manipulate others, "batting their eyelashes" to achieve objectives with the opposite sex.[16]

Highly attractive girls might seem to be under greater pressure to marry early, but the very fact that they have a high degree of appeal to many men appears to serve as a defense against premature commitment. Thus attractiveness does not seem to affect age at marriage.

Measured intelligence is not correlated with physical appearance, and it is only indirectly correlated with achieving high status through marriage. The combination of high intelligence and high socioeconomic status does, however, markedly increase the probability that a girl will attend college, at least for a year or two. Girls who attend college thereby associate with men whose occupational prospects are good. For this reason, college attendance itself provides a mechanism for achieving mobility through marriage, albeit a more indirect one than does physical attractiveness.[17]

[16] Oakland Growth Study data suggest, for example, that attractive middle-class girls were seen as more manipulative, affected, self-indulgent, and condescending toward peers. Only the last of these correlates of high attractiveness was found among working-class girls.

[17] Not surprisingly, physical attractiveness is more highly related to upward mobility through marriage for working-class than for middle-class girls. See Elder (1969a).

Our knowledge of the antecedents and correlates of early or late marriage for men is more meager. The primary preoccupation of a young man is likely to be his occupational goal, and in general it appears that men are subjected to less pressure to marry by a given age than are women. It is expected that a man will be somewhat older than his wife, so that deferring marriage does not markedly diminish a man's opportunity to select a mate whose attractiveness and other attributes are consonant with his social position and prospects. In general, men who become professionals remain in the student role until well after the mean age of marriage for nonprofessionals. Nevertheless, many marry while still in graduate or professional school. If few are early marriers, it nevertheless does not appear that most professionals defer marriage by more than a few years.

Men and women who do not marry are subject to much higher rates of mental disorder than are those who marry and remain married (see, e.g., Kramer, 1967). To some degree, the differences reflect higher levels of psychopathology among persons unwilling or unable to relate intimately to members of the opposite sex. It would appear, however, that something more than a difference in initial psychological health is involved. Rates of mental disorder among those who become separated or divorced are even higher than those among the never married. The emotional support and response afforded by marriage apparently protects against life stress. Men and women less than 65 years old who are widowed and remain unmarried are twice as likely as married persons of the same age to suffer from a functional psychosis, though only about half as likely to do so as are the separated or divorced. Beyond 65, however, married and widowed persons do not differ in the incidence of mental disorder, though both groups have a more favorable experience than either the never married or the separated or divorced.

THE NEWLY MARRIED COUPLE

For most men and women, marriage symbolizes a new definition of self. No other decision except entrance into a religious order entails so great a commitment of one's future life; and it is not mere coincidence that entrance into a religious order is characterized as marriage to the church. The changes in life patterns that marriage brings about are perhaps less abrupt now than they were a few decades ago, but they are by no means minor.

No matter how great their affection for each other, husband and wife have been participants in families with differing modes of communication, ways of sharing space, and achieving (or defending against) intimacy. The new couple has to work out a division of labor and mutually acceptable expectations for situations that they had never before encountered but that will now frequently recur. If both are to achieve full satisfaction in marriage, each must learn to recognize signs of distress in the other and to respond to them sympathetically, even if one does not fully understand the reason for the other's distress.

The change in identity brought about by marriage is likely to be greater for a woman, as previously suggested. She must now learn to respond to her new name. The reflected appraisals that she receives will in part depend upon connotations that her husband's name and reputation have for others. If her husband is employed and she is not, her daily round of activities will change markedly. Even if both husband and wife are employed, the demands of her job are likely to be secondary to the needs of her husband. If she does have a demanding job, a good deal of negotiation is likely to take place in achieving mutually acceptable expectations. The round of the husband's activities is more largely dictated by his job, which modulates the effects of marriage.

For both husband and wife, the first year of marriage is likely to be emotionally charged, with euphoria most prevalent. Viewed retrospectively, it tends to be a high point in life unless the initial adjustments are extremely traumatic. Much depends, of course, on what other events are taking place. Marriages made in time of war or under the threat of impending drafting into the army obviously face different stresses from those made in time of relative tranquility.

The initial stage of the family cycle that begins with marriage is, then, largely one of establishing complementarity and intimacy. As previously noted, the economic demands of setting up a new household are substantial, but prior to the birth of children most wives are employed at least part-time.[18] Sometime before the arrival of the first child, however, most working wives leave the labor force for a period of some years. Companionship between husband and wife tends to be maximal in the early period of marriage. There is relatively less division of labor in household tasks during this period than at any other. Husband and wife enjoy doing things together, and, especially when the wife works, they share household tasks (see Blood and Wolfe, 1960, pp. 70–72).

CHILDREN IN THE HOME

In many ways, the arrival of children tends to create greater changes in the lives of men and women than did marriage itself. The freedom of the couple is now sharply curtailed, especially during the infancy of the children. The young mother, in particular, tends to be cut off from recreational activities and community participation. Her dependence upon her husband for both economic and emotional support increases.

[18] See Lansing and Morgan (1955) for a thorough analysis of consumer finances over the life cycle. In the years covered by their analyses, nearly two-thirds of young wives without children worked. The proportion working dropped to less than one-fourth in families with a child under 6.

With the wife's withdrawal from the labor force, family income drops. Now it depends almost entirely on the husband's salary, a salary that is likely to be well below the ultimate peak of his earnings. At the same time there is pressure for more adequate living space. During the early years of the marriage, residential mobility is very high as the family seeks adequate quarters in a convenient location. Some couples are able to buy homes, but most must rent during the period when the children are small. As earlier noted, satisfaction with income and job tend to be lower in this period than in any other. Indebtedness reaches its peak; hence the frequency of moonlighting and of job shifts.

As the children reach school age, the mother increasingly takes over household tasks, or perhaps it would be more accurate to say that her husband's assistance tends to diminish. A sharper division of labor becomes manifest and the intensity of husband-wife interaction diminishes in many families.

Now neighborhood becomes as important as indoor space, and the need for outdoor play area sends many families to the suburbs to seek a home of their own. The tract house in a subdivision is hardly anyone's dream home, but it is all that many families can hope to own. Those who do acquire a home of their own tend to do so when the youngest child is still preadolescent.[19]

With the oldest child's entrance into school there begins a phase of social participation on the part of many parents that is predicated on the needs of their children rather than on their own interests. Supporting PTA activities, involvement in Cub Scouts or Bluebirds, serving as a teacher's helper on field trips, and chauffering children to and from movies, music lessons, and a host of other events and activities become part of the life of the middle-class suburban mother. Her working-class counterparts tend to be somewhat less involved, but middle-class mothers can more often count on assistance from their husbands.

Once all her children are in school, the mother can at least count on having some time of her own. Both parents are likely to feel less restricted and less burdened, though perhaps more concerned about financial problems because of the greater cost of clothing and feeding their rapidly growing offspring. Additional furniture is needed—beds, chairs, desks, or tables for children who need a place to do homework.

Some mothers return to work soon after their youngest child enters school.[20] Others may return when the youngest child is in high school. If they do go back to work, their husbands are likely to help with housekeeping

---

[19] The relation of housing choices and constraints to stage of the family cycle is discussed in detail in Abu-Lughod and Foley (1960, pp. 97–118).

[20] Longitudinal data on the mother's return to work are not available, but see Blood and Wolfe (1960, pp. 104–106) for family cycle comparisons within a cross-sectional survey.

duties. Wives and mothers work for a number of reasons, among which economic pressures certainly are important for all but upper-middle-class women. Especially if a woman has more education than her husband and if he is not upwardly mobile, a wife's expectations as to family standard of living are likely to exceed the level of her husband's performance.

Most of the available data that permit inferences about the wife's satisfactions at various phases of the family cycle are derived from cross-sectional data. These data suggest that satisfaction with standard of living is lowest during the children's preadolescent and adolescent years. In working-class families, the wife's satisfactions tend to increase if she takes a job. Her contribution to family income appears to strengthen marriage bonds that might otherwise be threatened by resentment of her husband's inability to earn more. Wives of upwardly mobile men, especially in the middle class, are in general better satisfied with their husbands' occupations and with their standard of living than are wives whose husbands have not moved upwards.

The parental role entails different duties and concerns as the children grow older. Adolescence of the children brings further freedom from restrictions but increased parental worry about the pitfalls that lie ahead for sons and daughters straining for more freedom. Reviewing their parental duties and concerns, parents whose children have passed puberty are likely to report adolescence as the most difficult phase of parenthood. Demands by the child for autonomy, conflict of values, and the sheer loss of power over the child in situations of conflict—often coupled with disagreement between the parents as to the best course to follow—may make this period extremely traumatic for some parents. More often, areas of conflict are offset by satisfactions with positive accomplishment. Children become resources to their parents, providing the mother with companionship and emotional support.

Stability of residence is much more likely during the later school years of the children than when they were younger, largely, of course, because many families will have bought homes by the time their children are adolescent.[21] Families of highly successful men may move to houses that permit a more gracious style of living, but on the whole the residential stability of the family with older children both encourages and is enhanced by putting down roots in a community. Informal participation with neighbors becomes an important part of the way of life of those who are not highly involved in formal associations.

As the children finish high school they tend to depart the family home, whether for college, marriage, or a job. The house that was bulging at the seams with three or four children begins to seem far more spacious. If the children are college-bound, the family income may still seem not quite ade-

[21] Abu-Lughod and Foley (1960, p. 106) note that three-fifths of the nonfarm houses sold in a given year were bought by married couples with husbands under 45 and children under 18.

quate, though by now most fathers will be well along toward peak earnings. Once the children are through college, however, the same income permits a higher standard of living for husband and wife.

A not insignificant number of marriages are dissolved or fade away when the children are launched. The period when there are adult children still at home seems to be a particularly low point in a wife's satisfaction with her husband's expression of love and affection.[22] Lacking adequate longitudinal data, we can only speculate as to the reasons. It seems safe to assume that when children over 18 remain in the parental home, they tend either to make the home primarily a base for sleeping and eating (and to be emotionally involved outside the home) or to be experiencing problems in finding their own identity and breaking their dependency upon their parents. In the former instance, they are less available to their mother for companionship and they do not provide any bond for mutual activity of husband and wife. In the latter instance, if they are experiencing difficulty in assuming full adult status, this is likely to lead to tensions and unhappiness on the part of their parents. We may assume that a certain proportion of families remain in the so-called launching stage, with children over 18 in the home, precisely because of the grown child's difficulties.

THE EMPTY NEST

Somewhere between the ages of 40 and 50, most couples now see the last of their children depart from everyday living under the parental roof. Children away in school and college will come home for vacations and married children will return for brief visits, but for the most part the children's rooms are unoccupied and the usual dinner is for two. A generation or two ago, the departure of the last child tended to come substantially later, often coinciding with the mother's menopause and sometimes with the father's incipient retirement or death. Now most couples can expect nearly two decades of life together after their children have left home.

The marked attenuation of the parental role that comes at this time will be for many parents the first experience of major role loss, but surprisingly few parents seem to dwell on this aspect.[23] With children on their own, parental worries greatly diminish. Even if parents are still closely involved with their children, they no longer need feel responsible for them. The adolescent's demands for autonomy and his tendency to challenge parental standards re-

---

[22] See Blood and Wolfe (1960, pp. 156 and 233–34). Their data were derived from a cross-sectional survey and may also relate to a somewhat atypical or even pathological group of families rather than to a phase of normal family development. Similar findings are, however, reported by Axelson, 1960, for both husbands and wives in a longitudinal study of couples married up to 20 years.

[23] This finding, reported first by Deutscher (1959), has been largely confirmed by Lowenthal and Chiriboga (1969), and by our Berkeley longitudinal research.

garding hours and activities made for a good deal of turmoil in many, perhaps most, families. Even where the parent-child relationship is basically a warm and satisfying one, both generations may feel a certain relief when the children are on their own.

The departure of the last child is likely to be most traumatic for the woman whose life has been completely centered on her children. For her, this stage may entail a degree of crisis, with feelings of loneliness and emptiness. Close emotional involvement with her children may initially have reflected a lack of satisfaction in the marital role, but once she has given her children substantially higher priority than her husband, the achievement of mutual understanding in the marriage may be far more difficult than before. Moreover, women who have devoted themselves almost exclusively to home and children are often less in touch with the larger social scene and less well prepared to establish new ties and interests outside the home. Even if they can look with satisfaction on the product of their maternal efforts, the hub of their round of activities is gone and they are likely to find this a difficult period.

For the most part, however, husbands and wives at this stage enjoy an increase in joint activity outside the home. Most wives derive zest from having a measure of freedom and independence that has not been theirs since the early years of marriage. They may perceive the departure of the last child less as a role loss than as an accomplishment. Visits of children and subsequently of grandchildren become highly satisfying events; a new periodicity, related to such visits and occasions when the house is temporarily filled, comes into being.

Among women who have been working during their children's adolescence, the departure of the children may end whatever feelings of guilt they may have had for not being fully available at home. Women who had not worked now tend in large proportion to look for an interesting activity. A surprising number of middle-class wives who had not been working begin or resume college in their 40's, either for the stimulus that it affords or to prepare for teaching or some other occupation. Some feel that they want to catch up with their husbands who were involved in stimulating activities while they experienced a period of relative stagnation at home. Some invest themselves heavily in community activities, although on balance it would appear that the peak of such investment for most women comes when their children are still in school. Many others simply relish the opportunity to do more things with their husbands and friends.

Whatever a woman's choice of activities when her children have left home, she is likely to be free from constraints that had been irksome. In the later years of marriage, it appears that the wife's power in decision-making is enhanced. At this stage of the family cycle, the nature of the marital relationship itself comes more sharply into focus, and the personalities of husband

and wife are likely to become more important than widely prevailing role definitions. The general satisfaction of husband and wife depend especially on the extent of their full acceptance of each other. Where each finds elements of the other's personality annoying, tensions may increase, especially after the husband's retirement and especially for the wife who is strongly home-oriented.

It is easier to reconstruct the sequence of role tasks and involvements at each stage of the family cycle than to assess meanings and satisfactions experienced by individuals. When one must rely on cross-age comparisons from surveys, life-course changes are obscured not only by cohort differences but by the fact that each advancing age group is a more select segment of the population. Marriages that endure thirty to fifty years almost certainly differed at earlier stages along the way from those that were dissolved in five to twenty years.[24] Particularly after the children are gone, husbands and wives seem either to achieve a realistic acceptance of one another or to recognize that their dissatisfactions will never end. At 50, very few husbands or wives expect that their partners are going to change. Nevertheless, the salience of various features of the marriage may change quite considerably.

What a man or woman wants in marriage and what gives him or her the greatest satisfaction about the marital relationship will depend upon their own early family experience and personal development, on the norms and values of their social milieu, and on their repertoire of role activities outside the family. Age clearly has important influence on each of these determinants. Blood and Wolfe (1960, p. 8) asked wives to select, from five alternatives, "the most valuable part of marriage" and found that "companionship" was so designated by a wide margin, followed by "the chance to have children," the husband's understanding, his expression of love and affection and, finally, the standard of living. These authors did not discuss changes in the importance of these aspects of marriage over the life span, but our longitudinal data suggest that such changes are quite striking. Once children are grown, they figure less importantly in the meaning of their parent's marriage. Mutual understanding appears to take on greater importance at this time for both husband and wife, and so does the comfort and security of a home. Overt affectionate display seems to drop off with sexual activity in the later years. After 25 years of marriage, a good many husbands and wives speak of no longer having romantic illusions and make clear that sensual and emotional delights in the relationship are minimal. A few, however, report that once the children are gone they can be more free in their sexual expression

---

[24] Of those Oakland Growth Study subjects who reported marital tensions at age 38, a considerable fraction had been divorced and remarried by age 49. Initial impressions of the data for ages 48–50 (just collected) is that self-ratings of marital satisfaction changed little but that expressions of acceptance and appreciation of the spouse (and of resignation to the less than ideal attributes of the spouse) increased substantially.

and that, indeed, for them the late 40's and early 50's have a honeymoon aura.

In this description of the stages of the family cycle, we have been describing modal patterns, largely from a middle-class perspective. But few individuals fall at the mode in all or even most stages of the family cycle. Some will have their children before 25 and enter the post parental phase in their early 40's; others may marry late and not have their children until they are well past 30, and for them the postparental phase is likely to have quite different meanings. Some marriages at all status levels end in early divorce, to be followed by a second marriage, with children now coming a good deal later than at the modal parental age. It is precisely because of such variations in parental age relative to the children's ages that the family cycle becomes an important adjunct to life-course analysis. Knowing the age of children, and especially of the youngest child, permits us to predict more accurately parental role involvement and activities than if we merely know the ages of the parents. It should be obvious, however, that marital and parental roles are negotiated among individuals who have other role commitments and personal involvements.

The changing meanings of marital and parental roles cannot be assessed without a knowledge of the other commitments and involvements and of the ongoing process of negotiation by which the partners in a family define and redefine their roles over the course of the family cycle. Prolonged or periodic unemployment of the father or his continual carrying over of job tensions to the family tends to lower a man's status in the eyes of his wife and children. Demands from outside the family on either husband or wife inevitably make them somewhat less responsive to the more subtle cues of difficulty or need for support on the part of other family members. Over the years, most husbands and wives develop ways of communicating their needs and recognizing signs of danger in other family members. Those who do not are likely to be numbered among the casualties who wind up in divorce proceedings or mental hospitals.

5 The middle and late years

During the period of maturity, when the individual is at the height of his physical and intellectual powers, life tends to be organized around occupational and family roles. As we have noted, these may be closely linked with other roles in the community and they anchor a man or woman in more or less stable networks of relationships, in patterns of activity and in a moral order. Major changes in occupational and family roles obviously threaten these anchorages. Even before major role changes occur, however, aging may pose problems both for instrumental performances and for self-conceptions.

For the most part, the physical changes of later life entail gradual diminutions of strength, vigor, visual acuity, and other capacities, though a serious illness may completely redefine one's status and future. The one clearly demarcated and predictable physical change is the female menopause, but in recent years both its timing and its impact have become less predictable.

IS THERE A MID-LIFE CRISIS?

Many writers have discussed the crisis of the middle years, whether or not they directly link the psychological developments to hormonal or other physical change. Some psychiatrists place the "mid-life crisis" much earlier, arguing that it tends to occur with the realization that life is half over and that one is no longer young.[25] But certain age thresholds hold great significance for some individuals while they mean almost nothing to others. The writer recalls the sense of despair evidenced by at least two friends when they became 40, while other friends seemed just to begin "blooming" at the same age.

Some men and women are acutely aware of aging at a period of life when others feel they are in their prime. Chronic poor health and loss of youthful looks are obvious cues that vigor and beauty are on the decline, but there may be more subtle cues as well. Declining response from members of the opposite sex can be devastating to the erstwhile Don Juan or his female counterpart. Response to evidences of aging will depend very much on dominant activity patterns and reference figures or groups. The athletic individual who took great pride in his ability to perform physical feats may experience a measure of despair when his manifest strength and endurance begin to drop off noticeably, even though he may still surpass most people in their prime. One man takes pleasure in seeing his son's powers surpass his own; another strongly contests his son because the son's ascendance can only mean his own decline.

Old wives' tales and clinical accounts of menopausal disturbances would lead one to expect major changes in the zest for life and self-conceptions of women at this time, but recent systematic research shows little evidence of such change. Indeed, the research of Neugarten and her associates (1963) suggests that the most upsetting thing about the menopause may be its anticipation. The hormonal changes taking place lead to nervous tension, headaches, and hot flushes, but most women seem to feel that these are unpleasant but not intolerable conditions to endure for a brief period. Although psychoanalysts have stressed the psychological significances of a woman's

[25] See Lowenthal and Chiriboga (1969) for a discussion of formulations of the "mid-life crisis."

no longer being able to bear children, very few women report themselves distressed by this fact. Indeed, considerably more are relieved that they no longer have to worry about becoming pregnant.

Women who have passed through the menopause frequently report themselves happier and healthier than they have been for some time. Perhaps the apparent decrease in the psychological stresses caused by the menopause is attributable to the fact that family pressures have now to a large extent abated by the time the wife enters this period of biological transition. A generation ago, as noted above, women were likely to be encountering menopausal symptoms at the beginning of the launching stage. Now at least some of the children are likely to have been launched a few years earlier. Moreover, we may assume that most women have come to terms, at least to some degree, with the fact of aging long before they pass through the menopause.

Thus it does not appear that any given age or the process of aging as such poses an inevitable crisis. At some time or another everyone must modify activities and adapt psychologically to the changes that age brings, but this need not involve general crisis any more than many previous adaptations did. To the contrary, the middle years often seem to bring a more realistic appraisal of one's world and one's self. Neither the young worker nor the young parent is, in general, minimally aware of the challenges to be encountered over the years. Marriage and parenthood entail the negotiation of relationships and situations that often cannot be defined in terms of any one actor's wishes. Even the most successful parent feels inadequate at times in the parental role. And many successful men have temporary encounters with the "Peter Principle" (that each man rises to the level of his incompetence, Peter and Hull, 1969) well before they reach their occupational ceiling. Personal growth in the adult years entails learning to mobilize all of one's resources to cope, accepting challenges, and learning from failures as well as successes. Indeed, until a person has a realistic conception both of the range of demands that may be made upon him in his major roles and of his strengths and weaknesses in dealing with such demands, it might be argued that he has not yet attained full integrity as a person.

In discussing the occupational role, it was noted that in the middle years many men re-evaluate their goals in the light of the work situation and their own experiences. Balanced against the gains of moving up are the costs in terms of pressures and tensions. Not the least of the sources of tension is the possibility that one may not be able to handle acceptably the pressures that a given job entails. As men with high capacities move up the ladder and encounter more diverse demands in their work, they become increasingly aware of their strong and weak points. By 50, most men are quite cognizant of the situations that give them difficulty and of the implications of such difficulties for further advancement. Failure to advance beyond a certain point or to aspire to advance is not, then, primarily a matter of having been "cooled out," nor are most men highly defensive against discussing their situations. Some, of course, do cloak their own shortcomings with denial and project upon others the reasons for their failure to go to the top. It is these men who are least well satisfied with their jobs and who, one suspects, are likely to be most threatened by the prospect of retirement.

Most men appear to be somewhat ambivalent about retirement, whether they have been highly successful in an occupation they enjoy or working at a job that affords little challenge or intrinsic satisfaction. For most workers retirement means a lower standard of living and a loss of valued social contacts. For some, the end of job involvement means loss of what has been the central purpose in life, as well as the loss of a sense of power and prestige. For those who have not achieved earlier aspirations, retirement may mean loss of the last chance to prove themselves. In general, though, one may assume that most men have come to terms with themselves on this dimension unless they practice massive denial as a means of ego defense.

On the positive side, nearly everyone likes the prospect of more leisure, freedom to travel, and freedom from job stress and worry. But these possibilities have existed for only a short time; much of the early research on attitudes toward retirement was conducted before the bulk of older persons could count on social security and other retirement provisions. Barring major, continuing inflation, those who retire in the 1970's are likely to be much better off in retirement than were their parents, and recent studies suggest that for many about to retire the economic aspect does not appear markedly problematic.

The prospect and initial readjustment posed by retirement tend to be more stressful for successful men highly involved in their jobs than for men who had earlier turned to family and leisure activities for their satisfactions. Nevertheless, retirement planning and high personal satisfaction later in retirement are most often found among the men for whom the occupational role had been rewarding. Adaptability is a function of multiple resources—personal, social, and economic—and not merely an attribute of personality.

The nature of the social matrix into which the older person retires can greatly influence the patterning of his subsequent activities. If prior social contacts can be maintained, if mutual psychological support and a round of meaningful activities can be arranged and sustained, adaptation to aging and retirement is likely to be much easier than if there are sharp disruptions of the individual's whole social network.[26]

In the later years, then, there are a number of losses and potential losses that must be coped with, and some of them may indeed constitute crises for

[26] This is strongly apparent in the recent research of Havighurst et al. (1969) on adjustment to retirement; and in the study of older women by Hochschild (1969).

the individual. For the most part, however, it does not appear that persons in their middle years regard this as a time of crisis or despair; it is a time for re-evaluation and review.

THE LATER YEARS

In time, of course, the burden of years is undeniable. The most vigorous person slows down, the healthiest becomes ill, and illness becomes more disabling as homeostatic mechanisms become less effective. Nevertheless, there is a tremendous variability as to when this occurs. Acute deficits may occur at 60 or may be staved off till 90. Actual age seems to affect performance at this stage only a little more than in the middle years. Consideration of individual life histories attests to enormous variability in role performance as in physical status in the later years. Some persons are largely detached from involvement in the community at 70, while others remain active well into the 80's.

Among well-educated persons who were active in community affairs, it does not appear that there is any decided decline in social activities and memberships until the 70's, when declining health begins to place substantial limitations on the activities of some persons. At all educational levels, political participation, at least to the extent of voting, remains high for men until the 70's. And for the man who continues to play a major role in business or government, old age may hardly be noticeable except in his need to pace himself.

Beyond retirement it is difficult to delineate modal patterns or typical sequences of life experience. Our society does not provide major new roles for the older person. To the extent that he can hold on to pre-existent roles, he tends to retain his identity. Role demands provide a structure and sustain the motivations to keep going when one might otherwise sit back in comfort. Some people much prefer to disengage and sit back in comfort, at least for a while. Most, however, seem to remain happier and more vigorous by remaining engaged.

Major social roles involve periodicities—periods of peak activity and of slack, for example—often having special social and emotional significance. In addition, occupants of roles that involve much responsibility benefit from a break or change in rhythm. The work year is sweetened by a vacation, and housewifely cares are lightened by an occasional day out. In the later years, when major occupational and parental responsibilities have been set aside, one day is likely closely to resemble another. One has relatively few demands upon his time and therefore is less likely to husband it and plan for different activities, even if sufficient energy is available. The major deviations from routine patterning are likely to be visits to children, particularly if these entail appreciable travel. The older person who can plan a varied round of activities apart from any firm role demands may be somewhat exceptional. Among those who manage to do so, many have younger friends with whom they are closely identified. They may still feel the pressure of time; time is still to be budgeted rather than to be "killed."[27]

Aging does not eradicate differences among individuals in tastes, values, and habits. If the later stages of the normal life course entail a measure of change in living arrangements, activities and relationships for almost everyone, those who still have the power to elect how the changes are to be made show great diversity in their choices. In this respect, modern industrial society seems to differ markedly from other societies. It does afford for many persons a wide range of choice, but as a corollary, it does not provide clear guidelines or supports for maintaining personal integrity.

THE LIFE REVIEW

During the developmental and early adult years, reviewing one's past seems to be a rather rare occurrence. In the later years of life, on the other hand, it becomes a major preoccupation.[28] Taking stock of one's past in the earlier adult years seems to serve different functions than in the later years. Initially, it is a way of integrating experience and evaluating one's performance with a light to improving that performance. One begins to take stock when he feels that he has fallen below expectations, particularly his own expectations. The sense of being "behind schedule" in some important way may lead to an attempt to explain why. Failure in a major role may serve the same function. It does not necessarily do so, of course. One may defend his self-esteem by denial or failure or by projection of blame on others rather than by stocktaking.

Review of one's past is likely to become much more urgent when one begins to realize that the years remaining are definitely limited. The death of loved ones, especially if they are not aged, or a serious accident or illness of one's own may bring this realization. Persons of a philosophical bent, concerned with the meaning of life, are likely to review their own lives at an earlier stage than those more oriented to action than to thought. A striking reference to such a life review is provided by an entry in the diary of the explorer Meriwether Lewis, while on his expedition with Clark in the unexplored West.

Sunday, August 18, 1805
This day I completed my thirty-first year, and conceived that I had in all human probability now existed about half the period which I am to remain in

[27] Calkins (1970) has provided a nice description of some of the uses of time.
[28] Butler (1963) discussing the life review from a psychiatric perspective, regards it as a universal occurrence in older persons. He notes reference to the process as long ago as in the works of Aristotle.

this sublunary world. I reflected that I had as yet done but little, very little indeed, to further the happiness of the human race, or to advance the information of the succeeding generation. I viewed with regret the many hours I have spent in indolence, and now soarly feel the want of that information which those hours would have given me had they been judiciously expended, but since they are past and cannot be recalled, I dash from me the gloomy thought, and resolve in future, to redouble my exertions and at least endeavor to promote those two primary objects of human existence by giving them the aid of that portion of talents which nature and fortune have bestoed on me; or in future to live *for mankind,* as I have heretofore lived *for myself.*[29]

In the later years, the life review serves to preserve an identity that can no longer be validated in the present. Lacking roles that bring respect and admiration, and lacking goals toward which he can strive, the very old person invokes the past to remind himself and his listeners that his life was meaningful and his identity worthy of respect. The success of one's children is another source of support; it provides evidence that one was a good parent and serves as a reminder of one's earlier competence.

This concludes our largely chronological discussion of salient elements in the life course in contemporary America. To a considerable degree, we have depicted the life course as seen from a middle-class perspective. In discussing adult role sequences, moreover, we have had much more to say about the occupational careers of men than of women and more to say about the family role satisfactions of women than of men. Obviously, some women have careers that not only afford major satisfaction but constitute the central cores about which they organize their identities. And equally obvious is the prime salience of marital and family roles for some men. Our treatment is biased both by the differential availability of adequate data and by the presentational strategy chosen in the light of space limitations.

Anyone who has read the earlier chapters will be aware that this treatment of the life course is biased in still another way: in many respects it is "cohort-centric." The longitudinal data drawn on have, for the most part, referred to a cohort entering adolescence in the depression and war years and only now confronting middle age. If we have been able to discern certain links and certain patternings in these life-course lines, they are by no means a basis for a general theory of the life course. Nevertheless, in the absence of any adequate theory of the life course, it has seemed desirable to consider available evidence and then to examine some theoretical issues. At this point it is time to turn from the chronological account to consideration of these issues.

[29] Quoted from Eide (1969, p. 93). The spelling appears to be partly idiosyncratic, partly that of the period.

6 *Cross-age relationships*

Age segregation is relatively low in early childhood, increases during the school years to a peak at adolescence, and then seems to decline gradually, becoming less and less salient in the middle years, only to increase (especially in institutional populations) in old age. A few years make a great deal of difference in abilities, interests, and activities during childhood and adolescence. Later on it is the nature of one's role involvements (age-linked, but not age-specific) that makes a difference: apprentices befriend apprentices; executives lunch and play golf with executives; mothers of small children tend to spend spare time with other mothers of small children and are probably most comfortable with those whose ages are close to their own.

Position within the family—whether one is an only child, or is first-born, for example—may itself influence early cross-age relationships. The first-born child tends to receive his initial socialization almost entirely from adults and to be more "adult-oriented" than his later-born siblings. The language he hears, and the activities he witnesses, are largely those of adults. Parental commentaries will be directed to him more than to his siblings, and it would appear that his role models will tend to be adults. Later-born siblings, on the other hand, will be subject to much more child-level interaction in the first year of life. The older siblings may serve as caretaker, pacesetter, and role model for the younger ones.

Harris (1964) has suggested that first-born, especially sons, are more concerned with "connectedness" in their cognitive styles. First-born children seem to be more interested in the family past, and they maintain closer ties with grandparents and with aunts and uncles than do their younger siblings. We do not know whether such cross-age ties tend to persist into adulthood or to generalize to other persons than relatives, but one might anticipate that first-born children would tend to relate to a wider age-span of friends than would later-born children.

At all stages of the life course, it appears that exceptional individuals have ties with relatively more persons outside their own age groups than do the relatively undistinguished. Older persons take an interest in the talented youngster, and the young and middle-aged constantly pass through the doors of the residence of the older person who has made a major impact on his time. Some great men who take young wives in the later years seem to keep going for decades longer than their peers, retaining the zest if not the full energy of youth. One thinks of a Casals or a Picasso as very old, yet ageless.

In times of relative stability of basic value orientations, age and generational differences occur but are not much more a source of friction than is the greater political conservatism of the older generation. Conventional morality tends to receive far stronger verbal backing by the older generation for a variety of reasons. Most older people are more securely anchored to the existing order precisely because it is orderly for them. The affirmation of general principles of morality and stability is a source of comfort and an expression of solidarity with one's peers, even if one has not always abided by those principles or if one feels that exceptions are sometimes warranted. Moreover, the older person has had many opportunities to witness the consequence of the flaunting of conventional morality.

Cleavages between generations that are as sharp as those existing at the present time seem rare, even granting that older generations have since time immemorial deplored the proclivities of their immediate successors. Issues such as violations of civil rights and the use of military aggression to serve "national needs" seem especially to separate the generations, and most sharply in the middle class. The issues that currently tend to divide the generations are especially emotion-laden because the position of the young is based precisely on the moral precepts that the older generation verbalizes (excluding precepts relating to patriotism). What the long-range effects of such changes in value orientation (at least for the cohort of students now in college) will be, we cannot predict. The current rejection of conventional career lines by many young people is also likely to modify their life course quite markedly from those of cohorts of the recent past.

Occupational groups vary considerably in the extent to which close cross-age relationships are fostered in the work situation. Teaching obviously entails the most highly structured cross-age involvement, with continual increase in the age-gap between teacher and student. To the extent that the subject matter taught deals with ideas and issues of contemporary society, as it does in the university, especially in the social sciences, teacher and student will be most actively engaged in dialogue about current issues and stratum differences in perspective. Under such circumstances, in times of marked changes in cohort perspectives, the teachers will be under strong pressure to take on or at least seriously entertain the new perspectives of their students. Few other occupational roles provide this kind of dialogue. Parenthood may do so, but in general parent-child communications are less likely to entail a rational analysis of the social order and more likely to be couched in terms of parental authority.

7 Aging, personality change, and identity

Data from long-range longitudinal studies that extend well into the adult years suggest that far more personality change takes place beyond childhood than had previously been recognized. The assessment of personality change over the life span is fraught with difficulties, for age-graded expectations influence to a substantial degree the salience of certain features of personality and the expression of underlying behavioral tendencies. Thus problems of dependency, aggression, and behavioral control are of considerable concern to the parents of small children; but the forms that these problems take in early childhood seem minimally related to dependency, aggression, and behavioral control in the adult years. To the extent that aspects of temperament are genetically determined, we might expect substantial continuity in tendencies toward temperamental expression, yet even here the overt manifestations may vary greatly.[30] Social roles modulate the expression of tendencies derived from constitutional make-up. Moreover, it is quite possile that the various components of genetic make-up exert differential effects at different periods of the life cycle. Thus we have seen that body build appears to have peculiar salience in the peer society of early adolescence, but intelligence seems to have far greater influence on outcomes in the adult years.

Moreover, socialization influences and role sequences have such great effects upon individual commitments and the forging of identity that we might anticipate relatively modest relationships between early measures of personality and those made in the later years. Few of the longitudinal studies have attempted to examine the effects of typical experiences and typical sequences on the development of personality. The small cohorts studied in most longitudinal research do not lend themselves to subgroup analyses that would assess the effects of intervening experiences. Also, few of the early founders of longitudinal studies were interested in research questions relating to adult outcomes. Therefore the relevant intervening experiences have been studied only haphazardly, for the most part.

CONTINUITY OF IDENTITY

It may be fruitful to consider briefly why many theorists have assumed more stability to personality beyond childhood than is warranted by research findings. The primary reason must be the individual's own sense of continuity and of identity. This sense is rooted in one's network of relationships with significant others; it first emerged in the years when those relationships had substantial continuity. The sense of identity is also based in part on our conception of our own appearance (something that surely changes slowly during the years from adolescence to old age), on our intellectual capacities and cognitive styles (again very stable elements of functioning), and on elements of temperament as these differentiate us from others. When we describe a person, we tend to think in terms of his appearance and his intelligence as well as his manner and relationships with others. If the latter ele-

---

[30] Personality continuity and change, the issues relating to their assessment, are discussed in a symposium reported in *Vita Humana* (1964).

ments are somewhat less stable than the former, they undoubtedly have high continuity when viewed by the individual himself.

Perhaps no one else has described with such precision and detail as Marcel Proust the realization that one has aged and changed when he had believed himself just as he had always been. Following World War I, the narrator, who had withdrawn from social gatherings for many years, went to a party where were gathered a large number of friends and social acquaintances whom he had not seen for more than a decade. At first he had the impression of a masquerade, so different were his friends from the memories he had been carrying:

> Then it was that I, who from early childhood had lived along from day to day with an unchanging conception of myself and others, for the first time, from the metamorphoses which had taken place in all these people, became conscious of the time that had gone by for them—which greatly perturbed me through its revelation that the same time had gone by for me. And, though of no importance to me in itself, their old age made me desperately sad as an announcement of the approach of my own (Proust [1927], 1951, p. 260).

> And I saw myself, as though in the first truthful mirror I had found, through the eyes of old folk who thought they had remained young (just as I believed I had myself) and who, when I pointed to myself as an example of an old man, hoping they would contradict me, showed no look of protest in their eyes, which saw me as they did not see themselves but as I saw them. For we did not see ourselves or our own ages in their true light, but each of us saw the others as accurately as though he had been a mirror held up before them (Proust [1927], 1951, p. 265).

A man's attitudes and values may change as imperceptibly (to him) as his appearance. We integrate our past into our present. Even though we may change our views substantially, we are aware of the basic ambivalences that underlie many attitudes and behaviors, which to an outsider seem to manifest unequivocal commitments or tendencies to response.

Another major source of the sense of stability is that derived from the centrality of certain roles and networks of relationship and the strain toward consistency in our perceptions of ourselves within these roles and networks. If value orientations shift within our larger reference groups, much of the change in our own values is absorbed, unnoticed, unless we go back and check against some benchmark left in the past.

More than just a sense of continuity is given by stable social networks. To a very considerable degree personality is anchored in the primary group memberships and major role commitments of the individual. Let these change significantly and the person will change. Once he is locked into a job, especially if it is in a large organization, and into the responsibilities of husband and father, a man's attention and energies are largely allocated. Even when many aspects of role definition are subject to negotiation by participants, stable expectations are evolved and then tend to be sustained. Many activities and relationships become routinized and in a sense "ingrained." If the role definitions achieved are congenial, costs are low and rewards high. If they are not congenial, the person is likely to feel himself trapped, yet with no alternative short of total revolt and the disavowal of much that constituted his identity. Under such circumstances, self-estrangement is likely to result; in the most extreme circumstances, suicide may seem the only possible escape route.

Sustained emotional commitment to a role requires either that one receive continuing direct satisfaction from role performance or that one be constrained to perform the role in order to achieve some related goal. One such goal may be an identity built upon the demonstrations of competence and success in a role that affords few intrinsic satisfactions. Failing success, one may still not be willing to acknowledge failure. A man may continue to strive after success in an occupation he does not really enjoy because he cannot acknowledge that he made a mistake in his original choice or in his assumptions about his own abilities. Or a couple may be constrained to remain married despite great dissatisfaction with their marriage if they feel a strong moral obligation to maintain an intact home for their children. In such instances, the role demands may not only be onerous but are also likely to create feelings of profound unhappiness and ambivalence about the incumbent's identity.

Alternatively, a nonsatisfying role will be given up, or, if that is impossible, will be performed in such a way as to minimize its salience. It is obviously much easier to give up roles that do not lock one into an integrated social network, for the relinquishment of such roles does not threaten one's position in the eyes of one's closest associates. This is undoubtedly a major reason for expecting far more personality change—change in values, in tastes, in activities—during the early adult years than during the middle years of life.

SOURCES OF DISCONTINUITY

No human life develops in a wholly orderly fashion. Childhood and adolescence offer opportunities for practice in making choices, making friends, making tentative commitments, but the adult years must also involve some trial and error, must witness ups and downs. Discontinuities may be culturally patterned or they may result from the vagaries of individual experience.

In her classic paper on continuities and discontinuities in cultural conditioning, Ruth Benedict (1938) emphasized the contrasts in our culture between the individual's role as son and father. She discussed three such contrasts, relating to responsibility, dominance-submission, and the sexual role. In the intervening 30 years we have seen an ever sharper contrast in expecta-

tions of responsible achievement for son and for father. The child and adolescent of the affluent 1960's had only the most meager opportunity for responsible social participation, yet were made aware as no previous generation
had been of the flaws in our society. There is both greater discontinuity and a
greater gap between generations.

Where Ruth Benedict noted the apparent discontinuity between norms
requiring a son's submissiveness and the demands of the work world for bold,
aggressive men, we might now wonder about reverse tendencies. A sizeable
fraction of our most capable young people are bitterly opposed to a political
and social system that has been, in their eyes, unresponsive to the needs of
large segments of its population. As fathers have become more permissive,
many sons have become more demanding and aggressive. They have committed themselves to certain values of the system while repudiating others to
which older people cling. In place of a balancing or mediating among conflicting values, many younger persons proclaim one set as absolute. They have
learned the power of nonnegotiable demands in limited academic circles. Once
they pass beyond those circles, however, they face severe problems; unless
they commit themselves to full battle against the system, they must find roles
that are part of the system, roles that bind them to reciprocity of privilege and
obligation.

Discontinuities in the sexual role, by contrast, seem far less today, even if
formal sex education lags far behind informal channels. About the only limitations of the child's exposure to the sexualizing of relationships and situations
is that imposed by the signs accompanying certain movies: "Persons under
18 not admitted." It is doubtful that the high level of exposure to sex as a
means of manipulating and exploiting others will lead to less problematic
sexual relationships in the life course of the present younger generation, although the movement for women's liberation and the efforts of many young
people to relate honestly to one another may serve as antidotes to the thrust of
the mass media.

Among today's other quite obvious discontinuities are those related to
deprivation of economic and educational opportunity at various developmental stages, especially discontinuity between preschool experience and
what the school offers the minority child; and discontinuity between the expectations that the child or adolescent acquires and what the job market
offers him.

Discontinuities of a different sort are encountered by the socially mobile.
The problem is particularly acute for minority group members who are
oriented toward majority group social circles, but is encountered by most persons who are markedly mobile, up or down. The upwardly mobile working-
class man who married early is likely to choose a girl from a background
similar to his own. She will very likely feel out of place in the social circles to

which her husband eventually becomes attached. In general, women are probably subject to greater discontinuities deriving from mobility than are men, since men more often get to choose the path they will take and women more often follow. The downwardly mobile man may be faced less with discontinuity than with a feeling of failure and dissonance vis-à-vis his former friends and associates. He is likely to avoid contacts that remind him of what he might have been.

Some discontinuities derive from the individual's own decision to call a halt to the course his life has been taking. The self is in part made up of reflected appraisals, but it is not merely a frozen reflection. Most persons come to know their own intentions, not fully but perhaps to a greater degree than psychoanalysts generally acknowledge. They also come to know the intentions and reputation that others ascribe to them. One does not always like what he sees. As Brim (1968) has noted, most persons recognize aspects of themselves they would like to change. They may derive their ideals for themselves from reference figures who differ greatly from the persons with whom they daily interact.

When they are free to shift associations and roles, young and even older adults may transform themselves. Such transformations have been noted not infrequently in long-term longitudinal studies. Thus, Jean Macfarlane, observing at age 32 the longitudinal subjects she had studied from infancy, noted that:

> Many of the most outstanding mature adults in our entire group, many who are well integrated, highly competent and/or creative, who are clear about their values, who are understanding and accepting of self and others, are recruited from those who were confronted with very difficult situations and whose characteristic responses during childhood and adolescence seemed to us to compound their problems (MacFarlane, 1964, p. 121).

Such changes in problem-plagued adolescents who had seemed destined to become problematic adults sometimes stemmed from dramatic re-evaluations and sometimes from the development of relationships and identifications that brought confirmation of worth and new goals. Many of these young people had been markedly deficient in their earlier resolution of the life cycle stages proposed by Erikson—the attainment of autonomy and industry, for example—yet once they had taken hold and found the direction in which they wanted to go, they quickly made up many deficiencies.

Changes in basic orientations and in personal attributes occur with sufficient frequency that formulations in terms of relatively invariant stage sequences simply do not seem to fit the facts of life. To cite another example, it may be recalled that Erikson postulated that an integrated sense of identity is prerequisite to the attainment of true intimacy. Some young adults do appear to be incapable of commitment to a fully intimate relationship before they have achieved a firm sense of who they are and where they are going. Others, however, seem to come to a firm sense of who they are by the route of a love relationship in which they are able to give themselves completely. Several of the highly principled young radicals studied by Keniston (1968) remarked on the great significance of deep attachments to members of the opposite sex in achieving a sense of their own identity.

8 The representation of the life course

As noted earlier, the life course is not easily encapsulated in a set of stages or in any single body of theory. At every period beyond early childhood, the individual has the potential to direct or modify large segments of his activities and relationships. He does this within a framework of roles and expectations that are often strongly age-linked, but they are not inexorable constraints. Individuals can and do differ in the extent to which they set themselves goals and invest themselves. The school dropout *may* become a highly creative, industrious, and successful rock musician, though obviously this is not the most likely result.

What we want to know perhaps more than anything else about a given life history is how that individual came to carve out the goals he pursues or how he came to abandon his incipient goals. Every life has turning points, though they may seem imperceptible either because the person never moved far enough to see where he was going or because a whole series of subtle influences escaped notice. Anselm Strauss (1959) writes of "status forcing" or transforming experiences by which an individual comes to redefine himself and the possibilities open to him. The art student whose efforts are singled out for favorable comment and encouragement by an eminent artist, or the unassuming underling who emerges as the only competent leader in the face of a disaster, may have new views of themselves and where they are going. Events that bring discontinuity into one life may actually bring meaning into another.

If we cannot encapsulate the life history, it is at least possible to focus on aspects that can be examined more systematically. One can examine how role priorities were established and how role conflicts have tended to be resolved. As noted in the discussion of occupational careers, many men acknowledge that their job comes first except for dire crises in the family. Many others would say that their families come first, an assertion that some wives and children might dispute. It would be helpful to have a schematic representation of a life in terms of the relative salience of various roles throughout the entire life course. Charlotte Buhler (see Volume I, p. 410; also Buhler and Massarik, 1968) has provided one form of schematic representation showing the duration of each major role commitment or salient activity by lines on a time grid. It is apparent at a glance how many major roles or activities the individual was engaged in at a given time and at what points in time roles were taken up or relinquished. What is lacking, however, is some feeling for the shifting importance of particular roles as one's identity becomes more fully involved or as one turns away from heavy commitment to a particular role. Such shifts are often the focal points of novels and of autobiographies.

Several investigators have experimented with the graphing of a life review as part of an interview. Subjects of whatever age are asked to "draw their lives" as they view the whole course or to evaluate for each year from early childhood to their current age the relative quality of their experiences. Back and Bourque (1970) have used the technique as part of a public opinion survey, thereby getting a large sample of persons at varied ages. Moreover, respondents were asked to evaluate their lives not merely up to the present but to project into the future what they think the quality of life will be like up to age 80. In general, the future looks more promising than the past, though a peak is reached between 50 and 70, after which decline is predicted.

In longitudinal studies at Berkeley, subjects have been asked periodically to discuss the most and least satisfying periods of their lives. In their late 30's, subjects in two of the studies were also asked to check "high-low charts," rating each year in terms of their recalled morale at the time, using a grid marked from 0 ("rock bottom") to 9 ("absolute tops"). Such graphs show great individual variation. Some cover the full range of ratings, with frequent shifts, while others show only minor variation from year to year. When the average ratings accorded each year of age are plotted, they reveal trends that reflect both aging and cohort patternings. Ratings by women indicate a relative positive evaluation of the first five years, then a drop during the early school years, reaching a low point early in adolescence, from which there was a steady climb until the early 20's. Most frequently mentioned as reasons for the low point of adolescence were feelings of not belonging or of lacking social skills. Men show less of a dip in adolescence but otherwise rather similar tendencies. (See Figure 11 · 1.)

The high points of early adulthood for both men and women tend to be marriage and the birth of the first child, though for men indications of occupational success were almost as frequently cited as the reason for life approaching "absolute tops." Most women who had several children in rather close proximity show a marked dip in morale for this period. The late 20's and early 30's show a slight drop, but for each of the cohorts with which we have used this technique, the average rating given the most recent year tends to be close to previous peaks.

Subjects currently being interviewed at age 48–50 who had completed "high-low charts" a decade ago are not asked to reconstruct the entire graph

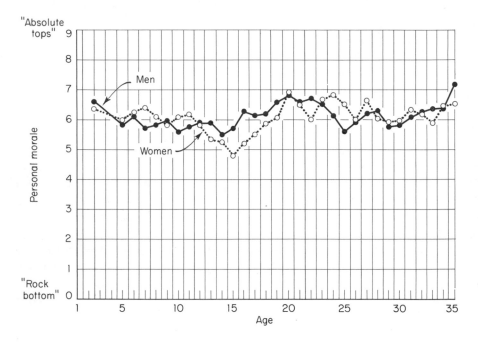

but to report on the most and least satisfying periods. A substantial proportion rate their 40's as most satisfying. Very, very few of our study members seem to feel that they are "over the hill" at 50. In general, retrospective reconstruction of high and low points in personal morale or life satisfaction over the life course seems reasonably consonant with the person's reported feelings at the time or relatively soon thereafter. That is, years marked by personal triumphs or tragedies, or years that were exceptionally pleasant (or on the contrary full of strife or other stress) were to a considerable degree subsequently reported as highs or lows. On the other hand, the general level at which various periods were subsequently rated seems to have relatively little relationship to feelings that the individual had reported at the time or to assessments of him by others at that time. For example, the professional whose life plot at age 37 is given in Figure 11 · 2 reports a rather favorable picture of his later high school years. They were undoubtedly less dismal for him than were the grade school and junior high school years, but at the time he could hardly have been characterized as sitting on top of the world. By contrast with what had been before and what came later, this period now appears in a most favorable light. This man, it may be noted, uses the full range of the scale. Others seem to be unwilling to rate any period "absolute tops" or "rock bottom." It is as if they were saying that they have yet to experience either extreme. Some laboriously plot year by year, keying to events that mark highs or lows or turning points. A few "draw pictures" of their lives, sketching the major trends rather than giving a set of points that might be connected as in Figures 11 · 1 and 11 · 2.

The reconstruction of one's past can be usefully combined with longitudinal data to indicate how features of past experience influence current perspectives. Figure 11 · 3 illustrates one such use. It is based on "high-low charts" at age 36–38 by subjects of the Berkeley Growth Study, a group studied from birth. Mother's behaviors toward these subjects during the first three years had been recorded and were subsequently rated along a number of dimensions. One such dimension was the mother's positive evaluation of the child (which correlated highly with expression of affection, attentiveness to the child, and nonpunitiveness).[31] The mother's positive evaluation of the child was in general correlated with positive behaviors on the part of the child (friendliness, cooperativeness, facility) throughout childhood. It is not entirely surprising, then, to find that more than thirty years later those women whose mothers had been critical and unaccepting of them in infancy recall their childhood years more negatively than do women whose mothers had been positively rated. Even for the small sample of subjects for whom all of the necessary data are available so that fixed samples can be compared over the entire period, the differences in reported morale are highly significant (reaching $p < .01$ at age 13, for example). It is interesting to note, however, that the differences largely disappear in the adult years, after the women are no longer in close contact with their mothers.

Assessment of the high and low points of one's life course not only permits one to single out crucial events and turning points, as perceived by the individual himself, but also gives clues as to the goals and values that have exerted a governing effect. Failure to achieve satisfying goals may sometimes be noted by the rating of the high school years as the peak of life satisfaction. This seems to occur especially often among those who were highly popular as young people. For example, in one sample the most popular girl in her high school class never again reached the peak achieved at age 17. Everything thereafter was anticlimactic, for she had little purpose except to be the center of a social whirl. As noted above, early adolescence is far more often viewed subsequently as a low point in life and subsequent movement up the scale of life satisfaction is closely keyed to developing purpose and commitments to particular goals and particular relationships.

There are, of course, many dimensions of individual performance and involvement that might be graphed, at least theoretically, if data were available.

[31] For details of the use of these ratings and their relationships to child behavior, see Shaefer and Bayley (1963).

FIGURE 11·2 *"High-low chart" of male professional, aged 37*

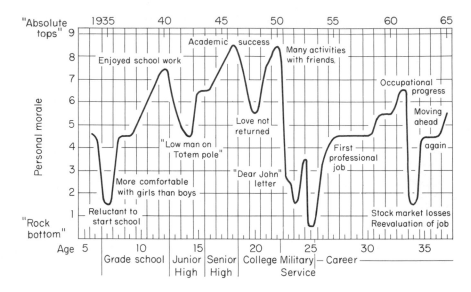

FIGURE 11·3 *Average morale scores assigned each earlier year of life, by women aged 36–38 whose mothers had been rated high or low in maternal evaluation of child in infancy*

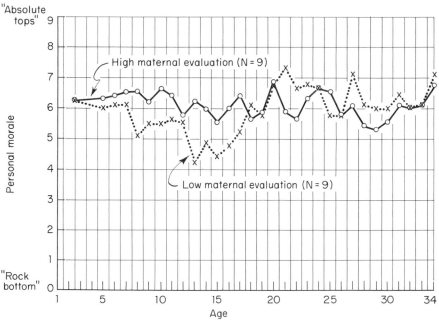

The dependency-power axis is one that is highly relevant, though not easily assessed by the individual himself except at times of marked shifts or desired shifts. In infancy the individual's only power is that which he exercises by virtue of the love his parents have for him; his dependency is absolute. Through the childhood years his dependency lessens and changes in nature, and his power to influence others increases. In adulthood, power is closely linked to occupational role, except as power over one's children is concerned; one is supposed to be self-dependent. For the infirm adult, or one who loses his source of livelihood, dependency again becomes a major problem. Now dependence tends to shift onto the succeeding generation.

Autonomy increases as dependency wanes, up to a point, but then come the commitments of adulthood—to occupational career and to family—and now autonomy is again sharply curtailed. Even though occupational and family roles often do not entail any substantial number of highly specific norms that are general to the whole population, normative expectations among members of a given role set tend to become consensual. When they do, it is the individual's commitment to the role and his conception of himself as performing that role adequately that holds him to the pressure of demands. Autonomy is not so much lost as constrained.

More interesting than the simple graphing of dimensions of change is the analysis of the meaning of change and the consequences of various modes of coping. Many role transitions are anticipated events toward which the individual is favorably (or unfavorably) oriented and more or less prepared. Others are a consequence of unforeseen events that lead to the opening up or closing off of opportunities, as occurs when a person receives high recognition or is publicly labeled as a deviant.

Transitions may be incremental, leading to expanded obligations and spheres of participation, or decremental, representing the loss of powers, opportunities, relationships. Marjorie Lowenthal and her associates are now in process of formulating a theoretical framework for the study of adaptation in adulthood by examining alternative responses to incremental and decremental transitions in the light of the individual's preexisting goals, especially as the latter are constricted or expansive in nature. By examining a number of transitions as different periods of the life course, data will be brought to bear on the theory. Only as this is done will we move toward more adequate conceptualizations of stability and change in the course of a life.

In this essay we have been concerned with the ways in which age gives patterning to the life space and to the sequences of roles, relationships, and activities that make up the life course. Within all segments of society the years provide a structure of expectations, opportunities and challenges. If these are to a considerable degree integrated by the individuals who experience them, they remain largely unintegrated insofar as a general theory of the life course is concerned. Perhaps it is unrealistic to think of a theory of the life course. Perhaps we can only look forward to more limited theories relevant to aspects of the life course—for example, more adequate theories bearing on types of role transition in different kinds of social settings. It is hoped that the present essay has at least indicated some of the elements that will be incorporated in more adequate formulations in the future.

Works cited in Chapter 11

Abu-Lughod, Janet, and M. M. Foley, 1960. "Consumer Strategies," in Foote, N. N., J. Abu-Lughod, M. M. Foley, and L. Winick, *Housing Choices and Housing Constraints*, New York: McGraw-Hill.

Axelson, L. J., 1960. "Personal Adjustment in the Postparental Period," *Marriage and Family Living*, 22, pp. 66–68.

Back, Kurt, and Linda B. Bourque, 1970. "Life Graphs: Aging and Cohort Effects," *Journal of Gerontology*, 25, pp. 249–255.

Baldwin, James Mark, 1913. *Social and Ethical Interpretations in Mental Development*, New York: Macmillan.

Benedict, Ruth, 1938. "Continuities and Discontinuities in Cultural Conditioning," *Psychiatry*, 1, pp. 161–167.

Blood, R. O., and D. M. Wolfe, 1960. *Husbands and Wives: The Dynamics of Married Living*, New York: Free Press.

Brim, Orville G., Jr., 1968. "Adult Socialization," in Clausen, John A., editor, *Socialization and Society*, Boston: Little, Brown, pp. 183–226.

Bronfenbrenner, Urie, 1970. *Two Worlds of Childhood*, New York: Russell Sage Foundation.

Buhler, Charlotte, and Fred Massarik, editors, 1968. *The Course of Human Life*, New York: Springer.

Butler, R. N., 1963. "The Life Review: An Interpretation of Reminiscence in the Aged," *Psychiatry*, 26, pp. 65–76.

Caldwell, Bettye M., 1964. "The Effects of Infant Care," in Hoffman, M. L., and L. W. Hoffman, editors, *Review of Child Development Research*, Vol. I, New York: Russell Sage Foundation, pp. 9–87.

Calkins, Kathy, 1970. "Time: Perspectives, Marking and Styles of Usage," *Social Problems*, 17 (Spring), pp. 487–501.

Deutscher, I., 1959. *Married Life in the Middle Years*, Kansas City, Mo.: Community Studies.

Eckland, Bruce K., 1965. "Academic Ability, Higher Education and Occupational Mobility," *American Sociological Review*, 30, pp. 736–746.

Eide, I. H., 1969. *American Odyssey: The Journey of Lewis and Clark*, Chicago: Rand McNally.

Elder, G. H., Jr., 1963. "Parental Power Legitimation and Its Effects on the Adolescent," *Sociometry*, 26, pp. 50–56.

————, 1968. "Achievement Motivation and Intelligence in Occupational Mobility: A Longitudinal Analysis," *Sociometry*, 31, pp. 327–354.

————, 1969a. "Appearance and Education in Marriage Mobility," *American Sociological Review*, 34, pp. 519–533.

————, 1969b. "Occupational Mobility, Life Patterns and Personality," *Journal of Health and Social Behavior*, 10, pp. 308–323.

————, 1970. "Marriage Mobility, Adult Roles, and Personality," *Sociological Symposium*, Spring.

————, forthcoming. *Children of the Great Depression.*

Erikson, Erik, 1950. "Eight Stages of Man," in Erikson, Erik, *Childhood and Society*, New York: Norton, pp. 219–234.

————, 1968. "Life Cycle," in Sills, David L., editor, *International Encyclopedia of the Social Sciences*, 17 vols., New York: Macmillan and Free Press, 9, pp. 286–292.

Flavell, J. H., 1963. *The Developmental Psychology of Jean Piaget*, Princeton, N.J.: Van Nostrand.

Ginsberg, E., et al., 1951. *Occupational Choice*, New York: Columbia University Press.

Goldner, Fred H., 1965. "Demotion in Industrial Management," *American Sociological Review*, 30, pp. 714–725.

Harris, I. D., 1964. *The Promised Seed: A Comparative Study of Eminent First and Later Sons*, New York: Free Press of Glencoe.

Havighurst, Robert I., J. M. A. Munnichs, B. Neugarten, and H. Thomae, 1969. *Adjustment to Retirement*, New York: Humanities Press.

Herzberg, F., et al., 1957. *Job Attitudes: Review of Research and Opinion*, Pittsburgh: Psychological Service of Pittsburgh.

Hill, R., and Joan Aldous, 1969. "Socialization for Marriage and Parenthood," in Goslin, D., editor, *Handbook of Socialization Theory and Research*, Chicago: Rand McNally.

Hochschild, Arlene, 1969. *A Community of Grandmothers.* Ph.D. dissertation, University of California, Berkeley, California.

Hughes, E. C., 1958. *Men and Their Work*, Glencoe, Ill.: Free Press.

Jones, Mary C., 1965. "Psychological Correlates of Somatic Development," *Child Development*, 36, pp. 899–911.

Keniston, Kenneth, 1968. *Young Radicals*, New York: Harcourt, Brace & World.

Kramer, Morton, 1967. "Epidemiology, Biostatistics and Mental Health Planning," in *Psychiatric Research Report 22*, Washington, D.C.: American Psychiatric Association, pp. 1–63.

Lansing, J. B., and J. N. Morgan, 1955. "Consumer Finances over the Life Cycle," in Clark, L. H., editor, *Consumer Behavior, Vol. II, The Life Cycle and Consumer Behavior*, New York: New York University Press.

Lidz, Theodore, 1968. *The Person*, New York: Basic Books.

Lowenthal, Marjorie Fiske, and David Chiriboga, 1969. "The Midlife Crisis," Paper presented at the Symposium, "The Context of Marriage," San Francisco Medical Center, University of California, November 8.

Macfarlane, Jean Walker, 1964. "Perspectives on Personality Consistency and Change from the Guidance Study," *Vita Humana*, 7, pp. 115–126.

Merton, Robert K., 1957. *Social Theory and Social Structure*, rev. ed., Glencoe, Ill.: Free Press.

Neugarten, B. L., Joan W. Moore, and J. C. Lowe, 1965. "Age Norms, Age Constraints and Adult Socialization," *American Journal of Sociology*, 70, pp. 710–717.

————, et al., 1963. "Women's Attitudes toward the Menopause," *Vita Humana*, 6, pp. 140–151.

Peter, Laurence J., and Raymond Hull, 1969. *The Peter Principle*, New York: William Morrow.

Proust, Marcel (1927), 1951. *The Past Recaptured*, New York: Modern Library.

Riley, Matilda White, J. W. Riley, Jr., and Mary E. Moore, 1961. "Adolescent Values and the Reisman Typology: An Empirical Analysis," in Lipset, S. M., and L. Lowenthal, editors, *Culture and Social Character*, New York: Free Press, pp. 370–386.

Roe, Ann, 1951. "A Psychological Study of Eminent Physical Scientists," *Genetic Psychology Monographs*, 43, pp. 121–239.

Sewell, William H., and Vimal P. Shah, 1967. "Socioeconomic Status, Intelligence and the Attainment of Higher Education," *Sociology of Education*, 40 (Winter), pp. 1–23.

————, 1968. "Parents' Education and Children's Educational Aspirations and Achievements," *American Sociological Review*, 33, pp. 191–209.

Shaefer, Earl S., and Nancy Bayley, 1963. "Maternal Behavior, Child Behavior and Their Intercorrelations from Infancy through Adolescence," *Monographs of the Society for Research in Child Development*, 28, No. 3 (Serial No. 87).

Strauss, Anselm, 1959. *Mirrors and Masks: The Search for Identity*, New York: Free Press.

Tausky, Curt, and Robert Dubin, 1965. "Career Anchorage: Managerial Mobility Motivations," *American Sociological Review*, 30, pp. 725–735.

Vita Humana, 1964, Vol. 7 (July).

Warner, W. L., and J. Abegglen, 1963. *Big Business Leaders in America*, New York: Atheneum.

Wilensky, Harold L., 1961a. "Orderly Careers and Social Participation," *American Sociological Review*, 26, pp. 521–539.

————, 1961b. "Life Cycle, Work Situation, and Participation in Formal Associations," in Kleemeier, Robert W., editor, *Aging and Leisure*, New York: Oxford University Press, pp. 213–242.

————, 1963. "The Moonlighter: A Product of Relative Deprivation," *Industrial Relations*, 3 (October), pp. 105–124.

Wilson, Monica, 1951. *Good Company: A Study of Nyakyusa Age-Villages*, London: Oxford University Press.

Yarrow, Marian Radke, John D. Campbell, and Roger V. Burton, 1970. "Recollections of Childhood: A Study of the Retrospective Method," *Monographs of the Society for Research in Child Development*, 35, No. 5 (Serial No. 138).

12

The succession of cohorts

Introduction
    The age-related processes
    Allocation and socialization
    Pressures for change
1   The flow of cohorts through the society
    Cohort flow and the age structure
    Reflections of social change
    Contribution to social change
    Implications for the future
2   Socialization
    Role relinquishment and role transfer
    Anticipatory versus tenancy socialization
    The socializer-socializee relationship
    Socialization and social change
3   Allocation
    Examples of the process
    Procedures and agencies
    Allocation and role transfer
    Allocator-candidate relationships
    Allocation and social change

The foregoing chapters have presented two equally dynamic, yet widely diverse, images: one, of the age strata in a changing society; and the other, of the individual as he changes over his life course. Chapter 10 has looked upon society as a shifting *age structure* of roles, in which age defines the social locations of individuals alive at any one time. Chapter 11 by Clausen has described these social locations, from the point of view of the aging person, as a *sequence* of roles—roles in which the individual makes continual adjustments during his lifetime, to which he brings his accumulated stores of past experience and future aspirations, and through which he seeks to preserve some sense of personal continuity and identity.

Pondering over these two images, we approach the topic of this final chapter; for it is not one man alone who is aging, but an endless flow of men, each pursuing his special course of life within a structure of roles that is itself changing. In short, we arrive at a problem underlying all these essays: the problem of the relationship between the tempo of mankind and the tempo of society.

According to the Scriptures, "One generation passeth away, and another generation cometh: but the earth abideth for ever" (Ecclesiastes 1 : 4). It is clear that generations (cohorts) of people follow one another in constant succession, even though particular races may eventually die out or may be preserved only by a Noah's Ark.[1] And the lifetime of man has a definite rhythm from birth to death (albeit with secular variations in longevity within an apparently fixed total span). But the timing of societal process has no comparable rhythm or periodicity. The diverse ideas, beliefs, and artifacts of culture have varying lifetimes of their own, from the newspaper tossed away after one reading to the pyramids of Egypt. The wide range of social structures (from tribes or cities to nation-states) that concern us as sociologists also endure over varying periods of months, years, or centuries. Poets and philosophers, each in his own way, have attempted to define the course and the periods of societal time, from Heraclitus or Aristotle, through Ibn Khaldūn or Herbert Spencer, to such recent instances as Mannheim's *Zeitgeist* ([1928], 1952, pp. 280 ff.) or the characterization of man in the 1950's as "other directed" (Riesman, 1950) or in the 1970's as "protean" (Lifton, 1970). And many

---

[1] Attributed to Mark Twain is a remark sometimes echoed today: "Often it does seem such a pity that Noah and his party did not miss the boat."

scholars, including Hume and Comte, have made varying attempts to measure societal time in quantitative terms, seeking cyclical or other rhythms. Nevertheless, both Mannheim ([1928], 1952, pp. 277 ff.) and Sorokin,[2] who have assiduously recounted such attempts, have characteristically dispatched them all as worthless.

Yet, even if no general rhythm is discernible in the processes of social stability and change, that these processes are operative is undeniable; there are, for example, economic fluctuations, technological breakthroughs, massive cultural diffusions, wars, or famines. And, whatever the nature of these societal processes—whether they are short-term or long-term, disintegrative or reconstructive[3]—societal processes are certainly not synchronized with the lifetimes of the men progressing through the social structure in endless succession.

In contrast to our view [*see Chapter 10*] of the full set of coexisting **age** strata moving concurrently across time, we now turn to the paths, staggered through the age strata, along which successive cohorts move [*see Figure 1 · 3 in Chapter 1*]. For it is these paths that describe the courses that men take in their lifetimes. The society, itself moving through time, is the composite of the several but unique cohorts—at varying stages of their journey, and often traveling divergent paths; only by understanding this fact can we also recognize the differing rhythms of individual and society and the sources of tension inherent in these differences in rhythm.

Thus we ask: How, within the age-stratified macrocosm of society, can we understand the fundamental processes of aging and cohort flow, and the processes that articulate this flow of people with the changing role structure of society?

THE AGE-RELATED PROCESSES

See Chapter 1, Figure 1 · 2

Of the four processes specific to our conceptual model, considerable discussion has been devoted throughout the book to two in particular: *cohort flow* (P1) and *aging* (P2). It is the special character of these two processes —when compared with social class mobility, for example—that reveals age stratification in its full uniqueness and in its intrinsicality to social change. For these processes are inevitable. Aging, or mobility through the age strata

---

[2] Sorokin (1941, pp. 505 ff.). See also Moore (1963) for a classification of various patterns of regularity in social change.

[3] These are the dimensions used by Smelser (1968, pp. 195 ff.). Throughout this book we take the position that, despite controversies over "functionalist" versus "conflict" theories of society, there are inherent in all societies (as recognized in the theoretical works of either Durkheim or Marx, Parsons or Simmel) processes operating both to maintain the stability of the system and to change it. Compare, for example, Nisbet (1969) with Parsons (1961). For fuller discussions, see, for example, Lipset (1968); Riley and Nelson (1971).

(P2), while its implications are commonly taken for granted, is universal, unidirectional, and irreversible. Everybody ages; everybody changes over his life course as personality develops, experience accumulates, and adjustments are made to new roles. And, although individuals may age in different ways and at different rates, nobody can ever go back.

Beyond this, knowledgeable as sociologists are about the inevitability of aging, they take much less cognizance of the inexorability of birth and death. Hence we have repeatedly stressed in this book how the graduated progression of many cohorts (P2) fit together at given times to form the changing age structure of young, middle-aged, and old strata in the society. A sociology of age stratification requires examination of the fact that cohorts are constantly replacing each other within these strata. However different these cohorts may be, all are mortal and follow a measured life span.

Indeed, it is in part the disparity between this inexorable cohort rhythm and the irregular timing of social change that forces upon our attention the second pair of processes, P3 and P4, that intervene between population and role structure and operate to synchronize their differing tempi. What is the nature of these intervening processes, and how are they central to a sociology of age stratification? One is *allocation* (P3), which continually distributes and redistributes a population of actors within the role structure (connecting elements 1 and 3). The other is *socialization* (P4), which continually ensures the training and motivation of actors in accordance with role requirements (connecting elements 2 and 4). Together they serve to bring people and roles into conjunction.

Socialization as role learning has long been an important construct in sociology, but the companion process, allocation, has received comparatively little sociological attention,[4] yet in every ongoing society some way is found for defining and conferring social membership upon new arrivals as they progress through various stages of their life course. A review of socialization and allocation in terms of our conceptual model throws their parallelism into sharp relief. This review reveals how both processes are intrinsically tied to age through the exigencies of aging and cohort succession. Individuals enter the society as relatively helpless infants, undergo a long maturation before they are ready for allocation to major adult roles, and must then prepare further for the role sequences of the later life course. As they age and their capacities become modified or elaborated, they experience a series of changes in role performance, relinquishing some commitments, adding others, and continually adjusting capacities and aspirations to societal expectations and opportunities. Moreover, these necessary accommodations

[4] Among the works that take note of the topic are Ryder (1965, p. 846); Levy (1952, p. 307). More extensive references appear in Section 3.

are endlessly repeated through the birth and death of successive cohorts. And, at the level of operation of the social system, our review makes clear that the process by which an individual is admitted to a role or extruded from it equals in importance the process by which he is prepared for role performance.

Thus allocation and socialization must be apprehended as integral components of the life course, linking the role sequences of individuals to age-graded changes in social expectations and rewards. Yet, as we shall see, they also contain seeds of social change.

ALLOCATION AND SOCIALIZATION

Although we shall discuss allocation and socialization separately in later sections of this chapter, we start by noting certain respects in which their joint operation requires common treatment. Both processes, in serving to synchronize societal time and cohort time, confront special sets of problems at the societal and the individual levels. Both tend to operate imperfectly, as they may, for example, be out of phase with one another. And both sometimes share institutional arrangements despite the differences in their respective emphases on assignment to roles and on development of motivations and capacities.

Levels of articulation   Socialization and allocation, working in conjunction, have somewhat parallel implications for the aging of the individual and for the dynamics of the society. For each *individual* in a cohort, these articulating processes are necessary if he is to perform in the sequence of life-course stages, achieving some sense of personal continuity and identity [*see Chapter 11 by Clausen*]. For the *society*, too, since it outlasts the lifetime of its members, these processes serve to maintain continuity insofar as they succeed in adjusting the available supplies of people and roles within each age stratum [*see Chapter 10 · 4*].

Yet personal identity and societal continuity are not always cognate. Hence the same articulating device that has positive consequences at one level may have negative consequences at the other. Thus allocation of manpower to military defense, while designed to maintain national stability, can at the same time create irretrievable disruptions for individuals in the affected cohorts. Or a disturbance at the societal level, such as incoming cohorts too small to fill personnel requirements in the labor force or the government, can be experienced by individuals in these cohorts as expanded opportunity through decreased competition for desirable positions. The consequences of articulation, then, can present divergent problems that depend upon whether societal or cohort time is the dynamic focus.

Phasing of the two processes   The consequences of allocation and socialization depend not only on the level of articulation being considered, but also on the ordering of the two processes over the life course of individuals.[5] Since skills and motivations can be utilized in role performances only as they have been acquired through socialization, the supply of able and willing role players in an age stratum is in part contingent upon whether or not the relevant kinds of socialization are provided. Yet, socialization without subsequent allocation is a not infrequent phenomenon—as is the case, for example, with trained engineers who cannot find jobs, or with women socialized for the occupational role who never find opportunity to work.[6] Conversely, allocation may take place without reference to whether the requisite capacities for role playing have been generated through prior socialization. For example, school attendance at age 6 or 7 is ordinarily compulsory for all children, though children of this standard age may vary widely in their earlier preparation for school.

Age structuring of articulation In addressing ourselves to allocation and socialization as processes inherent in life-course development, we also describe the arrangements and agencies present in every society (often located in particular institutions within the state, school, church, the family, or the occupational system), both for socializing individuals at various life stages and for determining which, and how many, individuals are to be assigned to which roles.[7] Interestingly enough, this concern with the social arrangements for articulation draws attention to a host of little recognized problems relating to the social structure, problems that remain elusive as long as only the processual aspects of allocation and socialization are emphasized. Both processes are essential to the progress of individuals through life (hence age-related in the dynamic sense). But both are also characterized by structured interrelationships among the age strata. Cross-sectional views of the society at particular time periods reveal not only an age distribution of roles, but also a multiplicity of role relationships among individuals who are in varying stages of socialization and allocation and who confront one another as candidates or allocators, or as socializees or socializing agents, for particular roles.

[5] Parsons (1951, pp. 236–243) maintains that the learning of broad orientations takes place during childhood, whereas "situational specification" of attitudes, cognitions, and skills can be developed only after assumption of particular roles. See also Brim (1966, pp. 24 ff.).

[6] Merton's observations (1957, Chapter 4) regarding "structured anomie" may be regarded as an instance of socialization without allocation. Though internalization of achievement-success values is generally regarded as a mark of successful socialization, there are often insufficient high-status roles available to absorb those motivated, and even some of those trained, to enter them.

[7] Sorokin ([1927], 1959, p. 207), indicating that many social institutions are not only the "agencies for education and transformation of human beings" but also perform "the functions of social selection and distribution of the members of a society," evaluates the importance of these latter functions as "scarcely less than that of education and training."

As long as the younger strata are small children, a "hierarchical" structure of age relations—with older strata assuming initial responsibility for the younger—is predictable because of the early dependency of the infant. Beyond this, the structuring of age relations in socialization and allocation remains open to theoretical and empirical inquiry, as these relations adjust to changes from one period of history to another in population, role structure, or environment. The extent of differentiation of these relations by age, and the potential for sequential shifts, at once raise critical questions. How, and how effectively, can the articulating processes operate, when participants typically differ both in life stage and in historical period of residence in the social system? What special tensions may be generated by these particular forms of relationship between participants from diverse strata?

Thus a serendipitous result emerges from our dynamic analysis of socialization and allocation: we detect a special synchronic structuring of members of the several age strata involved in these processes at given periods. We discover the implications of allocation and socialization, not only for the aging of individuals, but also for the impact of these special age-relationships on stability or change in the social system. For the processes of allocation and socialization would not be problematic could they operate as automatic regulators, responding to changes in people and roles much as Adam Smith's "invisible hand" was once thought to maintain stability in the market. But—as later economists were to discover regarding economic relations—processes of articulation, like other social processes, are embedded in and realized through a structure of social relations. And these structured relations, far from responding blindly to exigencies of the moment, may exhibit rhythms and create tensions of their own, reflecting their ties to other social structures and to the basic social values and personal interests of participants. Scrutiny of socialization and allocation as age-related phenomena thus points to a conclusion reached in varied ways by many social thinkers: the forces that preserve order and continuity in a society are more difficult to account for than the forces of conflict and disintegration. How, after all, could the articulating processes reach perfection in synchronizing the tempo of mankind and the tempo of society?

PRESSURES FOR CHANGE

Our discussion leads us, then, to the potentially innovative consequences for the society engendered by the ordering and structuring of these four processes of cohort flow and aging, allocation and socialization. Two broad types of strains and imbalances can be discerned: those deriving from operation of the processes *within* particular cohorts, and those deriving from the interplay *among* the coexisting cohorts that are subjected to these processes.

The first source of potential change inheres in each single cohort that confronts the prevailing social structure, as the cohort is characterized by a given size and composition, becomes articulated into this structure, and ages over its life course. Even if one could imagine no other source of change in society, intracohort sources of strains and imbalances would alone threaten social stability. Just as each individual endures continual tension throughout his lifetime because he must adjust to societal demands, learning new roles and relinquishing old ones, difficulties can also beset the society because each new cohort is born and requires continual allocation and socialization for the sequence of roles it must encounter (Moore, 1967). For example, a particular cohort can be disruptive of existing arrangements if it differs from neighboring cohorts in size, characteristics, or manner of response to early socialization or to historical events. Pressures for change can also be exerted by imperfections in the articulating processes, as allocation and socialization may be out of phase with each other, as socialization may qualify people inadequately for the roles available, or as allocation may fail to assign the numbers and kinds of people appropriate to meet current demands. In such ways, the age-related processes, interacting with one another and with the given role structure, can threaten social stability over the life course of any particular cohort.[8]

A second source of strain and imbalance, which enlarges the potential for change, derives from the fact of cohort succession. For, within the society as a whole [*as Chapter 10 has shown*], all the cohorts, though belonging to different age strata, coexist and are moving *together* through time. They live as contemporaries, but they are not coevals in age or experience. And age-incongruities in many types of relationships (including those particular to allocation and socialization) can be productive of tensions and conflicts.

Moreover, in addition to these changes that stem directly from the age structure and its distinctive processes, societal dynamics depend also upon exogenous factors and events outside our age-specific model. [*See Chapter 1 · 2 · A and 1 · 2 · B.*] Certain exogenous changes occur in the organism at the boundary between the social and the biological. Others occur in the general physical and social environment. Of special concern to us are changes in the environing structure of roles, as reflections of societal timing in contrast to cohort timing.

This final chapter deals with the four age-related processes and with their crucial relation to change. Social change presents ever-shifting sequences of roles through which each new cohort as it ages must be accommodated. And different cohorts, exposed to singular historical conditions, age in differing

---

[8] [*See the interrelationships among the age-specific processes, Chapter 1 · C.*]

ways that both *reflect* social change and, in turn, *cause* further changes. Section 1 of the chapter considers the succession of cohorts, as their similarities or differences yield patterned regularities in the size and characteristics of the age strata at different periods of historical time. Allocation and socialization are discussed separately in Sections 2 and 3. In reality, the distinction between these two is often blurred when both processes operate simultaneously within the same social structures—as, for example, when selection for socialization to a role is also a step in selection for allocation. The distinction, however, if not always visible, is valuable in enabling us to analyze those situations in which the two processes produce their own strain through failures of complementarity or coordination. The emphases of these two sections differ because of the marked discrepancies in previous sociological treatment. If Section 2 can only present selected aspects of the enormous literature on socialization, Section 3 discloses the entire topic of allocation as hitherto neglected, though both processes are revealed as intimately related to each other and to aging. Finally, Section 4 stresses some of the tensions and pressures for change implicit in the differences between cohort timing and societal timing—because the biologically rooted exigencies of cohort succession and aging must confront a social system that itself is undergoing change as alterations occur in the material and social environment, in the role structure, in the numbers and characteristics of the role players, and in the processes operating to articulate these elements.

1 *The flow of cohorts through the society*

See Chapter 1 · 1 · B; Chapter 2 · 2 and 2 · 3; and Chapter 3

Karl Mannheim once suggested a tantalizing mental experiment ([1928], 1952, p. 292). Imagine, he said, a society in which one generation lived on forever, and none followed to replace it. A few moments of thought are enough to dramatize once again the infrangible linkages among the succession of cohorts, aging, and age stratification. For, in contrast to Mannheim's imaginary society, each real society consists of successive cohorts, characterized by its own size, composition, and unique life-course pattern.

In this section, we shall illustrate certain of the connections between the flow of cohorts and the changing age structure of society. We return to the age-related societal patterns and changes in individual behaviors, attitudes, and relationships described in Chapter 10 as strata differences (Sd) and period differences (Pd); but we now look upon these societal patterns and changes as composites of the differing cohorts that form the age strata at particular periods. Here we are echoing the challenge to sociologists by Ryder (himself a follower of Mannheim in provocative formulation of the possibilities) to "exploit the congruence of social change and cohort differentiation."[9]

COHORT FLOW AND THE AGE STRUCTURE

Many changes in the age structure, and particularly the purely demographic changes, are widely familiar. Yet, the dynamics of such changes, as the macro-biographies of individuals form the history of society, are often elusive and can bear review.

Metaphor of the moving stairs As an aid to understanding the flow of cohorts through the society—reminiscent of Sorokin's metaphor of the elevator of social mobility ([1927], 1959, pp. 137–138)—imagine an escalator rising through the several floors (which bound the age strata) of a building. All entrants to the building move directly onto the bottom of this escalator (are born), ride steadily upward (grow older), and exit from the building once they reach the top (die). On the way up, the riders can view the scenes on each of the several floors.

If this were a *stable situation*, the entrants to the stairway at successive points in time (the cohorts) would always be alike in number and in kind, and all would remain in the building until they reached the top (would die at the same time). Thus, in a cross-sectional view, the numbers and kinds of people on each floor would be unchanging, even though the particular individuals on that floor are constantly moving out and being replaced.

In a *flexible situation*, by contrast, the numbers and kinds of people entering the escalator and continuing upward vary from time to time. Suppose that the number of entrants, instead of remaining fixed, rises steadily. This rise would produce ever-greater crowding on the stairs. [*Compare Principles 1 and 2 in Chapter 2 · 3.*] In addition, it would mean that, at any given period, the numbers of people on the lower floors would be greater than the numbers on the higher floors. Or suppose that the flow of entrants is interrupted completely for an interval of time. Then one section of the stairway would be completely devoid of riders, thereby emptying each of the floors in turn as this untenanted section travels upward. This metaphor suggests how the process of cohort flow ($P1$) can produce the age structure of a population (Sd) as the people on all the floors (the age strata) are viewed at one period. It also suggests how variations in this process can produce changes in the age structure (Pd). The figure might be elaborated with way stations to allow certain persons to enter or leave at each floor, corresponding to the migrations and the deaths at earlier ages that also affect the size and composition of particular strata.

[9] Ryder (1965, p. 861 and passim). See also the discussion by MacIver (1963, esp. pp. 110–111); Riley (1971).

At least one further elaboration is required to indicate differences among successive cohorts in the way they age (P2). Perhaps the scene on some of the floors is undergoing continual alteration. Then different riders, even though arriving at the same floor, are exposed to widely varied experiences on that floor depending on the time of their arrival.[10] This is the temporal feature of cohort succession that links the population processes to history.

Changing sizes of strata Let us consider in more detail the changing size and characteristics of the age strata suggested by this figure of speech. First, in regard to size, the metaphor is clearly connected to the demographic processes (natality, mortality, and migration). And these processes affect each separate cohort over its life course, thereby setting constraints upon the numbers (and the initial composition) of people available at particular periods in the age-stratified society.[11]

A *persistent trend* toward increases or decreases in the size of successive cohorts will be reflected in changing absolute numbers in the affected age strata. Thus steadily rising birth rates will mean increases in the younger age categories (as indeed the population under 15 years of age rose substantially with the fertility revival following World War II). Or continuing decreases in mortality at the older ages will tend to swell the size of the category 65 and over. Period changes in *proportionate* [*compare Chapter 2 · 1*] size of an age stratum are more complex, of course, since they reflect the composite of changes in all the age strata. For example, rising proportions of old people could result merely from decreasing proportions of younger people. In fact, the rising proportions of older people have been attributable largely (at least in the past) to the decreases in fertility rates.[12]

Sporadic changes in cohort size can also continue for many decades to exert effects on the age-stratified population, as the affected cohorts move through successive stages of their life course. If a particular cohort (or set of cohorts) is markedly different in size from its neighbors (as through fertility changes, war, epidemics, or sudden migration) this idiosyncracy will appear as a trough or a bulge in the age pyramid at a particular time (see Figure 12 · 1). When the pyramids depicting the same population are compared over time, this trough (or bulge) moves up the age strata as the particular cohort travels through its life course. As

[10] Despite the dangers of metaphor, one is tempted to embroider. For example, since chronological age is not coterminous with social aging, certain individuals may be able to linger on some floors. Or, since the age structure itself is changing, the building (that is, the society) must also be imagined as undergoing continuing alteration.

[11] Ryder (1965) speaks of the flow of cohorts as "demographic metabolism."

[12] Even though reductions in infant and child mortality have somewhat offset these decreases (Kiser, 1962).

FIGURE 12 · 1 *Changes in age structure, reflecting cohort flow, United States, 1900, 1940, and 1958 (whites only)*

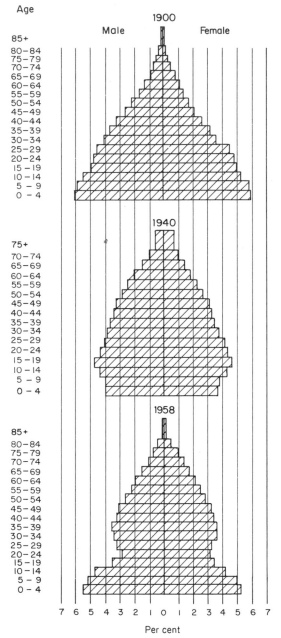

Source: Kiser, 1962, pp. 21–23.

can be seen from Figure 12 · 1, the cohort born in the 1930's was so small that the population trough (ages 0–9 in 1940 and 15–24 by 1958) is now reaching a period where the supply of personnel for the roles of middle life is actually smaller (in absolute numbers) than the previous complement for these roles [*compare Chapter 10 · 4*].

Differences among successive cohorts in composition as well as in size can also affect the age structure of the population—as wars change the sex ratio at particular ages, for example, or changing differentials in white-nonwhite fertility may influence the younger strata, or foreign-born immigrants can die out at the older ages.

We are, of course, interested here in the operation of the purely demographic factors primarily as surrogates for the associated social phenomena. To take a familiar example from the United States population, once the unprecedentedly large cohorts now in young adulthood are understood as a bulge moving up the age period over many decades, the historical accompaniments become clearer. Because these cohorts by far outnumber their predecessors, their early experience has been one of crowded housing and crowded schools. As they continue into the future, their impact will be felt in the labor market and in the marriage market, and in the numbers of children they in turn produce. Meanwhile the social structure, initially inadequate to absorb them, has felt the pressure to adjust at each of their life-course stages, providing more opportunities for children, more educational and military roles for adolescents, and so on. And again, adaptive difficulties or failures to make adequate adjustments constitute a major source of strain for both individuals and society.

In using such an illustration, our intention is to amplify Mannheim's thesis that demography alone, while providing opportunities for social process and social change, cannot account for particular features of any given modification. The relevance of the demographic facts of size and composition requires, as Mannheim put it, "proper attention to the formative layers of social and cultural forces."[13]

Changing characteristics of strata Cohort flow underlies changes not only in size and composition of the population but also in many age-related characteristics of sociological concern. Here the model of the moving stairs can be specified in terms of the method of cohort analysis described in Chapter 2. With a cohort defined as the aggregate of individuals within a society who are born at the same time and who age together,[14] then the changing age

---

[13] Mannheim ([1928], 1952, p. 312). Ryder (1965, p. 844) similarly asserts that demographic replacement, while providing the channel for societal transformation, cannot be regarded as the cause of social change.

[14] Not only total societies, but any social system that persists through the continual replenishment of personnel, can be effectively analyzed as a succession of cohorts. The cohort can be defined as an aggregate of individuals who share, not a common date of birth, but a

structure of society can be understood as comprising the overall succession of cohorts.

Three features of this method for studying the prevalence of a given characteristic can be recalled [*compare Table 2 · 5 in Chapter 2*]. First, cohort analysis can trace the life-course patterns of individuals *within* each cohort, as they undergo the processes of aging within the system. Second, it can compare the difference *among* cohorts in these life-course patterns. And third, the method can show how the sequential cohorts, each one lagging behind its precursor in the process of aging, all *fit together* to form the changing structure of the society.

Previous chapters have noted a number of cohort analyses that specify how *changes* in the characteristics and involvements of actors in successive cohorts relate to the dynamics of social systems. For example, Chapter 6 by Starr describes one such study in which Taeuber (1965), by using lifetime residence histories to reconstruct the migration patterns of successive cohorts, succeeded in determining whether individuals as they age have followed the societal trend of population away from the farm and toward the village or the city. In Chapter 2, rising levels of labor force participation by women are seen to be accompanied by changing life-course patterns of work among succeeding cohorts of females. Chapter 4 by Foner describes another analysis in which Crittenden (1962, pp. 651–654), was able to demonstrate, quite apart from the impact of general societal shifts, the individual's increasing identification with the Republican party as he ages.

Our present concern is not with the procedures of cohort analysis, which present many problems both of execution [*to be noted in the Appendix*] and of interpretation [*as discussed in Chapter 2, especially Section 4*]. Instead, our focus here is on the peculiar virtue of cohort analysis—on its translation into operations of the crucial differences between societal timing and individual (or cohort) timing. As an empirical approach, it takes cognizance of the society as a system—with its subcultures and its age-structure of roles—moving through historical time along its own path of stability and change. For example, the society may move through a sequence of states from 1955 to 1960 to 1965. Meanwhile, as the successive cohorts follow their special rhythm of aging over the life course from birth to death, cohort analysis views these cohorts, not only in the cross-sectional sequences that refer to the society, but along the paths of their respective lives and the respective portions of history in which their lives are inscribed. The method enables the researcher to deal over time both with the larger system and with the character-

---

common date of entry into the particular system (such as a college class, or persons admitted to a mental hospital in a given year); and the notion of "aging" can refer to duration of exposure to the system.

istics and behaviors of its constituent members.[15] In this way, cohort analysis can add to understanding of the subtle interplay between societal stability and change and the progress of individuals through their respective role sequences.

In effect, this method, by contrasting the life-course patterns of consecutive cohorts, shows how changes in the age structure of the society (Pd) are constituted by differences among cohorts—both differences in size or composition and also differences in the way cohorts age. At any *single* period, the cross-sectional pattern of similarities and differences among age strata (Sd) is produced jointly, as we have seen (Principle 1 from Chapter 2 · 3 · B), by intercohort differences (Cd) and by intracohort differences over the life course (Ld). Thus, as individuals change with aging, this process tends to affect the age structure, but would not produce permanent changes in this structure over historical time if individuals were to continue to age in exactly the same way [*Principle 2 from Chapter 2 · 3 · C*]. For, to repeat once again Ryder's epigrammatic statement [*from Chapter 3*], there can be no social change unless "successive cohorts do something other than merely repeat the patterns of behavior of their predecessors."

REFLECTIONS OF SOCIAL CHANGE

Let us now examine the implications for societal stability and change entailed by the central fact that cohorts do not all age in exactly the same way. While there is little actual evidence, and cohort differences interact with social change in complex ways, in principle certain differences can often be simply understood as primarily either reflecting social and environmental change or as contributing to it. [*See Chapter 1 · 2.*] We shall start with instances where it seems reasonable to interpret period differences in the age strata as the shifting mosaic of cohorts who have aged in differing ways because of their differing historical backgrounds. Later we shall suggest how cohort flow may actively initiate change. But we shall first treat this flow as a channel for alteration of society, following Ryder (1965) and Mannheim ([1928], 1952, pp. 309 and passim) before him. In Ryder's characteristically succinct phrasing, "Transformations of the social world modify people of different ages in different ways," and "The effects of these transformations are persistent" (p. 861).

Cohort differences in fertility   As one example of period changes that reflect intercohort differences in the way people have aged in our society, con-

---

[15] Cohort analysis is of special interest to the methodologist as a form of *social system analysis*, in the sense that it identifies the cohorts as parts of the society and traces their contributions to the changing system as a whole. See Riley and Nelson (1971); Riley (1963, Volume I, Unit 12).

sider past changes in fertility.[16] This example is interesting because, with biological and social changes running counter to each other, the latter seem to have had the greater impact on the age strata. On the one hand, epidemiologists tell us that, in comparison with women born a century ago, today's women have experienced menarche at earlier ages and menopause at later ages (Tanner, 1955; National Center for Health Statistics, 1966). That is, the period of potential fertility has appreciably lengthened. Moreover, the trauma of reproduction have been drastically reduced, as fewer women die in childbirth and fewer of their infants die. In practice, on the other hand, recent cohorts spend *fewer* years of their lives in childbearing. Women have telescoped the phase of actual reproduction, having fewer and more closely spaced offspring nowadays than did their mothers or grandmothers (see Glick and Parke, 1965). Thus, the limits on reproduction imposed by biology appear to have little effect here on cohort differences in fertility. Rather, these differences are responsive to social customs and attitudes concerning numbers and temporal arrangement of children in the family (see, for example, Westoff et al., 1964; Spiegelman, 1968, p. 479).

Cohort differences in education   Education, to which we frequently allude because of its high degree of age-grading in our society and its pervasive consequences, is also a noteworthy example of the significance of variations in cohort flow for cross-sectional differences among age strata.

The rapid pace of educational advance in the United States over a century is shown in Figure 12 · 2, which indicates the pronounced rise in rates of secondary school enrollment and the subsequent rise in college enrollment. [*Compare Chapter 7 by Parsons and Platt.*] These enrollment rates have set their mark upon the successive cohorts of young people involved, because of the practice in our society of compressing education largely into the early years of life, rather than spreading it over the life course. For education, once completed, tends to become a stationary characteristic (almost like sex or race) with which a person enters his adult roles [*see Chapter 2 · 2 · B*]. Thus marked by changing levels of education, the cohorts differ strikingly from one another. And, at any given time, these cohort differences set the age strata sharply apart from one another, with the young people dramatically better educated than the old.[17] These strata differences in education have in-

[16] An analysis of cohort patterns in general health would be important for understanding the linkage between biological and social factors in age stratification. Although we do not undertake such an analysis, there are undoubtedly important cohort differences in health reflecting social changes in standard of living, medical knowledge, or public health practices. See, for example, Eldridge (1968, pp. 383–384); and, for a discussion of cohort differences in relation to the health of older people, Chapter 5 by Susser in Volume II. A full analysis would involve changes at several levels—ranging as Strehler has suggested (1962, p. 20), from molecules and cells up to organ systems, individual persons, and populations.

[17] For data on strata differences in educational level, see Chapter 5 in Volume I. These strata differences are often used to illustrate the "life-course fallacy" described in Chapter 2 · 3 · B,

FIGURE 12 · 2 *Development of secondary and higher education in the United States*

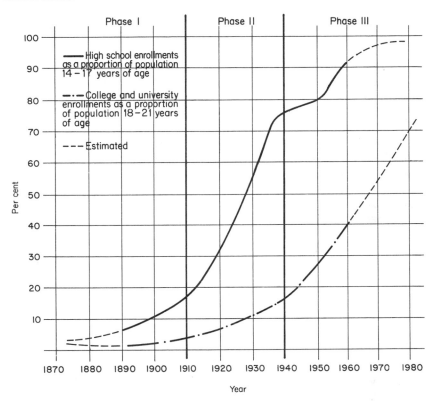

Source: Trow, 1966, p. 442.

calculable importance for many aspects of behavior and attitudes—for prejudice, feelings of powerlessness, narrow ranges of interests and friendships, and the like.

Many other changes in educational institutions and practices have produced wide variations among cohorts and forecast further variations. Indeed, the age pattern of education in the United States today is a reversal of that in earlier societies where the old were honored for their greater knowledge. Hu-

---

since this is an obvious case of strata differences that cannot be properly interpreted as changes over the life course of individuals. Less obvious, however, is the appropriate interpretation of changes in age-specific rates of school enrollment. As Beverly Duncan points out through a cohort analysis (1968, pp. 616–617, 629), the tendency for recent cohorts to spend more years in school than did earlier cohorts would be understated if the cross-sectional strata differences were interpreted directly, since there is a rising level of enrollment among the younger children too. [*Compare Principle 1 in Chapter 2 · 3 · B.*]

manitarian emphases on public education for the working classes goes back at least to Adam Smith who, reportedly influenced by Rousseau to regard the monotony of work as degrading, turned to education as a possible remedy (Viner, 1968, pp. 326–327). And if one looks ahead to the future from today's knowledge explosion, the information gap between the very young and even the not-so-young is deepening, creating pressures to change the entire structure of education if people beyond the earliest years are to maintain competitive equality.[18]

Other examples   These examples illustrate situations in which cross-sectional age patterns and changes may well be attributable, at least in part, to the impress of social trends upon consecutive cohorts. One can think of many other similar examples. Rates of drinking or smoking have been lower for older than for younger strata, and these structural differences are partially traceable to the past tendency for each new cohort to espouse these practices to an increasing degree (see Volume I, Chapter 11 · 6). The younger cohorts in the 1970's, however, may be introducing new habits, as lowerclassmen in some colleges, unlike the upperclassmen, reportedly prefer marijuana to beer. If such newcomers to college were to succeed in setting the pace for the cohorts that follow, such a change might drastically affect the earlier cross-sectional age patterns of drinking.

Or, in an example from another walk of college life, the analysts (Lipset and Ladd, 1970, p. 106) of a 1969 sample of professors expressed surprise at the large differences by age in support for student activism. In one discipline (political science), the range was from 76 per cent approving campus activism among professors in their 20's to 39 per cent among those in their 60's. The rates for the younger strata may have arisen, the authors think, from proximity in age and circumstance to the student dissenters. But why are the older strata so strikingly different? Is it only the fact that they are much farther along in years than the students? Or is this another of the age-specific findings that provoke further inquiry into the changes in *Weltanschauung* to which consecutive cohorts have been exposed during their early life?

CONTRIBUTION TO SOCIAL CHANGE

In contrast to situations in which social or environmental change sets its stamp upon the age strata, much as the changing seasons are reflected in the rings of a tree, there are other instances in which the age-related processes themselves appear to stimulate or contribute to change [*see Chapter 1 · 2 · B*]. Many of these contributions have repercussions through varied facets of the society. We shall reserve discussion of these contributions for Section 4

[18] The consequences of not effecting such a change may well be to encourage the increasing convergence of age and class stratification: see Chapter 10.

of this chapter, pausing now only to cite one example of the importance of cohort differences in *size* as a source of potential social change.[19]

We refer here to perhaps the most striking of all cohort differences, those in longevity [*as described in Chapter 10 · 2*]—that is, differences in the proportions of cohort members who survive through infancy and into the higher ages of the life course. The profound implications of such cohort differences in longevity can be intimated by just one of the many associated changes, the veritable revolution in the family structure (cf. Shanas, 1969, p. 146).

To produce this revolution (Volume I, Chapter 7) in the United States, the prolonged survival of all the family members has been coupled with changes in childbearing and in household living arrangements. Glick and Parke[20] have called attention to the striking alteration in the family cycle. Among couples born a century ago, the last child in the family was married, on the average, at about the same time as the death of one of the parents. But among recent cohorts, husbands and wives typically survive together as two-person families for a good many years after the last child has married and left home. Beresford and Rivlin (1964; see also Volume I, pp. 178–181), using records for the United States since 1940 and for Massachusetts since 1885, have uncovered trends in living arrangements that suggest a decline in the number of children (including young adult offspring) staying in the parental household. However, they find no evidence consistent with the widespread notion of extensive multigeneration living in the late nineteenth century; noting that only since 1940 has there been a decrease in the average number of households containing grandchildren or parents of the family head. In short, the single nuclear household of a century ago (parents and their children, sometimes including a grandparent) has been replaced by several generations of related nuclear households: the young couple with their dependent children, the middle-aged parents, the aged generation of grandparents, and the great-grandparent who also often survives.

Implicit in such a revolution in the age structure of the family are many and varied possibilities for social change. Does the extended period of husband-wife relationships in the middle years mean that couples in the more recent cohorts have learned greater independence from their offspring, or have they used the time to develop common interests or to accumulate assets for

[19] Interestingly enough, both Mannheim ([1928], 1952, p. 312) and Ryder (1965, p. 844) speak of cohort succession as "a constant," hence inappropriate as an explanation of social change. This argument appears, however, to overlook the fact that demographic replacement involves variations in cohort size which are certainly not constant; however, Ryder does state in the same article (p. 845) that "any extraordinary size deviation is lkely to leave an imprint on the cohort as well as on the society."

[20] Glick and Parke (1965, pp. 188–196); see also Glick's earlier (1955) formulation.

retirement? How does today's young adult offspring relate to the large number of his surviving relatives—to his parents and grandparents and (if he is married) to the parallel antecedents of his spouse? What are the consequences for child development and for the community of the dwindling proportions of little children who have lost one or both parents (Spiegelman, 1968, pp. 250–252)? Pitts (1961, p. 694), talking of the family as a unit for meeting the personality needs of both children and older members, makes the pregnant comment that it is

> . . . very likely that the nuclear family could not have developed as a tension-management center without a general increase in people's life expectancy. Because of this increase, the nuclear family in the Western world has attained much greater reliability as a protective and nurturant center for the personalities of its members.

Such speculations are enough to suggest the potentially fruitful hypotheses that can be derived from analyses of cohort differences as *sources*—not mere reflections—of social change.

IMPLICATIONS FOR THE FUTURE

Not all predictions about future implications of cohort differences are entirely speculative, of course. At any given time, a large proportion of the cohorts who will compose the age strata during the proximate future have already been born, so that much information is already in hand about cohort size, for example, sex, color, or place of birth.

Consider the oldest age stratum as the extreme case. All the cohorts who will reach 65 during this century or during the early decades of the twenty-first century are now alive. Thus, apart from unforeseeable changes (as through wars, depressions, or major shifts in migration or in values), fair estimates can be made about numerous characteristics of old people at particular dates in the future. The *size* of the aged stratum at the turn of the century will reflect the small numbers of babies in the Depression cohorts; but the size of the aged stratum will predictably increase again in the early decades of the coming century with the influx of the baby boom cohorts born after World War II.[21] In respect to *nativity*, the much-studied cohort who had passed age 65 or more by 1960 had contained a sizeable proportion of early immigrants who were largely illiterate and unskilled, whereas the more recent cohorts who will reach old age in subsequent decades contain fewer and better-educated immigrants. Or in respect to formal *education*, we have already noted that over 70 per cent of the cohort aged 75 or more in 1960 had had fewer than 9 years of school, contrasted with only 17 per cent of the cohort

[21] For a discussion of implications for public policy, see Spengler (1969).

aged 25 to 29, who will not reach age 75 before the year 2005 (Volume I, Chapter 5 · 1).

We are aware, also, of many changing societal or environmental conditions, not all of them salutary, that may influence in special ways the future life course of existing cohorts—as, for example, the spread of pollution might have the greatest effect on young cohorts subject to a full lifetime of exposure, or as the increase of smoking among women might bring female death rates more nearly into line with the currently higher male rates.

Over the long term, however, the cohorts alive today are gradually eroded away, becoming mere epiphenomena in the persistent current of cohort replacement. And the society, with its constant infusion of new cohorts and its exposure to the future course of history becomes increasingly unpredictable. For, while the aging of a cohort is inevitable, the "aging" of a population is not; indeed, trends in the proportions of old people, or in the proportions of "dependents" in the combined oldest and youngest strata, are far from irreversible, but can fluctuate markedly over time (Kiser, 1962, p. 18; Stockwell, 1968, pp. 375–376). And, as Pitts (1961, p. 694) suggests, in relation to certain social experiences (such as wars or depressions), cohorts are not a continuum but rather a discontinuity.

Moreover, it is not merely the changes in the total society that concern us, but the changes within the several age strata as different cohorts enter and leave the sequential stages of their life course. Just as each cohort is born into the society with its particular "enduring" traits, it also arrives at each of the transition points of life with additional accumulations of characteristics. At the starting point of adulthood, for example, the members of a cohort have not only the ascribed characteristics that were fixed at birth (such as sex or family background); but they have acquired also the experiences of youth, an educational level, a set of aspirations about occupational and marital roles, and so on. Thus at each stage, the cohort brings with it a definite form, that tends both to fashion and to constrain the remaining stages of its life. If, then, cohort differences are closely related to changes in society, they are also related to changes within the respective strata and within institutional fields as they too are stratified by age.

In this section, we have discussed the succession of cohorts that form the changing age strata, and we have begun to inquire into the interplay between cohort differences and social and environmental change. It is now apparent, however, that we can continue this inquiry only after we pause to examine in the two subsequent sections the articulating processes, socialization and allocation, which facilitate—though they sometimes impede—this flow of cohorts through the age structure of the society. How do these intervening processes operate in coordinating the changing life-course sequences of individuals with the changing age structure of society? And what strains are immanent in their operation?

2 Socialization

See Chapter 1, Section 1 · B · 4

Socialization, as one of the two major linkages between changes in people and changes in roles, has been widely discussed in the literature as a developmental process. Its age-relatedness is thus taken for granted. Although systematic attention has been devoted primarily to socialization of children rather than adults, the process is now widely recognized as continuing throughout the lifetime.[22] Not only must the individual, as he proceeds over his life course, learn new role complexes and unlearn old ones; but also each of the roles he plays is constantly shifting and must be endlessly relearned. Thus, aging becomes crucial for understanding socialization, and studies typically focus on clearly defined stages of individual development. A corollary of this life-course view of socialization, though seldom made explicit, is that socialization must be seen as a continuing aspect of role playing, not confined to those roles especially labeled as preparatory in the society. In the sequence of roles describing the lifetime of the individual, every role provides not only opportunity for expression of capacities learned in the past but also schooling (however adequate or inadequate) in the alteration or maintenance of current role performances and in anticipation of the performance of future roles.

Also not often made explicit, though essential to grasping the full importance of the process, is the fact that socialization is not merely a sequence of individual experiences in a social setting; it is also a societal phenomenon. On the one hand, the coexisting cohorts differ in the contributions the *individual* makes to the process: in his motivation and capacity to learn, in his willingness to adopt the status of learner and to apply learning strategies, and in his readiness to commit himself to new norms and loyalties. On the other hand, the *social* contributions[23] to the process are differentially accessible to members of different cohorts. For age, in affecting the availability of socially valued roles [*see Chapter 10*], at the same time affects the availability of rewards for successful learning, of opportunities for learning (such as sources of information, emotional support, or permissiveness), and of appropriate persons or agencies (socializing agents) for transmitting role expectations.

[22] In addition to the work of Erik H. Erikson and Harry S. Sullivan on the phases of personality beyond puberty, see, for example, Pitts (1961, pp. 698–701); Brim and Wheeler (1966); Brim (1968); Riley, Foner, Hess, and Toby (1969).

[23] For a discussion of individual versus societal contributions to the process, see Riley, Foner, Hess, and Toby (1969); Wheeler (1966); Clausen (1968); Inkeles (1969).

In addition, because the cohorts have entered the society at successive points in time, they differ both in their experiences of role learning and also in their locations in the process of socialization. Some have responsibility as socializers, others as learners, and still others occupy both positions simultaneously in their complex of roles. Thus, socialization is characterized by a set of structured age relations between socializees and socializing agents, each of whom is independently affected by age in the actions and attitudes of the one toward the other.

This section takes note of these little-discussed aspects of socialization where the emerging theory of age stratification suggests new insights both into the process itself and into its failures to bridge the gap between role expectations and individual motivations and capacities. [*See Chapter 10 · 4.*]

ROLE RELINQUISHMENT AND ROLE TRANSFER

A sociology of age inevitably draws attention to role relinquishment and role transfer as integral aspects of the socialization process. Learning the role of adult involves renouncing that of dependent child. Learning the role of retirement involves renouncing that of work. Such role transfers require not only adopting new behaviors and attitudes but also learning to relinquish former ones.[24]

Role relinquishment Socialization for relinquishing socially valued roles appears in many respects to reverse the process of socialization for role acquisition, so that the individual is faced with drastic changes in the expectations, facilities, and rewards afforded by society. For example, the individual, when widowed, is now *expected* (save for the later eventuality of possible remarriage) to learn to abdicate his earlier functions of looking after the physical and emotional needs of the spouse or (for the male) of supporting his wife. The available *facilities* and *resources* are no longer devoted to successful performance of the marital role, but to renouncing it. Although there may often be little advance socialization prior to actual bereavement (John Riley, 1968), husband and wife may sometimes prepare one another, and there may have been relevant role rehearsal on the occasion of earlier losses (e.g., of parents or other objects of affection). Former *rewards* are now withdrawn as the individual is deprived of the love and companionship of many years. Moreover, the subtle social approval accorded to the married state tends to be replaced with pity or indifference.

When, as in this example, the previously positive societal contributions to socialization are replaced by negative ones, resultant strains may create

---

[24] [*See Chapter 5 for examples.*] This topic is discussed in detail in Riley, Foner, Hess, and Toby (1969). The reduction of rewards for prior behavior as an incentive to conformity to new expectations has been specified by Bredemeier and Stephenson (1962, pp. 93–104).

pressure for change in the norms and definitions of the role. These strains stem from the central fact that socialization for role relinquishment persuades the individual to abandon former commitments while making new ones. Yet, the greater his commitment, the greater the difficulty of persuading him willingly to leave a role that he finds rewarding. If eventual relinquishment is necessary, then, should socialization for initial entry into the role attempt, as in the classical model of socialization, to secure maximum commitment of the individual? In general, it appears that the very existence of a sequence of roles to be played over the life course [see Chapter 11] marks a source of continual tension for both the individual and the society. The individual potentially faces a tug of war between existing demands and future expectations. For the society, accommodating the succession of personnel requires balancing the need for adequate performance from those occupying available roles against the need to loosen these individuals from their roles as they age.

One resolution to such problems might be in socialization for limited, rather than total, commitment to roles, since partial commitment can facilitate eventual exit from roles. However, limited commitment also enlarges the potential for deviant role behavior. And ultimately, limited commitment, as it reduces role expectations, can completely change the goals and norms of the role itself. One can begin to envision the effects through the mental experiment of what might happen if socialization for relinquishing the roles of worker or of spouse were to predominate over socialization for acquiring these roles.

Role transfer When socialization involves the dual processes of relinquishing one role and learning another (as the individual moves from worker to retiree, for example, or from student to teacher), several phases are involved. Van Gennep ([1908], 1960), in his classic description of the *rites de passage*, formulates three major phases of each life crisis: separation, transition, and incorporation. Throughout these phases of role transfer, the nature of the socialization process depends upon the degree of continuity in the role sequence [Chapter 10 · 1]. The role to be learned can be either a simple substitute for the individual's previous role, consonant with his previously learned values and attitudes, or it can differ from the previous role either in degree or in kind. Learning a substitute role can be a mere extension of prior socialization if, for example, the widower remarries or the retiree turns a hobby into a serious enterprise. Alternatively, however, where the expectations of the new role are incompatible with the self-expectations the individual has learned in earlier roles, new learning is required to resolve the internal conflict. Here he must find ways to implement his basic values in each new situation, while each new situation in turn contributes to the development of his basic value pattern.

Another important distinction in the phasing of socialization over the life course is that between anticipatory and tenancy socialization, between whether the individual learns his role before or after he is permitted to perform in it.[25]

Anticipatory socialization, either deliberate or unwitting, is often described as starting in childhood with the learning of broad value orientations and the acceptance of the legitimacy of particular roles and then as continuing in later life to specific learning of requisite attitudes and skills. Advance preparation of role players at various ages has special advantages (such as allowing optimal conditions for support or emphasis on progress in learning rather than on actual role performance), but age and time militate in certain ways against such advantages. One limitation is that socializing agents sometimes restrict or prohibit role rehearsal in order to prevent "premature" assumption of the role, since the learning of future roles can interfere with the demands of present ones. Another limitation is that the agents in anticipatory socialization are often neither the actual partners in the anticipated future roles, nor even the allocators to these future roles; thus they cannot be certain as to the ways in which sanctions for conformity or deviance will in fact be administered.

Perhaps the most important restrictions in terms of age and time is that anticipatory socialization always requires betting on the shape of the future.[26] Even in the situation of tenancy socialization, to the extent that future role requirements cannot be perfectly predicted and trained for in advance, older age strata may lose their advantage over the younger individual's age peers as socializing agents.[27] But the situation of anticipatory socialization is especially affected when the rapidity of change in a society increases the likelihood that older and younger age strata will have differing images of the future. An often-cited illustration is the disjuncture between parents with experience of severe economic depression, for whom occupational security and income are the central goals of adult careers, and offspring for many of whom the material standard of living is taken for granted while nonmaterial future career goals are central. Another, if more trivial, example of cohort differences in images of the future occurs in the initial frequent resistance by many parents and teachers to the "new math." Children taught under the more modern

[25] Compare Merton (1957, pp. 265 ff.). Neither of these types commonly exists in pure form, for even when a role is allocated without explicit prior socialization, many of the needed capacities for role playing have been acquired through previous experience in other roles.

[26] A form of betting widely impeded, according to 1970 accounts, by such reactions as "future shock," Toffler (1970); or "psycho-historical dislocation," Lifton (1970).

[27] [For a discussion of retraining of older workers, see Chapter 5 · 4.]

programs show higher performance in mathematical reasoning, problem solving, and conceptualization—but do less well in computation and routine operations than traditionally taught students. Since, however, the relative value of traditional skills becomes problematic in the computerized world of the future, one source of parental resistance to modern curricula may be the simple failure to understand future requirements in mathematical understanding.

An optimum situation for anticipatory socialization would be completely stable in the following purely hypothetical respects: (1) no change is foreseen by either candidates for future roles or by socializing agents; (2) no change in fact occurs subsequent to role assumption by candidates. To the extent that these hypothetical conditions are approximated (probably they are never fully met), older age strata are uniquely qualified to socialize the younger. Not only can the old teach expectations that coincide with the actual requirements of the role as oncoming cohorts will perform in it, but they can also offer competent role models for imitation.

Even when these ideal conditions are not approached, older cohorts do not necessarily lose their full competence as socializers as long as future changes in role requirements are foreseeable. To be sure, they suffer the disadvantage of presenting inadequate role models. Nevertheless, the *expectations* they hold out to the young can often incorporate norms that are entirely appropriate to future role performances. Thus mothers who themselves have not worked since marriage may still socialize their daughters to have careers; fathers with little formal education expect college attendance of their sons; age strata for whom little leisure exists may still manage to socialize the young for increased future leisure. Indeed, one study (Riley and Johnson, manuscript in preparation) of adolescents strongly suggests that such expectations on the part of socializing agents may have more influence than role models in shaping the self-expectations of individuals being socialized in anticipation, as older cohorts utilize a variety of sources for adjusting their expectations to the "norms of the future." In such manner the potential disruptions of social change may often be minimized as revised role definitions gain a measure of acceptance in the general society, becoming institutionalized as normative expectations prior to the time when they must be implemented.[28]

THE SOCIALIZER-SOCIALIZEE RELATIONSHIP

As we have noted, the fact of cohort succession means that the several age strata existing in a society will necessarily be found in varying relations of socialization with one another. Little is known, however, about the nature of these age relations and the consequences for socialization outcomes.

[28] Compare the discussion of reciprocal socialization that follows.

The extent to which the parent-child model of socialization has applicability when the older strata are being taught, for example, has still to be developed theoretically and tested empirically. In this model situation, the older, more competent, and more experienced parent is the socializer; the ignorant and dependent child is the object manipulated (though lovingly) to secure conformity to parental goals.[29]

Starting with the bizarre case studies (Davis, 1949, pp. 204–208) of children who, largely isolated from social contacts from birth, failed to develop most of the qualities commonly attributed to "human nature," such a model assumes certain contributions both on the part of the child who learns and on the part of the older, more experienced parents or teachers. The person being socialized contributes to the process varying degrees of motivation and capacity to learn. If the process succeeds, he gradually internalizes the role expectations as guides for his own behavior. Meanwhile the parent or other socializing agent (as in school or church) defines these expectations, utilizes societal facilities and resources in teaching, and controls the rewards and punishments that influence the learner in the desired direction. Moreover, to any situation of socialization beyond earliest infancy, the individual being taught brings not only his native abilities but also prior socialization experiences; hence the socializing agent confronts not a *tabula rasa*, but a person who already knows how to do certain things, who likes or prefers some people but objects to others, who views some things but not others as proper and good. (Here again we confront implications of the principle that aging of the individual coincides with his accumulation of experience.)

Reciprocal socialization If we were to apply this traditional model of parental socialization of the infant to later life stages beyond childhood, we would assume that those people who have gained experience in roles not yet taken by oncoming cohorts are inevitably the socializers of persons comparatively younger than themselves, regardless of their absolute age. Yet, in some situations the young socialize their elders. Consider the fact that socialization is not entirely asymmetrical, but may be to a degree reciprocal. Mannheim's early essay ([1928], 1952, p. 300) recognized the fact that each generation educates the other. Because the process *is* social, both the socializer and the socializee—and not only the latter—are dependent upon the performance of the other. As a consequence, the socializer is himself subject to many of the same mechanisms that he is applying to the person he is attempting to socialize. Nor does he control all the resources and rewards. Especially when the person being socialized is an adult, he too can control the general reward of approval and the punitive power of negative cathexis; often, too, he has the

---

[29] For a detailed description of the traditional model, see, for example, the work of G. H. Mead, Freud, K. Davis, Parsons, and the reinforcement psychologists.

choice of "opting out"; thus the older socializee is ordinarily able to offer rewards contingent on conformity to *his* expectations.

To be sure, the *responsibility* for socialization may be in the hands of the socializing agent. It is not, for example, the responsibility of children to teach the parental role. In practice, however, much reciprocal socialization occurs regardless of socially defined responsibilities. Even initial socialization contains some measure of reciprocity, helpless and malleable though the infant may seem. It has been suggested that the infant, with his imperious demands, socializes others perhaps even more than he himself is socialized (Rheingold, 1969): at the same time that the parents are caring for and teaching the infant, they are learning both how to be parents and how to forego many of their previous self-centered goals and gratifications. They learn that the infant "responds" to certain kinds of behavior on their part, and fails to respond to other kinds. Though their accumulated prior experiences may serve as anticipatory socialization to certain of the values and skills demanded by parenthood, it is actual tenancy in the role that can profoundly alter their definitions of parenthood and of themselves.

This potential for reciprocal socialization increases as the child gains ability consciously to manipulate his environment. And the greater this potential, the more uncertain the outcome, as the possibility increases that the individual being socialized will succeed in legitimating his own expectations—both for himself *and* the socializer—with the result that the goals and role performances for each are redefined.

The implications of reciprocal socialization for age relations in a *changing* society are especially notable. The facts of aging presuppose that those who have passed through certain life stages are best qualified to teach those who have still to enter them, despite the possibly superior organic condition of the younger cohorts. But the facts of cohort succession in a changing society oppose the experience of the older cohorts to the more recent training and the exposure to new values of the young.[30] As Margaret Mead puts it, people today who were born and bred before World War II are "immigrants in time" (1970, p. 72). When age strata differ in values and skills, the bilateral nature of relations of socialization may manifest itself in conflict and strain, as each side maneuvers to impose its own expectations as governing the relation. But reciprocal socialization also may function to bridge distances between age strata, as differences are resolved through "role negotiation," to use Goslin's term (1969, pp. 7–10), and as changes originating with, or largely manifested by, younger strata are disseminated through the larger society.

[30] In learning "new" values, the original sources are ordinarily older members of the society. But these older mentors (siblings, for example) frequently are not members of the same age cohorts as the "legitimate" socializing agents. When they are, they are frequently viewed by their age peers as deviant and not legitimate societal representatives having responsibility for socialization.

It may be that, in many respects, older cohorts currently possess superior power, authority, and competence in socialization of the young. But power (short of raw force), authority, and competence are characteristics to be defined and legitimated in the social system. When the younger and the older disagree on legitimacy in these respects, the situation of socialization is unstable and its consequences problematic. Thus, for example, whatever the sources and potential consequences of the demands of dissident students in a university, such students may function as socializing agents for other segments of the academic community.

The possibility for reversal of the traditional age hierarchy in socialization becomes especially real in a situation where the increasing education of successive cohorts produces societal upgrading with various potential consequences in the society. The very success of a society in improving the training of the young may tend to accelerate its time schedule for displacement of the old. Or, the young, by retraining the mature, may help these older people to adapt to a changing society.

Division of labor in socialization   The traditional parent-child model is further complicated when several socializing agents, who often differ in age, become involved. Socialization is essentially a two-person phenomenon only in the initial stages of the mother-child relationship. Even among the very young, role relations exist with father and siblings,[31] and often with grandparents and an array of other relatives. Moreover, in early childhood the child is likely not only to have a set of peer relations from the neighborhood and school but also to relate to adult representatives of these spheres. Beyond childhood, many other people become significant role partners, as the size and diversity of the role complex varies by age [*see Chapter 10 · 1*]. Each of these others is a potential agent of socialization. Since age differentiation can be an important source of variability in socialization outcomes, the fact is highly significant, though often overlooked, that the socializing agents often differ from each other in age even when the persons they are socializing all belong to the same age stratum.

If there is any truth to the sociological dictum that individuals located differently in society differ in social perspectives (see, e.g., Mannheim; W. I. Thomas), then age discrepancies among the socializing agents to which a person is exposed increase the possible diversity and conflict among the expectations governing particular roles. Even in a very stable and homogeneous society, people of varying ages have differential social locations because they are not at the same stage of their life course—stratum differences that may be

---

[31] The almost unmanageable complexity of age as a factor in socialization is illustrated by the fact that merely the effect of absence of younger or older siblings is the focus of a subspecialty in the study of family socialization.

vastly aggravated through special cohort differences generated in periods of change.

Though little is known empirically about the effect of age differences among socializers, one example may be suggestive for research on this topic. United States data for 1960 show the mid-40's as the median age of female elementary and secondary school teachers.[32] By contrast, the median age of parents of school children is considerably younger. What does such an age gap imply regarding relations between parents and teachers as agents in the socialization of the school-aged child? These questions cannot be decided in the absence of empirical data, though the prominence of school disturbances in the 1960's would in itself justify such research. On purely speculative grounds, the repeatedly stressed distinction between aging and cohort differences permits quite opposite lines of inferential argument.

On the one hand, teachers who are older than the parents of their pupils have more years of accumulated experience in other social roles. Many teachers are themselves parents and have already reared their own children. These factors—bulwarked by any prior socialization of the parents to official norms that may have stressed respect for teachers or conformity to teacher demands—may operate to build and reinforce an effective coalition between parents and teachers in the education of the young. In such a situation, any efforts by the child to reject the authority of teachers or to deviate from their expectations will be unrewarded in the home. Parents, even when they offer support and sympathy, will deny reciprocity, insisting that children obey the teacher. Should rebellion develop, either idiosyncratically or as a widespread condition among age peers in the school, then *both* sets of socializing agents, teachers and parents, are likely to present a united front.

On the other hand, consider the consequences of the possibility that the differing birth cohorts of which teachers and parents are members were exposed to sharply divergent experiences because of historical changes. For example, as children in family and in school, they may have had differing kinds of exposure in learning the roles for which they now as adults have become socializing agents. Parents with children in school in 1960 may well have reared their own children more permissively than did the earlier cohorts to which the teachers belong. Moreover, these parents, as members of the more recent cohorts, have received more formal education, on the average, than did the earlier cohorts of which teachers are members so that, in contrast to past historical periods, a sizeable proportion of parents today are the educational equals or superiors of their children's teachers. Since the age difference between parents and teachers, then, can index such differential

[32] Folger and Nam (1967, p. 84); Hughes (1970, pp. 17–18) comments on some telling paragraphs by Halbwachs on the increasing age gap between teacher and pupil.

exposure to historical trends and events, this difference may also distinguish parents from teachers in their values and their definitions as to the nature and purposes of the family and of educational institutions. Thus it may be possible that parents and children are now closer together in many respects than are parents and teachers, creating the potential for a coalition of home against school. In such a situation, parents may be the partners, whether silent or vocal, in their children's disobedience or in demands for educational changes resisted by teachers and school authorities.

Such alternative outcomes of patterned age differences between parents and teachers point to the need for an approach to socialization that emphasizes age relations in the society. Such an approach will require, however, considerable elaboration of the limited model of socialization as the learning of a single role within an asymmetrical relationship involving either a single socializer or an age-homogeneous aggregate of socializers. Though social scientists most certainly do not regard this oversimplified model as conforming to empirical reality, even the heuristic value of its restrictive assumptions must be weighed against the gaps in theoretical inquiry it can permit. Because individuals at every age have a multiplicity of role relationships, they are exposed to a multiplicity of socializing agents. And the mere fact of age differences among these socializers implies some measure of heterogeneity in the role models and expectations to which a person is exposed in the process of learning his culture. Given such heterogeneity as an intrinsic feature of society, the construct of a single set of societal norms against which to measure individual conformity and deviance, or social stability and change, is less acceptable as a theoretical anchor than as a hypothesis requiring careful empirical investigation.

A more realistic approach will take account also of the changes over the life course in the role complex, as these affect the division of labor among the socializing agents. At ages, for example, where roles must be learned that stress universalistic achievement, information and contingent rewards may be provided by one set of socializers in the school or workplace, while the requisite emotional support may be supplied by family or friends. Or, at ages where the constellation of roles to be learned is marked by conflicting expectations, there can be problems of integration among the several socializing agents, who may interfere or overlap with one another.

Age peers in socialization If socializing agents tend to differ in age among themselves, those in the process of learning particular roles often tend to be of similar age. In any age stratum, then, people may share role learning with their age peers, even while acting (beyond infancy) as socializing agents for people in other strata. One consequence may be a tendency for solidary relationships to develop among people in the process of learning particular roles.

That age peer groups, especially those of adolescence, do perform special functions in the socializing process has been the subject of extensive investigation.[33] Two functions of peer groups have been widely analyzed. The first stresses the expressive support offered by the peer group as respite from, or even as active defiance of, the efforts of socializers. The second notes the opportunities for anticipatory rehearsal of future roles that may accrue from the peer group's management of its internal affairs. Thus Parsons and Platt in Chapter 7 mention both these functions in examining the political activity of college students, and the relevance for age-graded friendship relations is examined in Chapter 9 by Hess.

In addition, it seems to us, there is a third function in which age peers serve directly, and often in purely instrumental fashion, to socialize each other. Peer groups often serve as clearinghouses for disseminating and organizing information received from diverse sources. Among the young, for example, sex education is reported to be largely a peer group phenomenon. Peers at any age can aid one another by comparing limited information received from the "outside," by exposing contradictory role expectations held out by "official" socializing agents, and by agreeing upon some measure of consistency in self-expectations.

Age peers seem most likely to act as the principal socializing agents where normative expectations for role performance are lacking or unclear, where socializing agents with prior role experience are unavailable, or where this experience is no longer relevant. The special situation of old age in these respects may encourage great reliance on peers. With old age marking the end of the life course, there are no older members of the society to act as agents of socialization. Many old people today did not have parents surviving to old age who could serve as role models in anticipatory socialization (Rosow, 1967). Moreover, old people are often residentially segregated from community affiliations with other age strata [see Chapter 6 by Starr]. And there are few clearly defined roles appropriate to old age in American society. Under such conditions, old people perforce must learn how to structure their social life through trial and error. And this learning can be greatly facilitated through peer communication about personal experience and the successes or failures of particular individual attempts.

SOCIALIZATION AND SOCIAL CHANGE

Our conjectures about age-related aspects of the socialization context, and about historical variability of this context, begin to emphasize certain connections between changes in socialization practices and in society at large. Other essays in this volume have alluded to relevant instances: for example,

---

[33] To some extent, these investigations have modified the parent-child model of socialization.

they have pointed to the decline of apprenticeship in occupational socialization [*Chapter 5*], speculated on the consequences of expansion and codification of knowledge in training for scientific professions [*Chapter 8 by Zuckerman and Merton*], focused on a new phase of socialization as marking the expansion of higher education [*Chapter 7 by Parsons and Platt*], or remarked upon variations in childrearing practices [*Chapter 11 by Clausen*]. Some of these changes in the structures and processes of socialization are easily traceable to related historical conditions. The causes of others are less apparent; trends in childrearing, for example, are somewhat differently explained by several competing theories. Indeed, we have suggested that the very structure of the socialization process itself may press for change as through the effect of reciprocal socialization or the vagaries of anticipatory socialization. Whatever the causes, such changes in socialization are not merely new techniques for teaching traditional roles. Rather, they represent both sources of, and responses to, alterations in the social structure of roles.

Even when changes in socialization are directed at the learning of particular roles, they are not entirely restricted in their consequences to the new cohort being socialized. Since these changes also affect the age strata playing complementary roles in the socialization process, they may tend to ramify through the society. The same individual, aging as he moves through the sequence of role complexes, shifts from socializee to socializer, or must act simultaneously in both capacities. Moreover, each change in socialization, though directed at a specific cohort, alters the role performances of this cohort throughout its life course and hence the age relations in the larger society for the time periods involved. For example, if early childhood socialization produces effects that endure through the life course, each of the co-existing age strata in the society continues to reflect those childrearing practices characteristic of its respective era.

All such considerations lead us to insist upon a view of socialization as a central vehicle for social change. Strangely enough, many widely noted theories focus on, or even define, socialization as a conservative process that merely preserves and transmits traditional values and practices. Since the society is made up of individuals, it seems curious that, by and large, conceptualizations of the "normal" process of socialization commonly overlook the counter-impact of these individuals upon society. Instead, a set of fixed norms is typically imagined, to which individuals as passive objects either conform or not. Nonconformity is then conceptualized as a *failure*[34] of socialization. In fact, however, departures in varying degrees from an imagined normative

---

[34] It is understood that socialization is used here to refer to socially approved (rather than deviant) roles and behaviors that are normatively consonant with dominant values in the society.

consensus are frequent, perhaps as frequent as conformity; thus the labels can be misleading.

In our view, a sociological theory of age leads inevitably to the recognition that inquiries into socialization must deal with elements of change, as well as elements of stability, as necessary to the preservation of social life. The continual replenishment of personnel in society (discussed in Section 1) has consequences far beyond the necessity of "bringing up baby." It means that, as individuals continue to age over their life span, their changing capacities and their responses must be channeled through a changing environment. It also relates to the fact that even comparatively stable societies consist at any given time of individuals who, because of their differing ages, make for normative heterogeneity.

Since societies only rarely approach stability, and change is a constant feature of social life (our hypothetical construct of a closed system, in which all the elements remain fixed, contradicts known reality), socialization theory must incorporate the fact of social change. Nor can such change be explained purely as a response to exigencies imposed from "outside" the social system. For the potential for a changing role structure can be seen to inhere in the very nature of the socialization process, once it is recognized that the people being socialized are invariably, though to different degrees, active agents in their own socialization.

3 *Allocation*

See Chapter 1, Section 1 · B · 3, Chapter 10 · 1, and Chapter 5

Like socialization, allocation is fundamental to both the life course of individuals and the age stratification of society, operating (though imperfectly) to redress the balance between people and roles in the coexisting age strata [*see Chapter 10 · 4*]. Just as the aging individual continually experiences socialization as preparation for leaving current roles and entering new ones, and as training in the roles he occupies, so also he experiences a continual sequence of role assignment, exit, and reassignment, confronting choices and opportunities as well as mandates and refusals. Let us now turn to the nature of the allocative processes with which the individual deals in assuming or leaving his successive roles.

Age structuring of allocation Intermeshed with the operation of allocation to facilitate the flow of individuals through the society, and the complex phasing between allocation and socialization as a companion process, is the operation of allocation as both reflector of, and contributor to, the age stratification in the society. We shall pay considerable attention in this section, not only to the dynamic, but also to these structural, facets. As noted in Chapter 10, incumbents of few social roles are distributed proportionately across all age strata. This differential age distribution is in part a result of the complex processes that bring into conjunction the supply of actors of a given age and the supply of roles open to that age stratum. And like socialization, this differential age distribution in social roles means that people of different ages often stand in varying relations of allocation to one another, most broadly as either candidates for roles or allocators to roles. Diverse arrangements and procedures are involved in this structuring of allocation, which can vary by institutional spheres. Often allocative agents can be identified as people who utilize age or age-linked criteria of assignment in determining whether a person (or category of persons) may appropriately occupy a status, perform in a role, or engage in some activity.

A caution   Of critical importance in avoiding confusion over the process, however, is a semantic warning, supplied by Parsons and Shils (1951, p. 198), to which heed must be given throughout our discussion:

> The term *allocation* should not be interpreted anthropomorphically. Allocation is a resultant that is only in part a product of deliberate decision; the total allocation in a social system especially may be the product of many processes that culminate in a distribution which no individual or collective actor in the system has sought.

Not only are the allocative processes in large measure nondeliberate, many of them are also obscure or unrecognized by the people involved—whether allocators or those being allocated. To be sure, certain aspects of allocation are open and explicit, and a degree of knowledge about how a person comes to occupy or leave particular social roles is commonly learned in the process of socialization and, when internalized, tends to be viewed as natural and appropriate. Often, however, people are not aware[35] that the ostensible arrangements available to them are not the only ones possible, nor immutable, but rather represent an implied selection from alternatives and are subject to alteration. Only when members of the society (or some significant segment of members) perceive the results of allocation as unfair or unworkable, are they likely to inquire more fully into the available alternatives, with a resulting potential for conscious change.

The intricacy of the process   Chapter 5 has already described in detail, as one familiar example of allocation, how the distinctive age patterns of work force participation stem from a variety of complex allocative procedures, many of which operate through institutions or agencies both inside the economic sphere and outside it in government, education, or the family. Thus the millions of individual decisions involving entry or exit from jobs occur, as

---

[35] For example, the fact that Irish peasants accept the sharp differences among age strata as "too natural a part of daily life to require explanation" is remarked by Eisenstadt (1956, p. 87).

Sorokin put it in discussing social mobility, not as a matter of chance, but under the firm control of "an enormously complex and inevitable machinery which controls the whole process of social testing, selecting and distribution of individuals within the social body" ([1927], 1959, p. 207).

A challenge   Despite its patent linkage to the much-studied topic of socialization, allocation is given remarkably little formal sociological attention outside of such basic pronouncements of its importance as those by Sorokin or by Parsons and Shils.[36] However, neither the age stratification of the society nor the succession of cohorts through the society, nor the life course of the individual can be understood without reference to the manner in which people come to occupy or to abandon various social memberships. Urgently needed is a theory of allocation parallel in breadth to that which has, over the decades, been accumulating regarding the process of socialization. Although formulation of a general theory of allocation is clearly outside the scope and intention of the present volume, consideration of the integral relation of age to allocation has led us to a tentative delineation of certain aspects of the process. In this section, then, we shall first offer some largely descriptive illustrations of allocation in selected institutional spheres as a means of communicating the kinds of allocative phenomena to which our developing theory of age has directed attention. These descriptive examples will be followed by a synopsis of the kinds of analytical concepts and principles that seem required for the development of a more adequate theory of allocation. We shall also note the nature and consequences of the structured age relations that enter allocation and shall begin to suggest certain implications of allocation for social change.

EXAMPLES OF THE PROCESS

A few additional examples of the ways in which the flow of personnel is regulated within the age strata seem necessary to illustrate the diversity that a general conceptualization of allocation must ultimately organize. These brief examples are intended to suggest the nature of Sorokin's "machinery"—the procedures and agencies of allocation, and the functions performed by the allocative processes (unintended and obscure as many of these processes are) in articulating people and roles within the age structure. Our hope is to stimulate the reader to imagine how an age-related approach can open broad vistas of little-explored sociological inquiry.

Allocation and school attendance   The public school system in the United

---

[36] The importance of age as a factor in allocative decisions has been stressed by Parsons and Shils (1951, pp. 198, 206–207, 221); and by Parsons (1951, pp. 114–117). However, such a general work as the *International Encyclopedia of the Social Sciences* (1968) indexes the term "allocation" only in relationship to inequalities and to apportioning economic resources.

States typifies one set of age-related processes whereby students are admitted, moved along from year to year, and finally relinquished. Almost all states have some form of compulsory school attendance, usually between the ages of 7 and 16 years. Here the law assigns a double responsibility, both to those being allocated and to the community as one agent in the process, by requiring not only that the individual attend, but also that the community provide educational facilities. Because the state mandates and enforces compulsory attendance, the allocative powers of the affected role players are severely limited. Self-selection of the role of student is not permitted.

Before *entry* into public school, prior socialization affecting the ability and motivation to perform in school is not evaluated. Moreover, though in many other instances the family retains allocative decision-making power for minor children, here it must submit to the law. The family's choice in determining the type of role assignment for its offspring is limited. It may choose between public and private school and, through choice of residence, from among public schools. Parents must inform themselves of the law and of the procedures for registering their offspring, must supply the necessary credentials such as proof of age and vaccination to school authorities, and must ensure subsequent attendance. Thus the family is merely given executive responsibility in carrying out the law, and may be prosecuted for violations.

Though schools (except private schools) have little or no choice in whether or not to admit members from the eligible cohort, they may have considerable latitude in the subsequent internal allocation. Even here, however, states often set restrictions regarding grade placement, special education for the handicapped, differentiation by race and sex, or—intervening in the socialization process—regarding curriculum and discipline of students. Internal allocation, once the child has entered school, tends to rest on a combination of strict age-grading and, within each grade, competitive academic subdivision. Various transition points—as from kindergarten to first grade, primary to middle school, middle school to high school—are often marked by quite elaborate ceremonies symbolizing past achievement and the progression of expectations.

Exit from the role of public school pupil may be made by individual decision once the upper age boundary for compulsory attendance has passed. The majority of students, however, are not "early school leavers" but remain long enough—twelve years or so—to receive a diploma certifying completion of the course of study, a completion marked once again by the ceremonial rituals characteristic of many allocative processes [*see Chapter 10*].

Allocation and college attendance   At later stages of the life course, school attendance presents a somewhat different set of allocative procedures, reflecting the different definitions of role requirements and institutional goals. Higher education, for example, is currently designed to accept and process an academic and cultural elite. Since allocation to higher education is not compulsory, self-selection—and hence prior socialization—plays a part, and the individual must take the initiative in applying for admission. However, opportunity for self-selection may be affected by prior claims on the individual's capacities. With males, for example, the state has the power to declare that military duty take precedence over student status.

Age enters into allocation to college in a way that differs from public school attendance. Some institutions set age boundaries, but more often the age boundaries are indirectly determined by educational prerequisites to admission and (for role exit) by limitations on the amount of time the individual may occupy the role of college student. Many colleges permit application by individuals of any age, but custom tends to restrict application and acceptance largely to late adolescence and young adulthood.

The size of incoming cohorts—and the number of applications coming out of these cohorts—can create pressures for expansion or contraction of college facilities. Even so, the number of role openings is not usually determined solely by the size of the cohort pressing for entry. Ordinarily, the college itself determines both the number to be admitted and the criteria governing competitive admission within the age stratum, such as the results of standardized tests, family ties, recommendations, geographical location, reputation of the high school, personality factors as presented in interview or application form, financial ability, extracurricular activities and interests, sex, or race.

Some of the difficulties of allocation in an achievement-oriented system are dramatized by the process of college admission. The multiplicity of criteria employed in college admission—and the difficulty, in demonstrating the relevance of some of these to high school training or to requirements for performance in college—illustrates the endemic problems of articulating allocative criteria at various life stages with prior socialization, on the one hand, and with requirements for role performance, on the other. One consequence is that it may become more important for candidates to satisfy allocators than socializers, potentially reducing control of the socialization process by those responsible for it. A second consequence is that socializers may direct their efforts toward allocation rather than toward role performance. Thus, unless there is a very high correlation between allocative criteria and performance expectations, or unless the role is such that performance is not markedly contingent on prior socialization and selection procedures, there is danger that optimal or adequate role performances will not take place. And this result, in turn, can press for changes in role definitions, socialization, or allocation.

Military conscription   Allocation to military service, as in the late 1960's in the United States, illustrates the complex and sometimes ambiguous procedures attached to a role that may be entered either voluntarily or involuntarily. Though the official norms stress "service to country," low social valuation of the role is manifest where the supply of vacancies is large enough to require conscription as a supplement to enlistment.[37] Draftees are assumed to be reluctant entrants (or else they would have enlisted, all apart

---

[37] The extent to which this is true has wide sociocultural variations, depending in part upon the degree to which the civilian economy offers employment opportunities.

from pressures of the draft) and, as a result, screening procedures tend to operate in somewhat contradictory ways.

All males of a given age must register for selective service with their local draft boards, but only a proportion of those reaching that age will perform military duties before eligibility expires at a specified older age. At various stages prior to induction, the original pool of candidates is successively narrowed. According to one arrangement candidates are selected as needed in an order determined by annual lottery of 19-year-olds based on date of birth. Local draft boards, composed of older citizens, are empowered to execute the succeeding phase of screening.

Officially, the local board merely applies a codified set of rules and regulations, but in fact it exercises considerable latitude in implementing allocative criteria. Goals of efficiency and effectiveness require that only those candidates qualified on intellectual, psychological, and physical grounds be inducted, and that candidates not be inducted if they have capacities for which civilian society has the "greater need." Such allocative procedures are designed to prevent induction of the unfit (and also, when possible, to give precedence to certain civilian priorities such as education, defense industries, health, or the ministry). In practice, however, potential draftees may manipulate the qualifying criteria (as by exhibiting their deficiencies in order to escape the role), and the official agents in turn tighten their screening procedures in order to supply the required personnel. In addition, selection for induction is sometimes used punitively (as when political dissenters are reclassified as draft-eligible), or used to rid civilian society of deviants (as when pardon for criminal offenses is made contingent upon agreement to enter military service). Thus candidates for induction must take a large measure of responsibility for informing themselves of their rights regarding exemptions, deferments, and disqualifications. In general, then, there may be an intrinsic tendency for agents of allocation to fill negatively evaluated roles by lowering qualifications beyond the official minimum.

The rituals accompanying conscription seem to reflect the nature of the allocative processes involved. Final selection for military service is validated by induction ceremonies in which administration of an oath is central. Then follows a period of intensive socialization, in which a variety of symbols, such as special hair cuts and uniforms, serve to remind neophytes that they have lost their old identities and assumed a new one.[38] For those completing their terms of conscription and not electing military careers,[39] role exit, unlike the ceremonial nature of induction, is attended by little ceremony. Indeed, the separation process for these individuals is almost entirely instrumental, consisting merely of record-keeping, final payments of monies owed, and dissemination of information about veteran status. The absence of expressive ceremony is not surprising since the individual by his voluntary exit is reject-

---

[38] Goffman (1961) supplies an unsurpassed description of socialization to roles in what he terms "total institutions."

[39] Processes of both entry and exit tend to differ for those who do elect to follow a career pattern; see Janowitz (1964).

ing the military role, and the military agents controlling allocation are unlikely to maximize the rewards of such rejection.

Allocation and voluntary association membership   Voluntary associations, while they vary widely in procedures for recruiting members, all share the special characteristic that role entry is based in part on self-selection by the individual applicant. Acceptance may be automatic and immediate, or it may be contingent upon strict criteria or upon a transitional period of trial membership.

Some procedures of allocation common among voluntary associations can be illustrated in the case of the Girl Scouts. For this organization, the age-related criterion of grade in school (such as the fourth grade) defines the lower limit of entry. Scouting is then organized at several age-graded levels (junior, cadet, senior), each of which may be entered without prior experience by a girl of the appropriate age. Exit may be accomplished through informal notification or simply by consistent failure to attend meetings. No normative upper age limit exists, since adult professional and volunteer roles are available for those who retain their membership. Thus the example points to an important source of structural elaboration of voluntary associations through the creation of new roles as an aging membership seeks to ensure the future of the organization by recruiting younger personnel while seeking, at the same time, to avoid relinquishment of their own memberships.

The number of vacancies is set by limits on troop size, availability of adults willing to play leadership roles, and the fusion of eligibility for membership in particular troops to community and neighborhood residence. As is frequently true with allocation of minors, parental permission is required to join, but the child herself must apply, thereby signaling motivation for membership. Application involves an area coordinator, who determines whether a vacancy exists. Particularistic considerations may enter at this point, when individual leaders are asked whether they will accept the applicant, or when the area coordinator passes judgment. Since it is difficult for individual applicants to assess the actual extent of vacancies, arguments are not uncommon over whether decisions have been "fair" in individual cases.

Acceptance is followed by a transitional period[40] of several weeks' attendance at meetings before full membership is conferred. Ostensibly, the initiation ceremony demonstrates the candidate's knowledge of scouting "laws," pledges, and rites as qualification for membership. In fact, initiation is ceremony, hence largely symbolic, and rejection rarely occurs at this point—a phenomenon that may be generally characteristic of initiation by voluntary association.

Allocation and friendship   Still another set of procedures is associated with friendship, which is, as we have noted, not only normatively voluntary, but is also one of the few roles in which each individual allocates the other to the complementary role. Whether or not third parties intervene varies with

[40] [*Compare the discussion of the varying span of the boundaries separating age strata in Chapter 10 · 1.*]

age, as Hess points out in Chapter 9. In childhood, parents exercise considerable direct control over their children's friendships, in addition to the indirect control represented by their choice of residence. In the middle years, the spouse may influence the friendship selections of his mate. And with the loss of spouse, widows must often rely largely on same-sex friendships. In general, third parties contribute to friendship allocation by performing introductions, by certifying eligibility (or suitability for friendship) of each member of the dyad to the other, and by vetoing "ineligible" selection.

Allocation to friendship is largely informal, with highly subtle forms of interaction replacing more formal techniques of disseminating information, application, certification, and acceptance. The allocative process is effected by various signals—such as greetings, conversational cues, invitations to parties, expressions of liking. Perhaps a common barrier to friendship formation is misinterpretation of such signals.

Exit from friendship, unlike entry, does not require consent of both parties or even notification. Indeed, many friendships are not explicitly terminated, since the norms encourage a gradual "drifting apart" rather than an abrupt rift. Moreover, social approval is often attached to having large numbers of friends and being able to retain them, so that the individual may seek to conceal any unilateral withdrawal.

Allocation to widowhood and parenthood   Allocation to these two roles is under a single heading because their age-relatedness derives in both instances from the operation of vital processes. On the surface, allocation might seem to be confined here to the occurrence of visible and unambiguous biological events—the death of a spouse or the birth of a child. Rituals for funerals and baptisms abound, and the people involved often perceive the social apparatus actually validating these events as mere formality or ceremony rather than as integral to the allocative process. Only on those relatively rare occasions when the biological event is invisible or ambiguous are the so-called formalities revealed as necessary mechanisms of allocation, attesting officially to the event and locating the affected individuals in their new roles. Since widowhood, for example, requires that death of the spouse be certified, widowhood must be legally defined when a body cannot be produced; and such legal definition requires certification of a valid marriage. Funeral ceremonies, death notices, or mourning attire serve as public announcements of the new status of the bereaved.

The special case of adoption, in which biological parenthood is separated from the social role, illustrates the extent to which parenthood is socially defined. For example, adoption agencies commonly set age limits for adoptive parents, in effect expressing socially acceptable ages of parenthood that may not coincide with the biological. Some agencies, faced with an oversupply of children needing foster care, have instituted the role of "foster grandparents," where the label emphasizes the age rather than the role of the nurturant individuals who actually function as parents. The considerable control by the state over the allocation of parenthood, despite biological events, is illustrated by provisions allowing birth certificates to be altered by striking the names of the biological parents and substituting those of the adoptive parents.

PROCEDURES AND AGENCIES

These examples, upon which we have dwelt because of the unfamiliarity of the topic, suggest some of the elements and principles essential to any methodical analysis of allocation. By starting with age-related aspects of the process —its inherence in the life course of individuals and its social function in continually replenishing roles with fresh cohorts—we are led toward a general formulation of allocation as a subject parallel to socialization, only brief allusions to which are appropriate for this book. We have seen that the nature of the process varies with the role in question, with, for example, the degree of compulsoriness attached to role assumption or with the age at which role assumption is typical or considered appropriate. The relations between allocative agencies and candidates for roles are governed by sets of diverse mechanisms (normative or factual procedures) for implementing criteria of role assignment. Mechanisms range from explicit and codified to informal and vague. Myriad rules, specific to each role, specify the conventions and even the social etiquette for interaction between allocator and candidate, such as: how to write a letter of application as a conscientious objector, how to dress for graduation ceremonies, or what constitutes an appropriate token of sympathy to the bereaved.

Bases of allocative procedures   Of special relevance to the place of age in allocation is the fact that, while allocation in general has a sociocultural character, certain procedures are rooted in nonsocial phenomena such as biological or vital processes, or territorial location of residence (cf. Parsons and Shils, 1951, pp. 207–208).

The purely *social* procedures of allocation, many instances of which have been noted repeatedly in our discussions, vary according to degree of formality: from highly formalized legal or bureaucratic processes; through market mechanisms involving hiring and firing, promotion and demotion; to informal customs and folkways. Within the family, for example, custom is both a positive pressure and a proscription for individuals not socially ready, or past the appropriate age, for becoming a spouse or a parent (see Pitts, 1964, pp. 67, 72). And custom, operating within the biological limits of fecundity, leads to the characteristic age gap between parent and offspring, and between an individual and his siblings.

Biological and vital processes contribute to allocation in a distinctive fashion. In previous discussions of these processes, we have emphasized either their effect on age criteria for role incumbency [*Chapter 10 · 1*]; or—as fundamental to our model [*Chapter 1 · 1*]—the ways in which, by entering into cohort flow (P1) and aging (P2), they affect the numbers and kinds of people in the several age strata (element 1) and the capacities and motivations (element 2) that qualify people at each age to be socialized for (P3) and allocated to (P4) appropriate roles. Now we want to emphasize a special consequence of these same processes: their operation in allocating an individual to certain roles (or removing him from others) by impinging upon his relationships to role partners.[41] For example, a person (an older person in the modal case) may be allocated out of the marital role and into widowhood via the death of a spouse. Or a younger person's allocation to the role of motherhood depends upon biological processes of producing a child.[42] Or a child becomes an orphan through the death of one or both of his parents. (This example is closely age-related. The proportions who are orphaned are markedly higher among older than among younger children today, but in general orphanhood has been rapidly decreasing because of the reductions in mortality at the ages when adults are parents of young children; Bogue, 1959, pp. 284–287; Spiegelman, 1968, pp. 250–252.) Other types of nonsocial allocative procedures include *territorial* dispersion, which, by separating a person from role opportunities or from role partners, can operate, for example, to terminate certain types of relationships—as between an individual and his job or between neighbors.

Even when allocation is mediated through nonsocial processes, however, *supplementary* procedures are widely used to symbolize or validate the social aspect of conferral (or withdrawal) of a role (as the foregoing illustrations of allocation to widowhood and parenthood attest). For example, registration and baptism legitimate the assumption of parenthood, at the same time marking the entrance of the child into state and church; or marriage ceremonies certify the mutual commitments of the nuptial pair to the roles of spouse.[43]

Phasing of allocative procedures   Many of the procedures for allocating individuals to (or out of) particular age-related roles, may also be classified according to the specific part each one plays in the process. Any functional classification would doubtless include (among others) mechanisms[44] for accomplishing such tasks as the following:

> *Dissemination of information* regarding available roles, available candidates, and appropriate means of application. Information may be circulated

[41] There are also purely social mechanisms, of course, which can result in allocation through impact on the individual's relation to his role partners, such as desertion or divorce in marriage or separation of a man from his job through dissolution of his firm.

[42] For a discussion of biological factors in family relationships, see Pitts (1964, pp. 57–59).

[43] In certain instances, social allocations may actually replace the biological process, as in the "ritual death" practiced in some cultures where, for example, parents may perform ritual death rites for a son who marries outside of his faith, thereafter refusing to admit his existence.

[44] [*For age-related examples applied to the role of worker, see Chapter 5 · 1.*]

through the mass media or by word of mouth, for example, or may be learned in advance during anticipatory socialization for the role.

Screening (by allocators) and presentation (by candidates) of *evidence of qualifications.* Candidates may merely express intent or desire to assume the role; but more often such devices are involved as standardized tests, proof of age, information given in interviews, letters of recommendation, portfolios of past achievement, and the like. Noncompetitive selection allows the applicant merely to show possession of the criteria (perhaps at some minimum level), whereas competitive selection requires him to demonstrate competence relative to others.

Validation and certification signifying the results of evaluating the evidence. These procedures range from elaborate rites of passage (bar mitzvahs, military inductions, weddings), to the issuance of official certificates or licenses, to simple verbal announcements or record entries. Some procedures extend over prolonged periods of time, as in trial membership or where the marriage ceremony progresses through several stages.

Types of agencies In assigning candidates to social roles, a variety of persons or groups—though not always identifiable—may act as agents in carrying out the allocative procedures. For some procedures, involving vital processes or formal legal-bureaucratic codes, allocation is likely to be perceived by the persons involved as an impersonal and automatic process. Even in such instances, however (as apparent from the earlier examples of widowhood, parenthood, or military conscription), personal agents or organizations often exercise a considerable degree of control over acceptance or rejection, or may stand behind the scene ready to exert such control when necessary. Agents, who operate differently for particular roles and in the several age strata, may be classified, like procedures, according to function into such categories as the following:

Controllers, who have actual power of acceptance or refusal at point of entry or exit.

Advisors, who make recommendations to controllers.

Screeners, who act to permit only selected members of eligible age cohorts to reach the point of entry or exit for evaluation by controllers.

Expediters, who are restricted to carrying out specific prescriptions, ruling on the evidence presented, facilitating the operation of impersonal procedures.

Certifiers, who carry out the validating procedures.

Self-selection, single agents, or constellations of agents Allocation is typically an interactive process involving at least the dyad composed of candidate and one role-partner. Despite common opportunities for *self-selection* through initiative in application or through the option to refuse proffered roles, role assumption is not merely a decision made by the candidate himself. It requires, also, acceptance and validation by some *other*—either by one or more role-partners with whom the candidate will interact in his new capacity, or by some representatives to whom allocative decisions have been delegated. These others must participate in the allocative process, if for no other reason than that any role performance requires the consent and complementary actions of reciprocal role players.

Exit from a role, by contrast, does not always require consent of an allocator. In certain roles—friendship, voluntary associations, employment—the individual may be permitted to resign by his own decision. In other roles, however, he may be compelled to resign at the discretion of those holding allocative power.

While for some roles, the allocative process is confined largely within the institutional sphere in which the role is organized, often some *third party* enters in. Indeed, it may appear upon careful scrutiny that constellations of several agencies participate in many roles. Marriage, for example, often involves not only proposal and acceptance between the couple but also state and church (and for minors, parents) as certifiers. Third parties, particularly those responsible for socialization, may also function as screeners in the allocative process. The family in the United States, except for control over procreation, has little power of direct allocation. However, few analysts dare ignore the importance of the family as screener in directing its members at appropriate ages to a variety of social roles. Thus, even though church officials may ultimately rule on church membership, initial religious affiliation is largely determined by the family. In like manner, political affiliations, occupational roles, mate selection,[45] and educational attainment tend to reflect screening processes that have taken place in the family.

The *multiple agencies* operating to facilitate entry into the work force by the young and exit from it by the old [*as set forth in Chapter 5·1 and 5·2*] exemplifies the differing *degrees of directness* with which different agents relate to the particular sphere of allocation. Within the employment sphere is the familiar entourage of agents: employers, personnel managers, employment services, labor unions, and so on. But many agents operate also from outside the economic realm. The government may manipulate the economy so as to control employment conditions, or may enforce conditions of age or citizenship, for example. Here again the family may intervene, by giving

---

[45] Alexis de Toqueville is reported to have said that, in New York State in the 1830's, men of 14 years of age and women of 12 could marry, and parents' consent was not necessary at any age.

advice and information, making referrals to influential friends and associates, or providing material or emotional support. Other systems, such as the educational or the military, may operate to *exclude* young people from the labor force, diverting them instead to competing types of activity.

Latitude in application of allocative criteria In applying allocative procedures, agents are permitted, normatively or de facto, varying degrees of latitude in using age or other characteristics as criteria. Agents are more likely able to select from among a variety of standards where these are not clearly specified, where multiple criteria are normatively approved without further specification of weighting procedures, where enforcement machinery is lacking, or where violations are difficult to detect. Thus in American society an individual may accept a spouse on the basis of a considerable number of characteristics. College admission officers, who utilize a diversity of indicants in deciding qualifications, may be free to give more or less weight to test results, grades, recommendations, athletic achievements, special interests, geographical location, race, sex, and familial ties. While such selections are typically made from within a roughly defined age stratum, admissions officers may also be free to use age criteria for excluding persons considered too old or too young. Employers and employment services may also utilize multiple criteria of allocation, contributing to difficulties in determining just which standards have in fact been applied to particular cases. Thus age discrimination in hiring, even when legally prohibited, may be difficult to establish and may well continue as a fairly widespread basis for assignment to occupational positions. Such latitude of implementation illustrates one way in which allocation may contribute to alterations in the age structure: changes in the modal ages for entering or leaving a role—the labor force, for example—can ensue not only from changes in the formal age criteria of assignment, but also from the particular ways in which the allocative process is carried out.

ALLOCATION AND ROLE TRANSFER

Allocation, like socialization, operates not only in role assignment but also in the role transfers, which, as we have seen, are brought into high relief by the facts of cohort succession and aging. Individuals are not allocated to one role at a time (as in our examples) but to a multiplicity of roles; and as they age, their passage through the changing sequence of roles involves successive reallocations. Each cohort over its life course supplies a continuously changing pool of potential role players; its size and composition changes, and the performance capacities of its members change. The roles too may change, as facilities and rewards are used up or wear out, as new situations develop, or as diminishing returns set in. Adjustments to such changes involve relinquishing old roles and assuming new ones. And the allocative procedures and agencies effecting the transfer combine to close (or render undesirable) one set of roles while enhancing the opportunities and rewards in the other.[46]

Sources of individual support   In addition to the types of procedures and agencies already discussed, special aspects of allocation are often involved in role exit and role transfer because of the strains imposed by leave-taking both on the individual and on the structure of the group.[47] To aid the individual first in relinquishment and later in initiation to the new role, support is provided in various forms, including modifications of the primitive rituals described by Van Gennep ([1908], 1960). (*Compare Section 1 of this Chapter.*)

In retiring from the work role, for example, the individual is given financial support by the employer or by the state in the form of a pension or social security. The retiree is relieved of the sense of personal failure in his job if retirement is defined as mandatory or customary. He is given emotional support both before retirement and afterwards by family, friends, or voluntary associations—agencies that often act also to assign him to new roles and activities in retirement.

In the case of widowhood, strong emotional support is afforded at the stage when an individual must relinquish the role of spouse. (Note that the age of onset of widowhood has been steadily postponed over the last decades, so that widowhood is typically associated with the aged, and also especially with women since they tend to outlive men.) Various agents stand by to aid the bereaved—not only relatives and friends, but also doctors, ministers, social workers, lawyers, insurance agents, funeral directors, and so on. However, the assistance available during the mourning period is often curtailed soon after the initial shock.[48] While to a certain extent relatives and friends step in to aid recovery, the individual is typically given little help in adjusting to the state of marital singleness and performing in the new role of widow.[49] (As in role transfer at earlier life stages, such as adolescence, it is through peer support that many individuals seek reassurance, release from stress, and a renewed sense of identity.)

Problems of group solidarity   Meanwhile, complementary mechanisms may be set in motion to restore the cohesion of the group when the social structure is disrupted by the loss of a member, as often occurs in small groups or through loss of a leader in groups of any size. The funeral is the

[46] [*For a detailed example, see Chapter 5 · 2 on the transfer from work to retirement.*]

[47] For an insightful analysis of the delicate behavior required in role transfer, especially in preventing retaliatory behavior by the individual who is leaving the group, see Goffman (1962).

[48] See, for example, the study of British mourning practices by Gorer (1965).

[49] Widows often use various denial mechanisms [*as suggested by Clausen in Chapter 11*].

prototype of the symbolic declaration of solidarity between the bereaved and the kin and community to which the deceased belonged (see, e.g., Malinowski [1925], 1948, pp. 29–35; Parsons and Lidz, 1967).

Social pressures to reconstruct the group take varied forms following losses of members through less drastic means than death. In instances where individuals leaving one group are in fact looking forward eagerly to the transfer to substitute roles, role exit may be interpreted as rejection of the former role. Hence, all sorts of *denial mechanisms* have been institution-alized as part of the relinquishment process. Witness the retirement party or the graduation ceremony in which expressions of sorrow over what must be ended are as much a part of the etiquette as are expressions of joy over future tasks. Often, denial takes the form of stressing continuities: friendships will remain; we'll be asking for your help; you'll always be welcome here; old soldiers never die. One example of denial of relinquishment is the elaborate ritual of a university alumni association that involves class insurance; club membership paid for over a period of ten years after graduation; annual reun-ions, symposia, and lectures designed especially for graduates; admission preference to sons of alumni; and a weekly magazine with undergraduate column and current faculty projects centrally featured.

In other instances, where individuals *resist exit* from a role, changes in the age composition of the group may ensue. In some organizations, the "old men" refuse to step aside (unless there are mechanisms compelling exit or unless equally rewarding alternatives are available), tending to increase the proportion of older members. Age-based voluntary associations, such as "young" Democrats or "junior" reading clubs, often find their upper age limits difficult to enforce, so that the entire organization "ages" with its mem-bers. Ordinarily, however, when role transfers are important for maintaining a system in operation, they may be made compulsory by the group; for ex-ample, the Social Security Act of 1935 provided aid to the aged as a device to remove them from the labor force in order to make room for the able-bodied family men who were thrown out of work during the Great Depres-sion (see, e.g., Cottrell, 1960, pp. 632 ff.).

ALLOCATOR-CANDIDATE RELATIONSHIPS

Much of our discussion to this point has either implicitly or expressly described aspects of the structuring of relations between allocators and candidates. We have stressed the diversity of these relations, as they may refer to varying institutional spheres and to situations of either role entry or exit. But certain general implications for allocator-candidate relations, and for changes in these relations, derive from a special feature of allocation: its reference to a *decision-making* process in which allocators often invite, compel, or refuse role assumption and role exit. Allocation to valued roles means distributing to certain candidates (but not to others) the typically scarce facilities and rewards associated with the role (Parsons and Shils, 1951, p. 25). Thus, to a far larger extent than with socialization, allocation defines a set of power relations in the society and relates directly to inequalities among the age strata described in Chapter 10. As such, allocation is far less likely than socialization to be a symmetrical process. Friendship (and, in some cultures, marriage) is one of the few fairly symmetrical social relationships in which each role player allocates the other to the complementary role. Far more frequently, the candidate lacks allocative power over the agent of allocation. Thus the applicant for a particular job or for admission to a university may be offered or denied opportunity to assume the role of employee or of student. To be sure, the applicant may choose whether or not he wishes to make specific applications. But he does not ordinarily have the reciprocal power to control personnel decisions or to appoint members of the admissions committee.

Age-relations in allocation   The dual facts that cohorts succeed one another through the role structure, and that experience in passing judgments may be associated with age, seem likely to produce a structure in which allocators tend to be older than candidates. Whether or not such an age structure exists is an empirical question.[50] And an important one. For, as we have seen, allocating an individual to a role means also assigning to him the rewards (or punishments) associated with that role. Hence age relations in allocation affect who has the power to decide who gets what and from whom. Allocators, having once attained power positions, doubtless attempt to retain (that is, to age in) these positions.

Systems in which such an age hierarchy seems least predictable are those, like friendships or ad hoc community movements, that do not survive the death or defection of their members. Or, to ponder this statement in its converse form, when allocation is concentrated in the hands of entering cohorts, the continuity of the system may be threatened by the potential for complete reconstitution of the membership with each new cohort.

Also of interest is the fact that particular allocator-candidate pairs, if they differ in age, reflect cohort differences that can set their stamp on the character of the relationship. Individuals as they age not only shift from candidates to allocators, and accumulate multiple experiences in both capacities; but their date of birth also affects the particular allocative processes to which they were exposed at each life stage. Thus, for example, the respective age strata to which allocators and candidates belong may have met different criteria for school attendance, labor force entry or exit, marriage or military conscription. They may have learned differentially effective practices of fer-

[50] Eisenstadt (1956) adduces much supporting evidence to this effect.

tility control or faced differing opportunities to marry rather than remain single. And indeed, younger cohorts today have been more widely exposed than their predecessors to various kinds of standardized testing (Brim et al., 1965, pp. 88, 133) and to the revolutionary changes in dissemination of information that can facilitate communication between allocators and candidates. All such cohort differences may be brought into play when the partners to the allocative process confront one another.

Relations among the candidates   Moreover, allocative processes, by directing the exclusion as well as the participation of role players, produce inequalities and affect the relations among the candidates themselves [*as described in Chapter 10 · 1*]. Exclusion may be experienced by the affected candidates as relative deprivation, depending upon the availability of substitute roles defined subjectively as having similar or superior reward value and socially as having similar utility for the group. When such roles are not available, the situation is ripe not only for individual strain, deviance, and alienation, but also for overt competition or conflict among the candidates.

Whether or not competition arises within an age stratum (as between privileged and underprivileged youth) or between age strata (as between young and old) depends partly on the use of age as the criterion for allocation/ exclusion. In either case, the processes of allocation themselves can be seen as often pitting candidates against one another, forcing them to compete for the scarce rewards controlled by allocators—in marked contrast to socialization which, as we have seen, tends to encourage solidary relations among persons being socialized together.

ALLOCATION AND SOCIAL CHANGE

Over the course of history, there have been enormous changes in the agencies and procedures of allocation, changes which only the social historians can adequately describe and document. Many of these changes in allocative processes parallel—or are simply restatements of—broad changes in social structure and shifts in centers of power among institutional spheres. In Western nations, school and firm have taken over many of the allocative functions formerly carried out by the family; the state has increasingly become a third party in licensing or certifying occupations, professions, marriages, births, and deaths; while the allocative control of the church as a third party has lessened. Along with changes in agencies of allocation have occurred changes in procedures that are equally striking. The development of mass media of communication has revolutionized the dissemination of information regarding available roles. The proliferation of formal, standardized, and bureaucratic techniques for presentation, review, and certification of qualifications has changed the entire character of the allocator-candidate relationship for many roles. A possible decline in the occurrence and elaborateness of ceremonial validation may, indeed, be the only aspect of allocative procedures that has not tended historically toward greater complexity. As a result of such increases in complexity, failure to acquire knowledge regarding allocative procedures may have become as great a barrier to role incumbency as failure to acquire the requisite skills for role performance.

Like most social phenomena, allocative processes are not merely reflective of and adjustive to social change, but may in special ways contribute to change. For the complexity of the processes carries an ever-present potential for malintegration. Some of these integrative problems represent those malfunctions and fallibilities to which any human system is subject: for example, allocative criteria may not be applied uniformly; communications may be blocked; screening procedures may represent invalid tests of qualifications. But many other problems inhere, not in allocation itself, but in the imperfect meshing between the rhythm of the individual's life course and the tempo of society. The quantitative and qualitative adjustment of the totality of people and roles in the society often fails to accord with the individual's "personal timetable" to which Clausen refers in Chapter 11.

Thus, to the individual, exit from a role represents either role transfer or role loss, a distinction of enormous significance to his life course, but one that may not enter into the societal exigencies dictating allocative decisions at a particular point in time. Or self-allocation, representing a decision by the candidate in the framework of his own life course, may run head on into contradictory decisions dictated by the larger social situation. A further source of strain is that the personal timetables of consecutive cohorts may be incompatible. Role assumption by members of one cohort may require role exit by an older cohort. The familiar difficulties of the old refusing to yield to the young are often compounded when the older role occupants are also the allocators.

Allusion to sources of strain in the allocative process takes on special significance as we repeat our contention that relations of allocation are relations of power; inequalities among the age strata represent to a large degree unequal access of the age strata to positions as allocators. And, as pointed out in Chapter 10, the legitimacy of inequalities is often vulnerable to challenge.

Thus, despite the sociological preoccupation with strains and conflicts inherent in socialization, we emphasize the process of allocation as involving even greater potential for cleavage. The demands of students in the 1960's for open admissions, abolition of grades, or participation in decisions regarding faculty hiring and tenure—to mention but a few examples—represent demands for positions as allocators and for rights to determine allocative procedures. To the extent that such demands are met, the result is an alteration of power relations within the university. The allocative process itself identifies an arena for potential change in societal relations of power.

4 Age and social change

See Chapter 1, Sections 1 · B · 6, 1 · C, and 2 · B; Chapter 10, Sections 3 and 4

The inescapable bond between age and time, a bond that gives age stratification its special character, leads inevitably to the final topic marked for exploration in these essays: the relation of age and social change. For, central to the foregoing discussion of the four processes of cohort flow, aging, socialization, and allocation is the axiomatic statement that bears frequent repetition: social change invariably involves differences among the life-course patterns of consecutive cohorts [*Principle 2 from Chapter 2 · 3 · C*]. In Section 1 of this chapter we showed how a great many cohort differences can be viewed as *reflections* of change, serving as a channel for societal transformation. In each of the foregoing sections we have hinted at, but not yet developed, the further strategic point: that certain cohort differences—through the interplay among the age-related processes—may serve to *generate* changes in society and in the larger environment. Section 1 described cohort differences in size as one source of social change. Sections 2 and 3 noted the potential for innovation inherent in the processes that articulate the successive cohorts with the changing social structures. Now, in this final section, we turn to a more explicit recognition of the complex interaction among the age-related processes, and shall close by indicating how this interaction can contribute to a wide variety of societal changes in norms, roles, and institutions. We shall raise more questions than we can answer—a fitting conclusion, we submit, to a book aimed to open a new field of sociology.

INTERPLAY AMONG AGE-RELATED PROCESSES

In first outlining our conceptual model [*see Chapter 1 · 1 · C and 1 · 2*] we described the four age-related processes as an intricate system of feedback loops, in which each process interacts with the others, with changes in the role structure, and with the changing environment. The three sets of processes represented in Figure 1 · 2—those affecting the age strata of people, those (extrinsic to our model) affecting age-stratified roles, and the articulating processes—are all interdependent with one another. They are also interdependent with the many additional environing factors, including the physical and biological factors, that impinge upon the social system from outside. These complex interdependencies can result in manifold disequilibria in the age structure. Although such disequilibria may in some instances persist in *similar* fashion through the lives of many cohorts, they are more likely to *distinguish* cohorts from one another either through temporary disturbances or through long-term change.

Examples of the interplay among age-related processes were listed in paradigmatic form in Chapter 1 and a wide variety of illustrations are scattered throughout the book. For example, changes in cohort size may affect socialization and allocation; changes in practices of socialization modulate capacities for performance over the life course; changes in allocation (as in work force allocation) may influence the motivation to control reproduction[51] (depending upon the demand for breadwinners in the family) or influence the will to live on in retirement; or changes in aging are incurred by modifications in the other three processes or in the role structure itself.

INTERACTION BETWEEN ALLOCATION AND SOCIALIZATION

In order to specify more fully the complex interactions among these processes, we shall discuss in detail here just one interaction—that between allocation and socialization—as the one that has been least explored in the sociological literature. More importantly, this particular interplay, upon which the articulation between people and roles depends, clearly holds high potential for strain and hence for change. (As Sorokin [(1927), 1959, p. 207] once said, in writing of social class, "a strong and prosperous development of the whole society" can depend upon the effective operation of the "selecting institutions.") Indeed, though allocation and socialization are the very processes often described as conservative of the social system, malfunctions and imbalances in them can occur in so many ways that the notion of balance between people and roles [*see Chapter 10 · 4*] is perhaps more aptly posed as an abstract reference for discussion than as a condition achievable in reality. Not only are there widespread incompatibilities between the shifting states of the society and the distributions of component actors, but as precursors of change, the integrative problems of coordinating and phasing the intricate elements involved in allocation and socialization become critical in a highly differentiated society.

Differentiation between allocation and socialization It is, of course, the fact of differentiation between these processes that creates the need to examine their coordination and phasing. The distinction between the two may remain latent or merely analytic until a society reaches a stage of differentiation where control is placed in the hands of separate agents. In the undifferentiated situation, those who socialize individuals in anticipation for a role are also those who determine when and whether role assumption may take place. Similarly, apprentices in tenancy socialization may expect to be trained by the

---

[51] Among the many modern reformulations of the Malthusian injunction to forestall the tendency of population to outrun the food supply, see, for example, Sauvy (1968, p. 355); Beshers (1967).

same people who select them. In differentiated modern societies, by contrast, socialization is often the responsibility of agents who have little control over allocation. For example, while the family has primary responsibility for ensuring the "readiness" of the child to attend school, it is not the family but the educational system (or the state through compulsory attendance laws) that allocates the child to a particular role in school. And, though the educational system is given primary responsibility for socialization to vocational and professional roles, the employing institutions (and often the state again as a third party) control the process of selecting and certifying job applicants. The school can only advise and recommend, not decide, whether an individual may be allocated to a particular occupational role.

Let us now draw together the previous scattered allusions to problematic aspects of coordinating or phasing these two differentiated processes. We have pointed out, for example, that allocation may take place without reference to prior socialization, with the result that those assigned to roles may not possess the qualifications needed for role playing. We have also noted that socialization is not invariably followed by role assignment, with the consequence that people motivated and trained to perform in particular roles may be prevented from assuming them. To repeat an example, we have indicated that one source of strain in allocation to the college student role lies in the fact that those responsible for preparation for college may introduce performance expectations that conflict with, or are unrelated to, the criteria employed by those responsible for allocation.

What we have not yet stressed is that many such problems have their locus, neither in allocation nor in socialization alone, but in the interaction between the two, and in their respective interdependency with other aspects of the social system. We shall now show how the tendency in modern societies for allocation and socialization to become distinct may be manifested in a variety of strains that introduce new questions of the efficacy of articulating processes producing role occupancy and role performance.

Problems of coordination and phasing   Among the strains and pressures for change arising from the failure of many diverse elements to mesh with one another are problems of coordination and phasing of these articulation processes. At any given time, failures of *coordination* can often intrude because of the separation of responsibility among allocators, socializers, and persons controlling actual performance in the role. Serious disjunctures can occur among the expectations governing the process of socialization, the criteria and procedures governing the process of allocation, and the capacities actually required for role performance. In addition to problems of coordinating these processes at given times, there are related problems of integrating them over time. Again we have previously noted various instances of the *phasing*, or temporal sequences of these processes as either one can precede the other. For example, we have discussed the relationship between anticipatory socialization and the later socialization that occurs during actual performance in the role. We have discussed the "situational specification" following role assumption of many of the broad orientations previously learned in childhood socialization. And we have called attention to the complex phasings resulting from the fact that both socialization and allocation extend over considerable portions of time and are characterized by differing, and often overlapping, stages of screening, processing, and controlling of candidates. More systematic consideration of phasing is needed, however, to lay bare the dynamic interplay between these processes which, even as they may be directed toward a single cohort, occur within a framework of a changing population, a changing role structure, and a changing history.

Socialization for unrealistic criteria Several types of disjunctures arise from failures of coordination among socializers, allocators, and persons controlling performance in roles. As one type, consider the plight of socializers in situations where the allocative procedures may not screen and test those capacities that are in fact needed for role performance. Certain types of college entrance examinations, for instance, may be poor predictors of college performance. How do socializers (to the extent that they are aware of such a situation) determine the kinds of expectations or the standards of evaluation they should use? They may attempt to train their charges to meet both allocative and performance requirements despite their divergence, but this explicit acknowledgment of inconsistency calls into question the legitimacy of the system. They may aim at generating capacities needed solely for actual role playing rather than those needed for allocation, with the risk that the allocative process may prevent role assignment and thereby label both socializer and socializee as failures. Or, they may aim their socialization practices at successful allocation rather than role performance. Numerous examples come to mind of teachers whose primary aim is to prepare students for college entrance examinations, or of parents who teach their daughters how to snare a mate but not how to be adequate wives. The obvious risk of this approach is that socializers may not prepare competent role players.

In such ways, inconsistencies between criteria of allocation and expectations for performance can lead to tensions and frustrations for those participating either as agents or objects in the processing of role players—tensions that may generate deviance, rebellion, or demands for change.

Dilemmas of control The separation of allocation and socialization also creates a second type of problem for the agents involved, dilemmas of control over the nature of the processes for which they are responsible.

Allocators, if they have the power of role assignment but are without the socializing power to shape directly the qualifications of candidates, must often "make do" with whatever capacities are at their disposal. They may be obliged to alter allocative procedures to accommodate the qualifications presented by candidates if they are to fill positions at all. Such alterations may eventually in turn change role expectations or the nature of the role itself. Thus personnel managers, though complaining that secretaries have inadequate stenographic skills, must often hire such people nevertheless. A latent consequence may be transformation of the role through development and introduction of substitutes for stenography such as dictating machines or electronic typewriters that respond to the recorded voice. In another instance, teachers complain that the family has failed to prepare its children for the disciplines of formal learning. Since school attendance is compulsory, the result may be restructuring of the role of pupil. Or college professors complain that students have not learned to compose an intelligible sentence. Yet, since there can be no professors without students, the consequence may be remedial courses in composition as a regular part of the college curriculum.

Socializing agents, because of the differentiation of socialization and allocation, may confront problems of control even more serious than those faced by allocators. Allocation to a role (or advancement in it) is, in one sense, *the* contingent reward to be manipulated in the process of socialization. Separation from socialization of this power to manipulate allocative sanctions raises questions of how socializers can control rewards sufficiently to secure conformity to their expectations. Deprived of power to prevent role assumption as a consequence of deviance, what substitute sanctions can they employ? One possibility is that socializers rely increasingly on the establishment of strong cathectic ties with their charges. In fact, we might speculate that the much-discussed development of permissive childrearing practices within the family is linked to this loss by the family of its former allocative controls. Should this speculation be correct, it has an important corollary: that is, that an authoritarian family structure is incompatible with contemporary forms of division of functions. Thus a little-heeded factor—the differentiation of allocation and socialization—must be taken into account in understanding the nature of relations in the modern family.

Allocation without socialization   The range of temporal disturbances encountered in the sequential phasing of the two processes can be suggested by considering two extreme situations: allocation without any reference to prior socialization, on the one hand, and socialization without subsequent role assignment, on the other. In the former case, there is often considerable uncertainty over just what kinds of capacities have been allocated. One consequent risk for the society may be widespread inconsistency or incompetence in role performance, and, for the individual, dissatisfaction in an uncongenial role. Phasing in this truncated form is especially likely to occur when assignment is compulsory rather than voluntary, as in school attendance, military service, or retirement; or where role assumption is rooted in biological events, as in widowhood or in unplanned or undesired parenthood. The strains entailed by such circumstances of allocation without reference to prior socialization may be minimized in various situations: for example, where wide variation in role playing is permitted (that is, where the role is not highly structured); where the relevant capacities are possessed by most or all of the population, making discrimination among candidates unnecessary; or where allocation is followed immediately by a period of deliberate and intensive socialization.

Socialization without subsequent role assignment Although much sociological concern has focused on "failures of socialization," in which individuals are allocated to roles for which they are totally or partially unprepared, perhaps equally common are "failures of allocation," in which individuals motivated or trained to perform in a role lack opportunities for role assumption. As we list some of the ways in which this latter situation may occur, it will become evident that socialization without allocation may operate both as effect and as cause of social change:

> *Structured imbalances [as in Chapter 10 • 4]*, reflecting basic social values or processes, may encourage socialization of too many people for the supply of roles known to be available. Competitive allocative procedures, for example, are designed for selection of only the few who are "best" among all those broadly qualified.

> Through *changes in the role structure*, the supply of vacancies available to a cohort may have dwindled or disappeared during the period of socialization. For example, a frequent complaint regarding vocational training is that it prepares people for obsolescent occupations.

> Demands of some *competing role* may intervene to prevent role assumption after socialization. For example, accidental pregnancy may prevent college attendance; the military draft may interfere with career advancement; family obligations may prevent or delay planned retirement.

> As already discussed under problems of coordination, allocative processes may represent *invalid screening mechanisms* thus preventing role assumption by those who have been appropriately socialized.

> Through *historical change*, or *duration* of the cohort in some prior role, the relative *reward value* of the role or the values of the cohort being assigned may change, so that technically trained individuals are no longer motivated to assume the new role. For example, students are sometimes reluctant to leave the university for the job market. Indeed, a variety of "employment avoidance" roles (involving volunteer or low-paid activities) may be emerging for the young, a trend that may reflect rejection of the traditional rewards associated with conventional careers.

Socialization, allocation, and response to societal crises The intricate problems of phasing socialization and allocation have broad consequences for the social system as a whole, in part because of the fact that many abilities required for role performances are not simply fixed at birth. These abilities are *created and altered* through the very processes designed to evaluate and select them. As Harry C. Bredemeier has pointed out:

> It is very probably more often the case than is generally realized that most people are technically able to play most roles, given the proper training and motivation. Getting roles played efficiently is not, then, as the American performance bias has it, entirely a matter of the accurate assessment of ability. Just as important probably is the process of socializing people into the skills and attitudes appropriate to the roles assigned to them (unpublished lecture).

Moreover, there are certain areas in which deficiencies in prior socialization can be rapidly corrected; for example, Zuckerman and Merton in Chapter 8 note that knowledge, even knowledge of a high order, can be transmitted rapidly if it is highly codified; or improvements in pedagogy, such as teaching machines or language laboratory techniques, can speed up training for particular competencies.

To the extent, then, that potential abilities in the population may exist far beyond their actual generation through socialization or their utilization through allocation, the operation of allocation to exclude some age strata from role performances creates, in effect, a "reserve pool" of personnel in the society.[52]

The existence of a reserve permits a measure of insurance against fluctuations in the level of mobilization needed to meet societal exigencies. The classic example is mobilization for warfare, in which large numbers of young men are diverted from the civilian labor force into military service, at the same time that the labor force may require expansion to meet the needs of defense industries. During such periods, previously excluded age strata may be admitted to the labor force, as young people may defer or accelerate education, while old people defer, or come out of, retirement.[53] Or, as another example, variation in the size of age strata customarily assigned to particular roles may trigger mobilization of previously excluded strata. Thus fluctuations in fertility resulting in abnormally small birth cohorts may tend to create for adjacent strata new roles from which they had previously been excluded, as the small cohorts pass through various stages of their life course.

[52] See, for example, the discussion of older retired people as a labor reserve (Goldstein, 1966).
[53] Similar tendencies may occur with segments of the population excluded on other bases. Thus women and blacks, in addition to young and old, found expanded employment opportunities in World War II.

Such interactions as those between allocation and socialization—and the similar interactions among the other processes involved—leave their imprint upon society [*see Chapter 1 · 2 · B*]. The foregoing example of societal response to *temporary* crises or fluctuations is indicative of how ad hoc responses can sometimes lead to *long-run* changes[54] or other basic consequences. Once the abnormal period has passed, the dislocation—in this instance, the allocative problem—is not always dealt with by a return of the society to the status quo ante. It may be resolved here, instead, by a continued incorporation into the role structure of the newly admitted age categories. During the intervening period, previously excluded strata will have acquired new motivations and abilities as a result of allocation to new roles. Are the affected age strata willing, then, to relinquish the roles in question? Or do they insist on remaining? Answers depend, of course, on a complex series of questions regarding prior socialization experiences, socialization subsequent to allocation, rewards of the role relative to others that may be open, the existing degree of integration in the individual's total role complex, and—as a consequence of all such factors—the extent of satisfaction experienced in the new role performances.

Needless to say, the aftereffects of mobilization for crises, or of many other responses to societal events through age-related processes, cannot always be foreseen. But it is likely that such responses are a not uncommon source of long-term change. These changes can occur in the role structure of the society. They can occur because individual role incumbents, as they age, change their own roles. And macrocosmic changes introduced by fluctuations in cohort timing and societal timing can affect the society, proliferating from one social sphere to another and from one age stratum to another.

Changes in role criteria The example of poor coordination or phasing between allocation and socialization illustrates how interplay between the age-related processes can alter role structure—in this instance through alteration of the age boundaries of roles [*as described in Chapter 10 · 1*]. The numbers and kinds of openings for particular roles may be changed, either temporarily or permanently, by adjusting the age criteria for role entry or exit. Pressure from young cohorts, socialized as they have been to norms of independence and equality, may have the consequence of lowering the voting age. Or the degree of rigidity of an age criterion may be adjusted (as, according to some reports, the provisions in many pension plans for compulsory retirement at age 65 may be becoming more flexible[55]).

---

[54] [*See the discussion of short-run versus long-run "period effects" in Chapter 2 · 4 · A.*]
[55] Unpublished report by William Pearl and Associates (1970), based on studies of 300 pension plans.

In a total social system such as England or the Catholic Church, the entire population of all strata form the pool of actors, and the entire role structure constitutes the supply of available roles. In such instances, the age boundaries differentiating the population of actors and the roles open to them may shift in response to historical changes in the population or in the role structure of the system as a whole, with broad consequences for relations among the age strata.

Impact of individuals   Interactions among age-related processes can have further consequences, far transcending the structures or boundaries of particular roles. Clearly, the society through which the "cohorts flow" is itself a complex system, comprising roles in many different types of collectivities and institutional spheres [*see Chapter 10 · 1*]. And, just as the individuals moving through these roles are subject to alteration, so too the concrete role units must continually undergo changes as the incumbent individual ages or is replaced.

Many of the strains exerted by society on the individual are, at the same time, placed upon the stability of role definitions. There are social counterparts to the tensions [*emphasized in Chapter 11*] that are aroused in aging individuals because they must pass through key transition points in the society —from infancy to childhood, for example, from one school grade to the next, from adolescence to adulthood, or from worklife to retirement. The strain between individual and role at such transitions is mutual—with the degree of impact upon the role, as upon the individual, depending upon particular social conditions (upon the continuity or discontinuity in the role sequences; upon how fully institutionalized a particular role may be; upon the internal consistency of role expectations, facilities, and sanctions; or upon how effectively people are trained or socialized at every stage of life). Not only the individual students, for example, but also the universities feel much of the stress entailed in our society because we crowd formal education almost exclusively into the younger stages of life rather than spreading it over the life course as individuals require it. A family must regroup itself after the marriage of its youngest child; or a community after the death of an elder statesman. Similarly, group adjustments are necessitated by the advent of new members like the birth of a child into a family, the entry of a new class of children into a school grade, or the move of a widowed old person into the household of her married daughter.

The extent to which individuals exert immediate influence upon the concrete roles they play depends upon how distinctively the roles and their incumbents are separated. For example, a particular nuclear family is inseparable from its members: it begins with the marriage of the concrete marital partners and ends with their death and with the dispersion of their children. But the first grade in a particular elementary school, even though its roles are somewhat modified during the course of the year as the first-graders progress, continues year after year, despite the replacement of its members. Or the role of head of state carries its own perpetuity. (The king is dead, long live the king!)[56]

While actual role incumbents influence their roles through the process of aging, however, this influence has an enduring structural effect only under special circumstances. The collective influence of many particular families would be required to affect the institution of *the* family. Yet a single man in a powerful position of leadership can often create permanent changes in his office (as, for example, it is said that President Washington's avoidance of consultation with Congress set precedents for the relationships between legislators and future chief executives).

Effects on other social spheres The long-range changes exerted on the social structure by individuals, and by differences among cohorts of individuals, take many forms. In one form, which suggests the potential for far-reaching societal consequences, life-course differences among cohorts in *one* social sphere can stimulate further changes in *other* spheres. For example, recent extensive shifts in the relations between men and women at various ages—the decreasing differentiation between the sexes or the greater freedom of sexual behavior—might be traced in part to the reversal in cohort patterns of female participation in the labor force. Many cohorts of women born during the late nineteenth century showed steadily declining rates of participation over the life course [*illustrated in Figures 2 · 6 and 2 · 7 in Chapter 2*]. But, following World War II, new life-course patterns began to emerge, as participation rates rose rapidly among married women during their middle years and—more recently—among young women in the childrearing ages also. The conjunction of these opposing trends meant that, for a considerable period, it was only the young mothers with little children whose labor force participation was notably low—a situation that may have prompted a classic observation (foreshadowing the full force of the Women's Liberation Movement) that "for the first time in the history of any known society, motherhood has become a full-time occupation for adult women" (Rossi, 1964, p. 615). Women at other times and places shared motherhood with demanding labor in the fields, the factory, or the household.

Can we expect that full-time motherhood is now institutionalized and will persist into the future? If so, we may be victims of our own cohort-centrism—one more proof that our understandings of society are influenced by our particular historical background. For this full-time preoccupation of American mothers with their young children seems already to be eroding as

---

[56] It has been reported that King Hussein of Jordan once said, "It is a weakness when a nation feels it must put all its hopes on the lifespan or the ability of one leader." (*New York Times*, September 23, 1970).

recent cohorts have developed a rather different pattern. Not only have the proportions of married women in the labor force during their middle years more than doubled, but there have been pronounced increases also among young married women, even those with little children (*Manpower Report of the President,* March 1970, pp. 46–48). Thus historians of the future may look back on full-time motherhood as a peculiar phenomenon, existing in American society only for a few decades of the twentieth century.

But whatever the future may actually hold, the example begins to suggest how the confluence of cohorts with differing life-course patterns in one respect (economic activity of women) can change society in other respects as well. Think, for example, of the mature women who no longer "retire" from major social roles many years before their husbands retire from work. Or think of the young husbands and wives who now share the work of homemaking and infant care. Such changing work habits may well result in entirely new modes of relationship in the family and—if only because of the widespread unavailability of working wives for daytime activities at home or in the community—in other social institutions as well.

Effects on other age strata   In addition to the spread of cohort changes from one social sphere to another, innovations emanating from a *single cohort* can sometimes ramify rather quickly through the *other age strata,* without awaiting the lag over a long series of cohorts. We have seen in Section 1 how the excessive size of the baby boom cohort born after World War II has required drastic adjustments throughout a society unprepared to absorb it— from the initial requirements for obstetrical facilities through the successive pressures on housing, schools, the job market, the marriage market, and so on into the future. Among the many other widely discussed instances are the increased financial burden borne (through transfer payments) by the remainder of society because so many retired old people have inadequate incomes;[57] or the potential changes in the ethos surrounding work and leisure as large numbers of old and young no longer participate in the work force.[58]

It has even been suggested that a completely revolutionary "consciousness," if it informs the values and behaviors of many young people, may affect the entire society (Reich, 1970). Indeed, there are several strands of sociological theory that, if brought together, might predict that many of the expressive emphases of today's younger cohorts, rather than being confined to the adolescent stage, may spread through the society. Bales (1950), for example, in his studies of groups set up for the specific purpose of solving

[57] See, for example, McConnell (1960, p. 505). See also the discussion in Volume II, Chapter 9, by Bernstein.
[58] See Chapter 5; also Donahue et al. (1960, pp. 359–361), and the related discussion in Riley, Foner, Hess, and Toby (1969).

instrumental tasks, demonstrated decades ago that the amount of instrumental activity is counterbalanced by expressive activity (which, he believes, serves to maintain group solidarity and to relieve strains and manage tensions engendered by the effort of problem solving). Parsons and Bales (1955), in another well-known strand of sociological thought, have emphasized the expressive character of the modern family—the reduction of family functions through societal differentiation to the point where the family has now become the central unit for filling the personality needs of individuals. Today the family provides not only material support and early socialization, but also social support, permissiveness, and management of tensions faced by each family member in the complex roles he must play in society at large.

What happens, then, to the offspring brought up in such a family when he is obliged to leave the sheltering, expressive environment for a bureaucratized adult society—a society that has, in practice, largely failed to absorb the Balesian wisdom? Eisenstadt [*like Parsons and Platt in Chapter 7*] has answered this question up to a point: In this circumstance, says Eisenstadt (1956), young people form youth groups. But what then? Will they ultimately become content to adjust to the achieving society (cf. McClelland, 1961), to absorb the "future shock" of rapid technological change (Toffler, 1970), to modify the Protestant Ethic to fit the notion of a "good society" in which each individual has opportunity to develop and exercise his capacities (White, 1961)? Or will they impose new sets of values which, though now regarded askance as "deviant" or "dysfunctional," may come to be institutionalized as the values of the future and to be implemented in a new structuring of social life? In such manner may the riders on the moving stairs, though pausing only briefly on the scene at each floor, permanently alter the view available to subsequent riders.

CONCLUSION

In this chapter we have stressed the potential for change intrinsic to the age-related processes. Over the life course of each new cohort, aging as a social phenomenon is made possible by the articulating processes that sort out individuals, train, and assign them to roles. And, as cohorts endlessly succeed one another, they respond to historical transformations in role sequences at the same time that they contribute to these transformations.

In sum, we are offering a special challenge to the oncoming cohorts of sociologists—not merely to pursue current lines of inquiry, but also to reorganize and re-examine existing knowledge in a new way. We suggest specifically a view of society stratified by age, which on the one hand, defines bases for inequality and conflict and, on the other hand, defines social positions that influence men in their performance of socially demanded operations. We suggest a review of social change and stability which, while merging Marxian emphases on conflict with Durkheimian emphases on integration,[59] focuses on still another dynamism: on aging and the succession of cohorts that follow their own rhythm, that entail special processes and structures for allocation and socialization of personnel, and that in themselves constitute strains and pressures toward innovation. Such an approach, we submit, can illuminate central aspects of the statics and dynamics of society, and at the same time suggest potential solutions to wide-ranging practical problems of great immediate concern. As sociologists, let us escape our own cohort-centrism!

Works cited in Chapter 12

Bales, Robert F., 1950. *Interaction Process Analysis: A Method for the Study of Small Groups*, Cambridge, Mass.: Addison-Wesley.

Beresford, John C., and Alice M. Rivlin, 1964. "The Multigeneration Family." Prepared for a meeting on the multigeneration family at The University of Michigan Conference of Aging, Ann Arbor, Michigan. Mimeographed.

Beshers, James M., 1967. *Population Processes in Social Systems*, New York: Free Press.

Bogue, Donald J., 1959. *The Population of the United States*, Glencoe, Ill.: Free Press.

Bredemeier, Harry C., and Richard M. Stephenson, 1962. *The Analysis of Social Systems*, New York: Holt, Rinehart & Winston.

Brim, Orville G., Jr., 1966. "Socialization Through the Life Cycle," in Brim, Orville G., Jr., and Stanton Wheeler, *Socialization After Childhood: Two Essays*, New York: Wiley, pp. 1–49.

————, 1968. "Adult Socialization," in Clausen, John A., editor, *Socialization and Society*, Boston: Little, Brown, pp. 183–226.

————, John Neulinger, and David C. Glass, 1965. "Experiences and Attitudes of American Adults Concerning Standardized Intelligence Tests," New York: Russell Sage Foundation.

————, and Stanton Wheeler, 1966. *Socialization After Childhood: Two Essays*, New York: Wiley.

Clausen, John A., editor, 1968. *Socialization and Society*, Boston: Little, Brown.

Cottrell, Fred, 1960. "Governmental Functions and the Politics of Age," in Tibbitts, Clark, editor, *Handbook of Social Gerontology*, Chicago: University of Chicago Press, pp. 624–665.

Crittenden, John, 1962. "Aging and Party Affiliation," *Public Opinion Quarterly*, 26, pp. 648–657.

Davis, Kingsley, 1949. *Human Society*, New York: Macmillan.

---

[59] Since we do not regard as incompatible the approaches to social explanation often designated as "conflict theories" versus "functionalist theories," we have strewn innumerable hints throughout the book as to how the two can be meshed to broaden understanding.

Donahue, Wilma, Harold L. Orbach, and Otto Pollak, 1960. "Retirement: The Emerging Social Pattern," in Tibbitts, Clark, editor, *Handbook of Social Gerontology*, Chicago: University of Chicago Press, pp. 330–406.

Duncan, Beverly, 1968. "Trends in Output and Distribution of Schooling," in Sheldon, Eleanor B., and Wilbert E. Moore, *Indicators of Social Change: Concepts and Measurements*, New York: Russell Sage Foundation, pp. 601–672.

Eisenstadt, S. N., 1956. *From Generation to Generation; Age Groups and Social Structure*, Glencoe, Ill.: Free Press.

Eldridge, Hope T., 1968. "Population: Population Policies," in Sills, David L., editor, *International Encyclopedia of the Social Sciences*, 17 vols., New York: Macmillan and Free Press, 12, pp. 381–388.

Folger, John K., and Charles B. Nam, 1967. *Education of the American Population* (A 1960 Census Monograph). Washington: Government Printing Office.

Glick, Paul C., 1955. "The Life Cycle of the Family," *Marriage and Family Living*, 17, pp. 4–9.

———, and Robert Parke, Jr., 1965. "New Approaches in Studying the Life Cycle of the Family," *Demography*, 2, pp. 187–202.

Goffman, Erving, 1961. *Asylums: Essays on the Social Situation of Mental Patients and Other Inmates*, Garden City, N.Y.: Doubleday, Anchor Books.

———, 1962. "On Cooling the Mark Out: Some Aspects of Adaptation to Failure," in Rose, Arnold, editor, *Human Behavior and Social Processes*, Boston: Houghton Mifflin.

Goldstein, Sidney, 1966. "Socio-Economic and Migration Differentials Between the Aged in the Labor Force and in the Labor Reserve." Presented at Annual Meeting of the Gerontological Society, New York.

Gorer, G., 1965. *Death, Grief, and Mourning in Britain*, Garden City, N.Y.: Doubleday.

Goslin, David A., 1969. "Introduction," in Goslin, David A., editor, *Handbook of Socialization Theory and Research*, Chicago: Rand McNally, pp. 1–21.

Hughes, Everett C., 1970. "Teaching as Fieldwork," *American Sociologist*, 5, pp. 13–18.

Inkeles, Alex, 1969. "Social Structure and Socialization," in Goslin, David A., editor, *Handbook of Socialization Theory and Research*, Chicago: Rand McNally, pp. 615–632.

International Encyclopedia of the Social Sciences, 1968, 17 vols. Sills, David L., editor, New York: Macmillan and The Free Press.

Janowitz, Morris, 1964. *The Professional Soldier*, New York: Free Press of Glencoe.

Kiser, Clyde V., 1962. "The Aging of Human Populations: Mechanisms of Change," in Tibbitts, Clark, and Wilma Donahue, editors, *Social and Psychological Aspects of Aging*, New York: Columbia University Press, pp. 18–35.

Levy, Marion J., Jr., 1952. *The Structure of Society*, Princeton, N.J.: Princeton University Press.

Lifton, Robert Jay, 1970. *History and Human Survival*, New York: Random House.

Lipset, Seymour M., 1968. "Stratification, Social: Social Class," in Sills, David L., editor, *International Encyclopedia of the Social Sciences*, 17 vols., New York: Macmillan and Free Press, 15, pp. 296–316.

————, and Everett Carll Ladd, Jr., 1970. ". . . And What Professors Think," *Psychology Today* (November), pp. 49–51, 106.

McClelland, David C., 1961. *The Achieving Society*, Princeton, N.J.: Van Nostrand.

McConnell, John W., 1960. "Aging and the Economy," in Tibbitts, Clark, editor, *Handbook of Social Gerontology*, Chicago: University of Chicago Press, pp. 489–520.

MacIver, Robert M., 1963. *The Challenge of the Passing Years*, New York: Pocket Books.

Malinowski, Bronislaw (1925), 1948. *Magic, Science and Religion*, Glencoe, Ill.: Free Press.

Mannheim, Karl (1928), 1952. "The Problem of Generations," in *Essays on the Sociology of Knowledge*, edited and translated by Paul Kecskemeti, London: Routledge and Kegan Paul, pp. 276–322.

Manpower Report of the President, March 1970. Washington: Government Printing Office.

Mead, Margaret, 1970. *Culture and Commitment: A Study of the Generation Gap*, New York: Doubleday, Natural History Press.

Merton, Robert K., 1957. *Social Theory and Social Structure*, rev. ed., Glencoe, Ill.: Free Press.

Moore, Wilbert E., 1963. *Social Change*, Englewood Cliffs, N.J.: Prentice-Hall.

————, 1967. *Order and Change*, New York: Wiley, pp. 234–250.

National Center for Health Statistics, 1966. "Age and Menopause, United States 1960–62," *Vital and Health Statistics*, Public Health Service Publication No. 1000—Series 11, No. 19, Washington: Government Printing Office.

Nisbet, Robert A., 1969. *Social Change and History*, New York: Oxford University Press.

Parsons, Talcott, 1951. *The Social System*, Glencoe, Ill.: Free Press.

————, 1961. "Introduction to Part 2: Differentiation and Variation in Social Structures," in Parsons, Talcott, et al., editors, *Theories of Society*, 2 vols., New York: Free Press, pp. 239–264.

————, and Robert F. Bales, 1955. *Family, Socialization and Interaction Process*, Glencoe, Ill.: Free Press.

————, and Victor Lidz, 1967. "Death in American Society," in Schneidman, E. S., editor, *Essays in Self-Destruction*, New York: Science House.

————, and Edward A. Shils, 1951. "Values, Motives and Systems of Action," in Parsons, Talcott, and Edward A. Shils, editors, *Toward a General Theory of Action*, Cambridge, Mass.: Harvard University Press, pp. 45–275.

Pitts, Jesse R., 1961. "Introduction to Part 3: Personality and the Social System," in Parsons, Talcott, et al., *Theories of Society*, New York: Free Press, pp. 685–716.

————, 1964. "The Structural-Functional Approach," in Christensen, Harold T., editor, *Handbook of Marriage and the Family*, Chicago: Rand McNally, pp. 51–124.

Reich, Charles A., 1970. *The Greening of America*, New York: Random House.

Rheingold, Harriet L., 1969. "The Social and Socializing Infant," in Goslin, David A., editor, *Handbook of Socialization Theory and Research*, Chicago: Rand McNally, pp. 779–790.

Riesman, David, 1950. *The Lonely Crowd: A Study of The Changing American Character*, New Haven: Yale University Press.

Riley, John W., Jr., 1968. "Death and Bereavement," in Sills, David L., editor, *International Encyclopedia of the Social Sciences*, 17 vols., New York: Macmillan and Free Press, 4, pp. 19–26.

Riley, Matilda White, 1963. *Sociological Research, Volume I. A Case Approach.* New York: Harcourt, Brace & World.

————, 1971. "Social Gerontology and the Age Stratification of Society," *The Gerontologist*, 11, No. 1, Part 1, pp. 79–87.

————, Anne Foner, Beth Hess, and Marcia L. Toby, 1969. "Socialization for the Middle and Later Years," in Goslin, David A., editor, *Handbook of Socialization Theory and Research*, Chicago: Rand McNally, pp. 951–982.

————, and Edward E. Nelson, 1971. "Research on Stability and Change in Social Systems," in Barber, Bernard, and Alex Inkeles, editors, *Stability and Social Change: A Volume in Honor of Talcott Parsons*, Boston: Little, Brown, pp. 407–449.

Rosow, Irving, 1967. *Social Integration of the Aged*, New York: Free Press.

Rossi, Alice S., 1964. "Equality between the Sexes: An Immodest Proposal," *Daedalus* (Spring), pp. 607–652.

Ryder, Norman B., 1965. "The Cohort as a Concept in the Study of Social Change," *American Sociological Review*, 30, pp. 843–861.

Sauvy, Alfred, 1968. "Population: Population Theories," in Sills, David L., editor, *International Encyclopedia of the Social Sciences*, 17 vols., New York: Macmillan and Free Press, 12, pp. 349–358.

Shanas, Ethel, 1969. "Living Arrangements and Housing of Old People," in Busse, Ewald W., and Eric Pfeiffer, editors, *Behavior and Adaptation in Late Life*, Boston: Little, Brown, pp. 129–150.

Smelser, Neil J., 1968. "Toward a General Theory of Social Change," in Smelser, Neil J., *Essays in Sociological Explanation*, Englewood Cliffs, N.J.: Prentice-Hall, pp. 192–280.

Sorokin, Pitirim A., 1941. *Social and Cultural Dynamics, Volume IV, Basic Problems, Principles, and Methods*, New York: American Book Company.

————, (1927), 1959. *Social and Cultural Mobility*, Glencoe, Ill.: Free Press.

Spengler, Joseph J., 1969. "The Aged and Public Policy," in Busse, Ewald W., and Eric Pfeiffer, editors, *Behavior and Adaptation in Late Life*, Boston: Little, Brown, pp. 367–384.

Spiegelman, Mortimer, 1968. *Introduction to Demography*, rev. ed., Cambridge, Mass.: Harvard University Press.

Stockwell, Edward G., 1968. "Some Notes on the Changing Age Composition of the Population of the United States," in Nam, Charles B., editor, *Population and Society*, Boston: Houghton Mifflin, pp. 373–378.

Strehler, Bernard L., 1962. *Time, Cells, and Aging*, New York: Academic Press.

Taeuber, Karl E., 1965. "Cohort Population Redistribution and the Urban Hierarchy," *Milbank Memorial Fund Quarterly*, 43, pp. 450–462.

Tanner, James M., 1955. *Growth at Adolescence*, Oxford: Blackwell Scientific Publications.

Toffler, Alvin, 1970. *Future Shock*, New York: Random House.

Trow, Martin, 1966. "The Second Transformation of American Secondary Education," in Bendix, Reinhard, and Seymour Martin Lipset, editors, *Class, Status, and Power*, 2nd ed., New York: Free Press, pp. 437–449.

Van Gennep, Arnold (1908), 1960. *The Rites of Passage*, translated by Monika B. Vizedom and Gabrielle L. Caffee, Chicago: University of Chicago Press, Phoenix Books.

Viner, Jacob, 1968. "Smith, Adam," in Sills, David L., editor, *International Encyclopedia of the Social Sciences*, 17 vols., New York: Macmillan and Free Press, 14, pp. 322–329.

Westoff, Charles F., Robert G. Potter, and Philip C. Sagi, 1964. "Some Selected Findings of the Princeton Fertility Study: 1963," *Demography*, Vol. 1, No. 1, pp. 130–135.

Wheeler, Stanton, 1966. "The Structure of Formally Organized Socialization Settings," in Brim, Orville G., Jr., and Stanton Wheeler, *Socialization After Childhood: Two Essays*, New York: Wiley, pp. 51–116.

White, Winston, 1961. *Beyond Conformity*, New York: Free Press.

Appendix

Some problems of research on age

Bernice C. Starr contributed to an early version of this Appendix.

Understanding the place of age in society requires research that is far-flung across time and space. In studies of fruit flies or rats, an investigator can comprehend the processes of aging and cohort succession over a small fraction of his own lifetime, and under controlled environmental conditions. In studies of human beings, however, the subjects and the researcher age at the same chronological pace; and environmental conditions—far from being readily controllable—are inseparable from historical and cultural diversity.

To be sure, a wide variety of sources, though still largely unexploited, is available for social research on age that would reach beyond a single contemporary society. Among such data are ethnographic reports on hundreds of different cultures containing pertinent materials, as evidenced by Simmons' (1945, 1960) analyses of the role of the aged in preindustrial societies. Other completed studies amenable to reanalysis reach at least as far back as LePlay's (1855) monographs on the family life of European workers or Booth's (1889–1891) house-to-house surveys of the life and labor of the people of London. The value of historical documents is illustrated in Chapter 5 · 1 through Smelser's (1959, 1968) analysis of age-related allocative mechanisms using data from factory legislation, union regulations, records of economic organizations, reports on agitation to limit child labor, and so on (see also Riley and Nelson, 1971, pp. 437–438). Letters, diaries, and other personal documents can be useful (note the studies by Thomas and Znaniecki, 1918, of relations between Polish émigrés and their families); as can tribal artifacts or works of literature, music, and art (note the analysis from portraits of the stages of childhood by Ariès, 1962). In several European countries, parish records of births, marriages, and deaths extend back for several centuries, or population registration has been maintained for over a century, permitting longitudinal studies of the linked biographies of successive generations (cf., e.g., Revelle, 1968; Knodel, 1970; and also the use in life-course analyses of uniform penal registers as cited in Volume I, Chapter 16 · B · 1). And, in more recent decades, many national and international organizations have developed massive statistical archives that contain age-specific information on numerous aspects of population, labor force participation, income, and the like (see, e.g., sources cited in Volume I, Part 1).

Ultimately, perhaps, a methodology of age stratification will specify systematic procedures for secondary analysis of these diverse data (cf. Riley, 1969). At present, however, much of the research on age as a social phenomenon is based on recently gathered (or still to be gathered) materials, hence constrained within narrow temporal and cultural limits. Moreover, much of the research (as we learned to our regret from the thousands of studies scrutinized in preparation of Volume I) is invalidated because of faulty procedures that lead to potentially misleading results.

In this Appendix we shall merely illustrate the nature of such faulty procedures (or the means of avoiding them). Because of the widespread use of sample surveys, many of our examples refer to population sampling and to data obtained by questioning. Of the three sections of the Appendix, the first two will deal with problems (related respectively to sampling and data collection) of *describing* age-specific phenomena as they actually exist at particular times, whereas Section 3 will mention problems of *analyzing* data in order to explain these phenomena.

1 *Problems of sampling*

The literature on age is replete with studies that aim to describe the age strata of particular societies or the life stages of particular cohorts, yet fail to meet criteria of representational sampling. Mere convenience often dictates which children to observe, for example, or which old people to interview. Or samples of old and young may be chosen by different criteria, as when tests are administered to aged patients in a hospital and to their youthful doctors without regard to divergences of each sample from its age stratum in crucial respects like intellectual functioning. Such imprecise procedures, though often fruitful of hypotheses, can interfere with the accuracy of the findings by misrepresenting the size and characteristics of age categories.

PHASES OF REPRESENTATIONAL SAMPLING

As in all representational sampling, age-related bias can occur at three phases: in designating the sampling frame, in selecting the sample from this frame, and in covering the entire sample once selected (cf. Riley, 1963, Unit 6). We shall cite a number of investigations aimed to assess the scope and nature of errors entailed in each of these phases by certain types of sample design.

The sampling frame　A major source of bias lies in failure to obtain a complete list of those empirical cases (the sampling frame) that correspond to the conceptual universe with respect to age or age-related characteristics.[1] Certain marginal segments of the relevant age strata are frequently omitted from the sampling frame—either unwittingly overlooked or deliberately excluded.

Securing a complete list of the population to be sampled may be quite feasible in certain instances, as in countries that maintain central registers of names and ages (see, e.g., Shanas et al., 1968, p. 457) or where biographical directories describe all the members of particular organizations under study. More often than not, however, listing involves difficulties. In a single community, Havighurst (1950), for example, using sugar rationing cards to list

---

[1] Clearly, neither probability nor judgment samples are immune from potential bias in this respect.

the old people, attempted to supplement the inadequacies of this list from numerous other sources (city officials, clergymen, neighbors, nursing homes, and so on). For the United States as a whole, even the Bureau of the Census recognizes undercounts that are proportionately large in certain age, sex, and color categories (C. Taeuber, 1968, pp. 47–48; Bogue, 1959, p. 94). While methods of measuring census inaccuracies are still comparatively crude, major sources of undercounts have been estimated. They can arise because certain living quarters are missed entirely from the listing; or because (prior to the use of mail in the 1970 Census) enumerators omitted some of the inhabitants of certain living quarters (Johnston and Wetzel, 1969). Such omissions can bias the census data as they tend to concentrate upon certain kinds of people within particular age strata: upon the "floating" population detached from family groups, the residents of overcrowded housing units, or those seeking (for whatever reason) avoidance of government. Moreover, erroneous census counts can be carried over to other analyses, such as age-specific labor force participation rates that are based on the census (Johnston and Wetzel, 1969, pp. 8–9), or surveys where census data are used as weights for correcting sample bias.

For a variety of practical research purposes, portions of the sampling frame are often deliberately omitted. Samples intended to represent all the age strata may eliminate people in institutions, rooming houses, and other group quarters. Yet certain age categories, notably young males in military barracks, college students, and the very old are more likely than others to live in quarters outside of households (see, e.g., 1960 Census of Population, Vol. I, Part 1, p. 453; also Volume I, Exhibit 6 · 19). A decision to restrict the sample to household dwelling units will result, then, in undersampling of octogenarians and of the strata (especially males under military draft) in their late teens and early 20's. In addition, when the frame excludes group quarters, the composition of these strata tends to be biased, not only by sex but in other important respects as well.

Captive populations are also frequently used as samples, despite obvious discrepancies from the complete population of interest. Many studies of adolescents, by depending on lists of students, omit important categories of high school dropouts or of those who do not go on to college. Yet college students, when contrasted with nonstudents of like age, hold quite different opinions and are clearly less likely to regard themselves as full-fledged adults (Smyth and Trainor, 1971). Research on old people often either over- or underrepresents the senile or the chronically ill, because it utilizes either membership lists of formal organizations or files of caretaking agencies. Mental disorder in particular is susceptible to these research problems, for the most complete data in this country pertain to patients in mental hospitals. However, psychiatric patients are far from representative, either in age or in socioeconomic status, of the population presumably in need of professional help.

Sample selection   Once the sampling frame is specified, the selection of cases from this frame affords a further source of potential error. Unless it is feasible to include *all* the cases, studies of age are not immune to the two major types of error possible in any sample. First, chance error is introduced whenever probability sampling is used; although appropriate statistical tests can make allowance for this type of error, its intimate relation to sample size presents problems in cohort analyses or compositional analyses where the numbers in the subcells are often too few to yield statistically significant results. Thus the researcher who would achieve representativeness through probability sampling will do well to consider the efficiency of his sample selection, not only for purposes of simple description of age distributions but also for purposes of analyses that may require considerable partitioning of the original sample.

The second type of error, which typically creeps into samples based on judgment or convenience, can bias the sample systematically in respect to size or composition of the age strata. Sampling bias, unlike chance error, is insidious and may be difficult to measure. Age-related sampling bias may be especially likely to occur when units of time and place, as well as population, are sampled. For example, the age composition of symphony audiences may vary by day or week; or users of public transportation by time of day. Even when probability sampling is used, bias may unwittingly be entailed if, as often occurs in research on human subjects, latitude is allowed in adherence to the probability model. In some situations, street addresses or small areas, but not specific individuals, may be chosen by probability procedures. And if investigators are free to question whoever answers the door or to select quotas of "types" of individuals within assigned areas, the size or composition of age strata may be misrepresented. In one study, interviewer selection of respondents apparently caused a severe distortion in sex composition within age strata.[2] Directly contrary to known changes in the sex ratio by age for the population at large, this sample displayed a consistent tendency for the ratio of males to females to rise with age (beyond age 30).

Sample coverage   In the third sampling phase involving data collection, still further misrepresentation of the age strata is possible unless information is obtained for all the cases selected. In a sample of ethnographic reports, for example, the relevant facts on age may have been overlooked by some of the investigators; or in sampling artifacts relating to life-course stages from primitive cliff dwellings, difficulty of access, if associated with the era of habitation, may cause age-biased omissions. In population sampling, errors

[2] National sample, drawn by the National Opinion Research Center, 1963, analysis unpublished.

of omission are mainly attributable to unavailability (subjects may have moved away or may be temporarily absent from home, office, school, or other location where they are sought); or to refusal (subjects may be negligent in returning mail questionnaires, unwilling to be observed or to talk with interviewers, or too ill or mentally incompetent to respond).

These two types of omission, unavailability and refusal, affect the age patterns of nonresponse in somewhat different ways. But just how far they bias the existing stores of data from cross-sectional surveys is not clear. There has been speculation that old people constitute the most neglected stratum, since many of them are incapacitated or, as lone widows, fearful of opening the door to investigators. For example, Wilensky (1962, p. 921) dramatizes the underrepresentation of the elderly, calling for a "sociology of isolation." However, the age-related patterns of nonresponse vary considerably from one survey to another. They vary in a critical—though often unreported— aspect of research procedure: namely, with the time and effort expended to locate and obtain information from the designated sample of subjects. Persons who respond at first approach differ in kind from those who are less available or who refuse.

The differences resulting from repeated callbacks in surveys based on personal interviews are examined in depth, for example, by Sharp and Feldt (1959).[3] These investigators utilize the University of Michigan's Detroit Area Study where no substitutions were permitted, no limits were set on the number or timing of the calls, and interviewers were supported by an intensive promotion campaign. On the first call, persons 65 and over proved considerably more likely than adults of younger ages to be found at home and to grant interviews (cf. Hilgard and Payne, 1944; Stephan and McCarthy, 1958, pp. 243–244). This pronounced difference in accessibility by age (as by sex or family income) depends in large part on whether the individual is working (the difference tends to disappear in the analysis when employment status is controlled). However, those old people who are *not* interviewed on the first call are far less responsive to subsequent attempts than are younger age categories. Indeed, the rate of refusal tends to increase progressively by age (as demonstrated also by Lowe and McCormick, 1955, p. 309; Stephan and McCarthy, 1958, p. 262), with incapacity and widowhood contributing importantly to nonresponse in the oldest stratum.

At the conclusion of this exhaustive research (in which 87 per cent of the total sample were finally interviewed), only 78 per cent of those aged 60 and over were reached, in contrast to 91 per cent of those aged 21 to 34 (see Table A · 1). But consider the results had the investigators stopped after the first call. For example, young women with little children would be overrep-

---

[3] Other investigations probing into the biasing effects of unavailability and refusal include Lowe and McCormick (1955); Mercer and Butler (1967).

TABLE A · 1 *Reasons for nonresponse in a cross-sectional survey*

Percentage distribution

		Nonrespondents			
Age	Re- spondents	Refusals	Not-at- home	Others	Total in sample
21–34	91	4	4	1	100
35–59	87	8	4	1	100
60 or older	78	12	3	7	100

Source: Sharp and Feldt, 1959, p. 659 (adapted).

resented in the data, as well as members of low-income families. Old people would also be overrepresented, not underrepresented, in the data. Moreover, the old people actually reached would indeed exclude Wilensky's "isolates"; but, at the other extreme, they would also exclude those active individuals not found at home because they were working or otherwise engaged.

This vulnerability of findings to variations in rigor of sample coverage is not restricted to surveys based on interviewing; for remarkably similar age patterns of nonresponse have been found in a very different type of survey (Hochstim and Athanasopoulos, 1970, pp. 74–76) carried on in a California county by mail questionnaire. Here the repeated follow-ups were conducted first by reminder letter, then by telegram, and finally through personal contact. Again, the older people 65 or over were overrepresented in the first wave of mail returns, whereas again the follow-ups were comparatively more effective in improving the representation of the younger strata.

Thus it seems clear that readily accessible respondents differ from stubborn cases both in age and in age-related characteristics. Samples that skirt the difficulties of follow-ups will be disproportionately composed of people with a special interest in the particular topic of investigation, people who spend long hours at home, or people who welcome the diversion of an interview. How many surveys, then, stop after the first interview or the first mailing? Or—with similar effect—how many allow the investigator to substitute other easy-to-reach cases whenever first attempts fail? Answers to such questions may be critical in interpreting the results of particular studies.

ASSESSING THE SAMPLING BIAS

Just how far our present understandings of the sociology of age are colored by inappropriate procedures in all three phases of sampling depends, then, both on the extent of sampling bias and on how closely this bias is associated with the variables at hand. (After all, an age-specific bias in the sex ratio, for example, no matter how pronounced, may be inconsequential in studying a topic where males and females react in similar fashion.)

If samples adhere to strict probability models, they can achieve fair degrees of overall representativeness even where nonresponse rates for some population segments are comparatively high (as in the studies we have been describing by Sharp and Feldt, 1959, pp. 660–661, or by Hochstim and Athanasopoulos, 1970, pp. 73–74).[4] Where errors exist, these can often be estimated by comparing respondents with nonrespondents (as in Shanas et al., 1968, p. 458); or by comparing sample data with "true" parameters from some outside source (such as ballots cast in an election, sales records, or government data on population characteristics). Estimated errors are sometimes corrected by weighting the observed data. In the Gallup polls, for instance, samples are balanced by education to fit the latest census projections (Irving Crespi, personal communication, 1971). Even after correction, there may still be hidden errors that mediate the apparent association between age and other variables of relevance to the analysis, or that misrepresent the ways in which such variables are related to each other.

STUDIES OVER TIME

We have been discussing age-related difficulties of achieving representativeness in single cross-sectional samples. When the research design involves repeated observations over time, sampling problems proliferate. Yet the crucial questions of individual timing and societal timing in our model of age stratification require longitudinal studies that refer to the life course, or sequences of cross sections that refer to the changing age strata of society. Thus the dilemmas inherent in both these types of design can be considered a challenge as well as a danger.

Longitudinal or panel studies The special strength of the longitudinal study, or the panel study of persons alike in age,[5] lies in the fact that the *same* persons are examined at successive stages of their life course [*as described in Chapter 11 by Clausen*]. Thus the physical, mental, and personality development of gifted children can be followed into the adult years (Terman and Oden, 1959); or the characteristics of couples can be reviewed after two decades of married life (Kelly, 1955). Important as such longitudinal studies are for research on aging as a process, however, the longitudinal design itself sets certain constraints upon the sample.

In some instances, respondents may be reluctant to participate if they are aware that their continued cooperation and availability is required. Here the sample is biased at the outset. Indeed, the researcher may even decide to

---

[4] A high degree of representativeness (within known confidence limits) has been demonstrated not only in the numerous samples of all age categories reported by the Bureau of the Census, for example, but also in such samples of old people as those reported by Shanas et al. (1968, p. 458) and by Epstein and Murray (1967, p. 194).

[5] Many panel studies are not age-specific, of course. [*See Chapter 2 · 2 · B.*]

set up his panel on the basis of convenience rather than probability in an effort to minimize subsequent losses. The Duke longitudinal study of aging, which involved bringing 250 older people into the hospital for clinical evaluation, affords an extreme example. As Maddox (1962, p. 281) puts it:

> It is difficult to get subjects living in the community into a clinic for a single examination, much less for a series of different examinations; and the problem is intensified with the increasing age of the subjects.

Still more serious than the problems of setting up the initial panel are the continuing problems of maintaining it intact. Panel loss, or "panel mortality" excluding actual loss of panel members through death, springs from a variety of sources. For example, those with the least *interest* in the investigation are especially likely to drop out (cf. Berelson et al., 1954, p. 384). *Migration* away from the research area, which tends to peak in the age stratum of young adults but persists among old people also (Volume I, Chapter 6 · C · 1), constitutes another problem, although follow-up can often be accomplished by mail (cf. Hochstim and Athanasopoulos, 1970). In the Cornell study of retirement, for instance, mail contacts were continued with a fair degree of success—among the original participants (approximately 64 years of age), 25 per cent were lost at the end of 18 months and another 10 per cent in the follow-up 2 years later (Streib, 1963, p. 31; Streib, 1966, pp. 201–203). *Health and intellectual functioning,* which tend to decline in the later years (see Volume I, Part 2) undoubtedly also interfere with continuing participation by the oldest panelists (see Maddox, 1962, p. 263). Moreover, these physiological changes with age, which can exacerbate the sampling bias, are closely associated with death. And death is a phenomenon that wreaks actual changes in the size and composition of the cohort under study, raising problems not of representational sampling but of analyzing the effects of mortality on the population from which the sample was drawn (discussed in Section 3).

Inherent in the longtitudinal design is the possibility of assessing both kinds of panel losses—those from research mortality and those from true mortality. Information from the early stages of a study permit detailed comparisons between panelists who continue their participation and those who eventually drop out for whatever reason (cf. Maddox, 1962, p. 283; Streib, 1966, p. 202). And because longitudinal studies do trace individuals through the vicissitudes of the life course, they have an advantage over other sample designs in contributing important research findings about the operation of death (in addition to migration, illness, and other major events), not as mere biasing factors but as aspects of the processes of cohort survival and aging that are central to our model.

Sequence of cross sections   While the essence of the longtitudinal study is the re-examination of the same persons, the repeated cross-sectional study uses a succession of different samples. Repeated sampling may be applied to a single cohort over its life course, or it may apply to all the age strata to allow period comparisons or life-course analysis of several cohorts [see Chapter 2 · 2 · B]. In either application, the sequence of cross sections is a design that, although it can no longer identify particular individuals over time, avoids the special difficulties of longitudinal designs in attracting and holding panelists.

Any sequence of cross-sectional studies loses comparability, however, unless the same sampling procedure is used at all the periods of observation. One type of sampling problem derives from changing definitions of the subpopulations within age strata. For example, the United States Census Bureau has redefined such terms as "urban" or "farm" to reflect the historic processes of urbanization (see Volume I, p. 121; C. Taeuber, 1968, p. 44). The result is that a sequence of age-specific samples of rural or urban residents, even though each may be representative for its period, requires various adjustments in the study of trends or cohort processes.

Lack of comparability in consecutive samples has been widely produced in survey research by changes from quota to probability sampling, and by the subsequent experience with practical means of approximating the probability model. A striking example of consequent changes in the degree of sample representativeness is adduced by Glenn and Zody (1970). Their example dramatizes the absurd results that can appear in a cohort analysis of education. The data (see Table A · 2) show an apparent marked decline in educational attainment as the cohort ages! Yet persons who at age 50 have completed more than 12 years of schooling have certainly not reduced this level by age 70. (In fact, the average education for a cohort as an aggregate tends to *rise* slightly over the years, since some individuals complete additional schooling and the oldest members with the lower education die; Glenn, 1969,

TABLE A · 2   *Years of school completed by a cohort of white males, 1945 through 1965*

Percentage distribution

Years of school completed	Year (ages in parentheses)					
	1945 (50–59)	1949 (54–63)	1953 (58–67)	1957 (62–71)	1961 (66–75)	1965 (70–79)
0–8	43.5	51.0	50.3	57.5	60.9	65.1
1–3 of high school	18.7	15.6	21.0	19.2	15.2	7.9
4 of high school	16.0	16.3	16.1	15.9	15.7	16.7
At least some college	21.9	17.1	12.6	7.4	8.2	10.2
Total	100.0	100.0	100.0	100.0	100.0	100.0
(N)	(771)	(812)	(366)	(365)	(440)	(430)

Source: Glenn and Zody, 1970, p. 234.

p. 23n). This anomalous finding can occur only because the data on successive life-course stages are drawn from completely different samples, reflecting the fact that the earlier quota samples tended to overrepresent higher-status persons (Likert, 1948). The example should serve as a caveat for researchers conducting secondary analyses of much raw data now stored in data banks. In recent years, with the greater standardization of sampling techniques, this type of error is less likely to occur.[6] Yet, as in this instance of educational composition of the age strata, changes in sampling technique can create factitious shifts that confound processes of aging or historical change.

As one means of offsetting these artifacts of research procedure, education may be controlled (or standardized) for each cross-sectional survey (Glenn and Grimes, 1968, pp. 565–566; Glenn, 1969, pp. 19–25). Such controls, which permit more adequate representation of people at the lower educational and socioeconomic levels, are similar in form to the compositional analyses [described in Chapter 2 · 4 · B] that examine education, sex, and other factors as explanatory variables mediating the relationship between age and particular dependent variables (see, e.g., the analyses by Crittenden, 1962; Miller, 1965).

In addition to procedural changes in sampling, historical events can disturb the comparability of samples used for dynamic analyses of age. In the United States, for example, postwar difficulties in 1870 prevented accurate census enumeration in the South (Taeuber and Taeuber, 1958, p. 27). Such problems are exacerbated in crises of various kinds, such as wars, internal upheavals or natural disasters which may involve large-scale and untraceable population movements within and across national boundaries.

SAMPLES DESIGNED FOR ANALYSIS

Although this section has emphasized the degrees of representativeness attained by various sampling procedures, many samples are not intended to represent the age categories but to analyze age as an explanatory factor (cf. Riley, 1963, Units 6, 11). Ideally, in experimental designs, random assignment of the presumed causal factor to experimental and control samples can be used to eliminate (within the limits of chance variability) the confounding effects of other factors. Because a person's age obviously cannot be assigned to him at random, however, quasi-experimental samples of different age strata often attempt to control certain confounding factors through matching. Thus samples of different age are drawn to resemble each other in sex or education, for example (see Schaie and Strother, 1968, pp. 262–263). Such

---

[6] The Gallup Organization, whose data are used in this example, use weighted samples to correct such errors in their published findings. Moreover, since 1965 the unweighted samples show close correspondence with census projections (Irving Crespi, personal communication, 1971).

matched samples can be highly useful for analysis as discussed in the next section of this Appendix, despite the impossibility of controlling *all* confounding factors and the fresh difficulties introduced by the built-in lack of representativeness. Unfortunately, some scholars, accustomed to taking for granted the benefits of randomization in experimental design, completely overlook the necessity for controlling interrelated variables in interpreting an observed difference as the effect of age. Thus comparison samples of young and old are unwittingly chosen in such fashion that they are drastically different from one another in many respects beside age. Several examples cited in Volume I on topics (especially in Part 3) where we failed to find more valid data suggest that the principles of designing samples to facilitate analysis of age may be more often honored in the breach than the observance.

This discussion is intended only to suggest the kinds of sampling problems entailed by research on age. Most of the examples assume individual, or some aggregate of individuals, to be the research case. The difficulties are compounded when sampling must permit analysis of an age structure of social relationships. Many of the theoretical problems posed in this book require, for empirical investigation, sampling of families, neighborhoods, organizations, and so on. For example, a study of age conflict or of solidarity in age-heterogeneous organizations might require a sample of organizations in which differing age distributions are controlled. Perhaps, by embarking upon a sociology of age, we may come to demand a new research methodology!

2 *Problems of data collection*

However painstaking the effort to eliminate or evaluate age-related errors in sampling, research results can still be called into question because of difficulties in the collection and use of data to represent the concepts under study. Age impinges in a variety of ways on attempts to gather complete and unbiased information. Simple specification of the size of strata in a society, for example, depends on the accuracy with which people report their age. And information about characteristics, attitudes, or behavior of age categories can be colored because subjects in different age categories are unlike in interpretation of stimuli, in response capacities, or in definition of the research situation.

AGE REPORTING

Errors due to inaccurate reporting of age can distort both size and age-related composition of the strata. In societies where illiteracy is extensive, people often do not know their age, and the usual practice is to instruct enumerators to estimate each person's age within broad categories (Hawley, 1959, p.

365). In the United States censuses, age reporting was inaccurate in the earliest years and in areas where illiteracy was prevalent; and there have been continuing tendencies to state age in round numbers rather than in precise years (Taeuber and Taeuber, 1958, p. 27; Bogue, 1959, p. 94; C. Taeuber, 1968, pp. 48–49). Older persons are especially prone to overstate age. Some say they are over 85 or over 100; others claim that they are 65 in order to advance their eligibility for social security; whereas persons at certain younger ages tend to understate. Census errors in age reporting seem to have been reduced by asking for year of birth rather than for age. Yet historical variations in method (in 1890, for example, the question referred to age at nearest birthday rather than completed age; Taeuber and Taeuber (1958, p. 27) introduce problems of consistency or comparability in the basic national data on age when strata, or rates based on these strata, are to be examined for the past or over time.

RESPONSE FRAME OF REFERENCE

In addition to inaccurate reporting of age itself, other types of error can invalidate the data intended to reflect the characteristics and composition of age categories in particular populations or particular cohorts. One type of error is possible because any given stimulus (a question, picture, or test item, for example) may have differing connotations for individuals depending on their age, their stage in the life course, or the historical events they have experienced. Thus, even when persons in several different strata confront the same data-gathering instrument, age may introduce systematic distortions in response.

People often have difficulty, for example, in identifying with stereotypes of an age decidedly different from their own. Veroff et al. (1960, p. 25) suggest that systematic age bias may be introduced into projective tests (such as the TAT or Thematic Apperception Test) where pictures are designed to reveal the subject's underlying perceptions of the world and his responses to it. Very old persons may be unable to identify with the images presented to them because the figures in the pictures are not clearly old in appearance. Or if the modes of dress or patterns of speech depicted in pictures or questions are specific to one age, individuals at other ages may have difficulty in making meaningful interpretations. Similarly, responses to a common stimulus may vary by age according to whether the situation presented is salient to the respondent's own stage of the life course. Adolescents and old people may be less likely than adults in the middle years to identify with descriptions or pictures of people engaged in work or in parental roles. This source of bias is also operative in intelligence tests. Although cross-sectional scores on many tests show peak scores among persons in their late teens or early 20's (Volume

I, Chapter 11 · 3), test items that involve practical tasks of adult life yield higher scores among middle-aged than among younger subjects (Demming and Pressey, 1957).

Thus data collection for a sociology of age stratification requires carefully designed indicants for measuring any concept that can take different forms at various stages of the individual's development. How, for example, is "social responsiveness" to be measured at the age of 1 year and at the age of 12 (Kessen, 1960)? Can the same questions probe the "morale" of students and retirees? Various ingenious devices have been invented for such purposes, ranging from the use of the completely projective Rorschach inkblot tests to compare interaction among children of varied ages (Smith, 1971), to the careful wording of questions about student-teacher friendships to compare fourth-graders with college seniors (Greenhouse, 1971).

More difficult to circumvent, perhaps, are the variations in meaning attributed to particular stimuli because persons of different ages, in addition to encountering different life course situations, have experienced different sociocultural environments. As Mannheim ([1928], 1952, p. 306) points out, members of the same cohort tend to share not only experiences but also perceptions and their linguistic expressions. But a question referring to the Depression, for example, or to farm life, or to particular types of warfare, when presented to cohorts with disparate historical backgrounds, would evoke different images and responses.

RESPONSE CAPACITIES

Apart from age-related variations in the meanings of questions and other data-gathering instruments, there are also age differences in people's ability to answer questions or respond to various kinds of tests. All such differences can bias the research findings. Young children and old persons handicapped by disability or illiteracy may be completely unable to handle questionnaires. Or the shortened attention span among the very young and the very old can prematurely curtail an interview or produce serious omissions in self-administered instruments. Cumming and Henry (1961, p. 240), for example, describe the special difficulties of interviewing persons over 80, due to inability to sustain interest in the content of the interview.

The capacity to provide clear and complete answers frequently depends upon familiarity with testing devices or upon skills developed in the educational process—factors that are linked to age both through life course changes and cohort differences. A national study by Brim et al. (1965, pp. 49–50) indicates that the majority of respondents over 50 had never taken a standardized test, whereas a majority of the younger adults did have testing experience. Particularly in self-administered questionnaires, response is likely to be associated with test-taking expertise.

Even when answers are recorded by an interviewer, inadequacies in the data may arise from age-related differences in verbal fluency. For example, the study of motivation by Veroff et al. (1960, esp. pp. 11–12), using thematic apperceptive measures on a national probability sample of adults, reports that inadequate protocols (that is, stories told with numerous or serious omissions) were more often obtained from older than from younger respondents. Hypothesizing that a crucial factor in the ability to answer questions is verbal fluency, the researchers analyze the data to discover a direct relationship between level of education (an indicant of verbal fluency) and adequacy of response. Thus, in studies relying on verbal measures, where the differences in education among the age strata may account for differences in response, the validity of the measure comes into question. If, for example, achievement motivation were measured by a method not dependent on verbal proficiency (hence on education), would the differences as observed between young and old remain the same?

Still another age-related difference is the failure to state an opinion in response to survey questions. Gergen and Back (1966) have shown an increase by age strata in "no opinion," "don't know," or indifferent answers, a finding that seems to indicate older people's noncommitment or inability to express clear views on a variety of topics. Here again the age differences in response are in part traceable to the mediating effects of education, as Glenn (1969, pp. 20–21) has shown by holding constant both education and sex in a reanalysis of data from sixteen Gallup Survey items.

THE RESEARCH SITUATION

Still another difficulty in data gathering relates to certain age-related circumstances that can distort the "ideal" structure of a research setting or disrupt the interactive process of an interview. The optimum structure typically excludes all persons except researcher and subject (or subjects). Yet interviews or observations involving persons at both extremes of the age scale are often disturbed by the presence of *intermediaries*. If mothers of young children or caretakers of the old invade privacy, sensitive areas of inquiry may be closed for research purposes. For example, are older persons questioned about living with their children likely to give full and candid responses in the presence of these children? Will adolescents venture honest opinions about drugs or sex if their parents are in the room? Are there aspects of peer group behavior that children are reluctant to enact or to discuss before their mothers?

In extreme cases, third parties intrude directly into the research situation, screening and interpreting the data presented. Research on an aged population often requires that a proportion of interviews be conducted entirely through intermediaries. Shanas et al. (1968, p. 458) report that about 3 per cent of the interviews completed in their cross-national survey of persons 65 and over were "proxy interviews." And in a study of Spanish-American War veterans (Richardson, 1966, p. 539), most of whom were octogenarians, approximately 12 per cent of the reports were characterized as "informant interviews." Similarly, data about very young children—and certainly about infants—are often obtained from their mothers, rather than directly from the subjects. Whether the intermediary participates in the research as proxy or as observer, there is the danger that his presence may exert unwanted controls over the reactions observed or may bias or truncate the information elicited.

With or without the presence of an intermediary, the *relative ages* of researcher and subject can affect the data-gathering process. A personal interview, for example, represents an interactive system where the behavior and orientations of each participant are contingent on the cues emitted by the other. It is well known that certain similarities or differences between interviewer and respondent, as in sex, color, ethnicity, or social class, may either inhibit or encourage responsiveness on particular topics (see, e.g., Katz, 1942; Hyman et al., 1954, pp. 153–170; Lenski and Leggett, 1960). It seems important to discover, then, how disparity in age may affect different types of investigation, either to improve rapport, or to constrain communication and interject age-specific differences in semantic patterns that can obscure or bias the meaning of the results (see Ehrlich and Riesman, 1961).

STUDIES OVER TIME

Just as studies that are repeated over time involve special problems of sampling, they also add complexity, as well as scope, to data collection and measurement. Again, because research on cohort-timing differs in certain respects from research on societal timing, problems of longitudinal studies can be considered separately from those of the sequence of cross sections.

Longitudinal or panel studies Data on the life course are collected in a variety of ways, each with its own weaknesses and strengths. *Panel studies*, for example, though they succeed in tracing the biographies of particular individuals, expose their participants to the special biases of being singled out for special attention or interviewed repeatedly. Such exposure can influence the behavior of subjects, sensitize them to previously unnoticed matters, or stimulate them to converse with others on unfamiliar topics (see, e.g., Glock, 1950). *Cross-sectional studies* of the same cohort at successive stages of life are similar in many respects to the cross-sectional sequences to be discussed shortly; while avoiding many of the special biases of panel studies, they lose the identity of individuals in focusing on the cohort as an aggregate.

Of special interest to the investigator seeking to extend his records into the past (or, through anticipation, into the future) are *self-reports* of the life course [*as discussed in Chapter 2 · 2 · B and in Chapter 11 · 1 by Clausen*]. Yet retrospective reports can be subject to errors of memory and recall. Such bias may be minimal in respect to certain major events in a person's life, as, for example, in the residence histories used by K. Taeuber (1967) to analyze rates of migration away from the farm at sequential life-course stages. Recollection of many other kinds of past events, however, is often interpreted in terms of subsequent experiences. A person views his past life differently as he ages, so that early occurrences may acquire new meaning or even be dropped from active recall if they are not supportive of his present frame of reference (cf. Yarrow et al., 1970; Goffman, 1961, pp. 145, 150–160; Berger and Luckmann, 1966, pp. 159–160). Moreover, unless direct observation is possible, the sole source of information about behavior in infancy and early childhood may be retroactive maternal reports. As we have suggested, the data from proxy interviews with mothers are filtered through the perspectives of a third person whose own identity is intimately entwined with that of the subject. And in the retrospective study, time also intervenes to add still further possibilities of distortion (see Webb et al., 1966, pp. 178–179).

This phenomenon of distorted remembrance of the past, though posing problems for research on the objective details of the life course, is not problematical when the focus is on the subjective meaning of earlier events for the person involved. As Clausen puts it [*Chapter 11 · 1*], retrospective reinterpretation forms "the sustenance on which our identities thrive." Thus one research procedure useful in self-assessments of the life history is to ask subjects to "draw their lives," a technique applied by Back and Bourque (1970) to a large sample of people of varied ages.

Sequence of cross sections   In studies designed to examine the changing age structure of society, rather than the life course of individuals or cohorts, a major issue is the comparability of the stimulus or the question wording not only across age categories but across historical time. Glenn (1969, p. 23) complains of the difficulties of reanalyzing opinion polls because of the "dearth of questions repeated with the same wording or the same meaning at intervals of several years on surveys which record the exact age data required for cohort analysis." Particularly frustrating to the researcher intent on examining age-related changes in attitudes is the discovery that survey questions on the topic of interest were worded differently at consecutive periods. To resolve this difficulty, it is often necessary to assume equivalence of meaning despite differences in wording. Thus Evan (1965, pp. 122–133) makes age-specific comparisons of responses at two time periods to such pairs of questions as the following:

> Should the government attempt to break up large business organizations? (1937)

> Do you think there are any monopolies in this country at this time? (1956)

Another pair to which Evan resorts is:

> Would you like to see a government agency furnish birth control information to married people who want it? (1938)

> Do you think birth control information should be made available to anyone who wants it, or not? (1959)

And Cutler (1968, p. 380), investigating the economic expectations of different cohorts, uses this pair to indicate negative expectations:

> Do you think there will be a serious business depression in the United States within the next ten years? (1946)

> Do you think the prices of most things you buy will be higher, lower, or about the same six months from now? (1951)

Short of abandoning efforts to use survey materials—a major source of data reflecting period or cohort changes in attitudes—social scientists may have no recourse but to utilize such ill-matched questions.

Even when surveys do include questions with the same wording (and, of course, the necessary age information) at several periods, unbiased comparability is not assured. As Evan (1965, p. 135) observes, identical questions may have different meanings to samples of respondents in different historical periods. Thus the variations in response due to age-specific connotations of questions that we have noted in a single cross-sectional study may be compounded in sequential cross sections by a period effect on the meanings of the questions themselves.

Period effects that are introduced into the research by the data-gathering instruments can be statistically controlled, just as other period effects are controlled [see Chapter 2 • 4 • A], for purposes of studying cohort differences or life-course differences.[7] In some studies, however, the fact that the meaning of a question changes over time is of intrinsic interest. In one example, a marked period change is reported by Agnello (1971) in responses to the statement, "Voting is the only way that people like me can have any say about how the government runs things." Having at first regarded this item as one of four reflecting political powerlessness, Agnello discovered that patterns of reaction to this item differed markedly from the other three over the electoral

---

[7] Such controls are effected by Crittenden (1962, pp. 651–654), by taking the difference between age-specific figures and the total for all the age strata in each period. Another procedure, though its use in the subsequent analysis is unfortunately obscure, is introduced by Cutler (1968, pp. 197–206), who standardizes the age-specific figures for each period by using a z-transformation.

years 1952, 1960, and 1968. Not only did the four items form differing Gutt-man scale patterns in the different periods; but, in addition, this particular item showed an unprecedented drop (from 79 per cent agreement in 1952 to only 38 per cent in 1968) among the youngest age groups (aged 21–28) entering the electorate. Such empirical configurations suggest various possi-bilities of changes in the relative import to the young of voting as compared with other types of political behavior.

THE NEED FOR GENERALITY

The possibilities of studying age and change across cultures and across his-torical time depend, then, upon improved comparability of definition and of procedures of data gathering. The feasibility of cross-national inquiry is evi-denced, for example, by some (though by no means all) of the wide-ranging compilations of the United Nations and its agencies, or by such a study as that by Shanas et al. (1968) where research teams in three different coun-tries employed common techniques for studying older people. The possibility of adjusting measures to correct for cohort differences or societal changes are suggested by the variety of precise formulas for stating income in constant dollars (cf. Volume I, Chapter 4 · A · 3), for example, or for separating short-term fluctuations from secular trends (see the early formulation by Ogburn and Thomas, 1927). A few types of records, such as those on body weight (Moore et al., 1962, p. 965) or on voting turnout (Tingsten, 1963; Volume I, Chapter 19 · 1), are available for sufficient times and places to begin to indi-cate the persistence of certain age-related patterns.[8] Yet, as Hyman (1970, p. 507) reminds survey researchers, dynamic analyses of social, political, and psychological patterns are in large part contingent on "an agenda of important and unfinished business." As he puts it:

> Repeating some of our old questions in future surveys, replicating the designs, and presenting fine age-breaks would yield invaluable, and now missing, evidence on the patterns as cohorts move through time and also experience social change.

3 Problems of analysis

The student of age stratification who is alert to the potential problems of *describing* the phenomena at hand must still confront the more serious prob-lems of *explaining* the observed data. Whether or not the procedures of sampling and data gathering reflect the "real" situation accurately, pitfalls

---

[8] It often seems plausible to interpret such persistent patterns as life-course differences be-cause of the varied conditions under which they occur. They could be explained as cohort (or period) differences only in the presence of unidirectional societal changes in overall levels of body weight or voting turnout. [*See Principle 1b in Chapter 2 · 3 · B.*]

still beset the analyst seeking clues from the data to causal connections and underlying processes.

The broad outlines of analysis for a sociology of age—its potential and its problems—have been described in Chapter 2. There we have shown how the life course of a cohort differs from the biographies of the individual cohort members, both because individuals shifting in opposite directions (in their opinions, for example, or the way they behave) can counteract each other in the collective data for the cohort; and because the size and composition of the cohort changes through the death and migration (as well as the role changes) of individuals. In this connection, we have pointed to a possible "compositional fallacy," where changes in the composition of a cohort are mistakenly interpreted as changes in the propensities or capacities of individuals. And, stressing the differing *levels* (individual, cohort, society) at which data can be analyzed, we have also noted that a possible "fallacy of proportional representation" can arise if, in dealing with the total society, variations in the size of the component cohorts are not taken into account.

Moreover, we have explained at length in Chapter 2 how period analysis (focused on our concept of societal timing) examines age-specific structural elements and changes in these elements; how cohort analysis (focused on our concept of cohort timing) examines changes with age over the life course (Ld) and differences among cohorts in life-course patterns (Cd); and how explanations of age-related findings may be sought in the impact of historical or environmental change. Here too we have defined certain possible fallacies—both derived from the principle that age-specific cross-sectional findings typically reflect a *combination* of life-course differences and cohort differences: a "life-course fallacy," where the analyst overlooks the possibility that cohort differences may be affecting the age strata he is examining; and a "generational fallacy," where he conversely overlooks the possible importance for his analysis of life-course differences [*see Chapter 2 · 3 · B*]. And we have noted the difficulties in particular analyses of phrasing the interpretation in terms of the appropriate factors—as "aging effects," for example, "cohort effects," or "period effects."

In this final section of the Appendix, we select for further emphasis and specification examples of a few stubborn problems of analysis, especially those where mistakes frequently occur in existing studies. We shall deal first with problems of the impact on research of mortality and migration, and second with problems of designating the appropriate explanatory factors.

THE IMPACT OF MORTALITY AND MIGRATION

It is well known that death operates selectively over the life course, reflecting systematic differences between those who survive and those who do not. These selective losses among the members of each cohort over its lifetime, coupled with changes through migration, demand special empirical procedures for research on one central process in our model, P1, which includes not only cohort succession but also survival [see Chapter 2 · 2 · A and Chapter 3].

Detailed studies by demographers of mortality (and its counterpart, longevity) (see Volume I, Chapter 2 · 3) already indicate certain population segments likely to be affected. First, the long-term decline in mortality has not affected all the age strata to the same extent. The most dramatic decreases in the United States have occurred in the groups under 55, especially in the youngest categories. Moreover, within each stratum, there are marked differences in mortality rates for various segments. For example, females at each age level generally have lower rates than males. Similarly, whites have consistently lower rates than nonwhites (although the difference is diminishing). Rates are lower for married persons than for the single, widowed, or divorced —a finding that holds for both sexes and at all age levels. Several studies also report an inverse relationship between age-specific mortality rates and occupational, educational, and income levels (e.g., Quint and Cody, 1970; Kittagawa and Hauser, 1967; Hinkle et al., 1968).

Basic dilemmas Two imponderable questions plague the analyst who would separate the effects of selective mortality (or migration) from the effects of age or other variables of major concern. First, what processes lead to long life among certain categories of people but not others? And second, how would the individuals who died have affected the research findings if they had lived (or the migrants if they had not moved)? While there are few definitive answers to such questions, unwarranted assumptions about them are frequently hidden in research reports.

In answer to the first question, one set of age-related factors in selective mortality is, without doubt, biological, including individual variations in health and physical functioning. But the further connections between such physiological differences and other selective factors are by no means clear. Physiological differences may, on the one hand, *contribute* both to mortality and also to educational attainment, earning power, occupational level, and other characteristics associated with mortality. On the other hand, biological differences affecting mortality may to an extent *result* from the differing ways of life, standard of living, or medical care associated with particular social, economic, and cultural backgrounds. To take sex and longevity as one example (see Volume I, Chapter 9 · 1 · c), a biological relationship is suggested by the persistent tendency for females to outlive males at most age levels (even in fetal life), under varied sociocultural conditions, and among animals. At the same time, variations in the ratio of male to female death rates are also in part responsive to environmental conditions that have contributed in the past both to maternal mortality and to deaths from tuberculosis among younger women, for example, or that contribute to high rates of lethal accidents or lung cancer among men.

These complex factors in selective mortality are often oversimplified in ill-considered research interpretations. For instance, it has been demonstrated repeatedly that mortality rates among old people in institutions exceed the rates for old people generally (Volume I, Chapter 25 · 5 · b). And this fact has often been attributed to insitutionalization as the "cause of death," even when no data were available to establish a causal connection (either through experimental assignment to institutions of some of the old people living at home, or through comparing death rates of institutionalized old people with rates of the noninstitutionalized having similar characteristics).

The second unanswerable question, in some ways akin to the first, asks: What would the deceased members of the study population have done if they had lived? If they outlived an illness, for example, would they have recovered their health? Would they have aged in similar fashion to others who, like themselves, were poor risks yet survived?[9] How valid is the principle that the nonsurvivors, had they escaped death, would have remained less fit than the survivors? And, if valid, to what characteristics and actions does it apply? Or, to consider the parallel question in respect to migration: How would the migrants have conducted their lives if they had remained at home?

Use of panels   If there are no full resolutions to these dilemmas, several research procedures can suggest clues or estimates. One such procedure uses the longitudinal or panel design to examine the prior history of dead panelists. Various panel studies, by describing events or attitudes prior to death, point to some of the links in the chain of selective mortality (our first question). Thus, in a sample of subjects aged 55 and over (with specific age controlled), performance on several tests showed differences between those who died in the following 5 years and those who survived and were retested. For example, those who subsequently died scored higher on tests of behavioral rigidity, but lower on certain verbal and intelligence tests (Riegel et al., 1967). In another study, in which senescent twins were given intelligence tests over an eight-year period, a mortality check 5 years later showed the lowest survival rates among those whose scores had declined in at least two out of three key subtests (Jarvik, Kallmann, and Falek, 1962; Jarvik and Falek, 1963). Still another finding, though the data are slight, evidences the potential value of this procedure: Maddox (personal communication, 1967) reports the highest rate of panel loss—due in large part to death) was among the "disengaged" members of the Duke panel (that is, those low in activity but

---

[9] There are clues, for example, that the mental functioning of institutionalized old people is related to background factors, such as education, that predate the ailments of old age (Kahn et al., 1961).

high in life satisfaction). Alternatively, in a somewhat different procedure, Lieberman (1966) tests a panel of old people known to be dying and then describes their approach to death (finding for instance, that those within a year of death tend to show more interest in others than in self, or to maintain a stable rather than an unstable self-concept).

Use of approximations In addition to panel designs for tracing biographies of individuals before their death, it is sometimes feasible to find supplementary information, or to specify reasonable assumptions, for approximating the hypothetical behavior of individuals if, contrary to fact, they had not died or moved (our second question). For example, in a study where detailed information is available on what kinds of people die, clues may be obtained by studying other persons who are as similar as possible but who do not die. Here the assumption is, of course, that the fact of death does not entirely vitiate the resemblance.

The value of additional information and carefully specified assumptions is demonstrated in an analysis by Sheldon (1958, pp. 56–59, 167–171), in which he estimates the "expected" labor force participation rates of migrants if they had not moved away from the farm. In this instance, the research problem was that trends in off-farm migration might impugn the widely held belief that farmers retire from the labor force at older ages than other workers (see Volume I, Chapter 3 · B · 2b). Cross-sectional census data for the United States in both 1940 and 1950 had shown that labor force participation rates in the oldest age strata fall off less sharply in the farm than the nonfarm population. But are these strata differences a mere artifact of a tendency for farmers to move, upon retirement, into a neighboring village? Sheldon attempts to answer this question by bringing in supplementary data (estimated migration rates for each of the cohorts between 1940 and 1950) and by an ingenious calculation[10] that approximates the numbers of migrants "expected" to have remained in the labor force if there had been no difference between farm and nonfarm rates. Since these approximations were well below the observed rates in 1950 for either the farm or the nonfarm population it seems likely that there is indeed greater occupational longevity for farming than for many other occupations. Thus out-migration, while it may have exaggerated the difference in the cross-sectional data, cannot entirely explain it away as a spurious finding.

Another example of a very different nature emphasizes again the utility of assumptions of *what might have been* in counteracting the absence from the study-population of certain individuals (in this instance, through death). Dennis (1966), in studying creative productivity in scholarly, scientific, and artistic fields, obtains his data from life records available through catalogues,

[10] See the original source for details.

bibliographies, library card files, biographical dictionaries, and so on (see Volume I, Chapter 18 · B · 2). He uses as his sample only biographies of men who had lived to age 79 or over. This selection is crucial: what it accomplishes is to prevent confusion in the analysis of individuals of differing longevity. Here again the assumption is obvious: if the men who died at younger ages had lived, their creative experiences would have related to the life course in similar fashion to the achievements of the long-lived men.

A famous example (Lehman, 1953), by contrast, fails to control the variations in longevity among individuals, and thereby tends to exaggerate the decrements with aging in several fields of scientific and artistic achievement (see Dennis, 1956, for a critique of Lehman's method). Spurious weight can be given by this procedure to the productivity of the earlier years through exclusion of those potentially productive men who did not live long enough to fulfill their promise. How this form of analysis can lead to fallacious interpretation is shown schematically in the hypothetical example in Table A · 3 (which for simplicity assumes that a man is either productive at one point in his life or is never productive). That is, with these imaginary numbers, those who died before reaching the productive age are excluded from the percentage base, thus artificially raising the rate of productivity of the younger age category.

Compositional fallacies   As such examples begin to suggest, one danger imposed by sample losses through mortality or migration lies in the attribution to *individuals* of characteristics or changes that are mere artifacts of the composition of the population being examined. Such "compositional fallacies"[11] can occur because certain characteristics are irreversible with respect to the individual, but are reversible on the cohort level because of selective mortality. For example, the level of education generally does not change (after adulthood) over the *individual* life course, but selective mortality could reverse the proportion who have a certain level of education over the *cohort*'s life course. Or individuals afflicted in early life with an incurable disease (cf. the classic analysis by Frost, 1939)[12] may later die—and, once these afflicted individuals have dropped out of the cohort, there will be decreases in death rates from this disease during the later life course of the cohort. In such instances, it would be fallacious, of course, to assume that *individuals* as they grow old are likely to recover from the incurable disease. Through such fallacies, which can occur in longitudinal[13] as well as cross-sectional studies, many life-course findings currently accepted as valid may

[11] For a more general formulation, see the discussion of "reification" of the group or aggregate in Riley and Nelson (1971).

[12] See also the relation between obesity and mortality rates suggested in Moore et al. (1962).

[13] This point has been emphasized by several critics; see, for example, Riegel et al. (1967).

TABLE A · 3 *Inappropriate analysis of relationship of productivity to age*

	Age of death			
	30–49		50–70	
Age of productivity	No.	%	No.	%
Under 50	100	100	100	50
Over 50	(100)[a]		100	
Total alive at productive age = 100%	100		200	

[a] Excluded because of death.

be vitiated by high rates of attrition and marked differences between survivors and nonsurvivors in relevant social or psychological characteristics.

These misrepresentations can often be corrected through compositional analysis [*described in Chapter 2 · 4 · B*], which holds constant those factors known to operate selectively upon mortality (or migration). In panel studies, moreover, it is possible to use each panel member as his own control in order to avoid the contaminating effects of selective mortality upon comparisons at consecutive time periods. That is, because the panel traces the same individuals over time, the analysis can compare the characteristics of survivors at time 2 with the characteristics of the same individuals at time 1, excluding from the sample at *both* periods those lost because of mortality or migration.

Maddox (1962) demonstrates the value of this panel procedure for avoiding spurious findings resulting from selective attrition in the sample. In a three-year analysis of old people, as long as individuals are used as their own controls, Maddox (1963, p. 199) finds a clear trend in the relationship between two variables: activity and life satisfaction. Thus those old people whose activity increased from time 1 to time 2 tended also to become better satisfied with life, whereas those whose activity fell off tended to become less satisfied. However, these findings would not have appeared—and indeed the trend would have been toward increasing independence of morale from activity—had the analysis simply compared the two cross-sectional studies without correcting for panel loss.

Through proper use of compositional controls, then, the researcher attempts to avoid compositional fallacies occasioned through the impact on his study population of mortality or migration. On the constructive side, the use of compositional analysis adds to his knowledge of the internal composition of the cohorts (or strata) themselves, thus serving as a major avenue for explaining why cohorts age in particular ways, why the life-course patterns of given cohorts are similar or different, or why the age structure changes as it does.

Such analyses of the internal composition of cohorts, or of cohort size, are not the only avenues open to the researcher who wants to explain the life-course differences in individuals or cohorts as they age, or the age-by-age differences among consecutive cohorts. He may examine the relationship between these differences and circumstances or changes in history and the environment [*as described in Chapter* 2 · 4 · *A*]. But such analyses are impeded by difficulties of designating which explanatory factors are relevant. Broadly, these difficulties center in logical questions of what assumptions to make in attributing particular findings to "aging effects," to "cohort (or generational) effects," or to "period effects" that cut across all age strata simultaneously. More specifically, the difficulties relate to details of those research techniques aimed to disentangle such effects.

Difficulties of designating pertinent factors One need peruse only a few of the studies concerned with the "effects" of aging or of generations to discover the logical confusion that is now rampant. Entirely contradictory interpretations may be placed on the same, or similar, sets of data. Thus identical patterns of difference among the strata at given periods of time (in consumption, for example, or in political attitudes) are attributed by some analysts to aging and by others to cohort differences in background or early socialization. And these conflicts in interpretations are exacerbated when studies extend over several time periods (see, e.g., the attack by Cutler, 1970, on the analysis by Crittenden, 1962).

Underlying such confusions and contradictions a difference in assumptions can usually be found. The difficulties are compounded because many researchers fail to make their assumptions explicit—indeed may be quite unaware of what assumptions are actually implied in their analyses.

Yet the logical model for any particular study typically requires explicit and often complex assumptions about the relations between societal timing (involving concurrent movement across time of strata of different ages) and cohort timing (involving the special rhythms of cohort succession and aging). The nature of such assumptions [*discussed in detail in Chapter* 2] has been set forth by various scholars. Above all, it has been made abundantly clear that no investigator should overlook in his conceptual model any one of the three major sources of variation that we refer to as "aging effects," "cohort effects," and "period effects" (see, e.g., Greenberg et al., 1950; Case, 1956; Schaie, 1965). Just to illustrate once again the pertinence of these factors, consider a complex situation where, for example, a characteristic—such as income from earnings—may be affected by differences in the value of labor due to age and experience, by increases in the wage levels at which each new cohort starts its work career, and by historical variations in inflationary pressures impinging upon all age strata simultaneously (cf.

Volume I, p. 8, and Chapter 4 · A · 4). In addition, many other kinds of assumptions are often required—regarding the signs or magnitudes of coefficients, for example, or certain kinds of nonlinear relationships (see Schaie, 1965; Cohn's Mathematical Note to Chapter 2 in this volume; Janson, 1971).

It should also be clear that failures to choose appropriate assumptions can result in fallacious interpretations, such as the common errors we have identified as the "life-course fallacy" and the "generational fallacy." Yet potential sources of such fallacies may be obscured by complex statistical operations, as when differences among the age-specific means computed from a series of cross-sectional samples are imputed solely to a "life stage" effect (Cutler, 1968, p. 207)—although here, as with all cross-sectional data, differences among strata are attributable to a *combination* of life-course and cohort-differences (except where the investigator makes explicit assumptions to the contrary).

Fortunately, there are many examples in the literature of simple or clearly explicated sets of assumptions that are useful as guides. Depending upon the research problem at hand, the analyst may assume (either a priori or on the basis of additional information) that only one (or perhaps two) of these three sets of factors has zero effect. For example, in a single cross-sectional study when the educational level of adults is observed to decline with advancing age, the researcher does not assume that this result is due to aging. Educational level (like many other characteristics that are irreversible over the life course) does not drop as people grow older. Nor can the researcher assume that the historical period of observation is producing the observed differences—since he is dealing with only a single period. In this instance, then, it is reasonable to assume that just *one factor*, the cohort factor, is operative. [*See Chapter 2 · 3 · B and also Volume I, p. 8.*]

In one cross-sectional study, Stouffer (1955, pp. 93–94) assumes the relevance of *two factors*. Starting with the finding that tolerance is more pronounced among younger than older people in the United States, he asks: Is this difference due to age? Does it mean that, as today's young people grow older, they will become less tolerant? Or is it a cohort effect due, not to aging, but to the differing attitudes to which each new generation was socialized? As the best available and most relevant index of cohort differences, Stouffer uses educational level, examining the joint relationships among age, education, and his dependent variable, tolerance. This procedure allows him to discover that each of the two postulated factors is independently related to tolerance. Or Miller (1965), in a cohort analysis of the relation of lifetime income to age and to period changes in economic growth, subdivides his sample by educational level, much as Stouffer does, as a means of controlling cohort differences. And, in still another explicit attempt to eliminate one of the three sources of variation (age, in this instance), Cecil (1971) asked a cross section of college alumni retrospective questions about their college days; this control of life stage—however imperfect the recollections—helped to improve the focus on cohort differences among the age strata.

Unlike these examples in which only one or two of the factors are assumed to operate, many research problems use models that involve all three. Where all three can be conceptualized as independent factors (as in our earlier example of income from earnings), no special difficulties should be involved *as long as each factor is measured directly*. Conventional statistical procedures are simply applied to the interrelationships of the three independent variables and the particular dependent variables under scrutiny.

The peculiar dilemma that does haunt much of the research on age stems from data in which the three factors are indexed, not by three measures, but by only two. The familiar table that lists dates on one axis and age on the other (often called a Lexis diagram; cf. Pressat, 1961) is widely used throughout this book and elsewhere for performing both period analysis and cohort analysis. And, as repeatedly shown, the two analyses of the same set of data can yield dramatically different results [*see Chapter 2, Section 3 · C*] through comparisons across the rows, down the columns, or along the diagonals. Yet it cannot be stressed too often that, while age, date of birth, and period of observation may superficially appear to reflect three variables, in fact they are always reducible to two (see, e.g., Ryder, 1964; Schaie, 1965; Janson, 1971; and the Mathematical Note to Chapter 2 by Cohn). Failure to recognize this essential fact is a major root of interpretative confusion and fallacy. Here the difficulty of identifying which theoretical factors correspond to which empirical elements becomes most acute. And here the necessity for explicit formulation of assumptions becomes most compelling.

Although serious problems of identifying the pertinent explanations remain unresolved in many analyses, the literature in a variety of disciplines reveals that research solutions to numerous specific problems have been reached, and that certain general principles are gradually being developed. Let us hope that this literature is now becoming cumulative!

Problems of implementation   Apart from the logical difficulties of designating which factors to use in interpreting findings from period and cohort analyses, the practical difficulties of conducting such analyses can themselves obscure the interpretation. Indeed, the unsuspecting researcher, setting out to test his conceptual model by a combined period and cohort analysis, may well find that he has opened a Pandora's box of annoyances—connected with the nature of the data available, the routines he must follow, or the methodological restrictions imposed. Case (1956, p. 161) dramatizes through comparison with studies of animals the vexations of studying human aging. Each batch of animals is kept separate from all the others and each is subjected to controlled conditions. Hence cohort changes, or experimental condi-

TABLE A · 4   *Overlap in age for three cohorts at five-year-intervals of observation*

	Period of observation			
	1910	*1915*	*1920*	*1925*
Cohort A	20–39	25–44	30–49	35–54
Cohort B	40–59	45–64	50–69	55–74
Cohort C	60–79	65–84	70–89	75 +

tions that cut across all the cohorts, can be readily observed. With people, however, aging, cohort succession, and environmental change are—apart from our abstract models—inextricably merged.

One of the many methodological constraints upon social research on age refers then, since the "batches" of human beings cannot be kept separate, to the criterion that age and date intervals should match. Social scientists must often rely upon data from opinion polls or demographic studies which do not meet this criterion. Imagine, for example, a set of data as in Table A · 4. Here the researcher has four observations for each of three cohorts— but the age groupings (20 years) are broader than the space between periods of observation (5 years). When, for example, Cohort A is traced from 1910 to 1915, a large portion of the persons observed at the first period are observed again at the second. Or, if the researcher should wish to compare characteristics of persons age 40–59 at different time periods, he would be unable to do so with data in this form. In such instances, numerous as they are, original sampling and coding decisions regarding age and time intervals thwart attempts at both cohort and period analysis.

Yet, in adapting available data, the researcher generally has little latitude in sampling time intervals. He can sometimes manipulate the size of age groupings (by combining information for adjacent ages), although not without resolving the dilemma created by two (often conflicting) criteria. On the one hand, a small age range may include too few cases to minimize sampling variability,[14] or to allow for introduction of control variables in analysis. On the other hand, too large an age grouping can conceal information about sensitive life-course shifts, blurring distinctions as to the specific age within a grouping at which change is most likely to take place (Glenn and Zody, 1970, p. 9; Cutler, 1966, pp. 141–145).

In addition to problems of matching age and time intervals, any series of cohorts artificially constructed from cross-sectional data (in contradistinction to a panel) contains a *shifting membership* as it moves through time. Case (1956, p. 161), in an example using five-year age and date intervals, shows

[14] In a study of intergenerational mobility, Duncan (1968, p. 711) refers to "the possibility that intercohort differences may arise from essentially arbitrary choices as to the grouping of birth dates, given sampling variability in the basic data."

in detail how the central year in a given cohort contributes more life-experience than any other and, unlike the other years, never appears in any of the other cohorts. The nature of this shifting membership, and the consequent need of a "separation factor" for interpreting it, can be suggested by the following example (cf. Pressat, 1961):

Suppose you are concerned with the infant mortality rate. You want to know what proportion of births in a given year are followed by death before age 1. You have the following information: number of births in a calendar year, and number of deaths in a calendar year, by single years of age. Suppose, now, you want to examine the birth cohort of 1970, who are aged 0–1 in 1970. How many of them die before reaching 1 year of age? First, you might look at the death rates in 1970 for those aged 0–1 at the time of death. These babies consist of *two* birth cohorts: (a) the 1970 birth cohort whose members did not live out the remainder of the year, and also (b) part of the 1969 birth cohort—those born in 1969 but who died in 1970 before reaching 1 year of age. The function of a "separation factor" would be to remove from the computation of cohort infant mortality for the 1970 birth cohort those belonging in category (b).

At the same time, you must also separate part of the 1970 cohort from the 1971 cohort in order to arrive at infant mortality for the 1970 cohort. To accomplish this, you now look at the number of babies who died in 1971 before reaching 1 year of age, who again must be separated into those belonging to the 1970 birth cohort and those belonging to the 1971 birth cohort.

Note that making the age-time interval extremely small does not remove the problem of shifting membership. If the analysis were done by *day* of birth and *day* of death, the splitting of the successive observations might still be done by using still finer intervals (hour of the day).

Among the many other technical difficulties of cohort and period analysis, in addition to those we have noted, the last example we shall cite is that of the *truncated form* in which the data typically occur. In contrast to short-lived animals, for whom many cohorts can be observed over the full life span, complete information for human beings is temporally bounded (cf. Schaie, 1965, pp. 93–94). A sequence of cross-sectional studies provides only partial information about most of the included cohorts [*see, as a typical example, the data in Table 2 · 6*]. Supplementary information about the past can sometimes be secured through recollection. But the future lives of cohorts not covered in the data are still largely unknown. The difficulties of analyzing truncated data become acute when, in place of age-by-age comparisons, the researcher uses averages or summary measures, for the cohorts are not comparable if the data for each one cover a different portion of the life course (cf. Cutler, 1968).

This account of the difficulties of period and cohort analysis, protracted as it is, is intended to alert the researcher, not to discourage him. For the method affords a main approach to understanding the sociology of age, and careful specification of the problems should form merely the first step toward their resolution.

CONCLUDING NOTE

Whether undertaking new research, analyzing available raw data, or evaluating the data of completed studies, the investigator of age (as of other topics) must inevitably deal with the question: Is it likely that the research findings are merely artifacts of the research procedure rather than a true reflection of the age-related elements and processes under study? In research on age, as on other topics, the steps in the procedure constitute a set of "hidden variables," the impact of which may be unknown and unsuspected but which may operate to confound the results of the study. Thus the problem of spuriousness in research findings and the problem of bias are essentially parallel, with the one representing a failure to incorporate the appropriate explanatory variables in the conceptual model, the other representing a failure in the application of research techniques.

The accumulating body of experience with age as a variable in the research design has begun to suggest the special patterns of age-related spuriousness and bias that may arise. We have suggested how these distortions may be introduced at each stage of the research process—sampling, data collection, and analysis—and, moreover, may be compounded in the dynamic designs, so often crucial to age research, that require repeated observations at several periods of time. Thus the examples reviewed in this Appendix illustrate the importance of assessing the nature and direction of age-related bias in interpreting research findings, and implicitly suggest ways in which such distortion may be anticipated and avoided in the research process.

Our discussion has merely hinted at the stupendous difficulties still to be overcome in an improved methodology for the sociology of age. But after all, as Ryder (1965, p. 861) has put it:

> . . . such difficulties are not so much those of the method itself as meaningful reflections of the research investment necessary to study a long-lived species experiencing structural transformation.

Works cited in Appendix

Agnello, Thomas, 1971. "The Effects of Aging on Feelings of Political Powerlessness," Senior Honors Paper, Rutgers University (unpublished).

Ariès, Philippe, 1962. *Centuries of Childhood: A Social History of Family Life,* New York: Knopf and Random House, Vintage Books.

Back, Kurt W., and Linda Brookover Bourque, 1970. "Life Graphs: Aging and Cohort Effect," *Journal of Gerontology*, 25, pp. 249–255.

Berelson, Bernard R., Paul F. Lazarsfeld, and William N. McPhee, 1954. *Voting*, Chicago: University of Chicago Press.

Berger, Peter L., and Thomas Luckmann, 1966. *The Social Construction of Reality*, Garden City, N.Y.: Doubleday.

Bogue, Donald J., 1959. *Population of the United States*, Glencoe, Ill.: Free Press.

Booth, Charles (1889–1891), 1902–1903. *Life and Labour of the People in London*, 17 vols., London: Macmillan.

Brim, Orville G., Jr., John Neulinger, and David C. Glass, 1965. "Experiences and Attitudes of American Adults Concerning Standardized Intelligence Tests," New York: Russell Sage Foundation.

Case, R. A. M., 1956. "Cohort Analysis of Mortality Rates as an Historical or Narrative Technique," *British Journal of Preventive and Social Medicine*, 10, pp. 159–171.

Cecil, Robert, 1971. Senior Honors Paper, Rutgers University (unpublished).

Crittenden, John, 1962. "Aging and Party Affiliation," *Public Opinion Quarterly*, 26, pp. 648–657.

Cumming, Elaine, and William E. Henry, 1961. *Growing Old: The Process of Disengagement*, New York: Basic Books.

Cutler, Neal E., 1968. *The Alternative Effects of Generations and Aging Upon Political Behavior: A Cohort Analysis of American Attitudes Toward Foreign Policy, 1946–1966*. Oak Ridge, Tenn.: Oak Ridge National Laboratory.

————, 1970. "Generation, Maturation, and Party Affiliation: A Cohort Analysis," *Public Opinion Quarterly*, 33, pp, 583–588.

Demming, J. A., and S. L. Pressey, 1957. "Tests 'Indigenous' to the Adult and Older Years," *Journal of Counseling Psychology*, 4, pp. 144–148.

Dennis, Wayne, 1956. "Age and Achievement: A Critique," *Journal of Gerontology*, 11, pp. 331–337.

————, 1966. "Creative Productivity between the Ages of 20 and 80 Years," *Journal of Gerontology*, 21, pp. 1–8.

Duncan, Otis Dudley, 1968. "Social Stratification and Mobility," in Sheldon, Eleanor Bernert, and Wilbert E. Moore, editors, *Indicators of Social Change*, New York: Russell Sage Foundation, pp. 675–719.

Ehrlich, June Sachar, and David Riesman, 1961. "Age and Authority in the Interview," *Public Opinion Quarterly*, 25, pp. 39–56.

Epstein, Lenore A., and Janet H. Murray, 1967. *The Aged Population of the United States: The 1963 Social Security Survey of the Aged*, Washington: Government Printing Office.

Evan, William M., 1965. "Cohort Analysis of Attitude Data," in Beshers, James M., editor, *Computer Methods in the Analysis of Large-Scale Social Systems*, Cambridge, Mass.: Joint Center for Urban Studies of the M.I.T. and Harvard University, pp. 117–142.

Frost, Wade Hampton, 1939. "The Age Selection of Mortality from Tuberculosis in Successive Decades," *American Journal of Hygiene*, Section A, 30, pp. 91–96.

Gergen, Kenneth J., and Kurt W. Back, 1966. "Communications in the Interview and the Disengaged Respondent," *Public Opinion Quarterly*, 30, pp. 385–398.

Glenn, Norval D., 1969. "Aging, Disengagement, and Opinionation," *Public Opinion Quarterly*, 33, pp. 17–33.

———, and Michael Grimes, 1968. "Aging, Voting and Political Interest," *American Sociological Review*, 33, pp. 563–575.

———, and Richard E. Zody, 1970. "Cohort Analysis with National Survey Data," *The Gerontologist*, 10, pp. 233–240.

Glock, Charles Y., 1950. "Participation Bias and Re-interview Effect in Panel Studies," Ph.D. dissertation, Columbia University.

Goffman, Erving, 1961. *Asylums: Essays on the Social Situation of Mental Patients and Other Inmates*, Garden City, N.Y.: Doubleday, Anchor Books.

Greenberg, B. G., John J. Wright, and Cecil G. Sheps, 1950. "A Technique for Analyzing Some Factors Affecting the Incidence of Syphilis," *Journal of the American Statistical Association*, 45, pp. 373–399.

Greenhouse, Richard, 1971. Senior Honors Paper, Rutgers (unpublished).

Havighurst, Robert J., 1950. "Problems of Sampling and Interviewing in Studies of Old People," *Journal of Gerontology*, 16, pp. 158–167.

Hawley, Amos H., 1959. "Population Composition," in Hauser, Philip M., and Otis Dudley Duncan, editors, *The Study of Population*, Chicago: University of Chicago Press, pp. 361–382.

Hilgard, Ernest R., and Stanley L. Payne, 1944. "Those Not at Home—Riddle for Pollsters," *Public Opinion Quarterly*, 8, pp. 254–261.

Hinkle, L. E., Jr., et al., 1968. "Occupation, Education, and Coronary Heart Disease, Cornell University Medical College and Bell System," *Science*, 161, pp. 238–246.

Hochstim, Joseph R., and Demetrios A. Athanasopoulos, 1970. "Personal Follow-up in a Mail Survey: Its Contribution and its Cost," *Public Opinion Quarterly*, 34, pp. 69–81.

Hyman, Herbert H., et al., 1954. *Interviewing in Social Research*, Chicago: University of Chicago Press.

———, 1970. Book review of Riley, Foner, and Associates, Vol. I, *Public Opinion Quarterly*, 34, pp. 506–507.

Janson, Carl Gunnar, 1971. "Longitudinal Studies: Note on Cohort Analysis." Mimeographed.

Jarvik, Lissy F., and Arthur Falek, 1963. "Intellectual Stability and Survival in the Aged," *Journal of Gerontology*, 18, pp. 173–176.

———, Franz J. Kallmann, and Arthur Falek, 1962. "Intellectual Changes in Aged Twins," *Journal of Gerontology*, 17, pp. 289–294.

Johnston, Denis F., and James R. Wetzel, 1969. "Effect of the Census Undercount on Labor Force Estimates," *Monthly Labor Review*, March, pp. 3–13.

Kahn, Robert L., Max Pollack, and Alvin I. Goldfarb, 1961. "Factors Related to Individual Differences in Mental Status of Institutionalized Aged," in Hoch, Paul H., and Joseph Zubin, editors, *Psychopathology of Aging*, New York: Grune & Stratton, pp. 104–113.

Katz, Daniel, 1942. "Do Interviews Bias Polls?" *Public Opinion Quarterly*, VI, pp. 248–268.

Kelly, E. Lowell, 1955. "Consistency of the Adult Personality," *American Psychologist*, 10, pp. 659–681.

Kessen, W., 1960. "Research Design in the Study of Developmental Problems," in Mussen, Paul, editor, *Handbook of Research Methods in Child Development*, New York: Wiley, pp. 36–70.

Kitagawa, E. M., and P. M. Hauser, 1967. "Education and Income Differentials in Mortality, United States, 1960," revised March 1967, University of Chicago. Mimeographed.

Knodel, John, 1970. "Two and a Half Centuries of Demographic History in a Bavarian Village," *Population Studies*, 24, pp. 353–376.

Lehman, Harvey C., 1953. *Age and Achievement*, Princeton, N.J.: Princeton University Press.

Lenski, Gerhard E., and John C. Leggett, 1960. "Caste, Class, and Deference in the Research Interview," *American Journal of Sociology*, 65, pp. 463–467.

LePlay, Frédéric (1855), 1877–1879. *Les Ouvriers Européens*. 2nd ed., 6 vols., Tours (France): Mame.

Lieberman, Morton A., 1966. "Observations on Death and Dying," *The Gerontologist*, 6, pp. 70–72, 125.

Likert, Rensis, 1948. "Public Opinion Polls," *Scientific American* (December 1948), pp. 7–11.

Lowe, Francis E., and Thomas C. McCormick, 1955. "Some Survey Sampling Biases," *Public Opinion Quarterly*, 19, pp. 303–315.

Maddox, George L., 1962. "A Longitudinal Multidisciplinary Study of Human Aging: Selected Methodological Issues," 1962 Proceedings of the Social Statistics Section of the American Statistical Association, pp. 280–285.

Maddox, George L., 1963. "Activity and Morale: A Longitudinal Study of Selected Elderly Subjects," *Social Forces*, 42, pp. 195–204.

Mannheim, Karl (1928), 1952. "The Problem of Generations," in *Essays on the Sociology of Knowledge*, edited and translated by Paul Kecskemeti, London: Routledge and Kegan Paul, pp. 276–322.

Mercer, Jane R., and Edgar W. Butler, 1967. "Disengagement of the Aged Population and Response Differentials in Survey Research," *Social Forces*, 46, pp. 89–96.

Miller, Herman P., 1965. "Lifetime Income and Economic Growth," *American Economic Review*, 55, pp. 834–844.

Moore, Mary E., Albert Stunkard, and Leo Srole, 1962. "Obesity, Social Class, and Mental Illness," *Journal of the American Medical Association*, 181, pp. 962–966.

Ogburn, William F., and Dorothy S. Thomas, 1927. "The Influence of the Business Cycle on Certain Social Conditions," in Thomas, Dorothy S., *Social Aspects of the Business Cycle*, New York: Knopf, pp. 53–74.

Pressat, Roland, 1961. L'analyse Démographique, Paris: Presses Universitaires de France.

Quint, Jules V., and Bianca R. Cody, 1970. "Preeminence and Mortality: Longevity of Prominent Men," *American Journal of Public Health*, 60, pp. 1118–1124.

Revelle, Roger, 1968. "Introduction to the Issue 'Historical Population Studies,'" *Daedalus* (Spring 1968), pp. 353–362.

Richardson, Arthur H., 1966. "Alienation and Disengagement Among the Very Aged," *Proceedings*, 7th International Congress of Gerontology, Vienna, 8, pp. 539–545.

Riegel, Klaus F., Ruth M. Riegel, and Gunther Meyer, 1967. "A Study of the Drop-out Rates in Longitudinal Research on Aging and the Prediction of Death," *Journal of Personality and Social Psychology*, 5, pp. 342–348.

Riley, Matilda White, 1963. *Sociological Research, Volume I. A Case Approach,* New York: Harcourt, Brace & World.

————, 1969. "Work in Progress on Aging and Society," *Sociological Inquiry,* 39, pp. 106–107.

————, and Edward E. Nelson, 1971. "Research on Stability and Change in Social Systems," in Barber, Bernard, and Alex Inkeles, editors, *Stability and Social, Change: A Volume in Honor of Talcott Parsons,* Boston: Little, Brown, pp. 407–449.

Ryder, N. B., 1964. "The Process of Demographic Translation," *Demography,* Vol. 1, No. 1, pp. 74–82.

————, 1965. "The Cohort as a Concept in the Study of Social Change," *American Sociological Review,* 30, pp. 843–861.

Schaie, K. Warner, 1965. "A General Model for the Study of Developmental Problems," *Psychological Bulletin,* 64, pp. 92–107.

————, and Charles R. Strother, 1968. "The Effect of Time and Cohort Differences on the Interpretation of Age Changes in Cognitive Behavior," *Multivariate Behavioral Research,* 3, pp. 262–263.

Shanas, Ethel, et al., 1968. *Old People in Three Industrial Societies,* New York: Atherton Press.

Sharp, Harry, and Allan Feldt, 1959. "Some Factors in a Probability Sample Survey of a Metropolitan Community," *American Sociological Review,* 24, pp. 650–661.

Sheldon, Henry D., 1958. *The Older Population of the United States,* New York: Wiley.

Simmons, Leo, 1945. *Role of the Aged in Primitive Society,* New Haven: Yale University Press.

————, 1960. "Aging in Preindustrial Societies," in Tibbitts, Clark, editor, *Handbook of Social Gerontology,* Chicago: University of Chicago Press, pp. 62–91.

Smelser, Neil J., 1959. *Social Change in the Industrial Revolution,* Chicago: University of Chicago Press.

————, 1968. "Sociological History: The Industrial Revolution and the British Working-Class Family," in Smelser, Neil J., *Essays in Sociological Explanation,* Englewood Cliffs, N.J.: Prentice-Hall, pp. 76–91.

Smith, H. W., 1971. "Interaction Process in Small Groups of Varied Ages," paper delivered at the meetings of the American Sociological Association.

Smyth, Daniel, and Douglas Trainor, 1971. Senior Honors Paper, Rutgers University (unpublished).

Stephan, Frederick F., and Philip J. McCarthy, 1958. *Sampling Opinions: An Analysis of Survey Procedures,* New York: Wiley.

Stouffer, Samuel A., 1955. *Communism, Conformity, and Civil Liberties*, Garden City, N.Y.: Doubleday.

Streib, Gordon F., 1963. "Longitudinal Studies in Social Gerontology," in Williams, Richard H., Clark Tibbitts, and Wilma Donahue, editors, *Processes of Aging*, New York: Atherton Press, II, pp. 25–39.

————, 1966. "Participants and Dropouts in a Longitudinal Study," *Journal of Gerontology*, 2, pp. 200–209.

Taeuber, Conrad, 1968. "Population: Trends and Characteristics," in Sheldon, Eleanor Bernert, and Wilbert E. Moore, *Indicators of Social Change: Concepts and Measurements*, New York: Russell Sage Foundation, pp. 27–69.

————, and Irene Taeuber, 1958. *The Changing Population of the United States*, New York: Wiley.

Taeuber, Karl E., 1967. "The Residential Redistribution of Farm-Born Cohorts," *Rural Sociology*, 32, pp. 30–36.

Terman, L. M., and Melita H. Oden, 1959. *The Gifted Group at Mid-life*, Stanford: Stanford University Press.

Thomas, William I., and Florian Znaniecki, 1918. *The Polish Peasant in Europe and America*, 2 vols., Chicago: University of Chicago Press.

Tingsten, Herbert, 1963. *Political Behavior: Studies in Election Statistics*, Totowa, N.J.: Bedminster Press.

United States Bureau of the Census, 1960 Census of Population, Vol. I, Part 1.

Veroff, Joseph, John W. Atkinson, Sheila C. Feld, and Gerald Gurin, 1960. "The Use of Thematic Apperception to Assess Motivation in a Nationwide Interview Study," *Psychological Monographs: General and Applied*, 74, No. 12, pp. 1–32.

Webb, Eugene J. et al., 1966. *Unobtrusive Measures: Nonreactive Research in the Social Sciences*, Chicago: Rand McNally.

Wilensky, Harold L., 1962. "Life Cycle, Work Situation, and Participation in Formal Associations," in Tibbitts, Clark, and Wilma Donahue, editors, *Social and Psychological Aspects of Aging*, New York: Columbia University Press, pp. 919–930.

Yarrow, Marian Radke, John D. Campbell, and Roger V. Burton, 1970. "Recollections of Childhood: A Study of the Retrospective Method," *Monographs of the Society for Research in Child Development*, 35, No. 5 (Serial No. 138).

Subject index*

Absolute size of strata, 33–34
Absolutism in student dissent, 270, 274–275
Academic value pattern, 242–243, 244, 260–261. SEE ALSO: *Cognitive rationality*
Accident rates of workers, 181
Accumulation of experience, 425–427, 459; and political partisanship, 126. SEE ALSO: *Aging; Duration; Commitment; Experience*
Achievement, component of instrumental activism, 271; differentiation in life course, 248–249. SEE ALSO: *Creativity; Productivity*
Achievement status, 96
Activity, community, 214, 216; in old age, 495–497; level, 428
Acute illness, 423
Adaptation and student dissent, 273–277
Adequacy, sense of, 431
Adjustment, personal, 431–432, 457–513 (*passim*)

Adjustments to societal imbalances, 451–452. SEE ALSO: *Change; Imbalances*
Administrative role, 254, 315–316, 318–322, 326–327
Adolescence, 240, 246, 471–475; and community, 216–219; and friendship, 359, 364, 368–370, 372–373, 380, 382–383, 385–387; and interaction potential, 437; and stratum solidarity, 436–437; as transitional stage, 436–437; differentiation of achievement, 248–249; differentiation of stage, 240–241, 414; disturbances, 240; peer group (SEE: *Peers, peer group*); sample biases in research, 586; structural features, 248–251; youth culture, 240–241, 255
Adulthood, and community, 219–221; boundaries of entry, 413; friendship in, 359, 364, 375, 383, 387–389; roles, 407. SEE ALSO: *Early maturity; Maturity; Middle age; Old age*
Advisors in allocation, 558

* Key concepts are set in boldface, as are the pages on which a particular concept is defined or most fully discussed.

Aestheticism in student dissent, 274
Affective neutrality in academic values, 271
Affective taboo, in studentry, 255
Age, 1, 19, 93; as a collective property, 14; as history, 19; as life course, 19–20; as relational, 14, 371; as social location, 398–399, 419; available data on, 584, 601
Age cleavage. SEE: *Conflict among strata;* SEE ALSO: *Student dissent; Youth culture*
Age conflict. SEE: *Conflict among strata;* SEE ALSO: *Student dissent; Youth culture*
Age-consciousness, 434–435
Age criteria of role allocation. SEE: *Allocative criteria*
Aged, and peers in socialization, 545–546; future cohorts, 534–535; mortality rates of institutionalized, 604; sample biases, 586; support from children, 439–440; withdrawal, 431–432. SEE ALSO: *entries beginning Old; Older*
Age discrimination in employment, 174–175, 176–177, 560
Age distribution of population, 33, 36, 38, 420–422, 424–425
Age grades, 207–208, 413, 462
Age groups, 435; female, 437; inclusiveness, 435, 438
Age-heterogeneous groups, 147–148, 399, 445–446. SEE ALSO: *Cross-cutting affiliations*
Age hierarchy. SEE: *Hierarchy in age relations*
Age-homogeneity, 203–206, 374–375, 399
Age-homophily, 205, 358, 371–374, 376–378, 390, 436–439
Age-incongruity, 189–191, 413–414, 442, 522
Age integration, 20, 338–345, 434–439
Age intervals in research, 611–612
Age mobility, 4, 8, 10, 22, 23, 517–518; and political orientations, 149–151; effects on interstratum relations, 443–444, 447. SEE ALSO: *Aging*
Agents of allocation. SEE: *Allocative agents*
Agents of socialization. SEE: *Socializing agents*
Age-oppression, 336
Age peers. SEE: *Peers, peer group*
Age polarization, 146, 411. SEE ALSO: *Conflict among strata*
Age processes. SEE: *Processes (age related)*
Age pyramid, 37, 39, 40, 41; and com-munity, 202, 204
Age related acts, 6, 7, 9
Age reporting, 594–595
Age research. SEE: *Research on age*
Age segregation, 20–21, 146, 203–206, 499–500
Age sets, 413. SEE ALSO: *Age grades*
Age-specific rates, 37, 40–42
Age status, 413
Age-status-deference, 335
Age-status-envy, 335
Age-status inconsistency, 189–191, 413–414, 442
Age strata. SEE: *Strata*
Age stratification, and environment, 15–18; and process, 517–518; bases, 398–401, 414–415, 452; model, 1–26, 395–455, 515–581; vs. class stratification, 22–23, 400, 414–415, 452, 532
Age-stratum-competition, 335
Age-stratum-solidarity, 335
Age structure, 1, 11, 54, 398, 420–422. SEE ALSO: *Population; Structure*
Age-time structure of population, 93–94
Aggregative fallacy, 103
Aging (P2), 2, 8, 9–11, 13–14, 17, 18, 29, 42–43, 46–53, 70, 517–518; and friendship, 358–359; and identity, 460–461, 497–498, 501–506, 519; and political attitudes, 72–73, 126, 133–140; and social change, 521–522; and voting, 123–124; as accumulation of experience, 459; as duration of exposure to system, 527–528; as sequence of roles, 458–459; awareness of, 493; changes in, 13–14; data, 46; of group membership, 562; of population, 119–120, 199, 206, 421–422, 535. SEE ALSO: *Age mobility; Life course; Life course stages; Role sequence*
"Aging effects," 22, 55, 69–80
Agricultural employment, decline in, 165
Allocation (P3), 8, 9, 11, 12, 13, 18, 22, 31, 43, 518–521, 535, 548–566, 567–572; agents of (SEE: *Allocative agents*); age structuring of, 520–521, 548–550, 562–564; aging of group membership, 562; ascriptive, 178, 249, 414, 551; asymmetry of, 563; biological processes, 556–557; certification procedures, 558; changes in, 13, 549, 552; church membership, 557, 559; cohort differences, 563–564; cohort vs. societal time, 565; college attendance, 551–552, 560, 568; community role in, 207–208; competitive vs. noncompetitive selection,

558, 564; compulsory vs. voluntary, 449,
550–551, 556, 570–571; criteria (SEE:
Allocative criteria); decision-making
process, 562–564; **denial mechanisms,**
561, **562; differentiation from socialization, 567–568;** distribution of rewards in,
562–564; faculty roles, 262–263; friendship, 370–377, 380–382, 554–555, 563;
Girl Scouts, 554; impersonal processes,
558; inequality in, 564, 565–566 (SEE
ALSO: *Inequalities among age strata*);
information in, 167–168, 557–558, 564;
interstratum relations, 520–521, 562–
563; marriage, 557, 559, 560, 563;
mechanisms, 556 (SEE ALSO: *Allocation, procedures; Allocative agents*);
military role, 519, 552–554, 571;
negatively evaluated roles, 553; nonsocial bases, 556–557; orphanhood, 557;
parenthood role, 555–556, 557; phasing
with socialization, 519–520, 522, 551–
552, 567–572; power relations in, 562–
564, 565–566; **procedures,** 167–168,
175–180, **556–566;** response to imbalance, 451; response to social crisis,
572; retirement, 172–184, 561; rituals
of, 551, 553–554, 555, 561; role complex, 560; role exit, 551, 553–554, 555,
559, 562; role transfer (SEE: *Role
transfer*); school attendance, 550–551,
568; scientific roles, 297, 299, 315–
330; screening procedures, 558; self-
selection in, 552, 554, 558–559, 565;
social change implications, 552, 564–
566; societal vs. cohort time, 565;
solidarity in, 561–562, 564; student
dissent over, 565–566; subjective assessment, 549; territorial location, 556, 557;
validation, 557, 558; vital processes in,
556–557; voluntary association membership, 554; voluntary vs. compulsory, 448–
449, 551, 556, 570–571; widowhood,
555, 557, 561; within-stratum relations,
564; work role, 161–162, 165–184, 189–
193, 414, 418, 519–520, 560, 568. SEE
ALSO: *Allocative; Articulating processes*
Allocative agents, 539, **549,** 556–560;
advisors, 558; as role occupants, 565;
certifiers, 558, 559; **controllers, 558;**
dilemmas of control, 569–570; **expediters,
558;** relations with candidates, 562–564;
screeners, 558, 559; separation from
socializing agents, 551–552, 568–572;
third parties, 554–555, 559, 564. SEE
ALSO: *Allocation (esp. specific roles)*

Allocative criteria, 7–8, 23, 29, **406**–411,
556; and role performance, 552, 569–
570; ascriptive, 178, 414–415; changes
in, 411, 573–575; **direct, 7, 408–409;**
factual, 7, 409–410; formal, 408; indirect,
7, 407–408; informal, 408; latitude in
application, 516; **normative, 7, 409–410;**
permissive, 409; political role, 120;
prescriptive, 409; relational age, 370–
371, **410–411;** violations, 413–414;
work force entry, 166–167; work force
exit, 174–175
Allocators. SEE: *Allocative agents*
Analysis, problems in age research, 601–
613. SEE ALSO: *Cohort analysis;
Interpretation of age data; Identification problem; Life course, analysis of;
Period analysis*
Analytical bases of sampling in age research,
593–594
Anomie in student dissent, 274
Anticipatory socialization, 417, 542, 546,
569; and social change, 547; for occupational role, 475–476; for old age, 384;
for relinquishing work, 186–187; **versus**
tenancy socialization, 539–540
Anti-intellectualism of student dissent, 274
Appearance, effect on life course, 469–471,
483–485
Apprentice-master relations in science, 315,
327–328, 338–345
Archives of age data, 584. SEE ALSO:
Available data on age
Articulating processes (P3, P4), 11, 12, 161,
162, 518–521, 535; age structuring of,
520–521; and social change, 521–522;
and societal crises, 572; coordination of,
519–520, 522, 551–552, 568–572;
levels of, 519. SEE ALSO: *Allocation;
Socialization*
Ascriptive allocation, 178, 249, 414, 551.
SEE ALSO: *Compulsory vs. voluntary
allocation*
Ascriptive status, 96
Aspirations, 181–182, 477–479
Asymmetry, in allocation, 563; in socializa-
tion, 245; of processes, 12, 21–22. SEE
ALSO: *Cohort vs. Societal time*
Atomistic fallacy, 103. SEE ALSO: *Fallacies*
Attrition of roles in science, 321–322
Authority, in college vs. high school, 251–
252; in faculty-student relations, 257–
258; in mature social relations, 248; in
science, 299–300, 343–345 (SEE ALSO:
Gerontocracy in science); relations
among strata, 441–442; versus cognitive

492; exclusion from parental solidarity, 266–267, 268–269; in work force, 163, 169–171; support by parents, 439–440. SEE ALSO: *Childhood*

China, family relations in, 441–442

Chronic illness, 423–425

Church membership, allocation to, 557, 559

Cigarette smoking, 73–75, 532

Citation analysis in science, 303–305, 309, 348–350

Clarity of role expectations, 416–417

Class, and community, 220–221; and peer group, 386–387

Class politics, and age conflict, 151–155

Class stratification vs. age stratification, 22–23, 452, 532

Cleavage. SEE: *Conflict*

Codification in science, 302–313; and discovery, 305–308; and evaluation, 336–337; and inter-science transfers, 311–313; and productivity, 306–309; and receptivity to new ideas, 308–310; and visibility of new ideas, 310–311

Coeducation, 277–278

Cognitive rationality, 237, 242–244, 253, 254, 261; and instrumental activism, 271–272; and student dissent, 275–276; commitment to, 259–261; disintegrative tendencies, 262; implementation in socialization, 263; vs. hierarchical authority, 252

Cognitive structure, and social structure, 302

Cohesion. SEE: *Solidarity; Integration*

Cohort, 4, 5, 9, 94, 527–528; characteristics of, 46; **individual shifts over time, 46–48,** 602; **lifespan, 9–10,** 98–99; unique history of, 9, 11

Cohort age structure, 94, 95

Cohort analysis, 46, **49**–53, 70, 79, 527–529, 602; attitudes toward unions, 134–135, 141; cigarette smoking, 73–75; identification problem, 75–80, 85–88, 610; migration, 528; political example (fictitious), 143–144; political orientation, 133–136; political party identification, 136, 528; problems of implementation, 610–613; problems of interpretation, 61–62, 66–88, 608–610; research problems, 599, 607–613; scientific roles, 317–320; separation factor, 611–612; truncated data, 66, 73–76, 612; vs. period analysis, 58–68, 70–76; voting (fictitious), 143–144; women in labor force, 54–56, 528

Cohort-centrism, **419–420,** 465, 498

Cohort change, ramification through age strata, 576–577; spread to other social spheres, 575–576. SEE ALSO: *Cohort differences*

Cohort composition, **9**

Cohort differences (Cd), **31,** 106, 516–517, 521–522, 524, 530–532, 534; and age relations in allocation, 563–564; and cohort flow, 527–529; and compositional analysis, 83; and future change, 534–535; and life course differences, 57–62, 64; and period differences, 62–67; and strata differences, 58–62; and structure, 58; as reflection of social change, 529–532; as source of social change, 532–534; drinking, 532; education, 530; faculty support of student activism, 532; fertility, 529–530; health, 530; immigration, 229–231; longevity, 533–534; maternal mortality, 530; menarche, 530; menopause, 530; migration, 226–229; political attitudes, 140–145; residential mobility, 226–230; size, 533–534; smoking, 532; voting, 123–124. SEE ALSO: *Specific subject entries*

Cohort effects, 22, 30, 53, **68–69, 75,** 68–80

Cohort flow, 4, **8–9,** 11, 13, 17, 18, 29, 42–44, 46, 53, 67–68, 69–70, 515–581; and age structure, 523–529; and change in sex roles, 575–576; and cohort differences, 527–529; and community, 191, 201, 230; and composition of strata, 524–527; and demographic processes, 524–527; and life course patterns, 527–529; and size of strata, 524–527; and social change, 521–523; changes in, 13–14; metaphor of moving stairs, 524–528, 577. SEE ALSO: *Cohort processes; Cohort succession; Population processes; Vital processes*

Cohort functions, 95

Cohort life tables, 66–67

Cohort processes, 43–45, 54, 56–57; and indirect age criteria, 408; and size of age strata, 44; and social change, 521–523; versus individual process, 93–94. SEE ALSO: *Demographic bases of age strata; Fertility; Mortality; Migration; Vital processes*

Cohort size, **9,** 46, 61, 154, 532–534. SEE ALSO: *Size*

Cohort succession. SEE: *Cohort flow*

Cohort trends, effect on cross-section data, 57–61

Cohort vs. societal time, **29,** 42–43, 53,
419–420, 516–517, 519, 528, 565, 573
Collaboration in science, 338–345
Collection of data in age research, 594–601
College, 244–245; analogy with family, 253–
269, 284–288; and specificity, 249; as
socializing agency, 253–269; differentiation of achievement in, 248–249; peer
solidarity in, 248–250; socialization
strains in, 245–246; solidarity of, 259–
265; vs. high school, 250–253. SEE
ALSO: *Faculty; Higher education;
Student; Studentry*
College attendance, 530; allocative processes, 551–552, 560, 568; and social
status, 246–247, 473–474; life course
effects, 472–474; socialization for, 472–
473, 551–552, 568
College faculty. SEE: *Faculty*
College student. SEE: *Student*
Commitment, **426–427;** academic value-
pattern, 259–261; and role relinquishment, 537–538; friendship role, 379;
political role, 125–126; science, 296–
297; **to society** (political implications),
129–130, 131, 139–140; work role, 181–
182, 186–187, 475–477
Community, 199–235, **201, 202;** activities,
214, 216; age structure, 199, 201–210,
224–230; aging of, 199, 206; and
adolescence, 216–219; and adulthood,
219–221; and change, 199, 224, 230;
and childhood, 211–216; and childrearing practices, 214–215; and cohort
succession, 199, 201, 230; and family
cycle status, 219–221; and fertility, 210;
and friendship, 365–367; and housing,
206–207, 208–209; and interaction,
213–214, 216–217; and later years, 221–
224; and life course, 199, 201, 210,
224, 487, 490; and migration, 210, 224–
230; and mortality, 210; and occupation,
219–221, 479–482; and peers, 213–214,
216–217; and school, 213–214; and
social class, 220–221; and socialization,
214–215, 218, 228–229; as allocative
agent, 207–208; as ecological structure,
199; as social structure, 199; as territorial
unit, 211–213; cosmopolitan vs. local
roles, 210–211, 213, 215, 216, 218–219,
220–221, 222–223; equilibrium model,
199; facilities, 209, 217–218, 226;
"fished out," 210; "gold rush," 210;
meaning of, 215–216, 218–219; roles,
207–208, 210–224, 365–367, 404, 479–
482, 487, 490; segregation of age strata,
203–206; "self-contained," 210; "self-

replenishing," 210; "single cohort,"
209–210; symbolic connotation, 218–
219; theme in student dissent, 270, 275;
typology of age structures, 209–210.
SEE ALSO: *Housing; Neighborhood;
Residence; Residential*
Competition between roles, **362;** and friendship, 369–370, 385–388
Competitive selection in allocation, 558–564
Complementarity of roles, **362, 404;** and
friendship, 368–369, 381–382, 385–389
Complex of roles. SEE: *Role complex*
Composite role patterns of scientists, 318–
322
Composition, 6; of cohort, 46; of community, 202–205; **of population, 91–92,**
95–98, 107, 421–423, 592–593; of
strata, 43, 45, 524–525, 527
Compositional analysis, 18, **81–84;** in
control for mortality, 607; of characteristics, 39–40; voting, 121
Compositional data, **35, 37**
Compositional fallacy, 61, **81–82,** 602, 606–
607
Compositional variables, 18, **40, 46;** as
controls, 107; demographic vs. nondemographic, 96; voting, 121–122
Compulsory retirement, 165–166, 174–175.
SEE ALSO: *Allocation, compulsory vs.
voluntary; Allocation, retirement;
Retirement*
Compulsory vs. voluntary allocation, 449,
551–555, 570–571
Conflict among strata, 117, 270, 401, 442–
448, 500; and social change, 445–448;
institutionalization of, 444–445; issues,
151–155; political, 145–155; segregation
of, 444–445, 447; values, 151–155, 446.
SEE ALSO: *Inequalities among strata;
Student dissent*
Conflict reduction, and age heterogeneous
memberships, 147–148; and political
socialization, 148–150; mechanisms of,
442–446
Confounding factors, control in age research,
593–594. SEE ALSO: *Compositional
analysis; Cohort analysis; Identification problem*
Consciousness, revolution of, 446, 576–577
Consciousness of age status, **434–435,** 493
Consensus among strata, 401, 443. SEE
ALSO: *Relations among strata;
Solidarity*
Conservatism, 132–146; and societal
commitment, 139–140; and socioeconomic status, 138; strata differences,
132–133

Distribution of rewards in allocation, 562–564

Division of labor in socialization, 543–545

Draft. SEE: *Military role*

Drinking, cohort difference, 532

Duration, as indirect age criterion, 408; **of experience, 426–427; of exposure to system as aging, 527–528;** of friendship, 370–371, 378–381, 390; of party identification, 126–127; of work role incumbency, 172–173. SEE ALSO: *Commitment*

Dynamic research on age, cohort analyses, 608–613; data collection, 42–43, 598–601; period analyses, 608–613; sampling problems, 590–593. SEE ALSO: *Cohort analysis; Longitudinal study; Panel study; Period analysis*

Early childhood, 466–468. SEE ALSO: *Childhood; Oedipal phase of childhood*

Early maturation, 461–462, 469–471

Early maturity (stage of life course), 238, 240, 246, 248–252, 255–256, 266. SEE ALSO: *Adulthood*

Early retirement, 177, 178. SEE ALSO: *Retirement*

Ecological correlation, 103

Ecological sectors of community, and age composition, 203

Economic attitudes, 132, 145

Economic base of community, and age composition, 203

Economic relations between strata, 440–441

Education (institution), and age as bases of stratification, 414; and differentiation of adolescence, 414; as structure for socialization, 237, 544–545; college, 237–291; expansion of higher, 242–244; for leisure, 188–189; higher, 237–291 (SEE ALSO: *College; Faculty; Student*); mass secondary, 240; process of institutionalization, 239; relational age in, 410–411, 544–545; structural changes in, 243–244. SEE ALSO: *Faculty; School; Student; Teaching role*

Educational attainment, 244, 425–426; and intelligence, 424; and mortality, 603; and party identification, 125; and political interest, 124–125; and retirement, 183; and unemployment, 177; and voting, 121, 122; and work force, 166, 190; and work role, 170–172, 181, 185; cohort changes in, 237–238, 530–532; in science, 299, 300–301; of future aged, 534–535. SEE ALSO: *College attendance*

Educational upgrading, 246; in science, 299–301

Effects in age interpretation, 68–80

Egalitarianism, as theme of student dissent, 270

Element 1. SEE: *Population; Strata; Structural elements;* SEE ALSO *Composition; Size*

Element 2. SEE: *Age-related acts; Capacities for role performance; Characteristics; Individual; Motivations; Structural elements*

Element 3. SEE: *Role(s); Role structure; Structural elements*

Element 4. SEE: *Allocative criteria; Role expectations; Role sanctions; Role performance; Structural elements*

Elements of age structure. SEE: *Structural elements*

Emigration, 100–101. SEE ALSO: *Immigration; Migration*

Empathic sharing of life course among strata, 443–444

Employing firm, and retirement, 176–177

Employment, 297, 298, 442; age discrimination, 174–175, 177, 560; allocation to, 560; and role exit, 559; change in age patterns, 440–441; decline of agricultural, 165; of women, 406, 486, 487–488, 490. SEE ALSO: *Career; Job; Labor force participation; Occupation; Women in labor force; Work force; Work role; Unemployment*

Empty nest stage, 482, 489–491

Environment and age stratification, 15–18

Environmental change, 16–18

Environmental effects, 51–53, 68–69; analysis of, 68–80; types of, 70

Equality in student peer group, 249–250

Equality of sexes, and student dissent, 278

Equilibrium model of community, 199

Ethnographic reports, and age research, 584

Evaluation of roles, 403–404

Exchange among strata, 439. SEE ALSO: *Relations among strata*

Exclusivity between roles, 404, 406

Exit from role. SEE: *Role exit*

Expectation of life, 66–67, 420, 422–423

Expectations (role). SEE: *Role expectations*

Expediters in allocation, 558

Experience, 425–427, 441–442; **accumulation of, 426–427,** 459; and political partisanship, 126; as indirect age criterion, 408; **duration of, 426–427.** SEE ALSO: *Accumulation; Aging; Commitment; Duration*

Experiential time dimension, 443–444

Experimental designs in age research, 553–554

Explanation, problems in age research, 67–85, 601–613

Expressive change, 576–577

Expressive component in faculty roles, 257

Expressiveness in student dissent, 270–271, 275–276

Expressive support of friends, 368–369

External migration, 100. SEE ALSO: *Immigration; Migration*

Extraneous factors, control in age research, 107, 593–594. SEE ALSO: *Compositional Analysis*

Facilities for role performance, 415, 416–418, 448, 450

Factual vs. normative criteria of allocation, 7, 409–410

Faculty, allocation to roles, 262–263; as *pater absconditus*, 254; differentiation of roles, 261–262; expressive component of role, 257; managerial tasks, 264–265; privacy as condition of solidarity, 263, 265–269; publication as value commitment, 260–261, 263; relations with students, 256–258, 262, 264–269, 281; research vs. private concerns, 264; role-set, 254; roles in socialization, 256-257; solidarity, 259–269; support of student dissent, 532. SEE ALSO: *Research role; Teaching role*

Failure of life goals, 429–430, 477–478, 494–495, 497

Fallacies, aggregational, 103; atomistic, 103; **compositional,** 61, **81–82,** 602, 606–607; **generational,** 602–609; **life course, 62,** 424, 602, 609; of interpretation, 61–63, 66–67; **of proportional representation, 84,** 602. SEE ALSO: *Interpretation of age data*

Family, age polarization in, 411; and democratic association, 264–265; and education (analogy), 253–269, 284–288; and peer group, 383–384, 386, 388; and political association, 148; and retirement, 175–176, 187–188; as allocator to work force, 169–171; as structure for socialization, 148, 187–188, 237, 253–269; differentiation from firm, 244–245; incest taboo, 255, 256, 259; managerial tasks in, 259; relations among strata in, 439–441; scope of childrearing stage, 412; solidarity in, 258–259

Family change, 253–254, 412, 575–576; and allocative powers, 570–571; and longevity, 532–534

Family cycle, 482–492; and community, 219–222; and housing needs, 200

Family roles, 404, 431–432; and career patterns, 479–482; and friendship, 363–364, 367; changes, 412; over life course, 482–492

Fantasy-ideology in socialization, 276–277

Father, as link to community, 256; differentiation of work-family role, 241, 253–254

Female age groups, 437

Female labor force participation, 54–57, 70–71, 165, 406, 442, 528; and changing sex roles, 575–576; changes in, 54–57, 163–164. SEE ALSO: *Employment of women; Women in labor force*

Fertility, 43–45, 93, 95, 98–100, 449; analysis, 102–103; and cohort flow, 525–528; and community age structure, 210; as age-time process, 94; cohort differences, 529–530; declines in, 421–422; differential patterns of, 45; period vs. cohort analysis, 67

Financial security, concern with, 432

"Fished out" community, 210

Fixed vs. changeable characteristics of population, 96–98. SEE ALSO: *Characteristics; Irreversible characteristics*

Flow of cohorts. SEE: *Cohort flow*

Foci of scientific interest, and age, 345–350

Foreign birth, 45, 100–101, 229–231, 422, 534

Formal criteria of allocation, 408

Foster grandparent role, 451, 555

Friendship, 357–393, 404, 417, 426; adolescent, 361, 364, 369–370, 372–373, 380–381, 382–383, 385–387; adult, 361, 364, 375, 383, 387–389; allocative processes, 370–378, 380–382, 554–555, 563; among married students, 376; and age dissimilarity, 359, 374–375; and age homophily, 371–374, 376–378; and aging, 358–359, 378; and community roles, 365–367; and family roles, 363–364, 367–368; and interaction, 379–380; and intimacy, 380; and length of residence, 366–367, 379–380; and neighborhood, 366–367, 368, 426; and parenthood, 363; and personal integration, 358; and propinquity, 213, 216–218, 219–220; and relational age, 359, 371; and retirement, 365; and role commitment, 379; and role competition, 369–370, 385–389; and role complementarity,

425. SEE ALSO: *Community; Residence*
Hypertension, 423

Identification problem in age research, 75–76, 610; and interpretation of data, 73–80; mathematical note, 85–88; need for assumptions, 78–80
Identities in age data, 62–65
Identity, and life review, 497–498; and occupation, 476–477; as aspect of aging, 460–461; continuity of, 501–503, 519; effects of maturational differences, 469–471; effects of peers, 469; over life course, 501–506
Ideology, cohort differences, 140–145; life course change, 133–140; of age in science, 320, 321–323; strata differences, 132–133
Ideology-fantasy, 276–277
Image of future in socialization, 539–540
Imbalances between poeple and roles, 13–14, 22, 32–33, 402, 448–452, 567–577; and cohort succession, 522–523; intracohort, 522. SEE ALSO: *Supply and demand for personnel*
"Immigrants in time," 542
Immigration, 45, 100–101, 229–231, 422, 534
Incest taboo, 255, 256, 259
Inclusiveness of age group, 435, 438
Inclusiveness of population data, 29
Income of older workers, 173–174, 178–179
Incongruity in age status, 189–191, 413–414, 442, 522
Inconsistencies in role sequences, 428–429
Inconsistency of age strata boundaries, 413–414
Incorporation, and role transfer, 538
Independence, 176; and family change, 533; in old age, 450
Indirect age criteria, 7, 407–408
Individual, and articulating processes, 519; contributions to socialization, 536, 548; differences, 457–513 (*passim*); impact on social structure, 548, 568–575; responses to role structure, 430–433; responsibility, 248, 431; self-initiated change, 505; self-selection in allocation, 551–552, 554, 558–559, 565; shifts within the cohort, 46–48, 602; vs. cohort process, 93–94; vs. population levels of analysis, 102–103; vs. societal time, 528, 565 (SEE ALSO: *Cohort vs. societal time*). SEE ALSO: *Life course*
Inequalities among strata, 191–193, 401, 415–418, 437, 443, 448, 562–563; and age conflict, 153–155, 445–448; and allocation, 565–566; as inequities, 430–432, 549; change in, 417–418; legitimation of, 417, 443, 445–446, 447–448; of opportunities, 404; of rewards, 404, 415–418, 448; responses to, 430–432; variability, 418. SEE ALSO: *Authority; Conflict among strata; Hierarchy in age relations; Relations among strata*
Inequalities within strata, 457–513 (*passim*), 564. SEE ALSO: *Composition(al)*
Inevitability of aging. SEE: *Age mobility*
Infancy, 240, 246, 465–467. SEE ALSO: *Childhood*
Infant mortality, research, 530, 611–612
Informal criteria of allocation, 408
Information dissemination in allocation, 167–168, 557–558, 564
Inheritance, cultural and genetic, 96–97, 466–467
Institutional care, 425
Institutional mortality rates, 604
Institutionalization of conflict among strata, 444–445
Instrumental activism and academic values, 242, 243, 271–272
Instrumental functions of friendship, 369
Integration, and student dissent, 274–275
Integration, social and friendship, 389
Integration of role complex, 128–129, 358
Integration of schools, 141, 142
Integration within strata, 20, 434–439
Intellectual functioning, 423, 424, 595–596, 604
Intellectual migration, 313
Intelligence tests, 424, 595–596, 604
Interaction, and community, 213–214, 216–217; and friendship, 379–380; potential, 437
Interaction between allocation and socialization, 567–572
Interactions among age processes, and social change, 12–14, 566–577
Intercohort differences. SEE: *Cohort differences*
Interdependence among strata, 439. SEE ALSO: *Relations among strata*
Intergenerational relations in family, 439–440; and socialization for retirement, 187–188. SEE ALSO: *Family*
Intermediaries in age research, 597–598, 599
Internal allocation, 551
Internal migration, 100–101. SEE ALSO: *Migration; Residential mobility*

Interpretation of age data, 61–62, 66–88; cohort and period analysis, 66–68, 70–76; identification problem, 75–80, 85–88, 610; mathematical note, 85–88; truncated time series, 66, 73–76, 612; use of models, 78–80. SEE ALSO: *Fallacies*

Interstratum relations. SEE: *Relations among strata*

Interviewer selection, as source of sample bias, 587

Intimacy, and friendship, 380

Intracohort differences. SEE: *Composition(al); Inequalities within strata; Life course; Life course differences*

Intracohort shifts, 46–49, 602

Intracohort sources of change, 522

Intraoccupational mobility, 173, 296, 316, 476–479, 481–482. SEE ALSO: *Career; Work role*

Intrastratum relationships. SEE: *Relations within strata*

Intrastratum solidarity. SEE: *Solidarity, within strata*

Irish peasants, 414, 434, 444, 549

Irreversibility of aging. SEE: *Age mobility*

Irreversible characteristics, 48, 96–98

Issues of age conflict, 151–155. SEE ALSO: *Student dissent*

Job, and community roles, 219–221, 479–482; and family roles, 479–482; commitment, 181–182, 186–187, 475–477; shifts, 476. SEE ALSO: *Career; Employment; Labor force participation; Occupation; Work role*

Job seeking, older workers, 177

Juvenescent population of science, 297

Juvenocracy in science, 331

Kinship-regulated societies, and age, 414

Kinship relations. SEE: *Family*

Labor force participation, 39, 41, 162–166; allocation, 162, 166–184, 189–193, 414, 418, 519, 560, 568; and migration, 605; changes in, 54–57, 163–166; effect of census undercounts, 585–586; of women, 54–57, 70–71, 163–165, 406, 442, 528, 575–576. SEE ALSO: *Career, Employment; Job; Occupation; Retirement; Work force; Work role*

Labor unions, and protection of work role, 173, 178; and retirement, 175, 178; and work force entry, 168; attitudes toward, 134–135, 141

Late maturation, implications for life course, 469–471

Latency, 239–241, 246, 248–249, 255. SEE ALSO: *Childhood*

Later years. SEE: *Aged; Old age; Older population; Old people*

Ld. SEE: *Life course differences;* also *Life course*

Leadership, 131

Learning, 424. SEE ALSO: *Intellectual functioning*

Legal barriers to voting, 126–128

Legitimation of inequalities, 417, 443, 445–446, 447–448

Leisure, 175, 182, 188–189, 192–193, 481, 495, 576–577

Length of residence, and friendship, 366–367

Level of social system in research, 28, 102–105

Lexis diagram, 610

Liberalism, 132–146

Life adjustment, 431–432, 457–513 (*passim*)

Life course, 19–20, 42–43, 457–513, **458–459;** analysis of, 104–105, 459–465; and age structure, 58–61; and cohort flow, 527–529; and community, 199, 201, 210–224, 487, 490; and higher education, 246–253; and indirect age criteria, 407–408; as sequence of roles, 459; as temporal dimension, 21–22, 419–420, 528–565 (SEE ALSO: *Cohort vs. societal time*); compositional analysis of, 82–83; determinants of, 462–463; differentiation of achievement, 248–249; empathic sharing among strata, 443–444; friendship patterns, 357–393; future, 427; identity, 460–461, 498, 501–506, 519; in science, 317–321; marriage, 482–492; migration, 224–225, 227, 228 (SEE ALSO: *Migration; Residential mobility*); of cohort vs. individual, 46–48, 602; parental roles, 486–492; peer relations, 382–389; political orientations, 72–73, 125–126, 133–140, 528; representation of, 506–511; residence, 210–214 (SEE ALSO: *Residential mobility*); socialization, 536 (SEE ALSO: *Socialization*); subjective appraisal, 506–511; transition points, 385–389, 429–430, 436, 437–438, 511, 551, 574–575; voluntary association membership, 481–482, 487, 490; voting, 123–124. SEE ALSO: *Aging; Cohort vs. societal time;*

P1. SEE: *Cohort flow; Cohort processes; Population processes; Vital processes*
P2. SEE: *Aging*
P3. SEE: *Allocation*
P4. SEE: *Socialization*
Panel study in age research, 47–49, 77–78, 590–591, 598–599, 604–607. SEE ALSO: *Longitudinal study*
Panel mortality in age research, 590–591, 604–607
Parental role, 404, 406, 416–417, 571; and community, 214–215, 229; and friendship, 363; allocative processes, 555–556, 557–558; in middle age, 494; over life course, 486–492. SEE ALSO: *Parents*
Parental solidarity in socialization, 258–259, 266–267, 268–269
Parental values, and work force allocation, 170–171
Parent-child model of socialization, 540–541, 543
Parent-child relations in adolescence, 472–473
Parents, and peer group, 388–389; and teachers, effects of age differences, 544–545; dependency relationship, 259; support of children, 439–440. SEE ALSO: *Parental role*
Parish records, 584
Parity cohort, 100
Participation, and student dissent, 270, 280–282
Participation in society, capacity, 246
Partisanship, 125–127
Part-time work, 183
Party identification, 72–73, 117, 125–127, 135–136, 138, 139, 528
Pater absconditus, 253–254
Patronage in science, 335–336, 342–345
Pattern maintenance, and student dissent, 275–276
Pd. SEE: *Period differences*
Peace vs. war, and student dissent, 279–281
Peers, peer group, adolescence, 249–250, 266, 281, 382–383, 385–387, 471–472; and community, 213–214, 216–217; and family, 383–384, 386, 388–389; and parents, 388–389; and role transition, 385–389; and social class, 386–387; and social control, 382, 383, 386–387; and socialization, 375–376, 382–389, 545–546; childhood, 385–386; commitment, 249–250; diffuseness, 249–250; effects of body build, 470; effects on identity,

469; loyalty, 250; over life course, 382–389; roles, 404; studentry phase, 248–250, 255, 257, 266
Pensions, 166, 175, 176, 177, 178–179
People and roles. SEE: *Supply and demand for personnel; Imbalances between people and roles*
Perceptual skills, 423
Performance. SEE: *Role performance*
Period age structure, 94, 95
Period analysis, 50, 53, 79, 602; and identification problem, 76–77, 85–88, 610; problems of implementation, 610–613; problems of interpretation, 75–80, 85–88, 608–610; truncated data, 66, 73–76, 612; vs. cohort analysis, 50–68, 70–78
Period data, 32
Period differences (Pd), 31, 32, 35, 42, **62–63;** as reflecting social change, 529–532; identical with cohort differences (Cd), 63–64; related to cohort differences (Cd) and life course differences (Ld), 58–62, 64
"Period effects" in interpretation, 30–31, 53, **55, 69,** 70, 144; and period vs. cohort analysis, 71–77; effort to isolate, 69–80; short run, 71–73
Period functions, 95
Periodicities of major social roles, 496–497
Period of history as temporal dimension, 419–420. SEE ALSO: *Cohort vs. societal time*
Period-specific event, 106
Permissive age criteria, 409
Personal and population time, 93
Personality, 239, 500–506
Personnel, supply and demand for, 3, 7, 22, 33, 402–406, 420, 427–428, **448–450,** 519, 520, 572
Person-years of exposure, 93–94
Physical mobility, and life course, 210–224
Physiological constraints on role performance, 423–424
Physiological differences, and age research, 603
Physique, effect on life course, 469–471, 483–485
Pluralism of American system, 271–272
Pluralistic loyalties in early maturity, 250–251
Polarization, 146, 411. SEE ALSO: *Conflict among strata*
Political activity, 119–132; extra-institutional, 130, 131–132. SEE ALSO: *Voting;*

Quasi population, 98–102. SEE ALSO: *Sub population*

Racial differences in mortality, 603
Racial integration, support, 141, 142
Racism, and student dissent, 278–279
Rationality, cognitive. SEE: *Cognitive rationality*
Rationalization of life, 247–248
Reaction time, 423
Receptivity to new ideas in science, 309–310, 348–350
Reciprocal socialization, 149–150, **541–543,** 547
Reciprocity of family support, 440
Reconstruction of past, 463–464, 599
Recreational facilities, 217–218
Re-enacted roles, scientific careers, 342–345
Referees in science, 316, 330–337
Reference group, and inequalities, 430–431
Rehearsal for retirement, 186–187
Relational age, 14, 410–411; and friendship, 359, 371; and performance expectations, 417; as criterion of allocation, 370–371, 410–411; **incongruities, 442,** 522; in research situation, 598
Relational roles, 21. SEE ALSO: *Relational age*
Relations among strata, 20–22, 433–448; allocation, 520–521, 562–564; authority, 248, 251–252, 257–258, 299–300, 343–345, 441–442; competition, 335; conflict, 117, 145–155, 270, 401, 442–448, 500 (SEE ALSO: *Student dissent*); conflict reduction, 147–151, 442–446; consensus, 401, 443, 446, 447–448; cross-cutting affiliations, 147–148, 445–446, 447; deference, 335, 441–442; economic, 440–441; effects of age mobility, 443–444, 447; empathic sharing of life course, 443–444; envy, 335; exchange, 439–441; familial, 439–440; hierarchy, 189–191, 245, 336, 383–385, 441–442, 521, 541–546, 562–564, 565–566; in science, 299, 327–337, 338–345; institutionalization of conflict, 444–445; interdependence, 439–441; political, 130–132, 145–155; **segregation, 20–21,** 147–148, 203–206, 499–500; segregation of conflict, 444–445, 447; solidarity, 335, 445–446 (SEE ALSO: *Solidarity*); value conflict, 151–155, 446 (SEE ALSO: *Student dissent*). SEE ALSO: *Allocation; Allocative agents; Inequalities among strata; Socialization; Socializing agents*
Relations within strata, 20–22, **148,** 205,

335, 434–441, 564. SEE ALSO: *Peers, peer group; Solidarity*
Relative deprivation, 430–431, 437
Relative size of strata, 34–35
Relinquishment of roles. SEE: *Role relinquishment*
Remarriage, 449
Repertoire of roles, 403, 404–405
Reported age, 594–595
Representational sampling in age research, 585–594
Republican party identification. SEE: *Party identification*
Research on age, age intervals, 611–612; age reporting, 594–595; analysis, 601–613 (SEE ALSO: *Cohort analysis; Life course, analysis of; Period analysis*); **cohort analysis** (SEE: *Cohort analysis*); **compositional analysis, 18, 81–84,** 606–607; compositional change, 592; **compositional fallacy, 61, 81–82,** 602, 606–607; composition as source of error, 602–608; control of extraneous factors, 107, 593–594; data collection, 594–601; data sources, 584, 593, 601; dynamic, 42–43, 589–593, 598–601, 608–613 (SEE ALSO: *Cohort analysis; Longitudinal study; Panel study; Period analysis*); experiments, 593–594; fallacies of explanation, 61–63, 66–67, 81–82, 84, 103, 424, 602, 606–607, 609, **fallacy of proportional representation, 84,** 602; **generational fallacy, 62,** 602, 609; **identification problem, 75–76,** 73–80, 85–88, 610; identities in age data, 62–65; intermediaries, 597–598, 599; interpretation, 27–89; interviewer selection of respondents, 587; **life course fallacy, 62,** 424, 602, 609; longitudinal studies, 47–49, 77–78, 590–591, 598–599, 604–607 (SEE ALSO: *Panel study*); migration, as source of error, 591, 602–608; mortality as source of error, 591, 602–608; need for generality, 601–602; nonresponse, 587–590; panel mortality, 591, 604–607; **period analysis, 50, 53,** 73–80, 85–88, 608–613; projective tests, 595, 596, 597; quasi-experiments, 593–594; relative age as source of bias, 597–598; response capacities, 596–597; response frame of reference, 595–596; retrospective reports, 463–464, 599; sampling, 585–594; separation factor, 611–612; sequence of cross-sections, 591–593, 598, 599–601, 612; stimulus meaning, 595–597, 599–601; testing experience,

596; time intervals, 610–612; truncated data, 66, 73–75, 612; verbal fluency, 597

Research role, 254; as private concern of faculty, 264; in science, 314–315, 317–327; vs. teaching role, 256–257, 314–315, 317–321

"Reserve pool" of personnel, 572

Residence, and job opportunities, 219; life course, 199, 210–224

Residential age segregation, 203–206

Residential mobility, and friendship, 367, 379–380; and voting, 127. SEE ALSO: *Migration*

Residential stability, and friendship, 366–367, 426; and life course, 488

Resistance to novelty, and age, 309–310

Respondent, frame of reference in age research, 595–596; refusal in age research, 587–590; unavailability in age research, 587–590

Response capacities in age research, 596–597

Responses to inequalities, 430–433

Responsibility, 248, 431

Retention of roles, in science, 322–330

Retirement, 404, 417, 418, 494–495, 571; allocation to, 172–184, 561; and education, 183; and employing firm, 176–177; and family, 175–176, 187–188; and friendship, 365–366; and government, 178–179; and health, 180–182; and housing needs, 200; and labor unions, 175, 177–178; and work commitment, 186–187; anticipatory socialization for, 186–189; compulsory, 165–166, 174–175; early, 177, 178; gradual, 183; income in, 178–179; personal reasons for, 182; plans for, 182; response to, 183–184, 432–433; unexpected, 183–184; voluntary, 184

Retirement communities, 205

Retraining of workers, 185–186, 190

Retrospective data, 463–464, 599

Retrospective longitudinal design, 47

Retrospective reconstruction of life course, 464, 507–511

Reversible characteristics, 48, 96–98, 120–121

Review of past, 497–498, 507

Revolution of consciousness, 446, 576–577

Rewards, and retirement, 173–174, 175; control in socialization, 570; distribution in allocation, 562–564, 565–566; inequalities in, 191–193, 404, 415–418, 430–432, 443, 445–448, 549; noneconomic, 192; subjective, 425, 430–

432; withdrawal in role relinquishment, 537

Rigidity, 604

Rites of passage, 385, 538

Rituals in allocation, 551, 553, 554, 555, 561

Role(s), 5; and biological constraints, 403–404; **and people, imbalances between, 13–14,** 22, 32–33, 402, **448–452,** 522–523, 567–577; as differentiating age strata, 399; availability to age strata, 6, 7, 9; changes, 11–14 (SEE ALSO: *Structural change; Change*); differences in social evaluation, 403–404; dimensions of differences, 403–404; in primary vs. secondary groups, 403; kinds available, 402–406; **mutually exclusive, 404,** 406; numbers available, 7, 402–406, 427–428; periodicity in performance, 496–497; priority among, 403–404; re-enactment, 342–345; **repertoire, 405;** rewards (SEE: *Rewards*). SEE ALSO *specific role references: Administrative; Community; Faculty; Family; Friendship; Gatekeeper; Science; Marital; Military; Neighborhood; Parental; Political; Research; Sex; Teaching; Voluntary association: Widowhood; Work*

Role allocation. SEE: *Allocation; Articulating processes*

Role allocators. SEE: *Allocative agents*

Role attrition, scientific research, 321–322; self-fulfilling prophecy, 327

Role candidates, 549, 562–564

Role commitment, 426–427; and friendship, 379; and political partisanship, 126; and role relinquishment, 537–538; in science, 296–297; work, 181–182, 186–187, 474–479

Role competition, 362; and friendship, 369–370, 385–389

Role complementarity, 362, 404; and friendship, 368–396, 381–382, 385–389

Role complex, 8, 20, 23, 366–367, 406, 427–428; and allocation, 560; and friendship, 358, 366–367, 373; and solidarity within strata, 436; in science, 314–330; integration, 128–129, 358; types of relations, 362, 404

Role data, 30–31, 108

Role entry. SEE: *Allocation*

Role exclusion, 410

Role exit, 551, 553–554, 555, 559, 561, 562. SEE ALSO: *Allocation; Role relinquishment; Role transfer; Role*

policy and gerontocracy, 330–337; referees, 316, 337; relations among strata, 299, 327–337, 338–345; role allocation in, 297–299, 315–330; socialization, 296–297, 338–345; **status judges in, 297, 299;** values and age structure, 299–300; visibility of new ideas, 310–311. SEE ALSO: *Scientist(s)*

Scientific personnel, age distribution, 297, 298

Scientist(s), 293–356; administrative role, 315–316, 318–321, 326–327; age distribution, 297, 298; cohort analysis of roles, 317–320; composite role patterns of, 318–321; delayed labor force entry, 297; discovery, 305–308, 311–313, 347; education, 299–301; eminence and persistence of productivity, 323, 325; foci of interest, and age, 345–350; in component sciences, 300–301; inter-science transfers, 296, 301, 311–314; intraoccupational mobility, 296; life course mobility, 296; mortality and productivity, 307–308; occupational commitment, 296–297; productivity, 299–300, 306–308, 321–323; receptivity to new ideas, 309–310, 348–350; re-enactment of roles, 342–345; research role, 314–315, 318–327; role-attrition, 321–322; role retention, 322–330; roles, 314–330; role sequence, 317–330; role specialization, 318–321; teaching role, 314–315, 317–321, 326–330. SEE ALSO: *Science*

Scope of age data, 72–76, 412–415

Screeners in allocation, 558, 559

Sd. SEE: *Strata differences*

Secondary education, 240, 243. SEE ALSO: *High School; School attendance*

Secondary school enrollment, 530–531

Second careers, 442

Segregation of age strata, 20–21, 146, 203–206, 499–500

Segregation of conflict among strata, 444–445, 447

Self-concept, and mortality, 604. SEE ALSO: *Identity*

"Self-contained" community, 210

Self-employment, 165

Self-fulfilling prophecy in role attrition, 327

Self-initiated change in life course, 505

"Self-replenishing" community, 210

Self-selection in allocation, 551–552, 554, 558–559, 565

Self-worth, 431

Seniority, 173, 178, 414

Sensori-motor skills, 423

Separation, and role transfer, 538

Separation factor, in cohort analysis, 611–612

Sequence of cross-sections in age research, 47, 76–77, 79, 591–593, 599–601, 612

Sequence of roles. SEE: *Role sequence*

Sequential characteristics of population, 97–98

Sequential relationships in family, 439

Sex, and age as bases of stratification, 414; and community orientation, 220; and friendship roles, 364; and labor force participation, 163–164; and mortality, 422, 449, 603–604; and residence, 204; and sampling biases, 587; and voting, 121–122; differentiation of roles, 452; role change, 575–576

Sexual activity, 423

Sexual equality and student dissent, 277–278

Sexual maturity, 461

Single vs. multiple cohorts in longitudinal research, 48–49

Situational specification, 569

Size of population, **6,** 84, 94, 95, 420–421; aged in future, 534; **cohort, 9,** 46, 61, 154, **533–534; strata, 33–36,** 37, 43–45, **525–527**

Smoking, 73–75, 532

Social change. SEE: *Change (also specific subject entries)*

Social class, and community, 220–221; and conservatism, 138; and peer group, 386–387

Social class stratification vs. age stratification, 22–23, 452, 532

Social control, and peers, 382, 383, 386–387

Social differentiation. SEE: *Differentiation*

Social evaluation of roles, 403–404

Socialist party membership, 140

Socialization (P4), 8, 9, **11,** 12, 13, 17, 18, 22, 31, 43, 93, **518–521,** 535–548, 567–572; age structure of, 237–238, 520–521, 536–537, 540–546; and affective solidarity, 257; and community, 214–215, 218, 228–229; and compulsory allocation, 551–552, 570–571; and friendship, 358, 375, 382–389; and future change, 539–540; and incest taboo, 255; and mass higher education, 284–288; and peers, 375, 382–389, 545–546; and role transfer, 537, 538; and social change, 546–548, 567–572; and student dissent, 276–277, 280–283;

anticipatory, 186–187, 384, 417, 475–476, **539–540,** 542, 546, 547, 569; apprentice-master relation in science, 315, 327–329, 338–345; as life course process, 238–239, 536; **as social structure, 536;** asymmetry of relations, 245, 384–385; changes in, 13, 237–291, 425–426; differentiated from allocation, 567–568; dilemmas of control, 570; division of labor in, 543–545; fantasies as expression of strain, 276–277; for college attendance, 472–473; 551–552, 568; for early maturity, 247–253; for retirement, 161, 186–189; **for role relinquishment,** 186–189, **537–538;** hierarchical age relations, 237–238, 245, 383–385, 540, 541–546; individual contributions, 536, 548; in college vs. family, 253–269; in early childhood, 465–468; in old age, 384; in school years, 468–474; in science, 296–297, 338; occupational, 475–476, 568; of college vs. non-college population, 250–253; parent-child model, 540–541, 543; phasing with allocation, 519–520, 522, 551–552, 567–572; political, 148–150; primary, 237; **reciprocal,** 149–150, **541–543,** 547; response to imbalance, 451–452; response to social crises, 576; role models for, 540; situational specification, 569; societal contributions, 536; studentry phase, 237, 240, 245, 246–247, 250–256, 266, 284–288, 412; tenancy form, 315, **539–540,** 542, 567, 569; to cognitive rationality, 263; work role, 161, 162, 185–192. SEE ALSO: *Articulating processes; Socializing agents*

Socializing agents, 537, 539–540, 541–546; age differences among, 543; as older strata, 540; dilemmas of control, 570; faculty roles, 256–257, 296; multiplicity of, 543–545; parental coalition, 258–259; peers, 375–376, 382–389, 545–546; separation from allocators, 567–572. SEE ALSO: *Socialization*

Social organization, demographic approach, 106–108

Social security, 175, 178–179

Social Security Act, 178–179

Social stratification and collaboration in science, 338–345

Societal commitment and political role, **129–130,** 131, 139–140

Societal continuity, 517, 519

Societal contributions to socialization, 536

Societal crises, responses of articulating

processes, 572

Societal divisions, and age strata, 398–400

Societal goals, and age conflict, 151–155

Societal time vs. cohort time, 29, 42–43, 53, 419–420, 517, 519, 528, 565, 573

Society, and articulating processes, 519

Socioeconomic status. SEE: *Social class*

Solidarity, across age lines, 335, 445; as requiring privacy, 263, 265–269; in early maturity, 266; in university, 259–265; of faculty as excluding students, 266, 267–269; of family, 258–259; of group and role exit, 561–562; of parents, as excluding children, 266–267, 268–269; of peers, and socialization, 545–546; of peers, in adolescence, 266; of students with faculty, impermanence, 262; organic, 271–272; within strata, 148, 205, 335, 401, 434–439, 564

Span of life, 422

Spatial mobility, and life course, 210–224

Specialization of role in science, 318–322

Specificity, in college, 249; in early maturity, 250; in friendship relations, 369–370, 389; in instrumental activism, 271

Sponsored mobility, 316, 342–345

Sponsorship, 335–336, 342–345

Stable population theory, 102, 105–106

Stage migration, 225

Stage of life course. SEE: *Life course stages*

Standardization, and compositional analysis, 82, 83

Status achievement, 96

Status ascription, 96. SEE ALSO: *Ascriptive allocation*

Status inconsistency. SEE: **Age incongruity**

Status judges in science, 297, 299

Status politics, and age conflict, 151–155

Stimulus meaning in age research, 595–597, 599–601

Stochastic models applied to life course, 47–48

Strata, 6, 9, 11, 397–455; and change, 401–402; and group memberships, 399–400; and other societal divisions, 398–400; and social relationships, 433–448; **as sub cultures, 420; boundaries, 398–399, 412–414;** changing characteristics, 527–529; changing size and cohort flow, 525–527; cross-cutting affiliations, 147–148, 445–447; **differences (Sd), 31, 32,** 44, 50, 51, 53, 54, 58–62, 64; **discontinuities between, 429–430;** interdependence of, 439–440; membership as social location, 398–399; relation to groups, 400; **scope of, 412; segregation, 20–21,** 146, 203–206, 499–500; size, 33–36, 37, 43–45, 525–527 (SEE ALSO: *Size*); solidarity within, 48, 401, 434–439, 564 (SEE ALSO: *Peer solidarity*). SEE ALSO: *Conflict among strata; Inequalities among strata; Inequalities within strata; Relations among strata; Relations within strata*

Stratification, age. SEE: *Age stratification*

Stratification, bases of, 22–23, 398–400, 414–415, 452, 532

Strength, 423

Structural change, 11–14, 16–18, 42, 54, 67–68; data, 32–37; related to processes, 62–67. SEE ALSO: *Change*

Structural data, 28–29, 58–61

Structural (or synchronic) elements, 5–8, 9, 15, 17–18, 28, 401; data, 32–37; polity, 119–121

Structural implications of age model, 20–21

Structural stabilities, 68

Structure, 1, 11, 54, 398, 420–421, 433–448; and cohort differences, 58–61; and cohort flow, 523–529; and demographic processes, 525–527; and life course patterns, 58–61; and process, 43, 53–67, 517–518; impact of individuals, 548, 568–575; of allocation, 520–521, 548–551, 562–564; of community, 199, 201–210, 224–230; of rewards, 175; of roles, 401–419, 427–428, 449–450, 451–452; of science, 295–302, 338–345; of socialization, 237–238, 520–521, 536–537, 540–546

Structured imbalances in age strata, 449–450

Student activism, faculty support, 532

Student culture vs. youth culture, 241

Student dissent, 237, 239, 258, 269, 283; absolutism, 270, 274–275; aestheticism, 274; and adaptation, 273–277; and allocation, 565–566; and goal attainment, 275–276; and integration, 274; and participation in university, 280–282; and pattern maintenance, 275–276; and socialization, 276–277; anomie, 274; anti-intellectualism, 274; community, 270, 275; constructive aspects, 276–283; dedifferentiation, 273–276; destructive aspects, 273–276; egalitarianism, 270; expressiveness, 271, 275; *Gemeinschaft,* 273–276; moralism, 269–270; participatory democracy, 258–259, 271; peace vs. war, 279–280; racism, 278–279; sexual

equality, 277–278; themes, 269–272; utopian concerns, 276. SEE ALSO: *Conflict among strata*

Student enrollment, 171

Student-faculty relations, and democracy, 281–282; bases of strain, 256–257; democracy as impractical, 264–265; exclusivity of faculty solidarity, 266, 267–269; hierarchy, 257–258; socialization, 257–258, 280–283; solidarity, 262

"Studentry," 237, **240, 246–247,** 412; affective attachments, 250–251; affective taboo, 255; as diffuse collectivity, 250; as phase of socialization, 284–288; differentiated value component, 250; peer solidarity, 248–250; repression of peer solidarity, 255–256, 266

Student role, 404, 406, 412, 415, 418; and work role, 171–172

Subjective reconstruction of past, 464

Subjective representation of life course, 506–511

Subjective responses to role structure, 430–433

Sub population, 101, 400. SEE ALSO: *Quasi-population*

Substitution of roles, 362, 451–452; and friendship, 367–368, 381–382

Suburbs, age composition, 202; and adolescence, 217; and age segregation, 203; and childhood, 211–215

Succession of cohorts. SEE: *Cohort flow*

Suicide rates, 71–72

Summary measures, 35, 37, 65

Supply and demand for personnel, 3, 7, 22, 33, 402–406, 427–428, **448–450,** 519, 520. SEE ALSO: *Imbalances between people and roles*

Support between generations in family, 439–440

Symbolic validation of allocation, 557, 558

Synchronic elements, 5–8, 32, 40. SEE ALSO: *Structural elements*

System level of research, 28

Teachers and parents, effects of age differences, 544–545

Teaching role, 254, 257–258; in science, 314–315, 317–321, 326–330; supply and demand, 449; vs. research role, 256–257. SEE ALSO: *Faculty; School*

Temporal dimensions. SEE: *Time*

Tenancy socialization, 315, 539–540, 542, 567, 569

Tenure provisions, 173

Territorial location, and allocation, 556, 557

Testing experience in age research, 596
Thematic apperceptive measures in age research, 545, 597
Themes of student dissent, 269–272
Third parties in age research, 597–598, 599
Third parties in allocation, 554–555, **559,** 564
Time, as central in sociology, 92; **cohort vs. societal, 29,** 43, 53, 419–420, 516–517, 519, 528, 565, 573; dimensions, 419–420
Time budgets, 432
Time intervals in age research, 610–612
Total rates, 40–42
Transfer of roles. SEE: *Role transfer(s); also Role transition*
Transfers of personnel, inter-science, 311–313
Transition between roles. SEE: *Role transition*
Transition matrix model of migration, 101–102
Transition points between life stages, 436, **437–438,** 511; and friendship, 385–389; in allocation, 551; life course, 429–430; strain and social change, 574–575. SEE ALSO: *Role transition*
Transition probabilities, 47–48, 101
Truncated time series, problems of interpretation, 66, 73–75, 612
Tuberculosis, death rates from, 50–53, 70
Turnover in occupations, 296–297
"Turnover" within the cohort, 47

Underdemanding roles, 449
Underenumeration in Census data, 585–586
Unemployment, 177–178, 432–433
Unions. SEE: *Labor Unions*
Universalistic component of instrumental activism, 271
Universalistic evaluations in education, 243
University. SEE: *College; Faculty; Higher education; Student; Studentry*
Upward mobility, and family roles, 480–482
Urban age distribution, 203
Urban residence, and adolescence, 217; and childhood, 213–215
Urban-rural migration, cohort differences, 226–228; life course, 225
Utopian concerns of student dissent, 276

Validation in allocation, **557, 558**
Value pattern, academic, 242–243, 244, 260–261, 271; instrumental activism, 271–273; of early maturity, 250; of studentry, 250
Values, and friendship, 378; conflict among

strata, 446–447; consensus among strata, 443; malintegration of, 448; of science, and age structure, 299–300
Verbal fluency in age research, 597
Villages, age composition, 202
Visibility of new ideas in science, 310–311
Vision, 423
Visiting, 380, 450
Vital processes, 8–9. SEE ALSO: *Cohort processes; Demographic processes; Population processes*
Vital statistics, records, 584
Voluntary association membership, 404; allocative processes, 554, 559; and friendship, 365–366; and life course, 481–482, 487, 490
Voluntary vs. compulsory allocation, 449, 550, 556, 570–571
Volunteer roles, 451
Voting, 117, 121–124, 417, 418, 450; and education, 121; and geographical mobility, 127; and life course, 123–124; and sex, 121–122; cohort differences, 123–124; compositional factors, 121–122; fictitious cohort analysis, 143–144; legal barriers, 126–128; obstacles, 124–130; trends, 123–124

Wallace, support for, 133
War issues, 45, 279–280
Weight, 601
Widowhood, 571; allocation to, 555, 557, 561; and friendship, 367–368; as relinquishment of marriage, 537; support in role transfer, 561
Withdrawal among aged, 184, 431, 432–433, 604–605
Within-stratum relations. SEE: *Inequalities within strata; Relations within strata*
Women in labor force, 53–57, 163–165, 406, 442, 528; and changing sex roles, 575–576; cohort analysis, 54–56, 70–71
Work force, 161–197; age hierarchy, 189–191; age strata, 163–166; allocation, 162, 166–184, 189–193, 414, 418, 519, 560; and age inequalities, 191–193; changes in participation, 162–166; children in, 163, 169–171; educational attainment, 166. SEE ALSO: *Employment; Labor force; Women in labor force; Work role*
Work role, 161–197, 404, 407, 416–417, 442, 476–477, 519; allocation, 162, 166–184, 189–193, 414–418, 519, 560; and community age structure, 207; and education, 171–172; and friendship,

Name index

Abegglen, James C., 185, 196, 481, 514
Abel, Neils, 308
Abel, Theodore, 391, 454
Abu-Lughod, Janet, 487, 488, 512
Adams, Bert N., 363, 390
Adams, C. W., 306, 351
Adler, Alfred, 328
Adorno, T. W., 252, 288
Agassi, Joseph, 346, 351
Agnello, Thomas, xvi, 600, 613
Aldous, Joan, 483, 513
Alexander, Paula, xvi
Altbach, Philip C., 148, 149, 156, 158
American Council on Education, 288
American Institute of Physics, 333
Anderson, C. Arnold, 107, 111, 290
Andrews, F. M., 350
Andvord, K. F., 50, 88
Aran, Lydia, 338, 351
Arensberg, Conrad M., 202, 232, 414, 453
Ariès, Philippe, 405, 453, 584, 613
Aristotle, 497, 516
Athanasopoulos, Demetrios A., 589, 590, 591, 615

Atkinson, John W., 618
Aurelius, Mildred G., xvi
Avorn, J. L., 258, 288
Axelbank, Rashelle G., 177, 193
Axelson, L. J., 489, 512
Ayres, Richard E., 127, 158

Babbitt, Irving, 193
Babchuk, Nicholas, 363, 380, 390
Back, Kurt W., 47, 88, 376, 391, 430, 453, 507, 512, 597, 599, 614, 615
Bailyn, Bernard, 355
Baldwin, James Mark, 467, 512
Bales, Robert F., 239, 244, 273, 285, 290, 385, 392, 576, 577, 578, 580
Baltes, P. B., 78, 88, 90
Balzac, Honoré de, 479
Bancroft, Gertrude, 168, 193
Banton, Michael, 452, 453
Barber, Bernard, 89, 272, 288, 309, 310, 351, 455, 581, 617
Barber, Elinor, 327, 354
Barfield, Richard, 173, 174, 178, 180, 182, 183, 184, 187, 193

Riegel, Klaus F., 604, 606, 617
Riegel, Ruth M., 617
Riesman, David, 242, 243, 254, 289, 516, 581, 598, 614
Riley, John W., Jr., xvi, 210, 388, 392, 423, 455, 514, 537, 581
Riley, Matilda White, 7, 8, 14, 23, 25, 28, 30, 47, 48, 57, 84, 89, 103, 110, 149, 158, 184, 189, 192, 195, 210, 258, 294, 299, 307, 310, 318, 329, 335, 355, 373, 382, 383, 385, 387, 388, 392, 429, 433, 451, 452, 455, 472, 514, 517, 524, 529, 536, 537, 540, 576, 581, 584, 585, 593, 606, 617
Rivlin, Alice M., 104, 110, 406, 407, 453, 533, 578
Robespierre, Maximilien, 276
Robinson, W. S., 103, 110
Roe, Anne, 323, 355, 472, 514
Roethlisberger, F. J., 365, 393
Rogoff, Natalie, 305, 355
Rokeach, Milton, 252, 290
Roper, Elmo, 119, 159
Rose, Arnold M., 194, 233, 442, 455, 579
Rose, Hilary, 302, 337, 355
Rose, Steven, 302, 337, 355
Rosenberg, George S., 220, 234, 368, 377, 393
Rosenberg, Morris, 253, 291
Rosow, Irving, 188, 195, 368, 377, 393, 546, 581
Ross, Edward Alsworth, 445, 455
Ross, Sir Ronald, 327
Rosset, Edward, 35, 89
Rossi, Alice S., 451, 456, 575, 581
Rous, F. P., 323
Rousseau, Jean Jacques, 193, 276, 532
Royal Society, 333, 348
Ryder, Norman B., 2, 4, 18, 24, 25, 42, 48, 57, 63, 66, 67, 89, 90, 91, 94, 95, 99, 100, 102, 107, 110, 111, 518, 523, 524, 525, 527, 529, 533, 581, 610, 613, 617

Saben, Samuel, 183, 195
Sagarin, Edward, xvi
Sagi, Philip C., 582
Saint-Simon (Comte de), 328
Salomone, Jerome J., 140, 157
Sanderson, Dwight, 202, 234
Santayana, George, 349
Sarton, George, 304, 355
Sauvy, Alfred, 567, 581
Sawyer, Jack, 373, 374, 376, 379, 392
Saxena, R. N., 354
Schachter, Stanley, 376, 391
Schaie, K. Warner, 59, 70, 76, 77, 78, 85, 90, 593, 608, 609, 610, 612, 617
Schmid, Calvin F., 204, 234
Schneider, David M., 259, 266, 291
Schneidman, E. S., 455, 580
Schnore, Leo F., 92, 95, 96, 103, 111
Schorr, Alvin L., 214, 234
Schrank, Harris, xvi, 160
Schrödingers, Erwin, 312
Schwartz, Morris S., 267, 291
Seeley, John R., 203, 208, 234
Sewell, William H., 473, 514
Shaefer, Earl S., 509, 514
Shah, Vimal P., 473, 514
Shakespeare, William, 459, 460, 461
Shanas, Ethel, 176, 196, 440, 456, 533, 581, 585, 590, 597, 601, 617
Sharp, Harry, 588, 589, 590, 617
Sheatsley, Paul B., 141, 142, 158
Sheldon, Eleanor Bernert, xvi, 193, 289, 453, 579, 614, 618
Sheldon, Henry D., 164, 196, 605, 617
Shepard, H. A., 350
Shepard, Paul, 219, 234
Sheppard Harold L., 119, 158, 162, 177, 183, 186, 196
Sheps, Cecil G., 615
Sher, L. H., 304, 348, 353
Shils, Edward A., 13, 25, 161, 185, 195, 260, 268, 273, 290, 291, 365, 392, 448, 455, 549, 550, 556, 563, 580
Shryock, Henry S., 219, 225, 234
Sills, David L., 25, 111, 159, 194, 195, 290, 454, 455, 456, 513, 579, 581, 582
Simmel, Georg, 107, 111, 359, 393, 428, 436, 438, 456, 517
Simmons, Leo, 131, 158, 442, 456, 584, 617
Simon, Bonnie, 366, 376, 391
Simon, Kenneth A., 243, 291
Slater, Philip E., 361, 393
Small, Albion W., 111
Smelser, Neil J., 12, 25, 108, 110, 169, 170, 195, 196, 253, 291, 441, 456, 517, 581, 584, 617
Smigel, Erwin O., 173, 196
Smith, Adam, 521, 532
Smith, Ernest A., 382, 388, 393
Smith, Clagett C., 350, 355
Smith, H. W., 596, 617
Smith, M. Brewster, 365, 393
Smith, Thomas S., 129, 158
Smyth, Daniel, xvi, 586, 617
Somers, Gerald G., 186, 196
Sorokin, Pitirim A., 12, 22, 23, 26, 107, 111, 146, 159, 202, 234, 276, 330, 355, 398, 400, 435, 438, 442, 444, 447, 456,

Washburn, Sherwood L., 233
Washington, George, 575
Watson, James D., 305, 306, 312, 352, 356
Watson, W., 220, 234
Webb, Eugene J., 599, 618
Webber, Melvin M., 221, 223, 234
Weber, Max, 23, 151, 152, 166, 192, 248, 400
Weinstein, Fred, 239, 240, 248, 254, 259, 276, 277, 291
Weiss, Paul A., 302, 303, 314, 356
Wells, W. P., 350
West, Patricia S., 364, 366, 376, 392
Westoff, Charles F., 530, 582
Wetzel, James R., 586, 615
Wheeler, Stanton, 157, 391, 453, 536, 578, 582
Whelpton, Pascal K., 83, 90
White, Winston, 243, 271, 290, 388, 392, 428, 456, 577, 582
Whitley, Richard D., 316, 348, 356
Whyte, William Foote, 219, 235, 253, 291, 368, 383, 393
Widdicombe, Stacey H., xvi
Wilensky, Harold L., 62, 90, 317, 356, 428, 456, 475, 480, 481, 482, 514, 588, 618
Williams, Richard H., 618
Williams, Robin M., Jr., 365, 393
Willmott, Peter, 202, 206, 209, 217, 220, 222, 235
Wilson, Monica, 462, 514

Wilson, Robert C., 265, 291
Wingo, Lowdon, Jr., 234
Winick, L., 512
Wirth, Louis, 208, 228, 229, 235
Wirtz, W. Willard, 174, 177, 196
Wolfbein, Seymour L., 176, 180, 188, 196
Wolfe, Donald M., 426, 453, 486, 487, 489, 491, 512
Wolff, Kurt H., 290, 393, 456
Woodward, Julian L., 119, 159
Wordsworth, William, 193
Wright, John J., 615

Yankelovich, Daniel, 157, 391
Yarmolinsky, Adam, 353
Yarrow, Marian Radke, 463, 514, 599, 618
Young, Donald R., xvi
Young, Michael, 217, 220, 235

Zeitlin, Maurice, 133, 159
Ziman, John, 302, 305, 344, 345, 356
Zimmerman, Carle C., 202, 234
Znaniecki, Florian, 584, 618
Zody, Richard, 83, 88, 592, 611, 615
Zola, Emile, 169
Zolbrod, Paul G., 258, 289
Zubin, Joseph, 615
Zuckerman, Harriet, 166, 173, 292, 293, 294, 306, 309, 316, 323, 326, 332, 333, 338, 339, 340, 342, 349, 356, 547, 572
Zulandt, Irene, xvi